Social Psychology
in Organizations

Social Psychology in Organizations

Advances in Theory and Research

J. KEITH MURNIGHAN, Editor

University of Illinois at Urbana–Champaign

Prentice Hall, Englewood Cliffs, NJ 07632

Library of Congress Cataloging-in-Publication Data

Social psychology in organizations : advances in theory and research /
J. Keith Murnighan, ed.
    p. cm.
  Includes bibliographical references.
  ISBN 0-13-374059-5 :
  1. Organizational sociology. 2. Social psychology.
HM131.S596 1993
302.3'5--dc20   92-33043
                                                            CIP

Acquisition Editor   *Alison Reeves*
Production Editor   *Maureen Wilson*
Copy Editor   *Patricia Daly*
Cover Designer   *Joe DiDomenico*
Prepress Buyer   *Trudy Pisciotti*
Manufacturing Buyer   *Patrice Fraccio*
Editorial Assistant   *Diane Peirano*

© 1993 by Prentice-Hall, Inc.
A Simon & Schuster Company
Englewood Cliffs, New Jersey 07632

Printed in the United States of America
10 9 8 7 6 5 4 3 2 1

ISBN 0-13-374059-5

Prentice-Hall International (UK) Limited, *London*
Prentice-Hall of Australia Pty. Limited, *Sydney*
Prentice-Hall Canada Inc., *Toronto*
Prentice-Hall Hispanoamericana, S.A., *Mexico*
Prentice-Hall of India Private Limited, *New Delhi*
Prentice-Hall of Japan, Inc., *Tokyo*
Simon & Schuster Asia Pte. Ltd., *Singapore*
Editora Prentice-Hall do Brasil, Ltda., *Rio de Janeiro*

Contents

The Contributors

Deborah G. Ancona	*MIT*
Robert A. Baron	*RPI*
Jean M. Bartunek	*Boston College*
Max H. Bazerman	*Northwestern University*
Joel Brockner	*Columbia University*
John S. Carroll	*MIT*
Robert Folger	*Tulane University*
Robert L. Kahn	*University of Michigan*
Roderick M. Kramer	*Stanford University*
Edward J. Lawler	*University of Iowa*
Joanne Martin	*Stanford University*
James R. Meindl	*SUNY Buffalo*
J. Keith Murnighan	*University of Illinois*
Margaret A. Neale	*Northwestern University*
Gregory B. Northcraft	*University of Arizona*
Barry M. Staw	*UC Berkeley*
Robert I. Sutton	*Stanford University*
Tom R. Tyler	*UC Berkeley*
Karl E. Weick	*University of Michigan*
Batia Wiesenfeld	*Columbia University*

Preface

As someone trained in social psychology, I have long claimed that it is the root of all knowledge. Philosophy, anthropology, political science, economics, sociology—they are all simple derivatives of social psychology. I have also felt for some time that the most important work in organizational behavior came from researchers trained in social psychology. Both ideas have something to do with personal preferences, professional commitment, and possibly a need for justification. While I have not made much headway with the first idea (no one seems to take it seriously), this volume is a result of the second.

My first impulse to shift these attitudes and beliefs into something behavioral and concrete was the result of a question posed by my friend and colleague, Dave Whetten. He was looking forward to the editorship of the *Academy of Management Review* and asked whether I had any ideas for a possible special issue. I suggested that we do one on social psychology in organizations. Dave soon realized that he controlled only 12 issues of the journal and precious few degrees of freedom, none of which could be devoted to my idea.

Things stayed in limbo until the spring of 1990. Two conference series—the Asilomar conference on organizations and the social psychological conferences at Nags Head, North Carolina—provided the spark for me to start thinking operationally again, this time in the form of a conference and a book.

We eventually held our conference at the Center for Advanced Study in the Behavioral Sciences in Stanford, California, in June of 1991. Since I thought that the book was the important thing, I viewed the conference primarily as a vehicle for ensuring that people would actually write their chapters. Thus, everyone was expected to have a first draft of their chapter at the start of the conference. Most people did. Those who did not felt considerable social pressure; one author even brought along a computer and a printer to continue writing.

Our conference became an important event itself. The atmosphere at the Center and the intellectual and social camaraderie that developed within the group far exceeded my expectations. The conference became an occasion for people who shared similar philosophies and professional goals to interact with one another—critically but constructively—and discuss topics near and dear to them. Although they sang different songs, their styles were much alike. Ideational discord was combined with and dominated by interpersonal and philosophical harmony, and the combined presentations made for a wonderful concert.

THE AUTHORS' TASKS

For the conference presentations and the chapters, I asked each author to present a conceptual summary of all of his or her research. Authors were directed to reflect on what they had done and try to make sense of it in a single, not-too-lengthy chapter. Chapters were supposed to be both reflective and substantive. I expected that they would naturally include basic issues from social psychology and their consequences in organizations.

Early in my contacts with the authors, I made the mistake of describing the chapters as "conceptual autobiographies." The mistake was in not emphasizing that I was much more interested in the conceptual than the autobiographical. As a result, it took several directives to move some people away from inclinations toward intense self-descriptions, from papers that might have been dominated by "The first study I ever did was . . ." and "What I did last summer." Some authors were tremendously responsive; others resisted the shift as they held out hope for the opportunity to write their autobiography before its time.

My actual intent was to encourage these productive, creative researchers to step back from their work and reflect on its conceptual contributions. This idea stemmed from my alternative career in photography, in which this kind of reflection is common since that field's dominant mode of discussion and instruction is critique. Although critiques can be gutwrenching experiences when people do not know how to be constructive, they compel you to consider seriously and thoughtfully why you have done what you have done—and to explain it convincingly. For many artists, the creative process can be so engrossing that it is easy to lose sight, at least momentarily, of the basic purpose. Critiques jar you back to a rediscovery or revision of your underlying idea. They force you to be self-critical and to conceptualize what you have actually produced rather than what you had hoped for when you started. They also provide an opportunity for your work to tell you something about who you are.

I hoped that a similar process of introspection and critique would be illuminating for this book's authors and, consequently, its readers. When presented with the idea, everyone was intrigued. After people had reflected on the possible enormity of the task, however, there were some different reactions. Potential impediments included the following: (1) Their work fell into several distinct areas, making it difficult for them to conceptualize everything in one chapter; (2) they had simply done too many projects to summarize them easily in a single chapter; (3) they had already completed a related summary of some or all of their work; and (4) they were so focused on one set of ideas that they wanted to continue to pursue them, even if this excluded much of their other previous work. Nevertheless, all of the chapters retained an approach that might be called "conceptual sensemaking." They all focus on important issues and, in addition to emphasizing and documenting their importance, show us how our knowledge base in these selected areas has progressed.

THE RESULTS

The final set of chapters, then, varies along several dimensions. Some authors took the task to heart and attempted a comprehensive conceptual summary of their research programs. Others wrote about issues that were most exciting to them at the time. Still others selected one cohesive portion from their body of work and presented a conceptualization of it.

Some chapters draw a direct, explicit tie between social psychology and organizations; others reveal these influences implicitly. Some chapters address a particular issue; others draw from several related areas to make a basic point. As a result, the chapters and their authors are consistent in many ways, including that they all reflect social psychology's methodological philosophies; they all address individual phenomena in organizations; and they all had to deal with the same strong-willed editor.

As a first-time editor, I learned that the improvements my colleagues could make from the first to the last drafts of their chapters were remarkable. The rough edges and disconnected but interesting ideas in the first versions of these chapters were magically transformed into cohesive, compelling chapters. (This never seems to happen with my own work.) As a result, the final version of this volume is a revelation. Just as the conference achieved far more than I had originally expected, so, too, do the last drafts of the chapters. The chapters are rich evocations of the latest thinking of each of the authors and stand at the forefront of the conceptual research in our field.

At the same time, some of my secondary hopes for the project were fulfilled. The authors themselves coordinated some of the material in their chapters, commenting on each other's drafts and providing constructive solutions to avoid potentially overlapping material. More importantly, when the project was almost over, one author said, "Writing it helped me understand what I do." I hope that this sense of discovery, which was one of my original goals for the project, will make the chapters fresh and exciting reading.

As a whole, the chapters document how a combination of creative theoretical insights and rigorous research can advance our basic knowledge base. These chapters represent the state of the field of social psychology in organizations, revealing where we have recently been and promising where we may soon be. At the same time, they provide models for what active research programs can accomplish.

A WORD OF THANKS

As with any project, many people contributed. Most of all, I would like to thank the people who wrote this book—they clearly contributed the most. They have been contributing important ideas and creative research to our field for many years. Hopefully, any additional attention they receive from their chapters in this volume will provide them with a little more recognition for their contributions to the field.

For the duration of this project, the contributors tolerated an editor who imposed strong standards on their thinking and particularly their writing, and they did not complain. They were easy to work with; they worked well with each other at the conference; they were fun to have dinner with; and they were on time (or close to it) with their drafts.

Several people and a couple of institutions were helpful in coordinating everything at the conference, including Bob Sutton, Kim Elsbach, the Hong Kong Flower Lounge, Hotel California, Linda Ginzel, Rod Kramer, Joanne Martin, and especially the staff at the Center for Advanced Study in the Behavioral Sciences (particularly Bob Scott, Kay Holm, and Shannon Greene). Dick Scott and Bibb Latane provided important role models for how to conduct a small conference. We received financial support from the College of Commerce and Business Administration here at the University of Illinois.

On the publishing side of things, Alison Reeves continues to be the model of the perfect editor. The writing of all of our chapters was superbly assisted by the editorial work of Frank Guthrie, Maureen Tan, Maureen Wilson, and Ruth Yontz. Elizabeth Keegan, Ruth Yontz, and Patricia Daly critiqued and sharpened the writing throughout. As with all good editors, they not only improved our English; they also improved our thinking.

I would like to finish by dedicating this book to its authors. As a group, they represent the best of academia. They do research that combines theory and empiricism. They have voracious curiosity, and they are socially conscious. In short, they are simply a fine group of people. Working with them has been a delightful task.

J. Keith Murnighan
Champaign, Illinois

Social Psychology
in Organizations

CHAPTER ONE

Theory and Research in Social Psychology and Organizations

J. Keith Murnighan
University of Illinois at Urbana–Champaign

Social psychology is a discipline that "attempts to understand and explain the thought, feeling, or behavior of individuals who are influenced by the actual, imagined, or implied presence of others" (Allport, 1985). As a field that draws from both psychology and sociology, it combines the study of individuals (their actions, cognitions, emotions, and fantasies) with an emphasis on context (other individuals, their immediate space, the greater society, etc.). The social psychology of organizations uses the theories, methods, and philosophy of social psychology to study organizations and organizational phenomena. As a multidisciplinary hybrid, its inherently holistic approach means that its research can fulfill our hopes of achieving comprehensive understandings of important social phenomena.

This volume documents some of the theoretical and empirical progress in this fledgling field. It provides a set of clear examples of the scientific advances a holistic approach can produce. The chapters include reviews, distillations, and conceptualizations of several noteworthy research programs in the social psychology of organizations. The authors all take a social psychological approach as they address the dynamics of organization. Collectively, they provide the basis for an argument that many of the best examples of theory and research in the field of micro organizational behavior come from the social psychological study of organizations.

Most of the authors have been trained as social psychologists; all have worked primarily within the social psychological tradition. They present a diverse set of ideas, theories, and empirical findings focusing on organizations and organizational phenomena. The underlying premise and driving force for this project was to use their work to show that combining the firm foundations of a basic discipline with a view toward potential application can generate ideas, conceptualizations, and findings that simultaneously contribute to substantial theoretical development *and* the possibility for societally relevant application.

SOCIAL AND THEORETICAL DISPARITY

The concept of disparity is a basic but unmentioned theoretical element in much of social psychology and in many of the chapters in this volume. (John Carroll's first draft, for instance, noted that the work on decision making in criminal justice organizations in the 1960s and 1970s often focused on disparities, particularly among and between juries' and judges' decisions.) *Social* disparity refers to the simple but essential social fact that people perceive the same situation differently. Broadly speaking, social disparities can be attributed to a variety of interpersonal, social psychological reactions, including different definitions, conceptualizations, or ideas of what is happening and why; different motives of varying strength that may influence reactions to the situation; and different strategies or styles to cope with internal and external forces. People are different; their views of a situation differ; and understanding the process and outcomes of these social disparities is an underlying force in the social sciences in general and in the social psychology of organizations in particular.

In strong situations (e.g., Mischel, 1977; Monson, Hesley, & Chernick, 1982), people react in similar ways: They are so affected by the situation and its contingencies that they seem to have little choice in how to react. In weak situations, on the other hand, people have considerable latitude and exhibit wide variation in their reactions. Thus, social disparities have their greatest effect in weak rather than strong situations, which limit the opportunity for disparity by stimulating more universal reactions. Organizations are a mix of strong and weak situations—a broader claim than Davis–Blake and Pfeffer's (1989, p. 387) assertion that "most organizational settings are strong situations." Weak organizational situations, then, give social disparities their greatest play and allow them considerable force in determining what eventually transpires.

Both strong and weak organizational situations, on the other hand, are open to *theoretical* disparities, in which our previous theoretical ideas about underlying social processes do not match our observations, leading to the necessity for new conceptualizations. Organizational behavior is a young science based on a set of preliminary theories that are, by their very nature, still developing. Thus, the fact that the chapters in this book repeatedly identify theoretical disparities is critical, as theoretical disparities are an essential element in the acceleration of the field's development. By highlighting where we have gone wrong, we have a better chance of more appropriately redirecting our efforts. In addition to identifying where and how our elementary theoretical conceptions do not apply, the authors have taken the next step and formulated new conceptualizations to replace them.

THE COUNTERINTUITIVE

During the 1970s, when many of this volume's authors were receiving their graduate training, social psychology placed great emphasis on the counterintuitive (e.g., Aronson & Carlsmith, 1968). Theories and results that were counterintuitive were considered more valuable and more important than theories and results that simply reiterated common sense. The most obvious example was the ubiquity of cognitive dissonance theory, and its relative, attribution theory, which constantly emphasized the counterintuitive.

Not surprisingly, counterintuitive theories and results began to take a foot-hold in organizational behavior as well. The early days of our field required a commonsensical enumeration of what was known and understood about the dynamics of organization. But later, particularly with the appearance of Weick's (1969) first edition of *The Social Psychology of Organizing*, counterintuitive ideas became both credible and valuable in organizational behavior.

Why such an emphasis on the counterintuitive? One reason is that counterintuitive events are another disparity, this time between what we intuitively expect and what actually happens. Counterintuitives are simply more interesting phenomena than those that conform to common sense. They also require a more elaborate, deeper understanding of complex social phenomena. If we assume that the social sphere is not unidirectional, that it is not simple, that understanding ourselves is difficult, and that understanding the social domain beyond ourselves is even more difficult, counterintuitive theories and research results become a necessary building block for social scientific advances. They also help to extend the boundaries of common sense.

Although the authors of this volume often focus on social disparities, their research has more frequently uncovered theoretical disparities, in which their ideas or findings have diverged from previous notions about the dynamics of organizational behavior. The key phenomena here are the informal structures of organizations—the thoughts, feelings, and behaviors that fall outside formal organizational rules and structures and outside the prescriptions for a rational economic person. In many cases, their observations have been counterintuitive. At a minimum, their work has stretched the bounds of what we know about organizations.

A PREVIEW

Karl Weick's discussion of the commitment and sensemaking process in organizations reinforces this emphasis on informal structures and exemplifies the tradition of the counterintuitive. Weick suggests that organizational structures are generated by early public acts that generate individual commitment and, ultimately, collective commitment by many of the individuals in an organization. This idea contradicts accepted wisdom (e.g., Thompson, 1967) that organizational structures respond to task contingencies (i.e., that organizational structures form consciously and purposively). Instead, Weick focuses on an individual's acts and their potential consequences for the collective. Can one person's early actions, based on little information of what might eventually follow, influence organizational traditions? Weick's chapter shows that they can. He documents the process and impact of individual action on subsequent individual commitment and its potential contagion throughout an organization.

In a similar way, John Carroll posits that utility and uncertainty models in decision making simply cannot predict how decisions are made in rich organizational environments. The rational, purposive view of human organization is seriously discrepant from the reality of organizational life and organizational decision making. Thus, in his chapter, rationality gives way to reality, and attributional analyses of the decision-making process incorporate multiple perspectives and dynamic interactions over time. In the process, he changes our conception of organizational decision making from a potentially overwhelming theoretical and empirical task to one that can benefit from incremental investigations that recognize the complexities of a particular context (in this case, parole decisions and nuclear power plants).

In like fashion, Robert Baron's chapter opens new vistas on the effects of subtle situational cues. Is it possible that lighting or fragrance can alter a work environment enough to make a difference in performance? The lighting question was one of the issues that drove the original Hawthorne study and, with today's advanced technologies, lends itself to socioorganizational theorizing at its most basic. The findings on fragrance—a topic that, until now, has been ignored in favor of the other senses—are truly surprising. In his chapter, Baron shows how what we might think of as the weakest aspects of a situation can still have significant effects on basic organizational processes.

James Meindl's chapter focuses on the processes of leadership attribution and notes another disparity from accepted wisdom. If organizational members and organizational researchers divest themselves of the idea that the antecedents of organizational outcomes are leaders and their personalities, and focus instead on the cognitions that organizational events generate, then, Meindl argues, we might be able to disabuse ourselves of the tremendously seductive romance of leadership. Meindl argues that our romantic cognitions are the major reason that leaders get credit for positive results. He suggests, in essence, that leadership attributions are like optical illusions. A leader's personality is much less important than us seeing him or her in the context of an organization. Thus, people's expectations of a leader are more critical in molding their attributions than any particular action a leader might perform. And these easy but essentially incorrect attributions (reinforcing the dominance of personal rather than situational attributions) drive organizational action more than any individual leader's particular behavior.

Joel Brockner and Batia Wiesenfeld's chapter addresses the important issue of employee layoffs. Rather than concentrating on the causes of layoffs or their effects on those out of work, their chapter focuses on those who remain in the organization and considers whether layoffs might have psychological consequences that will limit downsizing's effectiveness in turning around a floundering organization. Their work shows how basic social psychological theories (including those pertaining to procedural justice, attribution, intrinsic motivation, and stress) may help explain the variability in survivors' work performance and organizational commitment.

Tom Tyler addresses fundamental social disparities and how they naturally lead to social conflict and, ultimately, to the need for authority. The irony is that although people turn to authorities to regulate the interaction of their disparate preferences and desires, they simultaneously try to undercut these authorities whenever they can. Tyler points out how perceptions of legitimacy, organizational commitment, and group identification can act as alternatives to authority and still overcome the dysfunctions wrought by individual self-interest. His emphasis focuses on the influences of groups on individuals, particularly because individuals seek respect, status, resources, and self-esteem from their group memberships. He shows how standing (do you get respect?), trust (are authorities actually benevolent?), and neutrality (are authorities unbiased?)—all forces that can drive a group and its members away from destructive disparity—can lead to in-group contributions, organizational commitment, and social survival.

Robert Folger's chapter deals with the resentment and indignation that result from treatment that contradicts expectations. When disparities in outcome and procedure are both unexpected, people tend to react negatively. When the final, objective result would not have changed, however, even with more reasonable, fair, or considerate procedures, rancor and resentment may not surface so strongly. His Dual Obligations model—whereby people are expected or obligated to deal fairly with one another, even if the outcome is negative, and if it is unavoidably negative, to treat the victim with dignity—develops from a continuous mixing of theoretical inquiry, laboratory experiments, and field research. Folger's combination of theory with empirical work has allowed each to provide a strong foundation for the other. The result is a well-articulated model that can explain workers' reactions to mistreatment and when and why resentment may actually surface.

Max Bazerman shows how people's perceptions of outcomes can be inconsistent and personally dysfunctional. For instance, when conditions improve for everyone in a group, but more for some than others, people whose outcomes have not improved as much as others see the disparity between the two subgroups rather than the overall improvement. Thus, they feel unfairly treated. They do not stop to realize that on an absolute rather than a relative scale, their outcomes have increased. They take the other group's outcomes, rather than their own previous outcomes, as their referent.

Bazerman continues by discussing how people's utilities depend not only on their own payoffs but on the payoffs that others receive—contrary to standard formulations of utility theory and models of self-interest. In addition, they use these social utilities inconsistently. Even when people feel positively toward each other, they seem reluctant to sacrifice equality to maximize joint outcome: Equal outcomes have tremendous value and are often preferred to greater but unequal payoffs.

Gregory Northcraft and Margaret Neale take a decidedly different tack. Rather than identifying the dysfunctions of social and theoretical disparities, they celebrate social disparities and show how they can be turned to collective advantage. In their analysis, differences in abilities or work tendencies are essential for integration and problem solving in research (and other) collaborations. The key is recognizing these disparities as opportunities and structuring a relationship to take advantage of them—both eminently achievable goals.

Deborah Ancona's work on organizational groups highlights the theoretical disparities between longstanding models of group performance and the actual performance of effective organizational groups. Previous group research focused almost exclusively on internal group interactions without adequately considering a group's external environment. Observing both internal and external relationships—a straightforward application of systems theory (Katz & Kahn, 1978) that group research had consistently ignored—changes the picture dramatically. Different activities become necessary for effectiveness, and the inadequacy of the strict internal focus of previous models becomes readily apparent.

Roderick Kramer's chapter shows how social identity theory and research on social categorization processes can be used to understand the development of cooperation in organizations. Although our models of organizational behavior implicitly assume self-interest as a basic individual motive, Kramer notes that people who share a common group identity do not act as if they are strictly self-interested. Indeed, although society may be playing an expanded prisoner's dilemma game, where self-interest dictates noncooperation, we can look around and frequently see the exact opposite of selfish behavior. Thus, some cooperation must be occurring; people are not totally dominated by self-interest and its effects. As Kramer's chapter so aptly indicates, there is continued hope for humanity, even in organizations.

Edward J. Lawler's chapter identifies several disparities and their effects. Disparity in outcomes leads to the potential for revolution. Disparity in action or inaction among the unhappy gets resolved when people see mutual support for their revolutionary expectations. Our reactions to others depend more on our own contingencies than on the other person's—we respond to the structure of *our* situation rather than to the personal characteristics of the other actors, even as we make attributions personally. Thus, although organizational scholars and people in general may understand the interdependent nature of internal and external forces, we may not act as if we do, and we may restrict our focus inwardly.

Lawler's chapter moves from a consideration of revolutions to the use of power when disputants have more or less total power and/or when they have equal or unequal power. He contrasts the effects of two models (bilateral deterrence and conflict spirals) that generate markedly different predictions, even though each has considerable face validity. He shows how the interaction of two unequal but powerful parties can result in more conflict and more difficult conflict resolution, suggesting that powerful disparities can be particularly destructive.

Joanne Martin identifies some basic disparities in our theorizing about organizations. She suggests that our conceptions of interpersonal justice, which are firmly rooted in the restricted vision of the upper middle class, support potentially pervasive but inappropriate judgments of interpersonal equity and, simultaneously, preserve notions of organizational legitimacy—a frequent taken-for-granted in our society. The social differences between the disadvantaged and the well off (in outcomes, opportunities, etc.) cause the disadvantaged to perceive that equity is rare and that organizations are illegitimate—both viewpoints that our theories and much of our research have systematically ignored or distorted. Her chapter suggests that if we want to create *general* theories of organizational behavior, we need to broaden our focus to consider more diverse populations and philosophies.

Jean Bartunek's chapter takes social psychology to the macro level and investigates broad, complex issues of organizational change. Social disparities often lead to the initiation of change, and, ultimately, to conflict. Thus change processes illustrate the basic, central importance of social disparities. Managing multiple perspectives and their inherent conflict can become a gargantuan task for change agents and organizational researchers. This chapter includes descriptions of typical components of change. It also establishes a set of prescriptions to increase the chances that second-order change—wherein people's actions, expectations, and scripts change, along with organizational action patterns—can be planned and effectively implemented.

Barry Staw and Robert Sutton bring us full circle, carving out a new field, macro organizational psychology, and documenting how emotions and cognitions generate organizational structures. They highlight the social and theoretical disparities in our endeavor to understand organizational behavior. Rather than embracing multiple perspectives and wide-ranging outlooks, as many of our philosophies espouse, researchers tend toward territoriality and isolationalism, which sustain unnecessary distinctions between macro and micro organizational behavior. Their chapter is a clarion call for multidimensional approaches to organizational theory and research.

Staw and Sutton provide another important perspective on the power of broad-ranging social psychological processes to influence and establish organizational structures. For organizational behavior to achieve the status of a discipline, organizational researchers will have to become extradisciplinary and all-embracing in their empirical and theoretical approaches.

Finally, Robert Kahn's commentary chapter provides an additional perspective on this entire project. Kahn views the chapters from three distinct reference points: social psychology, the basics of organizations (e.g., work and satisfaction), and international relations. In addition to providing a wealth of insights, he outlines a research agenda for the end of the millennium. His chapter serves as a model of commentary, providing an excellent summary of many of the ideas in each of the chapters, extending these ideas further, and challenging readers to push these ideas even more. He provides a fitting cap to the book, particularly since his chapter, like the others, includes clear theoretical statements, new ideas, and new directions.

The study of social psychology in organizations resides, for the most part, in the field of organizational behavior. The study of organizational behavior, in turn, is rooted in the early traditions of scientific management (e.g., Taylor,

1911), industrial psychology (Tiffin, 1942), human relations (Follett, 1941; Roethlisberger & Dickson, 1939), administrative theory (Barnard, 1938; Fayol, 1916), theories of bureaucracy (Weber, 1947), and even in the writing of Adam Smith (1776). The early work of Lewin (1951) and March and Simon (1958) represent hallmarks in social psychology and in organizational behavior. In addition, both contributed to the beginnings of the social psychology of organizations.

The formal advent of the field came with *The Social Psychology of Organizations*, by Daniel Katz and Robert Kahn (1966), and *The Social Psychology of Organizing*, by Karl Weick (1969). In retrospect, we can easily see them as two of the most influential books in organizational behavior. Both published second editions in the late 1970s. Since then, research in this area has flourished. Until now, however, no systematic summary of the area has appeared. This volume is a first effort in that direction. It is based on the continuing notion that the grounding of a basic discipline with an interest in application makes for the best research, whether it is in the visual arts or mathematics or organizational behavior. Our collective hope is that the excitement that is implicit in each of these chapters will stimulate additional research, that the blending of social psychology and an interest in organizations will continue to flourish, and that, in so doing, we can build greater understandings for our mutual advantage.

REFERENCES

ALLPORT, G. (1985). *The Penguin dictionary of psychology* (p. 709). London: Penguin.

ARONSON, E., & CARLSMITH, J. M. (1968). Experimentation in social psychology. In G. Lindzey & E. Aronson (Eds.), *The handbook of social psychology* (Vol. 2, pp. 1–79). Reading, MA: Addison-Wesley.

BARNARD, C. I. (1938). *The functions of the executive*. Cambridge, MA: Harvard University Press.

DAVIS–BLAKE, A., & PFEFFER, J. (1989). Just a mirage: The search for dispositional effects in organizational research. *Academy of Management Review, 14*, 385–400.

FAYOL, H. (1916, 1949 translation). *General and industrial administration*. London: Sir Isaac Pitman.

FOLLETT, M. P. (1941). *Dynamic administration*. H. C. Metcalf & L. Urwick (Eds.). Bath, England: Management Publication Trust Ltd.

KATZ, D., & KAHN, R. L. (1966, 1978). *The social psychology of organizations*. New York: John Wiley.

LEWIN, K. (1951). *Field theory in social science*. D. Cartwright (Ed.). New York: Harper.

MARCH, J. G., & SIMON, H. (1958). *Organizations*. New York: John Wiley.

MISCHEL, W. (1977). The interaction of person and situation. In D. Magnusson and N. S. Endler (Eds.), *Personality at the crossroads: Current issues in interactional psychology* (pp. 333–352). Hillsdale, NJ: Erlbaum.

MONSON, T. C., HESLEY, J. W., & CHERNICK, L. (1982). Specifying when personality traits can and cannot predict behavior: An alternative to abandoning the attempt to predict single-act criteria. *Journal of Personality and Social Psychology, 43*, 385–399.

ROETHLISBERGER, F. J., & DICKSON, W. J. (1939). *Management and the worker*. Cambridge, MA: Harvard University Press.

SMITH, A. (1776). *The wealth of nations*. New York: McGraw-Hill.

TAYLOR, F. W. (1911). *The principles of scientific management*. New York: Harper.

THOMPSON, J. D. (1967). *Organizations in action*. New York: McGraw-Hill.

TIFFIN, J. (1942). *Industrial psychology*. New York: Prentice Hall.

WEBER, M. (1947). *The theory of social and economic organization*. (A. M. Henderson & T. Parsons, Trans., T. Parsons, Ed.). New York: Oxford University Press.

WEICK, K. E. (1969, 1979). *The social psychology of organizing*. Reading, MA: Addison-Wesley.

CHAPTER TWO

Sensemaking in Organizations: Small Structures with Large Consequences

KARL E. WEICK

University of Michigan

A key problem in organizational inquiry is to explain how microstabilities are produced in the midst of continuing change. It is proposed that the body of work on behavioral commitment can be reformulated as a prototype of sensemaking in organizations to solve this problem. The central concept is "committed interpretation," the use of binding social action to generate richer qualitative information that stabilizes a confusing flow of events. The concept of committed interpretation suggests that people become bound to interacts rather than acts, that the form of interacts is itself committing, and that justifications of commitment tend to invoke social rather than solitary entities. These three seeds of social order enlarge and diffuse among people through enactment, imitation, proselytizing, and reification, thereby imposing order on confusion. The concept of committed interpretation provides a synthesis of several lines of micro investigation, but more importantly specifies a possible mechanism by which structuration actually occurs.

When scholars evaluate their own work, they often apply unconsciously what I will call the "Schutz Test of Comprehension." In the book *Profound Simplicity*, William Schutz made the following observation about his own writing: "When I look over the books I have written, I know exactly which parts I understood and which parts I did not understand when I wrote them. The poorly understood parts sound scientific. When I barely understood something, I kept it in scientific jargon. When I really comprehend it, I was able to explain it to anyone in language they understood. . . . Understanding evolves through three phases: simplistic, complex, and profoundly simple" (Schutz, 1979, pp. 68–69).

When I applied that same test to the second edition of my book, *The Social Psychology of Organizing* (Weick, 1979), I discovered something that Richard Hackman anticipated on March 27, 1976. Richard and I were exchanging pencilled sketches at a meeting of social psychologists to help pass the time more quickly. One of Hackman's drawings shows two gravestones, one for each of us. On his stone is the epitaph, "He saved the world," and on mine is written, "He understood the world," and at the bottom of the diagram is written, "And they both were kidding themselves."

Whether we are kidding ourselves or not, Hackman is still trying to save the world and I am still trying to understand it. What happens in my case is that my own desire to understand the world has led me to attribute the same desire to the world itself. Thus, I view organizations as collections of people trying to make sense of what is happening around them.

The clearest parts of the organizing book (Weick, 1979) were about the process of understanding and included such ideas as (1) understanding involves the tradeoffs among generality, accuracy, and simplicity (pp. 35–42); (2) cause loops create predictability (pp. 74–77); (3) experience is stored in cause maps (pp. 138–143); (4) order is enacted into the world in ways that resemble self-fulfilling prophecies (pp. 159–164); (5) it takes a complex sensor to understand a complex world (pp. 188–193); and (6) sensemaking is a retrospective process (pp. 194–201).

Behind these ideas were remnants of a mindset that dates back to my dissertation. That mindset originated as an interest in cognitive dynamics (Markus & Zajonc, 1985, pp. 139–141), specifically the effects of cognitive dissonance on performance. Cognitive conflict was the independent variable that was hypothesized to have an effect on performance, because performance would be the means by which the conflict could be resolved.

In the study designed to test this idea (Weick, 1964), people agreed to do a difficult concept attainment task after they learned that they would get less reward for their participation than they expected (see Zanna, 1973 for a tighter version of this study). Those who were deprived most severely rated the subsequent task more interesting and were three times more productive at performing it than were people who felt less deprived. At the time, I felt that the severely deprived people had to resolve a disturbing set of cognitions: I came here to get the rewards they promised me, but I didn't get those rewards, yet I'm still participating. How come? Their answer was, because this is such an interesting task. That answer is actually a complex mixture of prospective and retrospective sensemaking. By working hard and solving more problems, they created a situation that confirmed the sensibleness of agreeing to participate in the first place. Ontology and epistemology were woven together out of cognitive necessity.

What continues to interest me about that study is that not only does it capture the effect of cognition on action, it also captures the effect of action on cognition. It does the latter more by accident than by design. Even though I designed the study to create cognitive dissonance, I also accidentally created the conditions later found to induce strong behavioral commitment. It will be recalled that three conditions are necessary for behavioral commitment: choice, an irreversible action, and public awareness of the action (Salancik, 1977). The dissertation experiment was designed so that people experienced several sources of dissonance. The study was built this way on the assumption that dissonant cognitions are additive and that the more dissonance, the stronger the pressure to do something about it. So negative features were added until the breaking point was reached, when a few people would refuse to participate.

At the time, I was more interested in the number of dissonant elements and did not pay much attention to their content. But now it is clear that the dilemma I created involved *choice* (the person could stay or leave, and four people chose to leave), *irreversibility* (once people agreed to stay, they could not back out halfway through the task), and *public awareness* of the decision (I, the experimenter, knew what the person chose to do, how that person performed, and could tell other people.) So the person made a clear commitment to work on a task, a commitment whose full content was not grasped at the beginning. The person gained a deeper understanding of what that original decision involved when he started to work on that task. Closer attention to the task accompanied by increased effort revealed unsuspected attractions that were given additional substance and credibility by hard work. Hard work literally built the convincing reasons that justified the choice to participate.

Notice the way in which the causal arrow is reversed when this study is reinterpreted as an instance of behavioral commitment. Now, cognition in the form of justification becomes the dependent variable and action is the independent variable from which the person draws inferences about what is happening. Having performed the concept attainment task successfully, the person infers that he must have liked the task, which then becomes the reason the person agreed to participate in the first place—even though he had no idea what the task would be when making the choice. Action affects cognition, which is the opposite direction of causality from that implied by dissonant cognitions affecting action.

The experiment mixes together the hot cognition of conflict resolution with the cold cognition of inference. That interpretation is obviously clearer in hindsight than it was at the time of execution. And both themes are largely buried by a rather heavy-handed set of experimental operations. Nevertheless, a prototype of sensemaking is implied in that study. The purpose of this chapter is to elaborate that prototype in context of organizations and show how it links with other work on sensemaking.

Before we explore the key ideas in depth, let's preview the argument. If we generalize the experiment, it suggests that behavioral commitment is a stimulus to build cosmologies and coherent world views out of whatever resources are at hand. Whenever people act, their actions may become binding if those actions occur in a context of high choice, high irreversibility, and high visibility. If action occurs under these conditions, then subsequent events may be enacted in the service of justification. Thus, justification can become an important source of social structure, culture, and norms. For example, Alan Meyer's (1982) important work on how hospitals adapted to the environmental jolt of a doctor's strike can be read as a series of commitments that were justified by the consolidation and articulation of a consistent culture, strategy, and structure. Each hospital became a more distinct, coherent entity after administrations chose publicly to cope with the strike by weathering the storm, experimenting with contingency plans, or monitoring controls more closely.

Organizations begin to materialize when rationales for commitment become articulated. Since the decisions that stimulate justification originate in small-scale personal acts, organizational rationales often originate in the service of self-justification. Only later does justification become redefined as collective intention. Justifications can easily be transformed into organizational goals because these goals themselves are so general. But collective goals can best be understood as embellishments of earlier direct efforts to validate the soundness of individual commitments on a smaller scale.

From the perspective of commitment, organizations are interesting for a specific reason. To see this, consider Daft's (1986, p. 9) definition of an organization as a social entity that is a goal-directed, deliberately structured activity system with an identifiable boundary. Like most scholars, Daft views an organization as a deliberately structured tool. What is left unspecified is the precise nature of that tool. And that is where commitment becomes important. Organizations are viewed as unique social forms that embody choice, visibility, and irrevocability. Goal direction itself takes on a different meaning: "Goals are discovered through a social process involving argumentation and debate in a setting where justification and legitimacy play important roles" (Anderson, 1983, p. 214).

Thus, organizational action is as much goal interpreted as it is goal directed, and the language of goals is indistinguishable from the language of justification.

Since binding choices can affect the tasks we are attracted to, the reasons that move us, the values we seek to realize, the plans we admire, and the people with whom we align ourselves, commitment helps us to understand organizational life. Organizations are filled with potential committing conditions. In most organizations, people do things that others see (e.g., Tetlock, 1985); people make choices and decisions (e.g., empowerment); choices commit resources to programs and structures that are not reversible; participation is used to raise ownership ("ownership" is simply a synonym for commitment); sunk costs are treated as a variable to be justified rather than a given to be dismissed; and the motivational backdrop for all employment is portrayed as a decision to participate, a decision to produce, and a psychological contract.

Despite the potential sweep of commitment and sensemaking, both concepts refer to events that have relatively small beginnings. Both commitment and sensemaking are promising concepts that can broaden the micro side of macro topics (O'Reilly, 1991, p. 449) and offset the current dominance of macro perspectives in organizational analysis.

To illustrate this promise, the remainder of this chapter addresses the following issues. First, we look more closely at the nature of sensemaking and at equivocality as the basic problem that organizations confront. After an overview of the nature of sensemaking we move, in the second section, to an elaboration of the idea of sensemaking as committed interpretation. After reviewing key ideas about interpretation and commitment, we propose a model by which these two processes interact. In the third section we take a closer look at the commitment process itself and show how interaction is inherently committing. We then look at justification in the fourth section and suggest that it creates social structure in a manner reminiscent of the documentary method of interpretation. In the fifth section, we examine the ways in which justifications are validated, a step that is crucial for organizational analysis even though it is usually ignored. We conclude with a brief discussion of implications.

THE NATURE OF SENSEMAKING

The central problem of sensemaking is best conveyed by an analogy between sensemaking and the game of Mastermind (Fay, 1990). The object of Mastermind is for a codebreaker to duplicate the exact pattern of colored pegs inserted into holes that has been created by a codemaker but is concealed from the codebreaker by a shield. The codebreaker ventures hypotheses as to what the pattern might be and, on the basis of information supplied by the codemaker, refines the hypothesis until the codebreaker's hypothesis exactly matches the codemaker's original pattern.

Mastermind is precisely what sensemaking is not. People cannot be sure there is a mastercode to be discovered, nor can they be sure what the nature of the code might be, nor even if there is some order in the first place. Even if people do discover the code, they can never be sure they have done so since there is nothing equivalent to the removal of the shield at the end of the game, which reveals the concealed code. Although the basic materials in the Mastermind game are pegs, colors, and holes, the person engaged in sensemaking does not know a priori what the exact building blocks are. "What the world is made of is itself a question which must be answered in terms of the available conceptual resources of science at a particular time" (Fay, 1990, p. 36).

People who try to make sense under these conditions have to differentiate and determine the nature of the materials they are working with, have to look for a unifying order without any assurance that there is a preexisting order in these materials, have to decide how to represent this order, and have to play indefinitely, never knowing whether they have discovered a unifying order.

The task of sensemaking resembles more closely the activity of cartography. There is some terrain that mapmakers want to represent, and they use various modes of projection to make this representation. What they map, however, depends on where they look, how they look, what they want to represent, and their tools for representation (Monmonier, 1991). The crucial point in cartography is that "there is no 'One Best Map' of a particular terrain. For any terrain there will be an indefinite number of useful maps, a function of the indefinite levels and kinds of description of the terrain itself, as well as the indefinite number of modes of representation and uses to which they can be put" (Fay, 1990, p. 37). The terrain is not itself already mapped such that the job of the sensemaker is to discover this preexisting map. "For mapmakers the idea of a pre-ordered world has no place or meaning" (Fay, 1990, p. 37).

It is the job of the sensemaker to convert a world of experience into an intelligible world. That person's job is not to look for the one true picture that corresponds to a pre-existing, preformed reality. The picture of sensemaking that emerges is not one of the tidy world of Mastermind. Instead, the picture that is suggested is "that there is nobody here but us scratching around trying to make our experience and our world as comprehensible to ourselves in the best way we can, that the various kinds of order we come up with are a product of our imagination and need, not something dictated to us by Reality Itself. There isn't any One True Map of the earth, of human existence, of the universe, or of Ultimate Reality, a Map supposedly embedded inside these things; there are only maps we construct to make sense of the welter of our experience, and only us to judge whether these maps are worthwhile for us or not" (Fay, 1990, p. 38).

The important points implied by the idea of sensemaking as cartography are the indefinite number of plausible maps that can be constructed, the role of imagination and need in the determination of the projections actually used, and the fact that the activity of sensemaking is largely social ("there is nobody here but *us* scratching around"). The problem of sensemaking is compounded because the terrain keeps changing and the task is to carve out some momentary stability in this continuous flow (Becker, 1986, p. 29). We expand on these points in the next section.

Equivocality in organizational life

Organizations resemble puzzling terrain because they lend themselves to multiple, conflicting interpretations, all of which are plausible (Daft & MacIntosh, 1981). In this equivocal situation of confusion, people are not sure what questions to ask, nor do they expect clear answers even if they do know the right questions (Daft & Lengel, 1986, p. 557). To reduce equivocality, people do not need larger quantities of information. Instead, they need richer qualitative information. "Information richness is defined as the ability of information to change understanding within a time interval. Communication transactions that can overcome different frames of reference or clarify ambiguous issues to change understanding in a timely manner are considered rich. Communications that require a long time to enable understanding or that cannot overcome different perspectives are lower in richness. In a sense, richness pertains to the learning capacity of a communication" (Daft & Lengel, 1986, p. 560). Information richness tends to covary with the extent of face-to-face personal interaction, which is why map making tends to be social.

The dominant form that equivocality takes in organizations is suggested by Gergen's (1982, pp. 62–65) three premises for constructivism, all of which focus on the multiple meanings of action.

1.   The identification of any given action is subject to infinite revision.
     There is no such thing as an ultimate definition, partly because events occur in a continually emerging context that changes the meaning of earlier events, and partly because events occur in an open-ended retrospective context in which all kinds of prior personal and societal history can be invoked to explain what is hap-

pening right now. There are no iron-clad rules or logics that guarantee that we will avoid the temptations to infinitely revise.

2.   The anchor point for any given identification relies on a network of interdependent and continuously modifiable interpretations.

What any action means is seldom self-evident; there is no such thing as a fixed unequivocal observable that allows for "proper identification." Since identification is determined by context, and since context is infinitely expandable into the future and the past, it is not clear which contextual indicators can be trusted among sensemakers. This issue is one that largely has to be negotiated. And whatever agreement people hammer out usually unravels as new events occur and old meanings crumble.

3.   Any given action is subject to multiple identifications, the relative superiority of which is problematic.

As the number of observers increases, so too does the range of contextual events in which an action can be embedded. And, in the absence of unequivocal observables, there are no grounds other than some kind of consensus or some exercise of power (Smircich & Morgan, 1982) to stabilize what people confront and what it means. To call something "a problem" is no more privileged and no easier to sustain than is the proposal that something is "an opportunity." To make things even more complicated, either proposal can set in motion responses that confirm the label.

Sensemaking in organizational life

If we begin to synthesize these separate images of commitment, retrospect, mastermind, map making, equivocality, rich communication media, and social construction into a coherent perspective on sensemaking, that synthesis would sound a lot like one developed by Morgan, Frost, and Pondy (1983). Sensemaking in the broadest sense is a metaphor that "focuses attention upon the idea that the reality of everyday life must be seen as an ongoing 'accomplishment,' which takes particular shape and form as individuals attempt to create order and make retrospective sense of the situations in which they find themselves. . . . [I]ndividuals are seen as engaged in ongoing processes through which they attempt to make their situations rationally accountable to themselves and others. . . . The sensemaking metaphor encourages an analytical focus upon the processes through which individuals create and use symbols; it focuses attention upon the study of the symbolic processes through which reality is created and sustained. Individuals are not seen as living *in*, and acting out their lives in relations *to*, a wider reality, so much as creating and sustaining images of a wider reality, in part to rationalize what they are doing. They realize their reality, by 'reading into' their situation patterns of significant meaning" (Morgan et al., 1983, p.24).

In the remainder of this chapter, we pay close attention to several themes in this description:

1.   Reality is an ongoing accomplishment: Sensemaking is about flows, a continually changing past, and variations in choice, irrevocability, and visibility that change the intensity of behavioral commitments.

2. People attempt to create order: Through social comparison, expectations, and action, flows become stabilized momentarily.
3. Sensemaking is a retrospective process: Remembering and looking back are a primary source of meaning.
4. People attempt to make situations rationally accountable: Justifications are compelling sources of meaning because they consist of socially acceptable reasons.
5. Symbolic processes are central in sensemaking: Presumptions about patterns that underlie concrete actions constrain interpretation.
6. People create and sustain images of wider reality: Maps are pragmatic images that provide temporary guides for action.
7. Images rationalize what people are doing: Images of reality derive from rationalizations of action, and this mechanism is a central theme in this chapter.

SENSEMAKING AS COMMITTED INTERPRETATION

The description of sensemaking constructed by Morgan, Frost, and Pondy imposed a preliminary order on elements of the sensemaking process. In this section, we impose additional order with the proposal that sensemaking is a process of committed interpretation.

This proposal enlarges on a mechanism first identified by Salancik and Pfeffer (1978), which they described this way: "Commitment binds an individual to his or her behavior. The behavior becomes an undeniable and unchangeable aspect of the person's world, and when he makes sense of the environment, behavior is the point on which constructions or interpretations are based. This process can be described as a rationalizing process, in which behavior is rationalized by referring to features of the environment which support it. Such sense-making also occurs in a social context in which norms and expectations affect the rationalizations developed for behavior, and this can be described as a process of legitimating behavior. People develop acceptable justifications for their behavior as a way of making such behavior meaningful and explainable" (p. 231).

Although this mechanism was discussed (and buried) within a larger discussion of a social information processing approach to job attitudes, I want to highlight and develop it because it provides a compact explanation of sensemaking in organizations. The elaboration developed in this chapter is labeled "committed interpretation," both to highlight the social, symbolic nature of sensemaking and to designate binding action as the object of sensemaking. The concept of committed interpretation combines two mindsets, one involving interpretation and the other involving commitment.

The interpretation mindset

The interpretation mindset is represented by the W. I. Thomas theorem: "If men define situations as real, they are real in their consequences" (Thomas & Thomas, 1928, p. 572). As Shalin (1986, p. 12) suggests, this theorem closely resembles William James's pragmatist dictum that, "We need only in cold blood

ACT as if the thing in question were real, and keep acting as if it were real, and it will infallibly end by growing in such a connection with our life that it will become real'' (1890, Vol. II, p. 321). In both cases an equivocal situation becomes more stable when definitions are imposed and one among many patterns in the flow of reality is isolated.

What is important to recall is that Thomas, unlike James, did *not* intend the theorem to portray reality construction as a process that varied from individual to individual. Instead, he emphasized that definitions should vary from one *group* to another, that different tribes should define the same situation in different ways, and that things should not have the same meaning for different people in different periods of time and in different parts of the country. The symbolic environment from which definitions arise is always a shared environment and the outlook itself is always a shared outlook that cannot be ignored. The sensemaker's ''actions always refer to the world that is already there, the intersubjective universe existing on the intersection of objectively established group perspectives'' (Shalin, 1986, p. 13).

The suggestion that the collective condition of human existence is the source of meaning is made explicit in Porac, Thomas, and Baden–Fuller's (1989, p. 398) summary of the four key assumptions in the interpretative approach. These four assumptions comprise the interpretation mindset. Paraphrased, the key ideas include the following:

1. *Activities and structures are determined partly by micro momentary actions of members.* We emphasize the justification of committed actions as our key micro momentary action.
2. *Action is based on interpretations of cues; these interpretations are externalized by concrete activities.* We emphasize that committed action sets the stage for interpretation by narrowing attention to those cues that suggest potential justification, and that justified action then serves to validate and support whatever justification has been chosen to interpret the committed action.
3. *Meaning is constructed when people link received cues with existing cognitive structures.* We emphasize retrospect and the documentary method as the means by which this interpretive process unfolds.
4. *People are reflective and can verbalize the content, and sometimes the process, of their interpretations.* We take seriously people's accounts of how they accomplish interpretation, mindful, however, that retrospective sensemaking involves biased reconstruction of antecedents since outcomes are known at the time reconstruction occurs. This very bias is the strength of retrospect as a method of sensemaking since it edits out false starts and imposes a spurious order on an indeterminate past. But this same editing requires that investigators observe sensemaking as it unfolds if they wish to counteract this bias, which often means that ethnography and use of personal experience are crucial sources of data about interpretation.

The problems in working with an interpretive perspective are not only those of a temptation toward subjectivism and mistaking hindsight bias for efficient information processing, but also, as Keesing (1987) has argued, underestimating the constraints imposed by context, distributed information, differentials in power, and vested interests. Each of these potential blindspots seems to have more effect on the content of justification than on the fact that behavior is the object of interpretation. Context affects the content of acceptable justifications and the choice of features of the environment that support the rationalizing. Context also has an effect on which behaviors are singled out for explanation. However, once the behavior is fixed, the process of sensemaking itself should unfold in essentially the sequence we propose in the next section.

The commitment mindset

Having specified what constitutes an interpretation mindset, we now turn briefly to an explanation of the commitment mindset. The bulk of this chapter elaborates the idea that commitment is a reference point for sensemaking. This idea was implicit in my concept attainment study (Weick, 1964) and in both editions of my organizing book (Weick, 1969, 1979) and was made more explicit by Salancik and Pfeffer (1978).

The basic ideas of commitment are these. Normally, when people act, their reasons for doing things are either self-evident or uninteresting, especially when the actions themselves can be undone, minimized, or disowned. Actions that are neither visible nor permanent are easily explained. As actions become more public and irrevocable, however, they become harder to undo; when actions are also volitional, they become harder to disown. When action is irrevocable, public, and volitional, the search for explanations becomes less casual because more is at stake. Explanations that are developed retrospectively to justify committed actions are often stronger than beliefs developed under other less involving conditions because the search to find these explanations requires more effort and more of the self is on the line. These justifications become tenacious and produce selective attention, confident action, and self-confirmation. Once formed, tenacious justifications then prefigure subsequent perception and action, which means they are often self-confirming.

Commitment focuses the sensemaking process on three things: an elapsed action, socially acceptable justification for that action, and the potential for subsequent activities to validate or threaten the justification. Thus, commitment drives interaction patterns by tying behaviors, explanations, social support, and expectations together in a causal sequence. This sequence can become a causal loop that either stabilizes or amplifies subsequent action patterns. It is these patterns that people come to label as organizational designs. Commitments lead to patterns and, ultimately, to what we see as designs.

To illustrate how the idea of commitment reshapes organizational theory, consider two examples. First, the influential garbage can model of organizations (Cohen, March, & Olsen, 1972) suggests that organizations consist of streams of people, choices, solutions, and problems that intermittently converge, more for reasons of timing than logic. The concept of commitment suggests the possibility of a third basis for order in addition to those of timing and logic. Choice may not be one of four equal determinants of organizational outcomes, as is suggested by the garbage can theory; instead, choice may be the occasion when the other three become organized. Problems, solutions, and people all are potential explanations that justify a binding choice (e.g., "I chose to fire him because he could not meet quality standards"; "We chose this line of technology because it will show the board we are serious about the future"; "We chose to move these people to Texas to bring more imagination to their operations.").

The second example hearkens back to the earlier discussion of equivocality. Staw (1980, p. 71) argues that organizations are often unclear about their goals and theories of causality, and that justification often removes some of this lack of clarity: "Under high levels of ambiguity, justification is necessary to both provide purpose for an organization's membership and rationale for parties external to the organization. In fact, organizations which face a great deal of ambiguity are frequently perceived as more effective when they have developed an elaborate or persuasive set of justifications for their particular goals and technology. . . . Thus, in many organizational settings justification can become reality: through justification, perceived sources of ambiguity can be explained away or replaced by shared meaning."

We show next how interpretation and commitment combine to produce sensemaking.

The process of committed interpretation

The model of committed interpretation is straightforward. We preview it here and explore its components in more detail in the remainder of the chapter.

Most action is social, even when the other party is only imagined or implied. This assumption has two immediate and important consequences. First, when people become bound to acts, those acts tend to be interacts rather than solitary acts (Sandelands & Weick, 1991). Second, interacts themselves generate their own conditions of commitment since each party's action is public, irrevocable, and volitional relative to the other party in the exchange. When an interact occurs in a committing context and also generates its own commitment, the action becomes bound to both parties and a search for justification intensifies.

Since the committed action is actually a committed interact, the appropriate justifications tend to invoke social entities (e.g., "We did it because our role demanded it, . . . because we are colleagues, . . . because we are in competition, . . . because we respect each other."). Social justification is the crucial step in the model for organizational theory. Commitments to interacts often are justified by explanations that reify social structure. Behavioral commitments tend to be justified by constraints and opportunities, and one of the most convenient and socially acceptable ways to package constraints and opportunities is (as in terms of) macro entities (e.g., "*They* hoped we would do it, hinted that it should be done, created the chance to do it.").

Once macro entities are invoked to justify a commitment, people continue to use them as explanations. And they urge others to use these same explanations. To support these explanations, people deploy them in a manner that resembles self-fulfilling prophecies. They expect the social world to be put together the way their justifications say it is put together, they act as if it is put together this way, and they selectively perceive what they see as if it were put together the way their justifications say. Through a mixture of reification, enactment, imitation, and proselytizing, incipient social structure is acted into the world and imposes order on that world. This process both creates new organization and reaffirms organization already in place.

Thus, straightforward, small-scale, micro behavioral commitments can have macro consequences, once we recognize five important properties of these commitments. First, they begin as commitments to social relationships rather than commitments to individual behaviors. Second, these social relationships often generate their own conditions of commitment. Third, since social relationships rather than behaviors are what people become bound to, justifications tend to invoke social entities rather than individual reasons. Fourth, reifications that justify social commitment tend to set up expectations that operate like self-fulfilling prophecies. And fifth, efforts to validate these social justifications tend to spread them to other actors.

Committed interpretation, therefore, is a sensemaking process that introduces stability into an equivocal flow of events by means of justifications that increase social order. Confused people pay closer attention to those interdependent acts that occur in conjunction with some combination of choice and/or publicity and/or irrevocability. (Commitment is an additive process that develops gradually [Salancik, 1977, p. 4].) As they become more fully bound to these interdependent actions, people are more likely to invoke some larger social entity to justify the commitment. This act of justification, which often resembles reification, invokes a presupposed order such as a role system, institution, organization, group, or imputed interest group that explains the action.

The residue from an episode of committed interpretation is a slight increase in social order plus a partial articulation of what that order consists of (e.g., role system, professional norms, group pressure, collective preference). When people act on behalf of these committed interpretations and their reified content, their actions become more orderly, more predictable, and more organized. As a result of this tightening, their actions have more impact on others and are more likely to be imitated. Thus, both the form and substance of organization become more distinct and the world momentarily becomes slightly less chaotic. And all because some action first stuck out as more public, more irrevocable, and more attached to a set of actors than were other actions.

In the remainder of this chapter, we expand on three themes mentioned in this overview of committed interpretation: interacts as the object of commitment, reification as the content of justification, and validation as the outcome of justification.

THE COMMITMENT TO INTERACTS

Commitment is a reference point for sensemaking, and the object of that commitment is a double interact, not an act. When an action by Person A evokes a specific action in Person B, an interact exists (e.g., author makes an assertion and editor criticizes assertion). If we then add in A's response to B's reaction, a double interact exists (e.g., author modifies assertion in response to criticism). Hollander and Willis (1967) argue that the double interact is the basic unit of analysis for social influence, because it can distinguish among conformity ($A_xB_yA_y$), anticonformity ($A_xB_xA_y$), independence ($A_xB_yA_x$), and uniformity ($A_xB_xA_x$).

The double interact is itself a committing context, because it contains all four variables that bind a person to action. *Volition* is present at two points, both when A takes an initial action and when A decides what to do in response to B's reaction. A's initial action is also *public,* because it is observed by B, and *explicit,* because B is able to see that a reaction is warranted. A's second action is *irrevocable* in that he or she had an opportunity to change the first act and has now responded to new information with the second action.

If we simply take the $A_1B_1A_2$ sequence one step further and add B_2 (a triple interact), we now have a sequence in which there should be more commitment to actions A_2 and B_2, because actions A_1 and B_1 created the conditions for commitment.

The potential for an interact to become a committing context when it extends to a double and triple interact may explain why it is so important to retain a *social* psychology of organizations. The smallest unit within which all four conditions of commitment can occur at the same time is the double interact. Conceivably, any action performed within this setting can dominate the actor's attention and draw justifications. If this is plausible, then whatever happens within double and triple interacts should have a disproportionately large effect on meaning and interpretation.

From interacts to collective structures

While the basic forms of interaction—the interact, double interact, and triple interact—have relevance to commitment because they embody conditions that can bind people to actions, we have said little about the content of the actions to which people become bound. This content is the sense that people feel and share.

Content becomes more salient if we reexamine the concept of collective structure (Weick, 1979, chap. 4). Allport (1962) argues that collective structure forms whenever "there is a pluralistic situation in which in order for an individual (or class of individuals) to perform some act (or have some experience) that he 'desires' to perform (or for which he is 'set') it is necessary that *another* person (or persons) perform certain acts (either similar or different and complementary to his own)" (p. 17).

Collective structures form when self-sufficiency proves problematic. This idea is the same starting point for organizational analysis that Barnard (1938) adopted in his famous analogy of men coordinating their actions to move a stone (pp. 86–89). If we translate Allport's description into the ABAB sequence of the triple interact, then all we need to do is argue that A_1 and B_1 are instrumental acts, A_2 and B_2 are consummatory acts, and that B must do B_1 if A is to enjoy A_2, and A must do A_1 if B is to enjoy B_2. Neither A nor B has direct control over their outcomes, and they must entice someone else to contribute a means activity to get their own desired outcomes. For example, editors need good manuscripts if they are to print issues of a journal on time, and authors need to have their work printed if they want to achieve wider dissemination of their ideas. The instrumental actions of writing manuscripts and providing journal space allow both parties to experience outcomes that they cannot control directly. Writing allows editors to print, and printing allows writers to influence.

When authors write and editors publish, these acts are part of longer strings of action. As writing proceeds, the author becomes bound, not just to the writing itself, but also to the subsequent steps of evaluation and dissemination. As editing proceeds, the editor becomes bound, not just to providing space for print, but to filling that space with interesting text and doing so in a timely manner. Thus, each party gets bound to a larger number of actions and contributions by other people.

These additional actions and people tend to be included in whatever justification is adopted. And this wider inclusion increases the possibility that justifications will invoke roles or other social forms as the explanation for the commitment. Commitment to interdependent behaviors, justified as roles in an emerging collective structure, sets the stage for these justifications to become entities.

In other words, people commit to and coordinate instrumental acts (means) before they worry about shared goals (Weick, 1979, pp. 91–95). But shared goals do emerge as people search for reasons that justify the earlier interdependent means to which they have become bound. And those reasons tend to be variations on the theme, "We did those things *because they were roles in a system*" (Katz & Kahn, 1978, chap. 7). Both the roles and the system that requires them (Wiley, 1988) are created and given substance when people justify a collective structure that was originally built around interdependent means.

From behavioral commitment to social commitment

Committed interpretation, thus, is distinctly social in at least three ways. First, the act that is the object of commitment tends to be a double interact rather than an act. For example, strategic conversations, defined as "verbal interactions within superior–subordinate dyads focusing on strategic generalities" (Westley, 1990, pp. 337–338), are double interacts in which top managers and middle managers co-determine strategic outcomes. Their joint efforts to synthesize feelings and frames into implemented strategy are volitional, public, irrevocable interacts that bind both parties and necessitate an explanation that justifies the relationship.

The second sense in which committed interpretation is social is that the justifications chosen to explain the committed interact are socially acceptable within the setting where the commitment occurred. For example, the interaction order among radiologists and technicians that Barley (1986) documented differed among hospitals and across time, and different rationales for dominance or cooperation were invoked in each setting.

The third sense in which committed interpretation is social is that social structure is often invoked to justify commitments. For example, social movement organizations often coalesce when "aggregates of individuals who share common grievances and attributional orientations" (Snow, Rochford, Worden, & Benford, 1986, p. 464) justify their actions by invoking silent constituents for whom they serve as agents of change. The justification lends form to these "unmobilized sentiment pools" and suggests the existence of an organizational base for expressing their discontent and pursuing their interests. The social movement becomes a social form constituted as justification for commitments to double interacts involving grievance.

In their description of sensemaking, Morgan et al. (1983) argued that images of reality tend to derive from rationalization. What we have suggested is that it is interacts rather than acts that are rationalized. This, in turn, suggests that the resulting images of reality will be social images. Previous work on individual commitment tends to overlook the degree to which commitment is grounded in social relationships and is justified by social entities. Once this possibility is entertained, then commitment becomes a more powerful tool to track sensemaking and the emergence of social structure in organizations.

THE JUSTIFICATION OF COMMITTED INTERACTS

When people justify interacts, those justifications routinely acknowledge the existence of interdependence (e.g., Zanna & Sande, 1987). The justifications lend substance to the interdependence and reify it into a social entity. For example, I can justify becoming bound to an interdependent sequence by arguing that it was expected; it was my role; it demonstrated that I trust you and am myself trustworthy; it accomplished something neither of us could have done alone; I am subordinate to you; it is our duty; we were told to do it; or we had the same interest. Each of these justifications affirms that a social act was the object of commitment, and each justification lends substance to that social entity.

The point is that reification of a collectivity justifies commitment. Having become bound to interdependent action, if the person says, "That's the way we do things in this culture, in this firm, in this family, or when women are involved," then cultures, firms, families, and gender are invoked as macro sources of micro contraints.

This line of argument resembles Knorr–Cetina's (1981) explanation of a possible linkage between micro and macro phenomena. The macro is not a distinct existential level that emerges from micro events. Instead, the macro is constructed and pursued *within* micro interaction. Micro interaction is constrained by representations of macro entities alleged to exist as a distinct layer of social reality (e.g., see avoided test in Weick, 1979, pp. 149–152). But aside from their effects as mediated through representations that are treated as if they were real, macro "entities" have no separate existential effects.

Participants "continually employ notions and engage in actions whose mutual intelligibility appears to be based upon their presupposition and knowledge of broader societal units" (Knorr–Cetina, 1981, p. 12). Thus a binding interdependent action is made intelligible and justified by presupposition of societal institutions and collective sentiments. Macro constructions such as organization, family, state, media, or market are created in micro situations, often in the form of justifications for interdependent actions ("We did it to preserve freedom, gain competitive advantage, create jobs, influence the market"), and then treated as if they were real constraints to be honored, resisted, bypassed, rationalized, reversed, or ignored.

As we will see later, reification is an *initial* move in an extended chain of validating actions, many of which lend substance to what originally was a mere presumption of social structure. As both Thomas and James made clear, presumptions taken seriously often become self-validating (see Weick, Gilfillan, & Keith, 1973, for a demonstration of this effect). When people presuppose societal institutions, expectations, constraints, and explanations that transcend the committed interact are activated and inform an institution's development.

Symbols and justification

To understand the role of reification in justification, we need to take a closer look at Morgan et al.'s (1983) suggestion that sensemaking involves "symbolic processes through which reality is created and sustained" (p. 4). To understand this phrase, we need to look both at symbols and at the way in which they become linked with concrete actions.

The content of sensemaking comes from preexisting symbols, norms, and social structures (Isaac, 1990, p. 6) that people reproduce and transform rather than create from scratch (Bhaskar, 1978, p. 13). Sensemaking itself is often described as sculpting done by a clever bricoleur (Harper, 1987, p. 74; Levi–Strauss, 1966) who uses whatever materials and tools are at hand to fashion whatever sense is needed. So, although we persist, as do Morgan et al. (1983) in using the verb *create* to describe sensemaking, we do so mindful that the activity itself is shaped by presuppositions and precedents (Smircich & Stubbart, 1985, pp. 732–733) as well as discoveries.

When Morgan et al. (1983, pp. 4–5) talk about symbols in the context of organizations, they emphasize the quality of bricolage: "The word *symbol* derives from Greek roots which combine the idea of sign, in the sense of a mark, token, insignia, means of identification, with that of a throwing and putting together. A symbol is a sign which denotes something much greater than itself, and which calls for the association of certain conscious and unconscious ideas, in order for it to be endowed with its full meaning and significance. A sign achieves the status of a symbol when it is interpreted, not in terms of strict resemblance with what is signified, but when other patterns of suggestion and meaning are 'thrown upon' or 'put together' with the sign to interpret it as part of some much wider symbolic whole. . . . Any object, action, event, utterance, concept, or image offers itself as raw material for symbol creation, at any place, and at any time."

Although organizational symbols can take many forms, the simple classification proposed by Czarniawska–Joerges and Joerges (1990) is a reasonable starting point. They suggest that people use at least three verbal tools to invest experience with meaning: labels, metaphors, and platitudes. "Labels tell *what* things are, they classify [e.g., decentralization, leadership excellence]; metaphors say *how* things are, they relate, give life [e.g., personal development as gardening, organization as garbage can]; platitudes conventionalize, they standardize and establish *what is normal* [e.g., democracy must be built anew in each generation]" (p. 339). Labels, metaphors, and platitudes link the present with the past, impose past definitions on present puzzles, and provide compelling images *if* those images are shared.

The probability of sharing is increased if socialization processes in organizations focus on language (Jablin, 1987; Louis, 1980). "Perhaps the most important context in which definitions of organizational reality are created and shaped is the socialization of new members" (Eisenberg & Riley, 1988, p. 136). Newcomers are exposed to a whole new vocabulary and grammar of symbols, jargon, ideology, attitudes, stories, private jokes, and restricted words, which shape their inclination to label events and which produce a trained incapacity to see the world differently.

Documentary method and justification

Once this vocabulary of symbols is in place, it becomes the language of justification. These symbols become linked with committed interacts through a process called the "documentary method" (Garfinkel, 1967, p. 78). Morgan et al. (1983) anticipated this process when they observed, "Symbols, when approached upon the basis of this perspective [sensemaking], assume principal significance as constructs through which individuals concretize and give meaningful form to their everyday lives" (pp. 24–25). The documentary method, which Heritage (1984, p. 84) has called the "constituent task of making sense," speaks to the linkage of concrete events with meaningful forms. The symbol simultaneously refers to the here and now and to the larger social scene, and the documentary method is the means by which these two worlds are connected.

Garfinkel (1967) defined the documentary method in the following manner: "The method consists of treating an actual appearance as 'the document of,' as 'pointing to,' as 'standing on behalf of' a presupposed underlying pattern. Not only is the pattern derived from its individual documentary evidences but the individual evidences, in their turn, are interpreted on the basis of 'what is known' about the underlying pattern. Each is used to elaborate the other" (p. 78).

Several parallels between the process of justification and the documentary method are suggested. The committed interact is the equivalent of the actual appearance or the document. The justification is the equivalent of an underlying pattern that presupposes a macro context. Neither the interact nor the underlying pattern are labeled initially. Instead, each fleshes out the other. The interact suggests a derived pattern, and the interact then takes its meaning from this derivation, which itself has become strengthened because there appears to be another tangible outcropping that exemplifies it; each is used to elaborate the other. The connection of a cryptic current interact with a presupposed pattern is the key interpretive procedure that reduces equivocality.

Leiter's (1980, pp. 165–189) extended discussion of the documentary method suggests the following nuances of this interpretive procedure. The method itself is deceptive in its apparent simplicity, since it appears to assert simply that people treat a set of appearances as standing on behalf of an underlying pattern. In the context of committed interpretation, we assert that the appearance that gets attention is a committed interact, that the pattern invoked to justify it is a feature of social structure consistent with the interact, that each elaborates the other through enactment into the world, and that through enactment into the world the pattern gains validity and the interact gains meaning. Precisely *which* pattern is likely to be invoked cannot be specified in advance simply because the content is sensitive to context and depends on which explanations are salient at the moment an accounting is required.

A subtle but crucial feature of the documentary method is that it lends factual character to a transient social world. The presupposed pattern creates a sense of stable social structure that is consistent across time and confers meaning on concrete acts that seem to occur under its aegis. The interacts literally become meaningful because they occur in a stable context, even though this stability is itself a construction. Precisely because the here and now can be "connected to the transcendent social scene" (Leiter, 1980, p. 168), the person is protected from having to deal with a continuing string of idiosyncratic, random appearances. "The members' sense of social structure involves, and depends upon, the stability of the object over and in spite of variations in situational appearances" (p. 169).

To use the documentary method is to presume and rely on the facticity of the social world while simultaneously creating that facticity. The world must be assumed to be real for it to be made real. Thus, the ability to assume a factual social world is necessary for facticity to be created. It is the joint effect of being bound to an interact and of being exposed to symbols that portray a presumably factual social world, which, in the case of organizational members, make it relatively easy to use this process of interpretation.

An important implication is that the documentary method is crucial for micro organizational analysis beyond its appropriateness for the concept of committed interpretation. The documentary method suggests a means by which organizational structure itself is created. Earlier, we suggested that justifications often reify social entities. Committed actions can be justified as macro necessities (e.g., "This is a partnership."). Once invoked as justifications, these macro entities then materialize when they are treated as if they are real constraints.

Although the earlier discussion of reification was confined to interacts, the relevance of reification for organizational sensemaking extends beyond these small units. A suggestion of this broader relevance is to be found in Hilbert's (1990) description of how skills used in the documentary method create the macro structures that make sense of micro events: "Microevents are classified into existence even as they are used to document the reality of macroevents of which they are examples. Macrostructures, then, are idealizations or typifications that are documented, filled out, and continually reproduced and modified by their microexamples, these examples being exactly what they are by affiliation with the very macropatterns they are used to document" (p. 803).

To return to the starting point for this chapter, sensemaking is an attempt to produce micro stability amidst continuing change. People produce micro stabilities by social commitment, which means that interacts become meaningful and that both the interacts and the meanings will be repeated. Stated more abstractly, micro stability is produced when people "orient to a presupposed social-structural order, reifying and reproducing it in the course of their activity and imposing its reality on each other as they do" (Hilbert, 1990, p. 796). Thus, reification starts with the documentary method. People presume that something concrete, often their own committed behavior, is a document of some larger pattern that, having been presumed, proceeds to flesh out both the particular and the general.

Illustrations of sensemaking using the documentary method are relatively common in the organizational literature. For example, Westley's (1990) discussion of middle managers and strategy presumes a mechanism similar to that of the documentary method: "Strategy is a meaning generating activity concerned with integrating and interpreting information. As such it is abstracted from specific tactics, policies, or operational procedures while being intimately concerned with relating these into an overall pattern" (p. 342). Strategy is the underlying pattern; tactics, policies, and procedures are the documents; and each relates to and integrates the other in the interest of meaning.

Westley describes a female middle manager who is excluded from the inner circle of people who know the strategic pattern thoroughly, and who, as a result of this exclusion, finds sensemaking difficult. When given a 2-inch pile of memos to digest and comment on, this person finds herself "searching for strategic generalities and the total picture so that she can make sense of the specific particular decisions that are passed along to her" (p. 343). She literally has documents in search of patterns. Having been excluded from strategic activity, she has not even a clue about the larger context of these memos.

Other examples of the documentary method can be cited. Daft and Weick (1984, p. 286) describe organizations as interpretation systems that tie external events (i.e., "documents") to internal categories (i.e., "underlying patterns"). Ranson, Hinings, and Greenwood (1980) state explicitly that "the 'rational' panoply of roles, rules, and procedures which make up organizational design is not pregiven in the organization but is the skilled, practical, and retrospective accomplishment of members. . . . Prescribed roles, rules, and authority relations are drawn upon retrospectively to locate and validate the emergent action within the wider context of meaning" (pp. 2, 5). Roles and rules are the underlying patterns that render the documents of "emergent action" more meaningful. Porac et al. (1989) suggest that specific transactions involving what to produce, what to purchase, and whom to target as customers are all documents that gain their meaning from a mental model of the environment that consists of identity beliefs and causal beliefs (p. 399). This mental model contains the underlying patterns that inform and explain the technical and material transactions.

The central role of justification in sensemaking has often been overlooked because traditionally the process has been labeled "*self*-justification" (e.g. Aronson, 1980, pp. 7–10). This phrase carries a connotation of defensiveness and distortion (e.g., Staw, 1980, p. 59), which deflects attention from the more neutral meaning that "a rational reason for doing something is merely rationalizing done within socially acceptable bounds" (Salancik & Pfeffer, 1978, p. 235, footnote 3). Furthermore, even the qualifier, "self" is misleading, since the self is socially defined and takes many forms (e.g., Simmel, 1971, pp. 10–11). If there are multiple selves, then the phrase *self-justification* specifies little.

The preceding analysis suggests that one way to understand the statement "symbolic processes create and sustain reality" is to argue that organizations begin to materialize when social rationales for social commitments are created. Not all justifications consist of reification, although all committed behaviors are social. This social character of commitment is always available as a cue that can guide the search for an underlying pattern toward social forms and macro entities. Since organizational settings are multiactor social forms, it seems safe to presume both that reification is a common route that justification will take initially, and that action initially explained by reification soon generates the reality that replaces the reification with substance.

THE VALIDATION OF JUSTIFICATION

Many justifications are not fully formed immediately after commitment occurs. Instead, they are worked out over time as the implications of the action are gradually discovered and new meanings of the action are created. Thus, the tendency for people writing about commitment to dwell on the immediate justification seems too limited because it focuses on too short a time interval. Key effects of commitment can also be observed later in the period, which we label postjustification action. There is evidence that once a justification begins to form, it exerts an effect on subsequent action (e.g., Penner, Fitch, & Weick, 1966; Weick & Prestholdt, 1968).

Justification is not a brief moment in sensemaking. Instead, it shapes and is shaped by action subsequent to the commitment. Thus, if a person justifies a decision to accept an unpleasant assignment with the explanation that it will be a challenge and an opportunity, that person often can create just such attractions and solidify the justification by the way he or she performs the assignment. The person acts so as to turn the assignment into an opportunity; these actions validate the rationale by actually creating opportunities, which further intensifies action; and the result is a justification whose validity is demonstrable and under the control of the actor. This scenario shows most clearly how justifications gain their tenacity and validity.

The way in which postjustification action contributes to validity can be illustrated if we extend a straightforward example of postaction justification. Salancik (1977, p. 27) describes a man who goes to a sales convention in Hawaii and justifies that action in different ways to different audiences. To himself he says he needed a vacation, to his wife he says it was a business obligation, and to his boss he says he wanted to survey the competition. The point we want to add is that, having made these justifications, he now will act more like vacations are important, conventions are a necessity, and surveying the competition is crucial. Justifications can turn into preferences that control subsequent attention and action (Weick, 1966, 1967). Detecting this outcome requires that we pay closer attention to the ways in which repeated use of a justification reaffirms its value and begins to transform it into a stable frame reference. Sensitivity to these outcomes requires, in turn, that we look for the ways in which actions following commitment are used to create and solidify an emergent justification.

Postdecision validation

Our focus on the postdecision period shows the continuing impact on organizational behavior of Leon Festinger and others who worked with cognitive dissonance theory. While dissonance theory per se has been increasingly bounded (e.g., Cooper & Fazio, 1989; Scher & Cooper, 1989), theorists of sensemaking continue to elaborate the basic insight that postdecision behavior differs markedly from predecision behavior (Jones & Gerard, 1967). During the predecision period, people pay equal attention to alternatives in an effort to reduce their ignorance. If there is differential attention to alternatives, they pay more attention to the alternatives they eventually reject. This is the pattern of information processing that Daft and Lengel (1986) associate with uncertainty.

Once the decision is made, the problem shifts from ignorance to confusion. This counterintuitive outcome—How can people be confused *after* a decision?— occurs because people temporarily face multiple, conflicting definitions of what their decision means. Not only does it mean that they will receive the positive features of their chosen alternative and avoid the negative features of their unchosen alternatives; it also means they will receive the negative features of their chosen alternative and forgo the positive features of their rejected alternative. Thus, when the decision means many different conflicting things, the problem is one of too many meanings, not too few, and the problem shifts from one of uncertainty to one of equivocality (Daft & MacIntosh, 1981). The decision has become an equivoque (Weick, 1979, p. 174), an event with two or more possible meanings. This may explain in part the much-discussed "regret" that often follows decision making.

We see that equivocality enters the sensemaking process at two points: before a committing action occurs, and immediately after a committed action becomes someone's responsibility but has not yet been justified.

Validation and action intensity

After the committed action has been chosen, there is little advantage to reflecting on the advantages of the rejected alternative or disadvantages of the chosen alternative. Once a decision is made, action is more effective when probabilistic information is treated as if it were deterministic and beliefs that are only relatively true are treated as if they were absolutely true (Brickman, 1987, p. 36). "Commitment marshals forces that destroy the plausibility of alternatives and remove their ability to inhibit action. These forces are nonrational, though their use is functional. . . . We may choose our actions in the first place on the rational basis of their standing in our informational system, but we drive them, energize them, and justify them on the nonrational basis of our motivational commitment to them" (Brickman, 1987, pp. 40–41).

Intensity facilitates the justification of commitments because it helps people accept activities that are not the best they might obtain and allows them to turn forgone possibilities into enhancement of the chosen alternative. People who pursue a chosen alternative unequivocally and with intensity often uncover unexpected attractions (Brickman, 1987, p. 54), with the result that the committed person is no longer greatly troubled by the thought that there might be more attractive alternatives.

Intense actions justify commitment by synthesizing positive and negative consequences of the chosen alternative. But intense actions also enable people to enact realities in which the justifications become accurate stories about how the world actually works. Consider an example proposed by Henshel (1987, p. 34).

Suppose a judge makes a public, irrevocable choice to dispose of juvenile delinquency cases on the basis of whether the defendant comes from an intact or broken home. The judge justifies this choice on the basis that broken homes produce delinquents who are incorrigible. The justification is a theory and a reification as well as a prediction that can be confirmed or disconfirmed. When the judge sends those from broken homes to prison more often than those from intact homes, this action exposes those in broken homes to prison experience, they find it harder to get jobs once they are released, and they resort more quickly to more serious crimes. As a result, official crime statistics now contain more cases that confirm the theory. Broken homes now do in fact correlate with a higher recidivism rate, which leads people to invoke the justification with more confidence. Judges resort to even more differential sentencing based on data about conditions at home because the "facts" show that home conditions make a difference.

A justification with little intrinsic validity comes to be seen as more valid because powerful people believe in it and act on these beliefs (Snyder, 1984). For these people, the world has become sensible. What they underestimate is their role in producing this sense. What has happened is that a justification has created a serial self-fulfilling prophecy that builds confidence in the prophecy through a deviation-amplifying causal loop (Maruyama, 1963). Under these conditions, both the justification and the action mutually strengthen one another, and the result is intense action that enacts a portion of the environment people confront. Thus, intensity guided by commitment can change the environment to resemble more closely the justification that was first imposed on it.

Similar scenarios are found throughout the organizational literature. Starbuck (1976, p. 1081), for example, argues that organizations play an active role in shaping their environments, partly because they seek environments that are sparsely inhabited by competitors, partly because they define their products and outputs in ways that emphasize distinctions between themselves and their competitors, partly because they rely on their own experience to infer environmental possibilities, and partly because they need to impose simplicity on complex relationships. A key mechanism in all of these scenarios is that perceptions and actions validate one another in ways that resemble self-fulfilling prophecies: "It is primarily in domains where an organization believes it exerts influence, that the organization attributes change to its own influence, and in domains where an organization believes itself impotent, it tends to ignore influence opportunities and never to discover whether its influence is real. . . . Moreover, it is the beliefs and perceptions founded on social reality which are especially liable to self-confirmation" (Starbuck, 1976, p. 1081).

Writing about political institutions, March and Olsen (1989) observed that "much of the richness of ecological theories of politics stems from the way in which the actions of each participant are part of the environments of others. The environment of each political actor is, therefore, partly self-determined as each reacts to the other. . . . When environments are created, the actions taken in adapting to an environment are partly responses to previous actions by the same actor, reflected through the environment. A common result is that small signals are amplified into large ones, and the general implication is that routine adaptive processes have consequences that cannot be understood without linking them to an environment that is simultaneously, and endogenously, changing" (p. 46).

Thus, political actors, as well as organizational actors in general, choose and create some of their own constraints, particularly when they justify committed interacts and then treat these justifications as prescriptive and factual and important.

CONCLUSION

A dominant question for scholars of organizing is, How do people produce and acquire a sense of order that allows them to coordinate their actions in ways that have mutual relevance? The answer proposed here is, by concrete communicative interaction in which people invoke macro structures to justify commitments. Thus, social order is created continuously as people make commitments and develop valid, socially acceptable justifications for these commitments. Phrased in this way, individual sensemaking has the potential to be transformed into social structures and to maintain these structures. Commitment is one means by which social structure is realized. This proposal suggests a possible mechanism by which structuration (e.g., Barley, 1986; Giddens, 1984) actually works.

The preceding analysis also implies the following:

1. Sensemaking is focused on those actions around which the strongest commitments form.

2. The content of sensemaking consists of justifications that are plausible to, advocated by, sanctioned within, and salient for important reference groups with which the actors identify.

3. Actions "mean" whatever justifications become attached to them. Committed actions are equivocal (Daft & MacIntosh, 1981) since they have multiple meanings; the justification process reduces this confusion (Daft & Lengel, 1986).

4. Organizing begins with moments of commitment. These moments determine the meanings that are available to make sense of events that fill the other noncommitting periods. The generation of meaning is a discontinuous process that is activated when important actions coincide with settings in which those actions are performed volitionally, publicly, explicitly, and irrevocably. Among our many actions, few occur under conditions that are binding. Most organizations, most of the time, activate few of these committing conditions. When they do, they activate them only for a handful of people. Since commitment is an additive process, commitments strengthen slowly and incrementally. Furthermore, new justifications and new meanings are slow to emerge as they are grounded in old meanings that persist even though they are outdated. As a result, organizational life may be experienced by many as empty and meaningless. This sense of anomie should decline the more action is encouraged and the more committing the context within which that action unfolds.

5. Presuppositions, expectations, and even faith are important engines in the sensemaking process, especially when actors are confident and environments are malleable. In understructured settings such as temporary systems, small firms, and entrepreneurial ventures, motivated presuppositions can exert influence and alter interaction patterns. Alteration is even more likely when the presuppositions and actions form a deviation-amplifying feedback loop. Micro dynamics have the potential to create sensibleness by actually stabilizing the environment, and this is the point of analyzing what happens *after* a justification is formulated. Justification is not just head work. Thoughts are acted into the world (Porac et al., 1989, pp. 398–401).

6. Organizations are ideal sites for committed interpretation because they generate action, champion accountability, make choices, value good reasons, and scrutinize everything. But organizations also exaggerate their intentional nature and thus often miss the fact that their interpretations are focused on their commitments. People *do* know best that to which they are committed, but not because they knew it and then became committed. It is just the opposite. Action leads the sensemaking process; it does not follow it. People need to be less casual about action since whatever they do has the potential to bind them and focus their sensemaking. Inaction, repetitive action, and idiosyncratic action all have direct effects on what people know and how well they know it. Action *is* intelligence, and until it is deployed, meaning and sense will be underdeveloped.

7. Social psychology is crucial for organizational analysis because it is the one discipline that does not fall prey to the error of assuming that large effects imply large causes. Social psychology is about small events that enlarge because they are em-

bedded in amplifying causal loops, are acted into networks where they spread (Porac et al., 1989), become sources that are imitated, resolve important uncertainties at impressionable moments, make discontinuous changes in performance (Chambliss, 1989), and so on. Organizations are not monoliths. Instead, they are loosely coupled fragments (Orton & Weick, 1990) just as individuals are. This fragmentation means that the relevant unit of analysis is small in size though not in influence, that small events spread intermittently and fortuitously, and that macro perspectives are hollow unless linked with micro dynamics.

It is important to reiterate the way in which commitments serve to guide organizational behavior. Our challenge as researchers is not to predict exactly what will happen in each organizational moment. To attempt that is to attempt to predict the path of a bouncing football (Kuhn & Beam, 1982, pp. xxi–xxii): It is neither necessary nor possible. Instead, what we need to understand are those events that give direction and meaning to the stream of organizational moments.

That is what commitments do. Once a person makes a commitment, then subsequent events often are interpreted in ways that confirm the soundness of that commitment. Thus, commitments constrain the meanings that people impose on streams of experience.

The picture of an organization that emerges from these ideas is that of a stream of problems, solutions, and people tied together by choices. What happens over time is that choices mobilize reasons and justifications, which people then use to make elements in these streams more orderly. Organizing starts with a set of choices and streams. When the streams converge, people pay attention and construct explanations for the convergence. Their explanations vary depending on their needs, their associates, and their prior choices. The stream of consciousness in organizations takes the tangible form of streams of people, solutions, and problems that become organized to justify choices. When we say that people construct reality, what we mean is that they use commitments to guide their efforts at sensemaking. Commitments are what they start with. And commitments are what shape their continuing search for sensible work in a sensible setting.

REFERENCES

ALLPORT, F. H. (1962). A structuronomic conception of behavior: Individual and collective. *Journal of Abnormal and Social Psychology, 64,* 3–30.

ANDERSON, P. A. (1983). Decision making by objection and the Cuban missile crisis. *Administrative Science Quarterly, 28,* 201–222.

ARONSON, E. (1980). Persuasion via self-justification: Large commitments for small rewards. In L. Festinger (Ed.), *Retrospectives on social psychology* (pp. 3–21). New York: Oxford.

BARLEY, S. (1986). Technology as an occasion for structuring: Evidence for observations of CAT scanners and the social order of radiology departments. *Administrative Science Quarterly, 31,* 78–108.

BARNARD, C. I. (1938). *The functions of the executive.* Cambridge, MA: Harvard University Press.

BECKER, H. (1986). Dialogue with Howard S. Becker. In H. S. Becker (Ed.), *Doing things together* (pp. 25–46). Evanston, IL: Northwestern University Press.

BHASKAR, R. (1978). On the possibility of social scientific knowledge and the limits of naturalism. *Journal for the Theory of Social Behavior, 8,* 1–28.

BRICKMAN, P. (1987). *Commitment, conflict, and caring.* Englewood Cliffs, NJ: Prentice Hall.

CHAMBLISS, D. F. (1989). The mundanity of excellence: An ethnographic report on stratification and olympic swimmers. *Sociological Theory, 7*(1), 70–86.

COHEN, M. D., MARCH, J. G., & OLSEN, J. P. (1972). A garbage can model of organizational choice. *Administrative Science Quarterly, 17,* 1–25.

COOPER, J., & FAZIO, R. H. (1989). Research traditions, analysis, and synthesis: Building a faulty case around misinterpreted theory. *Personality and Social Psychology Bulletin, 15*(4), 519–529.

CZARNIAWSKA–JOERGES, B., & JOERGES, B. (1990). Linguistic artifacts at service of organizational control. In P. Gagliardi (Ed.), *Symbols and artifacts: Views of the corporate landscape* (pp. 339–364). Berlin: de Gruyter.

DAFT, R. L. (1986). *Organization theory and design* (2nd ed.). St. Paul, MN: West.

DAFT, R. L., & LENGEL, R. H. (1986). Organizational information requirements, media richness and structural design. *Management Science, 32*(5), 554–571.

DAFT, R. L., & MacINTOSH, N. B. (1981). A tentative exploration into the amount and equivocality of information processing in organizational work units. *Administrative Science Quarterly, 26,* 207–224.

DAFT, R. L., & WEICK, K. E. (1984). Toward a model of organizations as interpretation systems. *Academy of Management Review, 9,* 284–295.

EISENBERG, E. M., & RILEY, P. (1988). Organizational symbols and sensemaking. In G. M. Goldhaber & G. A. Barnett (Eds.), *Handbook of organizational communication* (pp. 131–150). Norwood, NJ: Ablex.

FAY, B. (1990). Critical realism? *Journal for the Theory of Social Behaviour, 20,* 33–41.

GARFINKEL, H. (1967). *Studies in ethnomethodology.* Englewood Cliffs, NJ: Prentice Hall.

GERGEN, K. J. (1982). *Toward transformation in social knowledge.* NY: Springer-Verlag.

GIDDENS, A. (1984). *The constitution of society: Outline of the theory of structuration.* Cambridge, England: Polity Press.

HARPER, D. (1987). *Working knowledge.* Chicago: University of Chicago.

HENSHEL, R. L. (1987, September). *Credibility and confidence feedback loops in social prediction.* Paper presented at the Plenary Session of the VII International Congress of Cybernetics and Systems, University of London.

HERITAGE, J. (1984). *Garfinkel and ethnomethodology.* Cambridge, England: Polity Press.

HILBERT, R. A. (1990). Ethnomethodology and the micro–macro order. *American Sociological Review, 55,* 794–808.

HOLLANDER, E. P., & WILLIS, R. H. (1967). Some current issues in the psychology of conformity and nonconformity. *Psychological Bulletin, 68,* 67–76.

ISAAC, J. C. (1990). Realism and reality: Some realistic considerations. *Journal for the Theory of Social Behaviour, 20,* 1–32.

JABLIN, F. M. (1987). Organizational entry, assimilation, and exit. In F. M. Jablin, L. J. Putnam, K. H. Roberts, & L. W. Porter (Eds.), *Handbook of organizational communication* (pp. 679–740). Newbury Park, CA: Sage.

JAMES, W. (1890). *The principles of psychology. Vol. II.* New York: Holt.

JONES, E. E., & GERARD, H. B. (1967). *Foundations of social psychology.* New York: Wiley.

KATZ, D., & KAHN, R. L. (1978). *The social psychology of organizations.* New York: Wiley.

KEESING, R. M. (1987). Anthropology as interpretive quest. *Current Anthropology, 28,* 161–176.

KNORR–CETINA, K. D. (1981). The micro-sociological challenge of macro-sociology: Towards a reconstruction of social theory and methodology. In K. Knorr–Cetina & A. V. Cicourel (Eds.), *Advances in social theory and methodology* (pp. 1–47). Boston: Routledge & Kegan Paul.

KUHN, A., & BEAM, R. D. (1982). *The logic of organization.* San Francisco: Jossey-Bass.

LEITER, K. (1980). *A primer on ethnomethodology.* New York: Oxford.

LEVI–STRAUSS, C. (1966): *The savage mind.* Chicago: University of Chicago.

LOUIS, M. R. (1980). Surprise and sensemaking: What newcomers experience in entering unfamiliar organizational settings. *Administrative Science Quarterly, 25,* 226–251.

MARCH, J. G., & OLSEN, J. P. (1989). *Rediscovering institutions: The organizational basis of politics.* New York: Free Press.

MARKUS, H., & ZAJONC, R. B. (1985). The cognitive perspective in social psychology. In G. Lindzey & E. Aronson (Eds.), *Handbook of social psychology* (Vol. 1, 3rd ed., pp. 137–230). New York: Random House.

MARUYAMA, M. (1963). The second cybernetics: Deviation-amplifying mutual causal processes. *American Scientist, 51,* 164–179.

MEYER, D. A. (1982). Adapting to environmental jolts. *Administrative Science Quarterly, 27,* 515–537.

MONMONIER, M. (1991). *How to lie with maps.* Chicago: University of Chicago.

MORGAN, G., FROST, P. J., & PONDY, L. R. (1983). Organizational symbolism. In L. R. Pondy, P. J. Frost, G. Morgan, & T. C. Dandridge (Eds.), *Organizational symbolism* (pp. 3–35). Greenwich, CT: JAI Press.

O'REILLY, C. A., III. (1991). Organizational behavior: Where we've been, where we're going. *Annual Review of Psychology, 42,* 427–458.

ORTON, J. D., & WEICK, K. E. (1990). Loosely coupled systems: A reconceptualization. *Academy of Management Review, 15,* 203–223.

PENNER, D. D., FITCH, G., & WEICK, K. E. (1966). Dissonance and the revision of choice criteria. *Journal of Personality and Social Psychology, 3,* 701–705.

PORAC, J. F., THOMAS, H., & BADEN–FULLER, C. (1989). Competitive groups as cognitive communities: The case of scottish knitwear manufacturers. *Journal of Management Studies, 26,* 397–416.

RANSON, S., HININGS, B., & GREENWOOD, R. (1980). The structuring of organizational structures. *Administrative Science Quarterly, 25,* 1–17.

SALANCIK, G. R. (1977). Commitment and the control of organizational behavior and belief. In B. M. Staw & G. R. Salancik (Eds.), *New directions in organizational behavior* (pp. 1–54). Chicago: St. Clair.

SALANCIK, G. R., & PFEFFER, J. (1978). A social information processing approach to job attitudes and task design. *Administrative Science Quarterly, 23,* 224–253.

SANDELANDS, L. E., & WEICK, K. E. (1991). *Social commitment and organizing.* Unpublished manuscript, University of Michigan.

SCHER, S. J., & COOPER, J. (1989). Motivational basis of dissonance: The singular role of behavioral consequences. *Journal of Personality and Social Psychology, 56,* 899–906.

SCHUTZ, W. (1979). *Profound simplicity.* New York: Bantam.

SHALIN, D. N. (1986). Pragmatism and social interactionism. *American Sociological Review, 51,* 9–29.

SIMMEL, G. (1971). How is society possible? In D. H. Levine (Ed.), *George Simmel on individuality and social forms* (pp. 6–22). Chicago: University of Chicago.

SMIRCICH, L., & MORGAN, G. (1982). Leadership: The management of meaning. *Journal of Applied Behavioral Science, 18,* 257–273.

SMIRCICH, L., & STUBBART, C. (1985). Strategic management in an enacted world. *Academy of Management Review, 10,* 724–736.

SNOW, D. A., ROCHFORD, E. B., JR., WORDEN, S. K., & BENFORD, R. D. (1986). Frame alignment processes, micromobilization, and movement participation. *American Sociological Review, 51,* 464–481.

SNYDER, M. (1984). When belief creates reality. In L. Berkowitz (Ed.), *Advances in experimental social psychology* (Vol. 18, pp. 247–305). New York: Academic Press.

STARBUCK, W. H. (1976). Organizations and their environments. In M. D. Dunnette (Ed.), *Handbook of industrial and organizational psychology* (pp. 1069–1123). Chicago: Rand McNally.

STAW, B. M. (1980). Rationality and justification in organizational life. In B. M. Staw & L. L. Cummings (Eds.), *Research in organizational behavior* (Vol. 2, pp. 45–80). Greenwich, CT: JAI Press.

TETLOCK, P. E. (1985). Accountability: The neglected social context of judgment and choice. In L. L. Cummings & B. M. Staw (Eds.), *Research in organizational behavior: Vol. 7* (pp. 297–332). Greenwich, CT: JAI Press.

THOMAS, W. I., & THOMAS, D. S. (1928). *The child in America: Behavior problems and programs.* New York: Knopf.

WEICK, K. E. (1964). The reduction of cognitive dissonance through task enhancement and effort expenditure. *Journal of Abnormal and Social Psychology, 68,* 533–539.

WEICK, K. E. (1966). Task acceptance dilemmas: A site for research on cognition. In S. Feldman (Ed.), *Cognitive consistency* (pp. 225–255). New York: Academic Press.

WEICK, K. E. (1967). Dissonance and task enhancement: A problem for compensation theory? *Organizational Behavior and Human Performance, 2,* 189–208.

WEICK, K. E. (1979). *The social psychology of organizing* (2nd ed.). Reading, MA: Addison-Wesley.

WEICK, K. E., GILFILLAN, D. P., & KEITH, T. (1973). The effect of composer credibility in orchestra performance. *Sociometry, 36,* 435–462.

WEICK, K. E., & PRESTHOLDT, P. (1968). Realignment of discrepant reinforcement value. *Journal of Personality and Social Psychology, 8,* 180–187.

WESTLEY, F. R. (1990). Middle managers and strategy: Microdynamics of inclusion. *Strategic Management Journal, 11,* 337–351.

WILEY, N. (1988). The micro–macro problem in social theory. *Sociological Theory, 6,* 254–261.

ZANNA, M. P. (1973). On inferring one's belief from one's behavior in a low-choice setting. *Journal of Personality and Social Psychology, 26,* 386–394.

ZANNA, M. P., & SANDE, G. N. (1987). The effects of collective actions on the attitudes of individual group members: A dissonance analysis. In M. P. Zanna, J. M. Olson, & C. P. Herman (Eds.), *Social influence* (Vol. 5, pp. 151–164). Hillsdale, NJ: Erlbaum.

CHAPTER THREE

Out of the Lab and Into the Field: Decision Making in Organizations

JOHN S. CARROLL

MIT

The social psychological approach to decision making in the 1960s and 1970s tended to conceptualize decisions as within individuals, to keep each decision separate, to minimize context, and to conceptualize the decision maker as a mostly logical rule user. Using research on decisions by members of criminal justice organizations, an expanded framework is developed that situates decision making within an organizational context of tasks, alternatives, information, role relationships, and social systems. Further, the cognitive processes in decision making are refocused on purposive, knowledge-based processes including hypothesis testing, alternative-focused decision making, and the development and use of schemas. Finally, these processes are located in time by incorporating the dynamic feedback and learning processes that connect decisions. The framework is then used to examine how nuclear power plants learn from experience by a process of interpretation that involves causal reasoning and the social distribution of knowledge.

The 1960s were the zenith of laboratory social psychology. Researchers perfected a style exemplified by Leon Festinger and his students in their research on dissonance theory. This method included the creative manipulation of college students in the pursuit of counterintuitive results—surprises for existing theory that stimulated great interest in social psychology, propelled theory, and legitimated the laboratory technique.

The 1970s brought several changes. Each year at the American Psychological Association meeting, a symposium would address the "crisis" in social psychology. Much concern arose from the very elements that had made social psychology so successful during the previous 2 decades: the use of artificial situations and "naive" college students, the reliance on deception, and the tendency to use dependent measures that did not relate directly to "natural behavior" (e.g., Helmreich, 1975).

One of the first counterreactions was to make social psychology more "applied"—to use social psychology to study real-world social phenomena and contribute to society. Many of these efforts focused on social issues (e.g., crime, racism, conservation, war and peace, education) and public agencies' missions to address these issues. However, the broadening of social psychology also challenged theory in new ways.

This chapter begins by summarizing research on decision making and causal reasoning conducted within the experimental social psychological paradigm; it then develops a more *situated* understanding of decision making and causal reasoning in organizations. For the most part, the subject matter is the decision making and causal reasoning of persons in criminal justice organizations, such as judges, parole board members, and probation officers. The analysis, however, may be generalized beyond this particular context: The last section of this chapter extends these ideas to organizational learning in nuclear power plants.

1970s DECISION-MAKING RESEARCH IN CRIMINAL JUSTICE ORGANIZATIONS

Few social psychologists in the 1970s studied how decisions were made in real organizations. (There were some exceptions, such as Hackman & Oldham, 1975; Katz & Kahn, 1966.) The thrust of social psychological research was to test abstract theory about individuals or small groups. Researchers operationalized the few variables in the theory and controlled everything else, an approach that did not require much understanding of "everything else." For the most part, whatever organizational context was provided to subjects was intended to increase their involvement in the experiment. The typical social psychological study of juries, for example, provided minimal real-world context (Konecni & Ebbesen, 1979; Weitan & Diamond, 1979).

What was known about decisions in criminal justice organizations tended to come from outside social psychology. Much of this work focused on the issue of disparity as injustice—why individual judges differed in their decisions (Hogarth, 1971) or whether juries' decisions differed from judges' (Kalven & Zeisel, 1966). To study disparity, researchers used simple models relating case factors to decisions. Although some understanding of decisions in criminal justice contexts emerged from interviews and "policy capturing" studies of actual decisions, it was acknowledged that "the decision-making process is perhaps the most important—and least understood—single dimension of the correctional system" (Carter, 1967, p. 203).

Parole decisions and theory testing

Within the criminal justice system, a variety of decisions are made about the incarceration, release, and treatment of criminals. Prison officials, guards, and counselors talk readily about their "images" of kinds of offenders, their explanations for why people engage in criminal acts, and their understanding of what happens to various "types" of people in prisons. From the viewpoint of social psychology, these descriptions are practical examples of implicit personality theory (Schneider, 1973) and attribution theory (Heider, 1958) in action: The descriptions and typifications of offenders say as much about *perceptions* as about the *criminals* who are perceived.

Carroll and Payne (1976) approached one of these criminal justice decisions—the parole decision—from a psychological perspective. It is a parole board's responsibility to determine when offenders sentenced to prison will be released and what conditions of supervision and treatment will be required. In many states, the parole board has even greater discretion than judges over time in prison (Genego, Goldberger, & Jackson, 1975). For example, in Pennsylvania, judges sentence offenders to a range of prison time (e.g., 2 to 5 years), and the parole board determines the time of release within these limits.

The context of parole decisions provided a particularly attractive topic for research not merely for its intrinsic interest, but because it shared several features with laboratory decision tasks that made it more tractable for theoretical research: Parole decisions are based on written case material and brief interviews; decisions are repetitive; and the interviews take place at specified times and places and are open to researchers (unlike juries). Although the authority to decide is placed on the parole board as a group, in Pennsylvania individual parole interviewers conduct interviews and make recommendations as individuals. Furthermore, given the lack of prior social psychological research using parole boards, there were potential practical contributions and the challenge to extend available theoretical and methodological frameworks to a new domain.

Theory: causal attributions and information processing

Carroll and Payne (1976) developed a framework to permit theoretical research in the parole decision context. This framework was built from a few simple ideas: First, parole decision makers have to assemble case information into judgments that relate to their goals (Gottfredson, Wilkins, Hoffman, & Singer, 1973); second, some of these judgments involve causal reasoning, which can be analyzed using theoretical principles expressed in attribution theory (e.g., Heider, 1958); and third, assembling case information involves shortcuts or heuristics (Payne, 1973; Tversky & Kahneman, 1974) necessitated by the limitations of human information processing capabilities (Newell & Simon, 1972), leading to predictable errors or biases.

Attribution theory addresses how people interpret information about behavior in making judgments about the causes of events, and how these judgments affect a person's behavior. Attribution theory does not attempt to specify the "real" cause of behavior but how a person infers or attributes cause and what happens once he or she does.

Kelley (1967) interpreted Heider's (1958) work on attribution by theorizing that attributions are made to three types of causal factors: actors who take action, objects or stimuli that are the targets of action, and situations or circumstances. Further, Kelley suggested that attribution processes resemble those of a "naive scientist" who looks for covariation between causes and effects and assigns cause as a product of a "naive analysis of variance." The classic test of Kelley's model by McArthur (1972) presented students with such scenarios as "Mark is afraid of the dog; Mark has been afraid of the dog in the past; most other people are afraid of the dog," and requested students' inferences to possible causes, including Mark, the dog, the circumstances, and combinations of these.

Weiner and his colleagues (Weiner, 1974; Weiner et al., 1971) developed a dimensional model of attribution that enumerated and classified more kinds of attributions. Thus, "Jane got an A on the Math quiz" could be attributed to high intelligence, lots of study, an easy quiz, good luck, help from friends, and so forth. Attributions were classified as internal or external to Jane (the locus of control) and stable or variable over time. Behaviors attributed to internal causes led to more extreme rewards and punishments than the same behaviors attributed to external causes; compared to unstable causes, more stable causes produced expectations for similar behavior in the future. Other dimensions, such as degree of intention and generality across settings (Abramson, Seligman, & Teasdale, 1978), were also suggested by various researchers.

At the same time, decision-making researchers (e.g., Newell & Simon, 1972) were discovering that people solve complex problems and make difficult decisions by using shortcuts or heuristics. Repeatedly, research demonstrated predictable errors and biases resulting from limited information processing capabilities (Payne, 1973; Tversky & Kahneman, 1974). Such research suggested that an understanding of decision making would require both an understanding of the decision task characteristics and the heuristics or strategies that decision makers adopt to deal with the task.

Carroll and Payne (1976) used attribution theory and information processing theory to develop a framework for parole decisions. As illustrated in Figure 1, the framework divides the parole decision task into three major aspects: (a) task-specific information provided about the parole applicant (e.g., prior record) and about others (e.g., baserate information); (b) the decision maker's own information and cognitive processes—prior beliefs, attribution rules and decision heuristics, inferences, attributions, and other subjudgments made about the case, leading to judgments of *deservingness of punishment* and *risk of parole violation*; and (c) the final parole decision. The integral role of judgments about punishment and risk was suggested by a confluence of studies of parole decisions (Hoffman, 1973; Kastenmeier & Eglit, 1973; Wilkins, Gottfredson, Robison, & Sadowsky, 1973) and Weiner's (1974) attribution model, which separates rewards and punishments from expectations (i.e., risk).

In the aforementioned framework, causal attributions mediate parole decisions. Given the same crime, offenses attributed to internal causes should lead to judgments that offenders are more deserving of punishment than offenses attributed to external causes. Internal and intentional causes (factors people in-

FIGURE 1   Framework for the Parole Decision Process

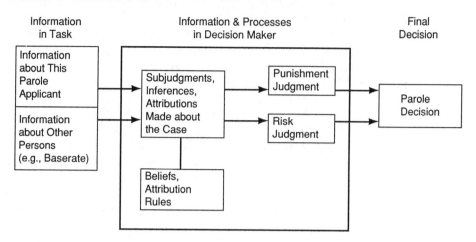

Note: Adapted from Carroll & Payne (1976), p. 17.

tend or control) should lead to the highest levels of punishment. Separately and orthogonally, attributions to more stable and enduring causes (whether internal or external) should lead to predictions of greater risk and a greater desire to further incapacitate the offender.

These predictions were first tested by having college students evaluate eight crime descriptions (e.g., robbery, rape, burglary, drugs) in all combinations of one crime and one of eight pieces of background information designed to suggest a causal attribution about the crime (Carroll & Payne, 1977a, 1977b). Background attributions formed a $2 \times 2 \times 2$ design of internal versus external, stable versus unstable, and intentional versus unintentional causes. The brief descriptions gave the offender's age, gender, charge, a brief narrative of the crime, and an apparent cause derived from "interviews"; all offenders had no previous record. The external, stable, unintentional cause was, "He could not find a good job because his skill had been replaced by mechanization. The circumstances around the crime had been acting on him for some time."

The results supported the theoretical framework. Attributions to internal causes led to more negative evaluations—more dislike; higher ratings of crime severity, responsibility, and the idea that the purpose of prison is punishment; and longer prison terms. Internal-intentional causes were judged the highest on responsibility. Attributions to stable, long-term causes led to higher expectations for recidivism, higher ratings of criminality, stronger feelings that the purpose of prison is incapacitation, and longer prison terms. Prison terms were assigned on the basis of punishment and risk factors and were an additive sum of internal–external and stable–unstable judgments.

After this initial study, similar materials were sent by mail to all persons in an expert decision-making capacity in the Pennsylvania State Board of Probation and Parole. Minor changes in wording were made in two of the cause manipulations to clarify their attributional implications; no subsequent differences were traceable to these changes. Experts were told that the cause manipulations were excerpts from interviews rather than summaries of interviews, since these materials were simply not credible enough as summaries.

In contrast to the college students, the experts treated internal-stable causes as distinct from other types of causes, leading to higher judgments of both crime severity and recidivism risk. For example, the experts' recommended prison term was 5.9 years for internal-stable causes, but between 3 and 4 years for all other causes. Thus, while attributional information was important to both students and experts, only the students clearly showed the predicted separability of the attributional dimensions in the resultant punishment and risk judgments. Further, the impact of the attributional information on nearly all the judgments was much greater for students than for experts (Carroll & Payne, 1977a). These differences presented an intriguing puzzle.

Experts and students had different reactions to the "same" decision task. The experts reported that they felt uncomfortable making decisions with so little information; a factor that may have lessened their reliance on the more subjective causal information. Although studies of parole boards had indicated that they *use* only a few pieces of information in making decisions (Wilkins et al., 1973), the experts *wanted* more complete case material. Thus, there was some question about whether this study demonstrated real differences in the attributional patterns of students and experts or was flawed by the use of controlled but artificial materials.

Some of the specific disagreements between students and experts suggested that the experts had different knowledge about criminals. Although there was high agreement on crime seriousness (a value judgment), there was considerable disagreement on risk of recidivism. For example, experts rated the murderer as least likely to commit another crime, while students saw him as third most likely. Actually, the experts' ratings reflected the fact that murderers are statistically good risks. In another instance, students treated the recent divorce as an excuse, but experts thought of it as a sign of social instability. Because some differences between students and experts may have arisen from the experts' contextual knowledge and experience, research would have to incorporate *more* context and elements of actual decisions to understand the role of causal reasoning in parole decisions.

A SITUATED FRAMEWORK FOR DECISION MAKING IN ORGANIZATIONS

The framework in Figure 1 contains many assumptions common to social psychology in the 1970s:

* Decision makers act as individuals, isolated from any organizational or institutional context.
* Decisions are "timeless": Changes over time through feedback or learning are ignored.

*   Differences among people are acknowledged without being described in any detail.

*   Decision makers apply a small set of general rules (logical and/or illogical) to convert case information into decisions.

The puzzle of why expert parole decision makers' judgments "failed" to support the theory stimulated research that developed gradually into a more "situated" framework of decision making in organizations. In contrast to the framework in Figure 1, this newer framework (illustrated in Figure 2) adds more detail about context, recognizes dynamics that unfold over time, and acknowledges in more detail different, individual cognitive processes among decision makers.

The context of the decision includes (a) the nature of the assigned decision task, including the formal division of roles, constraints on action, and decision procedures or aids; (b) the alternatives that are permissible and their presumed effectiveness; (c) the physical and organizational arrangements that create informal workgroups who cooperate to carry out the work; and (d) the information,

FIGURE 2   A Situated Framework for Decision Making in Organizations

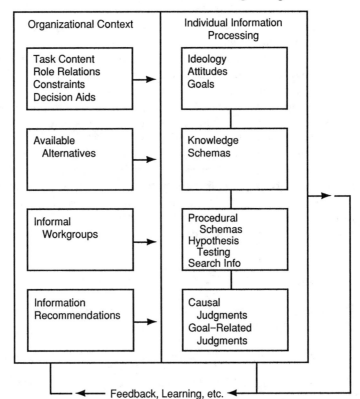

recommendations, and other opinions that flow formally or informally from actor to actor. Within the decision maker, the general decision rules are reconsid-
ered to include specific knowledge-based aspects such as goals and schemas,
and active processes such as hypothesis testing and searching for information.
These processes occur over time and may change with feedback. The following
sections of this chapter discuss research results that provide detail and evidence
for these features of the framework, beginning with studies of the parole decision task in Pennsylvania.

Parole decisions in the criminal justice system

Although parole decision making in Pennsylvania is the responsibility of the
five-person Parole Board, most decisions are not made by the board as a group.
The caseload is so large that parole decisions are, in effect, decentralized to a set
of parole interviewers. One interviewer reads case information and interviews
each offender prior to the expiration of the minimum sentence. This interviewer
may be a single board member or a hearing examiner. The recommendation of
the interviewer, along with a report, is then passed on to three board members
for their approval. Only cases that engender disagreement or have some special
significance are considered in a full board meeting. In a study of 250 cases, final
board decisions agreed with interviewer recommendations in 98 percent of cases
(Carroll, Wiener, Coates, Galegher, & Alibrio, 1982).

However, the parole interviewer is not acting alone in making decisions.
The case information consists of both facts and summary judgments and recommendations by members of the institution's correctional staff and the parole case
analyst, who works at the institution but is employed by the Pennsylvania Parole Board. Thus, the parole decision process involves a social transmission of
information and recommendations across several actors; it is not obvious "who"
is making the decision and how different people contribute different parts of the
decision.

Carroll, Wiener, et al. (1982) asked parole interviewers to fill out a questionnaire immediately following 1,035 actual interviews and coded extensive
information from the associated case files. They found that the interviewer
recommendation (usually the same as the board's decision) was best predicted
by four factors: the case analyst's recommendation, the interviewer's judgment
of conduct in prison, prognosis for supervision, and risk of future dangerous
crime. The case analyst's recommendation, in turn, was best predicted by the
institution's recommendation and the case analyst's judgments of conduct in
prison and participation in programs. The institution's recommendation was
best predicted by the institution's reports on conduct in prison. There was
strong reliance on others' judgments, but additional concerns were raised at
each level: The institution seemed primarily concerned with conduct; the case
analyst added concern with program participation; and the interviewer added
concern for the offender's future and community safety reflected in prognoses
for rehabilitation and judged risk of future crime. Crimes committed by paroled

inmates reflect more directly on the Parole Board than on the prisons. Interestingly, the case analysts who are *organizationally* part of the board but *located* at the prison seem to reflect the concerns of their institutional setting more than their reporting relationship to the parole board.

The importance of the interpersonal transmission of information and recommendations is echoed in studies of other criminal justice decisions. Konecni and Ebbesen (1982) found that judges primarily base their sentencing decisions on the recommendations of probation officers; Ebbesen and Konecni (1982) found that judges' bail decisions are based on the recommendations of the prosecuting and defense attorneys. In short, the courtroom workgroup (Jacob, 1978) of people who cooperate to process cases (judge, attorneys, probation officer, court clerk) is a decision unit. However, judges insist that they make the decision themselves and, for hypothetical cases, will pay much less attention to what the attorneys have recommended (Konecni & Ebbesen, 1982). Only in studies of actual decisions does the impact of the workgroup become evident: In the pursuit of efficiency and working harmony, judges accede to recommendations that they otherwise might have overruled.

The results in Carroll, Wiener, et al. (1982) also revealed that crime seriousness, crime type, and record were not related to parole release recommendations but strongly correlated with minimum sentence. Discussions with board members clarified the interpretation: The Pennsylvania board relies on the judge's minimum sentence for the punitive portion of the sentence and focuses more on predictions of the risks to the community and the benefits to the client as considerations in parole decisions. This finding conflicts with the Carroll and Payne (1976) framework that included both punishment and risk within parole decisions.

The degree to which parole decisions are based on punishment and risk should depend on the role played by the parole board within the criminal justice system; states distribute the responsibility for decisions differently. In Wisconsin, judges set a maximum sentence; the Parole Board begins reviewing the case early in the prison term and repeatedly reviews the case until parole is granted or the maximum sentence is reached. In this organizational arrangement, the punitive component of parole decisions should be more important than in Pennsylvania. Carroll and Burke (1990) presented hypothetical case materials with experts from the Wisconsin parole system and found, as expected, that issues relevant to punishment—crime seriousness and length of prior record—were of primary importance in determining parole decisions.

There is an interesting addendum to the considerations underlying parole decisions in Pennsylvania (Carroll, Wiener, et al., 1982). The results clearly demonstrate that the board was punishing inmates—not for their prior crimes, but for their misconducts and infractions in the prison. They perceived part of their responsibility, as a goal, to be "keeping the lid on the institutions" by making parole release contingent on good conduct. Presumably, this goal involves attributional judgments about prison behavior that have not been systematically studied.

Causal attributions in actual parole decisions

To capture actual decision processes in a naturalistic way, Carroll and Payne (1977b) collected verbal protocols from five experts examining actual parole cases. Attributions represented the single largest category of statements beyond factual information. Twenty-two percent of coded statements were attributions, demonstrating their prevalence in expert decisions.

As an illustration, one expert described the events around a crime of breaking into a food market and stealing 37 cartons of cigarettes in the following way:

> OK, you know, what he did was so, was done so impulsively, man. He was out. He had been drinking with this cat and uh, they were drunk, and they needed cigarettes. And he went into this place and he got the cigarettes.

This offender had a prior record but no offenses for 10 years prior to this crime. The expert felt that "the difficulties that the guy had in the past—the records would show that it was due to alcoholism, you know." He stated, "The guy has the ability to be stable out there," referring to his 10 years of staying straight and an expectation that he could do so in the future. Why, in the expert's view, did the alcoholism reemerge? "He indicated to the counselor that when he found himself out of work that he started hitting the bottle, which is, you know, that's his, you know, reason for doin' it. For going to the alcohol, as to why, why there would be some alcohol abuse."

This expert decision maker was concerned not only with the crime but also with the causes of the crime. He gradually built a picture of the offender as a person who had controlled an earlier alcohol problem but was set off by frustrations over losing his job. This causal attribution provided a consistent interpretion of the crime, the criminal record, participation in Alcoholics Anonymous in the institution; it even guided treatment plans: "I think the area that we're gonna be concerned with, or the parole agent should be concerned with this man, is that of his alcohol problems."

A more extensive study (Carroll, 1978) examined 272 actual parole hearings over a 2-month period (a subset of the questionnaires studied in Carroll, Wiener, et al., 1982). Nearly all the hearings were conducted by one of the five Pennsylvania board members. On the questionnaires completed by board members immediately after each decision, two open-ended requests for opinions addressed causal attributions: "opinion on underlying cause for offense committed" and "opinion on reason for criminal record/history."

Five hundred and fifty-seven attribution statements were produced from the questionnaires and grouped into categories. The most frequent causes given for offenses were, in descending order of frequency, (a) drug abuse problem, (b) alcohol abuse problem, (c) long-term greed, (d) sudden desire for money, (e) victim precipitation, (f) drunkkenness at time of crime, (g) influence of associates, (h) lack of control, (i) mental problems, and (j) domestic problems. The most frequent causes given for criminal history were (a) drug abuse problem, (b) alcohol abuse problem, (c) influence of associates, (d) long-term greed, (e) immaturity, (f) lack of control, (g) easy influencibility, and (h) aimlessness. Responses to the two attribution questions were coded on five-point scales for internality, stability, and intentionality.

The questionnaire also requested objective characteristics of the case such as minimum sentence, crime type, number of prior convictions, and the identity of the board member responsible for the case. The questionnaire also asked the parole board member to rate the importance of 22 decision considerations, the severity of the offense, the severity of the criminal record, risk of a new offense, and risk of a dangerous offense.

Analysis revealed that the stability of the cause of the offense was a significant determinant in judging the risk of future crime, thereby significantly influencing parole recommendations. Crimes attributed to more stable causes received higher ratings of risk and poorer parole recommendations. Contrary to predictions, the internality and intentionality of attributions did not influence parole decisions. However, because the Pennsylvania Board ignores punishment considerations, it is understandable that attributions of responsibility would have little impact.

Schematic knowledge

The foregoing analysis restricts the influence of causal attributions to a few dimensions such as locus of control and stability. Yet specific causal attributions such as "drugs" or "alcohol" carry additional distinct content. They are the conventional, pragmatic, meaningful categories (Rosch, Mervis, Gray, Johnson, & Boyes–Braem, 1976) that organize knowledge about criminals—what we will call schemas. Such schemas enable people to place their knowledge into a temporal sequence with a biographical past and prognoses for the future (as in the "story model" of Pennington & Hastie, 1988) and to generate inferences about missing information that may result in confusing case facts with expectations (cf. Taylor & Crocker, 1981).

One reason students and experts may have differed in their responses to the hypothetical crime-plus-attribution cases in Carroll and Payne (1977a, 1977b) is that the students had access to only the most general features of crimes and causes, whereas the experts had more detailed schemas that imbued these cases with more specific features and meaning. For example, the effect of unemployment on the experts' judgments of responsibility depended on the specific crime. An unemployed person who committed murder was not held very responsible (unemployment was an excuse for an isolated, emotional act); yet an unemployed person who sold heroin was held highly responsible (unemployment strengthened inferences about a pattern of drug dealing). A second example is the distinction made by board members between "criminal addicts" and "addict criminals": The former are "addicts" who support their habit by property crime; the latter are "criminals" whose rule breaking and thrill seeking include drug use.

The hypothesis that specific attributional categories have impact beyond their dimensional implications was tested with the Pennsylvania Parole Board data by recoding the attributions into five content categories: person, money, drugs, alcohol, and environment (Carroll, Galegher, & Wiener, 1982). After controlling for the previously coded attributional dimensions in a multiple regression analysis, attributional category still accounted for substantial variance in parole recommendations, prognosis for rehabilitation, and risk of subsequent offense. In fact, attributional category accounted for two to three times as much variance in these decisions and judgments as did attributional dimensions.

Lurigio and Carroll (1985) studied the schemas of another group of criminal justice experts—probation officers, whose job is to recommend treatment options to the court and supervise offenders placed on probation (usually instead of serving time in prison). A series of semistructured interviews inquired about "types of probationers" and the characteristics of each type. Probation officers reported between three and nine different schemas. Ten schemas were reported by at least one third of the officers; these are listed in Table 1. Follow-up studies showed that case information was spontaneously organized into schemas and that cases constructed to fit schemas were evaluated more consistently, confidently, and quickly than typical real cases or cases constructed to mix schemas.

These results suggest that decisions involve the interpretation of complex case material through the application of prior knowledge. The recognition of familiar "types" helps to speed up processing and create more consistency among decision makers and more distinctions among different case types. On the other hand, ascription of schemas to cases that do not fit could lead to incorrect decisions.

Hypothesis testing and alternative-driven decisions

Kelley's (1967) attribution model assumes that the perceiver is a naive scientist who collects information and uses general logical rules (a "naive analysis of variance") to produce an attribution. The attribution process is assumed to be inductive, data driven, and linear (i.e., the rules are applied once to produce a result).

Carroll and Wiener (1982) suggested modifications to the attribution process. They proposed that perceivers might leap to an attributional hypothesis on the basis of minimal information and then examine other information to confirm their hypotheses (Kruglanski, Hamel, Maides, & Schwartz, 1978). This process could introduce a confirmation bias (Snyder & Cantor, 1979).

Given an event such as "burglary," people generate plausible specific attributions such as "drugs" and "poverty" (Carroll & Wiener, 1982). As an example of the generation of attributional hypotheses, consider the first few statements in one verbal protocol collected by Carroll and Payne (1977a, p. 229): "Ah, ok, this summarization sheet says 22-year-old single man. Young, perhaps an immature kind of individual. Ah, charge?" Apparently, a potential cause of crime, immaturity, was generated merely by the offender's age *before* the crime (the charge) was even known. Another expert, while examining case material to un-

TABLE 1 Probation Officers' Schemas for Offenders

SCHEMA TYPE	BRIEF DESCRIPTION
BURGLAR	Early 30s, married, any race, intelligent, extensive burglary record, professional/expert, very poor prognosis (set lifestyle).
DRUG ADDICT	Early 20s, black, unintelligent, uneducated, lacking any social skills, parasite—uses people, varied crime background, crime to support habit, poor prognosis, some hope in a program.
GANGBANGER	Under 21, Hispanic, cocky at first, gang involvement causes crime, needs lots of supervision, prognosis good—matures out of gang activities.
UNCLE TOM	40–60s, black, sporadic history of petty crime, crime by impulse, excellent prognosis—fears prison, respectful, cooperative.
FEMALE WELFARE FRAUD	20s, black woman, unmarried but involved with male who controls her life, easily manipulated, feels forced to crime through concern for kids or her man, prognosis guarded to good depending on getting her away from the man.
CAREER CRIMINAL (CON-MAN)	Black, well-dressed, street-smart, manipulative, bad person, unreachable, no concern for others, extensive diverse criminal history, prognosis very bad.
VIOLENT MACHO-MAN	20s, Hispanic, short fuse—walking time bomb, assaults and bar fights when manhood challenged, may act out under supervision, prognosis—no change.
SUBURBAN KID	Teens, minor first offense, good kid in bad crowd, contrite, parents heavily involved in case, prognosis excellent.
DUMB HILLBILLY	Dumb, very easily influenced, impulsive, many petty crimes, cooperative, prognosis—guarded if controlled by probation officer.
WHITE-COLLAR CRIMINAL	White, 35–45, middle class, employed, family, businessman, looking for a fast buck, irresistible impulse, drug dealing, not a criminal type, prognosis excellent, cooperative although insulted by this process.

Note: From Lurigio & Carroll (1985), p. 1115.

derstand an offender's behavior, expressed and then rejected a "spoiled kid schema" hypothesis: "Sometimes, uh—the parents are overprotective and they've always covered him for everything he's ever done. And if that's indicated here, that would certainly be a, you know, somethin' that would you know—add—detract from him bein' able to make it when he hits the street. Nothing like that is indicated here" (p. 227).

Carroll and Wiener (1982) also proposed that attributional hypotheses could emerge from the decision alternatives; the perceiver's need to distinguish among response alternatives would tend to organize knowledge into schemas consistent with the alternatives. Schemas may arise, in part, because of the need to make distinctive responses to types of criminals. Not only is there a release decision, but different forms of treatment are available, including drug programs, alcohol programs, job training, and counseling. The major kinds of treatment programs and the major categories of attributions for criminal behavior are parallel: Drug problems are sent to drug programs, personality problems to counseling, and so forth. The availability of a treatment response may encourage the organization of knowledge around a schema that includes the treatment. Batson, Jones, and Cochran (1979) found that the availability of treatment options affected diagnoses for mental health patients: If psychotherapy was available, more patients were diagnosed with ailments that required that treatment. Forst and Wellford (1981) made a similar argument for judges' decisions among sentencing options.

Goals

Parole decisions involve a balancing of such goals as punishment and protection of the community. The different sentencing structures in Pennsylvania and Wisconsin change the responsibilities of the parole boards and thereby alter the degree to which their parole boards consider punishment as a goal. More generally, the typical sentencing goals or penal philosophies found in the literature on criminal justice decisions (e.g., Diamond & Herhold, 1981; Hogarth, 1971; McFatter, 1982) are (a) punishment, retribution, or just deserts; (b) rehabilitation; (c) incapacitation or protection of the community; (d) general deterrence or setting examples; and (e) special deterrence or direct punishment.

Individual decision makers tend to have consistent preferences for sentencing goals. Judges differ substantially in what goals they advocate for cases (Hogarth, 1971), even for identical cases (Forst & Wellford, 1981). Furthermore, goal preferences are strongly related to the type and severity of sentences. For example, both Hogarth and Forst and Wellford found that judges favoring incapacitation gave the longest sentences.

Goal preferences are associated with a variety of other individual characteristics. Hogarth (1971) found that judges' individual penal philosophies were related to their beliefs about the causes of crime. Those espousing rehabilitation attributed crime more to socioeconomic factors and believed many or most offenders to be mentally ill. Those low on rehabilitation (and high on punishment) downgraded socioeconomic causes, tended to see crime as due to lack of intelligence and alcoholism, and believed few offenders to be mentally ill. Judges favoring punishment believed that community resources are ineffective and that punishment is good for offenders; judges favoring rehabilitation believed that community resources are effective (Forst & Wellford, 1981; Hogarth, 1971). Hogarth interpreted this to mean that "punitive" judges come to believe that punishment works and rehabilitation does not; Forst and Wellford assumed that judges who think effective rehabilitation is unavailable become more punishment oriented. Clearly, both may occur (Staw, 1980).

Carroll, Perkowitz, Lurigio, and Weaver (1987) found that sentencing goals, attributions about the causes of crime, and measures of personality and ideology cluster together into two "resonances" (an extension of Alker & Poppen's [1973] terminology): punishment and rehabilitation. Those advocating tough treatment of criminals believe that such responses simultaneously provide just punishment, deter criminals, and protect society. These beliefs are associated with moral conservativism, authoritarianism, a belief in individual causation and a just world, and the ideology of the political right. Those advocating rehabilitation believe in economic causation and welfarism, the ideology of the political left. One conclusion from such research is that disparity in treatment is deeply rooted in mutually supporting beliefs—beliefs that are unlikely to change easily. Interventions intended to influence criminal justice decision makers (see next section) may fail to produce change if they do not recognize the resonance structure underlying judgments and decisions.

Carroll et al.'s (1987) results suggest that decision making is to some extent goal directed. That is, the characteristics of the case, the decision maker, and the setting make particular goals salient. Those goals then influence particular response possibilities and the pursuit of information. In short, decision makers engage in active hypothesis testing rather than a routine application of a fixed decision rule.

Decision aids

Since judgments of risk are central to parole decisions, accurate predictions by criminal justice experts are of central importance to rehabilitation and public safety. If they are not highly accurate, then an objective prediction device may be able to help. Parole boards and other criminal justice organizations have designed and implemented "guidelines" to assist decision makers in reducing disparity and enhancing effectiveness (Gottfredson & Gottfredson, 1980).

Carroll, Wiener, et al. (1982) obtained judgments of risk from Pennsylvania parole interviewers on a questionnaire immediately following 1,035 actual parole decisions. Case files provided 1-year follow-up data on 838 offenders paroled in Pennsylvania. Analyses were conducted on four outcome variables: (a) conviction of a new crime while on parole, (b) violation of the conditions of parole, (c) absconding, or (d) "failure" defined by the board as any of being recommitted to prison, absconding, dying during a criminal act, or being detained pending adjudication. These four outcomes were related to seven predictive judgments: (a) prognosis for supervision, (b) risk of future crime, (c) risk of future dangerous crime, (d) assaultive potential, (e) initial parole decision to release or deny, (f) initial institutional recommendation, and (g) initial case analyst's recommendation. None of these judgments significantly predicted any of the outcomes: the *largest* positive correlation was $r = .06$! The interviewers were more successful at predicting the seriousness of crime among the 88 parolees convicted of new crimes. Seriousness of new conviction correlated $r = .27$ with ratings of assaultive potential.

During the same time period, two clinical psychologists had established a reputation with one field office for astounding accuracy in predicting which parolees would commit crimes, the nature of the crimes, and the timing after parole. To more systematically test their accuracy, the psychologists were asked to evaluate a sample of case files of offenders released 1 year previously and to predict who would commit crimes. Their predictions were better than chance but not very good; they substantially overpredicted crime. This finding suggests that their reputation may have resulted from the classic illusory correlation or false learning effect (Chapman & Chapman, 1969; Einhorn, 1980), in which a few correct predictions of criminal behavior are so salient that people ignore incorrect or unknown outcomes.

Following the example of the U.S. Board of Parole decision aid system, the Pennsylvania Board developed their own set of guidelines focused on institutional conduct, parole prognosis, and adequacy of parole plan. There were explicit indicators for each factor: Institutional conduct was based on number of misconducts and rule infractions in the 12 months prior to release; subjective risk assessments were replaced by an empirical prediction based on prior convictions, offense type, and age (such predictions have correlations around $r = .3$ with outcomes but are better than subjective judgment; Gottfredson, Wilkins, & Hoffman, 1978). Combinations of these factors were related to presumptive decisions, using prior cases to examine past policy and consensus decisions regarding new policy. Since parole interviewers can go outside the parole guidelines but must give their reasons for doing so, the accumulation of such reasons form an input into a regular guidelines revision process.

The fundamental objective of parole guidelines was to assure fairness and equity. The guidelines helped make parole decisions predictable, understandable, and accountable to the public, the legislature, and the inmates. Guidelines strike a reasonable balance between consistency and autonomy, and objective and subjective factors.

Although guidelines have been adopted in a variety of criminal justice settings during the past 15 years, there has been wide variation in their success (Galegher & Carroll, 1983). In particular, whereas implementing guidelines with the U.S. Board of Parole is generally considered a successful model, implementing guidelines for judges is more problematic.

Rich, Sutton, Clear, and Saks (1982) conducted an impact analysis of sentencing guidelines used by judges in Denver, Chicago, and Philadelphia. In Denver, sentences were no more consistent with guideline recommendations after they were introduced than before. In Philadelphia, there was only slightly more consistency. Interviews with court personnel indicated that the guidelines were never effectively implemented because of the broader organizational context. In Philadelphia, heavy caseloads led to an avoidance of trials by encouraging guilty pleas. Defendants who demanded jury trials were especially discouraged by assigning jury trials to the harshest judges: Offenders sentenced by these judges received prison sentences 10 years longer than those who pled guilty or were convicted in bench trials. Thus, the guidelines (if they were followed) would have made sentence bargaining more difficult, encouraged charge bargaining, and increased the power of the prosecutors who typically set charges. In Chicago, some judges calculated the guideline sentences only after the actual sentence had been imposed; others ignored them. Within several months, judges had lost interest.

Galegher and Carroll (1983) suggested that successful implementation is affected by several factors: the fit between the guidelines and the goals of the decision makers; the advantages of guidelines over unassisted decision making; the perception of a performance gap in current practice; whether decision makers participate in guideline development; the mechanisms for monitoring the success of the implementation; and the complexity and centralization of the organization. The parole system tends to be more receptive than the judicial system, but the implementation process itself bears a great deal of responsibility for success. During the development of sentencing guidelines in Minnesota, careful attention to details, training, involvement of stakeholders, and perception of implementation as a continual process led to far more favorable outcomes (Blumstein, Cohen, Martin, & Tonry, 1983).

Dynamic decision making

Decisions are situated in a temporal context as well as an organizational context. Laboratory studies of decision making treat each decision as the unit; changes over time are a nuisance. In real organizations, however, feedback over time links a series of individual decisions and connects individual and organizational action (Brehmer, 1986; Kleinmuntz, 1985; Sterman, 1989). For example, experienced probation officers report fewer schemas than do novice officers, and their schemas are less idiosyncratic and more detailed (Lurigio & Carroll, 1985). Thus, officers learn which schemas of offenders are useful, enrich these schemas while weeding out useless ones, and become more knowledgeable and effective in their jobs (Lurigio & Carroll, 1985). Schema development and modification may result from direct experience with probation cases (Weber & Crocker, 1983); it may also result from the social transmission of information about cases through discussion and training.

Institutional policy, organizational practices, and individual decisions all play a crucial role in the decision guidelines process. As decision makers use the guidelines for the U.S. Board of Parole (Gottfredson et al., 1978), data comparing decisions to the guidelines are used to "tune up" decision makers who do not pay proper attention to the guidelines *and* to revise the guidelines when they are divergent from justifiable practices. Unfortunately, adequate monitoring and feedback mechanisms are rare in implementing *sentencing* guidelines (Rich et al., 1982).

Sentencing guidelines are frequently legislated to be more severe than judicial practice, resulting in more and longer prison sentences, gradual overcrowding of prisons, and more pressure on other parts of the system to release offenders earlier (and build more prisons). Because these dynamics unfold slowly and the consequences accrue to parts of the system distant from the guidelines' developers, these consequences can go unrecognized. In Minnesota, the law was written to keep the predicted incarceration rates with guidelines no higher than the predicted result of judges' preguidelines behavior (Martin, 1983).

The preceding discussion has touched on the elements in Figure 2 that provide an enriched framework for understanding decision making in organizational contexts. The framework adds additional detail about the context of task, organization, and interpersonal relations and about the purposive, knowledge-based cognitive processes that constitute individual decision making. Although the examples have been drawn from decisions within the criminal justice system, the framework should be applicable to other organizations. The next section examines how employees in nuclear power plants learn from their own experience (a dynamic decision task) by a process of interpretation that involves causal reasoning and the social distribution of knowledge.

LEARNING FROM EXPERIENCE IN NUCLEAR POWER PLANTS

The nuclear power industry focuses extraordinary attention on safety-related incidents. Because trial-and-error learning is too hazardous in this context (Perrow, 1984), there is emphasis on extracting information from any and all anomalies. Individuals and committees within plants and organizations in industry and government work very hard to gather and interpret information. Thus, the improvement of plant functioning and the enhancement of safe performance depend greatly on the ability to interpret experience from within and outside the plant. This ability derives from knowledge and expertise, the "cognitive capital" distributed through the organization and throughout the industry.

Causal analysis of events

Each incident or event in a plant is the product of a variety of causes. Thus, Three Mile Island, the worst disaster in U.S. nuclear industry experience, resulted from a stuck valve and operator misunderstanding, but also inadequate instrumentation, incorrect procedures and training, and failure to transmit information within the industry about this type of event (Kemeny, 1979; Perrow, 1984). Not only are there combinations of causes (e.g., operator error, mechanical failure), but each "cause" is embedded in a causal chain that includes some "deeper" causes (e.g., operator error by improper training, in turn caused by failure to transmit information; mechanical failure due to poor maintenance, which can be blamed on poor supervision, and so forth).

For decades, the hazardous consequences of technologies have been conceptualized primarily as technical problems, and the dominant conceptual analyses have been provided by engineers (Rasmussen & Batstone, 1991). Over time, with appropriate designs, models, and testing, these engineered systems were expected to become optimally safe. Indeed, a steadily improving trend though the past decade on various safety and performance indicators and current nuclear industry consensus suggest that nuclear power plants now operate plants more safely than comparable industries (e.g., chemicals).

When concern extends beyond the technical system to the human operators, maintainers, and designers who are essential to the safe functioning of the technical system, the convention has been to examine the immediate interface of people and technology. "Human error" is the first explanation of why things go wrong at the interface. Blame is laid on an incompetent or inattentive individual or on a confusing set of controls and indicators. The field of human factors, or human–machine interaction, is a logical extension of the technical view, and its emphasis on laboratory and experimental methods has yielded system designs with demonstrable success in improving safety and other aspects of effective performance.

A situated approach to event analysis

In both industry and academia, there is a growing realization that achieving the extraordinarily high level of safety demanded in hazardous technologies requires a further theoretical development (LaPorte & Consolini, 1989). Specifically, human–machine interaction must be considered in the context of social and cultural systems—that is, organizational forms, hierarchies, occupational cultures, recruitment, training, incentives and rewards, and management and supervision (Marcus et al., 1990; Moray & Huey, 1988; Rasmussen & Batstone, 1991).

The analysis of organizational decision making in criminal justice decisions (see Figure 2) can be used to analyze incidents in nuclear power plants. This analysis is divided into two parts: (a) causal reasoning and "mental models," and (b) the organizational context of causal reasoning.

CAUSAL REASONING AND "MENTAL MODELS."   Determining causes is not straightforward. Suppose, for example, that a mechanic skips a step in the procedure for repairing a valve and, as a result, the valve later fails. Although we may be tempted to lay the blame on a careless person, the analysis of this incident would be far more involved. Procedures may be out of date or incorrect; mechanics may do what they know to be correct instead of following procedures. There is pressure to do things quickly, so "carelessness" may be a symptom of work overload or conflicting organizational goals and incentives related to efficiency versus quality (or safety). Work is also checked by others, so that problems are partially attributable to failed quality control mechanisms. But each of these "causes" can be traced to other causes in communication, management, incentives, hiring and training practices, and even to demographics, educational systems, union structures, regulatory practices, and so on. *Any* causal analysis must be, in part, a construction of the analyst.

The causes attributed to various incidents and problems are constructed from *beliefs* about the causes of various events in the plant and ways to enhance plant functioning. These beliefs comprise "mental models" of plant functioning. Presumably, over time, mental models develop from occupational training, plant experience, and industry experience. However, the theories held by the most expert of plant employees, regulators, or consultants are not necessarily correct or complete.

In our framework, we consider that plant employees may have limited "mental models" for interpreting incidents and placing behaviors into causal stories, or a limited set of schema for understanding plant situations. The industry tendency to place individual human error at the forefront of incident analysis is an example of the "fundamental attribution error" (Nisbett & Ross, 1980). Because individuals act inappropriately or fail to act, it is natural to think of individual actors as primary causes. Thus, inattention to detail and carelessness are often used to describe errors. Or, the causes might be traced to different people who have trained others inadequately, developed incorrect procedures, or failed to communicate and enforce a "safety culture." These limitations are also consistent with attribution research literature on "functional blindness"—seeing the plant from a narrow perspective that makes only some causal factors salient—and "self-serving" attributions—reducing anxiety by blaming others for plant problems. (For a review of various biases, see Fiske & Taylor, 1984.)

Just as parole decisions may be structured by decision alternatives, the causal analysis of plant incidents may be response based. The search for causes is an instrumental process, oriented toward plant improvement and organized around actions that are believed possible. For example, the head of the International Atomic Energy Agency Incident Reporting System writes that "the root cause must be a cause that we have the power to deal with and solutions can be absurd if not limited" (Tolstykh, 1991, p. 2). "Limited" means within our control and consistent with other objectives (e.g., producing energy economically).

ORGANIZATIONAL CONTEXT.   What is difficult to see within the engineering world view of people and machines is the situating of these elements in social and cultural systems. For example, procedures that seem quite reasonable from an engineering standpoint may conflict with the social and cultural "logics" (Perin, 1990) of plant employees. In one plant, quality control over maintenance work was assigned to peers; in a worker team, one peer would check the work of his or her partner. However, it is disquieting to check the work of a friend because it implies hierarchy and "pulling rank" on a buddy. As a result, the checking did not always occur, and an incident was reported in which a worker's error went unchecked. Similarly, in a different plant, the shift supervisor was dealing with an emergency in the control room while the Nuclear Regulatory Commission Resident Inspector was looking over his shoulder and the Vice President of Nuclear Operations was on the phone from corporate headquarters. Although the shift supervisor had the authority to kick the resident out of the control room and hang up on the VP, this shift supervisor did not do so and, in the ensuing confusion, a mistake was made. Again, the procedural authority given to the shift supervisor to correspond with responsibilities and expertise may have been in conflict with the authority derived from hierarchy and institutional power.

Acknowledging complexity represents the beginning of what a recent international workshop on the science of safety and risk management called a paradigm shift in the science of safety toward a "social anthropology" of the organization "in its operational context" and toward learning how to "place a greater premium on cultural factors, heuristic rather than deterministic models, and working with incomplete and/or evanescent information rather than conceptually closed systems" (Rasmussen & Batstone, 1991, p. 9).

Measuring mental models

In a current research project, I am characterizing "mental models" in nuclear power plants. The goals of the project are to portray mental models not simply as a property of individuals but as socially distributed knowledge that is an organizational resource for interpreting experience and enhancing safe performance.

For the most part, "mental models" of the plant are implicit. They are rarely discussed or formally presented. They emerge as the foundation of the interpretive work that occurs around problems, incidents, or issues that create surprise, concern, or a need to know more. Mental models are revealed as they are used. As people in the plant discuss and analyze issues, they are exposed to each others' mental models, and each person's own model becomes more general, more comprehensive, and more consistent and closely linked with others' models.

Given the aforementioned reasoning, mental models should be assessed by evoking their use. In the project, interesting examples or scenarios from actual events in plants will be presented to a range of plant employees from several plants. To analyze these situations, they will be asked for more than a "right answer"; questions will request multiple implications, analyses, and suggestions to reveal mental models at work.

Two reasonable hypotheses about the capacity of a plant to learn from experience readily emerge from our framework: First, the variety and depth of the analyses produced by plant employees should be important to learning. Depth of analysis refers to system-based and temporally complex causes rather than simple human error, poor training, etc. Second, the overlap of analyses across functions and levels of plant employees should indicate employees' ability to communicate about incidents. The overlap is likely to index a past history of shared problem solving among a wide range of plant employees. The need for variety *and* shared knowledge suggests that specialization of plant employees into zones of expertise can be overdone, creating difficulty in working together to address complex problems that cut across areas of specialization.

SUMMARY

This chapter illustrates how the social psychological approach to decision making in organizations has broadened. Social psychologists in the 1960s and 1970s tended to focus on abstract behavioral principles centered on individual cognitions. Decisions were a property of individuals, were viewed apart from preceding and following decisions, were divorced from organizational context, and were made by individuals who used mostly logical rules.

Research on actual decisions by members of organizations acted as a stimulus to elaborate the fundamental concept of decision making. In the expanded framework that situates decision making within organizational place and time, the nature of the context is delineated more carefully to include the nature of the task, the available resources from which alternatives are created, the content and flow of information, the role relationships of the decision makers, and the informal social system that emerges from and contributes to decision making. Further, the cognitive processes in decision making are reexamined and refocused on purposive, knowledge-based processes including hypothesis testing, alternative-focused decision making, and the development and use of schemas. Finally, these processes are located in time by recognizing the dynamic feedback and learning processes that connect decisions.

The study of decision making in organizations is at a divergent stage of development, open to the phenomena that are being uncovered as more complex and less controlled decisions are examined, and breaking the boundaries that have traditionally kept individual decision making separate from the complexities of organizations and dynamic processes. The framework in this chapter is merely a step toward new theories of decision making that will guide and emerge from future research.

REFERENCES

ABRAMSON, L. Y., SELIGMAN, M. E. P., & TEASDALE, J. D. (1978). Learned helplessness in humans: Critique and reformulation. *Journal of Abnormal Psychology, 87,* 49–74.

ALKER, H. A., & POPPEN, P. J. (1973). Personality and ideology in university students. *Journal of Personality, 41,* 652–671.

BATSON, C. D., JONES, C. H., & COCHRAN, P. J. (1979). Attributional bias in counselors' diagnoses: The effect of resources. *Journal of Applied Social Psychology, 9,* 377–393.

BLUMSTEIN, W., COHEN, J., MARTIN, S. E., & TONRY, M. (Eds.). (1983). *Research on sentencing: The search for reform, Vol. 1.* Washington, DC: National Academy of Sciences.

BREHMER, B. (1986, November). *Feedback in dynamic decision making.* Paper presented at the 1986 annual meeting of the Judgment/Decision Making Society, New Orleans.

CARROLL, J. S. (1978). Causal attribution in expert parole decisions. *Journal of Personality and Social Psychology, 36,* 1501–1511.

CARROLL, J. S., & BURKE, P. A. (1990). Evaluation and prediction in expert parole decisions. *Criminal Justice and Behavior, 17,* 315–332.

CARROLL, J. S., GALEGHER, J., & WIENER, R. L. (1982). Attributional dimensions and schemas in expert parole decisions. *Basic and Applied Social Psychology, 3,* 187–201.

CARROLL, J. S., & PAYNE, J. W. (1976). The psychology of the parole decision process. In J. S. Carroll & J. W. Payne (Eds.), *Cognition and social behavior* (pp. 13–32). Hillsdale, NJ: Erlbaum.

CARROLL, J. S., & PAYNE, J. W. (1977b). Judgments about crime and the criminal: A model and a method for investigating parole decisions. In B. Sales (Ed.) *Perspectives in law and psychology, Vol. I: Criminal justice system* (pp. 191–239). New York: Plenum.

CARROLL, J. S., & PAYNE, J. W. (1977a). Crime seriousness, recidivism risk, and causal attributions in judgments of prison term by students and experts. *Journal of Applied Psychology, 62,* 595–602.

CARROLL, J. S., PERKOWITZ, W. T., LURIGIO, A. J., & WEAVER, F. M. (1987). Sentencing goals, causal attributions, ideology, and personality. *Journal of Personality and Social Psychology, 52,* 107–118.

CARROLL, J. S., WIENER, R. L., COATES, D., GALEGHER, J., & ALIBRIO, J. J. (1982). Evaluation, diagnosis, and prediction in parole decision making. *Law and Society Review, 17,* 199–228.

CARTER, R. M. (1967). The presentence report and decision making process. *Journal of Research in Crime and Delinquency, 4,* 203–211.

CHAPMAN, L. J., & CHAPMAN, J. P. (1969). Illusory correlation as an obstacle to the use of valid psychodiagnostic signs. *Journal of Abnormal Psychology, 74,* 271.

DIAMOND, S. S., & HERHOLD, C. J. (1981). Understanding criminal sentencing: Views from law and social psychology. In G. M. Stephenson & J. M. Davis (Eds.), *Progress in applied social psychology, Vol. 1* (pp. 67–102). London: John Wiley.

EBBESEN, E. B., & KONECNI, V. J. (1982). An analysis of the bail system. In V. J. Konecni & E. B. Ebbesen (Eds.), *The criminal justice system: A social-psychological analysis* (pp. 191–229). San Francisco: W. H. Freeman.

EINHORN, H. J. (1980). Learning from experience and suboptimal rules in decision making. In T. Wallsten (Ed.), *Cognitive processes in choice and decision behavior* (pp. 1–20). Hillsdale, NJ: Erlbaum.

FISKE, S. T., & TAYLOR, S. E. (1984). *Social cognition.* Reading, MA: Addison-Wesley.

FORST, B., & WELLFORD, C. (1981). Punishment and sentencing: Developing sentencing guidelines empirically from principles of punishment. *Hofstra University Law Review, 9,* 799–837.

GALEGHER, J., & CARROLL, J. S. (1983). Voluntary sentencing guidelines: Prescription for justice or patent medicine? *Law and Human Behavior, 7,* 361–400.

GENEGO, W. J., GOLDBERGER, P. D., & JACKSON, V. C. (1975). Parole release decision making and the sentencing process. *Yale Law Journal, 84*(4), 810–902.

GOTTFREDSON, D. M., WILKINS, L. T., & HOFFMAN, P. B. (1978). *Guidelines for parole and sentencing: A policy control method.* Lexington, MA: Lexington Books.

GOTTFREDSON, D. M., WILKINS, L. T., HOFFMAN, P. B., & SINGER, M. (1973). *The utilization of experience in parole decision-making: A progress report.* Davis, CA: National Council on Crime and Delinquency Research Center.

GOTTFREDSON, M. R., & GOTTFREDSON, D. M. (1980). *Decisionmaking in criminal justice: Toward the rational exercise of discretion.* Cambridge, MA: Ballinger.

HACKMAN, J. R., & OLDHAM, G. R. (1975). Development of the job diagnostic survey. *Journal of Applied Psychology, 60,* 159–170.

HEIDER, F. (1958). *The psychology of interpersonal relations.* New York: Wiley.

HELMREICH, R. (1975). Applied social psychology: The unfulfilled promise. *Personality and Social Psychology Bulletin, 1,* 548–560.

HOFFMAN, P. B. (1973). *Paroling policy feedback* (Supplemental Report 8). Davis, CA: National Council on Crime and Delinquency Research Center.

HOGARTH, J. (1971). *Sentencing as a human process.* Toronto: University of Toronto.

JACOB, H. (1978). *Justice in America: Courts, lawyers, and the judicial process* (3rd ed.). Boston: Little, Brown.

KALVEN, H., & ZEISEL, H. (1966). *The American jury.* Boston: Little, Brown.

KASTENMEIER, R., & EGLIT, H. (1973). Parole release decision-making: Rehabilitation, expertise, and the demise of mythology. *American University Law Review, 22,* 477–525.

KATZ, D., & KAHN, R. L. (1966). *The social psychology of organizations.* New York: Wiley.

KELLEY, H. H. (1967). Attribution theory in social psychology. In D. Levine (Ed.), *Nebraska symposium on motivation* (pp. 192–241). Lincoln, NE: U. Nebraska.

KELLEY, H. H. (1973). The processes of causal attribution. *American Psychologist, 28,* 107–128.

KEMENY, J. G. (1979). *The need for change: The legacy of Three Mile Island.* Report of The President's Commission on the Accident at TMI. Washington, DC: U.S. Government Printing Office.

KLEINMUNTZ, D. N. (1985). Cognitive heuristics and feedback in a dynamic decision environment. *Management Science, 31,* 680–702.

KONECNI, V. J., & EBBESEN, E. B. (1979). External validity of research in legal psychology. *Law and Human Behavior, 3,* 39–70.

KONECNI, V. J., & EBBESEN, E. B. (1982). An analysis of the sentencing system. In V. J. Konecni & E. B. Ebbesen (Eds.), *The criminal justice system: A social-psychological analysis* (pp. 293–332). San Francisco: W. H. Freeman.

KRUGLANSKI, A. W., HAMEL, I. Z., MAIDES, S. A., & SCHWARTZ, J. N. (1978). Attribution theory as a special case of lay epistemology. In J. H. Harvey, W. Ickes, & R. F. Kidd (Eds.), *New directions in attribution research* (Vol. 2, pp. 299–333). Hillsdale, NJ: Erlbaum.

LaPORTE, T. R., & CONSOLINI, P. M. (1989). *Working in practice but not in theory: Theoretical challenges of "high reliability organizations."* Unpublished manuscript, Department of Political Science, U. California, Berkeley.

LURIGIO, A. J., & CARROLL, J. S. (1985). Probation officers' schemas of offenders: Content, development, and impact on treatment decisions. *Journal of Personality and Social Psychology, 48,* 1112–1126.

MARCUS, A. A., et al. (1990). *Organization and safety in nuclear power plants.* Division of Systems Research, Office of Nuclear Regulatory Research, U.S. Nuclear Regulatory Commission, NUREG/CR-5437. Washington, DC: U.S. Nuclear Regulatory Commission.

MARTIN, S. E. (1983). The politics of sentencing reform: Sentencing guidelines in Minnesota and Pennsylvania. In W. Blumstein, J. Cohen, S. E. Martin, & M. Tonry (Eds.), *Research on sentencing: The search for reform* (Vol. 2, pp. 265–304). Washington, DC: National Academy of Sciences.

McARTHUR, L. Z. (1972). The how and what of why: Some determinants and consequences of causal attribution. *Journal of Personality and Social Psychology, 22,* 171–193.

McFATTER, R. M. (1982). Purposes of punishment: Effects of utilities of criminal sanctions on perceived appropriateness. *Journal of Applied Psychology, 67,* 255–267.

MORAY, N. P., & HUEY, B. M. (Eds.). (1988). *Human factors research and nuclear safety.* Washington, DC: National Academy Press.

NEWELL, A., & SIMON, H. A. (1972). *Human problem solving.* Englewood Cliffs, NJ: Prentice Hall.

NISBETT, R. E., & ROSS, L. (1980). *Human inference: Strategies and shortcomings of social judgment.* Englewood Cliffs, NJ: Prentice Hall.

PAYNE, J. W. (1973). Alternative approaches to decision making under risk: Moments vs. risk dimensions. *Psychological Bulletin, 80,* 439–453.

PENNINGTON, N., & HASTIE, R. (1988). Explanation-based decision making: Effects of memory structure on judgment. *Journal of Experimental Psychology: Learning, Memory, and Cognition, 14,* 521–533.

PERIN, C. (1990). *The social and cultural logics of nuclear power plants.* Unpublished manuscript, MIT Center for Energy Policy Research, Cambridge, MA.

PERROW, C. (1984). *Normal accidents.* New York: Basic Books.

RASMUSSEN, J., & BATSTONE, R. (1991). *Towards improved safety control and risk management.* Findings from the World Bank Workshops. Unpublished manuscript, Washington, DC: World Bank, 1988, 1989.

RICH, W. D., SUTTON, L. P., CLEAR, T. R., & SAKS, M. J. (1982). *Sentencing by mathematics: An evaluation of the early attempts to develop and implement sentencing guidelines.* Washington, DC: National Center for State Courts.

ROSCH, E., MERVIS, C. B., GRAY, W. D., JOHNSON, D. M., & BOYES–BRAEM, P. (1976). Basic objects in natural categories. *Cognitive Psychology, 8*, 382–439.

SCHNEIDER, D. J. (1973). Implicit personality theory: A review. *Psychological Bulletin, 79*, 294–309.

SNYDER, M., & CANTOR, N. (1979). Testing hypotheses about other people: The use of historical knowledge. *Journal of Experimental Social Psychology, 15*, 330–342.

STAW, B. (1980). Rationality and justification in organizational life. In B. Staw & L. Cummings (Eds.), *Research in organizational behavior* (Vol. 2, pp. 45–80). New York: JAI Press.

STERMAN, J. D. (1989). Misperceptions of feedback in dynamic decision making. *Organizational Behavior and Human Decision Processes, 43*, 301–335.

TAYLOR, S. E., & CROCKER, J. (1981). Schematic bases of social information processing. In E. T. Higgins, P. Hermann, & M. P. Zanna (Eds.), *The Ontario symposium on personality and social psychology* (Vol. 1, pp. 89–134). Hillsdale, NJ: Erlbaum.

TOLSTYKH, V. (1991). *Patterns in IRS event reports for 1990.* Unpublished reports, Vienna: International Atomic Energy Agency.

TVERSKY, A., & KAHNEMAN, D. (1974). Judgment under uncertainty: Heuristics and biases. *Science, 211*, 453–458.

WEBER, R., & CROCKER, J. (1983). Cognitive processes in the revision of stereotypical beliefs. *Journal of Personality and Social Psychology, 45*, 961–977.

WEINER, B. (1974). Achievement motivation as conceptualized by an attribution theorist. In B. Weiner (Ed.), *Achievement motivation and attribution theory* (pp. 3–48). Morristown, NJ: General Learning Press.

WEINER, B., FRIEZE, I., KUKLA, A., REED, L., REST, S., & ROSENBAUM, R. (1971). *Perceiving the causes of success and failure.* Morristown, NJ: General Learning Press.

WEITAN, W., & DIAMOND, S. S. (1979). A critical review of the jury simulation paradigm. *Law and Human Behavior, 3*, 71–93.

WILKINS, L. T., GOTTFREDSON, D. M., ROBISON, J. P., & SADOWSKY, A. (1973). *Information selection and use in parole decision making* (Supplemental Report 5). Davis, CA: National Council on Crime and Delinquency Research Center.

CHAPTER FOUR

Affect and Organizational Behavior: When and Why Feeling Good (or Bad) Matters*

ROBERT A. BARON

Rensselaer Polytechnic Institute

In recent years, a growing volume of research in social psychology has focused on the influence of *affect*—relatively mild, temporary shifts in current mood. With respect to social behavior, interest in affect has led to research on the *incompatible response hypothesis,* the suggestion that inducing affective reactions incompatible with anger can sharply reduce the likelihood or intensity of overt aggression. Research findings support this hypothesis, indicating that such reactions as empathy, humor, and even mild sexual arousal can reduce aggression among previously angered persons. The incompatible response hypothesis has recently been applied to the reduction of organizational conflict, with considerable success. Individuals exposed to positive-affect-inducing procedures (e.g., receipt of a small gift, humor, mild flattery) make more concessions during simulated negotiations and report stronger preferences for resolving future conflicts in relatively constructive ways than individuals not exposed to such affect-induction procedures. Other research in social psychology indicates that several aspects of the physical environment (e.g., ambient temperature, noise, air quality) can serve as important sources of positive and negative affect. Such reactions, in turn, have been found to enhance, respectively, prosocial and antisocial forms of behavior. These findings have recently been extended to organizational processes. Results indicate that such environmental variables as pleasant fragrances and certain types of indoor lighting induce positive affect and so influence organizational behavior in predictable ways (e.g., enhancing performance appraisals and reducing ongoing conflict). Together, these lines of investigation illustrate how progress in social psychology can stimulate valuable advances in the field of organizational behavior.

*I wish to express my sincere appreciation to Alice M. Isen for her insightful comments on an earlier draft of this chapter and for helping me to recognize that affect has, in fact, been one of the guiding themes of my own research.

In the beginning, many social psychologists (or at least those with a cognitive bent) would say, there was *dissonance*. And with its counter-intuitive predictions concerning the effects of making decisions, expending effort (the *suffering leads to liking* effect; Axsom 1989), and engaging in counterattitudinal behavior (*forced compliance;* Cooper & Fazio, 1984), it shook the field to its roots (Cooper & Scher, 1991). Then, just when all the excitement was finally beginning to wane, along came *attribution,* with its insightful analyses of the processes through which we seek to answer the question "Why?"—as in "Why do others act in the ways they do?" (Harvey & Weary, 1989). Finally, during the 1980s social psychology embraced *social cognition*—efforts to apply basic principles and findings of cognitive psychology to an impressively wide range of topics—everything from impression formation and stereotypes (Fiske & Taylor, 1991) through *counterfactual thinking* (the effects of imagining the opposite of what has actually happened in a given situation) (Wells & Gavanski, 1989). Truly, then, social psychology has undergone nothing short of what some have described as a *cognitive revolution.* During this transformation, the primary emphasis of the field shifted from social *behavior* (interpersonal relations and group processes) to social *thought*—how we think about others and interpret their characteristics, words, and deeds.

Given its close links to social psychology, it is hardly surprising that the field of organizational behavior has been influenced by this shift. The cognitive revolution experienced by social psychology has spread, in many ways, into organizational research. For example, dissonance theory and dissonance-based explanations have been applied to such varied organizational issues as the elusive relationship between job satisfaction and task performance (Baron & Greenberg, 1990) and to efforts to understand the nature and causes of escalation of commitment (Staw & Ross, 1989). Attribution theory has found even greater application and has added substantially to our understanding of such topics as leadership (Lord, DeVader, & Alliger, 1986), motivation (Klein, 1989), and performance appraisal (Dugan, 1989). Finally, knowledge about social cognition has been applied by organizational researchers to such key areas as decision making, influence, and ingratiation (Liden & Mitchell, 1988).

In short, the rising tide of interest in cognition, in social psychology, has reverberated through the field of organizational behavior. Looking back over the advances that have flowed from this perspective, one can hardly quibble with its ultimate value. But the story certainly does not end there. In recent years, the pendulum of scientific interest has begun to swing once again. And what it has swung to, in both social and cognitive psychology, is growing interest in *affect*—the mild, temporary shifts in current mood that virtually everyone experiences throughout each day (Isen, 1990). Research on affect began with a limited focus: efforts to understand its impact on specific forms of behavior such as helping (Isen, 1970) and aggression (Baron, 1977). But such work has expanded greatly in both scope and volume so that at present, affect is one of the major themes of research in virtually all major areas of social psychology (Isen, 1987). One topic currently receiving major attention from social psychologists is the complex interplay between affect and cognition—how feelings shape thought and thought shapes feelings (Fiedler & Forgas, 1988).

Consistent with growing interest in the role of affect, many organizational researchers have turned their attention to this topic (cf. Isen & Baron, 1991). Thus, in recent years, the influence of affective states on negotiation (Carnevale & Isen, 1986), performance appraisals (Cardy & Dobbins, 1986), prosocial behavior at work (Brief & Motowidlo, 1986), and even absenteeism and turnover (George, 1990, 1991) have all been investigated. Once again, therefore, a major trend in social psychology has been reflected in organizational research.

My own research over the past 25 years has been concerned with the ways in which shifts in people's feelings influence important aspects of their behavior and cognition. The purpose of this chapter is to summarize this work—to pull it together into a coherent whole not readily apparent in previous papers. Another, and perhaps more important, goal is to use research on affect by myself and others as a means of illustrating how progress in social psychology can both stimulate and form the basis for valuable advances in the field of organizational behavior.

The plan of this chapter is as follows. First, I describe two lines of investigation in social psychology concerned with the influence of affect. Following each, I indicate how such research encouraged conceptually related research on organizational topics. In a final section, I summarize the state of current knowledge concerning the role of affect in organizational behavior and call attention to important gaps and issues on which future researchers may profitably focus.

AFFECT AND SOCIAL BEHAVIOR: INCOMPATIBLE RESPONSES AND THE CONTROL OF HUMAN AGGRESSION

Can individuals experience two incompatible moods or emotional states simultaneously? Some clinical psychologists might contend that they can, and as evidence would point to sadists, for whom joy or intense pleasure mixes regularly with anger and the motive to harm others. However, two lines of research suggest that in general, sharply contrasting moods or emotions cannot coexist. One is the well-known research on *response incompatibility*. Such incompatibility occurs whenever organisms experience strong tendencies both to perform and avoid specific forms of behavior. The classic case, of course, is an animal who receives electric shocks at a place where it also finds food. As a result, it soon develops strong tendencies to both approach *and* avoid the same spot (Miller, 1959). The internal conflict between these incompatible tendencies is readily observed. Animals faced with this type of predicament can sometimes be seen running toward the food cup, screeching to a halt, reversing their direction, and then, when far enough away from the source of food (and shock), changing directions once again.

A second line of research suggesting that it is difficult, if not impossible, for human beings to experience two incompatible moods or emotions simultaneously is concerned with the treatment of *phobias*—intense and seemingly irrational fears. One highly effective treatment for phobias involves training in *relaxation*, within a process of *systematic desensitization* (Speltz & Bernstein, 1979).

Phobic individuals are first taught how to induce relaxation responses, generally by successively relaxing major muscle groups. Once they have mastered this technique and can induce relaxation at will, they are asked to imagine scenes relating to the source of their fears. The initial scenes are low in fear-evoking properties but gradually increase in this respect until, ultimately, individuals are asked to imagine scenes they initially find terrifying. For each scene, clients are told to indicate when they begin to experience fear and are instructed to stop thinking about the scene and to induce relaxation when this occurs. These procedures are based on the idea that feelings of relaxation are incompatible with feelings of fear and that as a result of such incompatibility, generalized fear reactions will decrease. Many investigations indicate that this is the case—fear *does* tend to decrease sharply as a result of such treatment. In fact, within only a few treatment sessions, many individuals reach the point where they can imagine previously terrifying events with little or no signs of fear.

Together, these two lines of research seem to suggest that it is difficult, if not impossible, for individuals to experience incompatible moods or emotions at the same time. What does this have to do with research on affect in social psychology? A great deal. In the late 1960s and early 1970s, research on *aggression* literally exploded in social psychology. One reason for this sudden increase was the development of a new methodology that permitted social psychologists to study physical aggression in the laboratory, under safe conditions in which no one, presumably, could actually be harmed. This procedure used a device known as the Buss *aggression machine*. By pushing buttons on this apparatus subjects could, presumably, inflict physical harm on another person. They could, supposedly, deliver electric shocks, loud noise, or intense heat to the recipient. In reality, of course, no shocks, noises, or heat were ever received by the supposed victim, who was actually an accomplice of the researcher. However, to the extent that subjects believed that they could harm the victim, their choice of highly numbered buttons on the apparatus could be interpreted as voluntary acts of aggression.

Does the *aggression machine* really provide a safe and effective means of measuring human aggression? Opinion remains somewhat divided on this issue (Berkowitz & Donnerstein, 1982). But in the late 1960s, the availability of this new methodology certainly stimulated a great deal of research. Some of this research was concerned with what soon came to be known as the *incompatible response hypothesis* (Baron, 1977).

This hypothesis, based on the previously mentioned two lines of research, suggests that it may be possible to reduce both anger and overt aggression by exposing individuals to stimuli or events that induce feelings (affective states) incompatible with anger and aggression (Baron, 1977). What feelings, precisely, might prove incompatible with anger and aggression? Several possibilities seemed feasible, but three were promising: feelings of *empathy*, feelings of *amusement* (generated by various forms of humor), and *mild sexual arousal* (generated by exposure to mildly erotic materials). In fact, all three were soon found to be effective in reducing anger and overt aggression (Baron, 1983). Since the work on empathy and humor has found most direct application in my subsequent organizational research, I focus primarily on these factors.

Empathy: compassion in response to the suffering of others

When human beings aggress against others, they are often exposed to signs of pain and suffering on the part of their victims. Successful aggression, after all, inflicts harm or injury on the intended recipient. What reactions will aggressors have to such responses? Two contrasting patterns seem possible. When aggressors are extremely angry and believe that their aggression is justified, exposure to such *pain cues* on the part of the victim may prove reinforcing—under such conditions, the suffering of one's enemy can be a positive outcome. When anger is intense, therefore, witnessing the discomfort of others may fail to deter subsequent aggression and may, in fact, increase it.

In contrast, when aggressors are not very angry, or when they perceive that assaults against others are not fully justified, a different reaction may occur. Under such circumstances, aggressors may experience feelings of *empathy* or *sympathy* toward their intended victim, vicariously sharing the discomfort experienced by this person. Such reactions may then prove to be incompatible with anger or aggression, hence reducing such reactions.

These predictions were tested in a series of studies using a device known as the *pain meter*. The pain meter contains a meter with labels ostensibly describing the amount of pain experienced by another person when he or she is subjected to unpleasant stimuli (Baron, 1971a, 1971b, 1979a). In fact, all readings on the meter are controlled by the researcher and are systematically varied to suggest contrasting levels of pain and discomfort.

In studies utilizing this apparatus, subjects in different groups were exposed to sharply contrasting levels of pain cues (i.e., meter readings) as they pushed various buttons on the aggression machine. For example, when subjects assigned to a *high pain cues* condition pushed button number 5 on the aggression machine, the meter yielded a reading of "Intense pain." In contast, when subjects in a *low pain cues* condition pushed the same button, the meter yielded a reading of only "Mild Pain."

To test the hypothesis that individuals who had been strongly angered would react to pain cues with increased aggression while those who had not been angered would respond to such stimuli with reduced aggression, subjects in these studies were either strongly angered or not angered by the accomplice prior to their opportunity to aggress. Strong anger was generated by exposing subjects to rude remarks and negative evaluations of their work on a preliminary task. Participants who were not angered did not hear such remarks and received more neutral evaluations of their work. Results offered clear support for the major predictions. Subjects who had not been angered responded to signs of intense pain on the part of the victim with reduced aggression. In contrast, those who had been strongly angered responded to such cues with increased aggression. Additional findings indicated that these contrasting reactions were indeed mediated by dissimilar emotional states. Subjects who had been angered reported positive reactions to pain cues on the part of the victim, while those who had not been angered reported more negative reactions. Those who had been angered reported feeling happier, more excited, and less tense in response to pain cues than those who had not been previously annoyed by the victim. Further, participants who had not been angered reported stronger feelings of sympathy and empathy than those who had been verbally abused by this person. These findings provided at least indirect support for the incompatible response hypothesis. As predicted, emotional states incompatible with feelings of anger and tendencies to lash out at others did appear to reduce overt aggression.

The effects of humor and feelings of amusement

Many people have had the following experience: They are annoyed or irritated by another person. Then, unexpectedly, this individual does or says something that they find amusing. When this occurs, their annoyance—or at least a substantial part of it—seems to vanish. Such informal experiences suggest that *humor*, and the pleasant feelings it generates, may be another reaction incompatible with anger and overt aggression.

This hypothesis was tested in another series of studies. In the first of these experiments (Baron & Ball, 1974), participants were either angered or not angered by an accomplice. Then, prior to an opportunity to aggress against him by means of the aggression machine, participants in both groups were exposed to one of two sets of stimuli. One set consisted of neutral pictures of scenery, furniture, and abstract art found, in pretesting, to produce very little impact on subjects' affective state. The other was a series of humorous cartoons, rated as very funny by subjects in pretesting. Results were clear: As predicted, angry subjects who examined the humorous cartoons later showed lower levels of aggression against the assistant than those who examined the neutral (nonhumorous) pictures (Baron & Ball, 1974). In addition, those who examined the cartoons reported significantly lower levels of anger and irritation and significantly higher levels of amusement and positive feelings (along such dimensions as good–bad, happy–sad, tense–calm).

While these findings seemed quite straightforward, other studies published at about the same time reported results that seemed, initially, to be opposite in nature (e.g., Berkowitz, 1970). In these experiments, subjects exposed to humorous materials actually showed *higher* levels of aggression than those exposed to neutral materials. What could account for this apparent discrepancy? One possibility was as follows: In these other studies, the humor employed contained hostile or aggressive themes. For example, it depicted one person denigrating another. In the Baron and Ball (1974) study, in contrast, the humor was essentially silly in nature; little or no hostility was present. According to the incompatible response hypothesis, only humor of the latter type would reduce aggression. Humor with a hostile, biting edge might, in fact, produce feelings or moods quite consistent with aggression.

To test this possibility, several additional studies were conducted—studies in which subjects were exposed to contrasting types of humor. Some participants viewed *hostile humor* while others examined nonhostile humor. Results indicated that hostile humor did *not* reduce aggression relative to a no-humor control condition (in which participants viewed the aforementioned neutral pictures of furniture and abstract art). Nonhostile humor, however, did reduce aggression.

In subsequent studies (e.g., Baron, 1978), similar findings were obtained with hostile and nonhostile *sexual humor*—humor based on sexual themes or situations. Again, nonhostile humor reduced subsequent aggression on the part of angry persons, while hostile humor failed to produce such effects.

Together, these two sets of studies provided additional evidence for the incompatible response hypothesis. Exposure to stimuli that induced positive feelings among subjects (feelings of amusement, other mild positive feelings) did reduce both anger and subsequent aggression. Exposure to stimuli that induced negative feelings or anger, however, did not produce such effects.

Additional research indicated that mild sexual arousal, too, could reduce overt aggression (Baron, 1974; Baron & Bell, 1977). Subjects exposed to mild erotic stimuli (photos of attractive members of the opposite sex either nude or partially clothed) showed lower aggression than subjects exposed to neutral stimuli (the same set of pictures of furniture, scenery, etc.). However, individuals exposed to more explicit erotic stimuli, and who reported more intense feelings of sexual arousal, did not demonstrate similar reductions in aggression. Since many participants reported feelings of frustration and even disgust in response to explicit erotica, these findings were not surprising. In fact, they, too, can be interpreted as consistent with the incompatible response hypothesis. Mild sexual arousal, it appears, generates primarily positive feelings or moods. These feelings, in turn, should decrease subsequent aggression. Stronger levels of sexual arousal generated by explicit erotica, however, present a more mixed pattern of feelings. Thus, it is not surprising that they do not reduce aggression and may, if negative reactions predominate, actually increase it (Baron, 1979b).

Several years of research and more than 20 different studies produced a substantial body of evidence consistent with the incompatible response hypothesis. Exposure to stimuli or events that generated feelings or moods incompatible with anger did reduce subsequent aggression. Affect, in short, seemed to play a key role in this form of social behavior; and interventions based on this fact appeared to provide a useful means for reducing the frequency or intensity of overt aggression. Subsequent research in several applied settings indicated that interventions based on the incompatible response hypothesis could be useful in several applied settings. For example, police have applied such techniques to the control of domestic violence. The development and use of such techniques, however, is not directly relevant to the purposes of this chapter. Instead, therefore, I turn next to ways in which the incompatible response hypothesis has contributed to research on organizational processes.

Affect and organizational conflict

Conflict is a serious problem for many organizations. Practicing managers report that they spend from 15% to 25% of their total time dealing with conflict or its effects (Baron, 1989; Thomas, 1992). In view of this fact, it seems important to identify effective techniques for reducing the frequency or intensity of conflict or, at least, for assuring that the potential positive effects of this process are maximized while its potential negative effects are minimized (Baron, 1991; Cosier & Dalton, 1990). Many existing frameworks for managing organizational conflict focus primarily on the *structural* or *organization-based* causes of conflict—such factors as actual conflicts of interest, disputes over jurisdiction and authority, and interdependence (Coombs & Avrunin, 1988). But it is increasingly clear that organizational conflict also stems in part from *interpersonal causes*—factors relating more directly to the individuals involved and their social relations. Such factors include anger, grudges, real or imagined loss of face, faulty attributions about others' intentions, stereotypes, and a host of other factors (cf. Fisher, 1990; Pruitt & Rubin, 1986). To the extent that organizational conflict actually stems from such factors, then an approach based on incompatible responses might prove helpful in this regard. In particular, exposing persons involved in a conflict situation to stimuli or events capable of inducing positive affect might be helpful in countering feelings of anger and annoyance and so might facilitate movement toward win-win, collaborative solutions (Tjosvold, 1990). This suggestion is consistent with the view that one of the key steps in resolving conflicts is to somehow *lower the volume*—reduce the strong emotional arousal and tension often present in such situations. This is crucial for strong arousal and often interferes with effective information processing (Mann, in press). Hence, it sometimes prevents individuals from recognizing their own long-term interests and proceeding accordingly.

To test this hypothesis, I conducted several related studies. In the first (Baron, 1984), subjects played the role of executives in a large organization and discussed two issues currently facing their company: Should it relocate to the Sunbelt and should it invest heavily in the manufacture of a new product? (This product was a telephone for airplanes that could be used in flight; interestingly, this product has subsequently been produced.) One of the two persons present was an accomplice of the researcher, specially trained to disagree with whatever positions the actual subject happened to adopt. The style in which the assistant disagreed, however, was systematically varied. In one condition, this person disagreed with the subject in a calm and reasonable fashion (e.g., "I can see why you feel that way, but I guess I disagree."). In another, in contrast, the assistant disagreed in an irritating and condescending manner (e.g., "Oh come on, you've got to be kidding! How could anyone possibly feel that way?"). A second aspect of the study took place after the discussion of both issues had been completed. At this time, the experimenter left the room for a few moments, presumably to get some needed forms. During this period, the assistant either sat quietly (a control condition) or engaged in one of three actions designed to induce among subjects positive feelings incompatible with anger. The assistant either offered them a small gift (a cherry "Lifesaver"), explained that he was very tense because of several important exams, or asked subjects to help him select the funniest cartoons out of an array of cartoons, for use in a class project.

When the experimenter returned, participants completed a questionnaire on which they rated the assistant on several dimensions (e.g., likability, pleasantness) and indicated how they would respond to future conflicts with him. They did this by rating their likelihood of using each of five different modes of conflict resolution: *avoidance, competition, compromise, accommodation* (surrender to the opponent), or *collaboration* (working together to maximize joint outcomes). These patterns have been found, in previous research, to represent basic modes of conflict resolution (Rahim, 1983; Thomas, 1991).

Results indicated that subjects assigned lower ratings to the accomplice and reported stronger feelings of anger when he behaved in a condescending manner than in a reasonable one. Second, and of greater importance, they reported greater willingness to collaborate with him and lower tendencies to avoid him when they had been exposed to the incompatible-response-generating procedures than when they had not. In other words, those given a small gift, exposed to humorous cartoons, or induced to feel sympathy for the assistant reported being more likely to collaborate with him and less likely to avoid him than those in the control condition.

These findings were extended in follow-up investigations in which additional procedures were used to induce incompatible responses among angry subjects (Baron, Fortin, Frei, Hauver, & Shack, 1990). As in the initial study, subjects were first angered through exposure to condescending treatment by an assistant. Then they engaged in negotiations with this person. During these negotiations, both persons played the role of executives in a large company and bargained over the division of $1,000,000 in surplus funds in the current budget and over the division of 20 necessary position cuts between the two departments. During these negotiations, the assistant adopted a very confrontational stance, demanding fully $750,000 for his own department and offering to accept only 6 of the 20 cuts. The accomplice then made only two small concessions with respect to each issue during the entire exchange of offers and counteroffers.

Procedures designed to induce incompatible responses among subjects were implemented during the negotiation session, on two separate occasions: during the second exchange of offers (Trial 2) and during the sixth exchange of offers (Trial 6; a total of eight trials were employed). In one condition, the accomplice offered the subjects some candy (again, a cherry "Lifesaver") on both occasions. In another condition, this person flattered the subject on these two occasions, making such remarks as "You're really doing a good job representing your department." In a third condition, the assistant made self-deprecating remarks on Trials 2 and 6, saying, for example, "I really have no experience in these things, so I don't know whether I'm making the right offers or not." In a fourth condition, the assistant engaged in excessive flattery, again at the same points during the negotiations, by making obviously ingratiating comments such as "Gee, my opponent makes a lot of sense . . . he/she is one of the sharpest people I've met recently . . . I like the way he/she handles himself/ herself. . . ." It was anticipated that subjects would react negatively to such flattery and that it would *not* serve to reduce subsequent aggression. Finally, in a control condition, no efforts were made to induce incompatible responses among subjects; the negotiations merely proceeded through to completion.

After negotiations were completed, subjects rated the accomplice on several personal traits (reasonableness, fairness, friendliness) and indicated their preference for resolving future conflicts with this person through the aforementioned five conflict-resolving modes (i.e., avoidance, accommodation, compromise, collaboration, competition). Results indicated that during the negotiations, subjects who heard the accomplice engage in self-deprecation made a larger number of concessions to this person than those in the control condition. Turning to reported preferences for solving future conflicts, male subjects (but not females) expressed stronger preferences for collaboration in the gift, self-deprecation, and flattery condition than in the control condition. Similar findings were *not* obtained for excessive flattery, however. Finally, subjects in the flattery condition reported weaker preferences for solving future conflicts through competition than subjects in any other group (see Figure 1).

A third experiment carried this research one step further by examining the impact of *timing* of procedures designed to generate incompatible responses. Here, two treatments for generating incompatible responses (flattery, exposure to humorous cartoons) were employed. These were presented by the accomplice either prior to simulated negotiations, during the negotiations, or after they had been completed. It was reasoned that efforts to induce incompatible responses among subjects during or after simulated negotiations would be viewed as spontaneous by recipients and might prove effective in generating positive affect, and so in shifting preferences toward collaboration and away from competition and avoidance. However, the same procedures might arouse considerable suspicion among recipients when introduced prior to the start of negotiations. Thus, they would fail to generate similar beneficial effects. Results offered support for this hypothesis. Both humor and flattery increased subjects' reported preference for handling conflicts through collaboration and reduced their reported preference for handling them through avoidance, relative to a no-treatment control condition. However, this was true only when these procedures were introduced during or after negotiations; similar findings did *not* occur when they were introduced earlier in the session.

In sum, the results of several studies suggest that procedures based on the incompatible response hypothesis can indeed be useful in resolving organizational conflicts. The positive affect generated by such procedures seems to encourage the adoption of relatively constructive approaches to conflict resolution

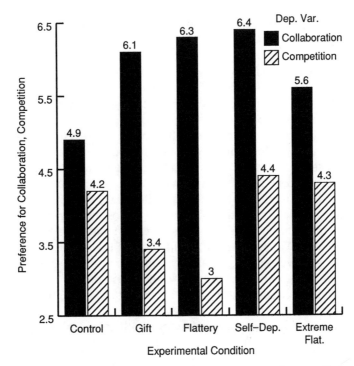

FIGURE 1   Reported Preferences for Collaboration and Avoidance in Four
Experimental Conditions

(collaboration) while discouraging approaches that are often less productive (avoidance, direct competition). At this point, it is important to note that other researchers have reported similar results. For example, Carnevale and Isen (1986) found that subjects exposed to humorous materials reached more integrative solutions in a simulated bargaining session and engaged in fewer contentious, conflict-generating tactics (e.g., the use of threats) than subjects not exposed to such materials. These findings, too, lend credence to the view that efforts to induce positive affect among the parties to organizational conflicts may yield important, beneficial effects.

All these studies on affect and organizational conflict were conducted under controlled, and relatively artificial, laboratory conditions. Whether, and to what extent, they generalize to actual conflict situations and actual negotiations remains to be determined. Still, the fact that professional negotiators often report the use of tactics designed to induce positive affect among their opponents suggests that such procedures can be effective in a wide range of contexts (Martin, 1991). Here, then, is a case in which research on affect conducted initially within the context of social psychology has found application to topics of direct concern to the field of organizational behavior. Now, I turn to a second illustration of the same general process.

ENVIRONMENTAL FACTORS, AFFECT, AND SOCIAL BEHAVIOR

Affective reactions can, obviously, be influenced by a very wide range of factors. One important category of such variables involves *social* causes of positive and negative affect, including all of the things people say and do to—or for—each other that induce shifts in current mood: praise or criticism, provision of gifts (or failing to provide them), accepting or rejecting requests—the list seems practically endless. Many of these factors, of course, apply equally to work and non-work settings, and many have already been investigated in research concerned with the impact of affective states on organizational behavior (e.g., George, 1990, 1991; Isen & Baron, 1991). But social factors, although of obvious importance, are clearly not the only source of positive and negative affect. Another set of factors that can produce shifts in current moods relates to aspects of the *physical environment*. Included here are such variables as ambient temperature, humidity, noise, crowding, air quality, lighting, and other features of the physical surroundings in which people work or interact (cf. Fisher, Bell, & Baum, 1990; Sundstrom & Sundstrom, 1986). Here, again, research on the impact of such factors started in social psychology but has recently been extended to important forms of organizational behavior. Both lines of research are now reviewed briefly.

Temperature and aggression: is the long, hot summer really hot?

One of my earliest memories is a very unpleasant one: It involves going with my father to the roof of the old apartment building in which we lived in search of a breath of fresh air. It was summer, and New York City was in the midst of a scorching heat wave. I vividly remember how miserable I felt, and I recall asking my father, with the perfect trust of a 4-year-old, "When will it end?" Not everyone shares such reactions, of course, but a large body of research indicates that most people do become increasingly uncomfortable—and experience growing levels of negative affect—as temperatures rise through the 80s and into the 90s Fahrenheit (Anderson, 1989; Baron, 1978). More importantly, both laboratory and field research suggests that such discomfort can sometimes contribute to the occurrence of aggressive actions.

In a series of laboratory studies, my colleagues and I (Baron, 1972; Baron & Bell, 1975; Baron & Lawton, 1972) investigated the effects of ambient temperature on aggression. Subjects were exposed to varying temperature (the low to mid 70s, 80s, and 90s Fahrenheit), and their level of aggression toward another person (an accomplice) via the aggression machine was observed. Initially, we anticipated that higher temperatures would lead to increased aggression. Instead, however, we found evidence for a more complex relationship—one in which the relationship between temperature and aggression is merely one reflection of an underlying relationship between negative affect and aggression.

Briefly, this relationship appears to be curvilinear in nature, so that initially, as negative affect rises, aggression, too, increases. Beyond some point, however, aggression actually begins to decline as the level of negative affect rises still further. This appears to be the case because at very high levels of negative affect, individuals focus primarily on *escape* or *minimization of discomfort*, and aggression is not always the most efficient means of attaining such results. The nature of this relationship between negative affect and aggression is perhaps most clearly illustrated by a study conducted by Paul Bell and myself (Bell & Baron, 1976).

In this investigation, subjects' affective state was varied through exposure to three different variables: the type of evaluation they received from another person (positive or negative), the extent to which this person agreed with them about various issues (high or low agreement), and ambient temperature (pleasantly cool or uncomfortably hot). A pilot study demonstrated that varying combinations of these factors did indeed influence affective states. Negative affect was lowest when subjects were exposed to positive evaluations, a high degree of attitude similarity, and cool temperatures but was highest when they were exposed to negative evaluations, a low degree of attitude similarity, and high temperatures.

In the main experiment, individuals were again exposed to one of these conditions but were then also provided with an opportunity to aggress against an accomplice by means of the aggression machine. Results offered clear support for the existence of a curvilinear relationship between negative affect and aggression.

Similar results were also obtained in an archival investigation that examined the relationship between ambient temperature and the occurrence of violent riots in the United States (Baron & Ransberger, 1978). Consistent with the curvilinear hypothesis, riots were most frequent not at extremely hot temperature but at more moderate ones (the mid to upper 80s Fahrenheit). Subsequent research, however, has not always confirmed this pattern of findings. In a series of studies focused on the relationship between temperature and violent crime, Anderson and his associates (e.g., Anderson, 1989) repeatedly found that violent crimes increase as temperature rises. Moreover, there does not appear to be a downturn in the rates of violent crimes at very high temperatures, as the curvilinear hypothesis would predict. In contrast, other researchers *have* found evidence for such a downturn (Bell & Fusco, 1990). At present, then, the issue has not been fully resolved. What does seem clear, however, is that there is indeed a link between ambient temperature and at least some forms of violent behavior.

Noise, crowding, air quality, and weather: other environmental causes of positive and negative affect

Temperature is not the only aspect of the physical environment that has been linked to aggressive behavior, however. Many other studies have examined the effects of such variables as noise, crowding, air quality, and weather on this important form of social behavior (Fisher et al., 1990; Rotton & Kelley, 1985). In general, these studies indicate that to the extent environmental factors generate negative affect, they also foster aggression. For example, in several studies, Rotton and his colleagues (e.g., Rotton, Frey, Barry, Milligan, & Fitzpatrick, 1979) found that exposure to highly unpleasant smells similar to those present in heavily polluted air can increase aggression. Similarly, Zillmann, Baron, and Tamborini (1981) found that nonsmokers report higher levels of negative affect and are more aggressive in the presence of cigarette smoke than in its absence. Several aspects of weather in addition to temperature have also been linked to accidents and hospital admissions as well as to violent crimes (Rotton & Frey, 1985). These include relative humidity, concentrations of positive and negative air ions, wind speed, and barometric pressure.

The impact of meteorological variables is not always negative, however. In fact, certain aspects of weather appear capable of enhancing *prosocial* as well as antisocial behavior. In ingenious research on this issue, Cunningham (1979) found that pleasant weather conditions (mild temperatures, sunny conditions) tend to induce positive affect among many persons and that such positive affect, in turn, is related to increased instances of helpful behavior. For example, Cunningham found that customers in restaurants left larger tips on sunny days than on cloudy or rainy ones.

In sum, it appears that many aspects of the physical environment can, and do, influence individuals' affective states. And the shifts in current moods produced by such factors, in turn, appear to influence several forms of social behavior.

ENVIRONMENTAL FACTORS, AFFECT, AND ORGANIZATIONAL BEHAVIOR

If environmental variables can influence key aspects of social behavior, it seems only reasonable to expect that they might influence organizational behavior as well. In fact, a growing body of evidence suggests that this is so. Much of this research has focused on the impact of environmental factors on task performance and can be viewed as a logical extension of the large body of research in human factors concerned with this basic issue (e.g., Kantowitz & Sorkin, 1983; Nagar & Pandey, 1987). Other studies, however, have sought to address the more general question of whether environmental factors, through their influence on affective states, can exert a somewhat wider range of effects on work-related behavior. This research is summarized in the next section.

Artificial fragrance and organizational behavior: the sweet smell of success?

Fragrance is a flourishing industry on a worldwide basis. Consumers in the United States alone spend several billion dollars each year on perfumes and colognes and on other products designed to "freshen the air" around them. Do such products induce positive affect? This is a trickier issue than it seems, for almost any scented product—even the most glamorous and expensive perfumes—can induce *negative* reactions on the part of some persons. Similarly, many fragrances that generate mainly positive reactions at low concentrations produce largely negative ones at higher doses (Baron, 1986). Under normal conditions, however, many commercial products are rated as fairly pleasant by most persons and do seem to generate at least small increments in positive affect among them (Baron, 1983).

If pleasant fragrances actually induce positive affect, then it seems possible that they will produce similar effects on behavior to those generated by other sources of positive affect—for example, praise, positive feedback, receipt of a small gift, and so on (Isen & Baron, 1991). This possibility has recently been tested in several studies. In one of these (Baron, 1990b), male and female subjects performed several tasks shown, in previous research, to be sensitive to shifts in affect. Half performed these tasks in the presence of pleasant artificial fragrances, while the remainder performed the same tasks in the absence of such aromas (Baron, 1990b). The fragrances employed were two commercial air fresheners identified, through pretesting, as ones to which a large proportion of subjects reported positive reactions. Among the tasks performed by subjects were (1) a clerical coding task identical to one employed in several previous studies (Baron, 1988); before actually performing this task, subjects indicated how many they thought they could complete in 5 minutes and their ability to perform the task (these provided rough measures of self-set goals and self-efficacy); (2) a simulated negotiation; and (3) a questionnaire on which subjects rated their preferences for resolving future conflicts with their opponent in the negotiations in each of five ways (collaboration, compromise, avoidance, competition, accommodation). In addition, participants also completed a questionnaire on which they rated the experimental rooms and their own affective states on several different dimensions (e.g., positive–negative; unpleasant–pleasant).

Subjects received their instructions and performed the clerical coding task in one room and the remaining tasks in a second room. This permitted the use of two fragrances, with one being sprayed into each room (in counterbalanced order) prior to the start of the experimental session. This was done to strengthen the manipulation of the scent variable, since sensory adaptation to such aromas occurs very quickly and is virtually complete within a few minutes.

Results indicated that the presence of these pleasant scents influenced several of the dependent measures. First, with respect to the clerical coding task, subjects reported higher self-set goals and greater confidence in their ability to perform this task in the scent than no-scent condition. Turning to negotiation, subjects set higher monetary goals in the scent than no-scent condition and made more concessions to their opponent. Finally, subjects in the pleasant scent condition reported weaker preferences than those in the no-scent condition for resolving conflicts through avoidance and competition.

Two findings indicated that these results were mediated by shifts in positive affect. First, subjects in the pleasant scent condition rated the experimental rooms more favorably on several dimensions and rated their own moods as more positive than those in the no-scent control condition. Second, analyses of covariance revealed that differences between the scent and no-scent conditions on several dependent measures totally disappeared when the influence of self-reported affect was removed statistically. In other words, the fragrance variable no longer exerted a significant impact on these dependent measures when the impact of differences in subjects' reported affective states was statistically controlled. In sum, the results of this study suggest that the presence of a pleasant fragrance did induce positive affect among subjects, and that such affect, in turn, influenced their behavior in several respects. It is important to note, moreover, that these effects were generally consistent in form with the findings of previous research in which positive affect was varied through other means (cf. Isen & Baron, 1991).

Lighting and organizational behavior:
Hawthorne revisited—with an emphasis on affect

If there is a "classic" study in organizational research it is, arguably, the famous Hawthorne project, carried out more than 50 years ago by Roethlisberger and his colleagues (Roethlisberger & Dickson, 1941). As a result, the term *lighting* has a special meaning in the field of organizational research. Yet there is reason to suggest that lighting may be another environmental variable that influences affective states. Research by Flynn and his associates (e.g., Flynn, 1977; Flynn, Spencer, Martyniuk, & Hendrick, 1973) indicates that individuals report contrasting reactions to various lighting conditions. For example, many report more favorable reactions to a given room in the presence of warm white light than cool white light (Flynn, 1977) and prefer diffuse lighting to direct downlighting. As Flynn (1977, p. 6) notes, "Without downgrading the obvious influence of light in facilitating visibility (and thus performance) of a visual task, it seems equally obvious that light contributes in other ways to the visual quality of a room and to the sense of well-being felt by the users of that room."

Statements such as these, plus a growing body of empirical evidence indicating that lighting has effects other than providing sufficient illumination for task performance, led my colleagues and I (Baron, Rea, & Daniels, 1992) to conduct a series of studies designed to determine whether two key aspects of indoor lighting—*illuminance* (the flux density of light on a surface measured in lux) and *spectral distribution* (the distribution of energy at different wavelengths)—could influence affect and, hence, performance on a wide range of work-related tasks. It was reasoned, in this research, that lighting conditions that induce positive affect would produce effects on various aspects of organizational behavior similar to those generated by other variables shown, in previous research, to influence subjects' affective states (e.g., Isen, 1990).

To test this hypothesis, we conducted several studies in which subjects performed several tasks previously shown to be sensitive to affective states, under one of several different lighting conditions. These lighting conditions were generated by systematic variation of two variables: illuminance (150 or 1500 lux) and spectral distribution (several different commercially available fluorescent bulbs that generated light that was relatively warm or cool in appearance; i.e., light containing relatively more red and yellow or green and blue wavelengths). The tasks performed by subjects included (1) a simulated performance appraisal, in which they read a folder providing neutral information about an imaginary employee and then rated this person on several dimensions (e.g., motivation, qualifications, responsibility); (2) word categorization, in which subjects were asked to indicate whether good and poor exemplars of various word categories belonged to these categories (e.g., pickle is a poor examplar of the word category *vegetable;* Isen & Daubman, 1984); (3) the clerical coding task described previously (see Baron, 1988; subjects also indicated self-set goals and rated their self-efficacy with respect to this task); (4) the MODE scale, which measures personal styles of resolving interpersonal conflict (relative preferences for avoidance, accommodation, compromise, competition, or collaboration); and (5) responses to a request for help, in which subjects were asked to volunteer their time, without compensation, for additional research projects. In addition, subjects completed a number of different scales designed to assess their affective states.

Results indicated that lighting conditions significantly influenced performance on virtually all of the tasks examined. With respect to simulated performance appraisals, subjects exposed to low levels of illuminance (150 lux) generally assigned higher appraisals than those exposed to high levels of illuminance (1500 lux). On the word categorization task, subjects exposed to low illuminance included more poor exemplars in various categories than those exposed to high levels of illuminance, thus indicating that they thought more inclusively under these conditions. Turning to scores on the MODE, subjects exposed to warm white light reported stronger preferences for resolving interpersonal conflicts through collaboration and weaker preferences for resolving conflicts through avoidance than subjects exposed to cool white light. Self-set goals and self-efficacy, too, were influenced by lighting conditions. In both cases, subjects exposed to warm white light set higher goals and reported high self-efficacy in the low than high illuminance condition. Similar results were not obtained with subjects exposed to cool white light, however.

Were these findings mediated by shifts in affective states? Unfortunately, the self-report measures employed did not yield clear-cut evidence that this was the case. A more refined measure, developed over the course of the several studies, and employed only in the final investigation, did indicate that subjects exposed to warm white light experienced higher levels of positive affect in the low than high illuminance condition; among those exposed to cool white light, the corresponding difference was not significant. However, in earlier studies, findings for self-report measures of affect were not consistent. This mixed pattern of results led us to adopt another tactic for investigating the potential mediating role of affect—an approach known as *converging operations* (Garner, Hake, & Eriksen, 1956; Isen & Baron, 1991). In this approach, different groups of subjects in an experiment are exposed to treatments that differ in external form but that are assumed to influence the intervening variable of interest (in this case, positive affect). To the extent that these contrasting but conceptually related treatments produce similar effects on dependent measures known to be sensitive to the intervening variable, it can be asserted that they are indeed exerting their impact through the operation of this variable.

In the final study in this series, subjects were exposed not merely to contrasting lighting conditions but also to another variable, as well: receipt of a small, unexpected gift (a small bag of assorted candies). This treatment has been found, in many previous studies, to generate positive affect among recipients (cf. Isen, 1987). Thus, it was reasoned that if certain lighting conditions, too, generate positive affect, then they should influence affect-sensitive dependent measures in the same direction as this variable (i.e., receipt of a small gift). This is precisely what was found. Both the receipt of a small gift and spectral distribution influenced ratings of an imaginary employee and willingness to volunteer one's time in a similar manner: The amount of time volunteered by participants was increased by receipt of a small gift and by exposure to warm white light (see Figure 2). These results suggest that lighting conditions did indeed influence performance on these tasks through the intervening variable of positive affect.

FIGURE 2   Minutes Volunteered (Helping) as a Function of Spectral Distribution and Receipt of a Small Gift

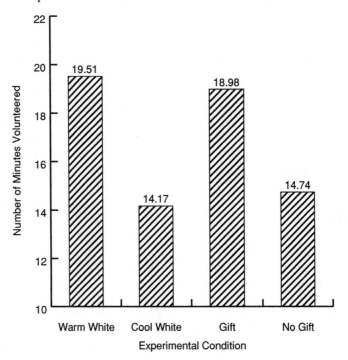

At this point, it should be noted that the pattern of findings obtained in these studies is *not* consistent with an interpretation based on the impact of heightened arousal. Lower levels of illumination, not higher levels, were found to enhance evaluations of a fictitious employee, to increase the range of stimuli included by subjects in various categories, and to enhance self-set goals and feelings of self-efficacy. Similarly, subjects volunteered more of their time under conditions of low illuminance, warm white light than under any others. Clearly, this pattern of findings is not consistent with an interpretation based on global arousal.

In sum, certain aspects of indoor lighting appear to constitute another set of environmental variables that can influence important aspects of organizational behavior. Moreover, lighting appears to exert such effects through its impact on affective states. Given that many millions of individuals spend a large part of their working lives in the presence of indoor illumination, further efforts to examine the potential impact of this aspect of work environments would seem to merit further, careful attention.

AFFECT AND ORGANIZATIONAL BEHAVIOR: AN OVERVIEW AND PROSPECTIVE

This chapter has covered a lot of ground. It has reviewed research conducted in social psychology and research focused more directly on organizational behavior. It has also traced diverse lines of investigation employing contrasting methods and dependent measures. A central idea behind this chapter has been that *affect* provides a unifying theme for all of this work. Given this assertion, it seems reasonable to conclude with two tasks: (1) summarizing what we currently know about affect and its impact on organizational behavior, and (2) identifying key issues requiring further clarification in future research.

Affect and organizational behavior: what we already know

Several recent reviews provide detailed summaries of literature bearing directly on the role of affect in organizational behavior (e.g., Isen & Baron, 1991). Thus, there appears to be little need to consider such evidence in detail here. Instead, it may be more useful to extract several key points suggested by this literature. These are as follows:

1. *Positive and negative affect do indeed influence important forms of organizational behavior.* An extensive and growing body of evidence indicates that both positive and negative affect can influence several important forms of organizational behavior, including performance appraisals, the outcome of job interviews, prosocial organizational behaviors, organizational conflict, influence, job satisfaction, leader–member relations, absenteeism, and voluntary turnover (e.g., George, 1990, 1991; Isen & Baron, 1991).

2. *Such effects can be produced by even relatively modest and temporary shifts in affect.* Consistent with literature on social behavior and cognitive processes, it appears that even small changes in individuals' affective states can influence key aspects of their work and organizational behavior. This suggests that shifts in affect may often "tip the balance" in situations where many different factors, operating together, influence complex judgments or patterns of social interaction.

3. *Affective states can influence organizational behavior even in the absence of clear recognition of such states.* Individuals are often largely unaware of mild shifts in their affective states, or at least cannot report on them accurately. Yet, despite this fact, such shifts seem capable of influencing important forms of organizational behavior. This is consistent with a large body of literature in social psychology indicating that individuals are often quite inaccurate in recognizing or gauging the cognitive factors that influence their overt behavior (cf., Nisbett & Ross, 1980; Zillmann, 1988).

4. *Positive and negative affect do not necessarily produce opposite effects on organizational behavior.* While positive and negative affect both appear to influence important aspects of organizational behavior, these effects are not necessarily parallel or opposite in nature. Growing evidence suggests that positive affect may exert more general and longer lasting effects than negative affect, perhaps because individuals are so adept at implementing techniques for countering or reducing negative affect.

5. *A wide range of social and environmental variables induce shifts in affect of sufficient magnitude to influence important forms of organizational behavior.* Mild and temporary shifts in affective state can be produced by a very wide range of social and environmental variables. Growing evidence indicates that the modest affective shifts produced by such factors are of sufficient magnitude to influence important forms of organizational behavior. This suggests that many aspects of work-related processes may be quite sensitive to shifts in individuals' affective states—perhaps as sensitive in this respect as various forms of social behavior, such as helping or aggression (e.g., George, 1990).

Affect and organizational behavior: issues for further research

While we already possess a considerable amount of information about the role of affect in organizational behavior, a number of important issues remain unresolved. Among the most crucial of these are the following:

1. *What are the mechanisms through which affect influences organizational behavior?* While affect has been shown to influence many important forms of organizational behavior, relatively little is currently known about the mechanisms through which it exerts such effects. Basic research on the interface between affect and cognition suggests that some of these mechanisms probably involve basic cognitive processes, such as memory and controlled/automatic processing (Isen, 1987). However, further research is clearly needed to delineate the precise manner in which mild, temporary shifts in affective states can influence such complex processes as performance appraisals, negotiation, conflict resolution, and leader–member relations. Specifying these processes is essential to the formulation of any comprehensive theoretical framework in this area.

2. *What is the relative importance of affective states in influencing various aspects of organizational behavior?* Research conducted to date indicates that positive and negative affect can sometimes influence several forms of organizational behavior. However, little effort has been made to determine the *magnitude* of such effects and to com-

pare their importance with that of other influential factors. For example, is affect more or less important in determining evaluations of others than key aspects of memory (e.g., priming, selective recall of information)? Is affect more or less important in determining strategies and actions during negotiation than perceptions of one's opponent or the significance of various issues and potential outcomes? Efforts to answer such questions must take careful account of the intensity of such factors. For example, powerful distortions in memory or information processing will probably exert stronger effects on performance appraisal than mild, temporary shifts in mood. In any case, it seems important to obtain information on the relative importance of affect as a variable influencing several forms of organizational behavior.

3. *What aspects of organizational behavior are influenced by positive and negative affect?* As noted previously, positive and negative affect have been shown to influence many forms of organizational behavior. The question of the generality or pervasiveness of this impact, however, remains largely unaddressed. Determining which aspects of organizational behavior are or are *not* influenced by mild shifts in affective states is an important task both for practical and theoretical reasons. From an empirical perspective, knowing which aspects of organizational behavior are influenced by affective states is important in determining those processes that can, potentially, benefit from efforts to reduce or eliminate the influence of affect. For example, knowing that affective reactions can bias performance appraisals or job interviews suggests the need for affect-oriented interventions in these areas. From a theoretical perspective, it seems clear that formulation of a comprehensive theory concerning the role of affect in organizational behavior can benefit from knowledge of the range of such effects. Such knowledge may help delineate the underlying mechanisms that mediate the influence of affect. Identification of these processes, in turn, is central to the formulation of a comprehensive theory of the role of affect in organizational processes.

4. *What factors in organizational settings exert the strongest or most consistent impact on affective states?* At present, we know that a wide range of social and environmental factors influence affective states. We do *not*, however, know the relative importance of these potential causes of affective shifts. Moreover, little attention has been paid to organizational factors as possible sources of positive and negative affect. Does organizational culture play a role in such reactions? Organizational design? The introduction of new technology? And what about cross-cultural differences—do they play a mediating or moderating role with respect to such factors? Growing evidence gathered in research on the problems faced by multinational companies indicates that cultural factors may well be of considerable importance in this respect (Black, Mendenhall, & Oddou, 1991; Boyacigiller & Adler, 1991).

5. *How can positive and negative affect best be measured in organizational settings?* Measuring shifts in affective states has been a continuing problem faced by laboratory researchers interested in the impact of positive and negative affect (cf. Isen, 1987). Such problems are compounded for organizational researchers, who wish to understand the impact of these affective states in the complex world of modern organizations. Self-report measures are notoriously unreliable and are often only marginally related both to procedures used to induce shifts in affective states and to relevant dependent measures (Isen, 1987). A more effective procedure, it appears, involves the use of converging operations, as described earlier in this chapter. Whatever procedures are employed, it seems crucial for researchers in this area to develop standard, agreed-on methods for measuring affect. In the absence of such standardization, it will remain difficult to determine whether seemingly inconsistent results in various studies are of theoretical importance and reveal useful information about the impact of affective states, or are merely the result of artifact and contrasting methods of measurement.

Admittedly, these tasks are daunting; they will require considerable effort by many talented researchers. Only if they are undertaken, however, can the crucial goal of developing a comprehensive theory of the role of affect in organizational behavior be attained. And the construction of such theories is, in the final analysis, what a science-based field of organizational behavior is all about.

REFERENCES

ANDERSON, C. A. (1989). Temperature and aggression: The ubiquitous effects of heat on the occurrence of human violence. *Psychological Bulletin, 106,* 74–96.

AXSOM, D. (1989). Cognitive dissonance and behavior change in psychotherapy. *Journal of Experimental Social Psychology, 25,* 234–252.

BARON, R. A. (1971a). Aggression as a function of magnitude of victim's pain cues, level of prior anger arousal, and aggressor-victim similarity. *Journal of Personality and Social Psychology, 18,* 48–54.

BARON, R. A. (1971b). Magnitude of victim's pain cues and level of prior anger arousal as determinants of adult aggressive behavior. *Journal of Personality and Social Psychology, 17,* 236–243.

BARON, R. A. (1972). Aggression as a function of ambient temperature and prior anger arousal. *Journal of Personality and Social Psychology, 21,* 183–189.

BARON, R. A. (1974). The aggression-inhibiting influence of heightened sexual arousal. *Journal of Personality and Social Psychology, 30,* 318–322.

BARON, R. A. (1977). *Human aggression.* New York: Plenum Publishing Co.

BARON, R. A. (1978). The influence of hostile and nonhostile humor upon physical aggression. *Bulletin of Personality and Social Psychology, 4,* 77–80.

BARON, R. A. (1979a). Aggression, empathy, and race: Effects of victim's pain cues, victim's race, and level of instigation on physical aggression. *Journal of Applied Social Psychology, 9,* 103–114.

BARON, R. A. (1979b). Heightened sexual arousal and physical aggression: An extension to females. *Journal of Research in Personality, 13,* 91–102.

BARON, R. A. (1983). The control of human aggression: An optimistic overview. *Journal of Social and Clinical Psychology, 1,* 97–119.

BARON, R. A. (1984). Reducing organizational conflict: An incompatible response approach. *Journal of Applied Psychology, 69,* 272–279.

BARON, R. A. (1986). Self-presentation in job interviews: When there can be "too much of a good thing." *Journal of Applied Social Psychology, 16,* 16–28.

BARON, R. A. (1987). Mood of interviewer and the evaluation of job candidates. *Journal of Applied Social Psychology, 17,* 911–926.

BARON, R. A. (1988). Negative effects of destructive criticism: Impact on conflict, self-efficacy, and task performance. *Journal of Applied Psychology, 73,* 199–207.

BARON, R. A. (1989). Personality and organizational conflict: The Type A behavior pattern and self-monitoring. *Organizational Behavior and Human Decision Processes, 44,* 281–297.

BARON, R. A. (1990a). Attributions and organizational conflict. In S. Graham & V. Folkes (Eds.), *Attribution theory: Applications to achievement, mental health, and interpersonal conflict* (pp. 185–204). Hillsdale, NJ: Erlbaum.

BARON, R. A. (1990b). Environmentally-induced positive affect: Its impact on self-efficacy, task performance, negotiation, and conflict. *Journal of Applied Social Psychology, 20*, 368–384.

BARON, R. A. (1991). Positive effects of conflict: A cognitive perspective. *Employee Rights and Responsibilities Journal, 4*, 25–36.

BARON, R. A., & BALL, R. L. (1974). The aggression-inhibiting influence on nonhostile humor. *Journal of Experimental Social Psychology, 10*, 23–33.

BARON, R. A., & BELL, P. A. (1973). Effects of heightened sexual arousal on physical aggression. *Proceedings of the American Psychological Association,* 81st Annual Convention, 171–172.

BARON, R. A., & BELL, P. A. (1975). Aggression and heat: Mediating effects of prior provocation and exposure to an aggressive model. *Journal of Personality and Social Psychology, 31*, 825–832.

BARON, R. A., & BELL, P. A. (1977). Sexual arousal and aggression by males: Effects of type of erotic stimuli and prior provocation. *Journal of Personality and Social Psychology, 35*, 79–87.

BARON, R. A., DANIELS, S. G., & REA, M. S. (1992). Lighting as a source of environmentally-generated positive affect in work settings: Impact on cognitive tasks and interpersonal behaviors. *Motivation and Emotion, 14*, forthcoming.

BARON, R. A., FORTIN, S. P., FREI, R. L., HAUVER, L. A., & SHACK, M. L. (1990). Reducing organizational conflict: The potential role of socially-induced positive affect. *International Journal of Conflict Management, 1*, 133–152.

BARON, R. A., & GREENBERG, J. (1990). *Behavior in organizations* (3rd ed.). Boston: Allyn & Bacon.

BARON, R. A., & LAWTON, S. F. (1972). Environmental influences on aggression: The facilitation of modeling effects by high ambient temperatures. *Psychonomic Science, 26*, 80–82.

BARON, R. A., & RANSBERGER, V. M. (1978). Ambient temperature and collective violence: The "long hot summer" revisited. *Journal of Personality and Social Psychology, 36*, 351–360.

BELL, P. A., & BARON, R. A. (1976). Aggression and heat: The mediating role of negative affect. *Journal of Applied Social Psychology, 6*, 18–30.

BELL, P. A., & FUSCO, M. E. (1990). Heat and violence in the Dallas field data: Linearity, curvilinearity, and heteroscedasticity. *Journal of Applied Social Psychology, 19*, 1479–1482.

BERKOWTIZ, L. (1970). Aggressive humor as a stimulus to aggressive responses. *Journal of Personality and Social Psychology, 16*, 710–717.

BERKOWTIZ, L. (1989). Frustration-aggression hypothesis: Examination and reformulation. *Psychological Bulletin, 106*, 59–73.

BERKOWITZ, L., & DONNERSTEIN, E. (1982). External validity is more than skin deep: Some answers to criticism of laboratory experiments. *American Psychologist, 37*, 245–257.

BLACK, J. S., MENDENHALL, M., & ODDOU, G. (1991). Toward a comprehensive model of international adjustment: An integration of multiple theoretical perspectives. *Academy of Management, 16*, 291–317.

BOYACIGILLER, N. A., & ADLER, N. J. (1991). The parochial dinosaur: Organizational science in a global context. *Academy of Management Review, 16*, 262–290.

BRIEF, A., & MOTOWIDLO, S. J. (1986). Prosocial organizational behaviors. *Academy of Management Review, 11*, 710–725.

CARDY, R. L., & DOBBINS, G. H. (1986). Affect and appraisal accuracy: Liking as an integral dimension in evaluating performance. *Journal of Applied Psychology, 71*, 672–678.

CARNEVALE, P. J. D., & ISEN, A. M. (1986). The influence of positive affect and visual access on the discovery of integrative solutions in bilateral negotiation. *Organizational Behavior and Human Decision Processes, 37,* 1–13.

COOMBS, C. H., & AVRUNIN, G. S. (1988). *The structure of conflict.* Hillsdale, NJ: Erlbaum.

COOPER, J., & FAZIO, R. H. (1984). A new look at dissonance theory. In L. Berkowitz (Ed.), *Advances in experimental social psychology* (Vol. 14, pp. 229–266). New York: Academic Press.

COOPER, J., & SCHER, S. J. (1991). Actions and attitudes: The role of responsibility and aversive consequences in persuasion. In T. Brock & S. Shavit (Eds.), *The psychology of persuasion* (pp. 216–233). San Francisco: Freeman.

COSIER, R. A., & DALTON, D. R. (1990). Positive effects of conflict: A field assessment. *International Journal of Conflict Management, 1,* 81–92.

CUNNINGHAM, M. R. (1979). Weather, mood, and helping behavior: Quasi-experiments with the sunshine Samaritan. *Journal of Personality and Social Psychology, 50,* 925–935.

DUGAN, K. W. (1989). Ability and effort attributions: Do they affect how managers communicate performance feedback information? *Academy of Management Journal, 32,* 87–114.

FIEDLER, K., & FORGAS, J. P. (Eds.). (1988). *Affect, cognition, and social behavior.* Toronto: Hogref.

FISHER, J. D., BELL, P. A., & BAUM, A. (1990). *Environmental psychology* (3rd ed.). New York: Holt, Rinehart & Winston.

FISHER, R. J. (1990). *The social psychology of intergroup and international conflict resolution.* New York: Springer-Verlag.

FISKE, S. T., & TAYLOR, S. E. (1991). *Social cognition* (2nd ed.). Reading, MA: Addison-Wesley.

FLYNN, J. E. (1977). A study of subjective responses to low energy and nonuniform lighting systems. *Lighting Design and Application, 7,* 6–15.

FLYNN, J. E., SPENCER, T. J., MARTYNIUK, O., & HENDRICK, C. (1973). Interim study of procedures for investigating the effect of light on impression and behavior. *Journal of the Illuminating Engineering Society, 3,* 87–94.

GARNER, W. R., HAKE, H. W., & ERIKSEN, C. W. (1956). Operationism and the concept of perception. *Psychological Review, 63,* 149–159.

GEORGE, J. M. (1990). Personality, affect, and behavior in groups. *Journal of Applied Psychology, 75,* 107–116.

GEORGE, J. M. (1991). State or trait: Effects of positive mood on prosocial behaviors at work. *Journal of Applied Psychology, 76,* 299–307.

HARVEY, J. H., & WEARY, G. (Eds.). (1989). *Attribution: Basic issues and applications.* San Diego: Academic Press.

ISEN, A. M. (1970). Success, failure, attention, and reaction to others: The warm glow of success. *Journal of Personality and Social Psychology, 15,* 294–301.

ISEN, A. M. (1987). Positive affect, cognitive processes, and social behavior. In L. Berkowitz (Ed.), *Advances in experimental social psychology* (Vol. 20, pp. 203–253). New York: Academic Press.

ISEN, A. M. (1990). The influence of positive and negative affect on cognitive organization: Some implications for development. In N. Stein, B. Leventhal, & T. Trabasso (Eds.), *Psychological and biological approaches to emotion* (pp. 175–194). Hillsdale, NJ: Erlbaum.

ISEN, A. M., & BARON, R. A. (1991). Affect as a factor in organizational behavior. In

B. M. Staw & L. L. Cummings (Eds.), *Research in organizational behavior* (Vol. 14, pp. 1–53). Greenwich, CT: JAI Press.

ISEN, A. M., & DAUBMAN, K. A. (1984). The influence of affect on categorization. *Journal of Personality and Social Psychology, 47,* 1206–1217.

KANTOWITZ, B., & SORKIN, R. (1983). *Human factors.* New York: Holt, Rinehart and Winston.

KLEIN, H. J. (1989). An integrated control theory model of work motivation. *Academy of Management Review, 14,* 1150–1172.

LIDEN, R. C., & MITCHELL, T. R. (1988). Ingratiatory behaviors in organizational settings. *Academy of Management Review,* 13, 572–587.

LORD, R. G., DeVADER, C. L., & ALLIGER, G. M. (1986). A meta-analysis of the relationship between personality traits and leadership perceptions: An application of validity generalization procedures. *Journal of Applied Psychology, 71,* 401–410.

MANN, L. (in press). Affect and decision making. In I. L. Janis & L. Mann (Eds.), *Decision making.* Hillsdale, NJ: Erlbaum.

MARTIN, K. B. (1991). *Interpersonal processes in complex negotiations.* Paper presented at Rensselaer Polytechnic Institute, Troy, New York.

MILLER, N. E. (1959). Liberalization of basic S-R concepts: Extensions to conflict behavior, motivation, and social learning. In S. Koch (Ed.), *Psychology: A study of a science* (Vol. 2, pp. 423–440). New York: McGraw-Hill.

NAGAR, D., & PANDEY, J. (1987). Affect and performance on cognitive task as a function of crowding and noise. *Journal of Applied Social Psychology, 18,* 1423–1442.

NISBETT, R. E., & ROSS, L. (1980). *Human inference: Strategies and shortcomings of social judgment.* Englewood Cliffs, NJ: Prentice Hall.

PRUITT, D. G., & RUBIN, J. Z. (1986). *Social conflict: Escalation, stalemate, and settlement.* New York: Random House.

RAHIM, M. A. (1983). A measure of styles of handling interpersonal conflict. *Academy of Management Journal, 26,* 368–376.

ROETHLISBERGER, F. J., & DICKSON, W. J. (1941). *Management and the worker: An account of a research program conducted by the Western Electric Company, Hawthorne Works, Chicago.* Cambridge, MA: Harvard University Press.

ROTTON, J., & FREY, J. (1985). Air pollution, weather, and violent crimes: Concomitant time-series analysis of archival data. *Journal of Personality and Social Psychology, 49,* 1207–1220.

ROTTON, J., FREY, J., BARRY, T., MILLIGAN, M., & FITZPATRICK, M. (1979). The air pollution experience and physical aggression. *Journal of Applied Social Psychology, 9,* 397–412.

ROTTON, J., & KELLEY, I. W. (1985). Much ado about the full moon: A meta-analysis of lunar-lunacy research. *Psychological Bulletin, 97,* 286–306.

SPELTZ, M. L., & BERNSTEIN, D. A. (1979). The use of participant modeling for claustrophobia: A case report. *Journal of Behavior Therapy and Experimental Psychiatry, 10,* 251–255.

STAW, B. M., & ROSS, J. (1989). Understanding behavior in escalation situations. *Science, 246,* 216–220.

SUNDSTROM, E., & SUNDSTROM, M. G. (1986). *Workplaces: The psychology of the physical environment in offices and factories.* London: Cambridge University Press.

THOMAS, K. W. (1992). Conflict and negotiation processes. In M. D. Dunnette (Ed.), *Handbook of industrial and organizational psychology* (2nd ed.). Palo Alto, CA: Consulting Psychologists Press.

TJOSVOLD, D. (1990). *Managing conflict: The key to making your organization work.* Minneapolis, MN: Team Media.

WELLS, G. L., & GAVANSKI, I. (1989). Mental simulation of causality. *Journal of Personality and Social Psychology, 56,* 161–169.

ZILLMANN, D. (1988). Cognition-excitation interdependencies in aggressive behavior. *Aggressive Behavior, 14,* 51–64.

ZILLMANN, D., BARON, R. A., & TAMBORINI, R. (1981). Social costs of smoking: Effects of tobacco smoke on hostile behavior. *Journal of Applied Social Psychology, 14,* 51–64.

CHAPTER FIVE

Reinventing Leadership:
A Radical, Social Psychological Approach

JAMES R. MEINDL

State University of New York at Buffalo

This chapter calls for more social psychological perspectives on leadership. In contrast to the conventional wisdom, the value of a social psychological approach to leadership inheres in the emphasis on followers and their contexts over factors associated with leaders themselves. I argue for a reinvention of leadership from a radical social psychological point of view. Ideas stemming from the "romance of leadership" notion are used to illustrate how a useful, anticonventional approach might be developed.

PART I

Introduction

Leadership is everything and nothing. Few topics in organizational behavior have inspired as much passion and polarization over the years. To many, leadership studies are indirectly connected to a number of important values, including national competitiveness in the global marketplace, political influence and military effectiveness, empowerment and humanity in the workplace, corporate ethics, morality, and social responsibility. For them, leadership is everything. But for others, the accumulated wisdom of literally thousands of studies on the topic is seen as irrelevant and uninteresting. For them, the study of leadership is, at best, of tangential concern; at worst, a colossal waste of energy and talent better spent on more direct efforts to study these important problems.

As it now stands, social psychologists whose research agendas focus on leadership run the risk of being defined as marginal participants in the mainstream of social psychology. This is somewhat ironic since leadership has had a prominent place in the history of social psychology. Major figures in the development of the field—including Lewin, Sherif and Sherif, Bogardus, Tannenbaum, and many others—have made significant contributions to social psychology via the study of leadership, particularly within the context of small groups. Some, such as Hollander, have spent the greater parts of their careers conducting significant, social psychological inquiries into the topic. I doubt that very many newly minted PhDs in social psychology would even be aware of this. The last revision of the *Handbook of Social Psychology* (Lindzey & Aronson, 1985) included a chapter on leadership, written by Hollander. It presented readers with an overview of the area, particularly as it relates to power and influence. A reading of that chapter reflects a fall-off of leadership studies by social psychologists in the 1970s and early 1980s. That trend has continued. In 1991, the contribution of social psychologists to leadership studies is quite modest. A part of that waning may reflect the general decline and interest in small group research in social psychology. But for whatever reasons, the net result has been a steady erosion of a social psychological perspective on leadership.

Fads come and go, interests wax and wane; and so do the intellectual heritages that guide the assumptions and beliefs of new generations of researchers. Students of organizational behavior, who might arguably have the greatest interest in the topic, are exposed to contemporary work that is largely being generated by researchers who collectively indulge in a narrow version of social psychology. In fact, much of the work is quite antisocial psychological. For some, this becomes the foundation and premise for their own work on the topic. For many others, it is a source of alienation since few topics in the so-called organizational sciences are as fruitfully explored from a social psychological perspective.

There are many avenues for developing a contemporary social psychology of leadership. The particular approach explored in this chapter flows in part from my earlier work on the "romance of leadership" notion. As the reader will see, it pushes, sometimes to an extreme, for a radical, social psychological approach to the study of leadership, insofar as the current and conventional leadership approaches are concerned. These approaches to leadership do not take enough advantage of a social psychological perspective. Thus, I have deliberately taken an anticonventional stance. Again, it is a lamentable irony that social psychology can be considered in any sense "radical" to the status quo.

A radical approach

Social psychology attempts to understand and explain how individuals are influenced, in their thoughts and their actions, by the real or implied presence of others (Allport, 1985). Too often, the meaning of a social psychological approach is reduced to an interaction between persons and situations. In the most limiting cases, the "interaction" implicates not a social process but simply a statistical interaction in an analysis of variance (ANOVA) design or a multiplicative term in a regression equation. Some of that comes from common knowledge associated with Kurt Lewin's celebrated dictum that $B = f(P, S)$. But as Allport notes, although social psychology invariably includes explicit or implicit theorizing about persons, that theorizing is strongly interested in the role of situational and contextual influences as perceived and interpreted by the persons involved. The Lewinian tradition attaches only secondary importance to personality and individual differences, being much more interested in situational effects. Thus, a strong social psychological lens on anything, including leadership, emphasizes situational, contextual influences above all else.

It is no accident that it was a social psychologist who discovered that when considering $B = f(P,S)$, there is an almost irresistible emphasis placed on P over that of S (Ross, 1977). And this is what has happened in contemporary leadership studies. Without the continued participation of social psychologists, person variables and individual differences—the stock and trade of many who are now studying leadership—have dominated over situational variables.

Hollander (1978) has viewed the "locus of leadership" as residing at the juncture of the leader, the follower, and the context that embeds them. Although this view is often espoused, contexts and followers have been of limited theoretical interest among contemporary leadership researchers. Of course, there are exceptions, but the field of leadership studies, if it can be characterized by anything, seems to have succumbed to sins of the intuitive psychologist (Ross, 1977), unable to fully appreciate the contextual priorities of social psychology. I am in complete agreement with Weick (this volume): Social psychology truly has a comparative advantage, that, I would add, is in danger of being lost in the conventional wisdom on leadership.

Alternative approaches to leadership can differ meaningfully from each other in terms of who and what is studied (see Table 1). One can focus on either leaders or followers, and on person or situation factors. Conventional approaches tend to be located at the leader/person end of who/what. Anticonventional, social psychological approaches to leadership are rightfully located in

TABLE 1 The Who and What of Leadership Studies

		Who	
		Leaders	Followers
What	Persons	Conventional Approaches	
	Situations		Anticonventional Approaches

the follower/situation end of who/what. In this chapter I describe one such approach. Before proceeding, however, it is necessary to engage in a brief tour of the leadership terrain over the last 2 decades—decades when leadership dropped from the intellectual domain and research agendas of most social psychologists.

A tour of the 1970s and 1980s

The 1970s and 1980s were turbulent decades for leadership studies. In the 1960s, contingency theories supplanted universalistic approaches. For example, the Managerial Grid program (Blake & Mouton, 1964), a practitioner-oriented, highly prescriptive elaboration of the earlier two-factor models that were empirically derived in the 1950s, waned as attention was drawn to the most popular contingency model of the day: Fiedler's LPC, leader-match program (Fiedler, 1964, 1967). Although some interest in this model continued into the 1970s (e.g., Fiedler, Chemers, & Mahar, 1976), its appeal was lessened, due in part to an intense and drawn-out debate over the adequacy of LPC concepts and instrumentation (e.g., Evans & Dermer, 1977; Fiedler, 1977; Kabanoff, 1981; Rice, 1978; Shiflett, 1973; Strube & Garcia, 1981; Vecchio, 1983). Other contingency models were proposed, such as Hersey and Blanchard's (1969, 1977) life-cycle theory. Whereas Fiedler posited that the effectiveness of directive/task-oriented or nondirective/people-oriented styles depended on certain situational and relationship factors, Hersey and Blanchard viewed the "maturity" (later relabeled "readiness") of followers—defined in terms of ability, motivation, and self-confidence—as the chief contingency variable to which a leader's style was to be matched, and overlaid it with a developmental philosophy. This model was widely marketed and used in many corporate training and development programs in the 1980s, despite a dearth of evidence regarding its scientific validity (e.g., Graef, 1983; Hambleton & Gumbert, 1982; Vecchio, 1987).

That kind of discontinuity between scientific and popular appeal was not uncommon, as a seemingly endless supply of leadership products was generated to service the needs of eager consumers. Indeed, during the 1980s the production and marketing of leadership development programs turned into a substantial industry in its own right. This was not surprising, given the sentiments expressed by many scholars and practitioners who considered leadership to be the most important topic in the kingdom of organizational behavior (Rahim, 1981). Specialized institutions, such as The Center for Creative Leadership, with its modest beginnings in the 1970s, boomed in the 1980s. It was during this decade that the "one minute manager" (e.g., Blanchard, 1989; Blanchard & Johnson, 1981; Blanchard & Lorber, 1984; Blanchard, Zigarmi, & Zigarmi, 1985) became a wildly successful series of quick-fix leadership tips that would capture corporate attention, rivaling the phenomenal success of Peters and Waterman's (1982) "In Search of Excellence" programs.

As a part of the growth of the business press in general, celebrations of leadership blossomed: "Ten Toughest Boss" awards, "Most Admired CEO" contests, and the like were regularly featured in magazines such as *Forbes, Fortune,* and *Business Week.* A remarkable bouquet of popular writings on leadership adorned the shelves of local bookstores. These flowerings were many and varied: from descriptions and testimonies of the effectiveness and styles of CEOs (e.g., Horton, 1986; Potts & Behr, 1987; Shook, 1981; Steiner, 1983; Stieglitz, 1985) to the prescriptions of renowned writers and consultants (e.g., Bennis & Nanus, 1985; Bradford & Cohen, 1984; Peters & Austin, 1985) from the leadership secrets of Attila the Hun (Roberts, 1985) to the practices of ancient Chinese generals (Cleary, 1988); from the leadership implications of Machiavelli (Buskirk, 1974) to the leadership philosophy reflected in Taoism (Heider, 1985; Wing, 1986). Biographies, autobiographies, and other, beatific descriptions of the captains of business and industry were also part of the mix (e.g., Iaccoca & Novak, 1984; Scully, 1987), being read by many an executive for their wisdom on matters of leadership as they hoped to move through corporate hierarchies.

By these standards, leadership was a huge success. But in many scholarly circles, the 1970s and early 1980s were plagued by serious reservations about the state of leadership research. A growing number of scholars were expressing disillusionment and dissatisfaction with the accumulation of knowledge in the area. Some even called for a moratorium on leadership research (e.g. Miner, 1975). Although research and theorizing did continue, on popular approaches such as path-goal theory (House, 1971; House & Mitchell, 1974; Indvik, 1986; Keller, 1989) and the vertical dyad linkage (VDL) model (Dansereau, Graen, & Haga, 1975; Graen, 1976) doubters found support for their views in several papers that dealt severe blows to conventional leadership wisdom.

The first blow was delivered by Staw (1975). Many areas of organizational research rely on people's reports of the objective behaviors of others and of organizational events, but leadership researchers had become particularly dependent on this methodology. Subordinates routinely reported on the occurrence and frequency of their supervisors' leadership actions. Staw demonstrated that such ratings were highly susceptible to what has become known as the "performance-cue" effect (e.g., Binning & Lord, 1980; Binning, Zaba, & Whattam, 1986): Groups with knowledge of their performance levels reported "objective" leadership behaviors that were consistent with performance levels (i.e., good leadership behavior was reported when performance was good; poor performance led to less flattering ratings) independent of the actual behavior of the leader. Dozens of conventional studies were now suspect, and a flurry of research on "implicit leadership theories," attributions, and performance cues ensued (e.g., DeNisi & Pritchard, 1978; Downey, Chacko, & McElroy, 1979; Eden & Leviatan, 1975; Gioia & Sims, 1985; McElroy, 1982; McElroy & Downey, 1982; Staw & Ross, 1980).

Calder (1977) delivered a second blow, bringing leadership into the domain of naive social psychology à la Heider (1958). Calder argued that the concept of leadership had more significance in the phenomenology of social actors and observers than it did as a scientific construct: Leadership was a part of social discourse, a way to talk about organizational events and processes. Leadership thus became an attributional problem, which Calder outfitted with a modified version of the classic "acts-to-disposition" model by Jones and Davis (1965). At about the same time, Pfeffer (1977) agreed with Calder, but arguing from a more macro rationale. Whereas Calder focused on individual actors, Pfeffer's analysis was at the level of the firm. He discussed the results of several disturbing studies, including one by Lieberson and O'Connor (1972), which indicated that the effect size of leadership (as measured by the stewardships of different management teams) on organizational performance (as measured by several common accounting measures) was far smaller than most people had expected. The vast bulk of performance variation in a firm was linked to variations in industry and more general economic conditions. An argument was developed suggesting that leadership was a concept whose significance was largely symbolic (e.g., Pfeffer, 1981; Pfeffer & Salancik, 1978).

A third blow came with Kerr and Jermier's concept of "leadership substitutes" (1978). They argued that many common prescriptions for effective leadership being offered by the conventional wisdom were misleading in that they lost sight of the idea that the principal function of leadership was the accomplishment of group purpose, and group purposes could be achieved through other means. Certain factors—organizational structures, task features, and subordinate's characteristics—allowed adequate task performance, and in their strong and full presence the exertion of leadership, along conventional lines, was redundant if not harmful and counterproductive.

These ideas were consolidated in one final blow in an article on the romance of leadership (Meindl, Ehrlich, & Dukerich, 1985). We argued that conceptions of leadership were deeply seated cultural expressions of a collective commitment toward understanding organizational performances in terms of the leaders. Studies showed that attributions to and collective interests in leaders and leadership were especially pronounced when performances were extremely good and/or extremely bad. In this view, leadership was seen as a simplified, biased, and attractive way to understand organizational performance (Meindl & Ehrlich, 1987).

The cumulative effect of these blows, serious as they were, appeared to have had little impact on conventional leadership studies. Many U.S. businesses and industries were simultaneously realizing that they were losing out to the Japanese, both in foreign and domestic markets. Leadership was first blamed for the erosion of U.S. competitive dominance and then credited with the hope of bringing about a more promising future. And it was in this era that leadership studies took an abrupt shift in emphasis.

About this time, Zaleznik (1977) wrote a controversial article in the *Harvard Business Review* in which he drew a distinction between real "leadership" and mere "management." The gist of this distinction was that managers and leaders operated on the basis of very different psychologies; that it was not surprising that most managers were not interested nor able to lead effectively. This caused quite an uproar, since one implication was that one could not be a good manager and a good leader at the same time. People actually fought, in print, over who was or was not a real leader. Despite the initial flap, this distinction eventually became commonplace and foreshadowed the widespread use of similar distinctions.

During these years, there were many bemoanings of a "leadership gap" and a "leadership crisis," referring to an absence of adequate leadership skills and opportunities in both the public and private sectors (e.g., Bennis, 1977; Zaleznik, 1983). This gap, however, was soon to be measured against a new kind of leader/savior whose characteristics were connected to one of the oldest traditions in leadership studies: charisma.

This "special gift," divine grace view of leadership was prominent in Weber's (1921, 1947) analysis of organizational authority and was resurrected for mainstream leadership researchers by Burns (1978) and House (1977). Burns distinguished between transactional and transformational leadership, with the latter referring basically to charismatic leadership. House summarized the sporadic history of work on charismatic leadership and proposed a definition of charismatic leadership in terms of its effects on followers. Bass (1985a) refined and popularized Burns's (1978) distinction. Bass and his colleagues (e.g., Hater and Bass, 1988) operationalized the differences between transactional (TA) and transformational (TF) concepts in the form of a paper-and-pencil questionnaire that subordinates typically complete about their leader. They showed that subordinates who score their leaders high, especially on the TF scales, are also the ones most likely to display charismatic effects, such as the exertion of extra effort and performance "beyond expectations."

By the late 1980s, issues of transformational leadership and charisma became the dominant objects of intellectual energy in leadership studies. Some writers focused on the connection between charisma and culture, and several case studies of prominent charismatic leaders were published (e.g., Trice & Beyer, 1986). Whereas charisma had in the past been thought to be a relatively rare occurrence in most organizational settings (Katz & Kahn, 1966) it was now considered potentially commonplace (e.g., Tichy & DeVanna, 1986). Various models and perspectives on charismatic and TF leadership were proliferated, many of them collected in a volume by Conger and Kanungo (1988).

A prominent theme running through much of the writing was an emphasis on the extraordinary endowments and/or behavioral displays of the charismatic leader (e.g., Conger & Kanungo, 1987; House, Spangler, & Woycke, 1991; Kuhnert & Lewis, 1987). For example, in the study by House et al. (1991), variations in the charismatic appeal of U.S. presidents was shown to be the direct result of their personalities, represented by the strength of various motives, such as the need for power and achievement. Howell and Frost (1988), in the only lab study on charisma up until that time, focused on the expressive actions of the leader in producing the kinds of charismatic effects that House and others had identified. Their results suggested that it might be possible to train leaders to display certain behavioral mannerisms that will then be registered in subordinates as charismatically appealing. Elaborating on that suggestion, a book by Conger (1989) focused on the special behavioral repertoires of charismatic leaders, highlighting the inspirational use of language and communication. New leadership training and development programs incorporating TF leadership were devised, such as the "Leadership Practices Inventory" (LPI) model (Kouzes & Posner, 1988). By the early 1990s, TF leadership had center stage. In fact, enough new work had been done to justify an updated version of House's 1976 theory of charismatic leadership (House et al., 1991).

Meanwhile, with all the noise about TF leadership, studies in the TA domain quietly continued. For example, earlier vertical dyad linkage (VDL) models of the 1970s were elaborated into more general and comprehensive leader–member exchange (LMX) models (e.g., Deinesch & Liden, 1986; Liden & Graen, 1980; Scandurra & Graen, 1984), and there was continued interest in contingent-reinforcement views of leadership (e.g., Klimoski & Hayes, 1980; Komaki, 1986; Podsakoff & Schreisheim, 1985). Paralleling the studies of charisma, the domain of TA leadership studies was characterized by a renewed interest in the special endowments of leaders. Fiedler's new cognitive resource theory (Fiedler, 1986; Fiedler & Garcia, 1987) and other work on the intellectual and creative abilities of leaders (e.g., Simonton, 1986, 1987, 1988) represent that trend. The long discredited "trait-based" approach to leadership began to make a comeback. Some reports suggested that earlier reviews were probably too pessimistic (Lord, DeVader, & Alliger, 1986).

So too, the "effect-size" of leadership debate that had been sparked by Pfeffer (1977), fueled by the external control models of organizations (Pfeffer & Salancik, 1978), and fanned by the attribution-oriented critiques (Calder, 1977; Meindl, Ehrlich, & Dukerich, 1985) dissipated. Several studies that had demonstrated no or small effect sizes were also criticized as overly pessimistic and as underestimating the real effect size, which was reestimated upward back into the comfort zones of most leadership researchers (Day & Lord, 1988; Smith, Carson, & Alexander, 1984; Weiner & Mahoney, 1981).

Optimism now reigns in the field, as major reviews by House (1988), Bass (1990), Hollander and Offerman (1990), and Yukl (1989) are all upbeat. By now, however, it is evident that the conventional wisdom in the area is being forged without the forceful participation of social psychologists. The earlier critiques, mainly social psychological, were swept away by the burgeoning interest in transformational, charismatic leadership.

Social psychology did have some impact in both the TA and TF domains during these years. This was apparent in the TA domain by attributional analyses of leadership (e.g., Martinko & Gardner, 1987; McElroy, 1982; McElroy & Schrader, 1986). In one popular approach (Mitchell, Green, & Wood, 1981; Mitchell & Wood, 1980), the mutual influence of a superior and subordinate's behavior on one another is considered, and the causal attributions by each are inserted into the loop as mediational variables—a straightforward application of Kelley's cube (Kelley, 1967).

Transformational researchers also injected attributional notions into their models of charisma. For example, Boal and Bryson (1988) put forth a model whereby the phenomenology of the follower intervenes between displays of charismatic behaviors by the leader and the subsequent displays of charismatic effects by the follower. Attributions of "charisma" are a part of that phenomenology.

Leadership studies became increasingly interested in the inferential processes associated with leadership phenomena (e.g., Ashour, 1982), and social psychology found some applications therein. This research was strongly influenced by the cognitive processing models that had become so important to mainstream social psychology (e.g., Foti, Fraser, & Lord, 1982; Lord, 1985; Lord & Alliger, 1985; Phillips & Lord, 1981). While influential in some respects, the impact of social psychology was circumscribed. Nowadays, social psychological perspectives on leadership are no longer broadly pervasive. The small group studies of leadership that social psychology had initiated decades earlier have all but vanished from the scene. The few that continue to be produced find audiences in secondary or highly specialized journals, where they are routinely ignored by both mainstream social psychologists and the producers of conventional leadership wisdom. Young scholars interested in organizational behavior who graduate from business and management programs have learned to see leadership through mostly nonsocial psychological lenses, manufactured by a recent intellectual heritage that has been impoverished by its disappearance.

The relevance of the romance of leadership

Since publishing our first piece on the romance of leadership, I have acquired the reputation of being somewhat of a naysayer regarding leadership; that I consider leadership to be unimportant (e.g., Yukl, 1989). In truth, though, I have never believed this, and the romance of leadership studies need not be taken to mean that leadership is trivial. The last edition of Bass and Stodgill's *Handbook of Leadership* (Bass, 1990) contained over 8,000 references. How can the sheer volume of such work be ignored? On the "central importance of leadership," as Hollander (1986) put it, I can agree with the established order. Where we part is on the objects of study and what objects are more significant than others. The romance of leadership calls into question the *conventional approaches* to the study of leadership. It suggests that current conceptualizations and modes of thought are probably providing a too narrow account of leadership's real significance. The romance of leadership studies established the prominence of leadership concepts in the way social actors address organizational problems. That is the significance of leadership, and that is one starting point for introducing a more radical, social psychological approach. A key to understanding and conceptualizing leadership must be built on the foundations of a naive psychological perspective. How leadership is constructed by both naive organizational actors and by sophisticated researchers should constitute the study of leadership. For it is those very constructions on which the effects of leadership, defined in conventional terms, are likely to depend. The romance of leadership defines leadership as an experience undergone by followers. In this view, the received wisdom is analyzed, in a sense, more for its expressive and symbolic content and less for its substantive truth about leadership. The initial work on the romance of leadership was a consciousness-raising endeavor. Some interpreted it as research on leadership research, not on leadership per se. I say it is the same thing.

All of the foregoing has been by way of introduction. The rest of this chapter outlines some ideas, speculations, and bits of research that may be useful to the development of an alternative approach to leadership. In keeping with a radical social psychological perspective, I try to answer the following kinds of questions: What if a view of leadership was not so directly dependent on the personas and behaviors of the leader? Could a more follower-centered approach be constructed? What sort of research agenda would it imply? What would such an approach teach us about leadership?

PART II

The importance of emergent leadership

Consistent with their situational/contextual bent, social psychologists have long understood that whether the position of leadership is bestowed on an incumbent by virtue of appointment or by election—top down versus bottom up—can create very different environments for leader–follower relations (e.g., Hollander, 1964; Hollander, Fallon, & Edwards, 1977; Hollander & Julian, 1970). In most organizational contexts the designations of supervisory and subordinate role are formally defined, and thus, appointment is a constant denominator. But appointment is simply a context from which leadership may or may not emerge. Leadership is not a given by virtue of the occupancy of hierarchical roles. It is a mistake to confuse the formal role designations with the emergence of leadership and the influence that might be attributed to one or the other aspect of the relationship that might develop between social actors. Leaders and followers are creations that, for the most part, describe the informal aspects of their relationship; subordination describes their formal aspects. Leadership is an overlay that followers place onto an otherwise formally defined hierarchical relationship with the supervisor. The emergence of leadership, then, implies more than subordination: It represents an enrichment in the conceptualization of the relationship. This can be understood in conventional terms by the kind or depth of social influence (e.g., Kelman, 1958) that occurs when followership develops beyond simple subordination (see Table 2).

TABLE 2   Leadership as Influence

CONCEPTUAL RELATIONSHIP	SOCIAL INFLUENCE
Insubordination	Noncompliance
Subordination	Compliance
Leadership (transactional)	Internalization
Leadership (transformational)	Identification

This is why social psychological analyses of emergent leadership, and the methods of leaderless group discussions, are vital to the study of leadership. Today, studies of this type are relatively rare in comparison to more mainstream topics in leadership, in part because of the mistaken view that they are not appropriate to understanding leadership in organizational contexts, where so-called leaders are appointed via their positions of legitimate authority within the hierarchical structure. The implication is that leadership does not have to emerge because it is already there. Of course, nothing could be further from the truth.

Leadership as ideology: an inside-out view

The current convention in leadership studies paints a portrait of leadership in terms of a process that the leader ultimately controls. Although mutual influence processes between leaders and followers are recognized (e.g., Crouch, 1987; Hollander, 1978; Zahn & Wolfe, 1981), leadership is mostly conceptualized as something seized on, and exerted, by the leader. It is something to be performed by the leader; it is dispensed to, and used on, followers to influence and control them. Such views naturally feed a leader-centered research agenda: what behaviors by the leader constitute good or bad leadership, and what personality traits and other endowments are conducive to the skillful exertion and effective application of leadership behaviors. The emergence of leadership, according to this view, is heavily dependent on who the leader is and what the leader does. Followers and subordinates are the ultimate targets of conventional leadership studies, but leaders are most definitely the objects of their study.

As an alternative to this convention, it is possible to define followers as the objects and leaders as the targets. In this view, the emergence of leadership depends heavily on the followers. Leadership then represents the emergence among followers of a state of mind, an experience they undergo. Leadership emerges in the minds of followers. Without the experience, without being in a state of leadership, followership does not exist, and hence leadership cannot be said to have emerged. Leaders are important only insofar as they may eventually become the targets of the followers' thought systems. This is an "inside-out" definition of leadership relative to conventional approaches. Thus, when I refer to the emergence of leadership, I am highlighting the development in group members of a particular way of thinking about their relationships to one another and to their tasks. In short, leadership is the emergence of an ideology. Its birth is not signaled by the exertions of the leader, but by the exertions of followership that accompany this ideology. The popular distinctions between TA and TF leadership domains have their meaning as two alternative forms of the emergence of leadership in the thought systems of group members. The task of leadership studies, then, becomes one of understanding the causes and implications of this ideology for organizational actors, systems, and structures.

Whereas early emergent leadership studies (e.g., Bass, 1954; Bass, McGehee, Hawkins, Young, & Gebel, 1953; Bavelas, Hastorf, Gross, & Kite, 1965;

Morris & Hackman, 1969; Strodtbeck & Mann, 1956) and more recent ones (e.g., Sorrentino, 1973; Sorrentino & Field, 1986; Stein, 1975, 1977; Zaccarro, Foti, & Kenny, 1991) have been concerned with understanding *who* emerges as leaders, dedicated to an understanding of how certain activities by individuals allowed them to emerge as leaders, the agenda should be revised. Instead, the ascension of a particular person as a leader can now be seen as a derivative consequence of the emergence of leadership. What is important is understanding *if and when* leadership emerges in the way group members think about themselves and each other. This focuses the issue at the very beginning of the process and provides a new focal point for emergent leadership research.

Process versus outcome measures of leadership

Conventional leadership approaches place considerable weight on the behavioral displays of the leader. Some evidence does suggest that social actors have formed implicit theories and cognitive prototypes of what is effective and ineffective leadership, defined in behavioral terms. When behavioral displays approximate, or perhaps activate, the prototypes held by observers, a definition of leader/leadership is more or less likely.

The relative strength of prototype matching and/or activation processes for the emergence of leadership must compete with contextual features that are likely to have their own effect. Here a distinction can be drawn between process and outcome measures of leadership effectiveness, defined in conventional terms. The behavioral displays of the leader are essentially "process" measures of effective leadership: They are not outcomes of value in and of themselves, but valuable in terms of their intended or likely impact on group productivity and the satisfactions of members. As process measures, leadership behaviors are less relevant for the emergence of leadership than outcome measures. A good example of an outcome measure is group performance. As I have already discussed, performance cues have been known to alter group members' reports of leadership factors. I view this as symptomatic of the emergence of leadership as a way of thinking on the part of group members. I would also submit that the behavioral displays of fellow group members, from the point of view of any focal member, can also be considered as significant "outcome" measures of leadership. Although the expressive reactions of other followers have not received much research attention in leadership studies, they are an important aspect of the social psychological context in which group members operate. One might speculate that just as leadership prototypes exist in the minds of group members (L-types), so too do prototypical images about the behavioral implications of followership (F-types). When the two images clash, I believe F-types will often win out, since L-types are process measures and naturally more subordinate to outcome measures. Thus, the L-prototype notions of conventional approaches suggest that when group members encounter its features, leadership will automatically emerge. Such an approach obviously overlooks the strength of social information in providing members with a sense of the meaning to be attached to their relations with the leader. Leader–follower relations are the property and domain of the group, and, as such, fellow group members carry much weight in how they are defined. These ideas are what underlie the social contagion view of charismatic leadership (Meindl, 1990).

Contagion and charismatic leadership

Charismatic leadership can be understood as a social contagion process (i.e., a phenomenon of the spontaneous spread of affective and/or behavioral reactions among the members of a group or social collective). Social contagion highlights the interpersonal processes and group dynamics that can plausibly account for the widespread dissemination of charismatic effects among followers and subordinates. Social contagion is characterized by a shared sense of arousal (e.g., stress, tension); some behavioral expressions of arousal; a definition of these expressions (symptoms) as being from some external source; and the acceptance of this definition and the dissemination of the symptoms in the group (Wheeler, 1966).

LEADERSHIP IS LIKE CATCHING A COLD.   Unlike approaches that emphasize the expressive behaviors of the leader, this analysis focuses on the expressive actions of followers. The core idea is that charismatic experiences are not newly and independently created in each follower as a function of dyadic interactions with the leader. Rather, any experience may be strongly dependent on the experiences of other individuals in the group. Charismatic leadership is possible because charismatic effects are re-created and transmitted among followers within the group.

This approach calls for examinations of the patterns and routes that charismatic attributions and charismatic effects follow within social networks. In short, charisma, as an emergent leadership phenomenon is treated as an epidemiological problem. One testable hypothesis is that the charismatic appeal of leaders and attributions of charismatic qualities are distributed along sociometric channels, being predicted by social network positions and parameters. This sort of hypothesis could be tested by examining the association, if any, between the charismatic appeal to followers of their leaders and their standing in the social network. Existing instrumentation (e.g., Bass, 1985a) could be adapted to assess charismatic appeal. Similarly, adaptations of social-network analysis (e.g., Bradley, 1987) and block modeling could examine the distribution and strength of the charismatic appeal of an organization's leaders and its correspondence with the sociometric locations of followers/subordinates, controlling for the frequency of direct interaction/contact with the target leaders. This kind of study would turn on the assumption that such distributions can be taken as the residue of a contagion process. It represents the logical precursor to a longitudinal study that would monitor charismatic appeal as it unfolds.

LEADERSHIP IS IN THE LAUGH TRACK.   Experiments could also examine the micro processes that would support a contagion model of emergent charismatic leadership. The main task would be to demonstrate that the charismatic appeal of a leader to followers is socially anchored by the expressive actions of other peers and co-workers who function as models. Charismatic reactions are contaged from such models. This idea is like the "laugh track" typical of U.S. television comedies, where something is apparently funny when we hear the "audience" laughing. One could examine if the charismatic appeal of a leader is more or less susceptible to social influence than other, more transactionally oriented aspects of leadership. This could be tested in a design where subjects are exposed to leadership stimuli and to an independent manipulation of expressiveness by other group members or observers.

Another approach might be to conduct a variation of the classical misattribution studies. The affect or arousal levels experienced by subjects at the time they are exposed to a leader may encourage the emergence of charismatic leadership as a way of thinking. For example, the general excitement and energy associated with large gatherings of people that involve a visibly salient leader (e.g., a political convention) may produce enough free-floating, unlabeled arousal to allow for misattributions of the type that would support charismatic contagion. Arousal might increase the likelihood that leaders will be evaluated in terms of their charismatic appeal, and would combine with the expressiveness levels among other group members or social models to produce charismatic appeal.

Crisis as context for the emergence of charismatic leadership

Most conventional approaches to charismatic leadership emphasize the personal endowments and activities of the leader to induce followership. A more social psychological approach would seek to understand the emergence of charismatic leadership as a result of the group members' context.

A part of the problem is that conceptions of personality are more highly developed than conceptions of the situational/contextual factors that might plausibly effect the emergence of leadership, a point that I discuss later. One of the few contexts that has been recognized as important is the existence of a crisis. Weber and others have talked about it, but almost no systematic data regarding the effects of crises on charismatic leadership exists. Furthermore, there is little to guide a researcher on what exactly is a crisis, or on what kind of crisis is likely to affect the emergence of leadership.

Many writings on the effects of crisis suggest a process whereby latent charismatic attributes and characteristics become manifested during the crisis, enabling the person to exercise control. Indeed, one reason that organizational researchers have turned to charismatic leadership is because of the promise that such leaders hold for the accomplishment of major organizational turnarounds. In the conventional approach, leaders are saviors who, as a result of their special endowments, rescue their organizations from disaster.

One of the most widely touted organizational examples of charismatic leadership is Lee Iacocca, whose dramatic and successful interventions to save Chrysler Inc. from bankruptcy were widely attributed to his strategic vision and charismatic (transformational) leadership. Such leadership, according to conventional wisdom, is the process of achieving major changes in the organization by affecting the attitudes and assumptions of the followers through the vision, inspiration, and charismatic displays of the transforming leader. Accordingly, extraordinary effects are thought to be achieved by the exertion of exceptional leadership.

In the anticonventional view, crisis affects followership, not as a result of the exertions of a leader but more directly through the emergence of leadership as a state of mind, which independently heightens the charismatic appeal of a leader and increases the probabilities of charismatic experiences developing within the group. In either case, though, the suggestion is that crises, and the emotional experiences associated with them, are potentially important precursors to the onset of charismatic leadership. Two recent studies (Pillai & Meindl, 1991a, 1991b) explored crisis as an aspect of the contextual features from which thoughts about charismatic leadership might arise in observers and group members. These studies appear to be the first to specifically test the idea that crisis events cause charisma to emerge.

Study 1

Research on TA leadership has consistently demonstrated that ratings of leadership behaviors are susceptible to the effects of performance cues. Pillai and Meindl (1991b) extended the performance-cue effect to the domain of charismatic leadership, considering the sorts of radical performance changes that are observed in the fortunes of some organizations. They introduced evidence of a "crisis" in addition to simple performance cues to examine the hypothesis that a crisis followed by good performance (i.e., turnaround) would heighten ratings of charismatic leadership more than just good performance alone.

In this study, subjects read different versions of a case about a fast food company, describing the industry, performance of the company over the last 10 years, and a profile of the CEO. Descriptions varied only in terms of information on company performance patterns, which were manipulated by crossing two factors: positive or negative growth and the presence or absence of a crisis. As a comparative baseline, a fifth scenario included no performance. In all versions, a constant profile of the CEO was included.

The results (see Figure 1) provided evidence that inferences regarding the charismatic appeal of a leader are influenced by performance and crisis cues. In the case of a performance turnaround (a crisis followed by recovery), perceptions of charismatic leadership appear to peak, whereas in the case of crisis followed by continued decline, perceptions of charismatic leadership seem to reach a nadir. The linear trend of this predicted ordering was statistically significant. This pattern suggests that a crisis combined with good performance (a turn-

FIGURE 1   Charisma Strength Across Conditions

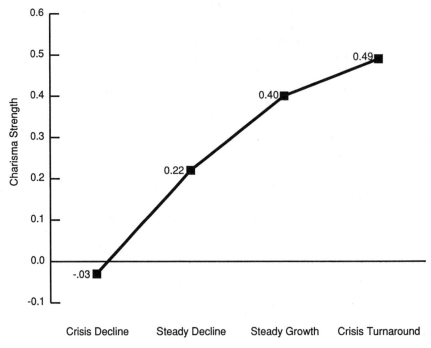

From Pillai & Meindl, 1991b

around) can add to a leader's stature; whereas a crisis combined with poor performance (no turnaround) may diminish it.

Study 2

Study 1 included rather distant observers who formed inferences about leadership after seeing summarized information about a CEO and his firm. Study 2 included more involved subjects whose ratings were made within the context of
ongoing tasks and performances. We were interested in generating something
akin to a crisis, specifically the mental state associated with a crisis, to demonstrate its effects on emergence of charismatic leadership.

We employed a classical emergent leadership paradigm. Student participants were assigned to groups and given an opportunity to interact with each
other, without the appointment of formal leadership roles. Immediately prior to
working together on a scheduled group activity, group members received bogus
feedback about the results of a test they had taken a few days before. Crisis
groups received low scores; no-crisis groups received high scores. Subsequently,
group members made leadership nominations and ratings on a shortened version of Bass's Multifactor Leadership Questionnaire (MLQ), focusing on charismatic (TF) and more mundane (TA) forms of leadership. Individuals also rated
the overall effectiveness of the leader they had chosen.

The group activity involved a business case analysis. The group members played the roles of Board members whose twin tasks were (1) to first select a Chairman of the Board after 20 minutes of discussion since the current chairman had resigned at the last meeting, and (2) to arrive at a consensus decision under the guidance of the new chairman following a further 30 minutes of discussion. They were led to believe that group performance would be evaluated on the extent of agreement between the group's decision and the actual decision and the quality of interaction among the members. The test score and the group activity counted for more than a third of their grade for the course.

The data indicated that crisis had a strong direct influence on the ratings of charisma, which in turn influenced global evaluations of leader effectiveness (see Figure 2). Furthermore, ratings of TA leadership were also affected by the crisis, but such ratings were not important influences on ratings of leadership effectiveness.

These results again suggest that conditions of crisis facilitate the emergence of charismatic leadership. Moreover, crisis appears to induce the use of charismatic appeal as a way to evaluate the effectiveness of leaders. One question that has not been answered is whether group members select someone who possesses inherently charismatic qualities or, alternatively, simply perceive any emergent leader as more charismatic. The present research is a beginning. But it also raises a number of additional issues as to the precise nature of the crisis and how crisis leads to the emergence of leadership in the minds of followers. Such questions and answers are not likely to emerge from conventional leadership studies. Some speculations along these lines follow.

FIGURE 2   Path Analysis of Crisis, Leadership, and Effectiveness

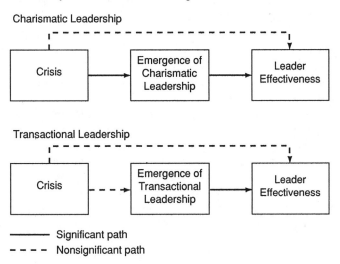

From Pillai & Meindl, 1991a

Leadership as aspirin:
a palliative view of leadership

The role of stress in the workplace has received considerable research attention because of its implications for employee performance and productivity. Work-related stress as it is commonly understood involves the arousal of disturbing emotional states in response to an external stimulus that places special physical/ psychological demands on the individual. These stimuli interact with an individual's personality to determine behavioral responses. Coping mechanisms, both individual and organizational, play an important role in controlling the strength of the response and its negative effects on the mental and physical health of the employee. The principal effect of a crisis on group members may be the stresses it creates for them. The conventional wisdom suggests that certain kinds of leadership may facilitate stress reduction by functioning as a powerful coping mechanism. Previous research has demonstrated that groups with leaders are better equipped to cope with stress than groups without leaders (Bass, 1990). Indeed, in certain contexts, behaviors by the supervisor may themselves be the cause of the stress and the crisis.

Although not explicitly discussed as such, at least two different views address the effects of leadership on the health and well-being of groups and individuals. In one, leadership creates the conditions that promote productivity, health, and well-being. An alternative view suggests that leaders buffer subordinates, protecting them from the effects of otherwise harmful organizational arrangements and difficult task environments. The former views leadership as a force that corrects environmental impediments to productive and satisfying work behavior; the latter views leadership as a way to alleviate the negative consequences of potentially destructive environments, providing symptomatic relief.

Both views imply that the exertions of leadership by the leader help subordinates cope. In the anticonventional approach, such exertions are of only indirect interest. When leadership is defined as a state of mind—as a thought system or ideology—it is possible to then search for the functions such ideologies serve; that is, how they are useful to actors, in the same way that social psychologists used to talk about the "functions" of attitudes and beliefs (e.g., Katz, 1960).

A palliative view is completely consistent with our present approach: The emergence of charismatic leadership may be a functional reaction; a sort of mental inoculation or at least a way of obtaining systematic relief from the otherwise unpleasant experiences associated with stressful events and circumstances. One can speak of leadership "agents" in a way that is analogous to the chemical agents found in medicinal drugs. These agents are not actors but are the beliefs and concepts that comprise the ideology of leadership. They ameliorate stress responses to the trials and tribulations of routine as well as crisis conditions. The task of the researcher becomes one of trying to understand the relative effectiveness of various leadership agents as they are represented in the emergent ideological system, and how such agents operate and interact with other factors, to relieve group members from the stresses and strains in their environments.

Given that TF leadership agents appear in contexts of crises or external threats, it seems plausible that they may be potent palliatives for reducing the experience of stress and strain. The emergence of leadership, insofar as it implies the development of various TA and TF agents, may be quite functional to followers, protecting them from the harmful effects of stressors, particularly during times of crisis. This protection would not be available to subordinates who, for some reason, have not developed such agents as a part of their thought systems.

Images of leadership

As Ross (1977) discovered, most of us are, at some level, closet personologists: We are inclined to think in terms of personality traits and characteristics, especially when it comes to processing information regarding symbolically meaningful figures such as those who occupy positions of power. The perspective in this chapter attempts to highlight the prospects for an alternative to the personological approach to the analysis of leadership in general, and charisma in particular. One can learn quite a bit about the occurrence of charismatic leadership in a system without much knowledge of the personality endowments of the leader. It is possible to examine charisma from the experience of followers and the social processes that occur among them.

If personality has a significant role in the phenomenon of charismatic leadership, then it is probably reflected in the personal attributes and characteristics of followers. They create the possibility for the emergence of leaders and ultimately surrender themselves to their creations (Katz & Kahn, 1978). If there is a psychology that is of singular importance to charismatic leadership, it is not to be found in the minds of leaders but in the minds of the followers. The charismatic relationship that develops between a leader and follower is symptomatic of larger social forces and system needs, which become integrated in the psychology and personalities of followers, transmitted, and amplified by the social interactions that take place among them. The personas of our leaders, and their relevance to the emergence of charismatic leadership, are simply one derivative component in a complex, integrated circuit-like system of social and psychological forces that create and sustain followership.

Although I have, to this point in the chapter, focused on the emergence of leadership within the context of groups, nowhere is the relevance of an alternative to the personological approach more apt than when it comes to understanding high-level targets in the public and private sectors, such as corporate CEOs and political party leaders. The endowments of a leader, as reflected in the force of personality on followership, are growing increasingly irrelevant. In many sectors, social/organizational life is changing in a way that undermines and erodes the conditions that enable the force of a leader's personality to have any bearing on how we respond as followers and subjects. I suspect that "personality signals," if they were strong in the past, are getting weaker. Sustained, repeated face-to-face interactions highlighted by the spontaneous behavioral expressions of a leader's own personality are being replaced with cursory, fragmented, mediated, and highly encumbered interactions. This is especially true in large organizations and in high offices where the behavior of the leader is often designed and constructed with a variety of constituents, interests, and purposes in mind. It is not just that such interactions are becoming more strategic; it is that the expressions and appearances of a leader are less under the control of the independent proclivities of a leader's own personality and increasingly under the influence and control of a differentiated social subsystem dedicated to certain production ends, irrespective of, in spite of, or even because of, the personal attributes of the leader. Their interest is more in a final product (some constructed image) than in the raw material (underlying personality). Thus, what remains increasingly in our exposure to and interactions with our leaders is less a connection with their personalities and, instead, more contact with the "strategic personality," if you will, of the social subsystem in which both leaders and followers are imbedded. I do not want to imply that such images are discounted and hence less effective in generating a sense of followership. On the contrary, such images can be carefully crafted so as to be extremely appealing (e.g., Keenan & Hadley, 1986).

Think of P as the personality of the leader. Think of B as the behavioral expressions of personality. Think of I as the image of leaders that is conveyed to followers, created by P through B, and that might foster charismatic followership. Perhaps under some circumstances the flow looks like this:

$P \rightarrow B \rightarrow I \rightarrow$ charismatic effects

Here the image projected to followers is a direct result of the expressive behaviors of the leader, reflecting his or her personality and psychology. One could argue, however, for an alternative concept, P' (P prime), and a flow that looks like this:

$I \rightarrow B \rightarrow P' \rightarrow$ charismatic effects

P' results from the social subsystem—the media, the image consultant, the political advisor, the strategist, the PR Department—who care about what I is presented and what behaviors must be performed to create that image. These behaviors are expressive of P', not of P. My contentions are as follows: (1) that often P and P' are not as congruent as they once were; and (2) that over time P', given highly mediated, encumbered interactions, is more powerfully transmitted and ascending in importance relative to P (see Figure 3).

It is not just the media, it is other forces as well. Systems have an interest in having leaders with visibly apparent endowments and attributes. They have an interest in circumventing, augmenting, producing, and symbolizing the qualities of a leader, whether or not such attributes truly express the leader's actual personality. At work is a process similar to that which gives rise to the exaggera-

FIGURE 3   Personality and Image

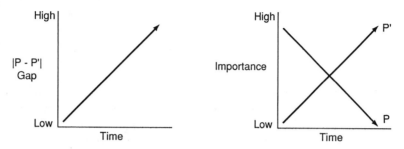

tion of physical (i.e., sexual) attributes of male and female rock idols. Indeed, many leaders respond and seek to fulfill the preferred images of their constituent followers. A part of the dynamics may be similar to that of the self-monitoring concept (Snyder, 1974, 1979), a concept that is now beginning to be examined within the domain of emergent leadership (Ellis, 1988; Ellis, Adamson, Deszca, & Cawsey, 1988; Garland & Beard, 1979; Zaccaro et al., 1991). The larger point here is that we ought to be examining the attributes and processes associated with P', instead of looking at P. We should be examining the conditions that encumber transmissions and convert P to P'. Studies along these lines are extremely rare (see, for example, Chen & Meindl, 1991) and will not easily grow out of more conventional approaches.

CONCLUSION

This chapter represents a call for more social psychological perspectives on leadership. The comparative advantage of social psychology, with respect to leadership studies, lies in its potential to generate theory and research that is juxtaposed against prevailing conceptions. Conventional approaches tend to study leadership in terms of leaders and their personal characteristics. A radical social psychological approach to leadership would emphasize followers as they are affected by their social contexts. I have presented some ideas along these lines, which stem from a consideration of the romance of leadership notion. In the particular anticonventional approach outlined, the focus has been on leadership as conceptualized by group members. In this approach, the social context and network of relations within the group will be important to understand, and these ought to be more fully explored. Such interfollower processes and dynamics are not easily appreciated within the confines of conventional conceptualizations of leadership.

Other social psychological perspectives on leadership can also be fashioned. Radical, anticonventional approaches might be inspired by the emphasis on followership in several older definitions of leadership (e.g., Bernard, 1927;

Bogardus, 1929; Dupuy & Dupuy, 1959; Jennings, 1944; Knickerbocker, 1948; Newcomb, Turner, & Converse, 1965; Redl, 1942) and in several analyses that deal with followers and their "propensity" to become involved in charismatic relationships (e.g., Madsen & Snow, 1983; Shils, 1965). In fact, some aspects of followership are implicit in a number of mainstream writings as well (e.g., Crockett, 1981; Gardner, 1987; Heller & Van Til, 1982; Kelly, 1988; Nolan & Harty, 1984; Zierdan, 1980); but the trick is to use them as a way to pursue a path of exploration that is unimpeded by conventional biases and assumptions. A few signs of this are now beginning to appear (e.g., Hollander, in press).

Some advances can be made by simply drawing on the wealth of theory and research in basic social psychology and applying it to issues of leadership. There are some signs of this occurring. And for those with little formal training in social psychology, that may be a reasonable way to make a contribution. Whatever the particular avenue explored, however, I suspect that the greatest contributions are likely to come from those who will treat leadership as a basic social psychological phenomenon and not an applied derivative of other, more legitimate or mainstream social psychological topics. Either of these options is preferable to the status quo. There are enough researchers, working within conventional mindsets, conducting leadership studies. What we now need are researchers, with or without formal training in social psychology, who are willing to break with convention. Of course, this presupposes that one is willing to endure whatever risks are associated with doing so. But, as some of my more investment-minded, MBA students are quick to point out, risk and return are often correlated.

REFERENCES

ALLPORT, G. (1985). In G. Lindzey & E. Aronson (Eds.), *The handbook of social psychology* (3rd ed., pp. 1–80). New York: Random House.

ASHOUR, A. S. (1982). A framework for a cognitive behavioral theory of influence and effectiveness. *Organizational Behavior and Human Performance, 30,* 407–430.

BASS, B. M. (1954). The leaderless group discussion. *Psychological Bulletin, 51,* 465–492.

BASS, B. M. (1985a). *Leadership and performance beyond expectations.* New York: Free Press.

BASS, B. M. (1985b). Leadership: Good, better, best. *Organizational Dynamics, 13,* 26–40.

BASS, B. M. (1990). *Bass & Stogdill's handbook of leadership* (3rd ed.). New York: Free Press.

BASS, B. M., McGEHEE, C. R., HAWKINS, W. C., YOUNG, P. C., & GEBEL, A. S. (1953). Personality variables related to leaderless group discussion behavior. *Journal of Abnormal and Social Psychology, 48,* 120–128.

BAVELAS, A., HASTORF, A. H., GROSS, A. E., & KITE, W. R. (1965). Experiments on the alteration of group structure. *Journal of Experimental Social Psychology, 1,* 55–70.

BENNIS, W. (1976). *The unconscious conspiracy: Why leaders can't lead.* New York: AMACOM.

BENNIS, W. (1977). Where have all the leaders gone? *Technology Review, 75*(9), 3–12.

BENNIS, W., & NANUS, B. (1985). *Leaders.* New York: Harper & Row.

BERNARD, L. L. (1927). Leadership and propoganda. In J. Davis & H. E. Barnes (Eds.), *An introduction to sociology* (pp. 296–315). New York: Heath.

BINNING, J. F., & LORD, R. G. (1980). Boundary conditions for performance cue effects on group process rating: Familiarity versus type of feedback. *Organizational Behavior and Human Performance, 26,* 115–130.

BINNING, J. F., ZABA, A. J., & WHATTAM, J. C. (1986). Explaining the biasing effects of performance cues in terms of cognitive categorization. *Academy of Management Journal, 29,* 521–535.

BLAKE, R. R., & MOUTON, J. S. (1964). *The managerial grid.* Houston, TX: Gulf.

BLANCHARD, K. (1989). *The one minute manager meets the monkey.* New York: Morrow.

BLANCHARD, K., & JOHNSON, S. (1981). *The one minute manager.* New York: Morrow.

BLANCHARD, K., & LORBER, R. (1984). *Putting the one minute manager to work.* New York: Morrow.

BLANCHARD, K., ZIGARMI, P., & ZIGARMI, D. (1985). *Leadership and the one minute manager.* New York: Morrow.

BLANK, W., WEITZEL, J., & GREEN, S. G. (1986). Situational leadership theory: A test of underlying assumptions. *Proceedings of the Academy of Management,* 384.

BOAL, K. B., & BRYSON, J. M. (1988). Charismatic leadership: A phenomenological and historical approach. In J. G. Hunt, B. R. Baliga, H. P. Dachler, & C. A. Schriesheim (Eds.), *Emerging leadership vistas* (pp. 11–28). Lexington, MA: Lexington.

BOGARDUS, E. S. (1929). Leadership and attitudes. *Sociologist and Social Research, 13,* 377–387.

BRADFORD, D. L., & COHEN, A. R. (1984). *Managing excellence.* New York: Wiley.

BRADLEY, R. T. (1987). Charisma and social structure: A study of love and power. *Wholeness and transformation.* New York: Paragon House.

BURNS, J. M. (1978). *Leadership.* New York: Harper & Row.

BUSKIRK, R. H. (1984). *Modern management and Machiavelli.* New York: Meridian.

CALDER, B. J. (1977). An attribution theory of leadership. In B. M. Staw & G. R. Salancik (Eds.), *New directions in organizational behavior* (pp. 179–204). Chicago: St. Clair.

CARLZON, J. (1987). *Moments of truth.* New York: Harper & Row.

CHEN, C. C., & MEINDL, J. R. (1991). The construction of leadership images in the popular press: The case of Donald Burr and People Express. *Administrative Science Quarterly, 36,* 521–551.

CLEARY, T. (1988). *The art of war by Sun Tzu.* Boston: Shambhala.

CONGER, J. A. (1989). *The charismatic leader: Behind the mystique of exceptional leadership.* San Francisco: Jossey-Bass.

CONGER, J. A., & KANUNGO, R. N. (1987). Toward a behavioral theory of charismatic leadership in organizational settings. *Academy of Management Review, 12,* 637–647.

CONGER, J. A., & KANUNGO, R. N. (1988). *Charismatic leadership: The elusive factor in organizational effectiveness.* San Francisco: Jossey-Bass.

CROCKETT, W. J. (1981). Dynamic subordinacy. *Training and Development Journal, 35,* 155–164.

CROUCH, A. (1987). An equilibrium model of management group performance. *Academy of Management Review, 12,* 499–510.

DANSEREAU, F., JR., GRAEN, G., & HAGA, W. J. (1975). A vertical dyad linkage approach to leadership within formal organizations: A longitudinal investigation of the role making process. *Organizational Behavior and Human Performance, 13,* 46–78.

DAY, D. V., & LORD, R. G. (1988). Executive leadership and organizational performance: Suggestions for a new theory and methodology. *Journal of Management, 14,* 453–464.

DEINESCH, R. M., & LIDEN, R. C. (1986). Leader-member exchange model of leadership: A critique and further development. *Academy of Management Review, 11,* 618–634.

DeNISI, A. S., & PRITCHARD, R. D. (1978). Implicit theories of performance as artifacts in survey research: A replication and extension. *Organizational Behavior and Human Performance, 21*, 358–366.

DOWNEY, H. K., CHACKO, T. I., & McELROY, J. C. (1979). Attribution of the causes of performance: A constructive, quasi-longitudinal replication of the Staw (1975) study. *Organizational Behavior and Human Performance, 24*, 287–299.

DUPUY, R. E., & DUPUY, T. N. (1959). *Brave men and great captains.* New York: Harper & Row.

EDEN, D., & LEVIATAN, U. (1975). Implicit leadership theory as a determinant of the factor structure underlying supervisory behavior scales. *Journal of Applied Psychology, 60*, 736–741.

ELLIS, R. J. (1988). Self-monitoring and leadership emergence in groups. *Personality and Social Psychology Bulletin, 14*, 681–693.

ELLIS, R. J., ADAMSON, R. S., DESZCA, G., & CAWSEY, T. F. (1988). Self monitoring and leader emergence. *Small Group Behavior, 19*, 312–324.

EVANS, M. G., & DERMER, J. (1974). What does the least preferred coworker scale really measure? A cognitive interpretation. *Journal of Applied Psychology, 59*, 202–206.

FIEDLER, F. E. (1964). A contingency model of leadership effectiveness. In L. Berkowitz (Ed.), *Advances in experimental social psychology* (pp. 150–191). New York: Academic Press.

FIEDLER, F. E. (1967). *A theory of leadership effectiveness.* New York: McGraw-Hill.

FIEDLER, F. E. (1977). A rejoinder to Schriesheim and Kerr's premature obituary of the contingency model. In J. G. Hunt and L. L. Larson (Eds.) *Leadership: The cutting edge* (pp. 45–50). Carbondale, IL: Southern Illinois University Press.

FIEDLER, F. E. (1986). The contribution of cognitive resources to leadership performance. *Journal of Applied Psychology, 16*, 532–548.

FIEDLER, F. E., CHERMERS, M. M., & MAHAR, L. (1976). *Improving leadership effectiveness: The LEADER MATCH concept.* New York: Wiley.

FIEDLER, F. E., & GARCIA, J. E. (1987). *New approaches to leadership: Cognitive resources and organizational performance.* New York: Wiley.

FOTI, R. J., FRASER, S. L., & LORD, R. G. (1982). Effects of leadership labels and prototypes on perceptions of political leaders. *Journal of Applied Psychology, 67*, 326–333.

GARDNER, J. (1987). Leaders and followers. *Liberal Education, 73*, 4–8.

GARLAND, H., & BEARD, J. F. (1979). Relationship between self-monitoring and leader emergence across two tasks. *Journal of Personality and Social Psychology, 64*, 72–76.

GIBB, C. A. (1954). Leadership. In G. Lindzey (Ed.), *Handbook of social psychology* (pp. 720–877). Cambridge, MA: Addison-Wesley.

GIOIA, D., & SIMS, H. P., JR. (1985). On avoiding the influence of implicit leadership theories in leader behavior descriptions. *Journal of Educational and Psychological Measurement, 45*, 217–237.

GRAEF, C. L. (1983). The situational leadership theory: A critical review. *Academy of Management Review, 8*, 285–296.

GRAEN, G., & CASHMAN, J. F. (1975). A role-making model of leadership in formal organizations: A developmental approach. In J. G. Hunt & L. L. Larson (Eds.), *Leadership frontiers.* Kent, OH: Kent State University Press.

GRAEN, G. (1976). Role making processes within complex organizations. In M. D. Dunnett (Ed.), *Handbook of industrial and organizational psychology.* Chicago: Rand McNally.

GREEN, S. G., & MITCHELL, T. R. (1979). Attributional processes of leader-member interactions. *Organizational Behavior and Human Performance, 23*, 429–458.

HAMBLETON, R. K., & GUMBERT, R. (1982). The validity of Hersey and Blanchard's theory of leader effectiveness. *Group and Organization Studies, 7*, 225–242.

HATER, J. J., & BASS, B. M. (1988). Supervisor's evaluation and subordinates' perceptions of transformational and transactional leadership. *Journal of Applied Psychology, 73*, 695–702.

HEIDER, F. (1958). *The psychology of interpersonal relations.* New York: Wiley.

HEIDER, J. (1985). *The tao of leadership.* Atlanta, GA: Humanics.

HELLER, T., & VAN TIL, J. (1982). Leadership and followership: Some summary propositions. *Journal of Applied Behavioral Science, 18*, 405–414.

HERSEY, P., & BLANCHARD, K. H. (1969). Life cycle theory of leadership. *Training and Development Journal, 23*(2), 26–34.

HERSEY, P., & BLANCHARD, K. H. (1977). *Management of organizational behavior: Utilizing human resources.* Englewood Cliffs, NJ: Prentice Hall.

HOLLANDER, E. P. (1964). *Leaders, groups and influence.* New York: Oxford University Press.

HOLLANDER, E. P. (1978). *Leadership dynamics.* New York: Free Press.

HOLLANDER, E. P. (1985). Leadership and power. In G. Lindzey & E. Aronson (Eds.), *The handbook of social psychology* (3rd ed., pp. 485–537). New York: Random House.

HOLLANDER, E. P. (1986). On the central role of leadership processes. *International Review of Applied Psychology, 35*, 39–52.

HOLLANDER, E. P. (in press). Leadership, followership, self, and other. *Leadership Quarterly.*

HOLLANDER, E. P., FALLON, B. J., & EDWARDS, M. T. (1977). Some aspects of influence and acceptability for appointed and elected leaders. *Journal of Psychology, 95*, 289–296.

HOLLANDER, E. P., & JULIAN, J. W. (1970). Studies in leader legitimacy, influence, and innovation. In L. Berkowitz (Ed.), *Advances in experimental social psychology* (Vol. 5, pp. 33–69). New York: Academic Press.

HOLLANDER, E. P., & OFFERMAN, L. R. (1990). Power and leadership in organizations. *American Psychologist, 45*, 179–189.

HORTON, T. R. (1986). *What works for me: 16 CEOs talk about their careers and commitments.* New York: Random House.

HOUSE, R. J. (1971). A path-goal theory of leader effectiveness. *Administrative Science Quarterly, 16*, 321–339.

HOUSE, R. J. (1977). A 1976 theory of charismatic leadership. In J. G. Hunt & L. L. Larson (Eds.), *Leadership: The cutting edge* (pp. 194–205). Carbondale: Southern Illinois University Press.

HOUSE, R. J. (1988). Leadership research: Some forgotten, ignored, or overlooked findings. In J. G. Hunt, B. R. Baglia, H. P. Dachler, & C. A. Schriesheim (Eds.), *Emerging leadership vistas* (pp. 179–199). Lexington, MA: D. C. Heath.

HOUSE, R. J., & MITCHELL, T. R. (1974). Path-goal theory of leadership. *Journal of Contemporary Business, 3*(4), 81–97.

HOUSE, R. J., SPANGLER, W. D., & WOYCKE, J. (1991). Personality and charisma in the U.S. Presidency: A psychological theory of leader effectiveness. *Administrative Science Quarterly, 36*, 364–396.

HOWELL, J. P., & FROST, P. J. (1988). A laboratory study of charismatic leadership. *Organizational Behavior and Human Decision Processes, 43*, 243–269.

IACOCCA, L., & NOVAK, W. (1984). *Iacocca: An autobiography.* New York: Bantam.

INDVIK, J. (1986). Path-goal theory of leadership: A meta-analysis. *Proceedings, Academy of Management*, Chicago, 189–192.

JENNINGS, H. H. (1944). Leadership—a dynamic re-definition. *Journal of Educational Sociology, 17*, 431–433.

JONES, E. E., & DAVIS, K. E. (1965). From acts to dispositions: The attribution process in person perception. In L. Berkowitz (Ed.), *Advances in experimental social psychology* (Vol. 2, pp. 220–266). New York: Academic Press.

KABANOFF, B. (1981). A critique of LEADER MATCH and its implications for leadership research. *Personnel Psychology, 34,* 749–764.

KATZ, D. (1960). The functional approach to the study of attitudes. *Public Opinion Quarterly, 24,* 163–204.

KATZ, D., & KAHN, R. L. (1966). *The social psychology of organizations.* New York: Wiley.

KATZ, D., & KAHN, R. L. (1978). *The social psychology of organizations* (2nd ed.). New York: Wiley.

KEENAN, N., & HADLEY, M. (1986). The creation of political leaders in the context of American politics in the 1970s and 1980s. In C. F. Graumann & S. Moscovici (Eds.), *Changing conceptions of leadership* (pp. 145–169). New York: Springer-Verlag.

KELLER, R. T. (1989). A test of path-goal theory of leadership with need for clarity as a moderator in research and development organizations. *Journal of Applied Psychology, 74,* 208–212.

KELLEY, H. H. (1967). Attribution theory in social psychology. In D. Levine (Ed.), *Nebraska symposium on motivation* (Vol. 15, pp. 192–238). Lincoln, NE: University of Nebraska Press.

KELLY, R. E. (1988). In praise of followers. *Harvard Business Review,* Nov./Dec., 142–148.

KELMAN, H. C. (1958). Compliance, identification, and internalization: Three processes of attitude change. *Journal of Conflict Resolution, 2,* 51–60.

KERR, S. M., & JERMIER, J. M. (1978). Substitutes for leadership: Their meaning and measurement. *Organizational Behavior and Human Performance, 22,* 375–403.

KLIMOSKI, R. J., & HAYES, N. J. (1980). Leader behavior and subordinate motivation. *Personnel Psychology, 33,* 543–555.

KNICKERBOCKER, I. (1948). Leadership: A conception and some implications. *Journal of Social Issues. 4,* 23–40.

KOMAKI, J. L. (1986). Toward effective supervision: An operant analysis and comparison of managers at work. *Journal of Applied Psychology, 71,* 270–279.

KOUZES, J. M., & POSNER, B. Z. (1988). *The leadership challenge: How to get extraordinary things done in organizations.* San Francisco: Jossey-Bass.

KUHNERT, K. W., & LEWIS, P. (1987). Transactional and transformational leadership: A constructive/developmental analysis. *Academy of Management Review, 12*(4), 648–657.

LAMB, R. B. (1987). *Running American business.* New York: Basic Books.

LIEBERSON, S., & O'CONNOR, J. F. (1972). Leadership and organizational performance: A study of large corporations. *American Sociological Review, 37,* 117–130.

LIDEN, R. C., & GRAEN, G. (1980). Generalizability of the vertical dyad linkage model of leadership. *Academy of Management Journal, 23,* 451–463.

LINDZEY, G., & ARONSON, E. (1985). *The handbook of social psychology* (3rd ed.). New York: Random House.

LORD, R. G. (1985). An information processing approach to social perception, leadership perceptions and behavioral measurement in organizational settings. In B. M. Staw & L. L. Cummings (Eds.), *Research in organizational behavior* (Vol. 7, pp. 87–128). Greenwich, CT: JAI Press.

LORD, R. G., & ALLIGER, G. M. (1985). A comparison of information processing models of leadership and social perception. *Human Relations, 38,* 47–65.

LORD, R. G., DEVADER, C. L., & ALLIGER, G. M. (1986). A meta-analysis of the relation between personality traits and leadership: An application of validity generalization procedures. *Journal of Applied Psychology, 71,* 402–410.

MADSEN, D., & SNOW, P. G. (1983). The dispersion of charisma. *Comparative Political Studies, 16*(3), 337–362.

MARTINKO, M. J., & GARDNER, W. L. (1987). The leader/member attribution process. *Academy of Management Review, 12*, 235–249.

McELROY, J. C. (1982). A typology of attribution leadership research. *Academy of Management Review, 7*, 413–417.

McELROY, J. C., & DOWNEY, H. K. (1982). Observation in organizational research: Panacea to the performance-attribution effect? *Academy of Management Review, 7*, 413–417.

McELROY, J. C., & SCHRADER, C. B. (1986). Attribution theories of leadership and network analysis. *Journal of Management, 12*, 351–362.

MEINDL, J. R. (1990). On leadership: An alternative to the conventional wisdom. In B. M. Staw & L. L. Cummings (Eds.), *Research in organizational behavior* (Vol. 12, pp. 159–203). Greenwich, CT: JAI Press.

MEINDL, J. R., EHRLICH, S. B., & DUKERICH, J. M. (1985). The romance of leadership. *Administrative Science Quarterly, 30*, 78–102.

MEINDL, J. R., & EHRLICH, S. B. (1987). The romance of leadership and the evaluation of organizational performance. *Academy of Management Journal, 30*, 91–109.

MINER, J. B. (1975). The uncertain future of the leadership concept: An overview. In J. G. Hunt & L. L. Larson (Eds.), *Leadership frontiers* (pp. 197–208). Kent, OH: Kent State University Press.

MITCHELL, T. R., & WOOD, R. E. (1980). Supervisor's responses to subordinates' poor performance: A test of an attributional model. *Organizational Behavior and Human Performance, 25*, 123–138.

MITCHELL, T. R., GREEN, S. G., & WOOD, R. E. (1981). An attributional model of leadership and the poor performing subordinate: Development and validation. In L. L. Cummings & B. M. Staw (Eds.), *Research in organizational behavior* (Vol. 3, pp. 197–234). Greenwich, CT: JAI Press.

MORRIS, C. G., & HACKMAN, J. R. (1969). Behavioral correlates of perceived leadership. *Journal of Personality and Social Psychology, 13*, 350–361.

NEWCOMB, T. M., TURNER, R. H., & CONVERSE, P. E. (1965). *Social psychology.* New York: Holt, Rinehart & Winston.

NOLAN, J. S., & HARTY, H. F. (1984). Followership > leadership. *Education, 104*, 311–312.

PETERS, T., & WATERMAN, R. H., Jr. (1982). *In search of excellence.* New York: Harper & Row.

PETERS, T. J., & AUSTIN, N. (1985). *A passion for excellence: The leadership difference.* New York: Random House.

PFEFFER, J. (1977). The ambiguity of leadership. *Academy of Management Review, 2*, 104–112.

PFEFFER, J. (1981). Management as symbolic action: The creation and maintenance of organizational paradigms. In L. L. Cummings & B. M. Staw (Eds.), *Research in organizational behavior* (Vol. 3, pp. 61–52). Greenwich, CT: JAI Press.

PFEFFER, J., & SALANCIK, G. R. (1978). *The external control of organizations: A resource dependence perspective.* New York: Harper & Row.

PHILLIPS, J. S., & LORD, R. G. (1981). Causal attributions and perceptions of leadership. *Organizational Behavior and Human Performance, 28*, 143–163.

PHILLIPS, J. S., & LORD, R. G. (1982). Schematic information processing and perceptions of leadership in problem-solving groups. *Journal of Applied Psychology, 67*, 486–492.

PILLAI, R., & MEINDL, J. R. (1991a). The effects of a crisis on the emergence of charismatic leadership: A laboratory study. *Best paper proceedings of the 1991 Academy of Management Meetings*, Miami, FL.

PILLAI, R., & MEINDL, J. R. (1991b). The impact of a performance crisis on attributions of charismatic leadership: A preliminary study. *Best paper proceedings of the 1991 Eastern Academy of Management Meetings,* Hartford, CT.

PODSAKOFF, P. M., & SCHRIESHEIM, C. A. (1985). Leader reward and punishment behavior: A methodological and substantive review. In B. M. Shaw & L. L. Cummings (Eds.), *Research in organizational behavior* (pp. 322–351). San Francisco: Jossey-Bass.

POTTS, M., & BEHR, P. (1987). *The leading edge: 10 CEOs who turned their companies around.* New York: McGraw-Hill.

RAHIM, A. (1981). Organizational behavior course for graduate students in business administration: Views from the tower and battlefield. *Psychological Reports, 49,* 583–592.

REDL, F. (1942). Group emotion and leadership. *Psychiatric, 5,* 573–596.

RICE, R. W. (1978). Construct validity of the least preferred co-worker score. *Psychological Bulletin, 85,* 1199–1237.

ROBERTS, W. (1985). *Leadership secrets of Attila the Hun.* New York: Warner Books.

ROSS, L. (1977). The intuitive psychologist and his shortcomings: Distortions in the attribution process. *Advances in Experimental Social Psychology, 10,* 174–220.

RUSH, M. C., THOMAS, J. C., & LORD, R. L. (1977). Implicit leadership theory: A potential threat to the internal validity of leader behavior questionnaires. *Organizational Behavior and Human Performance, 20,* 92–110.

SCANDURRA, T. A., & GRAEN, G. B. (1984). Moderating effects of initial leader-member exchange status on the effects of leadership intervention. *Journal of Applied Psychology, 69,* 428–436.

SCANDURRA, T. A., GRAEN, G. B., & NOVAK, M. A. (1986). When managers decide not to decide automatically: An investigation of leader-member exchange and decision influence. *Journal of Applied Psychology, 71,* 579–584.

SCHRIESHEIM, C. A., & KERR, S. (1977). Theories and measures of leadership: A critical appraisal. In J. C. Hunt & L. L. Larson (Eds.), *Leadership: The cutting edge* (pp. 51–56). Carbondale, IL: Southern Illinois University Press.

SCULLY, J. (1987). *Odyssey.* New York: Harper & Row.

SHERIF, M., & SHERIF, C. W. (1956). *An outline of social psychology.* New York: Harper.

SHIFLETT, S. C. (1973). The contingency model of leadership effectiveness: Some implications of its statistical and methodological properties. *Behavioral Science, 18*(6), 429–440.

SHILS, E. (1965). Charisma, order, and status. *American Sociological Review, 30,* 199–213.

SHOOK, R. L. (1981). *The chief executive officers, men who run big business in America.* New York: Harper & Row.

SIMONTON, D. K. (1986). Presidential Personality: Biographical use of the Gough Adjective Checklist. *Journal of Personality and Social Psychology, 51,* 149–160.

SIMONTON, D. K. (1987). *Why presidents succeed: A political psychology of leadership:* New Haven, CT: Yale University Press.

SIMONTON, D. K. (1988). Presidential Style: Personality, biography, and performance. *Journal of Personality and Social Psychology, 55,* 928–936.

SMITH, J. E., CARSON, K. P., & ALEXANDER, R. A. (1984). Leadership: It can make a difference. *Academy of Management Journal, 27,* 765–776.

SNYDER, M. (1974). The self-monitoring of expressive behavior. *Journal of Personality and Social Psychology, 30,* 526–537.

SNYDER, M. (1979). Self-monitoring processes. In L. Berkowitz (Ed.), *Advances in Experimental Social Psychology, 12,* 86–128.

SORRENTINO, R. M. (1973). An extension of a theory of motivation to the study of emergent leadership. *Journal of Personality and Social Psychology, 26,* 356–368.

SORRENTINO, R. M., & FIELD, N. (1986). Emergent leadership over time: The functional value of positive motivation. *Journal of Personality and Social Psychology, 50,* 1091–1099.

STAW, B. M. (1975). Attributions of the 'cause' of performance: A general alternative interpretation of cross-sectional research on organizations. *Organizational Behavior and Human Performance, 13,* 414–432.

STAW, B. M., & ROSS, J. (1980). Commitment in an experimenting society: A study of the attribution of leadership from administrative scenarios. *Journal of Applied Psychology, 65,* 249–260.

STEIN, R. T. (1975). Identifying emergent leaders from verbal and non-verbal communications. *Journal of Personality and Social Psychology, 32,* 125–135.

STEIN, R. T. (1977). Accuracy of process consultants and untrained observers in perceiving emergent leadership. *Journal of Applied Psychology, 62,* 755–759.

STEIN, R. T., HOFFMAN, L. R., COOLEY, S. J., & PEARSE, R. W. (1979). Leadership valence: Modeling and measuring the process of emergent leadership. In J. G. Hunt & L. L. Larson (Eds.), *Crosscurrents in leadership* (pp. 120–147). Carbondale, IL: Southern Illinois University Press.

STEINER, G. A. (1983). *The new CEO.* New York: Macmillan.

STIEGLITZ, H. (1985). *Chief executives view their jobs, today and tomorrow.* New York: The Conference Board, Inc.

STRODTBECK, F. L., & MANN, R. D. (1956). Sex role differentiation in jury deliberations. *Sociometry, 19,* 3–11.

STRUBE, M. J., & GARCIA, J. E. (1981). A meta-analytic investigation of Fiedler's contingency model of leadership effectiveness. *Psychological Bulletin, 90,* 307–321.

THOMAS, A. B. (1988). Does leadership make a difference to organizational performance? *Administrative Science Quarterly, 33,* 388–400.

TICHY, N. M., & DEVANNA, M. A. (1986). *The transformational leader.* New York: Wiley.

TRICE, H. M., & BEYER, J. M. (1986). Charisma and its routinization in two social movement organizations. *Research in Organizational Behavior, 8,* 113–164.

VECCHIO, R. P. (1983). Assessing the validity of Fiedler's contingent model leadership effectiveness: A closer look at Strube and Garcia. *Psychological Bulletin, 93,* 404–408.

VECCHIO, R. P. (1987). Situational leadership theory: An examination of a prescriptive theory. *Journal of Applied Psychology, 72,* 444–451.

WEBER, M. (1921). The sociology of charismatic authority. In H. H. Gerth & C. W. Mills (Trans. & Eds.), *From Max Weber: Essays in sociology* (pp. 245–252). New York: Oxford University Press.

WEBER, M. (1947). *The theory of social and economic organization* (A. M. Henderson & T. Parsons, Trans.; T. Parsons, Ed.) New York: Free Press.

WEINER, N., & MAHONEY, T. A. (1981). A model of corporate performance as a function of environmental, organizational, and leadership influences. *Academy of Management Journal, 24,* 453–470.

WEISS, H. M., & ADLER, S. (1981). Cognitive complexity and the structure of implicit leadership theories. *Journal of Applied Psychology, 66,* 69–78.

WHEELER, L. (1966). Toward a theory of behavioral contagion. *Psychological Review, 73,* 179–192.

WING, R. L. (1986). *The tao of power: Lao Tzu's classic guide to leadership, influence, and excellence.* New York: Doubleday.

YUKL, G. A. (1989). *Leadership in organizations* (2nd ed.). Englewood Cliffs, NJ: Prentice Hall.

ZACCARO, S. J., FOTI, R. J., & KENNY, D. A. (1991). Self-monitoring and trait-based variance in leadership: An investigation of leader flexibility across multiple group situations. *Journal of Applied Psychology, 76*(2), 308–315.

ZAHN, G. L., & WOLF, G. (1981). Leadership and the art of cycle maintenance: A simulation model of superior-subordinate interaction. *Organizational Behavior and Human Performance, 28,* 26–49.

ZALEZNIK, A. (1977). Managers and leaders: Are they different? *Harvard Business Review, 55*(5), 67–78.

ZALEZNIK, A. (1983). The leadership gap. *Washington Quarterly, 6,* 32–39.

ZIERDAN, W. E. (1980). Leading through the follower's point of view. *Organizational Dynamics, 8*(4), 27–46.

CHAPTER SIX

Living on the Edge
(of Social and Organizational Psychology):
The Effects of Job Layoffs
on Those Who Remain

JOEL BROCKNER   BATIA WIESENFELD

Columbia University   *Columbia University*

Layoffs are a pervasive downsizing strategy in corporate America, yet until recently there have been few attempts to understand their impact on the work behaviors and attitudes of the people who remain: the "survivors." This chapter identifies several psychological states and social psychological processes (perceived fairness, job insecurity, uncertainty, attributional instigation, peripheral vs. central social information processing, and intrinsic motivation) that explain survivors' reactions. Empirical research is presented showing how each psychological state (along with its accompanying theoretical framework) provides a partial explanation of survivors' reactions, such as work performance and organizational commitment. We attempt to integrate these separate explanations into a more unified framework: Lazarus and Folkman's (1984) model of stress, appraisal, and coping. The reciprocal relationship between social psychological theory and survivors' reactions is emphasized. Existing theory helps explain survivors' reactions, and the study of survivors' reactions (both present and future) may help sharpen our understanding of fundamental theoretical issues.

Job layoffs have long been of great interest to organizational scholars and practitioners (e.g., Eisenberg & Lazarsfeld, 1938). The bulk of theory and research has focused on the causes of layoffs (between and within organizations), or their consequences for the victims of job loss (Jahoda, 1982). Overlooked somehow was the practically and theoretically important question of how job layoffs affect the work attitudes and behaviors of the employees who remain (hereafter referred to as the "survivors"). Two facts highlight the practical significance of survivors' reactions. First, in the wake of foreign competition, technological developments, and mergers and acquisitions, layoffs pervaded the corporate landscape in the 1980s, and there is every reason to believe that this trend will continue (or even increase). For instance, more than half of the companies represented at the American Management Association (AMA) convention in 1989 had experienced layoffs within the past 4 years; a slightly greater percentage anticipated that they would downsize within the next few years (Right Associates, 1990). Second, from an organization's perspective, the success of the layoff depends to a great extent on how survivors react. In an extreme situation, the costs associated with unfavorable survivor reactions (e.g., reduced commitment to the organization or their jobs) could nullify the savings that the organization hoped to achieve by implementing layoffs.

Anecdotal evidence suggests that survivors' reactions, such as organizational commitment and work motivation, are highly variable, between and within downsizing organizations. For example, although the majority of companies at the AMA convention reported that survivors were fearful of future cutbacks and mistrustful of management, a sizeable minority said that survivors felt recommitted to the company's success and confident about the future.

This chapter seeks to provide a theoretical understanding of when and why survivors react to layoffs in different ways. The subject matter should also be of considerable interest to managers who must plan and implement layoffs to elicit the most favorable reactions among the remaining workforce. (For a more detailed discussion of the practical implications of this program of research, see Brockner, 1992.)

EXPLAINING SURVIVORS' REACTIONS: A SOCIAL PSYCHOLOGICAL ANALYSIS

Given the practical importance of layoffs, and the high variability in survivors' reactions, we have attempted to delineate the factors that affect survivors' reactions. At least three properties inherent to layoffs make social psychological theory relevant to this analysis. First, layoffs pertain to the *allocation of scarce resources*, which naturally elicits survivors' concerns about *justice and fairness* (Deutsch, 1985). Second, layoffs refer to *job loss*, which makes salient the effects of *job insecurity* (Greenhalgh & Rosenblatt, 1984). Third, layoffs often represent a source of sizeable organizational *change*, which arouses *uncertainty* in survivors and associated sensemaking processes (Festinger, 1954; Louis, 1980).

Social psychological theory is relevant to the analysis of survivors' reactions in another important sense. Although some social and psychological factors are extrinsic to layoffs, they are frequently associated with them. Layoffs may coincide with changes in survivors' career prospects, reporting relationships, and the size and nature of their workload. For example, survivors often find that their work has become more or less interesting after a layoff. Therefore, theory and research on job design (e.g., Hackman & Oldham, 1980) and intrinsic motivation (e.g., Deci & Ryan, 1985) may shed additional light on survivors' reactions.

In the next section of this chapter, we discuss some of the different determinants of survivors' reactions. The explanatory power of separate theories of fairness, job insecurity, social influence, and job design/intrinsic motivation can be conceptualized in several ways; we provide examples of each. The final section of the chapter attempts to provide a more integrated explanation of survivors' reactions, drawing on theory and research in the stress literature (Lazarus & Folkman, 1984). Throughout, we highlight the reciprocal relationship between social psychological theory and survivors' reactions, and we focus on important conceptual issues that merit further attention.

Determinants of survivors' reactions: toward differentiation

Once layoffs are conceptualized in terms of their inherent properties, several research questions emerge. For example, layoffs arouse survivors' concerns about fairness, which inevitably surround decisions pertaining to the allocation of scarce resources. Important research questions thus include (1) What factors affect survivors' judgments of the fairness of the layoff?, and (2) What factors moderate the relationship between survivors' fairness judgments and their attitudinal and behavioral reactions to the layoff?

THE ROLE OF FAIRNESS.   Many factors have been shown to influence survivors' judgments of the fairness of a layoff. Survivors may wonder, for instance, whether the layoff is truly necessary. Consider the case of Navistar, formerly International Harvester. When Navistar began downsizing in the late 1970s and early 1980s, many of its employees did not believe that layoffs were necessary. One worker commented that "the company could not be in financial trouble if it paid top executives millions of dollars a year, maintained a supervisor-to-employee ratio that was among the highest in the industry, and spent thousands of dollars to maintain the firm's grounds" (Jick, 1989, pp. 6–7).

The perceived legitimacy of a layoff may also be affected by the actions of other organizations in the firm's reference group and the corporate culture. If other organizations are initiating similar layoffs, then survivors are more likely to view layoffs in their own organization as fair. If layoffs represent a departure from the corporate culture, such as when a previously paternalistic organization that never laid off employees downsizes (e.g., Digital Equipment Corporation), then survivors are more likely to experience violated expectations and judge the layoffs as unfair.

Research has shown that survivors also are very sensitive to how fairly the layoff was implemented. They are affected by the fairness of both the *outcomes* associated with the layoff (distributive justice) and the *procedures* used to arrive at and implement the layoff (procedural justice). One determinant of perceived distributive justice is how well the organization provided for the layoff victims in concrete ways, such as severance pay and outplacement counseling. The more generously the organization took care of the victims, the more likely it is that the layoff will be perceived as fair. One antecedent of perceived procedural justice is the clarity and adequacy of the explanation the organization provided for the layoff; the more clear and adequate the explanation, the greater the perceived fairness (Bies, 1987; Rousseau & Anton, 1988; see Brockner & Greenberg, 1990, for a more comprehensive discussion of the determinants of survivors' perceptions of distributive and procedural fairness).

Survivors' reactions generally are more unfavorable (e.g., their organizational commitment and work motivation decreases) when they perceive the layoff to be unfair (Brockner, DeWitt, Grover, & Reed, 1990; Brockner, Grover, Reed, DeWitt, & O'Malley, 1987). Such findings come as little surprise in light of the vast amount of previous research attesting to the detrimental effects on employees of perceived unfairness (Greenberg, 1987). The more interesting question is whether survivors' fairness judgments are more strongly related to their work attitudes and behaviors under certain conditions rather than others.

Group value theory (Lind & Tyler, 1988) helps specify at least one moderator of the relationship between survivors' fairness perceptions and their work attitudes and behaviors. The basic assumption of the group value model is that people value their relationships with people, groups, organizations, and even social institutions. Relationships give people a way to evaluate the appropriateness of their beliefs and behaviors (Festinger, 1954) and offer a source of self-identity and self-worth (Tajfel & Turner, 1979). An important consequence of the value people attach to relationships is that they place a premium on being treated fairly in the context of those relationships. Fair treatment symbolizes that they are being dealt with in a dignified and respectful way, thereby heightening feelings of self-worth.

Although the group value theory assumes that people value their relationships, it is likely that in certain instances some people will value their relationships more than others and therefore place a greater premium on fair treatment. The group value model provides a theoretical basis for predicting that the association between survivors' fairness perceptions and their attitudinal and behavioral reactions to the layoff will be moderated by their prior commitment to the organization. Those who felt more committed to the organization prior to the layoff will be more influenced by the perceived fairness of the layoff than will their less-committed counterparts.

To test this hypothesis, Brockner, Tyler, and Cooper–Schneider (1992) studied the survivors of a layoff in a financial services organization. Participants rated their commitment to the organization prior to the layoff and the fairness of the decision rule that determined who would be laid off versus retained. Dependent variables included the change in survivors' organizational commitment and work effort. The results on the organizational commitment measure are shown in Table 1. (Similar results were obtained on the measure of work effort.) As predicted, the (positive) relationship between perceived fairness and survivors' change in organizational commitment was much stronger when survivors felt more committed to the organization prior to the layoff. In particular, survivors responded most negatively when they felt that the layoff was handled unfairly *and* they felt highly committed beforehand.

These results help explain some of the variability in survivors' reactions and broaden the domain of group value theory. Many empirical tests of the the-

TABLE 1   Survivors' Change in Organizational Commitment as a Function of Their Prior Commitment and Perceived Fairness of the Decision Rule

PRIOR COMMITMENT	FAIRNESS	
	Low	High
Low	103.23	98.82
High	82.40	103.69

Note: Score could range from 18 to 198, with higher scores reflecting more of an increase in organizational commitment, relative to before the layoff.

ory have been conducted in legal settings; in fact, results conceptually analogous to those shown in Table 1 were obtained in a study exploring citizens' reactions to their encounters with the police and the courts (Brockner, Tyler, & Cooper–Schneider, 1992).

Most pertinent to theory development, the study also raises important questions. For example, the prediction drawn from group value theory assumes that survivors will compare their prior beliefs about the organization with their experience of organizational actions during the layoff process. Those who were more committed to the organization presumably wanted and expected the organization to act fairly. When they perceived the decision rule to be unfair, we infer that their beliefs about the organization were violated. For theoretical purposes, however, it is important to specify the nature of the violated belief. Were survivors' *expectations* not met (i.e., they thought the organization would act fairly but found that not to be the case)? Or were survivors' *wishes or values* not fulfilled (i.e., they wanted the organization to act fairly but found that not to be true)? Of course, it is possible that both survivors' expectations and wishes were violated; what people want is often related to what they expect. Nevertheless, it is important to differentiate between what people *believe* will happen versus what they *want* to occur (Vroom, 1964).

The asymmetry of the results—those who previously were highly committed but perceived the decision rule to be unfair reacted quite negatively, while those who were relatively uncommitted but perceived the decision rule to be fair did not react especially positively—raises several important theoretical concerns. First, the findings suggest that the results did not simply reflect violated expectations. If they did, then those in the Low Prior Commitment/High Fairness condition should have reacted especially favorably, in that the organization's actions probably were more fair than they expected. As shown in Table 1, however, survivors did not react more favorably in the Low Prior Commitment/ High Fairness than High Prior Commitment/High Fairness condition. A second possibility is that negative discrepancies between prior beliefs and actual experience have more psychological impact than positive discrepancies; or, as Kahneman and Tversky (1984) have suggested in a different context, losses loom larger than gains. Further research investigating this possibility may have important implications for social judgment theory (e.g., Sherif, Sherif, & Nebergall, 1965), which is concerned with understanding the antecedents and consequences of assimilation and contrast effects.

In summary, a careful analysis of the properties inherent in layoffs helps to identify the mediators of the relationship between layoffs and survivors' reactions. One such mediator is perceived fairness. The important question, then, concerns when fairness will have a greater versus a lesser effect on survivors' reactions. Our research strategy relies on existing social psychological theory to help identify factors that moderate the relationship between perceived fairness and survivors' reactions. This strategy serves a number of purposes. First, it may help to explain the variability in survivors' reactions, which was the initial impetus for the research. Second, it provides a demonstration of the generalizability of the theory to a new domain. Third, the results of the study may shed light on an important theoretical matter, or may raise questions for future research, the pursuit of which may ultimately help extend theory.

THE ROLE OF JOB INSECURITY.   The multifaceted nature of layoffs suggests that factors besides perceived fairness will mediate the relationship between layoffs and survivors' reactions. One such factor is job insecurity. Greenhalgh and Rosenblatt (1984) suggested that job insecurity consists of two components: perceived threat and perceived control. Perceived threat is affected by such factors as survivors' expectations of the likelihood of future layoffs. Perceived control refers to survivors' beliefs that they will be able to counteract the negative consequences of job loss. According to this dual-component definition, job insecurity should be greatest when perceived threat is high and perceived control is low, least intense when perceived threat is low and perceived control is high, and moderately intense when perceived threat and control are both high or low.

We recently tested the hypothesis that survivors' job insecurity would influence their work effort in a nonlinear fashion—that is, that work effort would be greater at moderate rather than at low or high levels of job insecurity (Brockner, Grover, Reed, & DeWitt, 1992). Survivors with little job insecurity should be relatively complacent. At high levels of job insecurity, survivors also should be relatively unmotivated, but for different reasons. In particular, survivors are likely to feel helpless (Seligman, 1975) when perceived threat is high and perceived control is low. In fact, the results of the study supported the predicted inverted-U relationship between survivors' job insecurity and their work effort.

The study also examined whether survivors' economic need to work moderated the relationship between their job insecurity and work effort. Attitude theory and research suggests that people are more likely to act on beliefs that are of importance to them (Sivacek & Crano, 1982). Job insecurity should be a more important belief for those who have a high economic need to work; therefore, we predicted that the (inverted-U) relationship between job insecurity and work effort would be accentuated for survivors high in their economic need to work. As can be seen in Table 2, these are precisely the results we obtained. Among those high in their economic need to work, work effort was considerably lower

TABLE 2 Survivors' Change in Work Effort as a Function of Perceived Threat, Perceived Control, and Economic Need to Work

ECONOMIC NEED TO WORK	PERCEIVED THREAT	PERCEIVED CONTROL	
		Low	High
	Low	20.83	20.57
Low	High	19.55	20.29
	Low	24.94	18.70
High	High	19.93	23.25

Note: Scores could range from 3 to 33. Higher scores reflect a greater increase in work effort, relative to the pre-layoff period.

when job insecurity was low (i.e., when perceived threat was low and perceived control was high) or high (i.e., when perceived threat was high and perceived control was low) than when job insecurity was at a moderate level (i.e., when perceived threat and perceived control were both high or low). When economic need to work was low, survivors' job insecurity had no effect on their work effort.

One explanation of these results is cognitive, positing that survivors' judgments of threat and control influence their perceptions of complacency and helplessness, which affect their levels of effort. An alternative possibility is that the key psychological construct is survivors' level of arousal: The results are reminiscent of the age-old Yerkes–Dodson (1908) law of the (inverted-U) relationship between arousal and performance. Perhaps job insecurity served as a proxy for survivors' level of arousal and work effort reflected performance. Future research may separate these potential explanations and thereby make an important contribution to theory and research on the relationship between job insecurity and work motivation.

THE ROLE OF UNCERTAINTY.   A different conceptualization of the psychological consequences of layoffs focuses on the uncertainty layoffs produce. Survivors' uncertainty, in turn, instigates several social and psychological processes that influence survivors' work attitudes and behaviors. Two types of uncertainty are generated by layoffs. First, survivors will be uncertain about *how to define the situation.* They will attempt to define the situation at a surface, concrete level, by seeking knowledge about precisely what is happening. For example, survivors will likely want to know whether (a) there will be more layoffs and, if so, when; (b) the layoff (or management's handling of the layoff) was fair; and (c) their job responsibilities or career trajectories will change. At a deeper, more abstract level, survivors may investigate the *meaning or implications* of these events. For example, if a layoff has been interpreted as unfair, survivors may probe deeper to understand the symbolism associated with the unfairness. An unfairly managed layoff may mean that the organization cannot be trusted to act fairly in the future, even in matters unrelated to layoffs. Similarly, if survivors believe that more layoffs are likely, they may formulate ideas about the implications of working for a declining organization.

Second, survivors will also be uncertain about *how to respond to the situation.* For example, suppose that survivors feel considerably more job insecure than they did before. Does this mean that they should work harder, in the hopes of preserving their job, or less hard, on the grounds that they are likely to lose their jobs regardless of how hard they work? To what extent should they start looking elsewhere for employment? These issues reflect the "what should I do?" internal state that survivors are likely to experience.

Uncertainty should stimulate at least two social/psychological processes. In response to their uncertainty about how to define the situation, survivors may search for information that helps them make sense of what is happening. Part of this sensemaking process includes wondering why the layoffs occurred, or why they were implemented in the ways that they were. Survivors are also likely to look to each other for guidance about what to think and how to act. That is, uncertainty is likely to generate social interaction processes in which fellow survivors construct a definition of the situation and ways to respond to it.

UNCERTAINTY AND ASKING WHY.   Research on attribution theory (Kelley, 1973) has been primarily concerned with discovering the antecedents and consequences of particular causal explanations that people make for their own and others' behavior. An even more fundamental question for attribution theorists is, Under what conditions do people ask why? Several studies have shown that unexpected events lead people to wonder why they occurred (Pyczszynski & Greenberg, 1981; Wong & Weiner, 1981). Such findings suggest that attributional instigation is one way in which people try to make sense of events in their environments.

If attributional instigation facilitates sensemaking, then it may help explain the results of studies showing that people generally have better reactions to unfavorable resource allocation decisions if they are given a clear and adequate explanation of why the decision was made (Bies, 1987). Presumably, the explanation helps them to make sense of the decision.

To recap, survivors are likely to feel uncertain about how to define the layoff situation, motivating them to make sense of what is happening. As part of this sensemaking process, they are likely to initiate the attribution process, wondering why the layoffs occurred. Their reactions to the layoff—as measured by their work effort or organizational commitment—will depend on whether they accept the organization's explanation; the greater the adequacy and clarity of the explanation, the more likely it is that it will be accepted, and therefore, the more favorably survivors should respond.

We recently tested this hypothesis (Brockner et al., 1990). The notion that uncertainty instigates the sensemaking (and attributional) process led us to predict that the unusualness or unexpectedness of the layoffs will moderate the relationship between the clarity of the reasons for the layoffs provided by management and survivors' reactions to the layoffs. Survivors rated how clearly the organization had explained the reasons for the layoffs and how unusual the layoffs were in light of the prevailing corporate culture. The effects on survivors' work effort are shown in Table 3. A significant interaction effect emerged, such that clarity of the explanation was more positively related to work effort when the layoff was judged to be unusual.

These results not only provide additional evidence on the determinants of survivors' reactions, but also contribute to the emerging literature showing that employees react better to undesirable resource allocations when they are given a good reason for those decisions (Bies, 1987). None of the previous studies explored the role of explanations in attenuating survivors' hostile reactions to layoffs. Moreover, the moderating effect of unusualness suggests *why* people react more positively when they are given a reasonable explanation for an otherwise unpreferred decision; apparently, the explanation reduces peoples' uncertainty about why the decision occurred, thereby enabling them to make sense of (the meaning of) the decision.

UNCERTAINTY AND SOCIAL INFLUENCE.   A long and rich tradition of research has shown that in times of uncertainty, people take cues from relevant others about how to define and respond to the situation (Festinger, 1954; Schachter, 1959). The uncertainty inherent in layoffs makes the analysis of survivors' reactions particularly fertile ground for the study of social influence processes. Our basic premise is that survivors in a given work group will take cues from each other and therefore exhibit similar attitudinal and behavioral reactions to the layoff. This premise has been tested in two studies (Brockner, Wiesenfeld, Stephan, et al., 1992). In a laboratory experiment two subjects and a confederate were asked to work separately on a clerical task. After they worked on the first task a layoff was staged, in which the confederate was told to leave. Before working on the next task, participants learned the reactions of their fellow survivor. Surviving subjects were led to believe that their fellow survivor had either a fairly negative reaction to the layoff (Downbeat condition) or a much more positive reaction (Upbeat condition).

All participants then worked on another task; finally, they completed a questionnaire measuring their commitment to the experiment. The Downbeat condition led to consistently more negative reactions than the Upbeat condition.

TABLE 3   Survivors' Change in Work Effort as a Function of the Unusualness of the Layoff and the Clarity of Management's Explanations for the Layoff

UNUSUALNESS	CLARITY OF EXPLANATION	
	Low	High
High	19.32	21.13
Low	20.43	20.34

Note: Scores could range from 3 to 33, with higher scores reflecting more of an increase in work effort, relative to before the layoff.

The quality of participants' work performance decreased more in the Downbeat than Upbeat condition; moreover, survivors' commitment levels were significantly lower in the former than in the latter condition. Furthermore, these findings were moderated by participants' liking for the fellow survivor; the more they liked the fellow survivor, the more their reactions were influenced by their fellow survivor's.

These results were replicated and extended in a field setting. Independent variables included the reactions of fellow survivors in participants' immediate work groups, participants' attraction toward their fellow survivors, and their frequency of communication with fellow survivors about the layoff. When frequency of communication about the layoff was low, the results of the field study resembled those found in the laboratory: survivors were much more influenced by the reactions of fellow group members to whom they felt more attracted. (Frequency of communication was held constant at a low level in the laboratory experiment.)

However, as indicated in Table 4, when frequency of communication was high (as it tended to be for the vast majority of survivors), the results were quite different. Survivors tended to follow the reactions of their fellow group members, regardless of their level of attraction toward them. Those who communicated frequently with their co-workers seemed to pay more attention to what was said, rather than who said it, a tendency reminiscent of the sleeper effect in attitude change research (Pratkanis, Greenwald, Leippe, & Baumgardner, 1988).

Although both the laboratory and field studies showed that survivors' reactions were socially influenced, we suspect that the nature of the influence process varied across studies. Recent developments in information processing models in cognitive social psychology distinguish between two types, varying in the depth with which information is processed (Petty & Cacioppo, 1986). One model "encompasses deliberate and systematic cognitive manipulation of information. Theories in this group assume that people at times expend cognitive effort to evaluate information and to integrate it with prior information in forming an attitude or judgment" (Zalesny & Ford, 1990, p. 227). This is the central pro-

TABLE 4 Survivors' Change in Work Effort as a Function of Amount of Communication with Co-Workers, Attachment to Co-Workers, and Favorability of Co-Workers' Reactions

AMOUNT OF COMMUNICATION	ATTACHMENT TO CO-WORKERS	FAVORABILITY	
		Low	High
High	High	20.23 (99)	21.44 (118)
	Low	18.28 (119)	20.38 (68)
Low	High	18.95 (20)	21.53 (40)
	Low	22.57 (30)	19.93 (46)

Note: Scores could range from 3 to 33, with higher scores reflecting more of an increase in work effort, relative to before the layoff. Cell numbers are in parentheses. Thus, most participants had relatively high amounts of communication with their fellow survivors about the layoff.

cessing model. When centrally processing, people pay attention to the content of the social information.

The second model "proposes that often much less cognitive effort is expended in the development and expression of attitudes and judgments" (Zalesny & Ford, 1990, p. 227). This is the peripheral processing model. When peripherally processing, people pay less attention to the content of social information. Instead, "contextual cues surrounding the communication of information are seen as indirectly affecting an attitude . . . by directly influencing attention to and . . . acceptance of the information" (Zalesny & Ford, 1990, pp. 228–229).

Petty and Cacioppo's (1986) elaboration likelihood model discusses the antecedents and consequences of these two types of information processing. Because peripheral processing requires less cognitive work, they hypothesize that it is likely to occur unless people have the motivation or ability to engage in (more effortful) central processing. Moreover, judgments developed as a result of central processing are likely to be stronger, hence more likely to be expressed in behavior and more likely to influence the processing of future attitude-relevant information than are judgments resulting from peripheral processing.

Given the relative insignificance of the layoff in the lives of participants in the laboratory experiment, they should be relatively unmotivated to engage in central processing. Consistent with the notion that laboratory participants processed peripherally, it was found that a contextual factor—the fellow survivor's likeability—moderated the impact of the fellow survivor's reactions on participants' reactions. In contrast, the layoff in the field was highly significant to participants, which should have motivated them to search for cues from co-workers about how to respond. In response to a measure of how much they talked with their fellow survivors about the layoff, the average rating on a seven-point continuum was 5.58. This result is consistent with the notion that the majority of survivors were centrally processing their fellow survivors' reactions in the field study. High levels of communication should have heightened participants' ability to perceive the content of their co-workers' reactions.

Let us assume that frequency of communication with fellow survivors about the layoff was a proxy for the extent to which people centrally processed the information of how their co-workers responded. If so, then the relative minority of participants who had little communication (defined as those whose ratings were four or lower on the seven-point continuum) should have processed peripherally and thus reacted like those in the laboratory experiment (who generally were assumed to have processed peripherally). As can be seen in Table 4, this is exactly what happened; survivors who communicated relatively little with their fellow survivors were much more likely to follow the reactions of those to whom they felt more attracted. When frequency of communication was relatively high, survivors probably engaged in central processing, leading them to be influenced by their co-workers' reactions regardless of their attraction to them.

These studies provide further explanation of the variability in survivors' reactions; they also are the first to demonstrate the role of social influence processes among survivors. Furthermore, they are among the first studies to heed Zalesny and Ford's (1990) call to extend social information processing theory by distinguishing between peripheral versus central information processing.

THE ROLE OF ASSOCIATED CHANGES IN THE WORKPLACE.   The properties inherent in layoffs elicit a variety of psychological states, such as concerns about fairness, job insecurity, and uncertainty. Survivors' reactions also depend on other changes in the workplace associated with layoffs. These changes are not inherent to layoffs; nevertheless, they covary with layoffs frequently enough that, at the very least, they could be considered as control variables in studies of survivors' reactions.

Alternatively, these frequently associated changes could be the central focus of the study rather than being relegated to the status of control variables. For instance, if layoffs are accompanied by change in the perceived intrinsic appeal of survivors' jobs, then survivors' reactions should depend on the nature of the change. One fairly straightforward prediction is that survivors' job attitudes and behaviors should be more positive if the job is believed to have become more interesting. A more intriguing (and theoretically significant) task is to specify when this relationship is more or less pronounced. Hackman and Oldham (1980) found that the relationship between the intrinsic quality of job attributes and individuals' work motivation and satisfaction depends on dispositional and situational factors. People with strong growth needs, for example, exhibit a stronger relationship between perceived job attributes and work motivation/job satisfaction than their counterparts with weaker growth needs (Berlinger, Glick, & Rodgers, 1988).

Situational moderators include the favorability of the work context, including high job security, satisfying relationships with co-workers, and adequate levels of pay, which have led to strong relationships between perceived job attributes and work motivation/job satisfaction (Oldham, 1976; Oldham, Hackman, & Pearce, 1976). In other words, employees were less responsive to the perceived content of their jobs when the work context was discomforting.

We recently attempted to extend these findings to the analysis of survivors' reactions (Brockner, Wiesenfeld, Reed, Grover, & Martin, in press). In a field study, survivors indicated the extent to which their job attributes had changed (compared to the pre-layoff period), along the Hackman and Oldham (1980) dimensions of variety, identity, importance, responsibility, and feedback. Based on Oldham et al.'s (1976) findings, we expected survivors' organizational commitment to vary more as a function of change in job content when the context in which the layoff occurred was relatively favorable (e.g., when the layoff was viewed as more fair or fellow survivors reacted relatively favorably). The results of the study are presented in Table 5. As predicted, the relationship between perceived change in job attributes and change in turnover intention was more pronounced when the layoff was perceived to be more fair and when co-workers were believed to have responded in a more upbeat fashion.

A second study attempted to redress several deficiencies in the first study.

TABLE 5 Mean Levels of Change in Turnover Intention as a Function of Perceived Job Quality and Perceived Co-Workers' Reactions, and Perceived Job Quality and Perceived Fairness

PERCEIVED CO-WORKERS' REACTIONS	PERCEIVED JOB QUALITY	
	Low	High
Unfavorable	5.14	6.49
Favorable	5.75	8.02

PERCEIVED FAIRNESS	PERCEIVED JOB QUALITY	
	Low	High
Low	5.18	6.56
High	5.40	7.46

Note: Scores could range from 1 to 11. Higher scores reflect more of a *decrease* in turnover intention, relative to the pre-layoff period.

The correlational nature of the field survey made it very difficult to determine the causal relationship(s) between the independent and dependent variables. Furthermore, there was no independent verification that survivors' jobs had changed; we merely assessed their perceptions of how their jobs had changed. Study 2 was a laboratory experiment in which each subject and a confederate worked independently on a task designed to be moderately interesting. After the first task a layoff was staged, during which the confederate was asked to leave. All subjects then worked on a second task. For half of them, the task was deliberately made more intrinsically interesting than the first task (Interesting condition), whereas for the remaining half the task was reconfigured to be less interesting than the first one (Boring condition). Moreover, all participants were told that the change in their tasks had been made necessary by the layoff. To operationalize context favorability, half of the participants witnessed an unfair layoff, in which the laid-off person was sent home empty-handed, even though he had completed half of the study (Unfair condition). The remaining half saw that the confederate was treated more fairly; he was given partial course credit for the study (Fair condition). Dependent variables included participants' perceptions of the importance of the study as well as their overall reactions to having taken part. An interaction effect emerged, whose form was conceptually analogous to the field study results reported in Table 5. As can be seen in Table 6, the tendency for participants to respond more favorably in the Interesting than Boring condition was significantly more pronounced when the layoff was handled more fairly.

An important mandate for future research is to explain why job content and context combine interactively. Some useful leads may be offered by theory and research on intrinsic motivation (e.g., Deci & Ryan, 1985). For example, the initial studies on the overjustification phenomenon (Deci, 1971; Lepper, Greene, & Nisbett, 1973) suggested that people react less favorably to inherently enjoyable tasks if the context causes them to adopt an instrumental or "means-end" orientation (i.e., if they are given a monetary reward for working on the task).

TABLE 6   Mean Perceived Importance of the Purpose of the Study as a Function of Layoff Fairness and Type of Job Change

LAYOFF FAIRNESS	TYPE OF JOB CHANGE	
	Boring	Interesting
Unfair	4.71	4.86
Fair	4.00	5.83

Note: Scores could range from 1 to 7, with higher scores reflecting greater importance.

Several more recent studies suggest that contexts that reduce individuals' sense of freedom or control also reduce their responsiveness to the perceived content of the task. Ryan (1982) gave all subjects positive feedback for their task performance. In half of the cases, however, the feedback emphasized individuals' obligation (which probably reduced their sense of freedom); specifically, people were told, "You did well, just as you should." The remaining half were simply told that they did well. People were less appreciative of the positive feedback when it heightened their obligation to perform well.

Sansone (1989) had subjects rate the psychological significance of their task, which seems conceptually similar to the "importance" dimension in the Job Characteristics Model of Hackman and Oldham (1980). The expected positive relationship between perceived significance and liking for the task depended on an experimental manipulation of choice. Those who had some control over which task they worked on demonstrated a marked relationship between significance and enjoyment; no such relationship existed, however, for those who had the same task assigned to them.

One interpretation of the Ryan (1982) and Sansone (1989) findings is that contexts that foster a sense of control strengthen the relationship between the perceived attributes of, and peoples' liking for, the task. If this interpretation is correct, it further suggests *why* certain contexts led to stronger relationships between job attributes and work motivation in the original Oldham (1976) and Oldham et al. (1976) studies: The conditions in which the relationship was stronger (e.g., greater job security and satisfaction with pay) may have been those in which individuals felt a greater sense of control. In summary, our research on the effects on survivors of perceived change in the nature of their work may help us to better understand an important theoretical issue in the job design literature: how and why the content and context of jobs interactively combine to influence employees' work attitudes and behaviors.

Determinants of survivors' reactions: toward integration

Until this point, we have tried to analyze survivors' reactions in a psychologically differentiated way. Each of the psychological states of perceived fairness, job insecurity, uncertainty, and intrinsic motivation and the associated processes of sensemaking, attributional instigation, and social comparison offer partial explanations of survivors' reactions. A more complete understanding requires an integration of these various psychological states and processes.

This section provides such an integrative analysis, drawing on Lazarus and Folkman's (1984) theory of stress. Lazarus and Folkman argued against previous conceptualizations that emphasized stress as a stimulus residing in the environment (e.g., Holmes & Rahe, 1967) or as a response located within people (Selye, 1956). Such conceptualizations failed to account for the variability in peoples' reactions to identical environmental conditions. Lazarus and Folkman (1984) conceived of stress as "a particular *relationship between* the person and the environment that is appraised by the person as taxing or exceeding his or her resources and endangering his or her well-being" (p. 19, emphasis added).

The core concepts in Lazarus and Folkman's (1984) relational model of stress are (1) appraisal and (2) coping. Appraisal is the cognitive process of evaluating two questions: (1) "Am I in trouble or being benefitted, now or in the future, and in what way?" (primary appraisal), and (2) "What, if anything, can be done about it?" (secondary appraisal). If the appraisal leads people to conclude that the demands of the situation exceed their resources, then the coping process is initiated. Coping is defined as "constantly changing cognitive and behavioral efforts to manage specific external and/or internal demands" (p. 141), which emanate from the belief that the demands cannot be handled by the person's existing resources. The authors note four attributes in their definition of coping. First, coping is process oriented rather than trait oriented, hence the words *constantly changing* and *specific*. Second, coping refers to effortful cognitive and behavioral activity; automatized adaptive behavior falls outside the definition. Third, coping refers to the *attempts* people make to manage the stressful situation, regardless of their success. Fourth, the word *manage* in the definition should not be confused with mastery. Managing includes not only mastery, but also minimizing, avoiding, and learning to tolerate stressful circumstances.

Lazarus and Folkman (1984) suggested that different coping methods can be distinguished by their functions. Problem-focused coping "is directed at managing or altering the problem causing the distress," whereas emotion-focused coping "is directed at regulating emotional response to the problem" (p. 150). In other words, problem-focused coping attempts to redress the causes of stress (which may reside in the environment or the person), whereas emotion-focused coping tries to manage the symptoms produced by the causes of the stress.

Lazarus and Folkman's (1984) conceptualization provides a useful lens for analyzing survivors' reactions. First, we can expect that the post-layoff environment is potentially stressful to survivors. Lazarus and Folkman noted that situations that increase uncertainty are more likely to elicit stress than others. As suggested previously, layoffs often arouse considerable uncertainty in survivors. Further contributing to the potential stressfulness of a layoff is the element of duration. Survivors may need to cope for months and years rather than days or weeks. For example, one of our survivor samples reported feeling heightened stress 10 months after the onset of the layoff.

A second virtue of the Lazarus and Folkman (1984) framework is that it lends coherence to the results of separate studies. As we consider our results in retrospect, it is likely that some of our independent variables were pertinent to the appraisal process, others to the coping process, whereas some may have been relevant to both. For example, the study in which survivors reacted especially badly when they previously felt committed to the organization but felt that they had been treated unfairly (see Table 1) appears to have focused on primary appraisal. When people evaluate whether they are in trouble, two factors are important: (1) the magnitude of the threat, and (2) the personal significance of the threat to the individual. The perceived fairness variable probably influenced the magnitude of the threat (the greater the unfairness, the greater the magnitude), whereas prior commitment likely captured the personal significance of the threat (the greater the prior commitment, the greater the personal significance).

Primary and secondary appraisal may have been active when work effort varied as a function of perceived threat, perceived control, and economic need to work (see Table 2). Perceived threat was measured by asking survivors to indicate the likelihood that more layoffs would occur in the near future, whereas economic need to work was assessed by having participants indicate the extent to which they were the major breadwinners in their homes. The perceived threat and economic need to work factors probably affected survivors' primary appraisal. The higher the perceived likelihood of future layoffs, the greater is the magnitude of the threat; the greater the survivors' economic need to work, the greater is the personal significance of the threat. Perceived control was measured by having survivors indicate how well the benefits offered to the layoff victims (i.e., severance pay, help in finding another job, etc.) would provide for their needs if they were to face a layoff in the future. This measure seems related to secondary appraisal, in that it addresses the question of what can be done to deal with the threat. The greater the benefits, the more likely that survivors' secondary appraisal would reduce their felt stress.

Our studies dealing with the role of uncertainty seem particularly consistent with Lazarus and Folkman's (1984) framework. Previously, we suggested that survivors experience two types of uncertainty: (1) how to define the situation (e.g., what is happening, and what are the implications of what is happening?), and (2) how to respond to the situation (e.g., should I work harder, less hard, or no differently than before?). The resolution of these two uncertainties seems to be the central purpose of appraisal and coping, respectively. To appraise the significance of the layoffs, survivors may attend to the organization's handling of the process (as well as their fellow survivors' reactions). For example, whether the organization provided a clear and adequate explanation of the reasons for the layoff will influence survivors' reactions, particularly if the layoff was a relatively unusual (and thus unexpected) event (see Table 3). Moreover, uncertainty about how to respond (which includes coping behaviors) can be reduced by attending to the reactions of others.

The Lazarus–Folkman framework explains the results of studies on the effects of the inherent properties of layoffs as well as those studies that explored the effects of changes often associated with layoffs. For example, if the layoffs are accompanied by perceived change in the intrinsic appeal of their jobs, then survivors' reactions (e.g., commitment) will vary accordingly. Furthermore, as shown in Tables 5 and 6, the effect on survivors of perceived change in the job varies as a function of context favorability.

Our speculations concerning the reasons for this interaction effect—buttressed by several findings from the laboratories of experimental social psychologists (Ryan, 1982; Sansone, 1989)—centers on the role of perceived control. Not surprisingly, Lazarus and Folkman (1984) suggested that control is integral to appraisal and coping. Control as appraisal refers to beliefs that influence people's perceptions of the significance of the threatening situation. (Control as coping, in contrast, refers to the cognitive and behavioral steps people take to manage a stressful situation.) We suspect that context favorability influenced survivors' appraisals of control. If they perceived the context as favorable (e.g., if they perceived fairness, or that fellow survivors were upbeat), survivors may have appraised the situation as less threatening. This benign appraisal may have made coping a lower priority, leading them to be more psychologically available to be influenced by how they perceived the nature of their jobs. Clearly, our explanation of the results presented in Tables 5 and 6 is speculative. If it is confirmed in future research, however, we will be even more confident that Lazarus and Folkman's (1984) stress framework provides an integrative analysis of survivors' reactions.

A third advantage of the stress model is that by distinguishing between appraisal and coping, Lazarus and Folkman (1984) may help delineate the survivors' motivations. Not only do different survivor reactions reflect appraisal *and* coping, but the same behavior may also reflect appraisal *or* coping, depending on the circumstances. Consider the tendency survivors have to interact with their fellow survivors after the layoff. What is the purpose of their social interaction?

The Lazarus and Folkman framework suggests at least three possibilities. First, social interaction may serve appraisal purposes, either primary or secondary. Second, social interaction may be one step in the coping process. Survivors may choose to cope with the situation by leaving the organization. We have found that survivors' turnover intentions can be predicted by the turnover intentions of fellow survivors in their work group (Brockner, Wiesenfeld, Reed, et al., 1992).

Third, social interaction may be a means of coping in its own right. As Lind and Tyler (1988) pointed out, people value their interpersonal relationships for a variety of psychological and social reasons (e.g., to feel accepted, to define themselves). Layoffs could interfere with naturally occurring social interaction; survivors could feel isolated and thereby robbed of the social rewards in the workplace. Social interaction among survivors therefore may ward off isolation. We are not the first to speculate that stressful environmental conditions sometimes draw people together (e.g., Schachter, 1959). Unlike others, who have focused on the instrumental nature of affiliative behavior, we suggest that the tendency of survivors to interact may serve as its own reward, or at least as a coping method. More generally, the Lazarus and Folkman framework reminds us that the same phenotypical survivor reactions may be driven by different underlying genotypes.

That the stress-based analysis of survivors' reactions appears at the end (rather than beginning) of this chapter is quite deliberate. In looking at the various findings *after the fact*, we wondered whether the results could be subsumed by a single theoretical framework. Lazarus and Folkman's conceptualization seems promising, at least on a post hoc basis. The truer test of the framework, of course, is its ability to *predict* survivors' reactions.

Another indication of the utility of a theoretical framework is its ability to stimulate future research. In fact, several important and unexplored questions arise when one views survivor reactions in the more general context of stress theory. First, the stress framework suggests the need to broaden the scope of survivor reactions. Most of our research has focused on survivors' organizational commitment and work motivation/performance. However, many other beliefs and behaviors are likely to be influenced by the appraisal and coping processes. For example, survivors may deal with stress by blaming the victims of the layoffs, which seems reflective of the emotion-focused coping process known as distancing. If survivors believe that the layoff victms brought their fate on themselves (either through their negative behaviors or traits), then survivors can reassure themselves that they will not suffer a similar fate. In addition, survivors' nonwork behaviors and attitudes need to be investigated. Much has been written about the detrimental effects that layoffs have on the family lives of layoff victims (Jahoda, 1982). Are there spillover effects for the survivors as well? For example, to deal with the guilt of working overtime when many of their former co-workers were laid off, survivors may increase their contributions to charitable organizations. In short, the conceptualization of survivors' reactions as reflecting appraisal and/or coping facilitates the inclusion of new dependent variables in future research.

The notion that survivors are attempting to appraise and cope with their situations suggests at least two other possibilities for future research. First, we need to better understand whether a particular survivor reaction reflects appraisal or coping. Second, the stress framework strongly suggests that survivors' reactions need to be studied longitudinally. Lazarus and Folkman (1984) suggested that the manifestations of appraisal and coping may vary over time. They coined the term *reappraisal* to allow for the possibility that people may learn new information from the environment (or their own reactions to the initial appraisal). Inherent in their definition of coping is that the cognitive and behavioral efforts people exert to manage stress are "constantly changing." Thus, not only do survivors' reactions persist well beyond the onset of the layoff, but also the nature of their reactions may vary considerably over time.

Future research on survivors' reactions also may help clarify, extend, and define the limits of the Lazarus–Folkman (1984) stress framework. For example, survivors probably use some combination of problem-focused and emotion-focused coping. However, we need to move beyond the simple statement that both forms of coping are used. Under what conditions is one type used more than the other? How do these forms of coping relate to one another? Do they reflect a "hydraulic" process, such that the presence of one renders the other less necessary? Moreover, do they relate to each differently over time?

Another matter of fundamental theoretical significance is the nature of the relationship between primary and secondary appraisal. The perceived significance of the stressful encounter is likely to be most intense when (1) as a result of primary appraisal, people believe that they are in trouble; and (2) as a result of secondary appraisal, people believe that nothing can be done about it. Less clear, however, is whether these two components combine in an additive or multiplicative way. Our findings suggest the latter. As can be seen in Table 2, when survivors' economic need to work was relatively low (i.e., when a component of primary appraisal suggested that perceived danger was low), perceived control (a determinant of secondary appraisal) and work effort were essentially unrelated. However, when economic need to work was high, perceived control (in combination with perceived threat) was strongly related to survivors' work effort. More generally, our point is that future research needs to consider both the implications of the Lazarus and Folkman (1984) stress framework for the analysis of survivors' reactions and the implications of the specific research findings for the broader theoretical framework.

CONCLUSIONS

The premise of this chapter is that survivors show great variability in their reactions to the layoff, both within and across attitudinal and behavioral dimensions. Social psychological theory provides a set of conceptual tools to help explain survivors' reactions. Ideas from a broad array of literatures are germane, including fairness, perceived control, attribution theory, job design, intrinsic motivation, and social influence. Future research may pursue the leads suggested by these different bodies of theory and research. In addition, stress theory offers a promising integrative conceptualization that needs to be evaluated through further research. In the process, much may be learned not only about the determinants of survivors' reactions but also about basic theoretical issues in social and organizational psychology. Furthermore, this research stream (present and future) should help managers of downsizing organizations to plan and implement layoffs in ways that elicit the most positive (or least negative) reactions in the remaining workers (see Brockner, 1992).

REFERENCES

BERLINGER, L. R., GLICK, W. H., & RODGERS, R. C. (1988). Job enrichment and performance improvement. In J. P. Campbell (Ed.), *Productivity in organizations* (pp. 219–254). San Francisco: Jossey-Bass.

BIES, R. J. (1987). The predicament of injustice: The management of moral outrage. In

L. L. Cummings & B. Staw (Eds.), *Research in organizational behavior* (Vol. 9, pp. 289–319). Greenwich, CT: JAI Press.

BROCKNER, J. (1992). Managing the effects of layoffs on survivors. *California Management Review, 34*, 9–28.

BROCKNER, J., DeWITT, R. L., GROVER, S., & REED, T. (1990). When it is especially important to explain why: Factors affecting the relationship between managers' explanations of a layoff and survivors' reactions to the layoff. *Journal of Experimental Social Psychology, 26*, 389–407.

BROCKNER, J., & GREENBERG, J. (1990). The impact of layoffs on survivors: An organizational justice perspective. In J. S. Carroll (Ed.), *Applied social psychology and organizational settings* (pp. 45–75). Hillsdale, NJ: Erlbaum.

BROCKNER, J., GROVER, S., REED, T., & DeWITT, R. L. (1992). Layoffs, job insecurity, and survivors' work effort: Evidence of an inverted-U relationship. *Academy of Management Journal, 35*, 413–425.

BROCKNER, J., GROVER, S., REED, T., DeWITT, R. L., & O'MALLEY, M. (1987). Survivors' reactions to layoffs: We get by with a little help for our friends. *Administrative Science Quarterly, 32*, 526–542.

BROCKNER, J., TYLER, T. R., & COOPER–SCHNEIDER, R. (1992). The influence of prior commitment to an institution on reactions to perceived unfairness: The higher they are, the harder they fall. *Administrative Science Quarterly, 37*, 241–261.

BROCKNER, J., WIESENFELD, B., REED, T., GROVER, S., & MARTIN, C. (in press). The interactive effect of job content and context on layoff survivors' reactions. *Journal of Personality and Social Psychology*.

BROCKNER, J., WIESENFELD, B., STEPHAN, J., HURLEY, B., GROVER, S., REED, T., & DeWITT, R. L. (1992). *Social information, depth of processing, and survivors' reactions to layoffs: Evidence from the laboratory and the field.* Manuscript under editorial review.

BYRNE, D. (1971). *The attraction paradigm.* New York: Academic Press.

DeCHARMS, R. (1968). *Personal causation.* New York: Academic Press.

DECI, E. L. (1971). Effects of externally mediated rewards on intrinsic motivation. *Journal of Personality and Social Psychology, 18*, 105–115.

DECI, E. L., & RYAN, R. M. (1985). *Intrinsic motivation and self-determination in human behavior.* New York: Plenum.

DEUTSCH, M. (1985). *Distributive justice: A social psychological perspective.* New Haven: Yale University Press.

EISENBERG, P., & LAZARSFELD, P. F. (1938). The psychological effects of unemployment. *Psychological Bulletin, 35*, 358–390.

FESTINGER, L. (1954). A theory of social comparison processes. *Human Relations, 7*, 117–140.

GREENBERG, J. (1987). A taxonomy of organizational justice theories. *Academy of Management Review, 12*, 9–22.

GREENBERG, J. (in press). Stealing in the name of justice: Informational and interpersonal moderators of theft reactions to underpayment inequity. *Organizational Behavior and Human Decision Processes*.

GREENHALGH, L., & ROSENBLATT, Z. (1984). Job insecurity: Towards conceptual clarity. *Academy of Management Review, 9*, 438–448.

HACKMAN, J. R., & OLDHAM, G. R. (1980). *Work redesign.* Reading, MA: Addison-Wesley.

HOLMES, T. H., & RAHE, R. H. (1967). The social readjustment rating scale. *Journal of Psychosomatic Research, 11*, 213–218.

JAHODA, M. (1982). *Employment and unemployment: A social psychological analysis.* New York: Academic Press.

JICK, T. (1989). *Navistar: Managing change.* Boston, MA: Harvard Business School Press.

KAHNEMAN, D., & TVERSKY, A. (1984). Choices, values, and frames. *American Psychologist, 39,* 341–350.

KELLEY, H. H. (1973). The processes of causal attribution. *American Psychologist, 28,* 107–128.

LAZARUS, R. S., & FOLKMAN, S. (1984). *Stress, appraisal, and coping.* New York: Academic Press.

LEPPER, M. R., GREENE, D., & NISBETT, R. E. (1973). Undermining children's intrinsic interest with extrinsic reward: A test of the "overjustification" hypothesis. *Journal of Personality and Social Psychology, 28,* 129–137.

LIND, E. A., & TYLER, T. R. (1988). *The social psychology of procedural justice.* New York: Plenum.

LOUIS, M. R. (1980). Surprise and sense making: What newcomers experience in entering unfamiliar organizational settings. *Administrative Science Quarterly, 25,* 226–251.

MOWDAY, R. T., PORTER, L. W., & STEERS, R. M. (1982). *Employee-organization linkages: The psychology of commitment, absenteeism, and turnover.* New York: Academic Press.

OLDHAM, G. R. (1976). Job characteristics and internal motivation: The moderating effect of interpersonal and individual variables. *Human Relations, 29,* 359–369.

OLDHAM, G. R., HACKMAN, J. R., & PEARCE, J. L. (1976). Conditions under which employees respond positively to enriched work. *Journal of Applied Psychology, 61,* 395–403.

PETTY, R. E., & CACIOPPO, J. T. (1986). The elaboration likelihood model of persuasion. In L. Berkowitz (Ed.), *Advances in experimental social psychology* (Vol. 19, pp. 123–205). Orlando, FL: Academic Press.

PRATKANIS, A. R., GREENWALD, A. G., LEIPPE, M. R., & BAUMGARDNER, M. H. (1988). In search of reliable persuasion effects: III. The sleeper effect is dead. Long live the sleeper effect. *Journal of Personality and Social Psychology, 54,* 203–218.

PYSZCZYNSKI, T. A., & GREENBERG, J. (1981). Role of disconfirmed expectancies in the instigation of attributional processing. *Journal of Personality and Social Psychology, 40,* 31–38.

RIGHT ASSOCIATES. (1990). Managing change in the 90s. *The Right Research.* Philadelphia: Right Associates.

ROUSSEAU, D. M., & ANTON, R. J. (1988). Fairness and implied contract obligations in termination: A policy capturing study. *Human Performance, 1,* 273–289.

RYAN, R. M. (1982). Control and information in the intrapersonal sphere: An extension of cognitive evaluation theory. *Journal of Personality and Social Psychology, 43,* 450–461.

SANSONE, C. (1989). Competence feedback, task feedback, and intrinsic interest: An examination of process and content. *Journal of Experimental Social Psychology, 25,* 343–361.

SCHACHTER, S. (1959). *The psychology of affiliation.* Stanford: Stanford University Press.

SELIGMAN, M. E. P. (1975). *Helplessness.* San Francisco: W. H. Freeman.

SELYE, H. (1956). *The stress of life.* New York: McGraw-Hill.

SHERIF, C. W., SHERIF, M., & NEBERGALL, R. E. (1965). *Attitude and attitude change: The social judgment—involvement approach.* Philadelphia: W. B. Saunders.

SIVACEK, J., & CRANO, W. D. (1982). Vested interest as a moderator of attitude—behavior consistency. *Journal of Personality and Social Psychology, 43,* 210–221.

TAJFEL, H., & TURNER, J. (1979). An integrative theory of intergroup conflicts. In W. G. Austin & S. Worchel (Eds.), *The social psychology of intergroup relations* (pp. 33–47). Monterey, CA: Brooks/Cole.

VROOM, V. (1964). *Work and motivation.* New York: Wiley.

WONG, P. T. P., & WEINER, B. (1981). When people ask "why" questions, and the heuristics of attributional search. *Journal of Personality and Social Psychology, 40,* 650–663.

YERKES, R. M., & DODSON, J. D. (1908). The relation of strength of stimulus to rapidity of habit formation. *Journal of Comparative Neurological Psychology, 18,* 459–482.

ZALESNY, M. D., & FORD, J. K. (1990). Extending the social information processing perspective: New links to attitudes, behaviors, and perceptions. *Organizational Behavior and Human Decision Processes, 47,* 205–246.

CHAPTER SEVEN

The Social Psychology of Authority

Tom R. Tyler

University of California, Berkeley

This chapter examines the social psychological motivations underlying the willingness to voluntarily accept the decisions made by authorities in organizations. Two motivations are identified: the desire to gain valued resources from group membership and the desire to have the self-esteem-enhancing experience of being a high-status group member. Both motivations are shown to have important influences on workers' commitment to work organizations.

One of the most salient reasons why the study of authority is an interesting social psychological issue is the ambivalence that people display toward those who exercise authority. On the one hand, studies show that people create authorities in groups to deal with perceived problems, but, in those same groups, people also resist the authorities they have created. This chapter will show that the ability of authorities to overcome such resistance and gain cooperation from group members is based on both relational and resource links to the group.

A key finding of research on legal, political, and managerial organizations is that groups create authority structures to help them resolve their problems. For instance, in a study of how Californians responded to the 1974 energy crisis (Sears, Tyler, Citrin, & Kinder, 1978), people favored creating authority structures to restrict energy use. East Bay residents of Northern California responded similarly to the 1990–1991 water shortage in California (Tyler & Degoey, 1991). People respond to natural resource shortages by saying that more authority needs to be given to third parties. Further, the more serious the crisis is perceived to be, the more people want to delegate authority to third parties.

This desire to create authorities to regulate individual behavior in groups has also been demonstrated experimentally. In laboratory experiments, groups regulate access to renewable resource pools by delegating authority over that access to leaders (Messick et al., 1983). Other studies have also shown that group members faced with a crisis were more likely to embrace leaders (Pillai & Meindl, 1990; Willner, 1984).

Groups create authority structures in response to *social*, as well as resource scarcity, problems. For example, one response to the perceived threat of a crime wave is to give more authority to the police, allowing the police to stop people on the street and ask them for identification, to hold people without charge, to wiretap, and, generally, to take whatever actions they deem necessary to handle the crime problem.

Of course, the mere fact that an authority structure has been created does not mean that a group has effectively solved its problems. One of the most important conclusions to emerge from the psychological literature on group dynamics (Cartwright & Zander, 1953) is that the effectiveness of allocation decisions and conflict resolution efforts is strongly influenced by the *nature* of a group's authority structures. Different types of authority structures have varying degrees of effectiveness. The demonstration that different types of authority structures are differentially effective is one of the core findings of the classic study of autocratic, democratic, and laissez-faire authority structures by Lewin, Lippitt, and White (1939). Hence, we must be concerned with understanding how authority structures shape the ability of groups to function in ways that effectively solve group problems.

Several aspects of an authority structure might potentially influence its effectiveness. One is the form of the authority structure. Two important ways of establishing authority are the creation of rules and the empowerment of individual authorities. The effect of rules depends, among other things, on what those rules are. In addition, there are a variety of types of people who might be empowered as authorities. For example, recent studies of leadership have distinguished between charismatic and transformational leaders (Conger, 1989; Conger, Kanungo, & Associates, 1988; Meindl, 1990), while past studies have been concerned with the attributes of traditional and rational-legal authorities (Perrow, 1986). The key difference between rules and authorities is that a rule constrains the behavior of all members of a group, while empowerment of an authority constrains some group members but gives others (those in authority) discretion to determine both their own and the group's behavior.

Another concern is the amount of authority given to the rule structure or authority empowered. Too little authority leads to an inability to solve group problems. Too much authority can stifle the flexibility of a group and lead to an inability to respond quickly and flexibly to problems (Brickman, 1974). The difficulties resulting from having too much authority and/or too many rules are illustrated by the many problems of inefficiency and inflexibility associated with bureaucracies. Macauley (1963) demonstrated, for example, that businesses were reluctant to use the formal mechanisms of legal authority, such as trials, which they felt were too structured and rigid in their procedures, to resolve disputes and instead used more informal means such as mediation.

Giving too much authority to leaders raises the possibility of creating structures in which authorities take on too much power. In other words, people may overempower leaders, giving more authority to an individual or group of individuals than is required to resolve group problems. There is a tension between giving leaders enough authority to solve group problems and lessening the diversity of views that can influence the group. Since dissent and the influence of minority opinions can often facilitate effective group problem solving, the concentration of authority in one individual or subgroup can be antithetical to the long-term attainment of group goals (Nemeth & Staw, 1989). Under other circumstances, of course, conformity to majority views can be facilitative of the attainment of group goals, while attention to dissent can be disruptive (Nemeth, Mosier, & Chiles, in press).

An additional concern about authorities is the form of their influence over the group. Ever since the classic work of French and Raven (1959), it has been recognized that authorities could have a variety of potential forms of power or influence in groups. A central distinction is between reward and punishment power, which leads to overt compliance, and types of power linked to voluntary compliance (legitimate power, referent power, expertise). One key form that power takes in organizations is legitimacy. When people feel that authorities are legitimate, they are more likely to voluntarily accept their decisions (Tyler, 1990).

WHAT MECHANISMS CAN ENHANCE
THE EFFECTIVE EXERCISE OF AUTHORITY?

THE VOLUNTARY ACCEPTANCE OF DECISIONS.   For authorities to be effective in their role, they must be able to shape group behavior. Their ability to secure *voluntary* compliance with their directives is particularly important. While leaders typically have some power to reward and punish group members, their ability to govern effectively dissipates rapidly unless most people follow their decisions most of the time (Mechanic, 1962; Tyler, 1990). It is therefore important to examine why group members voluntarily accept decisions that give them less than they want or feel they deserve.

A finding common in all types of groups is that group members do not readily or easily accept decisions they do not like (Tyler & Lind, 1992). As a consequence, leaders cannot take the voluntary acceptance of their directives for granted. Although they may create authorities, people often then resist accepting third-party decisions. The same tension is found in dispute resolution. People resist or avoid the intervention of third parties (Rubin, 1980; Thibaut & Walker, 1975).

An interesting example of ambivalence toward authority is contained in a recent study on power imbalance (Tripp, 1991). In that study, students were assigned the role of manager or worker in a resource allocation task. The task was structured to give the manager greater power. Despite the legitimacy of having greater power, managers were reluctant to use their power and negotiated agreements that gave them less than they might have obtained. Tripp found that those acting as managers believed that workers would regard it as unfair for them to make full use of their authority in negotiations, even though that authority was legitimized by the structure of the task in which they were involved. Hence, even when authority has legitimacy, it may be only reluctantly exercised, because those with power think that exercising their potential power would lead to resistance by those over whom it is exercised.

The finding that people feel ambivalence about exercising authority parallels the findings of many studies on ultimatum games (see Bazerman, this volume). In ultimatum games one member of a dyad is given greater power to dictate the division of a resource. In such situations, high-power parties frequently take less for themselves than their power would seem to allow them to take. This self-restraint does not occur unless the high-power person believes that his or her decisions must gain the acceptance of the low-power person. Hence, it reflects anticipated difficulties in exercising power. This finding parallels that reported by Tripp (1991). In ultimatum games, however, the high-power position is not legitimized by a "managerial" role assignment.

In fact, leaders of all types of organizations are frequently regarded with suspicion and mistrust. For example, recent studies of public opinion about legal, political, and business leaders in the United States reveal widespread concerns about the integrity and competence of authorities in America (Lipset & Schneider, 1983). As a consequence, it is very difficult for these leaders to be authoritative.

LEGITIMACY AND COMMITMENT.   If people's actions are based primarily on individual self-interest, the prognosis for the voluntary acceptance of leaders' decisions is fairly grim. Because they allocate scarce resources and resolve conflicts that people cannot resolve on their own, authorities, by definition, must often give people outcomes that are less than they desire. Hence, we might expect widespread resistance to authority. Fortunately, people do not react to decisions in simple self-interest terms.

One source of evidence that people do not react to policy decisions in simple self-interest terms is the "symbolic politics" literature, which examines the basis of public reactions to political and social policies. That research shows that people's policy preferences are shaped by their political and social values (Sears, Lau, Tyler, & Allen, 1980).

One important set of these social values are social attitudes that lead people to react to groups in nonoutcome-driven ways. For instance, legitimacy is an important social attitude in the study of legal authorities. Legitimacy is linked to the perceived obligation to accept decisions and follow rules. The question of how authorities can legitimize their decisions is central to law (Tyler, 1990), because legitimate decisions are more likely to be accepted voluntarily.[1] A similar social attitude—organizational commitment—exists in work organizations.

---

[1]It is important to recognize that the desire to have decisions accepted voluntarily derives explicitly from the perspective of authorities. It is also possible to take a critical perspective on legitimacy, arguing that people would be better off not to accept the assumptions of the current situations (see Martin, this volume). Such a concern leads to an interest in identifying the antecedents of perceived injustice and illegitimacy.

Research has linked organizational commitment to a variety of positive behaviors (see Mathieu & Zajac, 1990, for a review), including rule following and organizational citizenship behavior (Graham, 1987). The key finding is that those who feel committed to their work organizations behave voluntarily in ways that facilitate the exercise of authority within those organizations.[2] Our concern is with the antecedents of such commitment.

PROCEDURAL JUSTICE.   One mechanism that can enhance legitimacy and commitment is the use of fair decision-making procedures (Thibaut & Walker, 1975). This mechanism of legitimation is very promising, from the perspective of group authorities, because, to the extent that it occurs, all parties to a decision can receive something that they value—procedural justice—from the third party.

The suggestion that justice might facilitate conflict resolution did not originate with Thibaut and Walker (1975). Earlier literature on relative deprivation (Crosby, 1976, 1982) and equity (Adams, 1965) also noted the importance of justice concerns. While they argued for the centrality of justice to conflict resolution, however, these reports focused on the importance of distributive justice—fair outcomes—rather than fair procedures (Deutsch, 1985).

Research has strongly supported the procedural justice hypotheses of Thibaut and Walker. It demonstrates that people evaluate authorities and institutions primarily in procedural justice terms. Studies of legal authorities (Tyler, 1984, 1990), political authorities (Tyler & Caine, 1981; Tyler, Rasinski, & McGraw, 1985), and managerial authorities (Alexander & Ruderman, 1987; Folger & Konovsky, 1989) all suggest that judgments about the fairness of procedures shape evaluations of authorities. Perceptions of procedures have also been linked to both general rule-following behavior (Tyler, 1990) and the acceptance of particular decisions (Lind, MacCoun, et al., 1990; MacCoun, Lind, Hensler, Bryant, & Ebener, 1988).

The sequence of judgments that has been outlined is summarized in Figure 1, in which all significant causal paths are shown. The numbers are the standardized regression coefficients (beta weights). When people in groups believe that the authorities are using fair decision-making procedures, they regard them as being more legitimate, and they become more committed to the organizations of which they are members. These supportive attitudes, in turn, increase willingness to accept voluntarily the decisions made by group authorities.

THE PSYCHOLOGY OF EFFECTIVE LEADERSHIP

Identifying the important role of procedural justice in enhancing organizational commitment, and through it the voluntary acceptance of third-party decisions, is central to understanding the effectiveness of authority. However, these findings do not explain the psychological underpinnings of organizational commit-

[2]Of course, organizational citizenship behavior is also linked to principled dissent, so loyal group members may also be disloyal in hope of improving the organization.

FIGURE 1   Conceptual Model

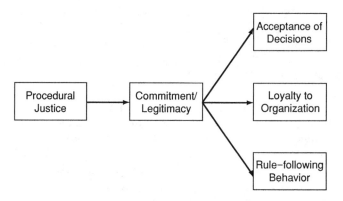

ment. They do not indicate *why* commitment develops and changes. Addressing this latter question requires a more direct focus on the psychology of organizational commitment.

Social exchange models

THE CONTROL MODEL.   One psychological model that can be used to understand commitment is the control model suggested by Thibaut and Walker (1975) to account for procedural justice findings: People are committed to organizations when they feel that they can control organizational decisions.

Thibaut and Walker's control model (Thibaut & Walker, 1975) is primarily an outcome model (derived from theories of social exchange; see Thibaut & Kelley, 1959) that proposes to explain their findings about procedural preferences and judgments of procedural justice. Their control model hypothesizes that the distribution of control between participants and a third party in a dispute resolution procedure is the key procedural characteristic shaping people's views about both fairness and desirability. Thibaut and Walker distinguish two types of control: process control—control over evidence presentation—and decision control—control over outcomes. Both their own and subsequent research have widely supported their suggestion that both types of control judgments influence assessments of procedural fairness (see Lind & Tyler, 1988, for a review).

The psychological perspective underlying the control model of procedural justice develops from interdependence models of social exchange theory (see Thibaut & Kelley, 1986, p. xi). Those theories suggest that people are primarily concerned with maximizing their direct or indirect control over the outcomes of third-party decisions so as to obtain as many *resources* through those decisions as possible. In other words, control theories suggest that disputants focus on the outcomes they receive, seeking to maximize their desirability. People want resources from others and evaluate their experience with others by the degree to which they provide them. Hence, control theory hypothesizes that the influence of control judgments on procedural justice is mediated by the impact of control on judgments about the favorability of the decisions made by the third party.

Studies of procedural justice typically find control effects. However, those effects are not of the type predicted by an instrumental view of control. First, people are found to care more about process control than about decision control. Second, people are found to care about process control when decision control is low. Most strikingly, people value the opportunity to present arguments even if it occurs after the decision has already been made (Lind, Kanfer, & Early, 1990). Also, open-ended studies in which people are asked to indicate what makes procedures fair or unfair do not find respondents talking predominantly about control (Lissak & Sheppard, 1983).

THE INVESTMENT MODEL.   The control model of Thibaut and Walker (1975) may not be complex enough to capture instrumental effects. A more complex alternative instrumental model is the investment model of commitment, loyalty, and exit based on exchange (Blau, 1964; Homans, 1961) and interdependence theory (Kelley & Thibaut, 1978; Thibaut & Kelley, 1959). Developed by Rusbult (1980, 1983), the investment model links loyalty and exit to people's satisfaction with the rewards they are receiving from their organization relative to what they might gain in other organizations. It suggests that people react to resource allocation and conflict resolution decisions by evaluating the consequences of those decisions for the rewards and costs of group membership.

The model identifies three potential elements of perceived investment: (1) satisfaction with the rewards received from an organization or a relationship (subjective gains); (2) the number of resources invested in the organization (investment), including time spent in the organization, friendships created, and the investment of self in the group;[3] and (3) evaluations of the rewards provided by the organization relative to available alternatives (relative gain; "CLalt" in Thibaut & Kelley, 1959, terminology).

The investment model has received support in studies of work settings (Farrell & Rusbult, 1981; Rusbult & Farrell, 1983; Rusbult, Farrell, Rogers, & Mainous, 1988; Rusbult & Lowery, 1985); in studies of romantic relationships (Rusbult, 1983; Rusbult, Johnson, & Morrow, 1986a, 1986b; Rusbult, Zembrodt, & Gunn, 1982); and in studies of friendship (Rusbult, 1980). In each case, an individual's loyalty to a relationship or an organization and his or her likelihood of exit were linked to investment evaluations.

Social identification models

THE RELATIONAL MODEL.   As an alternative to the control model, the relational model proposed by Tyler and Lind (1992) suggests that people are primarily interested in their status or standing in groups. People want high self-esteem and self-respect; they get it by feeling that they are valued members of groups.

---

[3]It is possible to argue about whether friendships at work and/or investment of self in one's job are a resource, as opposed to a relational, issue. However, for the purposes of this analysis the investment model is accepted as it is.

The relational model, like theories of social identification (Hogg & Abrams, 1988; Tajfel & Turner, 1979; Turner, 1987), hypothesizes that people value information about their *social status* or position within the group, information that is communicated to them through their experiences with third-party authorities.

In other words, the relational model suggests that people use the quality of their relationship with group authorities as an index of their standing in the group. From this perspective, people are not viewed as primarily concerned with the outcome they receive from the third party.

This model is like the models of Tajfel and Turner in that it links self-esteem to group status. However, unlike their models it does not focus on the status *of* the group of which one is a member intrinsically or in relationship to other groups. Instead, it focuses on one's position *within* a group as a source of status. In addition, people draw personal implications from the status of the groups to which they belong (Hogg & Abrams, 1988).

The relational perspective of Tyler and Lind (1992) was developed through studies of authority within legal, political, and managerial organizations. Such organizations are hierarchical in nature, with many levels of authority. In contrast, the work of Tajfel and Turner has focused heavily on "minimal group" situations in which small groups are artificially created. Such groups lack hierarchy and structure. In undifferentiated groups people focus on the status of their group, while in hierarchical/differentiated groups people focus on their status within the group.

Tyler (1989) states that a relational model predicts concern for three non-control issues: standing, trust, and neutrality. Each of these three dimensions of experience provides evidence about the degree to which a person is valued by the group.

Standing refers to the information communicated to a person about his or her status within the group. Information about status is communicated both by interpersonal aspects of treatment—politeness and/or respect—and by the attention paid to a person as a full group member. Polite treatment and respect for one's rights enhance feelings of positive social standing; undignified, disrespectful, treatment carries the message that one is not a full, valued member of the group (Lind & Tyler, 1988; Tyler, 1988; Tyler & Bies, 1990). Trust refers to the belief that organizational authorities are benevolent. This motive inference conveys information about the intentions of groups authorities, information that speaks directly to the social relationship between the person and the authority. Such motive inferences are especially important because they communicate information about future behavior. Finally, neutrality communicates information about whether the authority is attempting to create and maintain a "level playing field" within which all group members have equal opportunities.

Table 1 outlines the differing theoretical perspectives that have been developed and indicates the variables of importance within the models representing each theory. The basic theoretical distinction occurs between models that emphasize a desire for resources from third-party authorities and models that emphasize a desire for a positive relationship with group authorities.

TABLE 1 The Resource and Relational Perspectives

	RESOURCE PERSPECTIVE		RELATIONAL PERSPECTIVE	
Theoretical background	Social exchange		Social identity	
What do people want from authorities?	Favorable outcomes		Information about status	
Model	Control model	Investment model	Group-value model	Social identity model
Basis of evaluation	Direct and indirect control over outcomes	Satisfaction with rewards/resources invested/quality of alternatives	Status in group (reflected in neutrality/trust/ standing)	Status of group (intrinsic and relative to others)

EMPIRICAL RESEARCH

The influence of resource and relational concerns can be compared using several overlapping types of dependent variables. The first is the willingness to accept third-party decisions. The second is organizational commitment—a general attitude reflecting feelings about the organization. Third are general behaviors, including rule following and loyalty toward the organization. Loyalty is reflected in decisions to remain in the organization rather than accepting an offer elsewhere. The final dependent variable is judgments about the fairness of outcomes from third-party authorities and about the fairness of the procedures used by third parties to make allocations and/or resolve problems. These various types of attitudinal and behavioral reactions to organizations are distinct but interrelated.

Relational influences on affect and on the willingness to accept decisions voluntarily

Tyler (1991b) examined workers' willingness to accept their managers' decisions using a random sample of workers in Chicago ($n = 411$). The results indicated that relational concerns—neutrality, trust, and standing—significantly influenced both affect and the willingness to accept decisions. This study also investigated the possibility that investments might influence the willingness to accept decisions. In the same sample of workers in Chicago, willingness to accept managerial decisions was independently influenced by resource concerns. In other words, both affect and the willingness to accept decisions were affected, independently and significantly, by both the favorability of workers' relationships with their supervisors and by the extent to which they felt in control of valued resources.

Lind, Kulik, Ambrose, and Park (1991) extended this research to decisions made by legal authorities. In their study, litigants involved in civil cases in Federal courts ($n = 588$) had the option of accepting a court or arbitration decision or appealing to a higher court. They found that relational concerns had an important influence on litigants' willingness to accept the judges' decisions.

Relational influences on rule-following behavior

Tyler (1990) studied a panel of respondents who had a personal experience with legal authorities between two interviews in a panel study ($n = 291$). Rule-following behavior was affected by judgments about standing, but not by judgments of perceived control, neutrality, or trust. In the legal arena, when control and relational issues were contrasted, only relational issues matter. Tyler (1991b) found that the influence of interactions with a supervisor in a work setting on rule-following behavior was mediated by perceived trustworthiness, but not neutrality, standing, or control. Again, only the relational issue of trustworthiness mattered. However, in the work setting relational issues were also contrasted to investment issues. The results suggest that investment judgments of friendship at work were also influential, although length of time on the job, self-identification with work, and satisfaction with pay had no influence. Hence, relational issues and investment issues mattered, but control issues seemed to have little independent influence.

Relational influences on job satisfaction, organizational commitment, and turnover intention

Tyler (1991a) used the sample of Chicago workers already described to examine the influence of workers' interactions with their supervisors on workers' job satisfaction, commitment to their work organization, and their turnover intention.

In addition to examining the direct influences of control, neutrality, trust, and standing on the dependent variables, Tyler (1991a) directly investigated the mediating mechanisms hypothesized to underlie those effects. The control model hypothesizes that people value control because it leads to more favorable outcomes, suggesting that favorable outcomes will mediate control effects. The relational model hypothesizes that workers value standing, trust, and neutrality because those aspects of their experience reflect on the favorability of their relationship with their supervisor, which, in turn, reflects on their status in the organization.

Tyler (1991a) used a causal model in which judgments about personal experiences could influence (1) judgments of outcome favorability and judgments regarding relationships with the supervisor; and (2) evaluations of organizational commitment, intention to quit, and rule-following behavior. The model assumes that a variable on one level can influence any variable at a higher level (e.g., intention to quit can be influenced by organizational commitment, by outcome favorability, and/or by judgments of control).

THE EFFECTS OF EXPERIENCE.   The causal model can first be used to examine the influence of judgments about particular experiences. Such judgments are hypothesized to influence the favorability of workers' views about their relationship with their supervisor, their judgments about the outcome favorability (of the experience and generally), their organizational commitment, and their managerial evaluations. The results of the model are shown in Figure 2. Statistically significant paths ($p < .01$ or lower) are shown.

There are three primary findings of the analysis shown in Figure 2. First, the paths predicted by each model are found. Control influences judgments of the outcome favorability of the experience. If people feel that they have controlled outcomes, they judge them to be more favorable. In addition, standing, trust, and neutrality influence judgments about the quality of the worker–super-

FIGURE 2   The Effect of Workers' Experiences with Their Supervisors

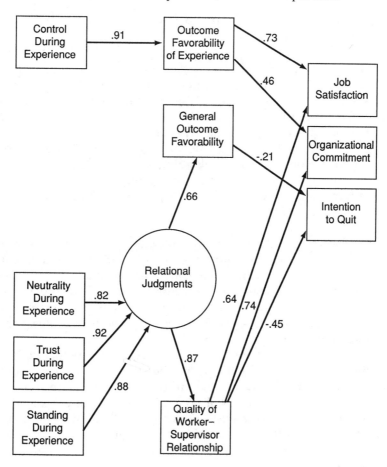

visor relationship. If people feel they were treated as if they have favorable standing in the organization during their recent experience; if they trust the intentions of their supervisor during their recent experience; and/or if they feel that their supervisor acted neutrally during their recent experience, they evaluated their relationship with their supervisor more favorably.

Second, Figure 2 shows that control over outcomes did not influence workers' views about the quality of their relationship with their supervisor. Hence, relational concerns appear to be distinct from control concerns. This independence is not reciprocal since relational judgments influence judgments of general outcome favorability. Hence, relational aspects of experience shape judgments of outcome favorability. However, relational concerns only shape general judgments; they do not influence experience-specific judgments.

Finally, experience ultimately influences job satisfaction, organizational commitment, and turnover intention through outcome favorability (both general and particular) and the quality of the worker–supervisor relationship.

Judgments about how the supervisor generally behaves

General judgments of control also affected evaluations of general outcome favorability (see Figure 3). In other words, the people who felt that they are generally able to control decisions evaluated the general favorability of organizational outcomes to them as greater. However, general outcome favorability is also affected by the relational judgments of neutrality, trust, and standing.

More importantly, relational judgments again dominate the influence of experience on organizational attitudes, influencing organizational commitment and turnover intention. General judgments of outcome favorability have no significant influence on evaluations of job satisfaction, organizational commitment, or turnover intention.

OVERALL EVALUATIONS OF THE WORKPLACE.   A direct comparison of instrumental and relational influences on organizational commitment, turnover intention, and rule-following behavior can also be made for overall evaluations of the investment and relational characteristics of one's workplace (length of employment; workplace friendships; rewards relative to alternatives; relationship with supervisor). Figures 4 and 5 present the results of a causal analysis for each of these two models.

The results shown in Figures 4 and 5 indicate that both resource and relational judgments influence the prediction of job satisfaction, organizational commitment, and turnover intention. Interestingly, the results shown in Figures 4 and 5 suggest a substantial separation of investment and relational concerns, just as the previous analysis indicated a substantial separation of control and relational concerns. None of the four investment indices significantly influenced judgments about the favorability of the worker's relationship with the supervisor.

FIGURE 3   The Effect of Workers' Overall Judgments about Their Supervisors

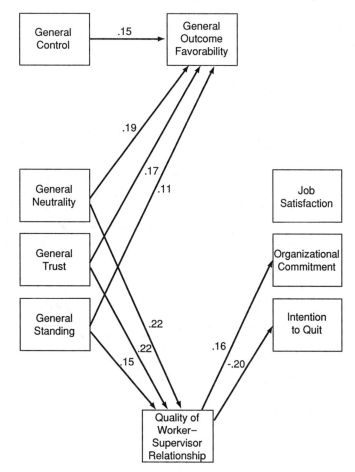

Relational influences on judgments about justice

The relational model has been supported by several recent studies of people's evaluations of the justice of their experiences with authorities. Tyler (1991c) found that workers' evaluations of the procedural justice of their experiences with managers were significantly influenced by control, neutrality, trust, and standing. Tyler (1989) also found that judgments of the fairness of the procedures used by the police and the courts were independently influenced by control, neutrality, trust, and standing.

Tyler (1991b) examined the influence of investment in the job on workers' judgments of the justice of their experiences with their supervisors. Evaluations of the distributive justice of decisions were significantly influenced by length of time on the job; by satisfaction with the resources received from the job; and by

FIGURE 4   The Effect of Investment Judgments on Reactions to Experiences with Supervisors

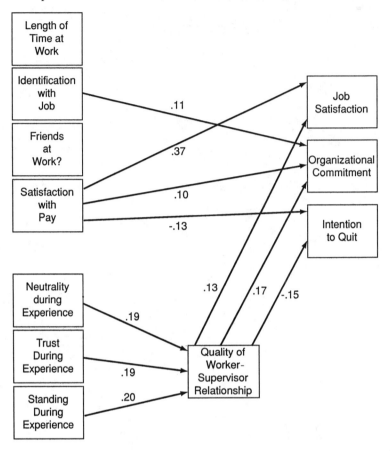

the favorability of the worker's relationship with the supervisor. Judgments of the procedural justice of decisions were influenced by self-identification with the job and by the favorability of the worker's relationship with the supervisor.

Judgments about the general fairness of the supervisor were influenced by length of time on the job; self-identification with work; satisfaction with the resources received from the job; and the favorability of the worker's relationship with their supervisor. Judgments of the overall fairness of the supervisor's procedures for solving workplace problems, however, were only responsive to relational judgments.

Implications

These studies reaffirm the important role of concerns about resources in shaping people's willingness to voluntarily accept third-party decisions; their organiza-

FIGURE 5   The Effect of Investment Judgments on Overall Judgments about Supervisors

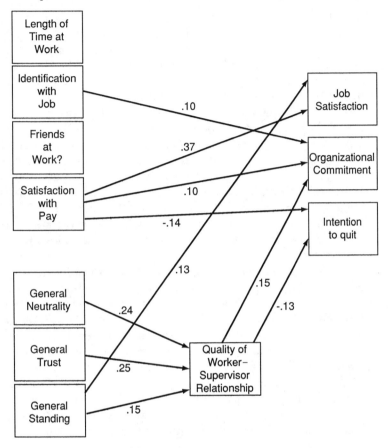

tional commitment, turnover intentions, and rule-following behavior; and their attitudes about justice.

These results are consistent with the conclusions of previous work on control, which links control to judgments about fairness and to the willingness to accept decisions (Lind & Tyler, 1988). Further, they support prior studies of organizational loyalty and exit that link investment judgments to commitment and loyalty. At the workplace level, the investment judgments identified by Rusbult as important to organizational loyalty are found to influence organizationally related attitudes and behaviors (Rusbult, 1980, 1983). People are more committed to and less likely to leave groups that provide them with more resources than they can obtain elsewhere.

This research further suggests, however, that resource influences do not provide a complete description of the psychology of organizational attitudes and behaviors. In work organizations and the legal system, relational influences have led to important effects on the voluntary acceptance of third-party decisions; on rule-following behavior; on job satisfaction, organizational commitment, and turnover intention; and on fairness evaluations. In addition, relational concerns have an important role in shaping organizational attitudes and behaviors irrespective of whether they are contrasted with evaluations of control over particular decisions, general evaluations of the workplace, or overall judgments about investment in the workplace.

Recent organizational theorists have argued that organizational loyalty could be better understood if an exchange perspective were supplemented with an attention to issues of social identification (Ashforth & Mael, 1989). These results support that suggestion. These findings provide strong support for the hypothesis that standing, trust, and neutrality independently influence commitment and loyalty. These observations are especially important because some of the studies provide direct evidence that the effects are mediated by judgments about the favorability of relationships with the group authority. Hence, they directly support the hypothesis that commitment and loyalty are responsive to relational factors.

The fact that people focus on social relationships in reacting to their experiences within groups parallels the findings of research by Kahnemen, Knetsch, and Thaler on public views regarding people's obligations to others (Kahneman, Knetsch, & Thaler, 1986a, 1986b). This research finds that the public regards many types of actions that a business might legally engage in as unfair (e.g., raising rents to market levels when they have an ongoing relationship with a tenant). Interestingly, these judgments frequently suggest a perceived obligation to people in an ongoing social relationship. It would, for example, be unacceptable to raise the rent to market levels for an existing tenant, but not to charge a new tenant what the market will bear. In other words, people may regard the maintainance of social relationships as more important than the maximization of resource gain.

A similar finding emerges in studies of social utility functions (see Bazerman, this volume; Loewenstein, Thompson, & Bazerman, 1989). When people are involved in a positive social relationship with another person, they willingly give up resources to the other party in the relationship. When people are involved in a negative relationship, however, they become more selfish. This suggests that people recognize independent relational concerns when they are in a relationship with others.

A third example of the importance of relational concerns is provided by the social dilemma literature. In that literature, group identification has often been found to have an important influence on voluntary progroup behavior (see Kramer, this volume; Kramer & Goldman, 1988). When people within groups identify with each other, they place the group's collective interests above their own self-interest. Again, maintaining their relational links may be more important to group members than maximizing the attainment of resources.

SUMMARY

Exchange theories (Blau, 1964; Homans, 1961) and interdependence theories (Kelley & Thibaut, 1978; Thibaut & Kelley, 1959) predict that people's loyalty toward groups is linked to the level of resources they provide their members. In contrast, a relational model links loyalty to groups to whether groups provide their members with a positive sense of identity and feelings of being respected, valued members of the group. The findings summarized in this chapter suggest that both theories are important to understanding loyalty toward work organizations and their authorities. These findings suggest the need for a model in which both resource and relational concerns are included.

REFERENCES

ADAMS, S. (1965). Inequity in social exchange. In L. Berkowitz (Ed.), *Advances in experimental social psychology* (Vol. 2, pp. 267–299). New York: Academic.

ALEXANDER, S., & RUDERMAN, A. (1987). The role of procedural and distributive justice in organizational behavior. *Social Justice Research, 1,* 177–198.

ASHFORTH, B. E., & MAEL, F. (1989). Social identity theory and the organization. *Academy of Management Review, 14,* 20–39.

BAZERMAN, M., LOEWENSTEIN, G. F., & WHITE, S. B. (1991). *Psychological determinants of utility in competitive contexts: The impact of elicitation procedure.* Kellogg Graduate School of Management, Northwestern University.

BLAU, P. (1964). *Exchange and power in social life.* New York: John Wiley & Sons.

BRICKMAN, P. (1974). *Social conflict.* Lexington, MA: D. C. Heath.

CARTWRIGHT, D., & ZANDER, A. (1953). *Group dynamics.* New York: Harper & Row.

CONGER, J. A. (1989). *The charismatic leader.* San Francisco: Jossey-Bass.

CONGER, J. A., KANUNGO, R. N., and Associates (Eds.). (1988). *Charismatic leadership.* San Francisco: Jossey-Bass.

CONLEY, J. M., & O'BARR, W. M. (1990). *Rules versus relationships.* Chicago: University of Chicago Press.

CROSBY, F. (1976). A model of egoistical relative deprivation. *Psychological Review, 83,* 85–113.

CROSBY, F. (1982). *Relative deprivation and working women.* New York: Oxford University Press.

CROSBY, F. (1984a). The denial of personal discrimination. *American Behavioral Scientist, 27,* 371–386.

CROSBY, F. (1984b). Relative deprivation in organizational settings. In B. M. Staw & L. L. Cummings (Eds.), *Research in organizational behavior* (Vol. 6, pp. 51–93). Greenwich, CT: JAI Press.

CROSBY, F., & NAGATA, D. (1990, July). *Denying personal disadvantage.* Paper presented at the annual meeting of the International Society of Political Psychology, Washington, DC.

DEUTSCH, M. (1985). *Distributive justice.* New Haven: Yale University Press.

FARRELL, D., & RUSBULT, C. E. (1981). Exchange variables as predictors of job satisfaction, job commitment, and turnover: The impact of rewards, costs, alternatives, and investments. *Organizational Behavior and Human Performance, 27,* 78–95.

FOLGER, R., & KONOVSKY, M. (1989). Effects of procedural and distributive justice on reactions to pay raise decisions. *Academy of Management Journal, 32,* 115–130.

FRENCH, J. R. P., JR., & RAVEN, B. (1959). The bases of social power. In D. Cartwright (Ed.), *Studies in social power* (pp. 150–167). Ann Arbor, MI: Institute for Social Research.

GRAHAM, J. (1987). *Organizational citizenship behavior.* Unpublished manuscript, School of Business, Loyola University, Chicago: IL.

HOGG, M. A., & ABRAMS, D. (1988). *Social identifications: A social psychology of intergroup relations.* New York: Routledge.

HOMANS, G. C. (1961). *Social behavior.* New York: Harcourt, Brace, and World.

KAHNEMAN, D., KNETSCH, J. L., & THALER, R. (1986a). Fairness as a constraint on profit seeking: Entitlements in the market. *American Economic Review, 76,* 728–741.

KAHNEMAN, D., KNETSCH, J. L., & THALER, R. (1986b). Fairness and the assumptions of economics. *Journal of Business, 59,* S285–S300.

KELLEY, H. H., & THIBAUT, J. (1978). *Interpersonal relations.* New York: Wiley.

KRAMER, R. M., & GOLDMAN, L. (1988). *Expectations that bind: Group-based trust, causal attributions, and cooperative behavior in a commons dilemma.* Unpublished manuscript, Graduate School of Business, Stanford University, Palo Alto, CA.

LEWIN, K., LIPPITT, R., & WHITE, R. K. (1939). Patterns of aggressive behavior in experimentally created "social climates." *Journal of Social Psychology, 10,* 271–299.

LIND, E. A., KANFER, R., & EARLEY, P. C. (1990). Voice, control, and procedural justice: Instrumental and noninstrumental concerns in fairness judgments. *Journal of Personality and Social Psychology, 59,* 952–959.

LIND, E. A., KULIK, C. T., AMBROSE, M., & PARK, M. (1991). *Outcome and process concerns in organizational dispute resolution.* Chicago IL: American Bar Foundation, working paper.

LIND, E. A., MacCOUN, R. J., EBENER, P. A., FELSTINER, W. L. F., HENSLER, D. R., RESNIK, J., & TYLER, T. R. (1990). In the eye of the beholder: Tort litigants' evaluations of their experiences in the civil justice system. *Law and Society Review, 24,* 953–996.

LIND, E. A., & TYLER, T. R. (1988). *The social psychology of procedural justice.* New York: Plenum.

LIPSET, S., & SCHNEIDER, W. (1983). *The confidence gap: Business, labor, and government in the public mind.* New York: Free Press.

LISSAK, R., & SHEPPARD, B. (1983). Beyond fairness: The criterion problem in research on dispute resolution. *Basic and Applied Social Psychology, 13,* 45–65.

LOEWENSTEIN, G., THOMPSON, L., & BAZERMAN, M. H. (1989). Social utility and decision making in interpersonal contexts. *Journal of Personality and Social Psychology, 57,* 426–441.

MACAULEY, S. (1963). Non-contractual relations in business: A preliminary study. *American Sociological Review, 28,* 55–67.

MacCOUN, R. J., LIND, E. A., HENSLER, D. R., BRYANT, D. L., & EBENER, P. A. (1988). *Alternative adjudication: An evaluation of the New Jersey automobile arbitration program.* Santa Monica, CA: RAND.

MARTIN, J., BRICKMAN, P., & MURRAY, A. (1984). Moral outrage and pragmatism: Explanations for collective action. *Journal of Experimental Social Psychology, 20,* 484–496.

MATHIEU, J. E., & ZAJAC, D. M. (1990). A review and meta-analysis of the antecedents, correlates, and consequences of organizational commitment. *Psychological Bulletin, 108,* 171–194.

MECHANIC, D. (1962). Sources of power of lower participants in complex organizations. *Administrative Science Quarterly, 7,* 349–364.

MEINDL, J. (1990). On leadership: An alternative to the conventional wisdom. In Barry M. Staw & L. L. Cummings (Eds.), *Research in organizational behavior* (Vol. 12, pp. 159–203). Greenwich, CT: JAI Press.

MESSICK, D. M., WILKE, H., BREWER, M. B., KRAMER, R. M., ZEMKE, P., & LUI, L. (1983). Individual adaptations and structural change as solutions to social dilemmas. *Journal of Personality and Social Psychology, 44,* 294–309.

NEMETH, C. J., MOSIER, K., & CHILES, C. (in press). When convergent thought improves performance: Majority vs. minority influence. *Personality and Social Psychology Bulletin.*

NEMETH, C. J., & STAW, B. M. (1989). The tradeoffs of social control and innovation in groups and organizations. In L. Berkowitz (Ed.), *Advances in experimental social psychology* (Vol. 22, pp. 175–210). New York: Academic.

PERROW, C. (1986). *Complex organizations* (3rd ed.). New York: Random House.

PILLAI, R., & MEINDL, J. R. (1991, August). *The effect of crisis on the emergence of charismatic leadership.* Paper presented at the Academy of Management meetings, Miami.

RUBIN, J. Z. (1980). Experimental research on third-party intervention in conflict. *Psychological Bulletin, 87,* 379–391.

RUSBULT, C. E. (1980). Satisfaction and commitment in friendships. *Representative Research in Social Psychology, 11,* 96–105.

RUSBULT, C. E. (1983). A longitudinal test of the investment model. *Journal of Personality and Social Psychology, 45,* 101–117.

RUSBULT, C. E., & FARRELL, D. (1983). A longitudinal test of the investment model. *Journal of Applied Psychology, 68,* 429–438.

RUSBULT, C. E., FARRELL, D., ROGERS, G., & MAINOUS, A. G. (1988). Impact of exchange variables on exit, voice, loyalty, and neglect: An integrative model of responses to declining job satisfaction. *Academy of Management Journal, 31,* 599–627.

RUSBULT, C. E., JOHNSON, D. J., & MARROW, G. D. (1986a). Determinants and consequences of exit, voice, loyalty, and neglect: Responses to dissatisfaction in adult romantic involvements. *Human Relations, 39,* 45–63.

RUSBULT, C. E., JOHNSON, D. J., & MARROW, G. D. (1986b). Predicting satisfaction and commitment in adult romantic involvements: An assessment of the generalizability of the investment model. *Social Psychology Quarterly, 49,* 81–89.

RUSBULT, C. E., & LOWERY, D. (1985). When bureaucrats get the blues: Responses to dissatisfaction among Federal employees. *Journal of Applied Social Psychology, 15,* 80–103.

RUSBULT, C. E., ZEMBRODT, I. M., & GUNN, L. K. (1982). Exit, voice, loyalty, and neglect: Responses to dissatisfaction in romantic involvements. *Journal of Personality and Social Psychology, 43,* 1230–1242.

SEARS, D. O., LAU, R. R., TYLER, T. R., & ALLEN, H. M., JR. (1980). Self-interest and symbolic attitudes in policy attitudes and Presidential voting. *American Political Science Review, 74,* 670–684.

SEARS, D. O., TYLER, T. R., CITRIN, J., & KINDER, D. R. (1978). Political system support and public response to the 1974 energy crisis. *American Journal of Political Science, 22,* 56–82.

TAJFEL, H., & TURNER, J. (1979). An integrative theory of intergroup conflict. In W. G. Austin & S. Worchel (Eds.), *The social psychology of intergroup relations* (pp. 33–47). Monterey, CA: Brooks/Cole.

THIBAUT, J., & KELLEY, H. H. (1959). *The social psychology of groups.* New York: Wiley.

THIBAUT, J., & KELLEY, H. H. (1986). *The social psychology of groups* (2nd ed.). New Brunswick, NJ: Transaction Books.

THIBAUT, J., & WALKER, L. (1975). *Procedural justice.* Hillsdale, NJ: Erlbaum.

TRIPP, T. M. (1991). *Authority, dependency, and fairness in negotiations.* Unpublished doctoral dissertation. Kellogg Graduate School of Management, Northwestern University, Evanston, IL.

TURNER, J. C. (1987). *Rediscovering the social group: A self-categorization theory.* New York: Basil Blackwell.

TYLER, T. R. (1984). The role of perceived injustice in defendant's evaluations of their courtroom experience. *Law and Society Review, 18,* 51–74.

TYLER, T. R. (1988). What is procedural justice?: Criteria used by citizens to assess the fairness of legal procedures. *Law and Society Review, 22,* 301–355.

TYLER, T. R. (1989). The psychology of procedural justice: A test of the group value model. *Journal of Personality and Social Psychology, 57,* 830–838.

TYLER, T. R. (1990). *Why people obey the law.* New Haven: Yale University Press.

TYLER, T. R. (1991a). *Comparing the investment and relational models of authority in organizations: The antecedents of commitment, loyalty and exit.* Unpublished manuscript, University of California, Berkeley.

TYLER, T. R. (1991b). *Investment influences on justice concerns.* Unpublished manuscript, University of California, Berkeley.

TYLER, T. R. (1991c). *A relational model of justice.* Unpublished manuscript, University of California, Berkeley.

TYLER, T. R., & BIES, R. J. (1990). Interpersonal aspects of procedural justice. In J. S. Carroll (Ed.), *Applied social psychology in business settings* (pp. 77–98). Hillsdale, NJ: Erlbaum.

TYLER, T. R., & CAINE, A. (1981). The role of distributional and procedural fairness in the endorsement of formal leaders. *Journal of Personality and Social Psychology, 41,* 642–655.

TYLER, T. R., & DEGOEY, P. (1991). *Support for the use of third-party authorities in allocating scarce natural resources: The case of the California water shortage.* Unpublished manuscript, University of California, Berkeley.

TYLER, T. R., & LIND, E. A. (1992). A relational model of authority in groups. In M. Zanna (Ed.), *Advances in experimental social psychology* (Vol. 25). New York: Academic Press.

TYLER, T. R., RASINSKI, K., & McGRAW, K. (1985). The influence of perceived injustice on support for political authorities. *Journal of Applied Social Psychology, 15,* 700–725.

WEBER, R., & CROCKER, J. (1983). Cognitive processes in the revision of stereotypic beliefs. *Journal of Personality and Social Psychology, 45,* 961–977.

WILLNER, A. R. (1984). *The spellbinders: Charismatic political leadership.* New Haven: Yale University Press.

CHAPTER EIGHT

Reactions to Mistreatment at Work

ROBERT FOLGER

Tulane University

Expanding my previous work on referent cognitions theory (RCT), I describe in this chapter a new theory concerning how employees come to feel mistreated. The new theory conceptualizes employment as both economic and social exchange, involving not only the material *things* exchanged (e.g., wages for hours worked) but also the relations of the *people* in the exchange (viz., how management treats employees on interpersonal dimensions such as politeness and respect). Two key management failures to fulfill implicit obligations thus comprise the core of employees' perceived mistreatment: (a) deficient reward from management for the labor *of* an employee (failing to provide enough things or the right things); and (b) wrongful behavior by management toward someone *as* an employee (failing to treat the employee as a person—instead, treating him or her as a thing). This approach emphasizes that procedures act not only as means to an end but also as ends in themselves (e.g., as signs of respect), whereas RCT had emphasized only the former (cause-and-effect) aspect of procedures. The revised theory provides a better fit to new field data and yet accommodates the same outcome-by-process interaction (obtained in lab and field) that RCT had predicted. I also discuss implications beyond the resentful reactions that had been the preoccupation of RCT, extending the focus to achievement motivation and topics such as entrepreneurship.

Thanks in part to Adams (1965), organizational scientists have long been aware of the important effects that can occur in the workplace when employees feel mistreated. Adams's formulation of equity theory, however, does not resolve some of the most crucial issues about the prediction of such effects. Consider, for instance, the employer who fears that employees may react with hostility toward management as the result of pay cuts, layoffs, or similar actions that reduce employee outcomes. Equity theory fails to provide explicit guidelines about what to expect in such situations. Underpay or harmful outcomes might produce attempts to resolve inequity by such negative behavior as sabotage or work restrictions aimed at lowering the employer's outcomes, the employee's inputs, or both. The same magnitude of disadvantageous inequity might instead, under some circumstances, produce more positive cognitive resolutions: The underpaid employee might, for example, shift attention from money to other on-the-job outcomes such as pleasant working conditions or friendly co-workers and might even work harder if those rationalizations make the work seem more enjoyable.

The theory and research I have pursued for several years reflects a divide-and-conquer strategy designed to attack these problems of prediction by first looking for the determinants of a single response category, and then moving on to other categories after the first has been adequately understood. Although my discussion concludes by touching on more than one response category, I focus primarily on the topic that has received most of my attention in the past—the events that evoke and sustain resentment.

Resentment is an emotion defined as "a feeling of indignant displeasure or persistent ill will at something regarded as a wrong, insult, or injury." "Righteous indignation" (cf. "moral outrage") is a phrase related to the word *indignant* that captures important aspects of this phenomenon. The etymological link to *dignity* suggests that a threat to, or attack on, one's dignity, self-worth, or self-respect tends to provoke retaliation.

An important category of an employee's reactions to the employment exchange thus centers on the antecedents and consequences of a psychological state with the following characteristics:

1.   From the employee's perspective, the precursor events have features that are captured by terms such as *provocation, slight,* or *affront* (cf. *wrong, insult,* or *injury*).
2.   The emotional experiences that accompany those events seem tied to perceptions that the dignity, worth, status, or socially recognized value of the employee has been placed in jeopardy (e.g., *indignant*).
3.   The employee develops a hostile inclination toward some social target (such as an employer, an organization, or "management") as the putative offender. Sometimes characterized as a desire for revenge or retaliation (e.g., "persistent ill will"), this inclination may also be adopted by others whose own standing has not been so directly jeopardized (e.g., the survivors of layoffs may identify with the victims).
4.   Aggrieved parties also tend to promote various expressions of hostility as being legitimate, condonable, or meriting approbation, by invoking normative standards such as those related to justice or morality (e.g., *righteous* indignation; *moral* outrage; injustice).

Adams (1965) suggested that employees who think they might have been mistreated at work can pursue any of several modes of inequity resolution, but his early work made only a few ad hoc suggestions concerning how to predict which mode might be chosen on a given occasion, thus leaving the prediction of reactions an uncompleted project. The study of resentment offers a relevant focus and starting point for part of that project. My own efforts represent attempts to expand our understanding of resentment and related phenomena, with the hope that new conceptualizations and phenomenological accounts will eventually lead to greater predictive success. To illustrate those efforts, I first review my previously proposed framework for understanding resentment—referent cognitions theory—and discuss some of the findings consistent with that framework. More recent findings are then used as a springboard for a revised conceptualization. Concluding speculations consider how further elaboration of these models might address a broader scope of possible reactions to negative (disadvantageous) outcomes from the employment exchange.

EARLY RESEARCH
ON REFERENT COGNITIONS THEORY

Resentment, as suggested by the dictionary definition cited earlier, implies anger directed toward a social target. When decisions are made or policies are implemented at work that affect employees' outcomes, we can refer to management decision makers and policy implementers as agents whose actions have been associated with those outcomes. If employees view their outcomes negatively, management agents become potential targets for resentment. Thus a focus on resentment helps emphasize the importance of distinguishing between employee reactions toward the outcomes received in an exchange and their reactions toward the exchange partner (agent). Negative reactions directed exclusively toward an outcome constitute outcome dissatisfaction. Negative reactions directed toward an agent who allocates outcomes may also stem from outcome dissatisfaction but must reflect some mechanism that permits or encourages dissatisfaction with a particular social target (rather than, for instance, oneself as an object of blame).

Determining the nature of this mechanism will allow us to predict when mere dissatisfaction with an outcome will occur but will remain associated with the outcome itself, versus situations when dissatisfaction will become a source of resentment. Consider, as an illustration, circumstances in which a pay increase—representing more money in the coming year than in the past—evokes the same negative psychological impact as an objective loss. Some employees might not compare the new pay amount with the old, but instead use some higher pay level that (for whatever reason) comes to mind as a comparative standard used for evaluative purposes; they will experience a sense of relative deprivation. Referent cognitions theory (RCT) gets its name from the term *referent outcome*, a generic label for these alternatively imaginable levels of outcome favorability (one of two factors central to the model—for more details, see Folger, 1987). In the example of a pay raise comparing unfavorably with a higher amount brought to mind, the latter constitutes a high referent outcome. High referent outcomes cause dissatisfaction with actual outcomes. But when do high referent outcomes lead to resentment of management agents?

Referent cognitions theory addresses that question by introducing process considerations as a second factor, namely the decision making and implementing conduct of the agent as a crucial part of the processes governing outcome allocations. Referent cognitions theory suggests that employees check management conduct for cues—comparing enacted behavior with normative standards about the appropriateness and legitimacy of procedures implemented and the character of related behaviors. Cues implying discrepancies from normative standards (e.g., arbitrary or capricious actions) tend to provoke outcome dissatisfaction and elicit resentment toward management. In this way, RCT combines equity theory's emphasis on outcome with the emphasis on process that characterizes research and theory on procedural justice (for reviews, see Folger & Greenberg, 1985; Greenberg, 1990; Lind & Tyler, 1988; Thibaut & Walker, 1975).

Referent cognitions theory thus represents a two-factor theory involving an outcome factor (dissatisfaction with actual outcomes as a function of higher referent outcome favorability) and a process factor (normative acceptability of management procedures and conduct). Resentment of an agent can stem from dissatisfaction with an outcome, but only in conjunction with the implementation of unfair procedures or other inappropriate conduct by the agent. The necessity of conjunctive conditions implies an Outcome × Process interaction as a fundamental RCT prediction.

Although the preceding summary is a general description of RCT, past theorizing and research has also stressed one particular mechanism as a key feature of the analysis. That cognitive mechanism, counterfactual thinking, refers to thoughts about imaginable alternatives; to think counterfactually is to undo an existing state of affairs in one's mind. In counterfactual thinking, outcome and process factors interact in a causal, means–ends fashion (at least according to the original version of RCT, which I modify shortly). Often the present end state of some sequence of events can be thought of as an outcome (e.g., the grade at the end of a course), and the prior events can be thought of as a contributory causal process (e.g., lectures, assignments, hours spent studying). To replay the sequence and its results in one's mind is to run a mental model of the world, starting from some selected point in the past and continuing to the present. In conducting *counterfactual* simulations, people act as directors of their own mental home movies by cognitively *undoing* some past event (by imagining it otherwise) and continuing the simulation to imagine how the end results *would have* turned out (e.g., if the lectures had not been so obtuse or if more studying had taken place).

Referent cognitions theory's original version emphasized mental undoing in the form of causal counterfactuals. Consider two very general types of independent variables in the research on procedural justice (cf. Greenberg, 1990): (a) actual procedures themselves, such as particular methods for arriving at decisions, and (b) information, such as explanations about those methods. The first is illustrated by structural features of procedures, such as voice and choice (cf. Greenberg & Folger, 1983); the second is illustrated by explanations in the form of excuses or justifications (cf. Bies, 1987). The effects of these variables can be understood by noting how they either encourage or discourage the following general counterfactual, which represents the conditions likely to produce maximum resentment: If only the agent had acted as he or she *should* have, then I *would* have received a better outcome.

Causal counterfactuals that mentally undo an existing procedure (creating an imaginable alternative) can be expected when choice or voice seems normatively appropriate but has played no role in the methods used for making an allocative decision. A salient counterfactual, in which the person imagines what would have happened if choice or voice had been granted, might easily simulate a high referent outcome for comparison (e.g., If only I had been allowed to argue for a proper interpretation of my performance, my performance ratings would have been good enough to earn me a better raise). Procedural differences such as the presence or absence of voice, therefore, can either encourage a resentful counterfactual by the absence of an appropriate structural element of fair decision-making practices (such as choice or voice) or discourage a resentful counterfactual by the presence of that element. When the procedural element of fairness is lacking, the recipient is more likely to think about what could and presumably would have happened if only the decision maker had implemented fair procedures.

An excuse, such as an agent's claim that mitigating circumstances prevented some form of action, also influences employees' thoughts about what could have happened. In this case, a convincing excuse tends to block counterfactual thinking because the person making the excuse has presented compelling evidence or arguments that he or she *could not* have behaved otherwise. When an allocator's "hands were tied" by precedent that could not be overturned, for example, the circumstances make it more difficult to think about what could have happened, reducing the salience of high referent outcomes.

Justifications represent appeals regarding what *should* be done. When justifying harmful actions, for example, the persuasiveness of the justification depends on the plausibility of an argument that some greater good was done or more important values were served. Once the justification proves worthy of acceptance, the tendency is to think that the decision maker *should not* have behaved otherwise. Sufficiently compelling justifications tend to inhibit counterfactual thinking.

A series of RCT experiments examined these three ways that the actions of an allocative decision maker can appear objectionable (through differences in excuses, justifications, or the procedures themselves), thereby evoking negative reactions that grow stronger the more a loss seems severe (see Figures 1, 2, and 3). Two experiments focused on explanations for outcome losses that occurred because one procedure had been used rather than another. In both, the experimenter introduced a change (essentially a procedural alteration) in the arrangements that determined outcomes. The experiments involved two types of explanations for the procedural change—differences in excuses or differences in justifications. In Folger and Martin (1986), loss occurred either when mitigating circumstances (equipment failure) provided an excuse for the experimenter's conduct, or when no such excuse existed (Figure 1). In Folger, Rosenfield, and Robinson (1983), an experimenter provided one of two different levels of justification for a change in scoring procedures. One fully exonerated the experimenter for the change by explaining why the new procedure improved on the old procedure. The contrasting communication provided no justification (Figure 2). Excuses and justifications produced similar effects: Each can influence an explanation's acceptability and exonerates an allocator's conduct. Clear and adequate excuses or legitimate justifications, as perceived by the person receiv-

FIGURE 1   Treatment Means Regarding "The Way You Were Treated by the Experimenter"

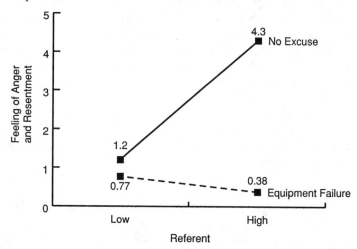

Note: Scores can range from 0 to 20; higher scores represent greater feelings of anger and resentment.

ing outcomes, prevent an allocator from being held accountable for an outcome loss—they exonerate or at least minimize vilification and corresponding hostility.

Similarly, procedures themselves can also mitigate or exaggerate others' reactions toward an allocator. For example, even people who think their own rewards do not fully reflect what they deserve may not respond unfavorably

FIGURE 2   Treatment Means for Ratings of "Angry" and "Resentful"

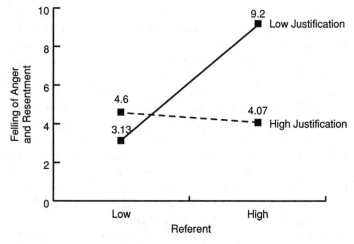

Note: The higher the number, the greater the extent to which subjects felt "angry" and "resentful."

FIGURE 3   Treatment Means for Ratings of "Fairly Treated"

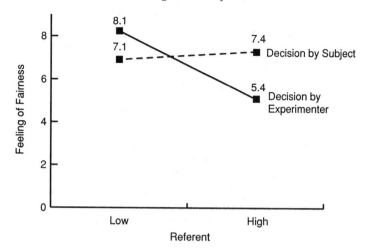

Note: The lower the number, the less the extent to which subjects reported having felt "fairly treated."

toward an allocator who uses a legitimate or acceptable decision-making procedure. Cropanzano and Folger (1989) provide an illustration: Experimental participants knew that their performance on one of two tasks would determine whether they received a reward. One procedure briefly described each task and gave participants the choice of which would determine the reward. The other procedure gave the experimenter the choice. After the task, participants learned that they had failed to obtain the reward because of their performance on the task that counted. In the high referent conditions participants learned that they would have won if the other score had counted; in the low referent conditions, participants understood that they would have lost either way. The results, as shown in Figure 3, reveal the same interaction as in Figures 1 and 2.

Thus, RCT laboratory studies published as of 1989 yielded results entirely consistent with the causal counterfactual version of that model. The next section describes subsequent field studies that provide evidence of the model's generalizability. However, after presenting those data I will argue that certain aspects of the results imply the need to rethink the original RCT approach. In particular, some of the data may not be so readily interpretable as instances of causal counterfactuals. My review of these more recent data thus provides the occasion for presenting a revised version of RCT that can encompass both a causal counterfactual mechanism and another, more general, basis for predicting responses.

FIELD STUDIES SHOWING RCT EFFECTS

Recent field studies (Folger, Konovsky, & Brockner, 1990; see also Brockner, Konovsky, Cooper, and Folger, 1992) have examined an employee's own or a co-worker's job loss. The first study involved people contacted at unemployment offices who had been laid off from a variety of firms. Two other studies included layoff survivors from two different companies. The common element in all three studies was a focus on the factors that would predict negative reactions to layoffs. With different operationalizations, the three studies focused on the same two underlying factors: (a) variations in the severity of the loss, and (b) variations in the implementation of the layoffs.

The 218 participants in the first study had been recently laid off. Two questionnaire items tapped their desire for regulation by asking whether companies should be required by law to use methods other than layoffs to reduce their work force, and whether the country needs more laws protecting the rights of workers to keep their jobs. The data in Figure 4 show how those reactions varied as a function of outcome severity (i.e., benefits they had received in connection with the layoff—the level of severance pay, and the extension of life and medical insurance coverage) and the extent of advance notice the employer had given. The means reflect a Benefits × Notice interaction in which the strongest desire for regulation resulted from the combination of poor benefits and little advance notice (i.e., layoffs conducted in a harsher manner than they might otherwise have been handled). Poor outcomes led to increased preferences for regulation only when the company had provided little advance notice.

The questionnaire also asked how employers treated people when they were laid off. These items measured interactional justice (the term coined by Bies & Moag, 1986) by assessing the extent of kind, considerate treatment and careful, adequate explanations for the layoffs. As before (where advance notice constituted the process-related factor), people reacted significantly more negatively to low benefits only when interactional justice was relatively low (see Figure 5).

FIGURE 4   Condition Means for Respondents Grouped by Level of Benefits and Advance Notice

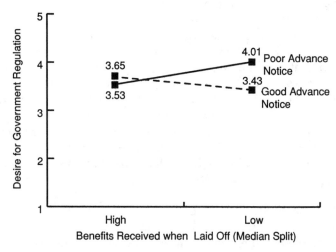

Note: Scores could range from 1 to 5; higher scores reflect a greater desire for governmental regulation of layoffs.

FIGURE 5   Condition Means for Respondents Grouped by Level of Benefits and Interactional Justice

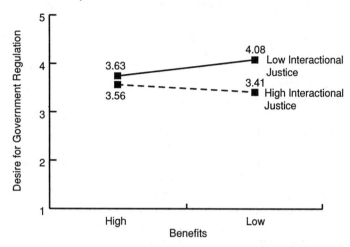

Note: Scores could range from 1 to 5; higher scores reflect a greater desire for governmental regulation of layoffs.

The second study (see Figure 6) surveyed 597 survivors of a recent layoff in a chain of small retail stores. They provided a retrospective self-report of the change in their organizational commitment (e.g., "I like working for this company"; "I am proud to tell my friends I work for this company") relative to what it had been before the layoffs. Again the study examined how reactions to the layoff would be affected by the severity of the loss and by the implementation of

FIGURE 6   Condition Means for Respondents Grouped by Outcome Negativity and Interactional Justice

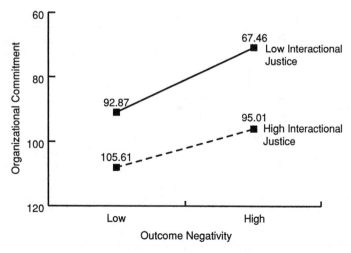

Note: Scores could range from 18 to 198; lower scores represent lower organizational commitment.

the layoff. Regarding the severity of the job loss, survivors were primed by being asked whether they agreed with a series of outcome-related statements (e.g., "The severance pay that the organization offered to the laid-off people was a generous amount"; "Management tried to help the laid-off people find a comparable job elsewhere in the organization"). Next came the outcome negativity assessment: "Suppose you were to be laid off. If so, how well do you think the assistance that management offered the laid-off people—severance pay, assistance finding comparable employment—would provide for your needs?" Respondents replied on a scale that ranged from "not at all" to "very much." They also answered items similar to those constituting the prior study's interactional justice index.

Figure 6 displays results that are similar to those from the first study, with additional effects for outcome negativity and interactional justice. The combination of conditions yielding the least organizational commitment—low interactional justice and low outcomes—bears a striking resemblance to the combination that produced the most negative reactions in our first field study. Once again, negative outcomes have a greater impact on employee reactions when layoffs are poorly administered.

A third study replicated the second with 150 full-time employees of a financial services company that had undergone layoffs 5 to 7 months earlier. Only the sample and operationalization were different. This time the outcome severity factor was objectively indexed by the proportion of employees who had lost their jobs within the organization's various subunits (which ranged from 6% to 40%). The results took the same general form. Notably, Figure 7 shows that organizational commitment did not vary when interactional justice was high but

FIGURE 7 Condition Means for Respondents Grouped by Layoff Severity and Interactional Justice

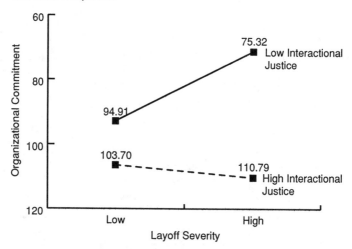

Note: Scores could range from 18 to 198; lower scores represent lower organizational commitment.

did when it was low. Again the most negative reaction to the layoffs occurred when interactional justice was low and the outcome was severely negative.

CONSOLIDATING THE FINDINGS AND EXPANDING THE FRAMEWORK

Because the field results show the same pattern as those from the lab studies, we might be able to consolidate them within a unified, parsimonious framework, using RCT as a starting point. The potential to capitalize on hindsight also presents a unique opportunity to expand and revise the framework. The emerging conceptualization has its roots in notions about obligations (i.e., duties and responsibilities). In particular, an important difference exists between *causal responsibility* and *moral obligation*. Causal responsibility means that a person's actions (or inaction) have contributed to producing a set of consequences. However, a person can be responsible for consequences in a strict sense of physical cause-and-effect but not be held morally accountable for any harmful effects. Others may conclude, for example, that although the person was a causal agent, she or he incurred no liability for the consequences and thus has no obligation to undertake restitution or related actions. Excuses and justifications, when deemed adequate, have precisely that effect—they absolve a person of a moral obligation to rectify harm even when causal responsibility cannot be denied.

Thus causal responsibility for harmful consequences entails a moral obligation to do something for the person harmed unless other considerations—such as superordinate justifications or mitigating circumstances—absolve the harmdoer. Even in the absence of causal responsibility, however, or when causal responsibility does not entail performing acts of restitution or rectification of harm, other types of moral obligations may still be implied; many follow the principle of not adding insult to injury. Students may deserve low grades, for example, and professors should not feel guilty about assigning low grades to students who deserve no better; nonetheless, professors ought to recognize a variety of obligations regarding issues such as privacy and confidentiality (some now protected by law), many of which reflect a duty to respect students' dignity and to avoid humiliating them publicly.

Consider how the following illustration relates to such moral obligations, whereas the RCT experiments focused more on causal responsibility in the sense of counterfactuals that mentally undo bad outcomes. Not long after Tom Landry had been fired as head football coach of the Dallas Cowboys, I met an avid fan who complained irately to me about the firing. He made it clear, however, that he thought Landry deserved to be fired. What incensed him was that Landry allegedly learned about his job loss by reading a newspaper account—the new owner of the team had not bothered to meet with Landry personally before releasing the news to the press. Although the fan was furious about the injustice of this action, Landry obviously would have been fired anyway: A change in the owner's behavior from misconduct to proper conduct (acting in a morally responsible manner by informing Landry personally) would not have changed the outcome Landry received—nor would the owner's causal responsibility for the outcome have changed. In contrast, participants in RCT experimental conditions that maximize resentment could say to themselves, "If only the experimenter's conduct had been different, I would have won." The experimenter *could* have been causally responsible for a *different* outcome—and *would* have, by acting in the appropriate, morally obligatory fashion (i.e., displaying the conduct that represents how a person *should* act under the circumstances).

In short, a difference exists between morally obligatory actions that have cause-and-effect consequences on exchange outcomes and those that do not. The broad category of moral obligation, which includes actions with or without causal implications for exchange outcomes, thus provides a more encompassing construct than causal responsibility. A close look at the measures used in the field studies suggests that they *do* cover a wider range of circumstances than the laboratory manipulations of RCT variables. This distinction becomes clearer after examining the two types of studies.

First consider the laboratory conditions—whether as a function of the procedure or the explanations provided—that reduced the experimenter's accountability for the student's outcome loss (i.e., made that loss not seem to have resulted from wrongdoing of the experimenter). Recall that in addition to referent outcomes, some aspect of the experimenter's conduct also was manipulated, thereby varying students' tendencies to exonerate the experimenter (via excuses, justifications, or differences in the procedure used to determine the outcomes). Regardless of the nature of that conduct, however, one distinctive feature was common to the conditions that involved an inadequate excuse, an insufficient justification, or an unfair procedure: When people were aware of a high referent outcome as an alternative, they not only realized that the experimenter's misconduct had led to their poor-by-comparison outcome, but also that better behavior on the part of the experimenter would have led to the better outcome. In other words, the experimenter was causally responsible for their poor outcome. Explanations of resentment based only on the laboratory evidence, therefore, might imply that negative reactions to an outcome loss occur *only* because mentally undoing a decision maker's conduct brings to mind thoughts about how better outcomes could have been a reality. This analysis limits RCT's explanatory power and potential generalizability by overemphasizing mechanisms of causal responsibility.

Evidence from the layoff studies also identifies limits to the original RCT formulation as a unifying framework. Consider, for example, the causal implications regarding advance notice for laid-off employees (see Figure 4, in which reactions to low benefits were more negative than reactions to high benefits only when employees received little advance notice). Although employees might consider the lack of advance notice to be employer misconduct, the absence of that particular form of misconduct (in a mental simulation of what would have happened if advance notice had been given) does not affect the outcome loss: Even in an alternatively imaginable scenario where advance notice might have been given, laid-off workers still would have lost their jobs.

The Landry example and the advance notice data suggest that when a severe loss coincides with adverse reactions toward a former employer, the employer's actions that trigger such employee reactions may have nothing to do with the causes of the outcome: Employees seem at least as concerned about whether management has met their moral obligations. By meeting those obligations, management tends to weaken connections between the negativity of an outcome and the negativity of the employees' reaction toward management.

Although only speculative, possible interpretations of the interactional justice items also support this analysis. Those items that referred to the adequacy of explanations have both causal and moral implications. Note that when employers lay off employees, notions about causal responsibility for layoffs can be ambiguous and subject to varying interpretations; even though employers might be regarded as causally responsible for the decision to implement layoffs, the need for such decisions might be linked to contributing factors such as a failing economy. The following possible interpretation of high scores on the explanation-related items of the interactional justice index, therefore, relies on a causal counterfactual mechanism: Employees accepted the excuses or justifications as legitimate and, in essence, agreed to believe that management responded to circumstances beyond its control or responded in the most correct manner under the circumstances.

An alternative or additional possibility, however, suggests that management could also have been seen as fulfilling a moral obligation by taking the time and trouble to provide adequate explanations and to articulate clearly the reasons for its actions. Employees (and others) might argue that employers who cause harm ought to explain why the harm was done. Employees who indicate that management provided an adequate explanation, therefore, might also believe that providing an adequate explanation fulfills some important moral obligations (not to add insult to injury). The absence or poor quality of explanations for harm might add the insult of poor or contemptuous treatment to a case of injury (e.g., job loss). Providing only the most perfunctory of explanations—or none at all—implies that an individual is insignificant and unworthy of respect. People feel obliged to explain their actions to those from whom they desire respect, those whose opinions matter, and those whose feelings they care about; with those so insignificant that we do not mind what they think, no such sense of obligation exists.

As an illustration of how explanations have implications for either causal responsibility, moral obligation, or both, consider layoffs by banks that have suffered from defaults on loans. If a bank's employees receive no explanation for layoffs, or an explanation that fails the test of adequacy, management has abandoned its moral obligation to say why the harm was done. At the same time, this lack of adequate explanation might imply that management was causally responsible, due possibly to a lack of business judgment that led to bad loans, or might suggest management's desire to avoid drawing attention to its causal responsibility for low-quality decision making.

Another interactional justice item, which referred to kind and considerate treatment, dealt the most directly with those moral obligations that are not related to undoing the counterfactuals of causal responsibility. As with the Landry example and the effects of advance notice, kindness and consideration have nothing to do with counterfactual variations in the causal events that preceded the layoffs. Whether managers show kindness and consideration or not, employees remain laid off.

Though the evidence can only be suggestive because survey items inevitably remain subject to more than one interpretation (and anecdotes about football coaches hardly count as conclusive evidence), the preceding discussion has raised enough questions to suggest the desirability of changes in the RCT framework. The original formulation still accounts for variations in perceived negativity and the severity of an outcome loss as a function of outcome-related influences on comparison standards (mental simulations of referent outcomes), but questions have been raised concerning the interpretation of the process-related factor. Referent cognitions theory's original description of process-related factors, which relied on an account of counterfactuals and "mental undoing," emphasized the instrumental nature of decision-making processes. Decision-making procedures help cause decisions: They are the means for determining outcome ends. The new view of process, however, includes actions that may have no effect on exchange outcomes (e.g., behavior after an allocation is finished) but nonetheless reflect important aspects of management conduct that can influence whether loss generates negative attitudes. The next section describes this second viewpoint in more detail and explores some of its implications.

TOWARD A DUAL-OBLIGATIONS MODEL

A remarkably consistent body of accumulated evidence (see Figures 1 through 7) suggests that two factors can predict when people will react most negatively to an outcome loss: the severity of the loss, and the inappropriateness of conduct by social agents in positions of authority (e.g., those whose decisions contributed to bringing about the loss). Previous descriptions of RCT (as well as the manipulations in RCT experiments) emphasized the means–ends relationship between a decision maker's conduct and the resulting outcomes. In contrast, a new version of RCT de-emphasizes the causal link between an agent in an authority role and the outcomes received by someone subject to that authority. This new version stresses the crucial elements that all interpersonal exchanges have in common—things being exchanged and persons doing the exchanging—rather than the causal role of the social agent who acts as decision maker.

The revision of RCT identifies things being exchanged as the first (outcome-related) factor of a two-factor model. The second (process-related) factor—the agent's role—requires greater attention in an expanded approach that focuses on the obligations of that role. I contend that in the context of employment, the agent's moral obligations toward the employee entail more than fair treatment with respect to the wages and benefits given in exchange for labor, and more than fair treatment with respect to the implementation of policies and procedures that determine those levels of compensation. In addition, a moral obligation exists to treat the employee with sufficient dignity as a person; doing so entails numerous aspects of conduct beyond those regarding compensation as ends or decision-making procedures as means to those ends. Rather, *all* aspects of the agent's conduct, whether or not they have a direct bearing on employee compensation or the means for determining compensation, can carry implicit messages about whether the agent views the employee as someone worthy of that minimal level of respect to which all humans should be entitled.

An employee's outcome loss will be seen as having come *from* this agent in some sense—especially because status and power differentials imply that the agent, by being in a position of greater responsibility, assumes more responsibility for decisions. Accountability characteristically goes along with responsibility, thus calling for consideration of the agent's *conduct*. Agents cannot act capriciously. Their role goes beyond their obligations for making and implementing decisions. Yet because of the natural link between processes and outcomes as means and ends, the literature on procedural justice—including RCT material—has focused primarily on the cause-and-effect aspects of the agent/process association (cf. process *control* vs. decision *control*; Thibaut & Walker, 1975).

Apart from their role in making decisions, managers may engage in a number of decision-related actions. Some managers may notify employees that a decision is about to be made; others may reveal nothing about the process until it is a *fait accompli*. After their decisions, some managers inform people affected by it immediately; others delay as long as possible; and some fail to communicate the decision at all. A distinction between outcome and conduct (rather than between outcome and process) more fruitfully captures the important aspects of things-being-exchanged and people-doing-the-exchanging. The differentiation of conduct from process emphasizes that an agent's conduct involves more than the process determining how much another person receives in an exchange. During an exchange relationship, conduct can convey messages about respect for an individual in a variety of ways; some conduct may have little to do directly with the things being exchanged or how the amounts to be exchanged will be determined.

Thus, one person's feeling about another is communicated in two ways, each with a set of moral obligations:

1. Some messages are communicated implicitly by the outcomes that are exchanged. When outcomes fall below what someone feels he or she deserved, the discrepancy may be viewed as a sign of disrespect, or worse. Outcome losses imply one form of unfulfilled obligations.
2. Messages are also conveyed by the decision-making procedure (e.g., timeliness, considerateness); here, too, affronts to human dignity can represent unfulfilled moral obligations.

Clearly, theories of organizational justice should incorporate each message and each set of implied obligations. Just as interpersonal exchanges by definition involve *people* (exchanging) and *things* (being exchanged), reactions to an exchange will be influenced by feelings about the outcome and the person from whom it was received. Furthermore, the nature of those feelings will tend to interact with one another: Models of justice should no longer treat the constructs of procedural and distributive justice as categories so distinct that their mutual influence on one another is overlooked.

A revision of RCT can begin by distinguishing between the impact of outcome-related and person-related factors:

1. Variations in the *things* exchanged influence not only whether the exchange is viewed as a loss, but also the severity of that loss. The variation in severity is perceptual, not objective, and reflects relative rather than absolute deprivation. The hedonic quality of the subjective loss experience, in other words, stems from whatever brings to mind some imaginable alternative outcome, as well as whether that referent outcome seems better than the one actually received.

2. Variations in interpersonal conduct influence perceptions about a given *person* associated with the outcome received (normally the exchange partner or that person's agent—such as a manager who acts as agent for an employer). We might assume that the stronger the negative feelings about the outcome, the stronger the negative feelings about a person associated with that outcome, but being upset about an outcome does not automatically entail being upset with the person who provided it, especially if that person's conduct fulfilled all expected moral obligations (e.g., honesty, integrity). Expressing moral outrage against individuals who have fulfilled their moral obligations is, surely, a socially unacceptable practice or at least highly questionable behavior.

Outcome negativity, therefore, is a necessary but not a sufficient condition for feelings of hostility expressed toward a person (as opposed to mere dissatisfaction expressed about a thing). The severity or negativity of an outcome loss provides evidence about the extent of exploitation; the exchange conduct indicates whether a person who is associated with a negative outcome should be exonerated or vilified, which depends on whether he or she fulfills moral obligations for correct conduct. Evidence about possible exploitation regarding outcome deprivation may be influenced by evidence about the morality (or social acceptability) of the suspected exploiter's conduct; the suspicion of outcome exploitation might in some sense be confirmed by indications that the person's other conduct is untoward. When a person's overall conduct is above reproach, doubt is cast on the suspicion that the outcome deprivation was exploitative.

This explanation focuses on the perceptions and interpretations of conduct as the key ingredient influencing whether negative outcomes translate into negative reactions toward an exchange partner or agent. Conduct governs a perceptual adhesive process: It can bind a not-so-good person to a bad outcome, or it can sever that link. Thus an exonerated exchange partner—dissociated from an outcome loss by means of virtuous, exemplary, or at least socially acceptable conduct and by acceptable fulfillment of moral obligations—may not necessarily be the focus of reactions that are more negative as the outcome loss becomes more severe. The partner whose conduct fails to exonerate, on the other hand, will be resented to suffer in direct proportion to the amount of damage done.

RELATIONSHIPS TO OTHER APPROACHES

This approach (see also Cropanzano & Folger, 1990) differs in certain respects from others. It broadens RCT's conceptual base by reducing the significance of causal actions by the alleged harmdoer. Exonerating behaviors (ethically responsive and socially desirable) that have no causal implications for outcomes (e.g., advance notice, apologies, timely information, courteousness, considerateness, honesty, and the like; cf. Folger & Bies, 1989) can keep the decision maker from being a target of resentment that increases as the perceived severity of the outcome loss increases. In other respects, however, the chief difference between this revision of RCT and alternative approaches is the greater parsimony of the former.

For example, this new approach draws from many recent sources that have emphasized the importance of impression-management concerns on the part of a putative harmdoer (e.g., Bies, 1987; Greenberg, 1990). These perspectives identify useful distinctions among actions that contribute to the sense of being treated unfairly (e.g., distributive, procedural, or interactional injustice), as well as useful distinctions among actions within each category of justice (e.g., excuses vs. justifications vs. apologies). The new approach suggests a parsimonious synthesis in highlighting the functional equivalence of actions that produce similar responses.

Space limitations permit only a brief discussion of one distinction between the RCT revision and the recent *group-value model* (Lind & Tyler, 1988; Tyler, 1989). As its name implies, the group-value model asserts that perceptions of fair treatment depend on a group context (although the model also contains other features). In particular, outcomes can connote one's standing in a group. More parsimoniously, however, standing can be an issue in any interpersonal exchange, including strictly dyadic single encounters between strangers. Although it would be impossible to ensure that a meeting between two strangers was not influenced by norms imported to that situation from each person's experience in groups beyond the dyad, if the *outcome* from that exchange will be unknown by a person's membership groups, then the standing in those groups is unaffected. What seems critical is the person's standing in the eyes of the other person (the partner in the dyadic exchange) at the time.

Even when we assert that the person wants his or her standing in the eyes of the partner to be commensurate with the standing achieved in primary groups, the invoking of "group values" represents some additional theoretical baggage I view as unnecessary from the current perspective. Deriving justice principles from an understanding about the basic nature of exchange thus seems more accurate than having to rely on the context of group values. Although groups have their own peculiar culture, historical past, and prospects for future involvement, a one-time-only exchange with a perfect stranger could have its fairness assessed on the basis of the two types of considerations (quality of the outcome and quality of the other's conduct) identified by the dual-obligations approach. For example, people who unknowingly buy merchandise that turns out to be shoddy can feel cheated by a merchant (i.e., will be dissatisfied with an outcome) without being a member of the merchant's "group" or thinking that the merchant will ever be seen again (i.e., will never become a member of one's own group). In the case of conduct, a merchant's behavior can be insulting without necessarily invoking any particular group context (e.g., if requests for assistance are rudely refused and completion of the transaction is needlessly delayed even though the customer is in a hurry).

In sum, the nature of exchange itself helps to identify why two very fundamental considerations—a perception of the things received in exchange (outcome) and a perception of the person with whom one is in an exchange relationship (conduct)—guide people's reactions in the aftermath of any exchange. The next section discusses some possible new directions for research and theorizing that take into account such considerations.

AN ADDITIONAL REACTION TO EMPLOYMENT EXCHANGE: ACHIEVEMENT STRIVING

This chapter has focused on negative reactions to outcome losses in an employment exchange, limiting discussion to a single potential reaction. The models presented here do not yet address reactions to exchange in general. Even in the restricted case of outcome losses, however, some prospects exist for an expanded treatment addressing other types of reactions. Achievement striving, for example, is another possible reaction to the frustration of a loss or unattained outcome: "If at first you don't succeed—try, try again." Achievement striving might accompany resentment under some circumstances, when a resentful person says "I'll show them" and then strives to prove that his or her loss was undeserved.

For example, Marris (1975) studied the emergence of small-scale industries in Kenya after independence. Many of the Kenyan men who became entrepreneurs had fought in the Independence movement and afterwards sought other "means of furthering economic development and national [economic] independence" (p. 114). The Kenyan career structure was tied closely to educational attainment, however, and their education did not match their aspirations: "Unlike the senior servants or political leaders with whom they identified, they were debarred from responsible and interesting work. . . . [and] excluded from careers which might have satisfied their desire to do something important and influential in their own eyes" (p. 114). These businessmen "compared themselves with the political and administrative elite, and felt deeply frustrated" (p. 113). Thus, Marris identified relative deprivation as a source that motivated their entrepreneurship. Similar experiences might motivate increased entrepreneurial activity by women, blacks, or other groups who feel disenfranchised by obstructions that restrict advancement in the world of work and are difficult to prove (i.e., a "glass ceiling").

Another example comes from a venture capitalist's account of the typical circumstances that led entrepreneurially inclined people to quit their jobs and start their own companies (Silver, 1983):

> [The] archetypal individual had been hired, he believed, for his creative potential, and was rewarded, he believed, for his creative contributions. . . . [but] as he became more energetic and needed increasing latitude . . . , the organization's commitment . . . and its willingness to invest in [him] . . . emerged as less than he wanted, less than he expected. . . . The workplace has not been satisfying, . . . and hasn't rewarded what he most respects in himself; the not-yet-active entrepreneur has put in a lot of time and has tried to contribute his best. He has become dissatisfied and to some extent disillusioned. . . . *Nevertheless,* though he resents the system, . . . *the true entrepreneur does not feel victimized.* (pp. 28–29, emphasis in original)

The experience of resentment-without-victimization obviously needs exploration as a possible reaction to outcome losses. Silver (1983) also suggested that outcome losses or perceived deprivation threatening self-esteem may be as motivating as slights and affronts whose insulting character drives a desire for revenge. Rather than saying "don't get mad, get even," people experiencing losses may say "I'll show them what I'm really worth."

Achievement striving accompanied by resentment-without-victimization provides an example of how reactions are directed toward the employer or agents of the employer (i.e., resentment as an emotion with a social target, feelings directed toward someone else). However, when people say "I really don't deserve anything this bad," the comment may refer to the nature of the outcome loss rather than to the conduct of another person. When circumstances do not involve misconduct by another person (i.e., other people's conduct was sufficiently legitimate, exonerating, and the like), what one "really deserves" functions as a high referent outcome that may not yield social resentment. People may even speak of having resentment or feeling resentful under such circumstances, but we should be clear that they do not mean resentment with a social agent as a target. For example, a runner who has trained hard and feels completely superior may in some sense feel "cheated" by not winning even when a loss is caused by tripping over his or her own shoelace. Notably, this runner need not resent the athletic association that sanctioned the competition nor the officials who implemented the procedures for conducting the race. The runner can still feel "resentful" (in the secondary sense noted earlier) without feeling victimized if losing a single race represents a minor setback—as when the pursuit of an Olympic gold medal remains intact despite the loss of one race during the years prior to the next Olympiad. Such examples affirm the importance of the exchange partners' conduct in the causal sense originally emphasized by RCT: People who scrupulously maintain fair systems for competition, after all, provide athletes with the best means for attaining their desired ends.

In the case of a frustrated, would-be entrepreneur, similar considerations apply. Leaving an employer to found one's own firm signifies that an outcome loss has not produced helplessness and despair. Instead it reflects a confidence in the fairness of the "tournament" (i.e., economic competition in the marketplace) along with a sense of hope for the future as a function of the chance to play in that fair tournament (cf. the "likelihood of amelioration" factor in the original RCT model). The fair conduct of the system, therefore, prevents *resentment* from being accompanied by the sense of *victimization*.

At the same time, an employer's conduct remains an important source of influence over an employee's achievement-oriented efforts because of its means–ends and moral obligations implications. Just as a runner can lose a race and not lose the desire to compete again, employees who suffer loss in the workplace (e.g., a missed promotion) need not turn against their employers in revenge nor seek to found their own businesses to accomplish desired ends. If employees perceive that their employer's conduct observes moral obligations for exchange outcomes by using fair policies and procedures to allocate rewards, they are less likely to seek alternatives outside the organization after a single instance of less-than-desired outcomes. Employers who observe the moral obligation of treating employees with dignity and respect will presumably earn added loyalty from their employees as well. Meeting both moral obligations—fair policies and dignified treatment—represents the greatest chance employers have to harness employees' entrepreneurial drives in the service of the firm.

In addition, fulfilled moral obligations can help distinguish between employees who will leave an employer and seek revenge through competition—and those who leave on better terms. Many new entrepreneurs do not shift industries. Indeed, some ex-employees work hand-in-glove with their previous employers; others go into ventures that serve a related consumer need but do not compete directly. Trends in downsizing will continue to displace large numbers of employees; some will start their own ventures. Potential new ventures represent another reason for employers to understand how their handling of a layoff can lead to differences in the extent of resentment experienced by ex-employees.

CONCLUDING THOUGHTS ABOUT DUAL OBLIGATIONS

The development of this new perspective, a revision of RCT, represents work in progress. Although couched in a form consistent with existing data, the present approach more broadly points to the overall importance of recognizing that different kinds of obligations exist.

Management representatives, as agents of the employer, can be said to have two broad categories of social obligations to employees: Fair policies and dignified treatment. These obligations have a social character that distinguishes them from the legal character of formal contractual obligations and reflects their grounding in social reality. A dual-obligations approach describes obligations from the perspective of employees or other citizens not employed by a given firm; it does not take the employer's perspective (i.e., employee reactions are determined by employee perceptions of an employer's obligations rather than by the employer's interpretation of those obligations. Managers, as agents of the employer, may or may not feel any sense of obligation of the type described by a dual-obligations model).

I would argue that employers are morally obligated to their employees as contributors of labor; in other words, the employee represents a *means* whereby the employer transforms capital and raw materials into goods and services. Exchange *partners* represent the *means* whereby interpersonal exchanges can take place; in the absence of a partner exchange, no exchange can occur. A potential partner needs an incentive or inducement to become an actual partner (i.e., compensation for participating in the exchange). The first social obligation, then, involves the duty to compensate an exchange partner when that partner has become the means whereby an exchange can take place. The shorthand label, *means* obligation, serves as a reminder of duties and responsibilities (such as not reneging on promised inducements or not failing to provide fair value in return) toward the exchange partner, who is considered only as a means to the ends of conducting the exchange (i.e., allowing an exchange for the sake of obtaining something that a person desired to receive-in-return from the exchange partner).

Although treating others *only* as means and never as ends-in-themselves implies exploitation, economic relations—such as the employment exchange—possess inherent features that can contribute to the perception that exploitation is permitted or even encouraged. Firms, just as people, profit from buying cheap and selling dear. Buying labor at the lowest possible price, therefore, only makes good business sense—a point that employers might expect employees to understand: After all, the market system of capitalism has, since the days of Adam Smith, been characterized as one in which unfettered individual self-interest can nonetheless work toward collective betterment (self-interest working as an "invisible hand" over time).

By fulfilling only its means obligations, management places itself precariously at the mercy of an inherent ambivalence in the eyes of employees and other citizens. Although socially sanctioned and culturally approved in capitalist systems, when management treats employees only as means to the ends of sustaining employment exchanges sufficient for the maximization of profit (i.e., keeping enough employees on the job at minimal cost), it runs the risk of alienating employees and causing them to think only in terms of *their* self-interest (treating the employer as means). Employees' self-interests, of course, focus on the outcomes they receive from the exchange, such as wages, promotions, and benefits. When management fulfills only its means obligations, its actions may foster tendencies for employees to react toward management and the organization solely on the basis of outcomes received. Under such circumstances, outcome losses can evoke hostility toward management and the organization, and the extent of the hostility would tend to vary as a function of the perceived severity of the loss (a reversal of means-based exchange reciprocity).

A dual-obligations orientation, however, stresses that employees (and observers of the employment exchange) expect to find more than means obligations being fulfilled by management. A second category of obligations exists, concerning the duty to treat people as ends-in-themselves. Both categories pertain to perceptions about organizational justice and fair treatment, as illustrated by their similarity to two broad categories within moral philosophy: teleological and deontological ethics. Teleological ethics seek to find the highest moral good in social ends such as the utilitarian maximization of collective welfare; individuals represent the means to such ends (by conducting the exchanges that allow Smith's "invisible hand" to operate). Deontological ethics, on the other hand, emphasize duties and obligations as ends-in-themselves (cf. Kant's categorical imperative, reflecting a translation of golden-rule principles for treating people as ends in themselves). Thus, though treating people as ends-in-themselves can involve relatively simple actions (e.g., courtesy and civility), those actions reinforce feelings of self-respect, dignity, and worth that are essential to the belief that one has been treated as a person rather than as a thing. Being treated *only* as a thing is an "insult" (to use a word from the definition of *resentment*) that becomes intolerable when added to the "injury" of an outcome loss.

Grounded in fundamental distinctions in ethics and in fundamental aspects of the exchange process itself, a dual-obligations approach seems to offer considerable promise for integrating and synthesizing a broad range of justice phenomena. Just as data from lab and field studies have converged to reveal a common form of interaction, this new approach suggests that various justice-related phenomena can be traced to the common roots of two types of obligations. Beyond the predictive value of a theory that can account for the particular form of interaction seen in Figures 1 through 7, the ultimate heuristic value of this new perspective may lie in exploring further implications of these two most basic reasons people may come to feel mistreated: (a) not receiving things (a respectable amount from an exchange) and (b) being treated as things (rather than feeling respected as humans and individuals).

REFERENCES

ADAMS, J. S. (1965). Inequity in social exchange. In L. Berkowitz (Ed.), *Advances in experimental social psychology*, (Vol. 2, pp. 267–299). New York: Academic Press.

BIES, R. J. (1987). The predicament of injustice: The management of moral outrage. In L. L. Cummings & B. M. Staw (Eds.), *Research in organizational behavior* (Vol. 9, pp. 289–319). Greenwich, CT: JAI Press.

BIES, R. J., & MOAG, J. S. (1986). Interactional justice: Communication criteria of fairness. In R. J. Lewicki, B. H. Sheppard, & B. H. Bazerman (Eds.), *Research on negotiation in organizations* (Vol. 1, pp. 43–55). Greenwich, CT: JAI Press.

BROCKNER, J., KONOVSKY, M. A., COOPER, R., FOLGER, R. (1992). The interactive effects of procedural justice and outcome negativity on victims and survivors of job loss.

CROPANZANO, R., & FOLGER, R. (1989). Referent cognitions and task decision autonomy: Beyond equity theory. *Journal of Applied Psychology, 74,* 293–299.

CROPANZANO, R., & FOLGER, R. (1990). Procedural justice and worker motivation. In R. Steers & L. Porter (Eds.), *Motivation and work behavior* (5th ed., pp. 131–143). New York: McGraw-Hill.

FOLGER, R., (1987). Reformulating the preconditions of resentment: A referent cognitions model. In J. C. Masters & W. P. Smith (Eds.), *Social comparison, justice, and relative deprivation* (pp. 183–215). Hillsdale, NJ: Erlbaum.

FOLGER, R., & BIES, R. J. (1989). Managerial responsibilities and procedural justice. *Employee Responsibilities and Rights Journal, 2,* 79–90.

FOLGER, R., & GREENBERG, J. (1985). Procedural justice: An interpretive analysis of personnel systems. In K. Rowland & G. Ferris (Eds.), *Research in personnel and human resources management* (Vol. 3, pp. 141–183). Greenwich, CT: JAI Press.

FOLGER, R., KONOVSKY, M. A., & BROCKNER, J. (1990, August). *A dual-component view of responses to injustice.* Presented at the National Academy of Management meetings, San Francisco, CA.

FOLGER, R., & MARTIN, C. (1986). Relative deprivation and referent cognitions: Distributive and procedural justice effects. *Journal of Experimental Social Psychology, 22,* 531–546.

FOLGER, R., ROSENFIELD, D., & ROBINSON, T. (1983). Relative deprivation and procedural justifications. *Journal of Personality and Social Psychology, 45,* 268–273.

GREENBERG, J. (1990). Organizational justice: Yesterday, today, and tomorrow. *Journal of Management, 16,* 399–432.

GREENBERG, J., & FOLGER, R. (1983). Procedural justice, participation, and the fair process effect in groups and organizations. In P. B. Paulus (Ed.), *Basic group processes* (pp. 235–256). New York: Springer-Verlag.

LIND, E. A., & TYLER, T. (1988). *The social psychology of procedural justice.* New York: Plenum.

MARRIS, P. (1975). *Loss and change.* Garden City, NY: Anchor Press.

SILVER, A. D. (1983). *The entrepreneurial life.* New York: John Wiley & Sons.

THIBAUT, J., & WALKER, L. (1975). *Procedural justice: A psychological analysis.* Hillsdale, NJ: Erlbaum.

TYLER, T. R. (1989). The psychology of procedural justice: A test of the group-value model. *Journal of Personality and Social Psychology, 57,* 830–838.

CHAPTER NINE

Fairness, Social Comparison, and Irrationality*

Max H. Bazerman

Northwestern University

The majority of research on fairness has focused on decisions concerning the distribution of scarce resources and the fairness of procedures for distributing scarce resources (Adams, 1963; Lind & Tyler, 1988; Thibaut & Walker, 1975). Most of this literature examines the objective nature of the distribution or actual procedures used. However, fairness is not an objective state. It is a judgment. This chapter examines how fairness judgments and social comparison processes account for the lack of explanatory power of economic models. Specifically, this chapter shows that judgments involving social comparisons deviate from the tenets of formal economic models, lead to inefficient outcomes, and create inconsistencies in decision preferences. Empirical research documenting these arguments is provided, and the implications for organizations are developed.

. . . Russians are long-suffering people who can bear misery, so long as they see others are sharing it. But let someone become better off—even if it is through his own honest labor—and the collective jealousy can be fierce.

. . . I came to see the great mass of Soviet people as protagonists in what I call the culture of envy—corrosive animosity that took root under the Czars in the deep-seated collectivism in Russian life and then was accentuated by Leninist ideology.

. . . what is ominous for Gorbachev's reforms is that this free-floating anger of the rank and file often settles on anyone who rises above the crowd. This hostility is a serious danger to the new entrepreneurs Gorbachev is trying to nurture. It is a deterrent to modest initiative among ordinary people in factories or on farms. It freezes that vast majority into the immobility of conforming to group attitudes.

*This chapter was supported by the Dispute Resolution Research Center at Northwestern University. Many of the ideas herein were developed in collaboration with a number of coauthors. Sally White and George Loewenstein have been especially central to research overviewed in this chapter. The extensive comments of Terry Boles, Joel Brockner, Claire Buisseret, Rob Folger, Pam Jiranek, Rod Kramer, Maggie Neale, and Tom Tyler have significantly improved the quality of this chapter.

. . . I heard of a farmer outside of Moscow whose horse and few cows were set free and whose barn was set afire by neighboring farm workers jealous of his modest prosperity.

. . . they are so jealous of other people that they want others to be worse off, if need be, to keep things equal.

. . . Nikolai Shmelvov, the radical economic reformer, has called this the syndrome of "equal poverty for all."

. . . Anatoly A. Sobchak (Mayor of Leningrad) said: "Changing that psychology is the hardest part of our economic reform. That psychology of intolerance toward others who make more money, no matter why, no matter whether they work harder, longer or better—that psychology is blocking economic reform."

. . . in the west, if an American sees someone on TV with a shiny new car, he will think "Oh, maybe I can get that someday for myself." But if a Russian sees that, he will think, "This bastard with his car. I would like to kill him for living better than I do."

> "The Russian Character," Hedrick Smith,
> *New York Times Magazine,* October 28, 1990

In these quotes, Hedrick Smith captures the dysfunctional aspects of social comparison. Invidious social comparisons create a barrier to economic development. Social comparisons can also create unhappiness, anger, inefficiency, missed opportunities, and dysfunctional conflict (Salovey, 1991). Smith's quotes capture much of what this chapter is about. Yet I disagree with Smith's implicit cross-cultural comparison and argue that the pattern of jealousy he describes is more universal. This chapter explores the common patterns of irrationality in how we make judgments of fairness via social comparisons.

The following story illustrates such irrational jealousy in academia:

> A subgroup of a department raised a significant amount of money for a research center. This money made the department financially better off; scarce resources no longer needed to cover the research expenses of the subgroup. In addition, the research center paid for a number of joint capital expenditures (fax machine, copying equipment, etc.). Overall, the research center made everyone objectively better off, but some were made better off than others. This led to anger and unhappiness among members of the department (faculty and doctoral students) not in the research center. The greater outcomes of the doctoral students and faculty members who worked in the center became the arbitrary basis for comparison. The extra resources did not make the department a happier place. Rather, jealousy and dysfunctional conflict followed.

In this story, dysfunctional consequences result from the differences in outcomes to organizational members. The center objectively improved everyone's resources. Yet many doctoral students and faculty who were not part of the center felt discriminated against. They perceived that their quality of life was worse because of the research center. They constantly compared what they received, not to an objective standard, past levels of support, or to what students or faculty received at other universities, but to the outcomes of those who were part of the research center. These social comparisons created anger, dysfunctional conflict, and perceptions of unfairness.

A number of authors have argued that fairness considerations account for the lack of explanatory power in economic models (Kahneman, Knetsch, & Thaler, 1987). Akerlof (1970) and Solow (1980) posit that fairness considerations inhibit employers from cutting wages during periods of high unemployment, despite changes in supply and demand. Okun (1981) has made similar arguments about the lack of price adjustment in the consumer domain.

Concerns for fairness have also been central to several theories in social psychology and organizational behavior. The majority of the behavioral research on fairness has focused on either the distribution of scarce resources (Adams, 1965; Messick, 1991; Rawls, 1971) or the fairness of the distribution procedures (Adams, 1963; Lind & Tyler, 1988; Thibaut & Walker, 1975).

In contrast to research on distributive and procedural justice, this chapter explores a new direction in the study of fairness and irrationality. I argue that neither distributive nor procedural fairness operates as an objective state. Rather, systematic and perverse characteristics of how we assess competitive environments—independent of the reality of procedures and the distribution of resources—create our perceptions of (un)fairness. This chapter develops a social cognitive model of how individuals evaluate fairness.

There have been other discussions concerning how judgments of fairness are inconsistent with rational action. Kahneman et al. (1987) demonstrate that social norms often dominate economically rational assessments in evaluations of fairness. Guth, Schmittberger, and Schwarze (1982) show that fairness considerations are important enough that individuals will reduce their own outcome state to maintain fairness. Similar arguments have been made about the level of effort provided by employees (Lawler, 1971). Fairness considerations lead to systematic departures from the predictions of economic models. This chapter provides an integrated assessment of how the social psychological influences of fairness considerations change individual behavior.

Fairness is not a value-free topic. Thus, I begin this chapter by discussing the values that I bring to this topic. Next, I provide a set of definitions of rational behavior and clarify why it is disadvantageous for individuals to act out of concerns for fairness that deviate from rationality. I then review a number of research streams that clarify how fairness considerations lead to systematic departures from rational action. Finally, I discuss the implications of these deviations from rationality for managing organizations more effectively.

MY RESEARCH VALUES

My past research fits with the theme of this volume in that it offers a social (and cognitive) psychological perspective to a topic relevant to organizations. Yet my research on decision making and negotiation departs in many ways from most micro organizational behavior research (cf. Bazerman, 1990; Neale and Bazerman, 1991). The perspective of fairness developed in this chapter is consistent with my earlier research on negotiation and is best understood within the context of my research values and assumptions. Thus, I try to specify these assumptions before presenting a behavioral decision perspective to fairness.

An overarching value that has guided my research is that research models should connect descriptive research to prescriptive and normative research. Behavioral researchers often make insupportable inferential leaps when we convert descriptive knowledge into advice. Our more analytical colleagues often make the reverse mistake, failing to realize that their false assumptions (typically about rationality) limit the power of their prescriptions. I hope that the four specific values and assumptions that have guided my research, which I discuss next, help me avoid these errors.

1. RESEARCH SHOULD ATTEMPT TO UNDERSTAND THE WORLD AS IT IS, NOT AS WE WOULD LIKE IT TO BE OR THINK THAT IT SHOULD BE.   Many researchers give advice based on insupportable assumptions. For example, economics is often distinguished from the other social sciences by the basic theoretical assumption that people have stable, well-defined preferences and make choices that are consistent with them. A central tenet of almost all economics is that a person will choose the course of action that maximizes his or her expected utility (Nash, 1950). Expected utility represents the transformation of psychological and material preferences into hypothetical units of outcome, which can be measured ordinally. Economists do not specify how this transformation is made: They contend simply that it can be made and, once it is, economists study how individuals can make optimal choices in complex decision environments.

In negotiations research, game theorists analyze games (negotiated, outcome-oriented interactions) by defining the specific conditions that constrain the interaction, such as the number of times that the players get to make offers and the exact order in which the players choose (Myerson, 1991; Shubik, 1984). Utility measures for the outcomes of each player are then attached to every possible combination of players' choices. Axiomatic analyses focus on predicting whether an agreement will be reached and, if one is reached, what its specific nature will be. Game theory's model of goal-oriented, fully informed, rational behavior has been the dominant economic theory of negotiation for almost a half century (Myerson, 1991; von Neumann & Morgenstern, 1947). While game theory has provided powerful analytic tools, catalyzed a vast amount of theoretical and empirical research, and provided many valid qualitative predictions, its basic approach (and that of much of theoretical economics) has been to study individuals as rationality suggests that they should behave, rather than as they actually do.

Many behavioral scientists also offer advice based on a set of normative values instead of the descriptive realities that organizational members face. Organizational development, for example, often gives advice based on the set of normative values that underlie the field (e.g., openness, participation, collectivism) rather than empirical evidence or a logical set of inferences. Similarly,

Fisher and Ury's (1981) *Getting to YES* is based on a set of beliefs, not a theoretical or empirical analysis. Ten years after its publication, no systematic empirical support exists for the book's ideas. Clearly, models of human behavior that involve two or more parties should start with a realistic, descriptive understanding of the behavior of individuals. Thus, a model of fairness and social comparison must first describe how individuals actually assess fairness.

2. DESCRIPTIVE RESEARCH IS STRENGTHENED BY A NORMATIVE BENCHMARK. While the accuracy of economic models is limited by their assumptions, such prescriptive and normative models can improve descriptive models by providing a goal and benchmark to evaluate actual performance (Bazerman & Neale, 1991, 1992; Kahneman, 1991). By having such a goal, the task of identifying behaviors that are inconsistent with the goal and developing prescriptions to counter dysfunctional limitations becomes more concrete. The most powerful descriptions need a normative anchor to provide a clear specification of the deficiencies and necessary corrections in the actual decisions and behaviors of individuals. This chapter defines rationality concretely so that irrational deviations resulting from fairness concerns can be clearly identified.

3. DESCRIPTIVE WORK CAN BE A POWERFUL TOOL FOR IMPROVING PRESCRIPTIONS. In interpersonal contexts, the optimal decision of one party is contingent on the decisions of other parties. Optimal system intervention or advice to one party is dependent on others' actions. When negotiating, Raiffa (1982) tells us that we must consider the actual, not necessarily rational, decisions of the other side. Much of the work of the negotiation group at Northwestern has focused on how negotiator judgment systematically deviates from rationality. Research on two-party negotiations suggests that negotiators tend to be inappropriately affected by the positive or negative frame in which risks are viewed (Bazerman, Magliozzi, & Neale, 1985; Neale & Bazerman, 1985); that they anchor their numerical estimates in negotiations on irrelevant information (Northcraft & Neale, 1987; Tversky & Kahneman, 1974); that they overrely on readily available information (Neale, 1984); and that they are overconfident about the likelihood of attaining favorable outcomes (Bazerman & Neale, 1982; Neale & Bazerman, 1985). In addition, negotiators assume that negotiation tasks are necessarily fixed-sum and thereby miss opportunities for mutually beneficial tradeoffs between the parties (Bazerman et al., 1985), escalate commitment to a previously selected course of action when it is no longer the most reasonable alternative (Bazerman & Neale, 1992), and overlook the valuable information that is available by considering the opponent's cognitive perspective (Bazerman & Carroll, 1987; Samuelson & Bazerman, 1985).

Understanding these pitfalls can facilitate the attainment of desired objectives and improve organizations (Bazerman, 1990; Dawes, 1988; Kahneman & Tversky, 1979; Tversky & Kahneman, 1974). One goal of highlighting irrationality in fairness and social comparison decisions is to help individuals and organizations move to a more preferred state. Descriptive research provides necessary information on impediments to an individual's attempts to follow rational courses of action. Thus, in judgments of fairness, better descriptions of actual judgments can improve training and contribute to systems that encourage individuals to make decisions that make themselves and society better off.

Ample evidence suggests that individuals fail to think carefully about the decisions of other parties even when it is in their interest to do so (Ball, Bazerman, & Carroll, 1991; Bazerman & Carroll, 1987; Samuelson & Bazerman, 1985). Most of the research in the social psychology of organizations is focused on the actions of the focal actor. When others are included in conceptual frameworks, they often play a passive or static role. As a result, many opportunities are lost. Descriptive work on interpersonal contexts can identify expected deviations from rationality in others' behaviors, improving the predictions generated by a purely rational analysis.

I argue that considering how others think about fairness and social comparison is essential to acting more rationally. One limitation of the existing justice literature is that it develops from a logical assessment of what should be seen as just and fair. However, insufficient attention has been given to the psychological processes of the recipients of an allocation as they cognitively assess the fairness of the action. Thus, researchers, like competitive decision makers, have given insufficient attention to the decisions of other parties.

4. DECISIONS OFFER POWERFUL LEVERAGE FOR CHANGING INDIVIDUAL BEHAVIOR IN ORGANIZATIONS.   Although the last decade has been described as the era of the cognitive revolution (Gardner, 1985; Ilgen & Klein, 1989), the field of organizational behavior may be only beginning to feel its impact. This field should care about cognition since decisions are the key mechanism by which members affect the organization. It is through decisions that organizational members enact the organizations that permeate our lives (Weick, this volume).

A central debate in the social psychology of organizations has been whether stable individual differences or situations are the primary determinant of behaviors in organizations (Chatman, 1989; Davis–Blake & Pfeffer, 1989; Staw, Bell, & Claussen, 1986; Staw & Ross, 1985). But both individuals' characteristics and the structure of the situation are relatively fixed. The greatest opportunity to influence organizational behaviors may lie in training members to make more rational decisions. While decisions can be conceptualized as either an individual difference variable or the result of the situation, I argue that the person–situation debate has hidden the decision perspective from the organizational arena. Thus, this chapter approaches fairness and social comparison as social psychological decisions that people make within organizations.

WHAT CAN BE IRRATIONAL ABOUT A JUDGMENT OF FAIRNESS?

Fairness is a perception. We are all entitled to our judgments about what we think is fair. As a result, most research on fairness has avoided any evaluative statements about the rationality of these judgments. Yet, this silence has inhibited our understanding of how our cognitive processes create anger, jealousy, and inefficiency (Salovey, 1991). If we are to reduce or eliminate dysfunctional perceptions of fairness, we need to confront the irrationality of these perceptions.

This section addresses what it means to be irrational in judging fairness. I propose three increasingly specific definitions of irrationality: (1) deviating from an economic model of behavior, (2) accepting a Pareto-inefficient agreement, and (3) having inconsistent preferences. These definitions are then used to understand the existing literature on irrational judgments of fairness.

Level 1 irrationality: deviating from an economic model of behavior

Economic theories have been built on the cornerstone of rationality (Coase, 1960; Myerson, 1991). Individuals are assumed to act out of self-interest and in accordance with the behavior specified in rational economic models. One simple definition of an irrational judgment of fairness is any judgment that deviates from the tenets of economic rationality (Kahneman et al., 1987). This definition is very broad. Thus, the next two are increasingly specific definitions that identify potentially harmful characteristics of how we think about fairness.

Level 2 irrationality: inefficiency

Pareto efficiency is a key concept for thinking about rationality in situations involving more than two parties. An agreement is defined as Pareto efficient when there is no other agreement that would make one party better off without decreasing the outcomes to any other party. If both sides would prefer an alternative agreement, the existing agreement is Pareto inefficient. For example, if a possible agreement existed that would give A $600 and B $800, an agreement that would give them each $500 would be Pareto inefficient—it should not be preferred by either party.

It is easy to see that society would be better off if all agreements were Pareto efficient. I argue that selecting a Pareto-inefficient agreement (which we often do, as described later) to obtain "fairness" (often defined as equality) is an irrational act that harms the individual and broader society. Forcing an equal outcome may make sense if the goal is to maintain a potential longer term relationship. However, choosing a Pareto-inefficient outcome to maintain equality in a single interaction is irrational.

Many individuals would argue that fairness has utility to decision makers (Messick, 1991). This reasoning would suggest that decision makers should be allowed to define their own rationality. However, this reasoning creates an unacceptable level of waste and is philosophically insupportable. Even the noted egalitarian philosopher Rawls (1971) suggests that social comparisons are dysfunctional in many situations. Rawls's theory of justice argues that resources should be distributed equally to all individuals or groups, *except* in cases where an unequal distribution works to everyone's advantage. Rawls allows for inequality to improve the outcomes of *all* societal members.

Pareto efficiency need not endanger the fair distribution of resources. People should always move from a Pareto-inefficient outcome to one that is better for both parties. Judgments of fairness are most useful when evaluating alternative efficient agreements. Judgments of inefficient agreements are often distracting and unnecessary. I argue that the discussion of the distribution of resources should occur along the efficient frontier.

Level 3 irrationality: inconsistency

An individual's fairness judgments are irrational when they are inconsistent. Inconsistency can take a number of forms. However, the integrating theme is that an individual's irrational perceptions of fairness are based on normatively irrelevant concerns. First, fairness evaluations are irrational if they are affected by the way in which a problem is framed (Kahneman & Tversky, 1982). Second, evaluations are irrational if fairness judgments are intransitive. That is, an individual should not prefer Outcome A over Outcome B, and then prefer Outcome B over Outcome A. Similarly, an individual should not prefer Outcome A over Outcome B, Outcome B over Outcome C, and Outcome C over Outcome A. Third, evaluations are irrational if individuals should change their preferences due to normatively irrelevant data. Finally, initial fairness judgments are irrational if people would change their preferences if they understood their decision processes more clearly. Evidence of such inconsistency is presented in the following section.

EVIDENCE OF IRRATIONALITY IN JUDGMENTS OF FAIRNESS

In this section, I review three streams of empirical work related to fairness judgments. Each stream indicates, in a different way, how fairness judgments are irrational and dysfunctional.

When do we accept the role of supply and demand?

In a provocative set of experiments, Kahneman et al. (1987) demonstrated that fairness considerations can dominate economically rational choices in decision making. For example, subjects were asked to evaluate the fairness of the action in the following example:

> A hardware store has been selling snow shovels for $15. The morning after a large snowstorm, the store raises the price to $20. Please rate this action as:
> Completely Fair—Acceptable—Unfair—Very Unfair

The two favorable and the two unfavorable categories were combined to indicate the proportion of respondents who judged the action acceptable or unfair. Despite the economic rationality of raising the snow shovels' prices, 82 percent of respondents ($N = 107$) considered this action unfair. In addition, informal research showed that many of the respondents who viewed the price increase as fair reversed their decisions when the commodity was generators after a hurricane—yet the problems were conceptually almost identical. Kahneman et al. (1987) did a thorough job of illustrating that individual judgment about fairness is inconsistent with the Level 1 definition of rationality—that judgments of fairness are not consistent with the basic economic theory of supply and demand.

Kahneman et al. (1987) also provided evidence for Level 3 irrationality by showing that judgments of fairness were not stable but were affected by the framing of the problem. Consider these questions:

> Question A: A company is making a small profit. It is located in a community experiencing a recession with substantial unemployment but no inflation. There are many workers anxious to work at the company. The company decides to decrease wages and salaries 7% this year.
> ($N = 125$)   Acceptable 38%   Unfair 62%

> Question B: A company is making a small profit. It is located in a community experiencing a recession with substantial unemployment and inflation of 12%. There are many workers anxious to work at the company. The company decides to increase wages and salaries 5% this year.
> ($N = 129$)   Acceptable 78%   Unfair 22%

Despite very similar changes in real income, judgments of fairness were starkly different. A wage cut was typically coded as an unfair loss; a nominal gain that does not cover inflation was more often acceptable. Whether the action is coded as a loss or as a gain clearly affects judgments of fairness.

A central issue in the work of Kahneman et al. (1987) is the anchoring role played by the status quo in judgments of fairness. This theme emerges across a number of related research programs. For example, Bazerman (1985) shows that arbitrators, in trying to award a fair wage in interest arbitration, typically accept the past wage as an appropriate benchmark from which to make an adjustment. However, to the extent that past wages were inappropriately high or low, this decision strategy simply perpetuates the inequity. Similarly, Martin (this volume) argues that the tendency to see past practice as legitimate leads to the acceptance and perpetuation of past inequities.

Ultimatum experiments

Fairness considerations also explain deviations from the expectations of rational models in a set of studies using ultimatum bargaining games (Guth et al., 1982; Roth, 1991). In Guth et al.'s (1982) study, player 1s divided a known, fixed sum of money any way they chose by filling out a form stating "I demand DM____" (the study was conducted in West Germany using Deutsche Marks). Player 2s could accept the offer and receive their portion of the money as divided by player 1, or reject the offer, leaving both parties with nothing. Game theoretic models predict that player 1s will offer player 2s only slightly more than 0, and that player 2s will accept any offer greater than 0. The results, however, showed that subjects incorporated fairness considerations in their offers and their choices. The average demand by player 1 was for less than 70 percent of the funds, both for first-time players and for players repeating the game 1 week later. This behavior is inconsistent with the Level 1 definition of rationality: Individuals are not acting according to an economic model of behavior that would dictate an offer of only slightly more than 0.

In addition, individuals in the role of player 2 rejected profitable offers and took zero 20 percent of the time. They were choosing a Pareto-inefficient result, violating the Level 2 definition of rationality. Guth et al. (1982) concluded that " . . . subjects often rely on what they consider a fair or justifiable result . . . subjects do not hesitate to punish if their opponent asks for 'too much.' " This result has been confirmed in a number of other experiments (Forsythe, Horowitz, Savin, & Sefton, 1988; Guth & Tietz, 1987; Ochs & Roth, 1989). Ochs and Roth (1989) studied a situation in which player 2 could reject player 1's offer, and then counterpropose. However, the amount of funds available was reduced if the first offer was not accepted. They found that 81 percent of rejected offers were followed by disadvantageous counteroffers, wherein the parties who rejected the initial offer demanded less than they had just been offered. Ochs and Roth (1989) argued that the players' utilities for fairness may explain the results. However, they also argued that a simple notion of equality does not explain the data, since in most cases player 1 asks for more than 50 percent of the resources. Rather, parties realize that the other side may very well refuse offers perceived as unfair despite the economic rationality of accepting them. Intuition tells us that the other party will not always follow the logic of Pareto efficiency. Bolton (1991) incorporates these findings within a formal model that argues that individuals behave as if they are negotiating over both absolute and relative money. This model is consistent with the model of social utility developed in the next section.

Ochs and Roth's argument is also consistent with Forsythe et al.'s (1988) results: Player 1 played either an ultimatum game as described earlier, or a "dictator" game in which player 1 could simply decide how the resources would be split without player 2's acceptance. They found that while many player 1s chose a 50–50 split in the ultimatum game, none proposed a 100%–0% split. However, under the dictator format, 36 percent of the player 1s took 100 percent. When acceptance was required, proposals became more equal (Ochs & Roth, 1989; Roth, 1991). Sixty-four percent of the subjects in the dictator game still chose to give the other party some portion of the resources. These results demonstrate that both a concern for being fair and the realization that being unfair can generate future costs led to choices that deviated from rational models in systematic and predictable directions.

Ongoing research on the ultimatum game also suggests that individuals are affected by normatively irrelevant information, thus violating Level 3 rationality. Kramer and Pradhan (1991), for instance, found that the effectiveness of the examples used to explain ultimatum games influences the subjects' aggressiveness. Tversky and Kahneman's (1974) experiments showed that a vivid example overwhelms a rational assessment of the ultimatum game. Subjects exposed to President Kennedy's successful ultimatum in the Cuban Missile Crisis were far more aggressive than subjects exposed to the air controllers' unsuccessful ultimatum in the PATCO strike. Loewenstein, White, and Bazerman (1991) and Boles and Messick (1990) also show inconsistency in how subjects respond to the ultimatum game. They find that when individuals are asked for the lowest amount they will accept in an ultimatum game, they specify a higher amount than the minimum they will actually accept when asked to make a choice between accepting or rejecting an ultimatum.

Someone who acts according to the economic model (e.g., increases the price of the shovels after a snowstorm or asks for 99 percent of the resources in the ultimatum game) may do worse than someone who considers norms of fairness, since others (e.g., the shovel customers, player 2s) may punish the unfairness of an economically rational action. Thus, following the economic model in a world in which others do not may not be rational. Rather, optimal decisions require consideration of other parties' expected decisions (Bazerman & Neale, 1992; Raiffa, 1982).

Instability and irrationality in social utility preferences

It is widely accepted that people exhibit concern for how their own rewards compare to the rewards of others. Roth and Murnighan (1982), for example, have observed numerous deviations from the predictions of normative game theory that appear to reflect the operation of social comparison. In organizations, elaborate job grade systems specify the compensation available to employees at each level within the organization. Salaries, bonuses, and benefits are carefully calculated within these specified parameters so that employees feel they are being fairly compensated relative to others in comparable positions (Mahoney, 1979). In addition, organizations fruitlessly try to keep pay secret to avoid social comparison (Lawler, 1971). Thus, across a broad variety of situations, individuals exhibit a concern for how their own rewards compare to those of relevant others.

Although the concern for equitable payoffs is pervasive, it is not constant across situations. Both the degree of concern for others' payoffs and the nature of that concern (e.g., whether it is positive or negative) have been shown to depend on a variety of factors. These include the nature of the relationship between the parties (Clark & Mills, 1979), the type of the dispute (e.g., personal or business) (Loewenstein, Thompson, & Bazerman, 1989), the information each side possesses (Roth & Murnighan, 1982), the preexisting needs of the disputants (Yarri & Bar–Hillel, 1984), the level of inputs each side contributes to the relationship (Adams, 1963; Homans, 1961; Walster, Walster, & Berscheid, 1978), the preexisting state of affairs (Kahneman, Knetsch, & Thaler, 1986a, 1986b), and other factors too numerous to list.

Loewenstein et al. (1989) asked subjects to assess their satisfaction from situations that presented them with an outcome to themselves and an outcome to another party in a dispute. Their relationship with the other party was either positive or negative. A social utility function (Messick & Sentis, 1985) for each subject was then computed by regressing the subject's satisfaction with each outcome on its value to the subject and on the difference between that value and the other person's outcome. The precise form of the estimated function, selected by goodness-of-fit tests over a variety of forms, was (as adapted from a model suggested by Messick and Sentis, 1985)

$$U = \beta_1 self + \beta_2 posdif + \beta_3 posdif^2 + \beta_4 negdif + \beta_5 negdif^2$$

where posdif indicates positive differences between one's own and the other's payoff (advantageous inequality) and negdif indicates the absolute value of negative differences (disadvantageous inequality). In general, disputants preferred equal outcomes over unequal outcomes, so that the signs of both β_2 and β_4 were negative. As expected, advantageous inequalities were preferred over disadvantageous inequalities: The absolute magnitude of the β_4 coefficient was greater than that of β_2. The major difference in social utility functions induced by manipulating the positive and negative relationship occurred in the domain of advantageous inequality. Modal subjects in the positive and neutral relationship conditions tended to dislike advantageous inequality ($\beta_2 < 0$); in the negative relationship condition, a majority derived positive utility from advantageous inequality ($\beta_2 > 0$).

Notice that this function is quite consistent with many of the violations of Level 1 and Level 2 rationality. If people are preoccupied with the difference between themselves and other parties, acting against the tenets of economic theory and violating Pareto efficiency are easily explained. However, this model still allows for consistency. That is, if an individual's utility was defined in a stable way within the model's parameters, consistency would exist. However, I present evidence later that indicates that Level 3's concern for consistency is also violated.

An additional study by Loewenstein et al. (1989) validated the foregoing results by comparing choice behavior in individual and interpersonal decision tasks. This experiment was designed to show that the social utility curves derived from the previous study could predict choices in risky environments that were (1) predictable based on the nature of the disputing relationship and (2) predictably different from those expected by individual decision models.

All subjects participated in two phases of this experiment. In Phase 1, they made three binary choices, each a selection between a sure thing and a risky alternative. In Phase 2 (the phases were presented in reverse order for half of the subjects), subjects also made three binary choices that offered the same choices to self as the first set but varied the implications for the other party. The only difference between the decision task in Phase 1 and Phase 2 was the social context—individual versus interpersonal choice.

In the individual choice condition, the risky choice involved gains/losses only to the self. In the interpersonal choice condition, the risky choice involved gains/losses to the self and another party, and subjects were randomly assigned to positive and negative relationship conditions. The individual questionnaire contained choices on a single page with the following instructions: "Below you are given choices between a SURE THING and a GAMBLE. Decide which option you prefer and indicate your choice to each question by circling either A or B."

The interpersonal choices began with the instructions, "Below you are given a description of an incident involving you and a neighbor. Please read the description and then answer each question." The description specified that either a positive or negative relationship existed between the disputants. The questionnaire then described situations in which the subject and neighbor either jointly owed or were to be paid $10,000. Subjects were then given a choice between accepting a settlement proposed by the neighbor or taking a risky option of arbitrating. The interpersonal choices involved payoffs to the subject that were identical to the three choices in the individual choice set. The first choice in both conditions was between a sure $5,000 or a risky alternative offering a .7 chance of $6,000 and a .3 chance of $4,000 (expected value = $5,400). In the individual decision condition, 81 percent chose the risky alternative and 19 percent chose the sure thing. In the positive relationship condition, 85 percent opted for the sure $5,000/$5,000 (self/other) split rather than a .7 chance of $6,000/$4,000 and a .3 chance of $4,000/$6,000. However, in the negative relationship only 27 percent opted for the sure, equal split. The choices in the interpersonal/positive condition were significantly different from those in the individual and interpersonal/negative relationship conditions.

These data are consistent with the predictions of the social utility functions described earlier. Subjects in the individual condition were willing to take risks to increase their expected values. However, in the interpersonal/positive condition, the equal split alternative predominated; both unequal outcomes, even the one offering a greater payoff to the subject, offered lower utility than the equal split. Subjects in the interpersonal/negative condition were willing to risk the disadvantageous inequality to maximize their own expected outcome and to increase the likelihood of obtaining (positively valued) advantageous inequality.

The social utility functions from the earlier study by Loewenstein et al. (1989) also explain the reversal of preference in the negative relationship condition. A negative relationship has two effects on the utility function: It causes a "selfish shift" that increases the desirability of the high-valued risky alternative, and it increases the slope of utility as a function of positive differences between the disputants' payoffs. Now, getting more than the other person is valuable; without the negative relationship, differences provided negative utility. Negative affect removes fairness barriers.

Another item in Loewenstein et al.'s third study involved losses rather than gains. In the individual decision condition, as Prospect Theory (Kahneman & Tversky 1979) predicts, 75 percent of subjects preferred a 50–50 chance of losing $10,000 or losing nothing over a sure loss of $5,000. However, in an interpersonal context, 85 percent of subjects in the positive relationship condition and 82 percent of the subjects in the negative relationship condition preferred equal losses of $5,000 over a lottery giving a 50 percent chance of either side paying the full amount. The positive and negative interpersonal relationship conditions differed significantly from the individual condition, but not from each other. In this situation, we see a pattern of concern for equality of payoffs dwarfing the general preference for risk in the domain of losses.

Prospect Theory describes a model of individual decision making in which losses and gains are evaluated in comparison to a neutral reference point. The reference point usually represents the status quo; in laboratory studies of choice, it is usually zero. In more natural contexts, the reference point may represent present wealth (Kahneman & Tversky, 1979). Loewenstein et al. (1989) argue that others' outcomes commonly act as a key reference point in interpersonal decision settings. Further, while losses and gains affect choice independently of the other party's payoff, the comparison to a relevant other is often a more important determinant of the utility of the focal decision maker.

A general conclusion of Loewenstein et al. (1989) was that interpersonal comparisons overwhelm concern for personal outcomes in rating potential resolutions of a dispute. For example, typical subjects rated $500 for the self and $500 for the other person as more satisfactory than $600 for the self and $800 for the other person. Yet it is not clear from this study that individuals would actually select the $500 for the self and $500 for the other person over $600 for the self and $800 for the other person if asked to choose between these two sets of outcomes.

An important methodological aspect of the Loewenstein study is that a *ratings* format was used. Subjects were asked to rate a large number of outcomes; each was described by the relevant payoffs to self and to another party. They lacked a mechanism to judge the quality of their outcome independent of the outcome of the other party. Consequently, the only obvious reference point for evaluating their outcome was the outcome of the other party. In contrast, in a *choice* context (when an individual is choosing between two or more different outcomes for himself or herself), the individual is more likely to use one option as a reference point against which to compare the other.

Consistent with this argument, Bazerman, Loewenstein, and White (1991) have shown that while individuals care far more about social comparisons when rating a specific outcome, absolute individual outcomes are more important in actual choice behavior. For example, while 70 percent rated the outcome of $400 for self, $400 for the other party as *more* acceptable than $500 for self, $700 for the other party when they evaluated these outcomes separately, only 22 percent chose the $400 for self and $400 for the other party over $500 for self and $700 for the other party when asked to choose between the two. This basic pattern is consistent across many other comparisons and a wide variety of contexts.

Bazerman et al. (1991) argue that when a series of joint outcomes are evaluated individually, others' outcomes become the reference point. When choosing between two outcomes for oneself, even when others' outcomes are available, the others' outcomes are not needed as a reference point, since outcomes to self can be easily compared. Others' outcomes become unimportant in most choices. The salient attribute in a choice task is outcome to self.

White, Loewenstein, and Bazerman (1991) have extended this result to a real situation involving real payoffs. They agreed to recruit subjects for a colleague's experiment. One group of potential subjects was offered $7 to participate in a 40-minute experiment, knowing that all subjects would be receiving $7. A second group was offered $8 to participate in a 40-minute experiment, knowing that some subjects were arbitrarily (based on the last digit of their social security number) being offered $10. A third group was given an opportunity (1) to participate in a 40-minute experiment in which everyone was being paid $7; (2) to participate in a 40-minute experiment in which some subjects, including themselves, would receive $8 and others would receive $10; or (3) not to participate. While significantly more subjects in the first group chose to participate (72 percent) than in the second group (55 percent), the majority of subjects (56 percent) in the third group chose to participate in the experiment that gave them $8 while some others were given $10 (16 percent chose the experiment in which everyone received $7; 28 percent chose not to participate in either). Thus, in evaluating whether to participate in one specific experiment, the outcomes of other potential subjects were critical. However, when multiple opportunities were available, the outcomes of others became less important. Subjects were able to simply compare what they would receive across the multiple experiments.

These results provide conclusive evidence that social utility preferences, which include concerns for the outcomes to other parties, are inconsistent. In violation of the third definition of rationality, judgments of fairness are affected by such normatively irrelevant concerns as the form of the elicitation.

CONCLUSIONS

Fairness judgments permeate organizational life. Comparisons of pay raises, the distribution of scarce budgets, promotions, grades, and prices are just a few of the many situations in which fairness judgments are made that affect our emotions and behavior. These judgments are based on more than reality. Crosby (1985) documents that relative comparisons are frequently more important predictors of feeling deprived than objective reality. This chapter has tried to provide an initial understanding of the cognitive patterns that lead to perceptions of relative unfairness.

The goal of this chapter has been to extend the logic of much of my past research to the domain of judgments of fairness, and in doing so to help define a new direction in fairness research. The judgments of the individuals who are allocated resources are central to understanding fairness. Extensive evidence has been provided to document that our judgments concerning fairness frequently violate the tenets of economic rationality, lead to Pareto-inefficient outcomes, and are based on inconsistent and unstable preferences. While additional research is needed to specify this irrationality, I want to conclude by discussing some of the implications of this work for creating more efficient and just organizations.

It is unrealistic to try to eliminate social comparisons. Ample evidence supports the argument that people will use social comparison information to interpret their world (Adams, 1965; Lawler, 1971; Wood, 1989). The department members that were not part of the research center in the story discussed in the introduction will care about the inequality of resources. But how much will they care, and how will their perceptions influence subsequent behaviors? By understanding our common judgment patterns, it may have been possible to shift these department members toward the choice condition of the Bazerman et al. (1991) study by including them in the decision, thus minimizing the adverse impact of fairness concerns. If the location of the research center had been presented as a choice (whether it was located in the department), perhaps the objective benefits would have been more salient than the inequalities that were created. This does not eliminate the need for organizations to create fair procedures and fair outcomes. However, it suggests that an understanding of how we judge fairness may help us better manage in a world that includes these constraints.

That choice preferences are different from ratings preferences suggests that if people were more aware of their obsession with social comparison in single evaluation contexts, they might reconsider the attention that they give to social comparison information. Dawes (1988) has suggested that one benefit of linear models is that they can be used to help inform decision makers about how they *actually* make decisions. I raise the question of whether it would be useful to create a diagnostic instrument that would allow individuals to see how social comparison affects their decisions, and whether this awareness would change social utility functions.

Culture is a topic of recent interest in organizational behavior (Martin & Siehl, 1983; O'Reilly, Chatman, & Caldwell, 1991; Rousseau, 1990). However, little attention has been given to the connection between organizational culture and specific cognitions and behaviors of organizational members. An interesting question is whether it is possible to create a culture of cooperation, shared happiness, and vicarious pride to replace our current culture of competition, jealousy, and envy (Chatman, personal communication).

Bies and Moag (1986; Bies, 1987) have suggested that an important added consideration to the justice literature is interactional justice. They argue that it is important to consider not only the procedures used to create justice but also how these procedures are implemented. I argue that effective implementation requires consideration of how the recipient will assess the procedures used, the implementation process, and the outcomes received. It is not only important that a justice system is fair but also that it appears fair (Greenberg, 1990). The evidence provided in this chapter suggests that many options are available and that different forms are likely to trigger very different social utility assessments.

The ideas in this chapter are not presented as an alternative to the existing literature on procedural and distributive justice. The justice literature is one of the most important and successfully developed areas of recent growth in the social psychology of organizations. Yet I am often struck that participants' perceptions of unfairness can easily develop in a situation that most others would see as fair. In many organizational environments, individuals will perceive unfairness no matter what decisions are made by the manager or organization. To understand these contexts, the justice literature can be further developed by creating better models of the cognitions of organizational members. This chapter offers an initial step in this direction.

REFERENCES

ADAMS, J. S. (1963). Toward an understanding of inequity. *Journal of Abnormal and Social Psychology, 67*, 422–436.

ADAMS, J. S. (1965). Inequity in social exchange. In L. Berkowitz (Ed.), *Advances in experimental social psychology* (Vol. 2, pp. 148–174). New York: Academic Press.

AKERLOF, G. (1970). The market for lemons: Qualitative uncertainty and the market mechanism. *Quarterly Journal of Economics, 84*, 488–500.

BALL, S. B., BAZERMAN, M. H., & CARROLL, J. S. (1991). An evaluation of learning in the bilateral winner's curse. *Organizational Behavior and Human Decision Processes, 48*, 1–22.

BAZERMAN, M. H. (1985). Norms of distributive justice in interest arbitration. *Industrial and Labor Relations Review, 38*, 558–570.

BAZERMAN, M. H. (1990). *Judgment in managerial decision making* (2nd ed.). New York: John Wiley & Sons.

BAZERMAN, M. H., & CARROLL, J. S. (1987). Negotiator cognition. In B. Staw & L. L. Cummings (Eds.), *Research in organizational behavior* (Vol. 9, pp. 247–288). Greenwich, CT: JAI Press.

BAZERMAN, M. H., LOEWENSTEIN, G. F., & WHITE, S. B. (1991). *Psychological determinants of utility in competitive contexts: The impact of elicitation procedure.* Working paper, Northwestern University, Kellogg School of Management.

BAZERMAN, M. H., MAGLIOZZI, T., & NEALE, M. A. (1985). The acquisition of an integrative response in a competitive market. *Organizational Behavior and Human Performance, 34*, 294–313.

BAZERMAN, M. H., & NEALE, M. A. (1982). Improving negotiation effectiveness under final offer arbitration: The role of selection and training. *Journal of Applied Psychology, 67*, 543–548.

BAZERMAN, M. H., & NEALE, M. A. (1991). Negotiation rationality and negotiation cognition: The interactive roles of prescriptive and descriptive research. In P. Young (Ed.), *Negotiation analysis* (pp. 109–130). Ann Arbor: University of Michigan Press.

BAZERMAN, M. H., & NEALE, M. A. (1992). *Negotiating rationally.* New York: Free Press.

BIES, R. J. (1987). The predicament of injustice: The management of moral outrage. In L. L. Cummings & B. M. Staw (Eds.), *Research in organizational behavior* (Vol. 9, pp. 289–320). Greenwich, CT: JAI Press.

BIES, R. J., & MOAG, J. S. (1986). Interactional justice. In R. J. Lewicki, B. H. Sheppard, & M. H. Bazerman (Eds.), *Research in negotiation in organizations* (Vol. I, pp. 43–56). Greenwich, CT: JAI Press.

BOLES, T. L., & MESSICK, D. M. (1990). Accepting unfairness: Temporal influence on choice. In K. Borcherding, O. Larichev, & D. M. Messick (Eds.), *Contemporary issues in decision making* (pp. 375–390). Amsterdam: North Holland.

BOLTON, G. E. (1991). A comparative model of bargaining: Theory and evidence. *American Economic Review, 81*, 1096–1136.

CHATMAN, J. (1989). Improving interactional organizational research: A model of person-organizational fit. *Academy of Management Review, 14*, 333–349.

CLARK, M. S., & MILLS, J. (1979). Interpersonal attraction in exchange and communal relationships. *Journal of Personality and Social Psychology, 37,* 12–24.

COASE, R. (1960). The problem of social cost. *Journal of Law and Economics, 3,* 1–44.

CROSBY, F. (1984). Relative deprivation in organizational setting. In L. L. Cummings & B. M. Staw (Eds.), *Research in organizational behavior* (Vol. 6, pp. 51–94). Greenwich, CT: JAI Press.

DAVIS–BLAKE, A., & PFEFFER, J. (1989). Just a mirage: The search for dispositional effects in organizational research. *Academy of Management Review, 14,* 385–400.

DAWES, R. M. (1988). *Rational choice in an uncertain world.* New York: Harcourt Brace Jovanovich.

FISHER, R., & URY, W. (1981). *Getting to YES.* New York: Houghton Mifflin.

FORSYTHE, R., HOROWITZ, J., SAVIN, N. E., & SEFTON, M. (1988). *Replicability, fairness and pay in experiments with simple bargaining games.* Working paper, University of Iowa.

GARDNER, H. (1985). *The mind's new science.* New York: Basic Books.

GREENBERG, J. (1990). Looking fair versus being fair: Managing impressions of organizational justice. In B. M. Staw & L. L. Cummings (Eds.), *Research in organizational behavior* (Vol. 12, pp. 204–235). Greenwich, CT: JAI Press.

GUTH, W., SCHMITTBERGER, R., & SCHWARZE, B. (1982). An experimental analysis of ultimatum bargaining. *Journal of Economic Behavior and Organization, 3,* 367–388.

GUTH, W., & TIETZ, R. (1987). *Ultimatum bargaining for a shrinking cake—an experimental analysis.* Mimeographed working paper.

HOMANS, G. (1961). *Social behavior: Its elementary forms.* New York: Harcourt, Brace, and World.

ILGEN, D. R., & KLEIN, H. J. (1989). Organizational behavior. *Annual Review of Psychology, 40.* Palo Alto, CA: Annual Reviews, Inc.

KAHNEMAN, D. (1991). Judgment and decision making: A personal view. *Psychological Science, 2,* 142–145.

KAHNEMAN, D., KNETSCH, J. L., & THALER, R. H. (1986a). Fairness and the assumptions of economics. In R. W. Hogarth & M. W. Reder (Eds.), *Rational choice: The contrast between economics and psychology* (pp. 117–141). Chicago: University of Chicago Press.

KAHNEMAN, D., KNETSCH, J. L., & THALER, R. (1986b). Fairness and the assumptions of economics. *Journal of Business, 59,* S285–S300.

KAHNEMAN, D., KNETSCH, J. L., & THALER, R. (1987). Fairness as a constraint on profit seeking: Entitlements in the market. *American Economic Review, 76,* 728–741.

KAHNEMAN, D., & TVERSKY, A. (1979). Prospect theory: An analysis of decision under risk. *Econometrica, 47,* 263–291.

KAHNEMAN, D., & TVERSKY, A. (1982). Psychology of preferences. *Scientific American,* 161–173.

KRAMER, R. M., & PRADHAN, P. (1991). The impact of availability on decisions in the ultimatum game. Ongoing research, Stanford University, Graduate School of Business.

LAWLER, E. E. (1971). *Pay and organizational effectiveness: A psychological view.* New York: McGraw-Hill.

LIND, E. A., & TYLER, T. R. (1988). *The social psychology of procedural justice.* New York: Plenum.

LOEWENSTEIN, G., THOMPSON, L., & BAZERMAN, M. H. (1989). Social utility and decision making in interpersonal contexts. *Journal of Personality and Social Psychology, 57,* 426–441.

LOEWENSTEIN, G., WHITE, S. B., & BAZERMAN, M. H. (1991). The role of elicitation procedure in the ultimatum game. Ongoing data collection.

MAHONEY, T. A. (1979). Organizational hierarchy and position worth. *Academy of Management Journal, 22*, 726–737.

MARTIN, J. (1992). Inequality, distributive injustice, and organizational illegitimacy. This volume.

MARTIN, J., & SIEHL, C. (1983). Organizational culture and counterculture: An uneasy symbiosis. *Organizational Dynamics, 12*, 52–64.

MESSICK, D. M. (1992). Equality as a decision heuristic. In B. Mellers (Ed.), *Psychological issues in distributive justice*, forthcoming.

MESSICK, D. M., & SENTIS, K. P. (1985). Estimating social and nonsocial utility functions from ordinal data. *European Journal of Social Psychology, 15*, 389–399.

MYERSON, R. (1991). *Game theory*. Cambridge, MA: Harvard University Press.

NASH, J. (1950). The bargaining problem. *Econometrica, 18*, 128–140.

NEALE, M. A. (1984). The effect of negotiation and arbitration cost salience on bargainer behavior: The role of arbitrator and constituency in negotiator judgment. *Organizational Behavior and Human Performance, 34*, 97–111.

NEALE, M. A., & BAZERMAN, M. A. (1985). When will externally set aspiration levels improve negotiator performance? A look at integrative behavior in competitive markets. *Journal of Occupational Behavior, 6*, 19–32.

NEALE, M. A., & BAZERMAN, M. H. (1991). *Cognition and rationality in negotiation*. New York: Free Press.

NORTHCRAFT, G. B., & NEALE, M. A. (1987). Expert, amateurs, and real estate: An anchoring-and-adjustment perspective on property pricing decisions. *Organizational Behavior and Human Decision Processes, 39*, 228–241.

OCHS, J., & ROTH, A. E. (1989). An experimental study of sequential bargaining. *American Economic Review, 79*, 335–385.

OKUN, A. (1981). *Prices and quantities: A macroeconomic analysis*. Washington, DC: The Brookings Institute.

O'REILLY, C. A., CHATMAN, J., & CALDWELL, D. F. (1991). People and organizational culture: A profile comparison approach to assessing person-organization fit. *Academy of Management Journal, 34*, 487–516.

RAIFFA, H. (1982). *The art and science of negotiation*. Cambridge, MA: Belknap.

RAWLS, J. (1971). *A theory of justice*. Cambridge, MA: Harvard University Press.

ROUSSEAU, D. (1990). Quantitative assessment of organizational culture: The case for multiple measures. In B. Schneider (Ed.), *Frontiers in industrial and organizational psychology* (Vol. 3, pp. 153–192). San Francisco: Jossey-Bass.

ROTH, A., & MURNIGHAN, K. (1982). The role of information in bargaining: An experimental study. *Econometrica, 50*, 1123–1142.

ROTH, A. E. (1991). An economic approach to the study of bargaining. In M. H. Bazerman, R. J. Lewicki, & B. H. Sheppard (Eds.), *Handbook of negotiation research: Research in negotiation in organizations* (Vol. III, pp. 35–68). Greenwich, CT: JAI Press.

SALOVEY, P. (1991). Social comparison processes in envy and jealousy. In J. Suls & T. A. Wills (Eds.), *Social comparison: Contemporary theory and research* (pp. 115–138). Hillsdale, NJ: Erlbaum.

SAMUELSON, W. F., & BAZERMAN, M. H. (1985). The winner's curse in bilateral negotiations. In V. Smith (Ed.), *Research in experimental economics* (Vol. 3, pp. 105–137). Greenwich, CT: JAI Press.

SCHMITT, D. R., & MARWELL, G. (1972). Withdrawal and reward allocation in response to inequity. *Journal of Experimental Social Psychology, 8*, 207–221.

SHUBIK, M. (1984). *Game theory in the social sciences*. Cambridge, MA: MIT Press.

SMITH, H. (1990). The Russian character. *New York Times Magazine*, October 28, 1990, pp. 31–71.

SOLOW, R. M. (1980). On theories of unemployment. *American Economic Review, 70,* 1–11.

STAW, B. M., BELL, N. E., & CLAUSEN, J. A. (1986). The dispositional approach to job attitudes: A lifetime longitudinal test. *Administrative Science Quarterly, 31,* 56–77.

STAW, B. M., & ROSS, J. (1985). Stability in the midst of change: A dispositional approach to job attitudes. *Journal of Applied Psychology, 70,* 469–480.

THIBAUT, J., & WALKER, L. L. (1975). *Procedural justice: A psychological analysis.* Hillsdale, NJ: Erlbaum.

TVERSKY, A., & KAHNEMAN, D. (1974). Judgment under uncertainty: Heuristics and biases. *Science, 185,* 1124–1131.

von NEUMANN, J., & MORGENSTERN, O. (1947). *Theory of games and economic behavior.* Princeton, NJ: Princeton University Press.

WALSTER, E., WALSTER, G. W., & BERSCHEID, E. (1978). *Equity: Theory and research.* Boston: Allyn & Bacon.

WEICK, K. E. (1992). Sensemaking in organizations: Small structures with large consequences. This volume.

WHITE, S. B., LOEWENSTEIN, G., & BAZERMAN, M. H. (1991). Toward the reduction of inconsistency in judgments of fairness. Working paper, Northwestern University, Kellogg School of Management.

WOOD, J. V. (1989). Theory and research concerning social comparison of personal attributes. *Psychological Bulletin, 106,* 231–248.

YAARI, M. E., & BAR–HILLEL, M. B. (1984). On dividing justly. *Social Choice and Welfare, 1,* 1–24.

CHAPTER TEN

Negotiating Successful Research Collaboration*

Gregory B. Northcraft

University of Arizona

Margaret A. Neale

Northwestern University

This chapter develops a framework for understanding scientific collaboration and coauthor selection. The framework proposes that successful scientific collaboration results when coauthors integrate their diverse skill capabilities and outcome preferences. Material from the judgmental heuristics-and-biases and negotiation literatures are used to explore why potentially fruitful collaborations often do not succeed. Some suggestions for managing coauthor relationships successfully— including fostering intellectual renewal over time within a collaboration—are derived from the framework.

In the eighteenth century, [chemical] mixtures were not fully distinguished from compounds by operational tests, and perhaps they could not have been. . . . That was the situation during the years when John Dalton undertook the investigations that led finally to his famous chemical atomic theory. But until the very last stages of those investigations, Dalton was neither a chemist nor interested in chemistry. Instead, he was a meteorologist investigating the . . . physical problems of the absorption of gases by water and of water by the atmosphere. Partly because his training was in a different specialty and partly because of his own work in that specialty, he approached these problems with a paradigm different from that of contemporary chemists. (Kuhn, 1970, pp. 131–133)

There is little doubt that coauthorship in scientific research has been on the rise for some time. For example, the mean number of authors for manuscripts published in American Psychological Association journals increased from 1.47 in 1949, to 1.72 in 1959, to 1.88 in 1969, to 2.19 by 1979 (Over, 1982). In the first 2 years of its existence (1958 and 1959), 95.4 percent of the articles published in the *Academy of Management Journal* were single authored. In its last two full years of

*The authors wish to thank Max Bazerman and Joe Moag for their helpful comments on earlier drafts of the manuscript.

publication (1990/1991), less than 22 percent of its articles were single authored, while more than 27 percent had three or more authors. However, not much is known about what makes coauthor teams successful, or why some researchers enter into stable, long-term publishing collaborations while others wander from one temporary partnership to another (Over, 1982).

In this chapter we develop a framework for understanding the processes of scientific collaboration and coauthor selection. We begin by considering a natural selection model of scientific contribution. We propose that successful scientific contribution results when collaborations optimize skill diversity, and that the optimizing of skill diversity in a coauthor team is much like negotiating an integrative agreement in bargaining. Material from the judgmental heuristics and biases (e.g., Kahneman, Slovic, & Tversky, 1982) and the negotiation literature (e.g., Neale & Bazerman, 1991) are used to explore why potentially fruitful collaborations often are not realized. Finally, some suggestions for successfully managing coauthor relationships—in particular, fostering intellectual renewal within a coauthor team over time—are derived from the framework.

A NATURAL SELECTION MODEL OF SCIENTIFIC CONTRIBUTION

Natural selection is the process by which a regulating mechanism allows entities possessing certain characteristics to survive and eliminates entities possessing other characteristics (Ashby, 1956). As shown in Figure 1A, there are four critical elements to the natural selection process. First, there must be a population of entities possessing a *variety of characteristics*. Second, there must be a *reproduction mechanism* that creates these entities such that the characteristics of the entities are a reflection of underlying capabilities of the reproduction mechanism. Third, there must be a notion of *survival* for these entities and their characteristics— some persist over time while others disappear. Finally, there must be a *regulating mechanism*—a filter that decides which entities (possessing which characteristics) will survive and which will disappear.

In biological terms, an organism possesses a variety of characteristics (the organism's phenotype) that reflects the organism's genes—the reproduction mechanism. The environment is the regulating mechanism. Phenotypes that are adaptive to the environment (e.g., heavy coats for cold climates) survive while phenotypes that are not adaptive die out. Survival of the adaptive phenotypes ensures that only the ability to reproduce adaptive phenotypes is retained in the population's gene pool.

Because this chapter is about scientific collaboration, the survival issue we address is survival of a research collaboration (rather than survival of the products—their articles, books, monographs, etc.) In the terms of scientific publication, the reproduction mechanism is the characteristics of the research team. As shown in Figure 1B, the population of entities the reproduction mechanism produces are potential scientific contributions, typically in the form of manuscripts.

There are several regulating mechanisms at work here. The most obvi-

FIGURE 1   Natural Selection and Collaboration

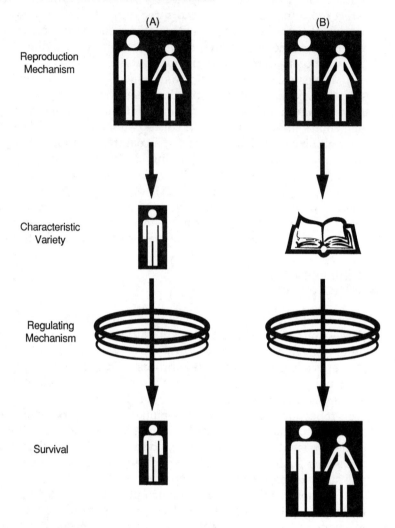

ous parallels to the biological model are journal reviewers and promotion-and-tenure (P&T) committees. Journal reviewers decide if the alleged scientific contributions that the research team produces (the phenotypes that reflect the underlying capabilities of the research team) are acceptable; P&T committees judge more globally the survival of individual research team members. A research team that produces viable entities (publishes scientific contributions) is more likely to survive, while research teams that do not publish are more likely to perish.

Research teams themselves no doubt exercise an additional *self*-regulating mechanism. While journal reviewers pass judgment primarily on the quality of a research team's outputs, the team's longevity probably reflects not only the success of its outputs but also the quality of its production *process*. High-quality outputs that come only at the expense of hair pulling, soul searching, teeth gnashing, and tantrum throwing are unlikely to promote any long-term survival of the team.

Variety is a cornerstone of the natural selection process. In biological terms, the more diversity there is in the parent gene pool, the more varied the phenotypes the reproduction mechanism can produce, and thereby the more likely that the reproduction mechanism will produce an adaptive phenotype. In terms of research teams, the more varied (diverse) the background and capabilities of the team members, the more likely that the combination of their talents and expertise will produce an insightful scientific contribution. Retreating to the biological example, the more diverse capabilities that a research team possesses, the more likely that all capabilities essential to its survival will be represented. There is a strong parallel here to "portfolio theory" (e.g., Sharpe, 1970) in investments. Portfolio theory suggests that investment diversity minimizes aggregate risk by spreading the risk over many different investments that are not under risk for the same reasons. In putting together a research team, diversity in the participants' capabilities minimizes the risk that an element critical to the research enterprise will not be represented on the team. In this sense, variety is more than the spice of research life; it is the very essence.

Dalton's derivation of chemical atomic theory—the vignette with which this chapter began—provides a graphic demonstration of the role of capability variety to the success of a research effort. Dalton brought a different perspective (meteorology) to the study of chemistry, in much the same way that colleageal interaction often brings different perspectives and backgrounds to bear on a research problem. The realization of creativity is based in part on a departure from typical associations and assumptions (e.g., Amabile, 1983). Thus, the interaction of diverse perspectives holds the promise of producing more creative and insightful contributions, or perhaps leading a research team to discover those insights more quickly than an individual might working alone.

At a practical level, diversity in research team capability has been volunteered as a prerequisite to scientific contribution because of the transition to "big science" (Price, 1963). As scientific fields have grown and expanded, the capabilities *and resources* needed to address new research issues increasingly may be falling outside the command of single individuals (Over, 1982).

Both arguments—the role of perspective diversity in scientific insight and the practical demand for skill diversity in a research team—may explain why multiauthored publications have more impact as measured by citation counts (Oromaner, 1974). These arguments certainly underscore why employment diversity may not only be in vogue in current society as a politically correct or moral imperative, but also as a logical precursor to success (Bantel & Jackson, 1989; Mandell & Kohler–Gray, 1990; Solomon, 1990). Increasing the diversity of the work force offers the organization the opportunity to respond more effectively to increasingly diverse environmental demands.

The biological example implies that capability diversity in the reproduction mechanism plays an even larger role if the regulatory mechanism is unstable. When the environment changes, new characteristics in phenotypes will be favored by the regulatory filter. The reproduction mechanism then must have enough variety to produce phenotypes that meet or match new adaptability criteria. As the frontiers of scientific knowledge and methodology move inexorably forward, two heads can keep pace better than one.

RESEARCH COLLABORATION
AS INTEGRATIVE AGREEMENT

The framework proposed in this chapter is something of a population ecology (Hannan & Freeman, 1977) of research teams. Research teams are formed and create products (typically, manuscripts); the environment (P&T committees, journal reviewers and editors) decides which products are acceptable, thereby selecting some research teams for survival and dooming others to extinction. The biological example suggests that capability diversity in the research team should be key in determining the acceptability of a research team's products. Does this simply mean that the more varied the background and capabilities of the research team, the more potentially successful the team? Or can something more precise be said about the form of diversity in a team that is most likely to promote its success?

More precisely, the building of scientific research teams should look very much like the negotiation of an integrative agreement. Negotiation has been defined as the process by which multiple parties decide what each will give and take in a relationship (Bazerman & Carroll, 1987). The "giving and taking" process can be thought to involve three kinds of elements (Thompson, 1990): distributive, congruent, and integrative issues. Distributive issues are those for which different individuals' needs, desires, or preferences are directly in conflict and equally valued by both sides. In the negotiation of the purchase price of an automobile, for example, the buyer would like to buy the car for the lowest price possible while the seller would like to sell the car for the highest price possible. If purchase price is an equally important issue to both sides, seller and buyer cannot both have their way. Thus, purchase price would be a distributive issue in this negotiation.

Congruent issues are those for which both sides' needs, desires, or preferences are identical. Returning to the automobile example, if the buyer were looking for a blue car and the seller had a blue car that he or she really wanted to sell, color of the car would be a congruent issue—both sides want the car that is sold to be blue.

Integrative issues are those for which the needs, desires, or preferences of the parties are in conflict but complementary. Integrative issues arise when parties have different needs, desires, and preferences. When parties' preferences differ, they can logroll, giving away what each considers less valuable in exchange for what each considers more valuable. In our automobile example, if the seller considered price to be more important than color while the buyer considered color to be more important than price, their preferences on these two issues would be complementary. The buyer would be willing to pay more for the desired color; the seller would be willing to take a higher price in exchange for conceding on color. Both sides give up something less important for something more important; both gain.

Research teams should be able to maximize the benefit of their capability diversity when that diversity is complementary (i.e., integrative). For example, imagine two researchers: Researcher A excels at data analysis but really is not very good at writing the first draft of the manuscript, while Researcher B excels at writing first drafts but really is not very good at analyzing data. If they collaborate, A should analyze the data and B should write the first draft. The resulting manuscript is better—or at least its production is more efficient—by virtue of having one expert analyze the data and having another expert write the first draft of the manuscript. Either researcher working alone on the same project would have had an expert doing only one of these two tasks. If the expert completion of both tasks is essential to the viability of the manuscript, the integrative nature of this collaboration increases the probability that the manuscript will be successful.

This integration of capability diversity in the research team also may occur at the level of theoretical (rather than methodological) expertise. Researcher A may be a judgment-and-decision-making expert, while Researcher B is a human resources management expert. Either might attempt to write a paper alone about judgmental biases in human resources management decisions; however, a joint paper would feature expert coverage of both halves of the research base.

The value of integrating the capabilities that coauthors bring to a research relationship is that integrating capabilities "expands the pie" (e.g., Pruitt, 1983). The reproduction process should be both more efficient (faster) and more effective (higher quality) when more elements of the process are accomplished by experts. Thus, researchers should be able to publish more *per capita* working together than working alone by virtue of logrolling their expertise, even despite some redundant effort and coordination costs.

Collaboration as diverse skill integration becomes even more compelling when the *outputs* side of coauthorship also is considered. Expanding the pie means that there will be more of something (cudos, accolades) to be divided among coauthors than will be realized by researchers working alone. The allocation process also raises the specter of distribution versus congruence or integration, and how a research team handles dividing up the spoils may well drive some of a research team's self-regulatory judgments (i.e., whether a coauthorship team decides to continue working together).

In the best of all possible worlds, the output preferences of research team members will be congruent (e.g., both collaborators will prefer that Researcher A be first author). Equally beneficial would be complementary (i.e., integrative) output preferences. If Researcher A believes that first authorship in manuscripts is most important for enhancing one's research reputation, while Researcher B believes that being the person who first presents the research publicly (e.g., at a national conference) is most important to enhancing one's research reputation, there is an obvious integrative division of the outputs. If their inputs have been similarly integrative—for example, Researcher A (the data expert) did the data while Researcher B (the expert writer) wrote the first draft—they will each be getting more or better outputs for contributing fewer inputs compared to their single-author colleagues.

THIS IS NOT THE BEST OF ALL POSSIBLE WORLDS

It all sounds so easy: You find someone who is your exact opposite and together you both become instantly, superhumanly productive. Obviously this is too simple. In addition, the dissolution of collaborations is common. Two major problems are practical and cognitive: The benefits of integration may be difficult to realize, and collaborators may not perceive the benefits of successful integration even when they are realized.

The practical angle

Why would the benefits of integration be difficult to realize? Again, the biological example in natural selection provides an appropriate reminder. Two organisms that are sufficiently different cannot successfully reproduce. There must be enough common ground (congruent elements, in the language of negotiation) to form the basis of a reproductive union. Two kinds of cattle can be mated to produce a new (and potentially integrative) variant, but only because different kinds of cattle are more alike than they are different. The trick is finding enough diversity to realize the benefits of integrative potential while retaining enough common ground to provide the basis for viable reproduction.

In the realm of research collaboration, there will need to be common ground (congruent elements) theoretically, methodologically, and stylistically. A physicist and an accountant might offer a universe of varied capabilities with which to attack research problems, but might not be able to agree on an appropriate problem or research paradigm. At the level of methodology, a survey researcher and a laboratory researcher might have difficulty finding a mutually satisfactory approach. At the level of research style, a "morning" person and a "night" person might have difficulty finding a time when both are adequately conscious to interact seriously.

While the optimal collaboration would include only congruent and integrative elements (and only enough congruent elements to ensure viable production), most research collaborations face distributive issues. When these differences can be compromised or accommodated (for instance, the "morning" and "night" researchers could meet in the afternoon, or take turns meeting in the mornings and evenings), the collaboration can proceed. However, the larger the proportion of distributive elements in the collaboration (issues where team members are giving up something important and only receiving equal if not less benefit in return), the fewer the benefits that are available from the collaboration.

The specter of distributive elements in a collaboration becomes even more discouraging in light of the likely differences in timing of distributive costs and integrative benefits. If one researcher uses IBM and the other uses Macintosh, if one models the world in terms of regression and the other in terms of analysis of variance, if one was trained in social psychology and the other in organizational behavior—these all present distributive barriers to entry into collaboration as well as the specter of immediate process losses (Hackman & Morris, 1975). As two researchers learn to work together, they can iron out the differences in their language and style, but at no small cost. Adjusted to and amortized over time, the costs to either party of accommodating or compromising these distributive elements in the collaboration eventually may seem small, especially if the collaboration is successful and lasting. But this assumes that the time horizon of the collaboration is sufficiently long. Compromising or accommodating on the distributive elements of a first collaboration will hardly prove worthwhile if that first collaboration is also the research team's last, or if the collaboration never produces anything. Taking turns only works as a distribution rule if there is a second turn to be taken.

The flip side of this concern is the time horizon for realizing integrative benefits. Discovering complementary abilities, contributions, needs, and preferences takes high aspirations, a problem-solving orientation, and especially *time* (Pruitt, 1983). The channels of communication must be opened (perhaps by first accommodating or compromising some of the distributive operational problems discussed earlier). At the most basic level, two researchers must learn to communicate with, trust, and respect each other before they can share the integrative potential of their differences. Eventually the specialization implicit in complementary abilities is likely to become a self-fulfilling prophecy (e.g., Rosenthal, 1973). The writer in the team will spend more and more time and become better and better at writing; the data analyst in the team will spend more and more time analyzing data and become better and better at analysis, providing additional integrative potential in the collaboration. As a result, their interdependence will increase.

However, the prospect of working through the pain (accommodating and compromising) to get to the gain (diversity integration) may be what prevents collaborations from surviving and maturing into long-term relationships. This seems especially true in light of the short-term lens through which participants typically evaluate their working relationships (Mannix & Loewenstein, 1991). This may also explain what Kanter (1977) has termed "homosocial reproduction"—the tendency for top management teams to select successors very much like themselves, thus decreasing (over time) the amount of diversity available in the corporate talent pool. As shown in Figure 2, similar others (who share more congruent elements in a collaboration) reduce the immediate cost of working together and increase the promise of quick benefits. The cost is a potentially lower ceiling on the ultimate benefits from integrative collaboration. Less complementary diversity and more congruence means fewer opportunities for integrative gains. If the costs of collaborating with dissimilar others are certain and immediate, while the benefits are uncertain and at best deferred, it should not be sur-

FIGURE 2   Costs and Benefits of Collaboration Over Time

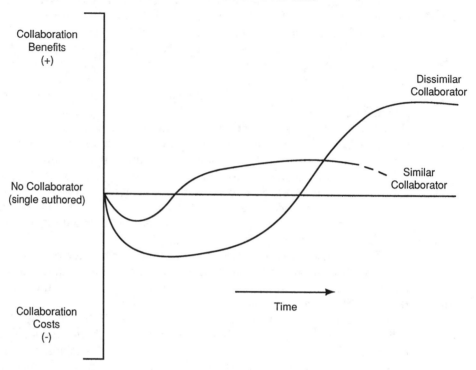

prising that more collaborations do not survive, or do not even start in the first place. First projects—even first attempts at first projects—are likely to make salient only the costs and not the benefits.

The cognitive angle

From a practical standpoint, the benefits of collaboration may seem too distant and uncertain for a research team to work together. A more pernicious possibility is that cognitive biases may blind researchers to integrative benefits even when they could or do occur in collaborative relationships.

Researchers might fail to perceive the benefits of collaboration because of the "fixed pie error" (Bazerman & Neale, 1983; Thompson & Hastie, 1990)—the tendency to assume that others' interests are completely opposed to one's own (i.e., to see all negotiations as distributive). Two related problems are the *incompatibility error* (Thompson & Hastie, 1990)—the failure of individuals to realize that others' preferences are congruent with their own—and *reactive devaluation* (Stillinger, Epelbaum, Keltner, & Ross, 1990)—the tendency to devalue concessions simply because someone with (ostensibly) opposing interests made them.

Given our earlier suggestions that successful collaboration is based on a core of congruency and a healthy accompaniment of complementary diversity, the inability of Researcher A to believe that another researcher's capabilities are complementary, or that another researcher's needs or preferences are congruent, would seem to doom Researcher A to a career of single authorship. The failure to perceive congruency raises the apparent costs of entering into a collaboration; the failure to perceive complementarity implies that there will be no benefit in doing so.

Many elements in collaborative relationships certainly appear, at first blush, to be distributive. For instance (and perhaps most obviously), a paper can have only one first author. This issue is both distributive and discrete—there is no possible compromise. Each researcher cannot be first author on half of the reprints. On this issue, one collaborator will "win" and the other will "lose."

There are some critical assumptions hiding in this "win/lose" perspective, however. Egocentric projection may lead researchers to assume that what they value most is also valued most by other researchers (Bazerman & Neale, 1983; Thompson & Hastie, 1990). As demonstrated by the example (mentioned earlier) of the tradeoff of first authorship for first public presentation, all researchers do not *necessarily* equally value all possible outputs of the research process. Interestingly, research has shown that Nobel laureates (Zuckerman, 1967) and American Psychological Association Distinguished Scientists (Over & Smallman, 1973) are significantly more likely than other researchers to be first authors on publications early in their careers and significantly *less* likely to be first authors on publications later in their careers. One implication of this finding is that first authorship becomes less valuable once a researcher's reputation is established (or full professorship is attained). Senior faculty also may come to value remaining active and contributing, mentoring others, and the social utility of collaborating, more than being first author. Also, with a sufficient reputation, a senior professor may realize that he or she will receive a large portion of the credit for a paper that is coauthored with junior colleagues, regardless of the order of authorship. Most fields, particularly the social, behavioral, and organizational sciences, typically distribute merit in line with reliable, consistent, and repeated contributions and the familiarity those contributions engender, rather than for isolated first authorships.

Integration does require an individual to give something up, but it means giving up something less valuable (first public presentation, perhaps) than what is received in return (for instance, first authorship). Reactive devaluation becomes a problem if a researcher believes he or she is conceding more than collaborators. As noted earlier, however, research suggests that multiauthored publications have greater impact (Oramaner, 1974). Further, the amount of this benefit personally sacrificed by not being first author is probably less than suspected. In one study, first authors received about 82 percent of the credit for a two-author article, while second authors were credited with about 68 percent; for three-author articles, the comparable figures were 74 percent, 62 percent, and 58 percent for first, second, and third authors, respectively (Nudelman & Landers, 1972). If a three-authored article receives as little as 20 percent more attention than a single-authored article (perhaps from the enhanced networking capabilities of its larger coauthor team), the third author's 58 percent share of the article's value would be worth about 70 percent of the value of publishing an article alone. Even assuming some collaboration processes losses (in the form of redundant effort, or accommodated or compromised elements), the third author of a three-authored publication still would be receiving more value per input than a single author working alone.

The failure of researchers to realize that their needs and preferences are congruent or complementary with those of potential coauthors is an example of a *prospective* "fixed pie" bias that might prevent researchers from pursuing collaboration opportunities. The flip side of this particular coin is *retrospective* "fixed pie" bias—the failure of researchers to realize that a successful collaboration has been integrative. Availability refers to the general tendency of individuals to overweight the value of information that is more available (Kahneman & Tversky, 1973). In jury decision making, for instance, vividly presented information is more available in memory and thereby given more weight in final judgments than equally probative information not presented vividly (Wilson, Northcraft, & Neale, 1989). In the case of research collaboration, most researchers see all the work they do but only a portion of that contributed by their coresearchers. A researcher's own contributions of ideas and insights probably are also more available than those of collaborators, as is the amount of time the researcher spent *thinking about* the work (e.g., Ross & Sicoly, 1979). It should not be surprising, then, that when researchers assess the proportion of their own contributions to a completed project, the total of their perceived contributions can be as high as 300 percent (Broad, 1981). Unfortunately, this availability bias can dramatically undercut the perceived integrative gain from collaboration. Even if a first author gets 70 percent of the credit for a three-author publication, it may still seem too little if the first author feels as if he or she has done 90 percent of the work.

Finally, some cognitive biases may lead to *both* prospective and retrospective beliefs that there is no "value added" in research collaboration. Overconfidence is a general tendency of individuals to have unwarranted levels of confidence in their judgmental abilities (Einhorn, 1978). A close cousin of overconfidence is the illusion of superiority (Taylor & Brown, 1988)—a general tendency of individuals to believe that they are better than average at almost everything. Research has repeatedly demonstrated that the probability estimates that individuals assign to uncertain events are unjustifiably high, with 98 percent confidence intervals covering as little as 60 percent of actual events (Alpert & Raiffa, 1982). Similarly, negotiators' mean estimates of the probability that an arbitrator will accept *their* final offer over their opponent's final offer is 67.8 percent—an impossibly overconfident estimate since the mean can only be 50 percent (Bazerman & Neale, 1982).

In the context of scientific collaboration, overconfidence and the illusion of superiority may surface prospectively when a researcher believes that he or she is capable of completing certain elements of the research enterprise just as efficiently or just as effectively as potential collaborators who are truly experts at those elements. A mediocre writer who believes that he or she can create a literary masterpiece is unlikely to see any value in adding an expert writer to the research team. In effect, this individual would perceive no integrative potential in collaboration and would be unlikely to pursue collaboration opportunities.

Overconfidence also might surface retrospectively as a "hindsight bias." Hindsight bias occurs when individuals alter their perception of the inevitability of an event once that event has occurred (e.g., Fischhoff, 1975). In research collaborations, hindsight bias occurs when a researcher honestly believes that he or she could just as easily have contributed all the winning insights and completed the project in the same time as the team. Again, the danger here is not that valuable collaboration has not occurred, but that collaborators have failed to perceive it.

All of these cognitive biases—the "fixed pie bias," the "incompatibility error," availability, overconfidence, and the illusion of superiority—represent barriers to the birth and growth of scientific collaboration. Unlike the practical problems discussed earlier, however, they are not real barriers to entry into collaboration, only illusory ones. Together with the practical problems, though, they do make one wonder: How do researchers ever end up working together?

FOSTERING INTEGRATIVE COLLABORATION

Entry into collaboration promises short-term costs, uncertain long-term benefits, and cognitive processes that work against perceiving favorable arrangements even when they do occur. One potential cure for these problems can be found in Hirschmann's (1972) consideration of why individuals do not exit organizations: *loyalty*. Loyalty is the willingness of individuals to remain in a relationship (e.g., a research collaboration) even when it looks like a good idea to leave. Furthermore, Hirschmann casts loyalty not as some "warm-and-fuzzy" psychological sense of attachment, but rather as formal arrangements (or procedures) that create costs of exit or nonparticipation. Loyalty incites dissatisfied participants to search for solutions to problems (what Hirschmann calls "voice"), rather than forfeiting the costs of exit or nonparticipation. This section of the chapter considers three such formal arrangements that increase the probability of collaboration success by inducing collaborative "loyalty": contracts, grants, and friendships.

Contracts

Contracts are formal, binding agreements that obligate parties to an exchange relationship involving specified inputs and outputs (Stinchcombe, 1986, p. 267). Contracts typically are undertaken to manage the uncertainty of future input commitments and output streams (Northcraft & Neale, 1990, p. 616). Contracts decrease uncertainty by specifying the future exchange relationship. A contract limits the maximum number of inputs required and the minimum number of outputs received by the parties. The downside of a contract is that it also may limit the parties' upside potential. This upside limit is the cost of decreased uncertainty in the exchange relationship.

Contracts, even informal ones, have implications for both the practical and cognitive barriers to successful coauthorship. At the practical level, contracting can alter the *time frame* of collaboration. Imagine, for instance, that three researchers agree to work together. As noted earlier, one important barrier to the birth of collaboration is researchers' perceptions of distributive elements with no middle ground. If these three researchers agreed to work only on one paper together, only one could be the first author; the other two might feel that they had lost in the transaction and would be less willing to try again. On the other hand, if they agree (contract) to work on *three* papers together, each can be first author once, second author once, and third author once. By extending the time frame of the collaboration (from one project to three), distributive elements of the collaboration (e.g., authorship) can now be compromised across time, rather than accommodated. No team member need suffer the uncertainty of making concessions that may never be reciprocated in the future.

The extended time frame provides other benefits. Working on multiple projects increases the probability that the collaborators will discover capability complements—they can move further along the time line shown in Figure 2, toward the point where incongruencies are well amortized and integrative benefits have been realized. The extended time frame also increases the possibility that the team members will realize that even the distributive elements of the collaboration (such as authorship) are not necessarily "win/lose" propositions. While contracts cannot decrease the certain costs of entry into collaboration, they do ensure that those costs will be amortized over a longer time frame—a time frame in which integrative benefits are more likely to be realized.

Contracts also can help collaborators deal with cognitive barriers to the perception of collaborative benefits. Coauthors can agree up front (contract) on the allocation of inputs and outputs among themselves. For example, Researcher A will write the first draft for manuscript 1 and be first author, Researcher B will only analyze the data for manuscript 2 and will be third author, etc. Discussing and specifying these arrangements *before* the work is done should help collaborators divide up the work so that no one later will feel overworked or undercompensated. Discussing these arrangements beforehand also offers a forum for discovering where capability or output complements in the research team may exist.

By definition, all contracts have a downside—namely, the loss of some upside potential. Contracts also may focus the attention or anchor the effort level of collaborators only on fulfilling the terms of the contract (e.g., Polzer & Neale, 1991; Staw & Boettger, 1988) rather than contributing (and achieving) more. In the research realm, the additional cost of multiple-study contracting is that a researcher may come to realize that a collaboration (to which the researchers are now committed) has little integrative potential, or that the costs of realizing the collaboration's integrative potential outweigh its benefits. This may be a cost of collaborating. If nothing else, multiple-study contracting decreases the probability that a researcher will prematurely and erroneously reach this conclusion.

Grants

Research grants provide an elegant extension to the idea of using multiple-study contracts to promote successful collaboration. Grants offer all the benefits of informal multiple-study collaborative contracting, with two bonuses.

First, at the practical level research grants make multiple-study contracting additionally beneficial by expanding the research"pie." Up-front multiple-study research contracting may sound like a tedious, "Let's-collaborate-but-I-don't-trust-you" approach to working together. When formally constituted as an accepted multiple-study research grant, however, authors can receive for the grant some of the same accolades accorded to completed publications. Two studies and an accepted grant proposal surely are worth more vita points than the same two studies without the accepted proposal.

The monetary resources offered by grants can provide "side payments" (Shubik, 1975)—benefits received outside of the researchers' input/output arrangements—that soften the short-term costs of working through the collaboration's incongruencies. Grant funding also admits others into a collaboration's integrative loop. Deans and department heads bask in the reflected glory of external legitimation of their selection decisions, at little expense to the researchers. The overhead dollars that grant acceptance brings may even help foster a conspiracy of cooperation among researchers and administrators. Given the influx of dollars to offset administrative costs, department heads and deans may be willing to grant the researchers' requests for more favorable teaching assignments, better access to facilities, doctoral student support, or other issues tangentially related to conducting the grant-supported research.

These are all essentially practical matters, however. At the cognitive level, research grants also improve on informal multiple-study contracting by making the contracting process *public*. Public commitment to multiple-study collaboration reduces researchers' uncertainty that the collaboration will continue. Perhaps more importantly, public commitment should activate self-justification processes (e.g., Salancik, 1976; Staw & Ross, 1978) that strengthen the value of working together.

Friendships

Both contracts and grants increase the probability of successful joint research by altering the perceived time frame of the collaboration negotiation. Contracts and grants extend the time frame to include multiple publications, thereby enhancing opportunities to trade off discretely distributive elements of the collaboration; by extending the time frame of the collaboration, they also increase the probability that early incongruencies in the collaboration will be ameliorated and the collaboration's potential will be realized. In contrast to the time-honored wisdom of "not mixing business with pleasure," cultivating personal friendships with prospective scientific collaborators also may serve these purposes.

Greenhalgh (1987) notes that casting a negotiation in the context of a long-term personal relationship (such as friendship) alters the nature of bargaining. Imagine two individuals negotiating the purchase price of a car—one a car dealer, the other a business school professor looking for a new car. Personal friendship between them would *extend the time horizon* of the negotiation, so that opportunities for reciprocation would increase and have a greater chance to be realized. The car dealer could give the professor a better deal than the typical buyer, perhaps in anticipation of later needing a favor (perhaps some consulting?). This concession does not have to be explicit; part of being friends is doing things for each other, in the integrative sense of trading favors. Collaborators who are friends may see their coauthorship negotiations within a longer time horizon, where first authorship and labor responsibilities can be traded off across multiple projects.

Within the context of negotiations, personal relationships also change the relative importance of disputed issues. Personal friendships offer a host of other issues that can be used as the basis for creating integrative agreements—including the social utility of the relationship. This is not to suggest that authorship might be bartered off for a few free dinners at a friend's house; nor would it justify the practice of simply adding names of friends (noncontributors) to publications (Broad, 1981). However, it might mean that in the context of a personal relationship first authorship for a particular paper might be conceded to a collaborator if it were especially important to his or her career.

Personal relationships also imply *trust*. Trust can be the basis for trading the information (either volunteering it or believing it when received) necessary for identifying integrative potential. Of the three considered to be prerequisites to identifying integrative potential—time, a problem-solving orientation, and high aspirations (Bazerman, Magliozzi, & Neale, 1985; Pruitt, 1983)—the first two clearly are enhanced by friendship. Interestingly, low aspirations may be a cost that being friends imposes on collaborators. Precisely because negotiations among friends occur against the backdrop of many other issues, friends may be less likely to push their individual agendas. This might lead to missed opportunities for integration—settling for inefficient or ineffective compromises to avoid conflict in the relationship (Valley & Neale, 1991).

Finally, evidence suggests that communication dividends can be reaped from collaborating with friends. Albrecht and Ropp (1984) note that people who communicate both at work and socially—"high multiplexity" communication—exchange *more* information about work than individuals who communicate only about work. Work-and-friendship communication relationships entail more communication episodes than work-only communication relationships; more communication episodes in turn provide more opportunities for work-related information to be exchanged. In the context of joint research, these additional communication episodes provide additional opportunities to work through incongruencies in the collaboration and to discover integrative potential. This suggests both a faster drop in the "process losses" of joint work and a shorter wait to realize integrative benefits.

Working with friends has the additional advantage of being wrapped in the illusion of superiority described previously. Self-worth is enhanced by believing that one's friends are better than most people (Tesser, Campbell, & Smith, 1984). The amount of reward and positive evaluation accorded friends is greater than that accorded equally performing strangers (Brewer & Kramer, 1985; Brown, 1986). Finally, in contrast to the usual application of the fundamental attribution error, friends are given more credit for success and less blame for failure than are most distant others (Hall & Taylor, 1976).

This is not to suggest that one should only collaborate with friends. Rather, it suggests that cultivating social relationships with collaborators can have value. Not only does all work and no play make Jack a dull boy; all work and no play between Jack and Jill may decrease the likelihood that their research collaboration will succeed.

THE RENEWAL FACTOR

The central theme of this chapter is that successful research collaboration involves a negotiation, one in which congruencies and complements need to be recognized and incongruencies worked out. Researchers who do not collaborate may miss valuable opportunities to enhance both the quality, scope, and efficiency of their work. However, once two researchers have established a successful collaboration, they must face a new problem: Over time the integrative benefits of the relationship may dwindle. The value of collaboration is its integrative potential. The paradox is that this integrative potential may block the addition of new collaborators, and new collaborators are key to renewing diversity in the relationship. Either member of a successful collaboration may find working with others difficult. Over time, the diversity that led the collaborators to come together successfully is replaced by ever-increasing, subtle, and potentially undetectable similarity. Maintaining initial levels of diversity runs counter to the increasing opportunities for developing similarities through continued interaction and mutual influence.

The reason for this apparent paradox is accommodation through specialization and assimilation. According to the model of collaboration described in this paper, a successful collaboration will be achieved when the incongruencies in a collaboration have been accommodated or compromised (for instance, a way of assigning authorship has been worked out), and complementary capabilities and needs have been recognized, so that the advantages of having experts working on each part of the task can be obtained. As noted earlier, the recognition of complementary capabilities may become a self-fulfilling prophecy (i.e., the better writer becomes a better writer by doing more of the writing). This same result may occur for accommodations in the collaboration. If neither collaborator likes to code data, someone has to and in doing so may become good at it (and even come to enjoy it!). Further, the disposition of benefits from the collaboration becomes assumed in the relationship—a settled issue.

In addition to specialization, accommodation has another, much less intended, influence on the collaboration—assimilation. If the research team is successful in producing manuscripts, they are likely to spend increasing amounts of time interacting. As the amount of interaction increases, the collaborators mutually influence the thinking and perspectives of each other. Over time, and especially to the extent that they are successful, collaborators not only assimilate each other's views but also develop a body of literature and a common way of thinking about research. They come to resemble the solitary researcher in the diversity they bring to research.

All of this suggests that the successful negotiation of an integrative collaboration can raise the barriers to entry for other prospective collaborators. New collaborators have to need an output from the collaboration that is not already spoken for; they need to contribute something not already provided. With elements already allocated (i.e., assigned inputs, claimed outputs), the degrees of freedom for discovering further integration with a new collaborator are limited, and the probability for success, therefore, lower. Further, the choice for the already-successful collaborators is between the efficiency of their current arrangements compared to the certainty of process losses from working through incongruencies with a new collaborator. This also would be the case for either member of a successful collaboration working outside the collaboration with someone else. Certainly, successful collaborators will know the benefits that can be obtained and may understand better how to obtain them; they also will be familiar with the costs. As a framing issue (Tversky & Kahneman, 1981), this resembles the choice between a certain benefit (the current collaboration) and a risky but potentially more valuable benefit (the additional collaborator).

Once two researchers have established a successful collaboration, the best candidates for adding to the relationship or working with either member individually are researchers *without* well-developed input specializations or output preferences. A new collaborator who would take over a collaboration's remaining incongruencies would be very attractive. Established researchers, with their output preferences and input capabilities already in place, are unlikely candidates to fit these requirements, especially when prospective collaborators are peers who value similar outputs.

Working in favor of new collaboration partners is the mobility of partners to a successful collaboration. Success generates new and better employment opportunities, and distance between established collaborators makes newly proximal researchers more attractive prospects. Changing locations, however, seems an extreme prescription for maintaining diversity in a collaboration.

Thus, *vertical* collaboration (for instance, between senior and junior faculty) may be the most likely way to add new collaborators. Senior faculty are likely to have less need for first-authorship, well-developed ability specializations and fixed output preferences. Further, junior faculty may find a particular department more attractive because senior researchers offer the opportunity to collaborate. Junior faculty have more to gain and lower status and therefore may be more adaptable to help begin a collaboration.

Working with doctoral students may promise an even greater likelihood of finding integrative potential. Doctoral students' premier output preference often is the opportunity to learn about the research enterprise and to develop as a researcher. These preferences/needs are a natural complement to a junior faculty member's high need for productivity and first authorship, or a senior faculty member's role as mentor. Further, doctoral students may be at an early enough career stage that capability (input) specialties or preferences are not yet developed. A doctoral student thus could assume, and develop as his or her unique competence, some element of research collaboration that has remained distributive for an extant research team. At the theoretical level this could mean becoming an expert in a topical area (e.g., agency theory) or methodological skill (e.g., LOGIT analysis) essential to a research team's upcoming project, and for which no current members of the team possess expertise. Doctoral students need to develop some unique competence—why not something that becomes integrative for the team and ensures their place on it?

The willingness of students or junior faculty to take on tasks that reduce the costs of conducting research for senior members of the team is not renewal. It simply reduces the costs of admitting new members into the collaboration. The renewal—fresh diversity—is provided when doctoral students and junior faculty are offered opportunities to incorporate different perspectives and new ways of conceptualizing and investigating interesting problems.

CONCLUSION

Our purpose in this chapter is to provide a framework for understanding successful research collaborations as well as identifying mechanisms through which the successful selection of collaborators takes place. The application of existing research in behavioral decision theory and negotiation provides the theoretical underpinnings for such mechanisms. A secondary goal of this chapter is to provide a creative application of basic research (such as that in behavioral decision theory and negotiation) to a real-world issue—research collaboration. While there has been a significant amount of empirical and theoretical work on collaborative research, the selection of collaborators has received little attention to date.

The framework proposed in this chapter—collaboration as the recognition of congruence, the management of incongruence, and the integration of complementary diversity—has applications beyond dyadic or triadic research collaborations. Diverse capability integration is probably a useful way of thinking about putting together *any* collaborative enterprise, from the conscription of volleyball teammates to the recruitment of new faculty members in an academic department. Certainly, business joint ventures and corporate diversification work best when partners bring unique expertise and diverse perspectives to the partnership (Bantel & Jackson, 1989), but only within the context of shared agendas and sufficient preference congruencies to achieve substantial economies of scale.

One issue that this chapter underemphasizes is that research collaborations often have goals other than successful research productivity. Collaboration is a social process, and for many researchers there is camaraderie in joint work that has value and social utility beyond its instrumental furthering of individual productivity. This is not to suggest that researchers use unproductive collaborations to satisfy social needs. It does suggest, however, that joint work might arise as a byproduct of socializing. If two people like spending time together, collaboration is one vehicle for doing so. It also suggests that the social utility of collaboration might help defray some of the entry costs (accommodations and compromises) that prevent the integrative potential of a collaboration from ever being pursued, let alone realized.

This chapter proved to be autobiographical in two ways for its authors: first, in reviewing and summarizing their research and that of their colleagues; and second, in applying this past work to understanding the successes and failures of their own collaborative research relationships. This chapter also proved to be integrative in three ways: first, in integrating the needs of the conference coordinator (for a research review paper) with the authors' need to do something new and different (anything but a research review paper); second, in finding a conceptual integration between decision-theoretic negotiation research and the process of research collaboration; and third, by (once again) integrating the input capabilities and output preferences of the coauthor team to produce a final product. The authors trust that the efficiency with which this product was produced and the quality of the insights it offers support the value of finding truly integrative collaborations, both at work and play.

REFERENCES

ALBRECHT, T. L., & ROPP, V. A. (1984). Communicating about innovation in networks of three U.S. organizations. *Journal of Communication* (summer), 78–91.

ALPERT, M., & RAIFFA, H. (1982). A progress report on the training of probability assessors. In D. Kahneman, P. Slovic, & A. Tversky (Eds.), *Judgment under uncertainty: Heuristics and biases* (pp. 294–305). Cambridge: Cambridge University Press.

AMABILE, T. M. (1983). The social psychology of creativity. *Journal of Personality and Social Psychology, 45,* 357–376.

ASHBY, W. R. (1956). *An introduction to cybernetics,* London: Methuen & Company, Ltd.

BANTEL, K. A., & JACKSON, S. E. (1989). Top management and innovations in banking: Does the composition of the top team make a difference? *Strategic Management Journal, 10,* 107–124.

BAZERMAN, M. H., & CARROLL, J. S. (1987). Negotiator cognition. In B. Staw & L. Cummings (Eds.), *Research in organizational behavior* (Vol. 9, pp. 247–288). Greenwich, CT: JAI Press.

BAZERMAN, M. H., MAGLIOZZI, T., & NEALE, M. A. (1985). The acquisition of an integrative response in a competitive market. *Organizational Behavior and Human Performance, 34,* 294–313.

BAZERMAN, M. H., & NEALE, M. A. (1982). Improving negotiation effectiveness under final offer arbitration: The role of selection and training. *Journal of Applied Psychology, 67,* 543–548.

BAZERMAN, M. H., & NEALE, M. A. (1983). Heuristics in negotiation: Limitations to dispute resolution effectiveness. In M. Bazerman & R. Lewicki (Eds.), *Negotiating in organizations* (pp. 51–67). Beverly Hills: Sage Publications.

BREWER, M. B., & KRAMER, R. M. (1985). The psychology of intergroup attitudes and behaviors. *Annual Review of Psychology, 36,* 219–244.

BROAD, W. J. (1981). The publishing game: Getting more for less. *Science, 211,* 1137–1138.

BROWN, J. D. (1986). Evaluations of self and others: Self-enhancement biases in social judgments. *Social Cognition, 4,* 353–376.

EINHORN, H. (1978). Decision error and fallible judgment: Implications for social policy. In K. Hammond (Ed.), *Judgment and decision in public policy formulation* (pp. 65–107). Denver: Westview Press.

FISCHHOFF, B. (1975). Hindsight $\neq$ foresight: The effect of outcome knowledge on judgment under uncertainty. *Journal of Experimental Psychology: Human Perception and Performance, 1,* 288–299.

GREENHALGH, L. (1987). Relationships in negotiations. *Negotiation Journal, 3,* 235–243.

HACKMAN, J. R., & MORRIS, C. G. (1975). Group tasks, group interaction process, and group performance effectiveness. In L. Berkowitz (Ed.), *Advances in experimental social psychology* (Vol. 7, pp. 127–169). New York: Academic Press.

HALL, J., & TAYLOR, S. E. (1976). When love is blind. *Human Relations, 29,* 751–761.

HIRSCHMANN, A. O. (1972). *Exit, voice and loyalty: Responses to decline in firms, organizations, and states.* Cambridge, MA: Harvard University Press.

HANNAN, M. T., & FREEMAN, J. (1977). The population ecology of organizations. *American Journal of Sociology, 82,* 379–398.

KAHNEMAN, D., SLOVIC, P., & TVERSKY, A. (1982). *Judgment under uncertainty: Heuristics and biases.* Cambridge: Cambridge University Press.

KAHNEMAN, D., & TVERSKY, A. (1973). On the psychology of prediction. *Psychological Review, 80,* 237–251.

KANTER, R. M. (1977). *Men and women of the corporation.* New York: Basic Books.

KUHN, T. S. (1970). *The structure of scientific revolutions.* Hyde Park: University of Chicago Press.

MANDELL, B., & KOHLER–GRAY, S. (1990). Management development that values diversity. *Personnel* (March), 41–47.

MANNIX, E. A., & LOEWENSTEIN, G. F. (1991). *Managerial time horizons and inter-firm mobility: An experimental investigation.* Working paper, University of Chicago.

NEALE, M. A., & BAZERMAN, M. H. (1991). *Cognition and rationality in negotiation.* New York: Free Press.

NORTHCRAFT, G. B., & NEALE, M. A. (1990). *Organizational behavior: A management challenge.* Hinsdale, IL: Dryden Press.

NUDELMAN, A. E., & LANDERS, C. E. (1972). The failure of 100 divided by 3 to equal 33⅓. *American Sociologist, 7,* 9.

OROMANER, M. (1974). Collaboration and impact: The careers of multi-authored publications. *Social Science Information, 14,* 147–155.

OVER, R. (1982). Collaborative research and publication in psychology. *American Psychologist, 37,* 996–1001.

OVER, R., & SMALLMAN, S. (1973). Maintenance of individual visibility in publication of collaborative research by psychologists. *American Psychologist, 28,* 161–166.

POLZER, J., & NEALE, M. A. (1991). *Updating the negotiator: Goal revision and rigidity in negotiations.* Working paper, Dispute Resolution Research Center, Northwestern University.

PRICE, D. J. (1963). *Little science, big science.* New York: Columbia University Press.

PRUITT, D. (1983). Achieving integrative agreements. In M. Bazerman & R. Lewicki (Eds.), *Negotiating in organizations* (pp. 35–50). Beverly Hills: Sage Publications.

ROSENTHAL, R. (1973). The Pygmalian effect lives. *Psychology Today, 7,* 56–63.

ROSS, M., & SICOLY, F. (1979). Ego-centric biases in availability and attribution. *Journal of Personality and Social Psychology, 37,* 322–336.

SALANCIK, G. R. (1976). Commitment is too easy! *Organizational Dynamics* (summer), 207–222.

SHARPE, W. (1970). *Portfolio theory and capital markets.* New York: McGraw-Hill.

SHUBIK, M. (1975). *The uses and methods of gaming.* New York: Elsevier.

SOLOMON, C. M. (1990). Careers under glass. *Personnel Journal* (April), 96–105.

STAW, B. M., & BOETTGER, R. D. (1978). Commitment to a policy decision: A multi-theoretical perspective. *Administrative Sciences Quarterly, 23,* 40–64.

STAW, B. M., & ROSS, J. (1978). Commitment to a policy decision. A multi-theoretical perspective. *Administrative Science Quarterly, 23,* 40–64.

STAW, B. M., & ROSS, J. (1987). Behavior in escalation situations: Antecedents, prototypes, and solutions. In B. Staw & L. Cummings (Eds.), *Research in organizational behavior* (Vol. 9, pp. 39–78). Greenwich, CT: JAI Press.

STILLINGER, C., EPELBAUM, M., KELTNER, D., & ROSS, L. (1990). *The "reactive devaluation" barrier to conflict resolution.* Working paper, Stanford University.

STINCHCOMBE, A. (1986). *Stratification and organizations.* Cambridge: Cambridge University Press.

TAYLOR, S. E., & BROWN, J. D. (1988). Illusion and well-being: A social psychology perspective on mental health. *Psychological Bulletin, 103,* 193–210.

TESSER, A., CAMPBELL, J., & SMITH, M. (1984). Friendship choice and performance: Self-evaluation maintenance in children. *Journal of Personality and Social Psychology, 46,* 561–574.

THOMPSON, L. (1990). An examination of naive and experienced negotiators. *Journal of Personality and Social Psychology, 59,* 82–90.

THOMPSON, L. L., & HASTIE, R. M. (1990). Social perception in negotiation. *Organizational Behavior and Human Decision Processes, 47,* 98–123.

TVERSKY, A., & KAHNEMAN, D. (1981). Framing of decisions and the psychology of choice. *Science, 211,* 453–458.

VALLEY, K., & NEALE, M. A. (1991). *The influence of relationship on achieving integrative agreements: The ups and downs of friendship.* Working paper, Dispute Resolution Research Center, Northwestern University.

WILSON, M. G., NORTHCRAFT, G. B., & NEALE, M. A. (1989). Information competition and vividness effects in on-line judgments. *Organizational Behavior and Human Decision Processes, 44,* 132–139.

ZUCKERMAN, H. (1977). *Scientific elite: Nobel laureates in the United States.* New York: Free Press.

ZUCKERMAN, H. A. (1967). Nobel laureates in science: Patterns of productivity, collaboration, and authorship. *American Sociological Review, 32,* 391–403.

CHAPTER ELEVEN

The Classics and the Contemporary: A New Blend of Small Group Theory

Deborah G. Ancona

MIT

This chapter summarizes the results of several studies aimed at developing an "external perspective" toward the study of effective group interaction. These studies of five consulting teams and 45 new product teams show that groups develop distinct strategies toward their environment that are related to managerial ratings of performance and to internal group process. The findings are moved to a more general theory of groups through the application of the work of George Homans and Kurt Lewin. This new theory argues that group behavior should be viewed as a series of escalating cycles of interaction between groups and their environment. Groups help "create" their environments through the permeability of their boundaries. Environments present a set of constraints to which the group must adapt. Different rates of revolutionary environmental change require that teams employ different strategies.

This chapter is about groups. Yet the research presented here differs from that usually found in the dominant social psychology paradigm. This research uses ongoing organizational teams, not one-time laboratory groups. The tasks of these organizational teams are complex and evolving, not simple and set. The task allocators are managers, not academics.

The key element that differentiates this research, however, is its focus. Rather than sitting on the group boundary and looking inward, the research lens includes both behaviors within the group and those directed outward, toward other parts of the organization (i.e., an "external perspective"; Ancona, 1987).

In a world of hypothesis generators and testers, this chapter is backwards. That is, it begins with data and ends with theory. This orientation follows our state of knowledge about groups' external activities. Since very little was known about external group activity prior to the work presented here, the first stages of research were necessarily description and classification (Gladstein & Quinn, 1985; Kerlinger, 1973). This early work allows us to move on to the task of inferring relationships among variables and positing hypotheses that go beyond the data and attempt to create a more general theory of groups.

My major sources in this movement from description to theory building are the classic works of George Homans and Kurt Lewin. Both were grand theorists who worked with real groups and modeled the interaction between internal and external group activity. Unfortunately, much of this early work has been either ignored or forgotten. Nevertheless, it provides an important guide to a more mid-range theory of groups. Thus, this chapter ends with a melding of data and classic theory, resulting in some new models of group behavior.

THE EXTERNAL PERSPECTIVE

The impetus for the first study on the external perspective came from a study of one hundred sales teams in the telecommunications industry (Gladstein, 1984). Following the dominant internal paradigm, the study tested two competing models of group performance: the humanistic model and the decision-making model. The humanistic school concentrates primarily on maintenance behaviors; that is, behaviors that "build, strengthen, and regulate group life" (Philip & Dunphy, 1959, p. 162). The school is characterized by a normative approach that encourages openness and the building of trust within a group (Likert, 1961). The decision-making school concentrates on particular task behaviors, behaviors aimed at solving the group's objective task. Decision theorists posit that behaviors such as weighting individual inputs according to knowledge and skill and discussing performance strategies for novel problems (Hackman, Brousseau, & Weiss, 1976; Hoffman, 1979) will improve group performance.

During preliminary interviews, salespeople frequently spoke of the importance of their interactions with their firm's installation and repair teams. Thus, several survey questions were added to pursue how teams interacted with other groups within their organization. It was hypothesized that these relationships would form another dimension to the task behaviors of the group.

The results were surprising. First, group members did not perceive process as separating into the traditional task and maintenance components (Bales, 1958; Philip & Dunphy, 1959; Schein, 1988). Instead, process was seen as divided into an internal and external component; behaviors taking place among group members versus those with outsiders. Second, while internal group process predicted solely team-member satisfaction and team-rated performance, external process was associated only with sales revenue (i.e. an objective, external measure of performance). Thus, an aspect of group process that had been virtually ignored in the literature facilitated organizational performance indicators in ways that internal processes did not. Unfortunately, we still knew very little about what those external activities were.

Our external perspective began with the simple realization that organizational group process was not fully represented by internal activities. Group members interact with one another, but they are also proactive with outsiders; seeking information and resources, interpreting signals, and molding external opinion. Common sense suggests that causal arrows move in both directions from the group to the environment and back again. Thus, although the environment does constrain action and shape beliefs, it probably is not deterministic. Similarly, the group is not omnipotent, but it can help determine external definitions of task and performance.

Several research questions guided a series of studies aimed at fleshing out this new approach to group behavior. In addition to asking the traditional question, "How does the group influence individuals?" we now asked "How does the organization influence the group?". Rather than asking "How do individuals attend to and map the group?" our question became "How does the group reach out to its environment?". In essence, we added the study of the dynamics between teams and their environment to the study of internal group dynamics.

A longitudinal study of five consulting teams (Ancona, 1990) and 45 new product teams in five high-technology organizations (Ancona & Caldwell, 1987, 1988, 1991, 1992) yielded four key findings. First, organizational teams develop a distinct set of external activities and strategies toward their external environment. Second, these activities are positively and significantly related to managerial ratings of performance. Third, there is a complex interaction between internal and external process that appears to change over time. Finally, just as teams show patterns of internal dynamics—for example, midpoint transitions (Gersick, 1988, 1989) and conflict over power (Schein, 1985)—so too do they display particular dynamics with their external environment. Each finding in our studies is explained in more detail later.

EXTERNAL ACTIVITIES AND STRATEGIES

Although the bulk of small group research has focused on internal dynamics, some researchers have examined external initiatives. Adherents of the information processing school have monitored the amount of information exchanged between teams and their environment, positing that groups must match their information processing capability to the information processing demands of the task environment (Allen, 1984; Gresov, 1989; Nadler & Tushman, 1988). However, by focusing primarily on the frequency, rather than the content, of this communication, these studies have not addressed the broader question of the purpose and nature of those interactions (Ancona & Caldwell, 1991).

In direct contrast to the information processing theorists, researchers examining particular organizational phenomena have concentrated on specific activities enacted by groups. For example, those studying innovation have focused on boundary spanning and the transfer of technical information across team boundaries (Allen, 1984; Aldrich & Herker, 1977; Katz & Tushman, 1979), those studying interdependence have focused on intergroup coordination (Malone, 1987), and those studying power and resource allocation have focused on political or persuasive action with external constituents (Dean, 1987; Pfeffer, 1981). Because they were studying specific organizational phenomena, these researchers did not use the group as a focal unit. As such, they have not tried to map the full range of external activities that groups use to deal with a broad set of environmental demands (Ancona & Caldwell, 1991).

Ancona and Caldwell (1987, 1991) attempted to complement existing theory by specifying the range of external activities new product teams use to meet environmental demands. The data included a log of all of the external activities of two teams for 2 weeks, interviews with 38 new product team leaders and managers, and surveys from 45 new product teams. Factor analysis results suggested three major styles of external action within the organization: ambassador, task coordinator, and scout.

Ambassador activity includes both buffering and representation. Examples of buffering include such things as protecting the team and absorbing outside pressure. One new product team leader said this activity was best explained by Tom West, a major character in the *Soul of a New Machine* (Kidder, 1981), who said "I don't pass on the garbage and the politics." Representational activities include persuading others to support the team and lobbying for resources. Members carrying out these activities communicate frequently with those above them in the hierarchy such as top R&D management, top division, and even top corporate management (Ancona & Caldwell, 1990).

Task coordinator activity is aimed at coordinating technical or design issues. Examples of activities in this set include discussing design problems with others, obtaining feedback on the product design, and coordinating and negotiating with outsiders. Individuals carrying out these activities show high levels of communication laterally through the organization with such groups as R&D and manufacturing (Ancona & Caldwell, 1990).

Scout activity involves general scanning for ideas and information about the competition, the market, or the technology. This activity set differs from previous ones in that it relates to general scanning as opposed to handling specific coordination issues. Individuals carrying out this activity show high levels of communication with marketing, sales, and R&D (Ancona & Caldwell, 1990).

External initiatives seem to be necessary for a group to obtain key resources in their environment. Ambassadorial activities establish access to the power structure of the organization and enable the group to manage vertical dependence. They protect the team from excessive interference from the top and facilitate the group's legitimacy and survival by identifying key threats, securing resources, and promoting the team's image. Task coordinator activities provide access to the work-flow structure; they enable the group to manage horizontal dependence. They fill in many of the gaps left by formal integrating systems. Through coordination, negotiation, and feedback, groups establish stronger relationships with other organizational units that can contribute to the group's performance. Scout activities provide access to information enabling the group to increase its expertise. They let the group update its information base, providing new ideas and up-to-date information about technologies and markets (Ancona & Caldwell, 1991).

While the first part of this research program documented and described a full set of external activities, it did not examine how teams organize themselves to carry out their external strategies. In other words, not all groups have the capacity or willingness to engage in all three activities. Some teams specialize, some are generalists, and others engage in no external activity at all. We use the term *strategy* to label these patterns of external activity. This is not to suggest that such patterns are necessarily intentional, just that they were exhibited consistently over a given period of time.

Our analysis suggested that groups clustered into four distinct strategies, having similar scores on the ambassador, task coordinator, and scout variables. The first strategy concentrates on ambassador activity and very little else; we labeled it Ambassadorial. The second combined scout activities with some task coordination; we called it Technical Scouting. The third strategy was low on all dimensions, with some minimal scout activity. We labeled this pattern Isolationist. Finally, the fourth strategy had members who felt responsible for both ambassadorial and task coordinator activities, but little scouting. This strategy avoided general scanning; it focused on external interaction to both persuade others that its work was important and to coordinate, negotiate, and obtain feedback from outside groups. We called it Comprehensive.

The four strategies that emerged in the new product team sample closely resembled those derived in the qualitative study of five consulting teams. While no ambassadorial teams were present in the latter, three other strategies were found. Informing groups, like Isolationists, remained relatively isolated from their environment. They made decisions using information that group members already had and defined their task themselves. Parading teams, like Technical Scouts, had high levels of passive scanning of the environment. They collected lots of information about the environment and were very visible to outsiders. Probing teams, like Comprehensives, sought outside feedback on their ideas and promoted their achievements within their organization. Probing teams also tested new ideas with outsiders to get early commitment and revised their knowledge of the environment through external contacts. This convergence of the two distinct data sets provides some support for the validity of the findings. Although different names were used to identify the strategies across studies, for the remainder of this chapter only the Ambassadorial, Technical Scouting, Isolationist, and Comprehensive are used.

ACTIVITIES, STRATEGIES, AND PERFORMANCE

Results from the new product teams (Ancona & Caldwell, 1991) indicated that external activities were definitely related to performance. Furthermore, external action was more strongly related to management ratings of performance than frequency of communication, the variable suggested by information processing theorists. The interaction of different team strategies provided important insights into the dynamics of performance. While ambassadorial activity was a key to external ratings of performance, its effects over the long term seemed to hold only when teams also engaged in task coordination. Pure ambassadorial and comprehensive teams moved along within budget and on schedule in the early months after they had formed. By the time their work was completed, however, the ambassadorial teams were rated as poor at innovation and team operations, while comprehensives continued to be the highest performers. This suggested that while managing the power structure alone may help speed a group along in its formative stages, as it formulates the work, contact with both the power and work-flow structures is needed to maintain performance. Not surprisingly, the process of moving through the complexity of producing a final product was facilitated when the teams got input from people throughout the organization. Thus, the combination of ambassadorial and task coordination activity allowed comprehensives to be effective both early and late in their life cycle.

Not all task activity was productive, however. Too much scout activity was related to low performance ratings. It may be that such teams constantly reacted to general environmental data and became unable to commit to producing a specific end product at a specific time. Alternatively, high levels of scouting may have reduced team members' efforts in the more performance-relevant external activities or into building effective internal processes (Ancona & Caldwell, 1991).

A very different pattern emerges when a team rated its own performance. Groups felt that they performed well when they concentrated their efforts internally; their perceptions of performance were negatively related to frequency of external communication and positively related to clear goals and priorities and high cohesiveness. Thus, as in the original study of sales teams, predictors of management-rated and team-rated performance were very different (Ancona & Caldwell, 1991; Gladstein, 1984).

Similar findings surfaced among the five consulting teams. The highest performers, as rated by top management 1 year after team formation, were the comprehensive teams, who combined upward persuasion with lateral feedback seeking, coordination, and testing of solutions. The lowest performer was the isolationist team, which remained isolated from both its external task environment (the customer) and top management. They were incorrect either in thinking that they had sufficient information to complete the task by themselves or in assuming that their performance would be evaluated independent of the process and visibility they displayed during the team's lifetime. In the middle were the scouting teams who were very visible in the external environment but were not viewed as achieving the task.

Although top management rated only the comprehensive teams as high performing, both the scouting and the comprehensive teams rated themselves as performing well at the end of 1 year. The comprehensive teams were quite satisfied because their efforts were recognized. The scouting teams, however, were angry because they felt unappreciated for all they had done.

The findings of the two studies support one another and suggest that external interaction that focuses on influencing top management and coordinating work across the organization will lead to the highest ratings of performance by top management. Furthermore, it is only in these teams that internal and external ratings of performance match one another and are positive.

INTERNAL AND EXTERNAL ACTIVITY

Most previous research suggests that external activities interfere with the development of effective internal operations. The internal cohesion that exists under conditions of groupthink (Janis, 1982, 1985) can promote external stereotyping and eliminate the import of external information that might damage group consensus. The intergroup literature (Smith, 1983, 1989) also suggests a negative relationship between internal and external activities. Groups can be underbounded—having many external ties but an inability to coalesce and motivate members to pull together their external knowledge—or overbounded—having high internal loyalty and a complex set of internal dynamics but an inability to reach out to the external world (Alderfer, 1976; Sherif, 1966). Finally, the conflict literature predicts intensified intragroup conflict when group members collect information from outsiders with different goals, cognitive styles, and attitudes (Schmidt & Kochan, 1972; Shaw, 1971).

Yet not all studies indicate a negative relationship. In a study of eight task forces, Gersick (1988) found that groups undergo a mid-point change where they fundamentally shift their basic assumptions and operating procedures. The study suggests that teams may deal with internal and external demands sequentially, first acting on initial information from the environment in isolation and then emerging to get further feedback and information from outsiders.

The studies discussed here show a complex relationship between external and internal process (Ancona & Caldwell, 1991). Frequency of external communication is not significantly related to internal task processes (e.g., the ability to set goals and priorities) but is significantly and negatively related to cohesiveness. Yet frequency measures group all types of communication together and mask the fact that not all external communication interferes with internal process. Ambassadorial action is significantly and positively related to internal task processes and marginally and positively related to cohesiveness. Task coordinator activity is not related to internal process, while scout activity is negatively related to both internal task process and cohesiveness.

Thus, while continuous general scanning seems to interfere with a team's ability to set goals and cohere, external activity aimed at influencing powerful outsiders facilitates internal action. An isolationist strategy is also positively related to internal process, particularly cohesiveness.

The consulting teams showed a change in the relationship between internal and external activities over time. Comprehensive team members were initially very dissatisfied with their teams. They were frustrated with poorly formulated goals, lack of direction, and the fact that the group often worked in small subgroups rather than as a whole. However, over time, as they pulled together their information about the environment and had positive feedback from the top management, satisfaction with internal processes increased. In contrast, scouting teams were extremely satisfied in the first few months but frustrated later because their work was not appreciated. The isolationist team in this study was very dissatisfied with their internal process throughout their history.

Thus, ambassadorial and comprehensive teams may not be cohesive initially, but they come together as they come to effectively interact with their environment. Results are more equivocal for scouting and isolationist teams. These teams seem to ignore their environment and enjoy cohesiveness and goal clarity, or suffer in their internal process due to negative external ratings of performance. It may be that scouting and isolationist teams are internally cohesive until they finally realize that they have failed to gain external legitimacy, after which their cohesion breaks down.

GROUP–ENVIRONMENT DYNAMICS

While the preceding sections describe a group as a free actor following a chosen strategy toward the environment, in reality this picture is too simple. The study of the five consulting teams (Ancona, 1990) shows that the environment reacts to a team, and then both team and context influence one another. The interactions between a group and its environment have patterns similar to the patterns of interaction between the members and the group itself in that there are struggles for identity and power. Just as individuals often spend time at the start of a group trying to determine what role they will play in the group, and which members will have power, so too do groups play out these same issues with key external constituents.

The themes of power and influence appear to play an important role in group–environment relations, with top management being a key player. Teams begin to act and, through their actions, top management clarifies what it wants the teams to do. For example, it was not until each of the consulting teams planned a different customer approach that the head of the organization realized that he wanted one unified approach. As top management begins to understand what it wants, it sets constraints and provides direction. Teams then react in a variety of ways; some welcome the direction, some try to shape the new directives, and others become resentful. For the latter, power struggles can occupy a great deal of time and energy and produce a lot of resentment.

Thus, an environment influences a team by setting limits on activity and by picking particular teams as models of effective performance. There is often a great deal of conflict as teams fight to maintain their autonomy in the face of these limits. A team can influence its environment by promoting its action as the model for effective task performance. Teams are not equally skilled in this influence process.

The external environment also plays the role of echo chamber (Ancona, 1990). Early in the consulting teams' existence, not much concrete information was available, so teams were not labeled by top management. Yet when the head of the organization felt that enough time had elapsed that output should have been visible, a review was set up. Afterward, information about how the teams performed and what top management liked got fed into the rest of the organization and amplified quickly. If a team was in trouble before the formal review, afterwards it was in bigger trouble because it now had a "problem" reputation. On the positive side, teams that were congratulated for their work developed a positive image, making it easier for them to continue on a successful track.

Thus, the first comparative, evaluative information—even if it is based on limited data—becomes big news. The environment changes whispers into roars, making it incumbent on groups to manage the information and images they send out early in their life cycle. These images appeared to get cast in concrete in the groups we studied: The initial reputations were intact a year later, despite efforts to change them; data were interpreted by top executives to support their original impressions. The inability to influence top management early on can be devastating to a team since they control resources and rewards. In short, early labeling creates self-fulfilling prophecies.

Finally, the environment acts as a selection mechanism. By creating a set of teams to meet new external market demands, the organization gets a wide variety of responses. This variety is useful to the organization for some period of time, until it becomes difficult to sustain. In choosing some responses over others, top management selects an organizational response. During the process some teams succeed and others fail. Indeed, two of the five consulting teams were finally disbanded and reconfigured to be more like the others. From a team standpoint this process is quite painful. However, from an organizational standpoint this may be an efficient way to discover new ways to meet environmental demands.

THE CLASSICS

While the research presented in this chapter has started to clarify some of the dynamics between teams and their environments, it remains highly specific and stays at the classification level rather than at the more general, abstract, theoretical level. To move in the latter direction, I examine the work of George Homans and Kurt Lewin. As was the style when they were writing, from the 1930s to the 1950s, both wrote at a very abstract level, creating a multitude of dissertation topics in paragraph after paragraph of hypothesis generation. Their style was to go back and forth between theory and data, slowly propelling the knowledge generation process. They both spent much of their long careers studying groups in their natural settings. They conceptualized the environment as a fundamental influence on a group, even though each is better known for his work on internal group dynamics. As I selected portions of their work to be presented here, I kept an external perspective on group action in mind. Therefore, I only summarize their theoretical work if it specifically highlights the nature of group–environment interaction.

George Homans

Homans believed that all of sociological theory could follow from a theory of the small group. In *The Human Group* (1950), he used the data from five case studies (the bank wiring room at the Western Electric Company's Hawthorne Works; the Norton Street Gang; a family in Tikopia, an island of Polynesia; Hilltown, a New England town; and an electric equipment company) to develop and illustrate a general theory of groups. After describing each group, Homans analyzed the description in terms of the theory he developed from all five cases. He attempted "to give one general form in which the results of observations of many particular groups may be expressed" (p. 21). He stated "the theory will show the group to be an organic whole; and the theory will be built up through careful examination of the link between social concept and social observation" (p. 17).

Homans first analyzed the group as a set of mutually dependent elements: activity, interaction, and sentiment. Activity refers to things that group members do, such as soldering metal or bowling. Interaction is independent of what group members may be doing, but instead refers to the fact that "some unit of activity of one man follows . . . or is stimulated by, some unit of activity of another" (p. 36). For example, when a wireman completes his work on one terminal and moves to the next, this is a signal to the solderman to begin work on the first terminal. Sentiment refers to the internal state of group members and must be inferred. The nature of the interdependence among the elements emerges from the data and is illustrated through a series of hypotheses, such as, "If the frequency of interaction between two or more persons increases, the degree of their liking for one another will increase and vice versa." In other words, activity, interaction, and sentiment feed on one another such that an increase (decrease) in one is often followed by an increase (decrease) in the other.

The internal workings of a group are further divided into an external and an internal system. The external system interacts with the environment and includes those behaviors that enable the group to survive in its environment. When members work together to produce output, their internal interaction is part of the external system. The internal system includes behavior that goes beyond the demands of the initial situation and changing environmental conditions. For example, the external system in the bank wiring room included communication patterns, physical positioning, and work allocation that was determined by the work flow and formal organizational rules. The informal cliques that developed as part of the group's internal system followed closely, but not directly, from this external system. Over time, the cliques deviated more and more from the external system as norms and rituals evolved that concerned interpersonal interaction and sentiment more than work.

But Homans did not solely model internal processes. He was quick to point out that the group is an organic whole surviving in an environment. Thus, the group is a system that "reacts on the environment and may to some extent change it, is itself to some degree modified by the environment, and is constantly adjusting and readjusting within itself" (p. 90). The group and the environment are therefore not cause and effect, but a dynamic equilibrium system. The basic elements of the group represent a nonunique solution on how to survive in the environment. The environment encompasses physical, technical, and social components. For the men in the wiring room it included the shape of the room and the location of benches, their tools, and other workers in the organization. According to the theory, if the environment were to change, the team's scheme of activity would change, as would its scheme of interaction and sentiment due to the mutual dependence of the basic elements with each other and with the environment. These changes in the external system would be elaborated by the internal system, which, in turn, would have an impact on the environment.

The elements of Homans's model encompass a complex series of interactions both within the group and between the group and its environment. The environment presents some initial and subsequent conditions to which a team must adapt. Adaptation is determined by the environment and by the interaction of the elements of the internal and external system.

Homans's contribution to the external perspective is this depiction of the group as a set of interdependent systems that interact with the environment. This depiction suggests that group behavior not be viewed in isolation at one time, but as continuing cycles of interaction between the group and its environment. After all, if all the elements of the systems within the group are interdependent, and the group is interdependent with the environment, then changes in any one system have ramifications for the other systems, creating feedback loops. Also, because of the mutual dependence of the elements, a relatively small departure can have relatively large results. The results are cycles of behavior. Homans's work goes on to suggest what the nature of some of those cycles might be.

Homans provides evidence to suggest that groups and their environments can enter positive or negative feedback cycles (for instance, cliques formed in the bank wiring room). Members then became increasingly bound to one another, developed increasingly complex and elaborate norms, and increasingly differentiated themselves from other cliques. Because these norms reinforced behaviors that also led to outcomes valued by the organization, interaction with the environment was positive and reinforced the continued elaboration of the internal system. As can be seen in the Hilltown example, however, this cycle can be turned around through a change in the group or its environment. As Hilltown developed, people had to band together to build the town. They were interdependent for their survival; as a result, complex bonds developed. Over time, however, people became more self-sustaining, lessening interaction, activity, and sentiment. This change in the reinforcing cycle was exacerbated by a change in the environment. Whereas early on the town was the center of most activity in the region, later, conditions around the town improved, attracting townspeople to outside organizations. This, in turn, fueled the decrease in the number and strength of interactions, shared activities, and sentiments until they "had become centrifugal rather than centripetal" (p. 360). Thus, the hypothesis that "interaction is accompanied by friendliness among the members only if the group as a whole is maintaining itself in its environment" is only one of many hypotheses that show this property of groups to have reinforcing positive or negative cycles of interaction with their environments.

The new product team and consulting team studies both offer support for Homans's cycles of interaction. Comprehensive strategies resulted in positive performance ratings from top management and, in turn, facilitated internal group process and cohesiveness. Positive feedback loops fueled a cycle of improving internal and external process and performance. The negative and escalating cycle is seen in scouting and isolationist teams. While these teams maintained positive internal processes in the short term, despite negative external evaluations (by being oblivious to the evaluations or banding together to fight them), internal processes eventually deteriorated.

Homans posits a cycle of increasing or decreasing complexity, in addition to the positive and negative feedback loops. In this cycle, increases in the complexity of the environment generate an increase in the complexity of the group's external activities, which, in turn, increases the complexity of interaction in both the external and the internal system and vice versa. This cycle can also move in the opposite direction of decreasing complexity.

This cycle could be used to explain the difficulties scouting teams had in completing their products. By continuously opening up their boundaries to diverse information and conflicting views, these teams had to develop complex internal mechanisms to process that information and resolve conflicts. These teams often got so caught up in the internal work needed to continuously coordinate activities to meet changing conditions that they failed to make adequate progress. Interestingly, although these groups had to adapt to the complex environment, they also created that environment by collecting information. This notion of the impact of boundary permeability is well developed by Lewin.

Kurt Lewin

Kurt Lewin, often referred to as the father of social psychology, was a key proponent of studying actors in relation to their environment. He argued that behavior and development depend on the state of the person and the environment, which are mutually interdependent. One of Lewin's major contributions was the concept of lifespace, where person and environment are one "constellation of interdependent factors" (Lewin, 1951).

According to Lewin (1951), the environment serves as a constraint to an actor. Physical and social conditions (e.g., lack of ability and social prohibition) limit the variety of life spaces by creating boundaries on the psychological field.

In addition, the field is personal in that it is seen through the needs of the individual. De Rivera (1976, p. 21) interprets Lewin's description of a landscape as seen by a civilian in peacetime versus a warscape as seen by a soldier in danger:

> Away from the front the horizon spreads out in all directions, and he notices the presence of homes. However, as he approaches the line of battle the scenery takes on a "directness". The horizon ends abruptly at the front, and instead of homes, he notices shelters from enemy fire. Within these shelters he sees "firewood" rather than the "furniture" he sees in homes. There is a corresponding change in behavior. It is not possible to march as rapidly toward the front as toward a distant horizon; it is possible to destroy a shelter, whereas it is impossible to treat a home in such a callous way. (p. 21)

Thus, Lewin, like Homans, does not create a deterministic environment. He posits that while behavior may be determined by the situation, people are also capable of making choices that determine the meaning of their situation. People can always choose to either take the responsibility of asserting meaning and accepting the consequences or of passively allowing someone else to determine the meaning of the situation (de Rivera, 1976). There is a continuum from free action to being completely controlled.

The aspect of Lewin's work that seems most pertinent to the external perspective is his notion of boundaries, their permeability, and whether there is resistance to influence or invasion from outside. One of Lewin's more vivid examples of boundary conditions is his comparison of U.S. and German culture (Lewin, 1936). He argued that differences among individuals are the cause of differences between groups. But differences in individuals are a result of living in a different social situation built by different histories. Thus, a dynamic between person and situation is established over time.

Lewin (1936) argued that the social distance between individuals was smaller in the United States than in Germany. Perhaps as an expression of democratic attitudes and the notion of equal rights, Americans were more open to others, more willing to share things, to talk to strangers, and to have an open door policy. But this openness was limited to peripheral areas of the personality. In intimate or core areas Americans were closed. Lewin observed that Americans quickly acquired friends but also easily said goodbye to one another after many years and picked up new friendships in other areas. Also, relationships often moved along speedily until they hit issues of commitment or marriage, when they suddenly slowed down as people became wary of the closeness.

For Germans only the most peripheral areas were accessible; they resisted invasion from outside; they were hard to know. Thus, in the United States you could learn all kinds of things about people easily, and very personal information was published in newspapers and magazines. This was not the case in Germany. Figure 1 illustrates the differences between the Americans and the Germans, with "O" representing the more open Americans and "C" representing the more closed Germans.

There were a great many speculated consequences to the differences. If the

FIGURE 1   Comparison of Two Models of Boundary Openness

Boundaries

Individuals and/or groups differ in
their boundary permeability or
resistance to invasion from outside.

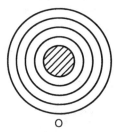 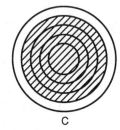

O   C

O = Open; much more open and accessible
     on a range of peripheral issues, but closed
     at core or central issues.

C = Closed; only the most peripheral area
     accessible, becomes hard to access
     quickly.

environment were to change, Americans would show more change since more layers were readily accessible and therefore more open to external influence. Germans would be more apt to behave the same way in each situation (e.g., to be formal even in bathing suits). The Germans had more private regions and thus their behavior was less modifiable. Social life in the United States was more homogeneous (fewer distinct classes and more fluidity across social status), since it was easier for Americans to get to know one another and become similar to one another. Newcomers would have found it easier to join a group of Americans than of Germans, although the relationship would only go so far.

Lewin's concept of boundaries can be applied to the group level of analysis and used to understand the behavior of the new product and consulting teams. How is it that some of these groups were able to understand and adapt to their environmental challenges—whether consciously or not—and others were not? Clearly, some enacted strategies are better than others. One answer is that those following the open model—the comprehensives—were better able to understand and change to match their environment. These teams maintained an open outlook and were receptive to new membership. Those following the closed model—the scouting and isolationist teams—maintained their world view, could not incorporate new information, and were less open to new ideas and members. Thus, through Lewin we are left with a kind of contingency model whereby different levels of openness to the environment are related to a group's ability to adapt to its environment.

BLENDING THE CLASSICS AND THE CONTEMPORARY

We have already seen some of the benefits of blending the external perspective with the work of Homans and Lewin. The concepts of escalating cycles of behavior over time and the degree of boundary openness shed new light on the group studies presented earlier. Now we move on to more general theory and try to extend the arguments made up to this point.

First, we revisit Homans's notion of cycles of behavior between the group and its environment. According to Homans, the cycle can start anywhere because all parts of the system are interconnected. Thus, effective internal processes can lead to successful interaction with the environment, which in turn can reinforce those internal processes, leading to more elaboration of norms and rituals. Or the cycle can start with successful interaction with the environment.

However, our data suggest that organizations evaluate work teams in the first few months of their development. Decisions label the teams, and a negative or positive escalating cycle begins. Teams that do not match this cycle may incur their own demise—even if they eventually carry out their task. Therefore, even though teams must fulfill both internal and external activities, the point in time at which they undertake those activities is not trivial. Obtaining support from the environment needs to come first for a team to enter a positive escalation cycle.

This matching appears to be similar to a process McGrath and Kelly (1986) call entrainment. This process occurs when the cycles or rhythms of one system become synchronized or coordinated with those of another. In our example, the environment has an evaluation cycle that resembles an on/off switch (Ancona & Chong, 1991). That is, there is a period in which an impression can be made, and following that period nothing can be done. For a group to entrain to that rhythm, it must make an impression in the allotted time frame.

Entrainment suggests that research on groups must study critical segments of group–context interaction. We must not only come to understand the cycles of escalating negative and positive interaction, we must also understand the other cycles to which a team must entrain and in what time frames these cycles occur. For example, we might hypothesize that teams must entrain some of their activities to cycles outside the organization, as well as those already illustrated inside the organization. Customers, suppliers, and competitors all operate along their own time lines that have consequences for teams that must interact with those groups. A team may develop a wonderful product, in the shortest time known in the organization, but if the competition has beaten them to market then the product may not sell to estimated levels. Similarly, a team may design a revolutionary product, but if it is introduced after a client has already been through a major change in technology, then that client may not wish to undergo another change required by the revolutionary product.

Thus, I hypothesize that groups and their environments each operate in cycles of activity that influence one another. I further hypothesize that groups will be higher performers to the extent that they entrain to critical aspects of their external environment, before developing their internal system. Groups must entrain to both the organizational environment and the external environment with which it is interdependent. Future research will have to identify those cycles that are the most critical to performance.

Second, like Homans and Lewin I hypothesize that although the environment has some objective component, it is also created by the perceptions and actions of the groups within them. More particularly, I borrow from Lewin in hypothesizing that a group's ability to entrain to its environment, and to adapt, is linked to its permeability. More specifically, groups that follow the open model are better able to entrain than those following the closed model. The difference is not solely openness to external input, but an ability to change world view, to incorporate new information and change member schemas, and to incorporate new members. Groups, like scouting teams, who collect lots of information but cannot use it flexibly to discover new solutions that meet external demands suffer in their performance. Groups, like comprehensive teams, that both mold, and mold to, external demands are better able to understand and predict external cycles and entrain to them. Thus, it is not solely amount of information that is let into the group but the type of information and how it is used by the group.

Third, the question must be raised as to whether the patterns presented here generalize to other situations. Are comprehensives always better performers? Are scouting and isolationist teams always doomed to enter negative cycles of performance and group disintegration? The answer is probably no. Both the consulting and new product teams existed in a time of change within their organizations and their external environments. New product teams exist in an environment of rapidly changing technology and market conditions. There are quick cycles of change in the environment's openness to particular products and services. In Tushman and Romanelli's (1985) language, there are frequent environmental discontinuities requiring major change for effective entrainment to changed conditions. In this case, teams are effective to the extent that they engage in the type of permeability that allows them to predict, adapt to, and shape environmental change. This same behavior would not be necessary under more stable conditions where the cycles of major change are less frequent and revolutionary.

I hypothesize that the external and internal behaviors needed for effective entrainment to an environment with frequent cycles of major change are costly but necessary. To engage in such behaviors when the environment is not rapidly changing is to expend energy uselessly (Ancona & Chong, 1991). Thus, I would hypothesize that in more stable environments, with few instances of revolutionary change and long periods of evolutionary change, isolationist teams will be better performers. These teams concentrate their energy on the internal group processes needed to effectively coordinate member effort toward the task. Once these teams have developed the appropriate view of their environment, this view can remain inertial. No change is necessary.

In conclusion, I call for a revision in our approach to group theory. The internal perspective should be joined by an external perspective with a research lens sitting on the group boundary and examining both internal processes and interaction with the environment. The reliance on one-time, correlational research needs to be replaced by studies over time, examining the interrelated cycles of activity between teams and their environments. The patterns of change in organizational and external environments must be examined to understand how teams can effectively entrain to those environments. Such changes may, in fact, shift the very nature of group research, leading to some exciting new directions that take off from both the classics and the contemporary.

REFERENCES

ALDERFER, C. P. (1976). Boundary relations and organizational diagnosis. In M. Meltzer & F. Wickert (Eds.), *Humanizing organizational behavior* (pp. 142–175). Springfield, IL: Charles C. Thomas.

ALDRICH, H. E., & HERKER, D. (1977). Boundary spanning roles and organization structure. *Academy of Management Review, 2,* 217–230.

ALLEN, T. J. (1984). *Managing the flow of technology: Technology transfer and the dissemination of technological information within the R&D organization.* Cambridge, MA: MIT Press.

ANCONA, D. G. (1987). Groups in organizations: Extending laboratory models. In C. Hendrick (Ed.), *Annual review of personality and social psychology: Group processes and intergroup processes* (pp. 207–231). Beverly Hills, CA: Sage Publications.

ANCONA, D. G. (1990). Outward bound: Strategies for team survival in the organization. *Academy of Management Journal, 33*(2), 334–365.

ANCONA, D. G., & CALDWELL, D. F. (1987). Management issues facing new-product teams in high technology companies. In D. Lewin, D. Lipsky, & D. Sokel (Eds.), *Advances in industrial and labor relations* (Vol. 4, pp. 199–221). Greenwich, CT: JAI Press.

ANCONA, D. G., & CALDWELL, D. F. (1988). Beyond task and maintenance: Defining external functions in groups. *Group & Organization Studies, 13*(4), 468–494.

ANCONA, D. G., & CALDWELL, D. F. (1990). Beyond boundary spanning: Managing external dependence in product development teams. *The Journal of High Technology Management Research, 1*(2), 119–135.

ANCONA, D. G., & CALDWELL, D. F. (1991). *Bridging the boundary: External process and performance in organizational teams.* Working paper 3305-91-BPS, MIT Sloan School of Management, Cambridge, MA.

ANCONA, D. G., & CALDWELL, D. F. (1992). Demography and design: Predictors of New Product Team Performance. *Organization Science,* forthcoming.

ANCONA, D. G., & CHONG, C. (1991). *Entrainment: Cycles and synergy in organizational behavior.* Working paper, MIT Sloan School.

BALES, R. F. (1958). Task roles and social roles in problem-solving groups. In E. Maccoby, T. M. Newcomb, & E. L. Hartley (Eds.), *Readings in social psychology* (3rd ed., pp. 437–447). New York: Holt, Rinehart & Winston.

DEAN, J. W., JR. (1987). *Deciding to innovate: Decision processes in the adoption of advanced technology.* Cambridge, MA: Ballinger Publishing Company.

de RIVERA, J. (1976). *Field theory as human-science.* New York: Gardner Press, Inc.

GLADSTEIN, D. (1984). Groups in context: A model of task group effectiveness. *Administrative Science Quarterly, 29,* 499–517.

GLADSTEIN, D., & QUINN, J. B. (1985). Making decisions and producing action: The two faces of strategy. In H. Pennings (Ed.), *Organizational strategy and change* (pp. 198–216). San Francisco: Jossey-Bass.

GERSICK, C. J. C. (1988). Time and transition in work teams: Toward a new model of group development. *Academy of Management Journal, 31*(1), 9–41.

GERSICK, C. J. C. (1989). Marking time: Predictable transitions in task groups. *Academy of Management Journal, 32*(2), 274–309.

GIBBS, J. P. (1977). Homans and the methodology of theory construction. In R. L. Hamblin & J. H. Kunkel (Eds.), *Behavioral theory in sociology* (pp. 27–48). New Brunswick, NJ: Transaction Books.

GRESOV, C. (1989). Exploring fit and misfit with multiple contingencies. *Administrative Science Quarterly, 34*, 431–453.

HACKMAN, J. R., BROUSSEAU, K. R., & WEISS, J. A. (1976). The interaction of task design and group performance strategies in determining group effectiveness. *Organizational Behavior and Human Performance, 16*, 350–365.

HOFFMAN, L. R. (1979). Applying experimental research on group problem solving to organizations. *Journal of Applied Behavioral Science, 15*, 375–391.

HOMANS, G. (1950). *The human group.* New York: Harcourt Brace Jovanovich.

JANIS, I. L. (1982). *Groupthink.* Boston, MA: Houghton Mifflin.

JANIS, I. L. (1985). Sources of error in strategic decision making. In J. M. Pennings & Associates (Eds.), *Organizational strategy and change* (pp. 157–197). San Francisco: Jossey-Bass.

JOHNSON, W. T. (1977). Exchange in perspective: The promises of George C. Homans. In R. L. Hamblin & H. H. Kunkel (Eds.), *Behavioral theory in sociology* (pp. 39–90). New Brunswick, NJ: Transaction Books.

KATZ, R., & TUSHMAN, M. (1979). Communication patterns, project performance, and task characteristics: An empirical evaluation and integration in an R&D setting. *Organizational Behavior and Human Performance, 23*, 139–162.

KERLINGER, F. N. (1973). *Foundations of behavioral research* (2nd ed.). New York: Holt Rinehart & Winston.

KIDDER, T. (1981). *Soul of a new machine.* New York: Avon.

LEWIN, K. (1936). Social psychological differences between the U.S. and Germany. Republished in K. Lewin (1948), *Resolving social conflicts,* pp. 3–33. New York: Harper & Brothers Publishers.

LEWIN, K. (1951). *Field theory in social science: Selected theoretical papers.* D. Cartwright (Ed.). New York: Harper & Brothers Publishers.

LIKERT, R. (1961). *New patterns of management.* New York: McGraw-Hill.

MALONE, T. W. (1987). Modeling coordination in organizations and markets. *Management Science, 23*, 1317–1332.

McGRATH, J. E., & KELLY, J. R. (1986). *Time and human interaction: Toward a social psychology of time.* New York: Guilford.

NADLER, D. A., & TUSHMAN, M. L. (1988). *Strategic organization design: Concepts, tools, and processes.* Glenview, IL: Scott, Foresman & Company.

PFEFFER, J. (1981). *Power in organizations.* Marshfield, MA: Pitman.

PHILIP, H., & DUNPHY, D. (1959). Developmental trends in small groups. *Sociometry, 22*, 162–174.

SCHEIN, E. H. (1985). *Organizational culture and leadership.* San Francisco: Jossey-Bass.

SCHEIN, E. H. (1988). *Process consultation: Its role in organization development* (Vol 1). Reading, MA: Addison-Wesley.

SCHMIDT, S. M., & KOCHAN, T. (1972). The concept of conflict: Toward conceptual clarity. *Administrative Science Quarterly, 17*, 359–370.

SHAW, M. (1971). *Group dynamics: The psychology of small group behavior.* New York: McGraw-Hill.

SHERIF, M. (1966). *In common predicament: Social psychology of intergroup conflict and cooperation.* Boston: Addison-Wesley.

SMITH, K. K. (1983). An intergroup perspective on individual behavior. In J. R. Hackman, E. E. Lawler, & L. W. Porter (Eds.), *Perspectives on behavior in organization* (pp. 397–407). New York: McGraw-Hill.

SMITH, K. K. (1989). The movement of conflict in organizations: The joint dynamics of splitting and triangulation. *Administrative Science Quarterly, 31,* 1–20.

TUSHMAN, M. L., & ROMANELLI, E. (1985). Organizational evolution: A metamorphosis model of convergence and reorientation. In L. L. Cummings & B. M. Staw (Eds.), *Research in organizational behavior* (Vol. 7, pp. 171–222). Greenwich, CT: JAI Press.

TUSHMAN, M. L., & VIRANY, B. (1986). Changing characteristics of executive teams in an emerging industry. *Journal of Business Venturing, 3,* 261–274.

TUSHMAN, M. L., VIRANY, B., & ROMANELLI, E. (1985). Executive succession, strategic reorientation, and organizational evolution: The minicomputer industry as a case in point. *Technology and Society, 7,* 297–331.

CHAPTER TWELVE

Cooperation and Organizational Identification*

RODERICK M. KRAMER

Stanford University

Organizational theorists have long recognized the important role cooperation plays in organizations. However, current theories say little about the antecedents of cooperative behavior in organizations. In this chapter, I present a conceptual framework for analyzing cooperation derived from social identity theory and social categorization theory. According to this framework, people are more likely to cooperate with other members of an organization when their identification with the organization is salient. The framework identifies several psychological processes mediating this link between organizational identification and cooperation, including group-based trust, social attraction, and self-presentational concerns. The framework also describes a number of structural and psychological determinants of organizational identification.

*The research reviewed in this chapter reflects many enjoyable collaborations. My close encounters with Marilynn Brewer and David Messick merit singular recognition. Jerry Davis, Linda Ginzel, Lisa Goldman, Len Greenhalgh, Robert Kahn, Chuck McClintock, Debra Meyerson, Elizabeth Newton, Pamela Pommerenke, Bob Sutton, Mark Weiner, and Stephanie Woerner deserve thanks for being wonderful coauthors. I also owe a debt to Jim Baron, Max Bazerman, Joel Brockner, Jane Dutton, E. Allen Lind, Maureen McNichols, Maggie Neale, and Tom Tyler for their comments and, even more, for their reliable and enthusiastic colleagiality. The generous financial support provided by the Dispute Resolution Research Center, J. L. Kellogg Graduate School of Management, Northwestern University; Graduate School of Business, Stanford University; Morris Management Company; and Fletcher Jones Foundation is acknowledged.

Any realistic picture of how real organizations operate . . . must take into account the importance of *identifications* in the utility functions of employees.

HERBERT SIMON (1986)

Organizational theorists have long appreciated the central role cooperation plays in organizations. In an early and yet still remarkably contemporary analysis, Chester Barnard (1938) characterized organizations as cooperative systems that depend on the coordinated activities of numerous interdependent actors. He went on to argue that the willingness of individuals to cooperate with other members of an organization is one of the major determinants of organizational effectiveness and efficiency. While recognizing the importance of cooperation, organizational scholars have also drawn attention to the paucity of theory regarding the determinants of cooperative behavior. Recent research has devoted considerable attention to the study of competitive processes in organizations. But, as Kahn and Zald (1990) cogently noted, theory and research on cooperation lags behind other areas of organizational research.

The purpose of this chapter is to present a social psychological perspective on organizational cooperation. This perspective attempts to blend and extend contributions from two streams of social psychological research: work on social identity (Tajfel, 1982a, 1982b; Tajfel & Turner, 1986) and work on social categorization processes (Rothbart & John, 1985; Turner, 1987; Wilder, 1981). While these two areas of research have exerted considerable influence on social psychological theory over the past decade (see, e.g., reviews by Brewer & Kramer, 1986; Hogg & Abrams, 1988; Messick & Mackie, 1989; Tajfel, 1982b), their impact on organizational theory has been limited. This chapter, accordingly, tries to make more explicit some of the organizational implications of this work.

Another aim of this chapter is to suggest the usefulness of laboratory-based approaches to studying cooperative processes in organizations. In this chapter, I summarize a number of findings from a program of research that investigates the antecedents of cooperative behavior using laboratory analogues of various interdependence dilemmas that arise in organizations. The primary aim of an analogue experiment is the "abstraction of the essential elements in a complex social situation . . . and their reconstruction in a different scaled down setting, such that an isomorphism is preserved between the original and the analogue situation" (Brewer, 1985, p. 163). Thus, by developing a suitable experimental analogue, it is possible to capture the critical structural and psychological features of a problem while removing the irrelevant cues and theoretically uninteresting sources of variation that often accompany research in organizational settings.

The central theoretical argument of this chapter can be stated quite simply. I argue that individuals' willingness to cooperate depends on their identification with other decision makers with whom they are interdependent. Individuals are assumed to possess multiple, co-occurring identities, including personal, group, and organizational identities. When personal identities are salient, individuals are more likely to focus on their own outcomes and, accordingly, cooperation is less likely. When organizational identity is salient, individuals are more likely to take into consideration the collective consequences of their actions. Accordingly, they are more likely to adopt cooperative orientations during decision making.

The emphasis of this chapter differs from previous theoretical work on cooperation in several important respects. First, previous work has often focused on structural determinants of cooperation. Sherif (1966), for example, examined the effects of introducing superordinate goals on cooperation. The present chapter, in contrast, focuses on social cognitive determinants of cooperative behavior. In particular, I discuss how the salience of organizational identity during decision making affects cooperation. Second, prior theory has explained cooperation primarily in terms of the objective patterns of interdependence among organizational decision makers. Resource dependence theory (Pfeffer & Salancik, 1978), for example, articulates a series of propositions regarding the relationship between decision makers' interdependence with respect to crucial resources and their incentive to cooperate. The present framework extends such arguments by considering how decision makers' subjective construal or perception of their interdependence affects cooperation. Finally, previous research on cooperation has assumed that decision makers are motivated by self-interests. Axelrod's (1984) influential work on cooperation, for instance, explicitly assumed that decision makers are egoistically motivated. I argue here that decision makers' motives are more complex than this assumption suggests. Specifically, I review evidence suggesting that people's motivational orientations are affected by the salience of different identities. Thus, self-interest is treated here as a variable rather than a constant. In laying the foundations for these arguments, I begin by providing a brief summary of several laboratory studies that investigated the relationship between group identification and cooperation.

GROUP IDENTIFICATION AND COOPERATION:
AN OVERVIEW OF THE EVIDENCE

Evidence that group identification affects cooperation is provided by a number of experimental studies (see Kramer & Brewer, 1986, for a review). Rather than attempt to review all of this evidence, I focus on a few illustrative studies.

Resource management dilemmas

One common form of interdependence found in organizations concerns the resources individuals need to complete their tasks. To achieve their goals, people require many different resources, including fiscal, space, personnel, and informational resources. In many instances, the aggregate demand for these resources exceeds the available supply. To the extent that such resources are perceived to be in short supply, competition for them may be acute. Consider, for example, the budget dilemma faced by many organizations. Because organizations have finite resources, their members realize that the organization as a whole will be better off if they request only those resources they actually need. They may also believe, however, that the more resources they request, the more they are likely to receive. Further, if future allocations are based on current use, they may reasonably predict that they will get more later if they use more now. Accordingly, individuals have incentives to consume more of an organization's resources than they actually need. If everyone reasons similarly, organizational resources will be seriously depleted and suboptimally allocated. Thus, decisions that are individually rational in the short term lead to highly undesirable long-term organizational outcomes.

Resource management dilemmas nicely illustrate the inherent tension between self-interests and collective interests. Actions that increase an individual's own gain are at odds with those that improve the welfare of others. Even if individuals prefer cooperating, however, they confront a dilemma. Individual restraint is ineffective if others do not reciprocate. In the absence of assurances that others will also cooperate, individuals have little incentive to cooperate themselves. Thus, individuals may abandon cooperation even when they prefer it.

Many theoretical predictions about how organizational actors will respond to dilemmas of this sort assume that individuals will act to further their self-interests (Fort & Baden, 1981; Olson, 1965; Ostrom, 1977). Marilynn Brewer and I, however, explored an alternative possibility. We hypothesized that increasing the salience of group identification would result in higher rates of cooperation (and less responding out of pure self-interest). In other words, we speculated that when decision makers focus on their common group identity rather than their distinctive personal identities, they would take less for themselves in order to preserve the collective resource.

To test this hypothesis, we used a laboratory simulation of a resource management problem. Small groups were told that they would be participating in a study involving the management of a shared resource pool and would interact with each other via computer. We asked participants to decide how many resources to take for themselves from the shared pool on a series of trials. At the end of each trial, the computer subtracted the total amount withdrawn by the group from the common pool. The remaining amount was then replenished by a random amount, determining the pool size for the next trial. Participants knew the average replenishment rate across trials, but did not know how much it would affect the pool for any given trial. Although the replenished pool could never exceed the original amount, it could be maintained at a high level if the total group demand did not exceed the average replenishment rate. Thus, if enough individuals cooperated by taking only moderate amounts from the pool, they could continue taking resources and accumulate more in the long run.

To vary the salience of personal and group identities, we used a procedure, adapted with some modifications, from Rabbie and Horwitz (1969). Participants knew they could earn money and that their pay would be based on the total number of resources they took from the pool. A lottery would determine the monetary value of these resources. To reinforce personal identity, separate lotteries determined each participant's payoff individually. To make group identity salient, a single lottery determined the value of resources for each member of the group simultaneously. This procedure manipulates participants' perceptions of their "common fate" and creates a minimal group identity.

We led participants to believe that they were interacting with each other so that their decisions were interdependent. In actuality, however, group members received false feedback so that we could systematically vary the information they received about decisions made by the other group members. This false feedback indicated that the pool level was being depleted as the trials progressed.

Our main prediction was that individuals for whom group identity was salient would reduce their consumption of the common pool more than individuals for whom a personal identity was salient. The results supported this hypothesis. We found that individuals' decisions as to how much was taken from the common pool depended on the level of salient identification. Specifically, individuals for whom group identification was salient were more likely to reduce their consumption of the common pool, especially as the pool level dropped compared to those in the personal identity condition.

The results of this experiment demonstrated that the degree of cooperation among decision makers increased, just as we had predicted, when group identity was salient. In an attempt to replicate and extend these findings, we conducted an additional experiment that investigated the relationship between group identification and cooperation in another kind of social dilemma known as a collective action problem.

Collective action dilemmas

Collective action problems are another important class of cooperation dilemmas that arise in organizations. Although collective action problems can take a number of different forms, including missing hero (Schelling, 1978), social loafing (Latane, Williams, & Harkins, 1979), and the free-rider or public goods problem (Olson, 1965), they all share a common logic. The benefits or rewards for many organizational tasks are often distributed equally among individuals, regardless of their contributions to the collective effort. Moreover, individual inputs may not be easily identifiable, especially when the costs of monitoring performance are high. For example, on many interdependent tasks, individuals' contributions are pooled, making it difficult to distinguish individual efforts. As a result, potential contributors know in advance that, regardless of their individual investments, they will all receive the same outcome. Because payoffs are not contingent on personal performance, people may be tempted to loaf or free ride on the efforts of others. They can, after all, enjoy the benefits of collective success while avoiding its costs.

Marilynn Brewer and I investigated whether group identification would increase cooperation on these tasks. We also examined how group identification interacted with two other aspects of the decision to cooperate, namely the way in which a decision is framed and the size of the group.

DECISION FRAME.   The decision to cooperate in collective action dilemmas is similar in some respects to the decision to cooperate on resource management dilemmas. In both cases, if individuals cooperate, they risk getting less for themselves than if they choose to act self-interestedly. If individuals are concerned only about the net outcomes of their decisions, then the rates of cooperation should be identical across both tasks.

Psychological research on decision making suggests that even though these decisions may be equivalent in terms of net gains and losses, they may not be regarded as psychologically equivalent by decision makers. According to Kahneman and Tversky's prospect theory (1979), individuals' preferences among choices are influenced by the way a decision is initially formulated. Specifically, when decisions are framed in terms of gains, decision makers tend to be risk averse, preferring a "sure bet" over a gamble. When decisions are framed in terms of losses, they tend to be risk seeking, preferring to gamble on a possible larger loss rather than accept an immediate and certain loss.

The decisions to cooperate in collective action and resource management dilemmas make salient different reference points with respect to gains and losses. In the case of providing a collective good, decision makers must decide how much to contribute of something of value already in their possession (e.g., workers may have to decide how much of their free time to give up to help launch a blood donor drive). In relation to what they start with, this decision entails enduring an immediate and sure loss to gain an uncertain future benefit (in the example, a blood bank that all can benefit from). Prospect theory predicts that individuals will be risk seeking (i.e., will prefer risking long-term loss to keep as much of what they have in the short run).

In the case of a resource management dilemma, decision makers start with nothing. In relation to this starting point, anything they accumulate represents a sure gain. This frame of reference should make them comparatively risk averse during decision making. In other words, they should prefer a smaller certain gain over a potentially larger but riskier gain (riskier because, if others do not cooperate, these long-term gains will never materialize). We theorized that group identification would increase individuals' willingness to take such risks because group identification might increase trust toward others and increase concern about others' welfare (the justification for these hypotheses is described in more detail later).

GROUP SIZE.   The second factor that we studied was group size. Previously, Olson (1965) had argued that the larger the size of a group of interdependent decision makers, the lower the level of cooperation among them. Olson's argument was based on the assumption that, as the size of a group increases, individuals have less incentive to cooperate. As group size grows, he reasoned, individuals will perceive their actions as having a diminished influence on others' decisions and a decreased impact on the collective outcome. Brewer and I reasoned, however, that group identification might offset these deleterious effects of group size. If group identification increases the concern individuals have for other group members, then increasing the salience of group identification might lead to higher levels of cooperation.

To test these ideas, we conducted an experiment using a computer-based task similar to that employed in our initial studies. We assigned participants to one of several conditions. First, to study the effects of decision frame, they were assigned to either a resource management dilemma task or a collective action task. Second, to examine how group size affects cooperation, we assigned them to conditions in which they believed they were in a group of either 8 or 32 individuals.

In the collective action version of the task, participants were given a certain number of resources at the start of each trial and decided how much to keep for themselves and how much to return to the common pool. If enough of the group members returned a sufficient number of their resources to the pool, they could sustain the pool and all would earn more than if they all kept their personal resources for themselves. In the resource management task, individuals had to decide how much to take from the common pool across trials. If enough of the group members exercised restraint on consumption, the common pool could be maintained and they could earn more in the long run than if they took the maximum allowable amount on each trial. False feedback was used so that each participant, regardless of task condition, received comparable information about the cooperation levels in their groups.

To manipulate the salience of personal versus group identification, we used the same common fate induction described earlier. The key test of our main hypothesis was individuals' response to evidence that the collective resource was declining. We predicted that, overall, individuals for whom group identity was salient would be more cooperative (give more in the collective action task and take less in the resource management task) compared to those in the personal identity conditions. Analysis of the data from the later decision-making trials, when the levels of the common resource pools were decreasing, revealed an interaction between group identification, task structure, and group size. Specifically, individuals in the resource management dilemma cooperated more when group identification was salient, irrespective of the size of their group. In the collective action task, this pattern was also observed in the small group condition. However, in the large group condition, individuals in the group identification condition kept more for themselves, contrary to our expectation.

In a series of other experiments, using different procedures and group identity inductions, we have replicated the general finding that increasing the salience of group identification enhances cooperation (Brewer & Kramer, 1984; Kramer & Brewer, 1984, 1986).

Other researchers have obtained compatible results regarding the relationship between group identification and cooperation. Wit (1989) examined the effects of group categorization on cooperation across several different forms of cooperation dilemmas. He employed a lottery procedure very much like ours. Participants were informed that there were not enough monetary resources for everyone to be paid for their participation. Therefore, a lottery was held to determine who would receive resources. In the personal categorization condition, separate lotteries were held for each person. In the group categorization condition, a single lottery was used for the group. Wit found higher rates of cooperation among people in the group categorization condition compared to those in the personal categorization condition in each of the dilemmas.

Dawes and his colleagues (Dawes, van de Kragt, & Orbell, 1988; Orbell, van de Kragt, & Dawes, 1988) found higher rates of cooperation when individuals' decisions were preceded by a group discussion. In interpreting their findings, they proposed that even a brief discussion lasting only a few minutes is sometimes sufficient to induce a sense of group identification.

SUMMARY.   Taken together, the evidence from these experiments supports the general hypothesis that group identification increases cooperation. The fact that this pattern has been replicated across a number of studies involving a variety of tasks and manipulations of group identification, as well as samples from at least two countries, enhances our confidence in the hypothesis.

WHY GROUP IDENTIFICATION MATTERS

The aforementioned evidence reveals that increasing the salience of group identity fosters more cooperative orientations. Thus, people do not always focus only on their own outcomes when deciding how to resolve interdependence dilemmas. Nor do they appear to draw the sharp distinctions between their own outcomes and others that many game theoretic and economic models of cooperation presume. While this evidence documents the relationship between group identification and cooperative behavior, I have said little about why identification affects behavior. Although our understanding of this relationship is far from complete, at least four processes appear to contribute to it: (1) group-based trust, (2) social attraction, (3) group-based empathy, and (4) self-presentational concerns.

Group-based trust

One reason why group identification might enhance cooperative orientations toward other group members is suggested by research on in-group bias. Numerous studies have shown that group members tend to attribute generally favorable traits such as friendliness, trustworthiness, honesty, and cooperativeness to other in-group members (Brewer, 1979; Brewer & Silver, 1978). Based on this evidence, Brewer (1981) proposed that trust may be one of the important "byproducts" of group formation. "Common membership in a salient social category," she argued, "can serve as a rule for defining the boundaries of low-risk interpersonal trust. . . . As a consequence of shifting from the personal level to the social group level of identity, the individual can adopt a sort of *depersonalized trust* based on category membership alone" (p. 356, emphasis in the original). Individuals may find it easier to cooperate with other group members, because presumably the fear of exploitation will be low in such encounters.

Trust linked with group membership may be particularly strong or binding for at least two reasons. First, group-based trust may not be contingent on the belief that a specific other toward whom an individual has been helpful in the past will return the favor. Instead, such trust is based on the confidence that group members will return other group members' beneficent acts. Consequently, group members can engage in long-term and diffuse forms of exchange with other group members. Second, trust linked with group membership may include a sense of duty or normative commitment, imposing an obligatory quality on an individual's decision to act cooperatively. As Rotter (1980) observed, trusting behavior may reflect more an individual's "belief in the moral rightness of trust [than] an expectancy of risk in trusting others" (p. 4). Thus, group members may engage in trusting behaviors independently of, and in some cases even despite, what other group members actually do.

Group-based trust can be distinguished from other conceptions of trust in several important regards. Previous psychological conceptions (e.g., Lindskold, 1978) have generally characterized trust as a generalized expectancy that individuals develop as a result of interactions with specific other individuals. In other words, trust is conceptualized as a learned response derived from the cumulative impact of exchanges or encounters with a specific other. Group-based trust, in contrast, is predicated on psychological salience of group membership and does not presume a specific history of interaction. It is conferred "ex ante" and is in this sense presumptive. In these respects, group-based trust differs from the highly contingent variant of trust implied by Axelrod's (1984) analysis of cooperation.

Group-based trust also differs from sociological conceptions of trust. Sociological perspectives have usually focused on the role of institutional mechanisms, contracts, and other means of social control to establish and maintain trust among interdependent parties (Shapiro, 1987; Zucker, 1986). According to such conceptions, trust is based on monitoring compliance and sanctioning violators. Group-based trust, in contrast, is not linked to institutional arrangements or contracts. Indeed, the sense of contract, if it exists at all, is tacit and psychological in character (cf. Rousseau, 1989).

Social attraction

Another reason why group identification might enhance other-regarding behavior is social attraction. Hogg and Abrams (1988) have proposed that social identification increases attraction among group members. Because it is predicated specifically on awareness of joint membership in a social group, they argued, this form of *social* attraction can be conceptually distinguished from interpersonal attraction "which is interindividual attraction based upon idiosyncratic preferences and firmly rooted in close personal relationships" (p. 107). Social attraction is thus presumed to be intimately linked to individuals' awareness of their common membership in a social group. Several studies support their argument (Hogg & Hardie, 1991; Hogg & Turner, 1985a, 1985b).

Group-based empathy

Several researchers have suggested as well that increasing the salience of group identification may affect the empathy individuals feel toward others in their group (Hornstein, 1976; Wilder & Cooper, 1981). When a common social identity is salient, according to this argument, there is a de-emphasis on the self as a reference point and, concomitantly, a decreased focus on self-interests as a standard for evaluating outcomes. As Turner (1987) suggested, when identification moves from the personal to the social level, there is a "shift towards the perception of self as an interchangeable exemplar of some social category and away from the perception of self as a unique person" (pp. 50–51). Some support for this argument is suggested by research on recategorization and cooperation (e.g., Gaertner, Mann, Murrell, & Dovidio, 1989).

Self-presentational concerns

Another reason that increasing the salience of group identification might enhance cooperative behavior is suggested by research on self-presentational concerns. People often desire to make favorable impressions on those with whom they interact (Tedeschi, 1981). These self-presentational concerns can assume many forms, however. In some situations, individuals may be motivated to establish an image of toughness, firmness, or competence, especially if they know their actions are being judged by individuals to whom they feel accountable (Carnevale, Pruitt, & Britton, 1979; Sutton & Kramer, 1990; Tetlock, 1985). When dealing with other members of their own group, however, they may be less concerned with being tough and more concerned about appearing fair and cooperative (cf. Greenberg, 1990; Kramer, Newton, & Pommerenke, 1991a; Reis, 1981; Reis & Gruzen, 1976).

IDENTIFICATION IN ORGANIZATIONS

The evidence reviewed thus far demonstrates that group identification increases cooperation among individuals, at least in the context of relatively small social groups. It also implicates a number of mediating psychological and social processes. Although these conclusions are based primarily on research using laboratory groups, the theoretical arguments seem quite general—and generalizable. Accordingly, in this section, I try to extend these arguments to organizational settings.

Organizational identification

Identification in organizations is a complex psychological and social process (see, e.g., discussions by Ashforth & Mael, 1989; Brown, Condor, Matthews, Wade, & Williams, 1986; Brown & Williams, 1984; Dutton, Dukerich, & Harquail,

1991; Kramer, 1991; O'Reilly & Chatman, 1986). Members of an organization possess many different identities, including personal, social, and organizational identities. Personal identities encompass those aspects of the self that individuals perceive as unique or distinctive (i.e., attributes that differentiate them from other members of the organization). Social identities are based on categories and attributes such as age, gender, or race (e.g., Alderfer & Thomas, 1988; Kanter, 1977; Lansberg, 1989).

Personal and social identities, by definition, exist independent of any particular organization. Other identities conferred on people reflect more organizationally specific distinctions. For example, within an organization, job titles, formal positions, roles, and work categories define various group and subgroup memberships. These memberships inform individuals both about who they are within the organization and, significantly, how they are related to other members of the organization (Baron & Bielby, 1986; Baron & Pfeffer, 1989; Kramer, 1991). In addition, membership in the organization itself creates an identity that, by definition, is common to all of the members of the organization. It provides a "superordinate" group identity that encompasses everyone within the organization.

Empirical research suggests several basic dimensions along which organizational identities vary. First, identities can vary in inclusiveness and exclusiveness. Organizational membership is an inclusive identity because it is common to all of the members of an organization. Group identities are more exclusive insofar as they represent distinctive or differentiating bases of identification. For example, "founder" and "CEO" are distinctive identities that separate one individual from all other members of the organization.

Identities can also vary in terms of their centrality. Some identities are central or core identities, exerting substantial influence on how individuals define themselves and how they construe their relationships with others. For example, research suggests that when individuals are labeled whistleblowers, this identity dominates both how they see themselves as well as how other members of the organization perceive them (Glazer & Glazer, 1989).

Similarly, identities can vary in their psychological status or dominance. Long-standing or enduring professional identities, for instance, may override organizational identities that might be perceived as more transitory. This can lead to complementary or conflictual relationships among identities. Several employees of Morton Thiokol reported feeling intense conflict over the decision to launch the space shuttle Challenger because they perceived a discrepancy between their organizational identity and their professional identity as engineers. Finally, identities can vary in terms of their positivity or negativity. Positive identities confer prestige and status for those who possess them; negative identities imply low status and may be experienced as stigmatizing (Goffman, 1963; Sutton & Callahan, 1987).

These dimensions are important because, as I argue in more detail later, they affect how much influence a particular organizational identity will have on decision making in a given context. Individuals often describe, and presumably experience, identity as a relatively stable entity, reflecting the existence of clearly defined preferences, values, attitudes, and dispositions (see Ross & Nisbett, 1991). They feel, for example, that they know who they are, what they are like, and can predict how they will act in a variety of situations.

This phenomenology is deceptive. Identification in organizations is neither stable nor fixed. Rather, it depends largely on the context in which the individual is embedded. A given identity may be highly salient in one context, exerting considerable impact on perception, judgment, and behavior. In another setting, the same identity may have low salience and exert little impact. Thus, organizational and psychological factors affect the dominance and positivity of different identities.

Effects of identity salience

Why should the salience of organizational identity affect individuals' cooperativeness? Social cognition research suggests several reasons. First, salience selectively focuses decision makers' attention. Because of salience, some attributes of a situation or problem stand out or "loom larger" during judgment and decision making. Thus, salience may direct attention inward toward the self, or outward toward others. As Fiske and Taylor (1991) have argued, salience affects whether perception is "self-focused" or "environmentally" focused. Extrapolating from this argument, when organizational identity is salient, individuals will be more organizationally focused.

Salience also increases the accessibility of congruent information, causing it to be overweighted during decision making. In contrast, information that is out of sight will remain out of mind (Kramer, Meyerson, & Davis, 1990). Finally, salience can lead to more polarized evaluations of individuals, accentuating within-category similarities and highlighting between-category differences (Fiske & Taylor, 1991; Messick & Mackie, 1989). Thus, individuals may overestimate their similarity to members of their own group, and overestimate their differences from members of other groups (Brewer, 1979; Kramer et al., 1989; Tajfel, 1969).

The particular identity that is dominant during decision making has two consequences. First, it affects how individuals categorize themselves. For example, when personal identities are salient, individuals will presumably categorize themselves in terms of the unique or distinctive attributes that set them apart from others. When organizational identity is salient, they will tend to define themselves in terms of attributes they share or have in common with others within the organization.

These "self-categorizations" (Turner, 1987), in turn, influence how decision makers construe their interdependence and relationships with others. Organizational identity, by its very nature, implies *relationship with* other members of the organization. Organizational membership, along with the social and psychological boundaries it defines, thus influences how individuals define themselves and interact with others. In short, they help locate and orient individuals, both in their intra- and interorganizational environments, in much the same way that perceptual boundaries orient organisms to their physical environments (Gibson, 1966).

The particular identity that is salient to an individual during decision making affects how he or she perceives or defines relationships with others. I assume that a set of distinct interests, beliefs, attitudes, goals, and values are associated with each of these identities. The interests associated with personal identity are relatively self-centered or egoistic. They may include, for example, enhancing one's own career or status. Personal identity increases the salience of interpersonal comparisons. The interests and values associated with group identity, in contrast, may include increasing the power of one's primary reference group within the organization. Group-level identity makes salient intergroup comparisons. Finally, the interests, values, and beliefs associated with organizational identity may include protecting or enhancing the image or welfare of the organization as a whole.

Turner (1987) hinted at the relationship between the identity that is salient to individuals during decision making and the interests and values underlying their decisions. Turner postulated that an inherent tension or antagonism exists between different psychological identities. When one identity is dominant, he suggested, the impact of the others will be recessive. When one becomes figure, the others become ground.

DETERMINANTS OF ORGANIZATIONAL IDENTIFICATION

A missing link in the analysis presented thus far is what structures and processes influence organizational identification. Empirical research on the determinants of organizational identification is, unfortuntely, rather sparse. However, researchers have identified or suggested a number of factors (Ashforth & Mael, 1989; Brown & Williams, 1984; Dutton et al., 1991; Kramer, 1991). Rather than attempt to review all of the theory and evidence relevant to this issue, I selectively focus on a few illustrative psychological and organizational processes that might be expected to increase or decrease organizational identification and, in turn, affect individuals' inclination to cooperate.

The analysis presented here has a strong functionalist bias. I assume that identification serves, among others, at least two important psychological functions. First, individuals have a need to make sense of their social and organizational environments (Weick, 1979). This drives them to engage in self and social categorization processes. Second, many people have a strong need to maintain positive personal and social identities (Taylor & Brown, 1988; Tesser, 1986).

Psychological determinants

SELF-CATEGORIZATION AND SENSEMAKING.   Organizational identification can arise, in part, from self-categorization processes. As noted earlier, organizational membership is an important psychological and social category, at least in many Western cultures. The cognitive consequences of self-categorization on judgment and interpersonal behavior have been documented in numerous experiments (Tajfel, 1982a; Turner, 1982; Wilder, 1981). In one of the first experimental demonstrations, Tajfel and Wilkes (1963) found that simply assigning objects to distinctive categories led people to overestimate the similarity of within-category objects and to overestimate the difference between objects from different categories. Subsequent studies showed that even categorization based on completely arbitrary and transient criteria is often sufficient to induce a sense of group identification (Brewer, 1979; Kramer & Brewer, 1984; Rabbie & Horwitz, 1969; Rabbie & Wilkins, 1971; Tajfel, 1982b; Tajfel, Flament, Billig, & Bundy, 1971).

Self-categorization at the organizational-identity level plays a positive functional role in interdependent decision making, insofar as it minimizes the costs of negotiating reciprocity with other individuals in the organization. In this respect, a parallel may be drawn between the function of organizational identification and the role networks play in lubricating and sustaining cooperative relations. As Powell (1990) noted, networks provide interdependent parties with a "mutual orientation—knowledge which the parties assume each has about the other and upon which they draw in communication and problem-solving" (p. 303). Networks thus obviate the need for negotiating reciprocity with specific network members on an organization-by-organization basis. In a similar way, shared organizational identification provides a basis for mutual orientation that the parties can rely on during intraorganizational exchanges.

SELF-ENHANCEMENT AND ORGANIZATIONAL IDENTIFICATION.   A great deal of evidence indicates that individuals are motivated to maintain positive identities (Taylor & Brown, 1988; Tesser, 1986). To do so, they may use a variety of cognitive and behavioral strategies to enhance their self-images. When necessary, they will try to defend themselves against information or events that threaten their positive images. Numerous studies have shown, for example, that individuals distort information about the self in a self-enhancing direction (e.g., Brown, 1986; Brown, Collins, & Schmidt, 1988; Greenwald, 1980; Kramer, Newton, & Pommerenke, 1991b; Taylor, 1989; Taylor & Brown, 1988).

One reason for self-enhancement is the need to protect self-esteem (Taylor, 1989). Tajfel and Turner (1986) extended this self-esteem argument to group-level identification, arguing that individuals can use their membership in social groups to maintain and bolster self-esteem. Through their association with prestigious groups, people can enhance their social images and status. Empirical support for this argument has been provided by a number of studies (Abrams & Hogg, 1990; Crocker & Luhtanen, 1990; Lemry & Smith, 1985; Luhtanen & Crocker, 1991; Oakes & Turner, 1980).

Organizational determinants

The functionalist argument raised in the preceding paragraphs implies that organizational events should influence organizational identification. For example, organizational identification should increase when the public attractiveness of an organization is high and decrease when its attractiveness is low (Dutton et al., 1991). This suggests that organizational identification may wax and wane as the status of the organizational identity increases or decreases (see Dutton et al., 1991; Kramer, 1991, for more extended discussion of this issue).

IDENTITY-ENHANCING EVENTS.   Research on impression management has shown that people who experience identity-enhancing events often try to claim closer association with those events (Tedeschi & Reiss, 1981). It seems reasonable to argue from this research that when groups or organizations experience successful outcomes or positive events, individual members will identify more strongly with them. People will want to take credit and bask in the reflected glory of the organization (Cialdini et al., 1976; Kramer, 1991; Sutton & Kramer, 1990; Tedeschi, 1981). Some evidence of this could be observed following the recent military victory of the United States in the Persian Gulf. Following this conflict, many organizations published announcements in local newspapers thanking those employees who had been involved in the conflict. While ostensibly aimed at expressing appreciation, doing so also provided an opportunity for them to indirectly assume some credit for and association with that success.

IDENTITY-THREATENING EVENTS.   Conversely, a parallel prediction concerns the effects of identity-threatening events on identification. When negative events happen to an organization, individuals might try to distance or dissociate themselves from the organization or its predicament (Sutton, 1990; Sutton & Callahan, 1987; Tedeschi & Reiss, 1981). Stigmatizing events, therefore, should lead individuals to eschew organizational identity in favor of more flattering individualistic or group-level identities. Under such circumstances, employees of a stigmatized firm may draw sharper boundaries between themselves as employees and top management as decision makers. "*They* (top management) messed this up, but *we* (the employees) did all we could to warn them."

Although the logic of this argument seems straightforward, the relationship between threats and identification may be more complex. Individuals' responses to identity-threatening predicaments may depend, for example, on the nature of the threat and how it is construed. Specifically, individuals' attributions about the cause of the threat and the responsibility of the organization for the problem may mediate their responses. If threats are attributed to factors beyond the organization's control, organizational identification may actually increase. The threat may be perceived as a collective problem increasing attraction and cohesiveness among those threatened (Janis, 1963; Staw, Sandelands, & Dutton, 1981). Moreover, repairing the damage to the organization's image may be viewed as a superordinate goal, binding organizational members more tightly together as a group (Sherif, 1966; Sherif et al., 1988).

DIRECTIONS FOR FUTURE RESEARCH

The conceptual framework presented in this chapter does not provide a complete theory of organizational cooperation, nor was that the intent of the chapter. Rather, the goal of the chapter is to illustrate some conditions under which cooperation is likely to emerge in organizations. With this in mind, future research might take several directions. First, most of the empirical results reported in this chapter are based on laboratory experiments designed to simulate cooperation dilemmas commonly found in organizations. In one of the few field studies, Mael (1988) reported that identification of alumni with their alma mater was positively correlated with donations to that institution (cited in Ashforth & Mael, 1989, p. 26). This finding is consistent with the theoretical arguments presented in this chapter, but there is clearly a need for additional field studies.

In most laboratory studies, group identification has been manipulated by the experimenter. By doing so, the causal relationship between group identification and cooperation can be established. However, studies that directly measure individuals' organizational identification are also clearly needed. As Dutton et al. (1991) noted, "not all organization members identify equally with their organizations. There may also be significant organizational differences in the degree to which organizational identifying occurs" (p. 33). Thus, there is a need for research that measures both intra- and interorganizational differences in identifying.

Central to the argument presented in this chapter is the assumption that self-esteem needs and the desire to maintain a positive identity affect organizational identification. While some evidence supports the self-esteem arguments advanced here, alternative claims have been put forward as well. Brewer (1991), for example, suggested that "ingroup bias may not be a method of *achieving* self-esteem so much as an extension of self-esteem at the group level" (p. 8, emphasis in the original). Similarly, Crocker and Luhtanen (1990) argued that in-group enhancement, rather than reflecting an indirect attempt at self-enhancement, may sometimes "simply represent an attempt to enhance the ingroup, in the service of collective rather than personal esteem needs" (p. 66). Insofar as enhancement can be in the service of both goals simultaneously, I would argue that neither of these positions is inherently incompatible with the arguments presented in this chapter. However, it is clear that more empirical work is required to clarify these issues.

The analysis presented in this chapter is distinctive in its emphasis on identification as a determinant of cooperative behavior. However, the general arguments underlying this analysis seem compatible with a number of other recent perspectives. Accordingly, one direction for future research would be to investigate the relationship between organizational identification and the central variables associated with other theoretical perspectives. For example, Lowenstein, Thompson, and Bazerman (1989) recently described the results of several experiments that investigated the social utility functions underlying interpersonal decision making. They found that the perceived relationship between the parties is an important determinant of such functions. Individuals who perceived their relationship with another party in positive terms cared more about that party's outcomes. Organizational identification may also affect the form these social utility functions take. In particular, it seems straightforward to argue that, as organizational identification increases, individuals may experience greater concern about the welfare of other members of the organization.

The relationship between organizational identification and organizational citizenship behavior is another area that merits more sustained attention from researchers. Organ (1988) described organizational citizenship behavior as "individual behavior that is discretionary, not directly or explicitly recognized by the formal reward system, and that in the aggregate promotes the effective functioning of the organization" (p. 4). Organizational identification may be an important predictor of organizational citizenship behavior and other forms of prosocial behavior.

Lind and Tyler (1988; Tyler, 1989; Tyler & Lind, 1990) have written a series of thoughtful papers concerning the relationship between group membership and procedural justice. They propose that individuals' justice concerns are shaped by the value that individuals attach to membership in social groups. In particular, they argue that group membership influences the expectations people have about just treatment. "People expect an organization to use neutral decision-making procedures . . . so that over time, all group members will benefit fairly *from being members of the group*" (p. 837, emphasis added). Presumably, the more strongly individuals identify with an organization, the greater such expectations might be about fair treatment.

IMPLICATIONS AND CONCLUSIONS

The analysis of cooperation presented in this chapter has a number of implications. One implication is that organizational actors will cooperate with each other far more than theoretical perspectives based on egoistic assumptions forecast. This point is not trivial. The implicit assumptions about human motivation and decision making that are built into our organizational theories are not only descriptive, they are *prescriptive* as well. Theoretical models shape, both subtly and explicitly, our research agendas, affecting how questions are framed and determining which topics and problems receive sustained examination from researchers.

In addition to affecting how problems are framed, the kinds of solutions to organizational dilemmas that researchers consider may also be anchored by their implicit assumptions about what motivates decision makers. Solutions predicated on Hobbesian assumptions that presume that individuals perceive sharp disjunctions between their own welfare and others' welfare may focus attention on negative forms of control (e.g., sanctions) to deter self-interested behavior. Such assumptions assume a baserate of noncooperation and imply that organizational systems must inhibit and constrain self-interested behavior.

In contrast, solutions predicated on more socialized conceptions of motivation and decision making imply the efficacy of more positive approaches to managing interdependence. Structures and processes that increase organizational identification may prove just as efficacious as more coercive mechanisms, while generating fewer side effects such as reactance. Recall that Dawes et al. (1988) found that even a 10-minute discussion was sometimes sufficient to induce a sense of group identification and increased cooperation.

Another potential contribution of this framework is that it provides the foundation for a more general theory of interdependent decision making in organizations. There are, at present, few conceptual frameworks for linking micro and macro level conceptions of cooperation; instead theory-building efforts and empirical results in the macro and micro realms have remained largely fragmented and unintegrated. While structural and social psychological theories of interdependence enjoy a number of natural conceptual affinities, these affinities have remained largely unexplored and unexploited (see Kramer, 1991, for a more extended discussion of this issue).

This lack of integration, of course, is not unique to research on cooperation. It has been described as symptomatic of organizational research in general. Cappelli and Sherer (1991), Rousseau (1985), and Staw and Sutton (this volume) have drawn attention to this impasse and have suggested some constructive strategies for moving beyond it. Cappelli and Sherer (1991) have proposed that what is needed are more conceptions that connect micro and macro level explanations of organizational behavior. "Efforts to develop links between micro and macro theories," they suggest, "fortunately do not require abandoning existing paradigms, but instead rely on 'bridge statements' which develop theoretical relationships between existing macro and micro laws" (p. 88). One aim of this chapter has been to suggest a framework for generating such bridging propositions.

While far from perfect or complete, the conceptual framework outlined in this chapter tries to suggest how organizational and social psychological processes might be combined in explaining cooperation. On a broader level, the framework presented in this chapter was motivated largely by a disenchantment with prevailing conceptions of interdependent decision making in organizations. Current conceptions imply that individuals are calculative rather than affiliative; rational rather than emotional; and individualistic rather than communal. In explaining how organizational actors respond to interdependence, previous theories have assumed that behavior is motivated primarily by self-interests. For example, agency theory, transaction-costs perspectives, and theories of collective action all share the assumption that individuals act to further their own interests (Eisenhardt, 1989; Hirsch, 1990; Olson, 1965). Similarly, many of the problems that have preoccupied organizational scholars, such as moral hazard, adverse selection, and free riding, reflect the dynamics and dilemmas generated by the interaction between interdependent actors who are presumed to be unboundedly self-interested.

The prominence afforded the assumption of self-interest in theories of organizational behavior is not altogether surprising. Even casual observation is sufficient to suggest that individuals' behavior is often directed toward the achievement of personal goals, even when doing so compromises the goal attainment of other members of the organization or undermines the welfare of the organization itself. Indeed, recent popular accounts of contemporary organizational life are replete with tales of the unmitigated pursuit of self-interest (e.g., Bach, 1985; Burrough & Helyar, 1990; Lewis, 1989).

In contrast to its easy assertion, however, the assumption that human behavior is motivated by self-interests is less easily reconciled with many organizational behaviors. For example, individuals frequently help other organizational members, even when doing so does not seem to further their self-interests (Brief & Motowidlo, 1986; Organ, 1988). Moreover, individuals often express concern about others' outcomes as well as their own (Loewenstein et al., 1989; MacCrimmon & Messick, 1976; Ochs & Roth, 1989). Finally, people cooperate far more than theories predicated on the assumption of self-interest suggest (Dawes & Thaler, 1988; Kramer & Brewer, 1986). Thus, although behavior in organizations is sometimes self-regarding, it is often *other*-regarding (Perrow, 1986).

Despite empirical evidence of such "other-interested" behavior, however, organizational theory provides few conceptual frameworks to account for this behavior. As Granovetter (1985) cogently observed, current theories have been largely dominated by "atomistic, *undersocialized* conceptions of human action" (p. 483, emphasis added). Such conceptions cannot readily explain the many forms of cooperative behavior observed in organizations. Organizational identification is a useful construct for accounting for such other-interested behavior. It also provides a fruitful way to conceptualize the tension between these divergent views about human motivation and decision making. In other words, rather than assume self-interest as invariant, it should be regarded as a dependent variable much like any other. As Perrow (1986) suggested, "Self-interest is still a problem worthy of investigation *if it is posed as a variable, rather than a fixed property*" (p. 232, emphasis added). The interesting empirical question then becomes under what circumstances will people act self-interestedly rather than other-interestedly. This chapter has tried to suggest that a theory of cooperation grounded in a social psychological conception of organizational identification can shed light on this important question.

REFERENCES

ABRAMS, D., & HOGG, M. A. (1990). *Social identity theory: Constructive and critical advances.* New York: Springer-Verlag.

ALDERFER, C. P., & THOMAS, D. A. (1988). The significance of race and ethnicity for understanding organizational behavior. In C. L. Cooper & I. Robertson (Eds.), *International review of industrial and organizational psychology* (pp. 1–41). New York: John Wiley.

ASHFORTH, B. E., & MAEL, F. (1989). Social identity theory and the organization. *Academy of Management Review, 14,* 20–39.

AXELROD, R. (1984). *The evolution of cooperation.* New York: Basic Books.

BACH, S. (1985). *Final cut: Dreams and disaster in the making of Heaven's Gate.* Beverly Hills, CA: Morrow.

BARON, J. N., & BIELBY, W. T. (1986). The proliferation of job titles in organizations. *Administrative Science Quarterly, 31*, 561–586.

BARON, J. N., & PFEFFER, J. (1989). The social psychology of inequality. Unpublished manuscript, Stanford University.

BARNARD, C. (1938). *The functions of the executive*. Cambridge, MA: Harvard University Press.

BREWER, M. B. (1979). In-group bias in the minimal intergroup situation: A cognitive-motivational analysis. *Psychological Bulletin, 86*, 307–324.

BREWER, M. B. (1981). Ethnocentrism and its role in interpersonal trust. In M. B. Brewer & B. E. Collins (Eds)., *Scientific inquiry and the social sciences* (pp. 345–360). New York: Jossey-Bass.

BREWER, M. B. (1985). Experimental research and social policy: Must it be rigor versus relevance? *Journal of Social Issues, 41*, 159–176.

BREWER, M. B. (1986). Ethnocentrism and its role in intergroup conflict. In S. Worchel & W. G. Austin (Eds.), *Psychology of intergroup relations* (pp. 88–102). Chicago: Nelson-Hall.

BREWER, M. B. (1991). The social self: On being the same and different at the same time. *Personality and Social Psychology Bulletin, 17*, 475–482.

BREWER, M. B., & KRAMER, R. M. (1984, August). *Subgroup identity as a factor in the conservation of resources*. Paper presented at the American Psychological Association annual convention, Washington, DC.

BREWER, M. B., & KRAMER, R. M. (1985). The psychology of intergroup attitudes and behavior. *Annual Review of Psychology, 36*, 219–243.

BREWER, M. B., & KRAMER, R. M. (1986). Choice behavior in social dilemmas: Effects of social identity, group size, and decision framing. *Journal of Personality and Social Psychology, 50*, 543–549.

BREWER, M. B., & SILVER, M. (1978). Ingroup bias as a function of task characteristics. *European Journal of Social Psychology, 8*, 393–400.

BRIEF, A. P., & MOTOWIDLO, S. J. (1986). Prosocial organizational behaviors. *Academy of Management Review, 10*, 710–725.

BROWN, J. D. (1990). Evaluating one's abilities: Shortcuts and stumbling blocks on the road to self-knowledge. *Journal of Experimental Social Psychology, 26*, 149–167.

BROWN, J. D., COLLINS, R. L., & SCHMIDT, G. W. (1988). Self-esteem and direct versus indirect forms of self-enhancement. *Journal of Personality and Social Psychology, 55*, 445–453.

BROWN, R., & WILLIAMS, J. (1984). Group identification: The same thing to all people? *Human Relations, 37*, 547–564.

BROWN, R. J., CONDOR, S., MATTHEWS, A., WADE, G., & WILLIAMS, J. A. (1986). Explaining intergroup differentiation in an industrial organization. *Journal of Occupational Psychology, 59*, 111–129.

BURROUGH, B., & HELYAR, J. (1990). *Barbarians at the gate: The fall of RJR Nabisco*. New York: Harper & Row.

CAMPBELL, D. T. (1958). Common fate, similarity, and other indices of the status of aggregates of persons as social entities. *Behavioral Science, 3*, 14–25.

CAPPELLI, P., & SHERER, P. D. (1991). The missing role of context in OB: The need for a meso-level approach. In L. L. Cummings & B. M. Staw (Eds.), *Research in organizational behavior* (Vol. 13, pp. 55–110). Greenwich, CT: JAI Press.

CARNEVALE, P. J., PRUITT, D. G., & BRITTON, S. D. (1979). Looking tough: The negotiator under constituent surveillance. *Personality and Social Psychology Bulletin, 5*, 118–121.

CIALDINI, R. B., BORDEN, R. J., THORNE, A., WALKDER, M. R., FREMAN, S., & SLOAN, L. R. (1976). Basking in reflected glory: Three (football) field studies. *Journal of Personality and Social Psychology, 34*, 463–476.

CROCKER, J., & LUHTANEN, R. (1990). Collective self-esteem and ingroup bias. *Journal of Personality and Social Psychology, 58,* 60–67.

DAWES, R. M., & THALER, R. H. (1988). Anomalies: Cooperation. *Journal of Economic Perspectives, 2,* 187–197.

DAWES, R. M., van de KRAGT, A. J. C., & ORBELL, J. M. (1988). Not me or thee but we: The importance of group identity in eliciting cooperation in dilemma situations: Experimental manipulations. *Acta Psychologica, 68,* 83–97.

DUTTON, J. E., DUKERICH, J. M., & HARQUAIL, C. V. (1991). *The organizational self: Linking organizational identity and image to individuals through the process of organizational identifying.* Unpublished manuscript, University of Michigan.

EISENHARDT, K. M. (1989). Agency theory: An assessment and review. *Academy of Management Review, 14,* 57–74.

FISKE, S., & TAYLOR, S. (1991). *Social cognition* (2nd ed.). New York: Random House.

FORT, R. D., & BADEN, J. (1981). The federal treasury as a common resource pool and the development of a predatory bureaucracy. In J. Baden & R. L. Stroup (Eds.), *Bureaucracy vs. environment: The environmental costs of bureaucratic governance* (pp. 9–21). Ann Arbor: University of Michigan Press.

GAERTNER, S. L., MANN, J., MURRELL, A., & DOVIDIO, J. F. (1989). Reducing intergroup bias: The benefits of recategorization. *Journal of Personality and Social Psychology, 57,* 239–249.

GIBSON, J. J. (1966). *The senses considered as perceptual systems.* Boston: Houghton Mifflin.

GLAZER, M., & GLAZER, P. (1989). *The whistleblowers.* New York: Basic Books.

GOFFMAN, E. (1963). *Stigma: Notes on the management of spoiled identity.* Englewood Cliffs, NJ: Prentice Hall.

GRANOVETTER, M. (1985). Economic action and social structure: The problem of embeddedness. *American Journal of Sociology, 91,* 481–510.

GREENBERG, J. (1990). Looking fair versus being fair: Managing impressions of organizational justice. In B. M. Staw & L. L. Cummings (Eds.), *Research in organizational behavior* (Vol. 12, pp. 111–158). Greenwich, CT: JAI Press.

GREENWALD, A. G. (1980). The totalitarian ego: Fabrication and revision of personal history. *American Psychologist, 35,* 603–618.

HIRSCH, P. (1990). Rational choice models for sociology: Pro and con. *Rationality and Society, 2,* 137–141.

HOGG, M. A., & ABRAMS, D. (1988). *Social identifications: A social psychology of intergroup relations and group processes.* London: Routledge.

HOGG, M. A., & HARDIE, E. A. (1991). Social attraction, personal attraction, and self-categorization: A field study. *Personality and Social Psychology Bulletin, 17,* 175–180.

HOGG, M. A., & TURNER, J. C. (1985a). Interpersonal attraction, social identification and psychological group formation. *European Journal of Social Psychology, 15,* 51–66.

HOGG, M. A., & TURNER, J. C. (1985b). When liking begets solidarity: An experiment on the role of interpersonal attraction in psychological group formation. *British Journal of Social Psychology, 24,* 267–281.

HORNSTEIN, H. A. (1976). *Cruelty and kindness: A new look at aggression and altruism.* Englewood Cliffs, NJ: Prentice Hall.

HOWARD, J. A. (1990). A sociological framework of cognition. In E. Lawler & B. Markovsky (Eds.), *Advances in group processes* (Vol. 7, pp. 75–103). Greenwich, CT: JAI Press.

JANIS, I. L. (1963). Group identification under conditions of external danger. *British Journal of Medical Psychology, 36,* 227–238.

KAHN, R. L., & ZALD, M. (1990). *Organizations and nation-states: New perspectives on conflict and cooperation.* San Francisco: Jossey-Bass.

KAHNEMAN, D., & TVERSKY, A. (1979). Prospect theory. *Econometrica, 47,* 341–350.

KANTER, R. M. (1977). *Men and women of the corporation.* New York: Basic Books.

KRAMER, R. M. (1991). Intergroup relations and organizational dilemmas: The role of categorization processes. In L. L. Cummings & B. M. Staw (Eds.), *Research in organizational behavior* (Vol. 13, pp. 191–227). Greenwich, CT: JAI Press.

KRAMER, R. M., & BREWER, M. B. (1984). Effects of group identity on resource use in a simulated commons dilemma. *Journal of Personality and Social Psychology, 46,* 1044–1057.

KRAMER, R. M., & BREWER, M. B. (1986). Social group identity and the emergence of cooperation in resource conservation dilemmas. In H. Wilke, C. Rutte, & D. M. Messick (Eds.), *Experimental studies of social dilemmas* (pp. 205–234). Frankfurt, Germany: Peter Lang Publishing Company.

KRAMER, R. M., MEYERSON, D., & DAVIS, G. (1990). How much is enough? Psychological components of "guns versus butter" decisions in a security dilemma. *Journal of Personality and Social Psychology, 58,* 984–993.

KRAMER, R. M., NEWTON, E., & POMMERENKE, P. (1991a). *Bounded individuality and bargaining in organizations: A social identity perspective.* Unpublished manuscript, Stanford University.

KRAMER, R. M., NEWTON, E., & POMMERENKE, P. (1991b). Self-enhancement biases in negotiator judgment: Effects of self-esteem and mood. *Organizational Behavior and Human Decision Making,* forthcoming.

LANSBERG, I. (1989). Social categorization, entitlement, and justice in organizations: Contextual determinants and cognitive underpinnings. *Human Relations, 41,* 871–879.

LATANE, B., WILLIAMS, K., & HARKINS, S. (1979). Many hands make light the work: Causes and consequences of social loafing. *Journal of Personality and Social Psychology, 37,* 822–832.

LEMRY, L., & SMITH, P. M. (1985). Intergroup discrimination and self-esteem in the minimal group paradigm. *Journal of Personality and Social Psychology, 49,* 660–670.

LEWIS, M. (1989). *Liar's poker: Rising through the wreckage of Wall Street.* New York: W. W. Norton & Co.

LIND, E. A., & TYLER, T. R. (1988). *The social psychology of procedural justice.* New York: Plenum.

LINDSKOLD, S. (1978). Trust development, the GRIT proposal, and the effects of conciliatory acts on conflict and cooperation. *Psychological Bulletin, 85,* 772–793.

LOEWENSTEIN, G. F., THOMPSON, L., & BAZERMAN, M. H. (1989). Social utility and decision making in interpersonal contexts. *Journal of Personality and Social Psychology, 57,* 426–441.

LUHTANEN, R., & CROCKER, J. (1991). Self-esteem and intergroup comparisons: Toward a theory of collective self-esteem. In J. Suls & T. Wills (Eds.), *Social comparison: Contemporary theory and research* (pp. 211–236). Hillsdale, NJ: Lawrence Erlbaum.

MacCRIMMON, K. R., & MESSICK, D. M. (1976). A framework for social motives. *Behavioral Science, 21,* 86–100.

McPHERSON, M. S. (1984). Limits on self-seeking: The role of morality in economic life. In D. C. Coldander (Ed.), *Neoclassical political economy* (pp. 121–130). Cambridge, MA: Harvard University Press.

MESSICK, D. M. (1974). When a little "group interest" goes a long way: Social motives and union joining. *Organizational Behavior and Human Performance, 12,* 331–334.

MESSICK, D. M., & MACKIE, D. M. (1989). Intergroup relations. *Annual Review of Psychology, 40,* 45–81.

OAKES, P. J., & TURNER, J. C. (1980). Social categorization and intergroup behavior. *European Journal of Social Psychology, 10,* 295–301.

OCHS, J., & ROTH, A. E. (1989). An experimental study of sequential bargaining. *American Economic Review, 79,* 355–384.

OLSON, M. (1965). *The logic of collective action.* New Haven, CT: Yale University Press.

ORBELL, J. M., van de KRAGT, A., & DAWES, R. M. (1988). Explaining discussion-induced cooperation. *Journal of Personality and Social Psychology, 54,* 811–819.

ORGAN, D. W. (1988). *Organizational citizenship behavior: The good soldier syndrome.* Lexington, MA: D. C. Heath.

ORGAN, D. W. (1990). The motivational basis of organizational citizenship behavior. In B. M. Staw & L. L. Cummings (Eds.), *Research in organizational behavior* (Vol. 12, pp. 43–72). Greenwich, CT: JAI Press.

O'REILLY, C., & CHATMAN, J. (1986). Organizational commitment and psychological attachment: The effects of compliance, identification, and internalization on prosocial behavior. *Journal of Applied Psychology, 71,* 492–499.

OSTROM, E. (1977). Collective action and the tragedy of the commons. In G. Hardin & J. Baden (Eds.), *Managing the commons* (pp. 173–181). San Francisco: W. H. Freeman & Co.

PERROW, C. (1986). *Complex organizations* (3rd ed.). New York: Random House.

PFEFFER, J., & SALANCIK, G. R. (1978). *The external control of organizations.* New York: Harper & Row.

POWELL, W. P. (1990). Neither market nor hierarchy: Network forms of organization. In B. M. Staw & L. L. Cummings (Eds.), *Research in organizational behavior* (Vol. 12, pp. 295–336). Greenwich, CT: JAI Press.

RABBIE, J. M., & HORWITZ, M. (1969). Arousal of ingroup bias by chance win or loss. *Journal of Personality and Social Psychology, 13,* 269–277.

RABBIE, J. M., & WILKINS, G. (1971). Intergroup competition and its effects on intragroup and intergroup relations. *European Journal of Social Psychology, 1,* 215–234.

REIS, H. T. (1981). Self-presentation and distributive justice. In J. Tedeschi (Ed.), *Impression management theory and social psychological theory* (pp. 269–291). New York: Academic Press.

REIS, H. T., & GRUZEN, J. (1976). On mediating equity, equality and self interest: The role of self-presentation in social exchange. *Journal of Experimental Social Psychology, 12,* 487–503.

ROSS, L., & NISBETT, R. E. (1991). *The person and the situation.* New York: McGraw-Hill.

ROTHBART, M., & JOHN, O. P. (1985). Social categorization and behavioral episodes: A cognitive analysis of the effects of intergroup contact. *Journal of Social Issues, 41,* 81–104.

ROTTER, J. B. (1980). Interpersonal trust, trustworthiness, and gullibility. *American Psychologist, 35,* 1–7.

ROUSSEAU, D. M. (1985). Issues of level in organizational research: Multi-level and cross level perspectives. In L. L. Cummings & B. M. Staw (Eds.), *Research in organizational behavior* (Vol. 7, pp. 1–38). Greenwich, CT: JAI Press.

ROUSSEAU, D. M. (1989). Psychological and implied contracts in organizations. *Employee Responsibilities and Rights Journal, 2,* 121–139.

SCHELLING, T. C. (1978). *Macromotives and microbehavior.* New Haven, CT: Yale University Press.

SHAPIRO, S. P. (1987). The social control of impersonal trust. *American Journal of Sociology, 93,* 623–658.

SHERIF, M. (1966). *In common predicament: Social psychology of intergroup conflict and cooperation.* New York: Houghton Mifflin.

SHERIF, M., HARVEY, O. J., WHITE, B. J., HOOD, W. R., & SHERIF, C. W. (1988). *The robbers cave experiment: Intergroup conflict and cooperation.* Middletown, CT: Wesleyan.

SIMON, H. A. (1986). *Organizations and markets.* Unpublished mimeograph, Carnegie-Mellon University.

STAW, B. M., SANDELANDS, L. E., & DUTTON, J. E. (1981). Threat-rigidity effects in organizational performance. *Administrative Science Quarterly, 28,* 582–600.

SUTTON, R. (1990). Organizational decline processes: A social psychological perspective. In B. M. Staw & L. L. Cummings (Eds.), *Research in organizational behavior* (Vol. 12, pp. 205–253). Greenwich, CT: JAI Press.

SUTTON, R., & CALLAHAN, A. (1987). The stigma of bankruptcy: Spoiled organizational image and its management. *Academy of Management Journal, 30,* 405–436.

SUTTON, R., & KRAMER, R. M. (1990). Transforming failure into success: Impression management, spin control, and the Iceland Arms Control Talks. In R. Kahn & M. Zald (Eds.), *Organizations and nation-states* (pp. 221–248). San Francisco: Jossey-Bass.

SWINGLE, P. G. (1976). *The management of power.* Hillsdale, NJ: Erlbaum.

TAJFEL, H. (1969). Cognitive aspects of prejudice. *Journal of Social Issues, 25,* 79–97.

TAJFEL, H. (1982a). *Social identity and intergroup relations.* Cambridge: Cambridge University Press.

TAJFEL, H. (1982b). Social psychology of intergroup relations. *Annual Review of Psychology, 33,* 1–39.

TAJFEL, H., FLAMENT, C., BILLIG, M. G., & BUNDY, R. P. (1971). Social categorization and intergroup behavior. *European Journal of Social Psychology, 1,* 147–175.

TAJFEL, H., & TURNER, J. C. (1986). The social identity theory of intergroup behavior. In S. Worchel & W. G. Austin (Eds.), *Psychology of intergroup relations* (pp. 7–24). Chicago: Nelson-Hall.

TAJFEL, H., & WILKES, A. L. (1963). Classification and quantitative judgment. *British Journal of Social Psychology, 54,* 101–114.

TAYLOR, S. E. (1989). *Positive illusions: Creative self-deception and the healthy mind.* New York: Basic Books.

TAYLOR, S. E., & BROWN, J. D. (1988). Illusion and well-being: A social psychological perspective on mental health. *Psychological Bulletin, 103,* 193–210.

TEDESCHI, J. T. (1981). *Impression management theory and social psychological research.* New York: Academic Press.

TEDESCHI, J. T., & REISS, M. (1981). Identities, the phenomenal self, and laboratory research. In J. T. Tedeschi (Ed.), *Impression management theory and social psychological research* (pp. 3–22). New York: Academic Press.

TESSER, A. (1986). Some effects of self-evaluation maintenance on cognition and action. In R. M. Sorrentino & E. T. Higgins (Eds.), *Handbook of motivation and cognition: Foundations of social behavior* (pp. 121–135). New York: Guilford.

TETLOCK, P. E. (1985). Accountability: The neglected social context of judgment and choice. In L. L. Cummings & B. M. Staw (Eds.), *Research in organizational behavior* (Vol. 7, pp. 297–332). Greenwich, CT: JAI Press.

TURNER, J. C. (1982). Toward a cognitive definition of the group. In H. Tajfel (Ed.), *Social identity and intergroup relations* (pp. 123–137). Cambridge, England: Cambridge University Press.

TURNER, J. C. (1987). *Rediscovering the social group: A self-categorization theory.* Oxford: Basil Blackwell.

TYLER, T. R. (1989). The psychology of procedural justice: A test of the group-value model. *Journal of Personality and Social Psychology, 57,* 830–838.

TYLER, T. R., & LIND, E. A. (1990). Intrinsic versus community-based justice models: When does group membership matter? *Journal of Social Issues, 46,* 83–94.

WEICK, K. E. (1979). Cognitive processes in organizations. In L. L. Cummings & B. M. Staw (Eds.), *Research in organizational behavior* (pp. 43–64). Greenwich, CT: JAI Press.

WILDER, D. A. (1981). Perceiving persons as a group: Categorization and intergroup relations. In D. Hamilton (Ed.), *Cognitive processes in stereotyping and intergroup behavior* (pp. 214–260). Hillsdale, NJ: Lawrence Erlbaum.

WILDER, D. A., & COOPER, W. E. (1981). Categorization into groups: Consequences for social perception and attribution. In J. H. Harvey, W. Ickes, & R. F. Kidd (Eds.), *New directions in attribution research* (pp. 79–92). Hillsdale, NJ: Erlbaum.

WIT, A. (1989). *Group efficiency and fairness in social dilemmas: An experimental gaming approach.* Dissertation. The Netherlands: University of Leiden.

ZUCKER, L. G. (1986). Production of trust: Institutional sources of economic structure, 1840–1920. In L. L. Cummings & B. M. Staw (Eds.), *Research in organizational behavior* (Vol. 8, pp. 53–111). Greenwich, CT: JAI Press.

CHAPTER THIRTEEN

From Revolutionary Coalitions to Bilateral Deterrence: A Nonzero-Sum Approach to Social Power*

EDWARD J. LAWLER

University of Iowa

This chapter reviews a program of work investigating how social power, defined as a structurally based capability, affects the tactics chosen in a conflict. A nonzero-sum approach to power stipulates that the total amount of power in a relationship can have effects distinct from those of relative power or power difference. This assumption is grounded in Emerson's power dependence theory and reminiscent of Tannenbaum's concept of control. The basic ideas are that (1) higher total power in a relationship has an integrative effect on that relationship, resulting in more conciliatory and less hostile responses to conflict; and (2) larger power differences have divisive effects on a relationship, making conflict resolution less conciliatory and more hostile. Research on revolutionary coalitions, power dependence processes in bargaining, and bilateral deterrence exemplify and support the importance of the nonzero-sum approach to power.

When individuals, groups, or organizations experience a conflict of interest, they can respond in a variety of ways. One common response is to attempt to influence the other party by choosing among some set of available tactics; another is to avoid the relationship or situation in which the conflict can occur; still another is to do nothing right away except work to improve one's power position in preparation for one of the first two options. Threatening or damaging action is an example of the first option; leaving the scene, an example of the second; and forming a coalition with others, of the third. Along with a variety of other social psychologists (e.g., Deutsch, 1973; Kipnis, 1976; Kipnis & Schmidt, 1983;

*The author expresses appreciation to Samuel B. Bacharach, with whom many of the projects described herein were developed jointly. In addition, Rebecca Ford has contributed to the author's thinking about this theory and research program in important ways.

Tedeschi, Schlenker, & Bonoma, 1973), my program of research has taken the concept of power as central to understanding how actors respond to a conflict and in particular how they react to an opponent's response. This chapter reviews the conceptual odyssey of this research program (e.g., Bacharach & Lawler, 1980, 1981a; Lawler, 1975a&b, 1986, 1992).

Virtually all parts of the program—from the early research on revolutionary coalitions (Lawler, 1975) to more recent work on bilateral deterrence (Lawler, 1986)—should be interpreted as an effort to understand power processes, in particular when people use power and how they use it (see Bacharach & Lawler, 1981a). One fundamental question has consistently driven this program of work: *How does power, defined as a structurally based capability, affect the tactical use of power*? This chapter presents the abstract, theoretical position on power that has emerged in the work over the last 20 years. More specifically, it presents the theoretical framework, analyzes the central themes or theoretical propositions, and shows how these themes are stimulating work on some new issues (see also Lawler, 1992; Lawler & Ford, in press).

Broadly construed, the framework on power embedded in our work pulls together ideas, somewhat selectively, from sociology, social psychology, and the study of organizations. A few examples help set the stage for what follows. From sociological analyses, we adopt a social structural perspective on the sources of conflict (Dahrendorf, 1959). From some organizational theory, we adopt the notion that social structure is an objective, external phenomenon that has both a horizontal and vertical dimension (e.g., Blau, 1977). From Emerson's power dependence theory, we extract a nonzero-sum conception of power, which emphasizes structurally based, rather than interpersonally based, power. From social psychological research, such as that treated by Rubin and Brown (1975) and Pruitt (1981), we adopt a tactical approach to the use of power in conflict. Overall, the terms *social structure, power,* and *tactics* capture the theoretical content of the research program. Revolutionary coalitions and two-party bargaining have been the major substantive topics.

In this conceptual biography, I focus very heavily on the conceptual, as opposed to the empirical, side of the research program. The conceptual side of the program is treated in terms of two elements: the metatheory and the set of testable propositions or theories spawned by the metatheory. A metatheory refers to a set of fundamental assumptions that orient and shape theorizing about some phenomenon, often in subtle, nonconscious ways (Wagner & Berger, 1985). Field theory and social exchange theory are examples of basic metatheories found in the literature on power. A theory is essentially a set of abstract, testable claims or propositions about the causes or effects of a phenomenon (Wagner, 1984). Power dependence theory (Emerson 1962, 1972) is an example of a theory of power falling within a social exchange metatheory.

Metatheories are important because they define the substantive problems of theoretical interest, indicate how those problems should be investigated, and establish boundaries around the sort of theoretical solutions deemed satisfactory (Berger, Wagner, & Zelditch, 1987; Lawler & Ford, in press; Wagner, 1984).

Much can be learned by teasing out metatheories and juxtaposing them with testable parts of theorizing. We believe, along with a growing number of sociologists (e.g., Berger et al., 1987), that more explicit metatheorizing can promote better theorizing. Thus, one purpose of this chapter is to use the distinction between metatheory and theory to present and analyze my own program of work; a second purpose is to illustrate how more explicitness about metatheories might stimulate interesting and important theoretical shifts (see also Lawler & Ford, in press).

The chapter is divided into five sections, corresponding to several distinct stages of development within the theory and research program. The *first stage* consisted primarily of research on revolutionary coalitions. This work focused on the determinants of a single tactic; it was highly problem driven. The *second stage* was a series of empirical papers using power dependence theory to understand how actors evaluate and choose among a set of tactics. In this work, a revolutionary coalition is but one among a set of possible tactics suggested by power dependence theory. The *third stage* was essentially a theoretical interlude, in which Bacharach and I produced books on *Power and Politics in Organizations* (1980) and *Bargaining* (1981a). This was the point at which the metatheory crystallized, and the research became more theory driven. The *fourth stage* was to develop and test theoretical notions that relate power capability and power use. The *fifth stage* is taking the main ideas (e.g., theoretical propositions) and using them to address other issues, such as the effectiveness of unilateral initiatives in bargaining and commitment in social exchange relations.

STAGE 1: REVOLUTIONARY COALITIONS

The research on revolutionary conditions developed from the early work of Caplow (1956) and Gamson (1961) on coalition formation. The Caplow/Gamson tradition asked *which* of the possible winning coalitions will form, assuming that a coalition is virtually inevitable (see Murnighan, 1978, for a review). Our research asked a different question—namely, under what conditions will two or more subordinates in a status hierarchy mobilize a coalition against a group leader (Lawler, 1975a, 1975b, 1983; Lawler & Thompson, 1978; Lawler, Youngs, & Lesh, 1978; Michener & Lawler, 1971; Michener & Lyons, 1972). This work focused on a particular type of coalition and addressed its capacity to mobilize.

The research assumed a status hierarchy in which three or more actors work on and receive a group outcome from a collective task. The leader had the authority, legitimized on the basis of merit, to allocate group outcomes. The major focus was on the conditions determining when subordinates will engage in a collective revolt in response to an inequitable allocation of group outcomes by the leader. In this context, a series of experiments conducted from the early 1970s to the early 1980s yielded several important findings.

First, inequity produced revolts, not by simply generating the emotional or attitudinal responses emphasized in equity theory such as dissatisfaction or anger, but by creating mutual expectations among the subordinates that they are likely to share dissatisfaction (Lawler, 1975a, 1975b). To put it another way, collective responses to inequity were mediated by expectations of mutual support. Presumably, such expectations were fostered by a "sense of common position" produced by a leader's inequitable action. The most exciting implication of these results was that expectations of support from other subordinates were actually more important than negative individual feelings or attitudes toward leaders (see especially Lawler 1975a).

The second finding was closely connected to the importance of expectations of mutual support. Specifically, we found that a leader could treat subordinates inequitably and forestall a revolt with a co-optation tactic, involving an offer to promote one of two subordinates to an intermediate position in the social structure or hierarchy (Lawler, 1983; Lawler, Youngs, & Lesh, 1978). Through a subtle process of tacit bargaining, revealed by interaction data, such an offer by the leader to one of two subordinates made the favored subordinate a bit more reluctant to form a coalition and the other disfavored subordinate more hesitant to push for a revolt in anticipation of opposition from the favored subordinate. Through such a tacit-bargaining process, inequitable reward allocations by the leader produced revolts about 20 percent of the time when such a tactic was used by the leader and roughly 80 percent of the time in the absence of a co-optation tactic (see Lawler, et al., 1978). Figure 1 summarizes the implications of the research.

Other findings of this research indicate that subordinates were more inclined toward a revolt in response to inequity if the leader was perceived as highly responsible for the inequitable allocation of group benefit (Lawler & Thompson, 1978), or if the coalition had the power to redistribute outcomes rather than simply to punish the leader (Lawler & Thompson, 1979). In addition, the co-optation tactic was effective only if it provided significant benefits to the recipient and if the promotion offer from the leader was stated in fairly definite rather than probabilistic or "maybe" terms; that is, the leader conveyed that the promotion was virtually assured if there was no coalition by subordinates (Lawler et al., 1978).

FIGURE 1 Implications of Research on Revolutionary Coalitions

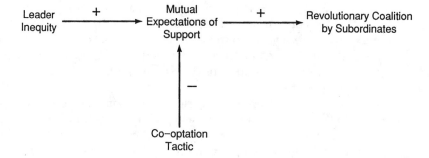

Overall, the research on revolutionary coalitions produced a coherent body of findings, but not a theory. The closest this work came to a theory was the identification of three necessary conditions for a revolt: a normative or moral justification for upsetting the status hierarchy or acting contrary to it, a perception that a revolt would successfully influence or depose the leader, and an expectation that it would be possible to mobilize joint action with the other subordinates (see Lawler et al., 1978). These normative, utilitarian, and organizational factors subsumed the specific conditions found to affect the occurrence of revolts in this series of experiments.

STAGE 2: EARLY RESEARCH ON POWER DEPENDENCE

The search for a better theory led to Emerson's (1962, 1972) power dependence notion and a related shift in the research focus. Emerson offered a concise, appealing concept of power and, more important at the time, a multidimensional conceptualization of tactics, one of which was a coalition. Emerson's theory put coalitional action in the context of other, individual-based tactics that could be available. Thus, the theory raised questions, such as when do subordinates choose a coalition from among a variety of tactics and, more generally, how do subordinates in a hierarchy choose among a range of tactics? The research agenda was expanded accordingly.

The basic principle of power dependence theory is that the power of party A is based on party B's dependence on A and vice versa. More specifically, B's dependence on A is a function of how highly B values the outcomes or benefits from the relationship with A and the availability of those outcomes in other relationships. The theory, therefore, suggests four dimensions of dependence in a dyad: the availability of alternative persons or partners to A, the value or importance that A attributes to the benefits received in the relationship with B, the availability of alternative persons or partners to B, and the value of the benefits to B. These four dimensions of dependence imply a broad set of tactics for influencing another or for improving one's power position (see Bacharach & Lawler, 1980, chap. 7; Blegen & Lawler, 1989). A revolutionary coalition, for instance, is conceptualized in this scheme as an effort to reduce the alternative sources of benefit for the other (see Emerson, 1962). Power dependence theory provides a few parsimonious ideas with broad applicability.

Bacharach and I initiated the power dependence research of the program in a series of papers on how a subordinate (employee) in conflict or disagreement with a superior (employer) evaluates and chooses among the four tactics specified by power dependence theory (Bacharach & Lawler, 1976, 1981b; Lawler & Bacharach, 1976, 1979). To address these issues, we used vignettes in which an employee of a small business store wanted a pay raise but knew the employer was against it. We investigated both the employee subjects' tendencies to use each tactic and also their expectations concerning the employer response to their attempts at influencing the decision about pay.

To make the transition from what is essentially a social structural theory to the choice of tactics, we adapted the "treatment of choice" metaphor used quite effectively by David Kipnis (1976). The resulting hypothesis was that actors would use the dimensions of dependence to identify points of strength or weakness in their own or the other's power position. Different tactics (of the four suggested) deal with or respond to different sources of strength or weakness. Actors ostensibly would attach probabilities of success to each tactic based on whether it uses a strength or mitigates a weakness (Bacharach & Lawler, 1980, 1981b; Lawler & Bacharach, 1976, 1979). For an obvious example, a threat to leave would be used more if the employee had many alternatives; similarly, a coalition would be most likely when the employer had many alternatives. In sum, this work took Kipnis's idea that an actor facing resistance from another will diagnose the reasons for the resistance and apply the "treatment" (i.e., tactic) with the highest probability of success. The prime differences are that in our approach, the *reasons* are structural, not motivational, and the *treatments* explicitly use this structure in some fashion. It is also important to note that our purpose here was to elaborate and test the implications of a particular theory, Emerson's power dependence theory, not to comprehensively identify and examine the sort of tactics used by an employee to influence an employer. In this sense, the work had and continues to have different purposes than that of Kipnis and Schmidt (1983).

The empirical results supported many of the hypotheses developed from power dependence theory. First, in a study of perceptions of power, Bacharach and Lawler (1976) found that each of the four dimensions of dependence did affect a subordinate's perceptions of self and other's power as predicted (Bacharach & Lawler, 1976). Second, in a study of how the subjective expected utility of attempting influence is affected by the power dependence relation, Lawler and Bacharach (1979) found that subordinates attached a higher subjective utility to influence when they had many alternatives and the employer had few. Third, we found that different dimensions of dependence affected different tactics— or, more precisely, each of the four tactics as a function of different dimensions of dependence. The mapping of the tactics on the dimensions of dependence, however, was not completely consistent with Emerson's (1962) version of power dependence theory.

The departure from power dependence theory took one basic form. When assessing the four tactical options suggested by the theory, actors attributed more importance to their own dependence on the opponent, rather than the opponent's dependence on them. In fact, all four tactics of a subordinate were a function primarily of the subordinate's own dependence on the superior. The broad implication was that people did not interpret the power relationship solely in relative terms. They treated their own and the other's power partly in absolute terms and somewhat independently. This led us to question prevailing zero-sum conceptions of power and triggered a shift toward a nonzero-sum conception (see Gamson, 1968 for a discussion). Reexamining Emerson's power dependence formulation, we found important justification for such a shift. In fact, it became evident that power dependence theory had an implicit nonzero-sum feature left undeveloped by Emerson and his colleagues (Cook & Emerson, 1978; Emerson, 1972, 1981). At this point, we set out to develop the nonzero-sum side of Emerson's writings. The basic metatheory of the program began to crystalize, and this led to the third stage of the program.

The transition to the third stage is in part a transition from a "problem-driven" to "theory-driven" research enterprise. The first two stages emphasized a particular substantive issue (i.e., the determinants of a revolutionary coalition or the choice among a range of tactics). By the third stage, we had become more interested in the abstract social processes connecting a wide variety of substantive phenomena and committed to elaborating and developing power dependence notions beyond their previous boundaries. It was at this point that we began explicitly to "zero in" on the relationship between power capability and power use.

The basic difference of emphasis between problem-driven and theory-driven programs is worthy of note. Problem-driven programs are oriented to producing a substantial accumulation of information or data on a particular topic (e.g., inventories of effects or causes). Review articles exemplify the culmination of such research programs. Theory-driven programs tend to produce more theoretical formulations and much less concrete information or data over time (i.e., a higher ratio of theory or ideas to data (see Berger & Zelditch, in press). One can certainly argue about the merits of each approach, yet there is clearly an imbalance in favor of problem-driven programs, not just in social psychology but across the social sciences.

STAGE 3: DEVELOPMENT OF A METATHEORETICAL FRAMEWORK

The metatheory took initial shape in Bacharach and Lawler's books of 1980 and 1981, one on political processes in organizations and the other on two-party bargaining. The metatheory has continued to evolve and, at this point, is captured by three basic assumptions about power.

The power-process assumption

The research program adopts very sharp distinctions between power as a capability, the use of that power, and actual or realized power (Lawler, 1992). Analyses of power—in the larger sociological, psychological, and political science literatures and in the more specific literature on conflict and bargaining—tend to reveal three emphases. First, some analyses treat power as a potential or capability to influence the opponent (Bierstedt, 1950; Chamberlain, 1955; Emerson, 1972). These tend to reflect a structural emphasis. Second, some analyses focus on how people use power or the tactics directed at influencing another (Blalock, 1989; Kipnis, 1976; Strauss, 1978; Tedeschi et al., 1973). These tend to reflect a behavioral or tactical emphasis. A tactic is defined as a move or set of moves directed at influencing another's cognition or behavior (Lawler, 1992). Third, some analyses essentially reduce power to the result of an influence process (Dahl, 1957; Dunlop, 1950; Gray & Tallman, 1987). These reflect an outcome or "who really has it" emphasis. The three conceptions of power, of course, are complementary, and all are important to an understanding of power relations (for supporting evidence, see Molm, 1990).

Our framework treats power capability, power use, and actual power as distinct moments in a power process (Lawler, 1992). In any power process, actors ostensibly have a structurally-based capability to affect each other's resources, an option to use or not use that capability, and an uncertain probability of success. Thus, it is clear that a power capability may or may not be used and, if used, it may or may not be effective. This sort of conceptualization is consistent in general with many others, especially the social exchange formulations of Cook (Cook & Emerson, 1978) and Molm (1987) and the organizational perspective of Pfeffer (1981).

A sharp distinction between these three parts of a power process raises a number of important research questions (Lawler, 1992): When do parties use a power capability available to them? If a power capability is used, what tactical form does the power use (i.e., tactics) take? When does the use of a power capability result in actual power? Are there conditions under which a power capability itself—without the mediation of action—produces actual or realized power? All of these questions are important. But some or all of them are neglected by conceptions of power that dismiss one or more of the moments in the assumed power process. Furthermore, with approaches—or measures—that equate power with effective or successful power, such theoretical questions are virtually defined away (e.g., Dahl, 1957; Dunlop, 1950). Our framework keeps all three questions very much alive.

The social structure assumption

The second assumption is a fairly subtle one about the foundation of the conflict likely to activate a power process. Specifically, we assume that most conflicts—whether between individuals, groups, organizations, or societies—have some social structural basis (Lawler, 1992). Power capabilities are grounded in structure. Our focus on power capability and power use is, therefore, tantamount to a focus on social structure and social action. The principal units of structure are sets of interrelated positions, abstractly representing the places that people or groups can come to occupy. Structure should have both a horizontal and vertical dimension in most contexts, and following the macrostructural theory of Blau (1977), these represent heterogeneity and inequality, respectively.

The structural positions, formal or informal, that convey a power capability have associated interests. Occupants represent these interests, and the interests are likely to be passed on to successive occupants. For example, conflicts of interest between sales and production managers over product lines tend to persist even when the occupants of these positions change. All of this may sound familiar and obvious, but in the social psychological literature on bargaining, there is a fairly subtle difference between structural and interpersonal interpretations or assumptions about the sources of conflict. An interpersonal approach is implied by Dean Pruitt's (1981) conceptualization of negotiation. He indicates that "negotiation is a process by which a joint decision is made by two or more parties [with opposing interests]," . . . (Pruitt, 1981, p. 1). To say that parties have opposing interests is to say that they have different individual needs leading to incompatible preferences. Pruitt (1981, p. 4) indicates further that "interests should never be regarded as inherently opposed." From such an interpersonal view, bargaining or negotiation becomes a form of primarily cooperative decision making, and the task of conflict resolution is primarily to reconcile individual needs and opinions (Lawler, 1992).

In contrast, the social structure assumption stresses the competitive side of the mixed-motive dilemma. It indicates that conflict will continually resurface even if position occupants change (Dahrendorf, 1959; Ury, Brett, & Goldberg, 1988), and it suggests that the resolution of conflict requires a change in the social structure of which the individuals or groups are a part. A structuralist premise sees conflict resolution as more problematic and temporary in ongoing relations such as those created by organizational structures (see Kanter, 1977). While structuralist and interpersonal premises are each useful for some purposes, it is important to recognize that our program comes down on the structural side, and this is one reason for its emphasis on distributive rather than integrative bargaining (Bacharach & Lawler, 1981a).

The structural assumption must be tempered, however, to accommodate parties' capacities to define and redefine relevant power capabilities. Bacharach and Lawler (1981a) emphasized the cognitive nature of power, distinguished various imageries of power, and suggested that actors' responses to power depend on their imagery. Parties interpret, translate, and otherwise make concrete the interests and power embedded in their social structural positions. They can bridge differences, find common ground, and otherwise reduce the conflict emanating from the social structure, or they can risk escalation of the conflict, attempt to intimidate their opponent, or engage in aggression. Structural positions create and frame the conflict, but it is the occupants of positions in the structure who decide specifically how to deal with it (Lawler, 1992).

The importance of position occupants is reflected in the fact that parties with smaller power capabilities can sometimes achieve greater influence than those with larger power capabilities; the use of some forms of power (especially coercion) over time can undermine the power of the user (Emerson's notion, "to use power is to lose it"); and tactics designed to gain advantage in the immediate situation may produce integrative rather than divisive effects on the relationship in the long run—for example, by increasing the mutual dependence of actors as we have shown elsewhere (Bacharach & Lawler, 1980; Lawler, 1992). This suggests the importance of the tactical dimension of behavior.

Power use is defined as a tactic chosen by an actor in the context of a structurally determined power capability. Tactics have an impression management facet and flow ostensibly from conscious or nonconscious deliberation in which power is estimated, options assessed, and consequences anticipated. While this implies a rational choice process, it is highly bounded and subjective. For most purposes in our program, a simple and common two-fold classification of tactics, as conciliatory and hostile, is sufficient (see Pruitt, 1981; Lawler & Ford, in press). Conciliatory tactics are positive acts, communicating a willingness to coordinate or collaborate; hostile tactics are negative acts, communicating an intention to compete or resist.

The nonzero-sum assumption

The most central assumption guiding recent theoretical work is a nonzero-sum conception of power (Lawler, 1986, 1992; Lawler & Bacharach, 1986; Lawler & Ford, in press). Zero-sum approaches to power take for granted a fixed sum of power in a relationship or set of relationships, such that a change in one party's power capability will produce an equal and opposite change in the other's. In contrast, a nonzero-sum conception indicates that the absolute or total amount of power in a relationship is not fixed, but variable. Given that the total or absolute amount of power in a relationship can vary, both parties in a relation could experience an increase in power; both could experience a decrease; or, of course, one might gain power while the other's remains constant (Lawler, 1992). Nearly all approaches to power adopt a zero-sum conception in practice if not always in principle (see Gamson, 1968, Tannenbaum, 1968, and Kanter, 1977 for exceptions).

Emerson's power dependence theory provides the basis for a nonzero-sum approach to power. Recall that from power dependence theory, the power capability of A is based on the dependence of B on A for valued resources, and vice versa (Emerson 1962, 1972). Thus, given the dimensions of dependence, the power of party A is a function of B's value and alternatives, while the power of B is a function of A's value and alternatives. *Each party's power is based on the other's dependence on them, not their own dependence on the other*. This is the ultimate source of the nonzero-sum premise found in power dependence theory. The implication is that the absolute power of each party in a dyad is not interrelated a priori in a specified way. The amount of power in the relationship can vary as can the distribution across the actors. This conceptualization is consistent with the notion of Tannenbaum and Kahn (1958) that the total control in an organization can vary independent of its distribution across hierarchical levels.

From a nonzero-sum conception, we have developed a contrast between the total power in a relationship and the relative power of the parties (or power differences) in that relationship. This contrast was initially proposed in the 1981 bargaining book. I have developed it further (Lawler, 1986) in theory and research on bilateral deterrence and conflict spiral (Lawler, 1986; Lawler, Ford, & Blegen, 1988). With the unit of analysis being a single relation or dyad, total power refers to the sum of each party's absolute power (i.e., Pab + Pba); relative power refers to the power difference or ratio of each party's absolute power (i.e., Pab/[Pab + Pba]). Increases or decreases in total power involve changes in the degree of mutual dependence, or what Emerson (1972) termed "relational cohesion." Shifts in relative power occur either through a redistribution of existing power, or when total power changes and these changes are distributed unequally within the relationship.

The importance of the distinction between total and relative power is implicit in Kanter's (1977) case study. She shows, for example, that increasing the power of middle managers does not necessarily decrease the power of lower level managers. If middle managers are "empowered" by becoming more involved in strategy planning and external subunit relations, then their subordinates might also be "empowered" through greater discretion and autonomy over the day-to-day activities of the subunit. The power of both middle and lower managers, thus, can move in the same direction. An expansion of the tasks or uncertainties faced by an organization or its subunits is a condition facilitating the growth of total power and essentially the empowerment of each party to the relationships (Kanter, 1977; Ch. 7). In a similar vein, Tannenbaum shows that enhanced participation in organizational decision making can increase actors' control over others but also their receptivity to control by them, thereby enhancing total control (see Tannenbaum, 1968).

The main point is that relative and total power can change in a variety of interesting and somewhat independent ways. If two organizations over time become the exclusive providers of valued commodities, then the total power in the relationship has grown without a change in the relative power, as long as the net growth of each party's absolute power is equal. If labor and management jockey for position between contract negotiation periods by successfully increasing the other's dependence, then the result of this power struggle will be a growth of mutual dependence in their relationship (Lawler, 1992). In an interpersonal context, if actors with a close relationship each develop their own set of friends, then total power—and, hence, relational cohesion—declines without necessarily changing their relative power. Yet if only one person develops a set of friends, a change in both total and relative power occurs, though in this case all of the change in total power would be an artifact of the change in relative power. The contrast of relative and total power disentangles two facets of a power relation that are typically confounded in research on power (see Lawler, 1986, for more discussion of this point).

To take a more abstract illustration, assume that each party's absolute power can vary from 1 to 20 units and that the total power in the relationship can vary from 2 to 40 units. A nonzero-sum conception leads us to ask whether a relationship in which each party has 5 units of power capability produces different rates of conflictual behavior than a relationship in which each party has 15 units of power capability. Furthermore, if a relationship with a distribution of 5 units for A and 20 for B changes to one with a distribution of 10 for A and 15 for B, then relative power has changed but total power has not. A more complex situation is one in which A has 5 units of power and B 15, but the change is to a situation in which A has 10 units and B 30—in this case, total power has increased from 25 to 40 and the power difference has increased from 10 units to 20. A non-zero-sum conception of power takes account of such patterns of change, while a zero-sum conception attends only to the power differences.

From metatheory to theory

The major research questions stem from the distinction of relative and total power: First, how does the total power in a relationship affect the use of conciliatory and hostile tactics in a conflict? Second, how do equal versus unequal power affect the use of conciliatory and hostile tactics in conflict? The general answers to these questions are expressed in two propositions, which represent the common themes around which much of the specific theory and research can be organized (Lawler, 1992):

* *Total-power proposition:* If parties have an equal power relationship and conflict occurs, a relationship with higher total power will produce more conciliation and less hostility than a relationship with lower total power.
* *Relative-power proposition:* If each party has a "significant" amount of absolute power and conflict occurs, a relationship with unequal power will produce more hostility and less conciliation than a relationship with equal power.

The argument of the 1981 bargaining book was that the effect of power depends on the degree that actors' imagery of power stresses absolute, relative, or total power. If actors adopt a nonzero conception of power, then they should respond to variations of the total power in their relationship; if they adopt a zero-sum imagery, then their tactical responses should be consistent with traditional models of power.

The total-power proposition captures an implication of Emerson's power dependence theory as well as selected theorizing on deterrence in international contexts (Blalock, 1989; Emerson, 1972; Lawler, 1992; Morgan, 1977). In Emerson's terms, total power constitutes the level of mutual dependence or "relational cohesion" in the relationship. Higher total power in a relationship essentially produces an increase in the opportunity costs associated with leaving the relation (Lawler, 1992; Lawler & Bacharach, 1987); parties have a larger stake in the bargaining and, more specifically, in bringing it to a reasonable conclusion. Thus, bargaining in relationships with higher, rather than lower, total power generally should be more cooperative and produce more mutually satisfactory agreements. While counterexamples to this general pattern can be identified, this is the basic idea implied by power dependence theory (Emerson, 1962, 1972).

The relative power proposition expresses the notion that relationships with unequal power tend to be less stable than ones with equal power (cf. Emerson, 1972; Rubin & Brown, 1975). A major reason, particularly important in explicit bargaining, is disagreement over the legitimacy of power differences or, specifically, how such differences should affect a negotiated solution. With an unequal power relationship, the disadvantaged party may resist solutions that reflect their power differences, while the advantaged party may advocate those solutions that provide them with payoffs proportional to their power advantage (Bacharach & Lawler, 1981a, chap. 6; Lawler, 1992; Lawler & Ford, in press). If power capabilities are unequal and parties face a conflict, then the legitimacy of the power difference is likely to be contested, because an equal split is generally a highly prominent solution (see Pruitt, 1981, and Schelling, 1960, for more discussion of "prominence"). Thus, unequal power tends to complicate the issues faced by parties to explicit bargaining, thereby reducing the prospects of conflict resolution.

Focusing primarily on absolute and total power, we posed two primary hypotheses about bargaining. First, concession behavior of an actor would be a function of that party's own dependence, not the other's; and second, the greater the total power (i.e., mutual dependence) in the relationship the greater the likelihood of conflict resolution. The Bacharach and Lawler (1981b) experiments provided parties information on each other's alternatives, and results generally supported these predictions. Concession behavior was primarily (though not exclusively) a function of whether the actor could expect a good agreement from an alternative bargaining partner; and greater total power in the relationship produced higher average rates of concession across actors. Moreover, in several experiments, agreements were more likely when both actors had alternative bargaining partners who were likely to offer poor rather than good alternative outcomes. These results can be interpreted as "relational cohesion effects" in Emerson's (1972) terms, and they probably reflect the opportunity costs of leaving the current relationship to negotiate with another from whom a poor agreement is likely (see also Lawler, 1992). Overall, Bacharach and Lawler's (1981a) research supported a nonzero-sum conception of power, because parties in conflict did respond to the total power dimension.

STAGE 4: BILATERAL DETERRENCE AND CONFLICT SPIRAL

The fourth stage of the program not only fleshed out the different effects of total and relative power, but also dealt with a problem that we stumbled into while doing the book on bargaining. Emerson (1972) began with the fairly standard notion that power is the ability of an actor to levy costs on another, yet power dependence theory actually encompassed only one form of cost—*opportunity costs* (i.e., the value foregone when a choice is made). Retaliation or punishment costs were not easily incorporated, and this assumption made it difficult to directly connect power dependence theory to the use of hostile tactics, such as threats and punishments (see Bacharach & Lawler, 1981a; Lawler & Ford, in press; Molm, 1987).

Following the 1981 book, I offered a simple theory of bilateral deterrence and conflict spiral (Lawler, 1986). The focus was still limited to the impact of power capabilities on power use. In this sense, it was designed to understand the deterrent and spiral-like effects of power capabilities, per se. We assumed a situation where both parties in a dyad have a capability to damage each other punitively (e.g., see also Hornstein, 1965; Michener & Cohen, 1973). There were four steps in the development of this theoretical stage (see Lawler & Ford, in press, for a similar analysis).

The *first step* involved the explication of two classic arguments, about the link between the magnitude of a punitive capability and the use of that capability through threats or punishments, one by Deutsch (1973) and the other by Tedeschi and associates (Tedeschi et al., 1973). The trucking-game tradition of Deutsch and Krauss (1962) and related work suggests that, when available, a power capability tends to be used and, by implication, the larger the capability the greater the frequency of use. Use ostensibly leads to counteruse, giving rise to a conflict spiral from which everyone loses (Youngs, 1986). The central argument is that, all other things being equal, where parties have larger punitive capabilities, a conflict between them should produce greater hostility.

The alternative argument is based on other social psychological research that implicitly or explicitly incorporates principles of deterrence. For example, Tedeschi's analysis of threats (Tedeschi et al., 1973) indicates that a large power capability for A decreases B's use of hostile tactics (see also Hornstein, 1965; Michener & Cohen, 1973). These different lines of research represent a complicated disjuncture between underlying perspectives, which had been overlooked in reviews of this literature (e.g., Pruitt, 1981). My purpose was to reconstruct these classic arguments in a way that revealed their incongruencies. Figure 2 contains this reconstruction. An equal-power relationship is assumed at this point.

The classic deterrence argument is that each actor's use of punitive tactics will be an inverse function of the other's (absolute) power capability (Lawler, 1986). The other's capability produces a "fear of retaliation" that is crucial to effective deterrence. The conflict spiral argument, in contrast, indicates that larger power capabilities create more temptation to use power. Overall, the classic arguments specify different mediating processes—fear of retaliation versus temptation—and indicate that an actor's use of punitive tactics is a function of different absolute power dimensions within the relationship.

This characterization of the two arguments, however, also points to a theoretical problem. Each implicit theory traces power use to either an actor's own or the other's power capability, but not both (Lawler, 1986). The conflict spiral argument suggests that parties use power simply because they have some, while the deterrence argument suggests that parties do not use power because of the opponents' power. Neither theoretical position traces the punitive tactics of parties to *both* their own power capability and that of others. This did not make sense, intuitively, and it was important to have a theoretical formulation that tied the punitive tactics of a party to both their own and the opponent's power capability, without reverting to a zero-sum conception of power.

The *second step* proposed a solution to this problem, which built the "expec-

FIGURE 2   Classical Views

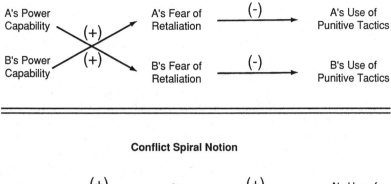

tation of attack" into each theory. The idea for this came from Schelling (1960), who had proposed that successful deterrence was contingent on two factors: a high fear of retaliation on the part of both actors and a perception that this fear will reduce the other's inclination to attack. Notice that this implicitly involves an inference from both one's own and the other's absolute power capability. Furthermore, a variety of social psychological work had documented that parties who formed expectations of attack in a conflict act more competitively even in advance of anticipated attacks (see for example, Pruitt, 1981; Rubin & Brown, 1975; Tedeschi et al., 1969). This fits our early hypotheses about cognitive imagery. Treating expectation of attack as a mediating cognition also had the advantage of incorporating an important facet of each actor's perception of the other's perception.

In the revised formulation (see Figure 3), each actor's use of punitive tactics is now a function of both their own and the other's power capabilities, and the intervening cognitive processes expand (Lawler, 1986; Lawler & Ford, in press). Bilateral deterrence theory predicts that higher punitive power for both actors results in each having a higher fear of retaliation (due to the other's high power) and lower expectations of attack (due to their own high power). These conditions, in turn, produce lower frequencies of punitive action on the part of both parties. In contrast, conflict spiral theory predicts that higher total power will increase the temptation of each actor to use his or her power (due to each actor's own power) while also increasing the expectation of attack (due to the other's power). These conditions enhance the frequency of punitive action in the dyad.

Overall, the competition of the theories is somewhat "friendlier" because

FIGURE 3   Reformulation of Classical Views

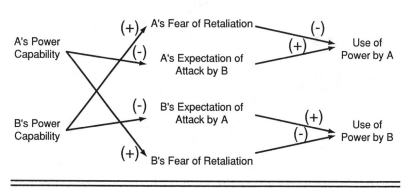

Bilateral Deterrence Theory

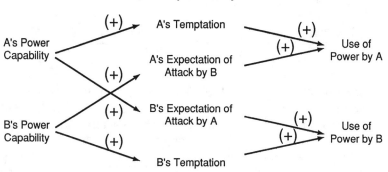

Conflict Spiral Theory

of the addition of an identical intervening cognition (i.e., expectations of attack), but the differences between them also are sharpened because expectations of attack are based on a party's own power in bilateral deterrence theory and the other's power in conflict spiral theory (Lawler & Ford, in press). As this formulation developed, I also made the simplifying assumption that actors would expect each other to use the underlying power dimensions in the same way. In other words, if A's fear of retaliation is based on B's power, then A will expect B's fear of retaliation to be based on A's power. A's expectation of attack, therefore, is tantamount to A's perception of B's fear of retaliation.

Having developed bilateral deterrence and conflict spiral predictions for total power in the relationship, the *third step* was to consider equal versus unequal power. To this point, the focus had been on each actor's absolute power and on the total power in the relationship. If the predictions of each theory for equal power relationships (see Figure 3) are simply transposed to an unequal power relationship, the conclusion is that both theories predict no difference in the rate of punitive tactics (at the level of the dyad) between equal and unequal power relationships. In the case of unequal power, the rate of power use by the lower power party would diminish while the higher power party's power use would increase proportionately.

For example, assume both A and B begin with a capability to reduce each other's outcomes by 50 percent, but then A's power increases to 60 and B's decreases to 40. Bilateral deterrence theory suggests that A's fear of retaliation and expectation of attack would decrease, and B's fear of retaliation and expectation of attack would increase. Assuming that changes in the fear of retaliation and expectation of attack are proportional, any increase in A's use of punitive tactics would be offset by a corresponding decrease in B's use of punitive tactics. A similar conclusion is reached from conflict spiral theory. Thus, without additional assumptions, both theories predict no difference between equal and unequal power at the dyad level as long as the total power in the relationship remains constant. This implication is inconsistent with Emerson's (1962, 1972) analysis of power-balancing tactics and Bacharach and Lawler's (1981a) analysis of instability within unequal power relationships.

By thinking more about how actors might interpret absolute power levels in the context of unequal power, this issue was resolved. From bilateral deterrence theory, the prediction was that unequal power relationships would generate more use of punitive tactics, while from conflict spiral theory the prediction was the opposite. The theoretical reasoning underlying these predictions focused on the relative weight parties would give the mediating cognitions in Figure 3. I assumed that when actors are in an equal power relationship, they give equal subjective weight to the fear of retaliation and expectation of attack in the case of bilateral deterrence, and equal subjective weight to temptation and expectation of attack in the case of conflict spiral (Lawler, 1986). But in an unequal power relationship, bilateral deterrence assumes that the higher power party gives greater weight to the fear of retaliation (now lower, given the other's lower power) and that the lower power party gives greater weight to the expectation of attack (now higher, given the other's higher power). The result is that both parties in an unequal power relationship will be inclined toward more use of punitive tactics, but for different reasons. These are the conditions especially likely to produce high levels of hostility in a conflict. Extrapolating from the bilateral deterrence formulation, unequal power relationships are particularly prone to conflict escalation as long as the lower power party has significant absolute power.

The conflict spiral formulation makes the opposite prediction, less punitive action under unequal power than equal power. The lower power party ostensibly submits due to lower temptation; while the higher power party forms corresponding low expectations of attack and anticipates that the difference in power capability will produce the desired outcomes without having to actually use the capability. You might say that, from conflict spiral theory, deterrence in its *unilateral* form of one actor deterring another occurs under conditions of unequal power. Thus, one finds a bit of conflict spiral logic within deterrence theory and a bit of deterrence logic within conflict spiral theory.

The *fourth step* was empirical research. We pitted bilateral deterrence and conflict spiral theories against one another (Lawler, et al., 1988) using a fairly standard two-party laboratory setting in which participants (1) exchange offers across a series of bargaining rounds (e.g., Chertkoff & Esser, 1976; Komorita & Barnes, 1969; Siegel & Fouraker, 1960), (2) represent the interests of a group in conflict with another group, and (3) could levy punitive damage against each other on each round (e.g., Michener & Cohen, 1973). Instructions encouraged an individualistic orientation (i.e., maximization of the payoffs for their own group without regard to the payoffs of the opposing group). Punitive capability was manipulated by varying the maximum amount (i.e., capability) of an opponent's resources that the subject could destroy, that is, 10 percent versus 90 percent (e.g., Lawler et al., 1988). Punitive behavior was measured by the frequency of inflicting damage (with the magnitude fixed) summed across both actors, while conciliatory behavior was measured by the total magnitude of concession making in the dyad and the likelihood of agreement.

The empirical evidence supported the predictions of bilateral deterrence theory over those of conflict spiral theory. In two studies, the total punitive capability had a negative impact on the use of punitive tactics; one study indicated that this effect occurred mainly in the later phases of the bargaining after subjects experienced the negative consequences of power use (Lawler & Bacharach, 1987; Lawler et al., 1988). Furthermore, punitive tactics were used more frequently in unequal power relationships than in equal power relationships, and there were no differences between high- and low-power actors' use of punitive tactics. Similar (though weaker) support for bilateral deterrence occurred for conciliatory tactics. Parties in relationships with high total power made larger concessions overall than those in relationships with low total power, and they made larger concessions when in relationships with equal, compared to unequal, power. Significant effects were not observed for the likelihood of agreement across the two experiments (Lawler et al., 1988).[1]

In summary, the theory of bilateral deterrence extends the idea of total power from dependence-based to coercive-based power (see Lawler, 1992; Lawler & Bacharach, 1987). Beyond our experimental evidence, some corroboration for the extension to coercive power can be found in the deterrence literature on international relations, in particular, research dealing with war in bilateral and multilateral power systems (e.g., Houweling & Siccama, 1988; Thompson, 1986). From such literature, if two or more parties develop and maintain high levels of coercive power (i.e., capability to damage each other), then each will either not use that capability or will use it less frequently, because they fear the costs of retaliation. This is termed a "general deterrence" process by Morgan (1977). Theories of dependence and coercive power emphasize different types of cost but incorporate the same total and relative power proposition.

---

[1]While research evidence currently supports bilateral deterrence theory over conflict spiral, it would be premature to reject the conflict spiral formulation. The conflict spiral predictions are likely to obtain under some conditions (for example, if there is a "first strike" incentive for power use). Further theoretical and empirical work is needed on the conditions under which conflict spiral effects occur (see Lawler & Ford, in press).

The distinct lines of research on power dependence and coercive power in the program each support the usefulness of a nonzero-sum conception of power. In the case of both dependence and punitive forms of power, total power has cohesive or integrative effects on the relationship, and these effects are distinguishable from the effects of relative power or power differences. Both power dependence and bilateral deterrence formulations indicate that the primary reason higher total power produces less use of that power is the cost associated with power use: opportunity costs for power dependence and retaliation costs for bilateral deterrence. In both lines of specific research, furthermore, unequal power engenders more hostility and less conciliation in the context of a conflict. Bilateral deterrence clarifies the role of unequal power by suggesting why lower power parties with substantial power capability may resist efforts at intimidation and use power as much as the higher power actor. An effort is needed to understand further the conditions under which unequal power relationships produce such resistance rather than compliance by the lower power party.

STAGE 5: THEORETICAL EXTENSIONS

Currently, I am addressing several new issues that follow from the nonzero-sum approach to power. The first concerns the effectiveness of unilateral initiatives in two-party bargaining. The primary question is whether total and relative power in a relationship affects the success of the conciliatory tactic (unilateral initiatives) proposed by Osgood (1962) and empirically examined by Lindskold (1978), Patchen (1987), and Boyle and Lawler (1991). This project integrates ideas from Osgood's (1962) notion of GRIT with Lawler's (1986) bilateral-deterrence formulation (see Lawler & Ford, 1991). The second issue concerns the emergence of a commitment in dyads within a larger exchange network building from the work of Cook and Emerson (1978, 1984). We have modified Emerson's concept of "relational cohesion" to incorporate both the total and relative dimensions of power, and we explain commitment in social exchange from this reformulation (Lawler & Yoon, 1990). Each of these theoretical extensions is summarized next.

Power and unilateral initiatives

This project (Lawler & Ford, in press) addresses the following specific question: Given a pattern of conflict between two groups or organizations, how does power in the relationship affect the ability of a party to generate mutual conciliation in explicit bargaining through unilateral initiatives? To answer this question, we focus on how the power relationship should affect the impressions "given off" by unilateral initiatives once parties have reached the bargaining table.

According to Osgood's (1962) original formulation, unilateral initiatives are a method of enhancing trust and, thereby, reversing the direction of a conflict escalator from upward to downward. The danger of unilateral initiatives, however, is that they will be interpreted as a sign of weakness and, thus, result in less rather than more conciliation by the opponent (e.g., see Benton, Kelley, & Liebling, 1972; Boyle & Lawler, 1991; Komorita & Brenner, 1968; Seigel & Fouraker, 1960). The implication is as follows: If unilateral initiatives enhance trust more than they give off impressions of weakness, then such tactics should increase the opponent's conciliation; but if unilateral initiatives convey weakness more than they enhance trust, then such tactics should backfire and reduce conciliation by the opponent. This simple idea is the starting point for analyzing the impact of the power relationship.

By extending bilateral deterrence predictions to concession behavior, we propose how total and relative power capabilities should affect each actor's response to unilateral initiatives. To accomplish this, it is first necessary to consider how total and relative power affects perceptions of trust and impressions of weakness. Two implicit assumptions are extrapolated from bilateral deterrence theory (Lawler, 1986; Lawler & Ford, 1991); (1) Given equal power between two parties in explicit bargaining, higher total power in the relationship reduces the degree that unilateral initiatives create impressions of weakness; and (2) relationships with unequal, compared to equal, power reduce the degree that unilateral initiatives create trust.

Elaborating the first assumption, if each party has considerable coercive capability and these are known to each, then it is difficult for either party to sustain an inference of weakness (or softness) when the opponent engages in unilateral concession making. Bilateral deterrence implies that the higher the total power in the relation, the quicker and more receptive a party becomes in accepting an opponent's unilateral initiatives. This is because higher total power produces greater fear of retaliation and lower expectations of unprovoked attack. Thus, in relationships where each party has high, rather than low, levels of power capability, unilateral initiatives should not create impressions of weakness or softness (Lawler & Ford, 1991). This reasoning leads to the following proposition:

* *Proposition 1:* Given equal power in explicit bargaining, if parties have higher rather than lower levels of power capability, then the effectiveness of unilateral initiatives increases.

Turning to relative power, unequal power complicates the interpretive task of parties facing another who uses unilateral initiatives (Lawler & Ford, 1991). From bilateral deterrence theory *(ceteris paribus)*, conflict within an unequal power relationship should generate more distrust than conflict in an equal power relationship, posing serious problems for unilateral initiatives by either party. These problems would be compounded if, as suggested by bilateral deterrence notions, the higher power actor argues for solutions that reflect their higher power, while the lower power actor argues for more equal solutions (Lawler, 1992). The upshot is that parties with an unequal power relation should have a more difficult time creating minimal levels of trust in explicit bargaining, especially after an initial period of mutual resistance and hostility. Thus, the basic proposition is as follows:

* *Proposition 2:* Given fixed total power in the relationship, if parties in explicit bargaining have unequal rather than equal power capability, then the effectiveness of unilateral initiatives decreases.

Research on these propositions is underway, and it should provide more indication of whether the contrast between total and relative power is useful to understand tactical behavior in bargaining.

Commitment in exchange networks

A "transaction" in social exchange theory is a negotiated solution to a mixed motive problem (Cook & Emerson, 1978). One often cited difference between social and economic exchange is that exchanges in social contexts are not independent (Emerson, 1972, 1981). Repetitive exchanges between the same parties tend to emerge, and these have social effects that cannot be accounted for by economic-exchange models. Various theoretical and empirical efforts have attempted to understand the sources and consequences of repetitive exchange, frequently conceptualized as "commitment processes" (Cook & Emerson, 1978, 1984; Tallman, Gray, & Leik, 1991; Williamson, 1975). We are developing a line of research that utilizes the nonzero-sum concept of power to elaborate how the power relationship affects the likelihood of commitment formation (Lawler & Yoon, 1990). Commitment formation in dyadic relations is important in part because it can produce power balance (i.e., equality) throughout the network (Cook & Emerson, 1984) but also fragment a social network, breaking it down into a series of disconnected dyads (see Markovsky, Willer, & Patton, 1988; Willer, Markovsky, & Patton, 1989).

Commitment is defined broadly as an obligation to maintain a relation over time (Tallman, et al., 1991), with continuous repetitive exchange between the same actors being the behavioral indicator of that obligation (Cook & Emerson, 1978, 1984). Our approach is to treat commitment as a property of a relationship and focus on mutual or bilateral forms of commitment; in addition, our approach is behavioral rather than attitudinal, and the negotiated transaction is the joint behavior of primary concern. The longer sequences of repeated exchange signify stronger commitments, especially if negotiated exchanges continue despite better alternatives.

To understand the structural sources of commitment, we propose to use the contrast of relative and total power to modify Emerson's idea of "relational cohesion" (see Lawler & Yoon, 1990). The problem is to combine or integrate the effects of relative power with those for total power, such that relational cohesion is a result of both higher total power and more equal relative power. One way to characterize the combined effect is as a function of the geometric mean of two actors' absolute power, as follows:

$$\text{Relational Cohesion (C)} = \sqrt{P_{ab} \times P_{ba}} \text{ or } \sqrt{D_{ba} \times D_{ab}},$$

where

P_{ab} is the power of A over B
P_{ba} is the power of B over A
D_{ba} is the dependence of B on A
D_{ab} is the dependence of A on B

A geometric-mean specification of relational cohesion is similar to Molm's (1987) concept of average power since it uses the notion of a mean to capture the mutual dependence of actors in a dyad. However, our specification also takes into account the effect of relative power. This is important because while arithmetic average power, adopted by Molm (1987), varies only as a function of the sum of the two values of power (i.e., total power), the geometric-mean specification varies as a function of both total power and relative power. More specifically, the relationship of relational cohesion to total power and relative power in the geometric-mean specification can be treated in terms of first partial derivatives as follows (see Lawler & Yoon, 1990):

$C = f(TP, RP)$
$\partial C / \partial RP < 0$
$\partial C / \partial TP > 0$

where

C is relational cohesion
RP is relative power ($| P_{ab} - P_{ba} |$)
TP is total power ($P_{ab} + P_{ba}$)

As the preceding inequalities in first partial derivatives indicate, relational cohesion in our specification is an increasing function of total power if the power difference (relative power) effect is constant, while it is an inverse function of power difference if the total power effect is constant. Verbally, assuming that relational cohesion underlies commitment formation, the geometric-mean specification leads to the following proposition:

* *Proposition 1:* If total power in a relationship increases and the power difference decreases, then greater commitment will develop.

Some evidence in support of this idea can be found in Lawler and Bacharach (1987). In that study, two actors bargained over a single, distributive issue in a fairly standard two-party bargaining context, except that each could also negotiate with an alternative person. Relative and total dependence was manipulated by varying the probability of a good agreement from the alternative. Coercive capability (i.e., potential to punish) also was manipulated. The results indicated that the likelihood of conflict resolution (agreement) was significantly higher when parties had both high total and equal power in their relationship. The implication is that in an exchange network, commitments are most likely in relations with higher total power and lower power difference. Research in progress is developing and testing such implications of relational cohesion.

CONCLUSION

The nonzero-sum approach to power contains the same fundamental message as Tannenbaum's (1968, 1974) concept of control. Both the distribution and the total amount of power can vary in a relationship, group, or organization. The total amount of power or control is essentially the integrative dimension of social power, or the degree that parties are dependent on one another to achieve valued goals (Bacharach & Lawler, 1980). Relative power is the distributive dimension of social power, reflecting differential dependencies among parties who are often embedded in organizational hierarchies. These two dimensions capture the variable-sum and fixed-sum aspects of social power, respectively, and by incorporating them into a single framework, we direct attention to both the divisive and cohesive effects of power in relationships.

The five stages of the program reflect the development of the nonzero-sum conception of power from an implicit to an explicit theme. In work on revolutionary coalitions, the co-optation tactic can be construed as enhancing the influence of both the leader (who reduces the inclination of the target to form a revolutionary coalition) and the target subordinate (who influences the other subordinate). Applying Tannenbaum's (1968, pp. 12–20) theory, an increase in total control underlies the effectiveness of the co-optation tactic. Turning to the early empirical work on power dependence, parties evaluated tactic options based on their own dependence (i.e., the other's power) more than the other's dependence (i.e., their own power); they treated power dependence in absolute rather than relative terms (see Bacharach & Lawler, 1981b). Thus, parties to a conflict seemed to adopt a nonzero imagery of power somewhat inconsistent with prevailing zero-sum conceptions offered by scholars.

The nonzero-sum approach to power was developed explicitly in the 1981 bargaining book (Bacharach & Lawler, 1981a) and in the theories of bilateral deterrence and conflict spiral (Lawler, 1986). Assuming a conflict, two primary predictions reflect the core ideas: First, the greater the total power in a relationship (i.e., mutual dependence of parties or bilateral coercive capability), the greater the use of conciliatory tactics and the lower the use of punitive tactics in the relationship. These propositions have received empirical support from relatively distinct empirical work on dependence and punitive forms of power (see Bacharach & Lawler, 1981a; Lawler & Bacharach, 1987; Lawler, et al., 1988).

The nonzero-sum approach is being developed further in current work. One line of research applies our nonzero-sum approach to the question of what power conditions will make unilateral initiatives (Osgood, 1962) more or less effective in explicit bargaining (Lawler & Ford, 1991). A second line of research elaborates the integrative side of social power by reconceptualizing Emerson's

(1972) concept of "relational cohesion" as a joint function of high total and highly equal power (Lawler & Yoon, 1990). Parties to social exchange should develop stronger commitments over time if structural conditions involve high versus low relational cohesion. Both emerging lines of work emphasize the integrative effects that a power relationship can have in conflict and bargaining.

REFERENCES

BACHARACH, S. B., & LAWLER, E. J. (1976). The perception of power. *Social Forces, 55,* 123–134.

BACHARACH, S. B., & LAWLER, E. J. (1980). *Power and politics in organizations.* San Francisco: Jossey-Bass.

BACHARACH, S. B., & LAWLER, E. J. (1981a). *Bargaining: Power, tactics, and outcomes.* San Francisco: Jossey-Bass.

BACHARACH, S. B., & LAWLER, E. J. (1981b). Power and tactics in bargaining. *Industrial and Labor Relations Review, 34,* 219–233.

BENTON, A. A., KELLEY, H. H., & LIEBLING, B. (1972). Effects of extremity of offers and concession rate on the outcomes of bargaining. *Journal of Personality and Social Psychology, 24,* 73–83.

BERGER, J., WAGNER, D. G., & ZELDITCH, M., JR. (1987). Theory growth, social processes, and metatheory. In J. Turner (Ed.), *Theory building in sociology* (pp. 19–42). Beverly Hills, CA: Sage Publications Inc.

BERGER, J., & ZELDITCH, M., JR. (In press). *Theoretical research programs: Studies in theory growth.* Stanford University Press.

BIERSTEDT, R. (1950). An analysis of social power. *American Sociological Review, 15,* 730–738.

BLALOCK, H. M., JR. (1989). *Conflict and power.* Beverly Hills, CA: Sage Publications.

BLAU, P. M. (1970). *Inequality and heterogeneity: A primitive theory of social structure.* New York: Free Press.

BLAU, P. (1977). A macrosociological theory of social structure. *American Journal of Sociology, 83,* 26–54.

BLEGEN, M. A., & LAWLER, E. J. (1989). Power and bargaining in authority-client relations. In R. Braungart & M. Braungart (Eds.), *Research in political sociology* (Vol. 4, pp. 167–186). Greenwich, CT: JAI Press.

BOYLE, E. H., & LAWLER, E. J. (1991). Resolving conflict through explicit bargaining. *Social Forces, 69,* 1183–1204.

CAPLOW, T. (1956). A theory of coalitions in the triad. *American Sociological Review, 21,* 489–493.

CAPLOW, T. (1968). *Two against one.* Englewood Cliffs, NJ: Prentice Hall.

CHAMBERLAIN, N. W. (1955). *A general theory of economic process.* New York: Harper & Row.

CHERTKOFF, J. M., & ESSER, J. K. (1976). A review of experiments in explicit bargaining. *Journal of Experimental Social Psychology, 12,* 464–486.

COOK, K. S. (Ed.). (1987). *Social exchange theory.* Beverly Hills, CA: Sage Publications.

COOK, K. S., & EMERSON, R. (1978). Power, equity, and commitment in exchange networks. *American Sociological Review, 43,* 721–739.

COOK, K. S., & EMERSON, R. (1984). Exchange networks and the analysis of complex organizations. In S. B. Bacharach & E. J. Lawler (Eds.), *Sociology of organizations, volume 3: The social psychological processes* (pp. 1–30). Greenwich, CT: JAI Press.

COOK, K. S., EMERSON, R., GILMORE, M. R., & YAMAGISHI, TOSHIO. (1983). The distribution of power in exchange networks: Theory and experimental results. *American Journal of Sociology, 89,* 275–305.

COOK, K. S., & GILMORE, M. (1984). Power, dependence, and coalitions. In Edward J. Lawler (Ed.), *Advances in group processes* (Vol. 1, pp. 27–58). Greenwich, CT: JAI Press.

DAHL, R. A. (1957). The concept of power. *Behavioral Science, 2,* 201–218.

DAHRENDORF, R. (1959). *Class and class conflict in industrial society.* Stanford, CA: Stanford University Press.

DEUTSCH, M. (1973). *The resolution of conflict.* New Haven, CT: Yale University Press.

DEUTSCH, M., & KRAUSS, R. M. (1962). Studies of interpersonal bargaining. *Journal of Conflict Resolution, 6,* 52–76.

DUNLOP, J. T. (1950). *Wage determination under trade unions.* New York: A. M. Kelly.

EMERSON, R. (1962). Power dependence relations. *American Sociological Review, 27,* 31–40.

EMERSON, R. (1972). Exchange theory, part II: Exchange relations, exchange networks, and groups as exchange systems. In J. Berger, M. Zelditch, & B. Anderson (Eds.), *Sociological theories in progress* (Vol. 2, pp. 58–87). Boston: Houghton Mifflin.

EMERSON, R. M. (1981). Social exchange theory. In M. Rosenberg & R. H. Turner (Eds.), *Social psychology: Sociological perspectives* (pp. 30–65). New York: Basic Books.

GAMSON, W. A. (1961). A theory of coalition formation. *American Sociological Review, 26,* 373–382.

GAMSON, W. A. (1968). *Power and discontent.* Homewood, IL: Dorsey Press.

GRAY, L., & TALLMAN, I. (1987). Theories of choice: contingent reward and punishment applications. *Social Psychology Quarterly, 50,* 16–23.

HORNSTEIN, H. A. (1965). The effects of different magnitudes of threat upon interpersonal bargaining. *Journal of Experimental Social Psychology, 1,* 282–293.

HOUWELING, H., & SICCAMA, J. G. (1988). Power transitions as a cause of war. *Journal of Conflict Resolution, 32,* 87–102.

KANTER, R. M. (1977). *Men and women of the corporation.* New York: Basic Books.

KIPNIS, D. (1976). *The powerholders.* Chicago: University of Chicago Press.

KIPNIS, D., & SCHMIDT, S. (1983). An influence perspective on bargaining within organizations. In M. Bazerman & R. J. Lewicki (Eds.), *Negotiating in organizations* (pp. 303–319). Beverly Hills: Sage.

KOMORITA, S. S., & BARNES, M. (1969). Effects of pressures to reach agreement in bargaining. *Journal of Personality and Social Psychology, 13,* 245–252.

KOMORITA, S. S., & BRENNER, A. R. (1968). Bargaining and concession making under bilateral monopoly. *Journal of Personality and Social Psychology, 9,* 15–20.

LAWLER, E. J. (1975a). An experimental study of factors affecting the mobilization of revolutionary coalitions. *Sociometry, 38,* 163–179.

LAWLER, E. J. (1975b). Impact of status differences on coalition agreements: An experimental study. *Journal of Conflict Resolution, 19,* 271–277.

LAWLER, E. J. (1983). Cooptation and threats as "divide and rule" tactics. *Social Psychology Quarterly, 46*(2), 89–98.

LAWLER, E. J. (1986). Bilateral deterrence and conflict spiral: A theoretical analysis. In E. J. Lawler (Ed.), *Advances in group processes* (Vol. 3, pp. 107–130). Greenwich, CT: JAI Press.

LAWLER, E. J. (1992). Power processes in bargaining. *Sociological Quarterly, 33,* 17–34.

LAWLER, E. J., & BACHARACH, S. B. (1976). Outcome alternatives and value as criteria for multistrategy evaluations. *Journal of Personality and Social Psychology, 34,* 885–894.

LAWLER, E. J., & BACHARACH, S. B. (1979). Power dependence in individual bargaining: The expected utility of influence. *Industrial and Labor Relations Review, 32,* 196–204.

LAWLER, E. J., & BACHARACH, S. B. (1986). Power-dependence in collective bargaining. In D. B. Lipsky & D. Lewin (Eds.), *Advances in industrial and labor relations* (Vol. 3, pp. 191–212). Greenwich, CT: JAI Press.

LAWLER, E. J., & BACHARACH, S. B. (1987). Comparison of dependence and punitive forms of power. *Social Forces, 66,* 446–462.

LAWLER, E. J., & FORD, R. (1991). *Power and unilateral initiatives.* Grant proposal, National Science Foundation.

LAWLER, E. J., & FORD, R. (in press). Metatheory and friendly competition in theory growth: The case of power processes in bargaining. In J. Berger & M. Zelditch, Jr. (Eds.), *Theoretical research programs: Studies in theory growth.* Stanford, CA: Stanford University Press.

LAWLER, E. J., FORD, R., & BLEGEN, M. A. (1988). Coercive capability in conflict: A test of bilateral deterrence vs. conflict spiral theory. *Social Psychology Quarterly, 51*(2), 93–107.

LAWLER, E. J., & THOMPSON, M. E. (1978). Impact of a leader's responsibility for inequality on subordinate revolts. *Social Psychology Quarterly, 41,* 264–268.

LAWLER, E. J., & THOMPSON, M. E. (1979). Subordinate response to a leader's cooptation strategy as a function of the type of coalition power. *Representative Research in Social Psychology, 9,* 68–80.

LAWLER, E. J., & YOON, J. (1990, October). *Power and ritual behavior in social exchange.* Paper presented at the Iowa Workshop on Theoretical Analysis.

LAWLER, E. J., YOUNGS, G. A., JR., & LESH, M. D. (1978). Cooptation and coalition mobilization. *Journal of Applied Social Psychology, 8,* 199–214.

LINDSKOLD, S. (1978). Trust development, the Grit proposal, and the effects of conciliatory acts on conflict and cooperation. *Psychological Bulletin, 85,* 772–793.

MARKOVSKY, B., WILLER, D., & PATTON, T. (1988). Power relations in exchange networks. *American Sociological Review, 53,* 220–236.

MICHENER, H. A., & COHEN, E. D. (1973). Effects of punishment magnitude in the bilateral threat situation: evidence for the deterrence hypothesis. *Journal of Personality and Social Psychology, 26,* 427–438.

MICHENER, H. A., & LAWLER, E. J. (1971). Revolutionary coalition strength and collective failure as determinants of status reallocation. *Journal of Experimental Social Psychology, 7,* 448–460.

MICHENER, H. A., & LYONS, M. (1972). Perceived support and upward-mobility as determinants of revolutionary coalition behavior. *Journal of Experimental Social Psychology, 8,* 180–195.

MOLM, L. (1987). Power dependence theory: Power processes and negative outcomes. In E. J. Lawler & B. Markovsky (Eds.), *Advances in group processes* (Vol. 4, pp. 171–198. Greenwich, CT: JAI Press.

MOLM, L. (1990). Structure, action, and outcomes: The dynamics of power in social exchange. *American Sociological Review, 55,* 427–447.

MORGAN, M. P. (1977). *Deterrence: A conceptual analysis.* Beverly Hills, CA: Sage.

MURNIGHAN, J. K. (1978). Models of coalition formation: Game theoretic, social psychological, and political perspectives. *Psychological Bulletin, 85,* 1130–1153.

OSGOOD, C. A. (1962). *An alternative to war or surrender.* Urbana, IL: University of Illinois Press.

PATCHEN, M. (1987). Strategies for eliciting cooperation from an adversary. *Journal of Conflict Resolution, 31,* 164–185.

PFEFFER, J. (1981). *Power in organizations.* Boston, MA: Pitman Publishing Co.

PRUITT, D. G. (1981). *Negotiation behavior.* New York: Academic Press.

RUBIN, J. A., & BROWN, B. R. (1975). *The social psychology of bargaining and negotiations.* New York: Academic Press.

SCHELLING, T. C. (1960). *The strategy of conflict.* New York: Oxford University Press.

SIEGEL, S., & FOURAKER, L. E. (1960). *Bargaining and group decision making.* New York: McGraw-Hill.

STRAUSS, A. (1978). *Negotiations: Varieties, contexts, processes, and social order.* San Francisco: Jossey-Bass.

TALLMAN, I., GRAY, L., & LEIK, R. K. (1991). Decisions, dependency and commitment: An exchange based theory of group formation. In E. J. Lawler, B. Markovsky, C. Ridgeway, & H. A. Walker (Eds.), *Advances in group processes* (Vol. 8, pp. 227–253). Greenwich, CT: JAI Press.

TANNENBAUM, A. S. (1968). *Control in organizations.* New York: McGraw-Hill.

TANNENBAUM, A. S. (1974). *Hierarchy in organizations: An international comparison.* San Francisco: Jossey-Bass.

TANNENBAUM, A. S., & KAHN, R. L. (1958). *Participation in union locals.* Evanston, IL: Row Peterson.

TANNENBAUM, A. S., KAVCIC, B., ROSNER, M., VIANELLO, M., & WIESER, G. (1974). *Hierarchy in organizations.* San Francisco: Jossey-Bass.

TEDESCHI, J. T., & BONOMA, T. V. (1972). Power and influence: An introduction. In J. T. Tedeschi (Ed.), *Social influence processes* (pp. 1–49). Hawthorne, NY: Aldine.

TEDESCHI, J. T., LINDSKOLD, S., HORAI, J., & GAHAGAN, J. P. (1969). Social power and the credibility of promises. *Journal of Personality and Social Psychology, 13,* 253–261.

TEDESCHI, J. T., SCHLENKER, B. R., & BONOMA, T. V. (1973). *Conflict, power, and games.* Hawthorne, NY: Aldine.

THIBAUT, J. W., & KELLEY, H. H. (1959). *The social psychology of groups.* New York: Wiley.

THOMPSON, W. R. (1986). Polarity, the long cycle, and global power warfare. *Journal of Conflict Resolution, 30,* 587–615.

URY, W., BRETT, J. M., & GOLDBERG, S. B. (1988). *Getting disputes resolved: Designing systems to cut the costs of conflict.* San Francisco: Jossey-Bass.

WAGNER, D. (1984). *The growth of sociological theories.* Beverly Hills: Sage.

WAGNER, D., & BERGER, J. (1985). Do sociological theories grow? *American Journal of Sociology, 90,* 697–728.

WILLER, D., MARKOVSKY, B., & PATTON, T. (1989). Power structures: Derivations and applications of elementary theory. In J. Berger, M. Zelditch, Jr., & B. Anderson (Eds.), *Sociological theories in progress: New formulations* (pp. 313–353). Newbury Park: Sage.

WILLIAMSON, O. E. (1975). *Markets and hierarchies.* New York: Free Press.

YOUNGS, G. A., JR. (1986). Patterns of threat and punishment reciprocity in conflict settings. *Journal of Personality and Social Psychology, 51,* 541–546.

ZELDITCH, M., JR., HARRIS, W., THOMAS, G. M., & WALKER, H. A. (1983). Decisions, nondecisions, and metadecisions. In L. Kriesberg (Ed.), *Research in social movements, conflicts in change* (Vol. 5, pp. 1–31). Greenwich, CT: JAI Press.

CHAPTER FOURTEEN

Inequality, Distributive Injustice, and Organizational Illegitimacy*

JOANNE MARTIN

Stanford University

This chapter analyzes the ways some organizational theories reflect the viewpoints of the relatively prosperous, while ignoring the perspectives of the less advantaged. For example, research on institutional theory, internal labor markets, and occupational gender segregation often assumes that common organizational arrangements are perceived as legitimate (right and just), even by those who benefit the least. Distributive justice research suggests that these legitimacy assumptions may sometimes be invalid. For example, when inequality between groups is large, disadvantaged people may feel that their entire group is unjustly treated. If sufficient mobilization resources are available, they may engage in collective action to change the system. If collective action is not feasible, they may continue to feel unjustly treated and show those feelings via individual reactions, such as drug dependency, exit, mental illness, etc. Distributive justice research suggests that the legitimacy assumptions that lie at the heart of many organizational theories should be empirically tested, with a focus on the viewpoints of members of disadvantaged groups. Under some conditions, they expect their rewards to be low and find this dissatisfying and unjust.

MANAGERIAL BIAS IN ORGANIZATIONAL RESEARCH

Organizational research has been repeatedly criticized for attending to the viewpoints of the relatively prosperous, such as managers, while ignoring the perspectives of those who are less advantaged, such as the truly destitute, the working poor, and victims of discrimination (e.g., Calás & Smircich, 1992; Clegg & Dunkerly, 1977; Gouldner, 1970; Israel & Tajfel, 1972; Mumby, 1988; Ossow-

---

*Helpful comments were offered by James Baron and Jeffrey Pfeffer, as well as the other authors of this volume. Any residual errors of omission or commission are my own fault.

ski, 1963; Stablein & Nord, 1985; Stark, 1958). For example, Jermier argues that the apparent value neutrality in organizational research draws attention away from its managerial bias:

> Most of the undesirable features of modern capitalistic society are not mentioned by organization theorists, presenting the appearance of value neutrality, but in actuality masking a politically conservative bias. This compromises the social function of the field to the point where organizational theory serves primarily the dominant interests of capital, rather than the society at large. (Jermier, 1982, p. 204)

One prevalent form of this managerial bias is the assumption that an organization's customary methods of operation are considered legitimate by all its members. This same assumption can be seen in studies of other kinds of social structures.

The distributive justice research reviewed in this chapter examines two issues: why assumptions of legitimacy may be inaccurate or misleading and under what conditions members of a group might consider customary methods of allocating rewards to be unjust. This research has broad implications for theories that have legitimacy assumptions at their core.

Before proceeding, it may be helpful to define legitimacy and discuss its relevance to particular organizational theories.

LEGITIMACY ASSUMPTIONS IN ORGANIZATIONAL SOCIOLOGY

For a set of organizational arrangements to be considered legitimate, it is not enough that they be implemented in a similar manner in a wide variety of contexts. In addition, according to the definition of legitimacy used in this chapter, these similar practices must be considered "right and just" (i.e., Frug, 1986, p. 1285; Habermas, 1979, p. 178). This definition acknowledges the possibility that individuals and groups might have different beliefs about the legitimacy of commonly observed arrangements.

Such a definition does not make legitimacy an empirical impossibility, but it requires that researchers define and measure belief in the legitimacy of a particular set of arrangements to demonstrate that this belief is widely shared. If a specified degree of consensus does not exist within the boundaries of an organization (or a society), organization-wide (or society-wide) legitimacy cannot be said to exist. However, a specified consensus criterion may be met within the narrower boundary of a hierarchical level or other subgroup within the organization (or the society). This approach requires that claims of legitimacy be restricted to a specified set of social actors who empirically exhibit the required degree of consensus about the legitimacy of the relevant arrangements.

Sociologists tend to define legitimacy differently. They are usually concerned with the properties of collective phenomena, such as social structures, rather than with the thoughts, beliefs, or behavior of individuals within these structures. To summarize Mayhew's (1980) version of this viewpoint, individuals can replace each other with little effect on a structure. A focus on individuals is therefore seen as having less explanatory power than an analysis of a collective phenomenon. Individual-level thoughts, beliefs, and behaviors are viewed as a reflection of sociostructural conditions and, as such, need not be measured. This line of reasoning consigns assumptions about the legitimacy of a social structure to a "black box" containing unmeasured variables. This black box is at the core of many sociological theories, such as institutional theory and research on internal labor markets.

Institutional theory argues that some environments pressure organizations to become similar (e.g., DiMaggio & Powell, 1983; Meyer, Scott, & Deal, 1981; Powell & DiMaggio, 1991; Scott, 1987; Zucker, 1988). When organizations use a similar structure or practice (even if that similarity is mandated by law), institutional theorists often assume that the similarity reflects shared beliefs about the legitimacy of these arrangements. For example,

> Once a single element becomes institutionalized in a formally organized collectivity, other associated roles, acts, and even procedures become "infected" with legitimacy. The more tightly integrated the structure, the more rapidly the legitimacy spreads (Hernes, 1976, pp. 540–544). Thus, a few stable legitimate elements tend to proliferate over time through a contagion of legitimacy to other elements tightly coupled to them. (Zucker, 1988, p. 24)

Although such assumptions about legitimacy are central to many versions of institutional theory (Elsbach & Sutton, 1991), they are rarely elaborated, questioned, or tested empirically. Indeed, one of the few institutional theorists to advocate empirical exploration of legitimacy issues notes that institutional research has usually focused on similarities in formal structure, in part because structures are supposedly considered legitimate by all:

> Institutional theory [focuses] on the taken-for-granted nature of organizational forms and practices, on precisely those aspects of organization that are unaffected by the particular interests of politically conceived actors. (DiMaggio, 1988, p. 4)

Legitimacy assumptions also lie at the core of most theories of internal labor markets (Baron, 1988). Firms have internal labor markets when new employees are usually hired to fill entry-level positions and most higher level positions are filled by promoting current employees. High status and high pay, then, are primarily reserved for insiders. Recent studies have examined whether particular aspects of internal labor markets strengthen employees' commitment to and economic dependence on the firm, decrease turnover, save the firm the cost of training new employees, and maximize use of employees' firm-specific skills (e.g., Baron, 1988; Bielby & Baron, 1983; Blinder, 1990; Doeringer & Priore, 1971; Halaby, 1986; Peterson, Spilerman, & Dahl, 1989; Price, 1981; Rosenbaum, 1984; Williamson, 1975). These studies usually go beyond documenting the existence of these effects and attempt to explain why such effects might occur. These explanations emphasize employees' greater economic dependence on a firm with an internal labor market or they offer a legitimacy explanation: Supposedly, the promise of upward mobility encourages lower paid employees to believe in the legitimacy of the higher status and pay levels of top managers.

Scully (in preparation) is testing the validity of these legitimacy assumptions by surveying the employees of two relatively large firms known for having internal labor markets. Scully observes that in most firms with internal labor markets it is virtually impossible for clerical or blue-collar employees to move into managerial positions, in effect suggesting the existence of multiple, separate internal labor markets within a single firm. Scully hypothesizes that blue-collar and clerical employees will be less likely than managerial employees to believe in the legitimacy of internal labor market practices. According to Scully, increased economic dependency on a firm, rather than legitimacy, will explain turnover and retention rates of lower level employees in companies with internal labor markets. Such results would suggest limits to the accuracy of legitimacy-based explanations of internal labor market effects. Even if these predictions are not confirmed, this study offers one feasible approach to testing the validity of the legitimacy assumptions that lie at the core of many organizational theories.

OVERVIEW

If assumptions about the legitimacy of organizational arrangements were tested empirically, some customary practices and structures would probably be judged to be illegitimate, particularly by those who are not managers. Organizational theories that assume legitimacy would therefore have to be reformulated, contextualized, or elaborated. Such theories would have to rely on non-legitimacy-based explanations, such as increased economic dependence on a firm, or be reformulated in some other way to include the needs, interests, and beliefs of those who do not consider common arrangements to be legitimate. Such an approach could increase our understanding of the underlying mechanisms that lead

*   power inequalities to affect the interpretation and effects of organizational practices;
*   groups and individuals to perceive organizational practices differently;
*   people to resist pressures toward homogeneity; and
*   institutions to foster dissent, intergroup conflict, and internally generated change.

The empirical analysis of legitimacy requires an investigation of what members of a collectivity, an organization, or a society would consider just and right. This is precisely the focus of psychological studies of justice. This chapter critically reviews what has—and has not—been learned from recent distributive justice research. (Other chapters in this volume cover procedural justice research and related studies of commitment, satisfaction, and attachment.) Questioning assumptions about legitimacy requires crossing disciplinary boundaries, bringing sociological insights to psychological research, and psychological concerns to sociological studies. First, I discuss the legitimacy implications of distributive justice research; then, I return to the broader questions raised earlier.

DISTRIBUTIVE JUSTICE

Since the early 1970s, equity theory has been a dominant view of distributive justice in the United States (Berkowitz & Walster, 1976). According to equity (social exchange) theory (e.g., Adams, 1963; Homans, 1974), people decide if they are being rewarded fairly by calculating the ratio of their contributions (such as education, seniority, skill) to their outcomes (such as pay). They then compare their own ratio to that of another person. If the two ratios are equal, the relationship is said to be equitable, or just. Equity researchers, drawing on social comparison studies, have found that their subjects generally prefer to compare themselves to people with similar qualifications and jobs and are satisfied if they are being rewarded similarly.

When organizational sociologists invoke untested assumptions about legitimacy, they sometimes use equity research to support their interpretations because it explains why those who earn less, such as lower status employees and victims of discrimination, might find their lower pay levels just. For example, in a series of studies of public and private sector organizations, Baron and his colleagues have found that over 90 percent of men and women are segregated into different job title categories, with different opportunities for advancement, even when they do identical work; similar patterns of racial segregation have been found. Furthermore, as job titles proliferate, men and women and whites and nonwhites within the same general line of work experience greater inequality in pay and promotion opportunities (Baron & Bielby, 1986; Baron & Newman, 1990; Bielby & Baron, 1984; Strang & Baron, 1990).

Baron and Pfeffer (1991) suggest one possible explanation for these findings. They draw on social comparison and equity research to suggest that the proliferation of job titles that are segregated by race and gender may facilitate similar comparisons and feelings of distributive justice, even among lower paid women and blacks:

> Social psychological studies show that individuals tend to make reward comparisons against those in the same job categories and social groups. Therefore, by contributing to ascriptive segregation, specialized job titles conveniently reduce the tendency for women and nonwhites to compare their outcomes to white males' . . . [thereby inhibiting] the ability of incumbents to make straightforward comparisons between their wages and those received by members of other groups and job categories. (Baron & Pfeffer, 1991, pp. 23–24)

This interpretation is as yet untested because these studies of gender and race segregation do not include people's choices of comparative referents or their judgments about whether particular arrangements are legitimate. Baron and

Pfeffer suggest (p. 38) that the proliferation of job titles, assigned according to gender or racial identity, prevents employees from questioning the "wisdom, value, and legitimacy of these differing employment relationships" so that "differing employment and compensation regimes are more easily justified for workers who also differ in other ways besides the mere category of how they are employed" (p. 38).

In these and other studies, the results of equity research have been used to argue that customary rules of reward allocation—even discriminatory ones—will generally be considered legitimate, even by those who are disadvantaged by these rules. Although legitimacy explanations (such as those offered by Baron and Pfeffer) are plausible, recent distributive justice research suggests very different patterns of reaction, with important implications for organizational theories that rely on untested legitimacy assumptions.

A critique of equity and social exchange research

In the years since Berkowitz and Walster's definitive summary of equity research (1976), different aspects of equity theory have been challenged. Deutsch (1975) showed that equity's exclusive focus on the contribution rule of distributive justice precluded an exploration of other kinds of distributive justice claims, such as need- and equality-based rules. Brickman, Folger, Goode, and Schul (1981) examined macro level concerns about distributive justice that equity theory did not consider, such as the shape of an outcome distribution and the magnitude of variance within it. Pettigrew (1967) drew attention to the limitations of equity's approach to social comparison and produced a theoretical integration of equity, social comparison, reference group, and relative deprivation research under the rubric of social evaluation theory.

Because these critiques do not explore the ramifications of the managerial bias inherent in equity research, we reviewed this work, with a special emphasis on the ways this theory reflects and reinforces a managerial point of view (Martin & Murray, 1983). Next I highlight some of our review's legitimacy-related conclusions.

In many equity studies, methodological choices make it more likely that results will reflect an assumed belief in the legitimacy of an organization's customary methods of distributing economic outcomes. For example, as in most psychological research, participants in experimental studies of equity tend to be college students or managers. If, instead, these participants had come from populations where middle-class levels of prosperity were virtually unattainable, the results of these studies might have been different. For instance, undergraduates or managers might choose to compare themselves with those of similar background and thus find customary reward inequalities to be just; poorly paid custodians or the chronically unemployed might choose to compare themselves with those of dissimilar, more prosperous backgrounds, such as managers, and conclude that the customary reward inequality is unjust. Evidence supporting this contention comes, for example, from bargaining literature. Negotiators who are formulating bargaining strategies tend to choose and invoke the social norm that puts them in the best light (Komorita, 1977; Komorita & Chertkoff, 1973). Thus, advantaged bargainers (e.g., managers and the middle class) would choose equity, while disadvantaged bargainers (e.g., blue-collar workers and the relatively poor) would prefer equality or need-based rules of distribution.

Studying relatively tepid forms of injustice increases the likelihood that equity predictions will be supported. Experimenters, for sound ethical reasons, are reluctant to upset the people who participate in their studies. Organizations are also understandably reluctant to let researchers foment trouble by asking their employees personally relevant, potentially emotional ("inflammatory") questions about possible injustices. Thus, equity researchers tend to study relatively uncontroversial contexts and relatively unemotional reactions. For example, when a student gets slightly lower pay than expected for part-time work, this may be upsetting, but a slight shortage of spending money is less serious than a pay cut that threatens a family's ability to pay the rent and put food on the table. When researchers limit their methodological choices to role plays and pencil-and-paper measures, they also limit the theoretical issues that can be addressed and the results that can be obtained (Lerner & Lerner, 1981).

This focus on the uncontroversial and unemotional is reinforced by the wording of dependent measures in equity studies. Rather than permitting participants to make free, less constrained comparison choices, an experimenter will often present them with a set of relatively similar comparative referents. Questions usually ask what is "expected" or what would be "satisfying." Even questions about what would be "fair" are placed in a context that tacitly encourages participants to interpret the question with reference to how rewards are usually distributed, rather than whether the distribution itself is "just." The problem is that what is considered expected, satisfying, and even "fair" may not be the same as what would be considered just. Restricting comparisons to similar others and refraining from measuring perceptions of justice are methodological choices that make it more likely that equity research will conclude that customary economic inequalities are perceived to be legitimate.

A few equity studies have avoided some of these methodological constraints. For example, frequently cited field studies by Blau (1964), Homans (1974), and Patchen (1961) examined blue-collar workers' reactions to pay for full-time work. A detailed examination of these data (Martin & Murray, 1983) revealed that, contrary to equity predictions, roughly one third of the workers in these studies made upward, dissimilar pay comparisons to managerial-level employees and concluded that their own compensation was unjust. The authors of these studies sometimes ignored or "explained away" this evidence of chronic discontent with an expected pay inequality. For example, "Such attitudes laid them open to charges of mere envy towards those who were better off. . . . Envy is indeed often rationalized as injustice" (Homans, 1974, pp. 256–257). Blau (pp. 155–156) and Homans (p. 263) blurred the important conceptual distinction between the rewards that blue-collar workers expected, given current distribution norms, and the rewards that they would consider just. Homans implied that a long-established economic system that is expected to continue should come to be perceived as just: "A man does not go on forever making comparisons that show him to be unjustly treated, if he can do nothing about it" (Homans, 1974, p. 253).

Because the present chapter focuses on assumptions of legitimacy, these field studies are particularly germane. Unlike most experimental studies in this area, field research often explicitly discusses the links between equity theory and the legitimation of current economic systems. For example, Homans (1974) dismisses charges that managers exploit workers as "matters, so to speak, of taste" (p. 251) and argues that jobs involving drudgery or "mere dirt" are unimportant and are "wholly compatible" with low pay (p. 247–248). Blau (1964) is somewhat more sensitive to the perspectives of the less prosperous. He does not dismiss evidence of exploitation as a matter of taste (p. 158), and he discusses the physical difficulty and low status of manual labor as important costs associated with these jobs. Even Blau, however, justifies these kinds of unfair exchanges as a necessary evil, "the human cost that helps equilibrate the system of occupational supply and demand" (p. 162). He minimizes the effects on the severely disadvantaged by using the meritocratic language of mobility:

> Mobility of various types makes it possible for competitive conflicts to persist and serve their functions without serious, permanent injury to the individuals innocently caught up in them. (Blau, 1964, p. 162)

To the extent that Blau acknowledges limits to mobility, these limitations are blamed on the social attachments of individuals, rather than on obstacles in a system that supposedly permits the most skilled people to reap the highest rewards.

Thus, in their methodological choices and in their interpretation of data, equity and exchange researchers have favored conclusions that reinforce a belief in the legitimacy of contribution-based economic allocation norms. These theories imply that people who earn relatively little will restrict their comparisons to similar others and be content, as long as similar others are equally impoverished. According to this approach to distributive justice, current systems of reward distribution and the economic inequality that they entail will be considered just, even by those who earn the least. This is a legitimacy argument.

Evidence of the prevalence of working-class conservatism in the United States supports this point of view (e.g., Lane, 1962; Sennett & Cobb, 1972). However, not all people in disadvantaged positions are content with their outcomes and not all find the system that allocates those rewards to be just. Equity theory has failed to explore the implications of this alternative viewpoint. In the last 2 decades, researchers have become increasingly critical of the restrictive assumptions of equity theory and have begun to explore alternative distributive justice theories, such as relative deprivation, that can explain both the legitimation and delegitimation of allocation norms.

Relative deprivation: an alternative approach

There are important similarities between equity and relative deprivation theories. In each, individuals compare their contributions and outcomes with those of others to determine whether they are being justly rewarded. If they decide their compensation is unjustly low, feelings of deprivation are said to occur. Differences between equity and relative deprivation are made salient by Runciman's (1966) distinction between personal/egoistic deprivation (based on comparisons between two similar individuals) and group/fraternal deprivation (based on comparisons between two dissimilar groups). Personal deprivation is similar to the judgments studied by equity theorists. In contrast, group deprivation permits the study of enduring inequalities between, for example, labor and management, the poor and the rich, blacks and whites, women and men; this intergroup focus draws attention to enduring income inequalities likely to cause chronic discontent.

The study of group deprivation is, in essence, the study of the potential delegitimation of a system of reward distribution. For example, blacks who felt deprived as a group, in comparison to wealthier whites, were more likely to participate in civil rights protests (Caplan & Paige, 1968). Whites who felt that white economic gains had been less than those of blacks (another form of group deprivation) were more likely than other whites to vote for segregationist politicians (Vanneman & Pettigrew, 1972). In studies such as these, members of less prosperous groups make upward, dissimilar comparisons between two groups, judge the inequality that exists between the two groups to be unjust, and engage in collective behavior designed to change the system of reward distribution. These results are inconsistent with equity predictions.

Methodological choices explain, in part, why equity and group deprivation studies come to such different conclusions. Before the 1980s, most group deprivation research was conducted outside the laboratory, with subjects drawn from somewhat less prosperous groups. Particularly in studies of race riot participation, the contexts were decidedly emotional and controversial. Comparison choices were often severely constrained or left unspecified. In addition, feelings of deprivation were often measured with questions that referred to violated expectations or dissatisfaction, rather than feelings of injustice.

In the United States, race riots and civil disobedience diminished in the 1980s. During this decade most distributive justice research moved from the streets into laboratories and organizations (e.g., Crosby, 1976; deCarufel, 1981; Folger, 1977; Greenberg & Cohen, 1982; Jasso, 1983; Martin, 1982; Messick & Cook, 1983; Tyler & Bies, 1990; as an exception see, for example, Guimond & Dubé–Simard, 1983). At the same time, distributive justice researchers began trying to combine theories, drawing on equity theory's more complex treatment of comparison processes and relative deprivation theory's greater attention to the group level of analysis. Moving deprivation research into laboratories and organizational settings affected the kinds of conclusions that could be drawn: It was more likely that results would legitimate the status quo, as equity research had done, rather than focus on processes of delegitimation, as earlier group deprivation research had done.

The discontent of the disadvantaged

My own interests were more specific. I could not understand why members of less properous groups (such as blue-collar workers, women, and blacks) would legitimize a system of reward allocation that consistently placed them in a disadvantaged position. Under what circumstances would they consider their disadvantaged status to be unjust?

When expectations and justice do not coincide

In one of three studies to be described here, I addressed these questions directly, using a simple survey design (Martin, 1986b). Survey respondents were blue-collar workers (mostly white men) from seven plants of a manufacturing corporation. After watching a documentary videotape that described a managerial job and a blue-collar job at a large utility company, these participants designed three pay plans for managers and workers at the utility company: one that was expected, one that would be satisfying, and one that would be just.

In addition, I included a measure of meritocratic ideology, using items from Patchen (1961) (e.g., "For people who grew up when you did, how much would you say a person's chances for getting ahead in life depended on himself/herself and how much on things beyond his/her control?"). These ideology scores were split at the median into two groups, labeled believers and skeptics. Those who endorse meritocratic ideology (believers) attribute lack of prosperity and upward mobility to an individual's lack of effort or ability. I predicted that believers would conform to the predictions of equity theory and confine their perceptions of injustice to comparisons with others of similar, blue-collar status and that skeptics would make upward, dissimilar comparisons to managers and find blue-collar/management inequalities to be unjust.

The data confirmed these predictions. Believers expected relatively small inequality between the blue-collar workers and management. They also expected relatively large inequality within the blue-collar group and thought that in a just organization, it should be even larger. In effect, these believers wanted a higher ceiling on blue-collar wages, perhaps because they thought that this pay could be theirs if they worked hard enough. In contrast, skeptics tended to focus their discontent on the inequality between blue-collar workers and management. They expected this between-group inequality to be relatively large and thought that, in a just world, it should be much smaller. In summary, subjects who endorsed meritocratic ideology designed pay plans that fit the predictions of equity theory; those who were skeptical of meritocratic ideology found expected labor/management pay inequalities to be unjust, as predicted by theories of group deprivation.

Participants also drew strong distinctions between what they expected, what they would consider satisfying, and what would be just. Both believers and skeptics agreed that satisfying pay plans fell between what was expected and what would be just (see also Messick & Sentis, 1983). Clearly, in distributive justice research these three variables must be kept conceptually and empirically separate. Furthermore, legitimacy cannot be assumed: What was expected was significantly different from what was considered just.

Labor/management inequality: an expected injustice

In this study I addressed similar questions about inequality and injustice, using experimental rather than survey methodology (Martin, 1982). Blue-collar participants (mostly white men) evaluated one of four pay plans for managers and blue-collar workers at a utility company. The pay plans included manipulations of two kinds of pay inequality: The inequality between management and the blue-collar workers was either large or small, and the inequality within the blue-collar group was either large or small. Blue-collar pay levels were relatively high in all of these pay plans, compared to the norms in this geographic area. Meritocratic ideology was also measured, using Patchen's items.

These participants freely selected upward, dissimilar comparisons to managerial pay levels. They were generally unaffected by inequality within the blue-collar group but were very sensitive to the inequality between management and blue-collar workers. When this inequality was large, these participants found the labor/management pay differential to be expected, dissatisfying, and unjust. This pattern was particularly strong among subjects who were skeptical of meritocratic ideology. These results provide additional evidence of group deprivation rather than the individual-level concerns of equity and personal deprivation theories.

The results of these two studies are due, in part, to the fact that these participants were blue-collar workers. Group deprivation is more likely to occur among members of groups that usually earn less, such as blue-collar workers, women, and blacks. In contrast, white male managers will be more likely to restrict their comparisons to other, similar managers. From this privileged perspective, large magnitudes of inequality between groups will tend to be seen as expected, satisfying, and just.

Secretarial reactions to managerial salary levels

In another experiment, participants were women (mostly white) holding secretarial jobs at two large insurance companies (Martin, Price, Bies, & Powers, 1987). They watched a slide and tape show that described the responsibilities and pay levels for secretaries and sales managers at a hypothetical oil company. Pay was based on industry norms, which subjects agreed were realistic and congruent with the norms at their own companies. In the slide show, the gender of the sales managers was manipulated. There were two conditions: total occupational segregation (all managers were men; all secretaries were women), and partial occupational segregation (within the managerial group, two thirds were men and one third women; all secretaries were women).

In this context, the relevant ideology concerned attitudes toward the employment of women in jobs traditionally reserved for men. This ideology was measured using the "Attitudes Toward Women in Business Scale" (Spence, Helmreich, & Stapp, 1973). Scores were split at the median, creating two groups, labeled traditionals and feminists. We predicted that traditionals would prefer substantial inequality between managerial and secretarial pay levels. In accord with equity theory, we expected that they would restrict their comparisons to other secretaries and be content when similar secretarial contributions yielded similar rewards. We expected that feminists would react in an opposite pattern, selecting upward, dissimilar comparisons to managers and finding substantial inequality between these groups to be expected, dissatisfying, and unjust—consistent with group deprivation predictions.

The results were more complex than we had anticipated. The participants in all conditions (total segregation: feminists; total segregation: traditionals; partial segregation: feminists; partial segregation: traditionals) freely chose both similar comparisons (to secretaries) and upward, dissimilar comparisons (to managers). The reactions of feminists in the totally segregated condition differed from all others. They were more likely to find secretarial pay levels expected, dissatisfying, and unjust (personal deprivation) and were more likely to find the inequality between secretaries and managers to be expected, dissatisfying, and unjust (group deprivation). These subjects were also more likely to consider promotions into the managerial ranks more desirable and less likely than subjects in the other three groups.

The implications of these findings become evident when the responses of feminists in the partially segregated condition are considered. This second group of feminists expressed less individual and group deprivation and rated promotions out of the secretarial ranks as *more* likely and *less* desirable—as if they were saying, in accord with reactance theory (Wortman & Brehm, 1975), "Now that I can have it, I don't want it." These findings suggest that attempts to integrate occupations may have the paradoxical effect of depressing the aspirations of those who might be most likely to want promotions: the feminist women who remain, at least for the time being, in low-paid, sex-segregated positions (Martin, 1986a).

Several explanations for these results are possible. Perhaps the secretaries realistically considered the costs associated with promotion into management positions (longer hours, more tension and responsibility, etc.) only when they thought those promotions were possible. Or perhaps the managerial job became devalued once it seemed accessible; other jobs have lost prestige once they were made accessible to women and minorities (e.g., Touhey, 1974; Worchel, Lee, & Adewole, 1975).

In the two studies of blue-collar workers, expected labor/management inequalities were considered dissatisfying and unjust. In contrast, the results of this experiment suggest that people may adjust to their circumstances by legitimating a system of reward distribution that places them in a disadvantaged position. The secretaries with traditional attitudes about the roles of women expressed little discontent with low secretarial pay levels and showed little desire for promotion. In effect, they were defining their lower status and pay as legitimate. The feminist secretaries felt discontent with secretarial pay levels only when opportunities for promotion seemed unlikely. When advancement seemed possible, feminists were more likely to find low secretarial pay levels more just and promotions less desirable. In all these patterns of adjustment, the secretaries rationalized their situations in a way that enabled them to live with—not change—their disadvantaged status.

Catalysts for violence: the injustice debate

The studies of blue-collar workers specified some conditions when members of a less prosperous group found their situation to be unjust (illegitimate); the study of the secretaries, both feminist and traditional, suggested the opposite—these employees found ways to rationalize and legitimize their less prosperous status. These contradictory results are not anomalous; the cumulative results of other justice studies have also found evidence of both patterns of behavior.

In an attempt to understand reasons for these contradictory results, Martin and Murray (1984) reviewed the previous psychological and sociological research on the relationship between feelings of injustice and collective violence, such as riots and protests. Four explanations of violence were examined: (1) triggering incidents, such as policy brutality (a variation of the frustration-aggression hypothesis); (2) economic competition between disadvantaged groups, such as blacks and Hispanics; (3) resentment about inequality between advantaged and disadvantaged groups; and (4) absence of expected increases in prosperity levels (see, for example, Davies's [1962] J-curve hypothesis concerning rising expectations). Empirical evidence clearly disconfirmed the first two explanations for collective violence, but the evidence concerning the last two was mixed.

Methodological choices (including a common failure to measure freely chosen comparative referents or to use measures of justice other than expectations or satisfaction) could account for these mixed results. Recent field studies of collective action (e.g., Tougas, Beaton, & Veilleux, in press) have used more appropriate measures of comparison choices and feelings of injustice, finding support for group deprivation predictions. Although it is difficult to administer an attitude questionnaire in the midst of a protest or riot, it is easier to do so in an organization, where collective actions (such as work slowdowns, coordinated sabotage, and strikes or protests) would be relevant. This was the focus of our next study.

Moral outrage and pragmatism: is injustice irrelevant?

The foregoing review of the collective action literature failed to consider an important theoretical possibility: Feelings of injustice may not predict willingness to engage in collective behavior. This is the point of view of many sociologists and is congruent with the generally weak relationship between attitudes and behavior (e.g., Azjen & Fishbein, 1980). Sociologists are not surprised when distributive justice researchers fail to find a consistent relationship between feelings of group deprivation and willingness to engage in collective behavior. From a sociological point of view, individual ideologies and feelings of injustice are irrelevant as predictors of collective behavior. Only when structural conditions are ripe, and potential members of a movement have the requisite material resources (such as contact with each other, money, and weapons), will they rebel (e.g., McCarthy & Zald, 1977; Oberschall, 1978; Skocpol, 1979; Smelser, 1980). Others find this resource mobilization perspective implausible, agreeing instead with relative deprivation researchers (e.g., Gurr, 1970), revolutionary leaders (e.g., Fanon, 1968), and historians of revolution (e.g., Moore, 1978) that anger about injustice is an essential precursor to collective action.

We put these conflicting group deprivation and resource mobilization arguments to an experimental test (Martin, Brickman, & Murray, 1984). A sample of working women, drawn from a wide variety of occupations and organizations, read a case description of the secretarial and sales management positions at a hypothetical oil company. A "supplemental fact sheet" contained experimental manipulations of pay inequality and resource availability at this company: Men and women holding the same sales manager position at Cal. Oil were paid unequally; the magnitude of this gender inequality was large, moderate, or small; and mobilization resources available to the women sales managers (opportunities for contact with each other, indispensability to the functioning of the firm, and knowledge that underpaid women executives at another firm had successfully mobilized) were either all present or all absent.

The participants were asked to react from the point of view of a woman sales manager at the oil company who was earning the mean pay level for a woman in that position. (This was a realistic request, given the participants' job experience and the requirements for the hypothetical job). When gender inequality was large, participants expressed significantly stronger personal and group deprivation; the presence or absence of mobilization resources had no impact on their feelings.

Participants were also asked if they would be willing to engage in a variety of collective behaviors designed to change the firm's system of pay allocation. Feelings of injustice—even group deprivation—had no effect here. Instead, in accord with the resource mobilization perspective, willingness to engage in collective behavior was influenced only by the availability of resources. When the resources necessary for mobilization were present, the subjects said they were willing to act collectively, regardless of the intensity of their feelings of injustice.

Tolerance of injustice

These studies all address questions of (il)legitimacy. The results suggest that when inequality between groups is large, members of the disadvantaged group will judge that inequality to be expected, dissatisfying, and unjust. These feelings of group deprivation will be particularly strong among those who share an ideology that delegitimizes the inequality. Such ideological differences may account for observed differences in justice reactions among citizens of different nations. For example, Runciman (1966) reported little group deprivation among English blue-collar workers; Wedderburn (1974) replicated Runciman's findings with English blue-collar workers but found strong group deprivation in a comparable Scandinavian sample. Crosby (1976) found little personal deprivation among middle-class working women in the United States, even though they earned less than men with similar qualifications in similar positions. In contrast, Tougas et al. (in press) found strong group and personal deprivation among Canadian women who had experienced sex discrimination.

There are strong pressures against translating feelings of group deprivation into collective action. For example, in the aforementioned studies, secretaries rationalized their low-status, low-paid position as either just or more desirable than a promotion to a managerial job; women with a wide range of working experiences considered pay inequities between men and women managers to be unjust but were unwilling to translate their feelings into action to change the system. People may have a strong tendency to adjust to a system of reward allocation, even when they are paid unequally and find that inequality unjust.

What happens to these feelings of injustice, then, if they are not translated into collective action? Hirschman (1970) suggested three responses to discontent: exit, voice, and loyalty. The group deprivation studies add a variant of Hirschman's voice option: Those who feel group deprivation may be more likely to engage in collective behavior (such as voting or joining protests, riots, work slowdowns, strikes, or revolutions) designed to alter systems of reward allocation.

Even this expanded formulation, however, is too simplistic, especially for members of disadvantaged groups (Martin, 1986a). The resource mobilization research suggests that, in many circumstances, people lack the power and resources necessary to undertake collective action. The exercise of "voice," as in a grievance procedure, may bring no results because the management of an organization may feel its system of reward allocation is sufficiently "just" as long as other organizations reward members of a disadvantaged group in a similar way. Exit may not be an option for members of disadvantaged groups because moving to a different area may not be possible (particularly for those who lack the funds to move or whose spouses are reluctant to relocate). Knowledge of other job options may be absent or other job opportunities may be no better. For example, if more than 90 percent of the jobs in any industry sector are racially segregated, voice is unlikely to have an effect on a company's race segregation policies, and exit to another organization is not likely to bring much improvement.

Under such conditions, according to Hirschman, the only option left is loyalty. In other words, an employee must decide that a system is legitimate. Strauss (1974, quoted in Jermier, 1982, p. 205) acknowledges this by noting that people can adapt to unchallenging work and relatively low pay by "lowering expectations, changing need structures, and making the most of social opportunities on and off the job." This is certainly one option, but another response is possible. Jermier reconceptualizes the loyalty/legitimation option in more critical terms, suggesting that adjustment "is at the expense of crushed aspirations, excessive consumerism, drug dependency, political indifference, family disintegration and generally lower life satisfaction and fulfillment" (Jermier, 1982, p. 205). Taking Jermier's argument one step further, personal deprivation research suggests that members of disadvantaged groups may react to an expected inequality with chronic anger, unhappiness, and alienation. If these people feel there is no hope for improvement, and that collective action would be futile or too costly, they may respond to their chronic discontent by engaging in self-destruction or alienated behaviors, such as drug dependency and alcoholism.

All these behavioral options have been combined (Crosby, 1976) and reformulated (Martin, 1986a) as follows: Personal and group deprivation can lead to positive individual behaviors (such as self-improvement efforts) or to negative individual behaviors (such as drug and alcohol dependency, mental or physical illness). Group deprivation is more likely to lead to collective efforts to change an entire system—either through voice (by voting or utilizing grievance procedures, for example) or through protest (by sabotage or strikes, for example). Although this conceptual framework integrates a broad range of behavioral reactions to injustice, the fact remains that collective action is a relatively infrequent choice—one that is at best imperfectly correlated with feelings of group deprivation.

Several lines of investigation would be useful to explore in future research. When members of a disadvantaged group are confronted with a large inequality, it is not clear why some focus on within-group comparisons and find their rewards to be just while others focus on between-group comparisons and find their rewards to be unjust. The aforementioned studies suggest that relatively small inequality between groups and belief in an inequality-legitimating ideology facilitate a within-group focus. Research reviewed in other chapters of this volume (for example, studies of equity, procedural justice, and personal deprivation) suggests other reasons why people might restrict their comparisons to similar others and be content, as long as similar inputs were associated with similar outcomes and fair procedures for allocating rewards were followed (Bies, 1987; Brockner, 1990; Brockner, Grover, Reed, DeWitt, & O'Malley, 1987; Crosby, 1976; Folger, 1977; Gartrell, 1987; Greenberg & Folger, 1983; Halaby, 1986; Lind et al., 1990; Tyler, 1990). However, because most of these studies do not focus on those who are clearly disadvantaged, the relevance to situations where between-group inequalities are large is unclear. These studies explain why organizations should be considered legitimate, even by those who earn the least pay, but they do not fully explain why intense feelings of group deprivation and system illegitimacy sometimes arise.

We also do not understand the relationship between feelings of injustice and behavior. It is not clear why personal deprivation is sometimes channeled into positive rather than negative behaviors or why group deprivation is sometimes associated with negative individual behaviors rather than with collective action. We do not understand why feelings of personal or group deprivation sometimes have no apparent behavioral effects. Existing research provides some answers. For example, the availability of resources is certainly important. Nevertheless, this is an area where other literatures (on collective behavior, organizational change, and social movements, for example) might make useful contributions. Exploring these behavioral issues would help us understand how the legitimacy of a system of reward allocation is questioned, challenged, and changed.

Counterbalancing financial and socioemotional rewards

Critical theory offers a fresh approach to some of the questions raised earlier, suggesting that when members of a disadvantaged group consider their low status and low rewards legitimate, they are exhibiting a kind of false consciousness or are being co-opted. More specifically, perhaps some people are content with low pay because an organization has "bought them off" or distracted them by offering nonfinancial rewards such as warmth and friendliness. If so, perhaps managers use a counterbalancing strategy when distributing rewards, supplementing unequal distributions of financial rewards (according to equity rules) with more equal distributions of socioemotional rewards (based on need or equality rules).

In an experiment testing this hypothesis (Martin & Harder, 1990), participants were MBAs. They studied a case description of a small start-up firm, which included the characteristics of its employees (e.g., seniority, performance ratings, age, number of dependents) and their pay levels. Salary inequality, across all levels of the company's hierarchy, was manipulated to be either relatively large or small, compared to local industry norms. The participants completed an "in-box" exercise that required them to allocate seven types of financial rewards (such as profit sharing and access to company cars) and nonfinancial rewards (such as relocation counseling for spouses, friendliness, etc.) to the company's employees. For each type of reward, the participants rated the appropriateness of seven distributive justice rules, including various equity, equality, and need-based alternatives.

The results supported the counterbalancing hypothesis: Participants were more likely to distribute the financial rewards unequally (using equity rules based on individual performance and status), while socioemotional rewards were distributed more equally (using need, individual-equality, or group-equality rules). The manipulation of pay inequality had no effect on these allocations. Participants had managerial experience and were being trained for high-level executive positions. Had they been destined for poorly paid positions, pay inequality may have had a stronger effect, with the distribution of all kinds of rewards being more equal when pay inequalities were large.

Injustice and the legitimation of revolutionary violence

Jermier's criticisms of relative deprivation theory suggest an alternative approach. Rather than studying the process of legitimating inequality, he focused on the delegitimation of extremely large magnitudes of inequality:

> We produce more than people need, strictly speaking, to live. Because those goods are not distributed equally, some are truly deprived, so they are hungry and do not have a home. These are often the unemployed, and so conveniently they generally are considered to fall outside the purview of organizational theory, which focuses on those who are employed by organizations. The very rich [the leisured classes who do not work], the very poor, and the economically dependent [children, spouses, other relatives] are not included. For the very rich and the very poor, absolute amounts of economic goods are what is salient; relative deprivation as a psychological construct would not be meaningful. (Jermier, 1982, p. 204)

Jermier's observations are even more powerful when the methodological limitations of most justice research (including my own) are considered. Justice has usually been studied in laboratories, corporations, and traffic courts, where severe deprivation is not an issue. In addition, the methodological choices discussed in the beginning of this chapter (reliance on students or managers as participants, the difficulty of gaining organizational entry to ask controversial questions, reliance on paper-and-pencil measures, etc.) have limited our ability to study delegitimation where it is most likely to occur.

To escape these limitations, we turned to the rhetoric of twentieth-century revolutionary leaders to see whether their ways of speaking about inequality and injustice would suggest ways of extending psychological theories of justice (Martin, Scully, & Levitt, 1990). We analyzed the content of the speeches and writings of leaders such as Castro, Mao, Fanon, and Luxemborg to determine how these "experts" talked about injustice during the early years of a struggle, when they were trying to mobilize participation in violent collective action. The outcome of the revolution (success or failure), country or region, gender of the leader, and political orientation of the movement (left or right wing) had no effect on the results.

Although our coding system anticipated complex social comparisons and distributive justice rules, much of the leaders' rhetoric was unexpectedly simple. They described their enemies in starkly simplified, totally dissimilar terms. They also justified bloodshed in simple language: The enemy's violence was always unjust, but that of the revolutionary group was almost always just. Their use of distributive justice rules was also simple: There was too much inequality. Given the revolutionary contexts we were studying, we expected that equity theory's contribution rules would be seldom used. We did not expect, however, that the leaders would never use the plethora of other distributive justice rules we were prepared to code. In addition, leaders mentioned only one procedural justice concern: representation in government. These results suggest that members of a disadvantaged group may consider procedural justice less important when out-comes are distributed in a very unequal fashion.

The leaders' portrayal of the future was also starkly simple. The enemy was never mentioned (killed or converted?), and any sources of dissimilar-ity within the revolutionary group—even ethnic dissimilarity—were unmen-tioned. This ominous form of simplicity suggests that homogeneity may be a necessary component of a vision of justice; diversity may be tolerated during a revolution, but not afterward.

These results also suggest that our conceptions of procedural and distribu-tive justice should incorporate a complex and detailed consideration of emo-tional and ideological concerns. When the revolutionary leaders spoke to their followers about the necessity of bloodshed, they stressed the group's past emo-tional suffering and anticipated its future emotional solidarity. In addition, they spoke of ideological bonds such as a shared history and political consciousness. They mentioned the unequal distribution of emotional well-being as often as the unequal distribution of material goods. Previous research has focused on mate-rial resources for mobilization (guns and butter), but these leaders stressed ideo-logical resources, such as moral righteousness and historical inevitability, to offer a favorable portrait of the balance of power. Clearly, our theories of justice can and should incorporate deeply held emotions and ideological convictions, so that they become theories of the heart as well as of the pocketbook.

INSIGHTS FROM CROSSING
DISCIPLINARY BOUNDARIES

The studies discussed in this chapter draw on a broad range of psychological and sociological theories of justice. The results contribute to our understanding of belief (and disbelief) in the legitimacy of the economic inequalities created by organizational systems of reward allocation. A sociological perspective looks be-yond the individual level of analysis to

* focus on inequality between, as well as within, groups;
* consider comparisons between dissimilar groups as well as similar individuals;
* study members of relatively less prosperous groups, such as blue-collar workers, women who hold clerical positions, and the truly destitute;
* examine highly emotional contexts, such as pay disputes and racial conflicts;
* assess whether some behavioral options, such as voice or exit, may be unavailable or impractical for members of disadvantaged groups;

*   include collective responses to injustice, such as tactics that challenge the legitimacy of entire systems of distribution (e.g., sabotage, wildcat strikes, protests, riots, and revolutions).

A social psychological perspective suggests that it is essential to

*   measure freely chosen comparative referents, rather than assume that people will only make comparisons to other, relatively similar individuals;
*   use separate measures of what is considered just, what is satisfying, and what is expected; do not assume that measures of "fairness" tap feelings of justice, rather than expectations of customary distribution norms;
*   measure ideologies (such as meritocracy, racism, or attitudes toward women's roles) that may legitimate or delegitimate particular economic inequalities;
*   include a wider range of individual behaviors, such as drug use, mental illness, and efforts at self-improvement.

Opening the black box of legitimacy assumptions

The studies discussed in this chapter illustrate the importance of crossing disciplinary boundaries when studying legitimacy, bringing sociological insights to psychologically oriented research and psychological concerns to more sociological studies. Results suggest that psychological studies of justice might draw different conclusions if they examine the same phenomena in different contexts. For example, justice researchers could study the severely deprived in contexts that are perceived as illegitimate.

Procedural justice research has begun to do this. Early procedural studies focused on contexts, such as traffic courts and the distribution of grades or pay, where the legitimacy of the context itself was seldom questioned by study participants. In this research, participants' satisfaction was usually determined by the perceived justice of the procedures used to allocate outcomes, even if those outcomes were low. These findings were interpreted as evidence of the greater importance of procedural rather than distributive justice.

In response to criticisms that procedural justice might be important only for relatively trivial outcomes, such as traffic tickets or exam grades, more recent studies have focused on more consequential outcomes, in circumstances that might well be considered illegitimate by members of disadvantaged groups. For example, Casper, Tyler, and Fisher (1988) examined the reactions of defendants charged with felonies, where penalties included long periods of incarceration and substantial fines. When defendants received these more serious outcomes, both procedural justice and distributive justice concerns were important.

These results suggest that distributive justice may become more important as outcomes become more serious, disadvantaged status is more permanent (i.e., race, gender, or lengthy prison term), and the reward allocation context is considered less legitimate. For example, when black defendants are charged with raping or murdering white victims, they are more likely to receive a long prison term or death sentence than white defendants charged with the same crimes. How would black defendants rate the relative importance of procedural and distributive justice in this context?

As a second example, consider Bies's (1987) study of the ways managers frame the delivery of "bad news" to dissipate discontent, for example by stressing fair procedures or how much worse things might have been. (See also Brockner's studies of layoffs, in this volume.) Such explanations for a job loss or layoff would not be so soothing if study participants had little chance of obtaining minimally decent jobs. To summarize, there probably are boundary conditions to procedural justice—points at which no procedural improvement would dissipate discontent with severe deprivation. These examples suggest that recent justice research, like earlier studies of equity, may have inadvertently found evidence of legitimacy because we have studied contexts where deep feelings of injustice do not surface.

These distributive justice findings have implications for some organizational research. For example, as described earlier, Baron and Pfeffer (1991) use equity research to explain how women and blacks might react psychologically to occupational segregation. They argue that those who are segregated by race or gender in lower paying job categories will make comparisons only to similar others (same race or gender, same job title), thus restricting their perceptions of injustice to pay inequalities within their own group. Some of the research reviewed in this chapter and elsewhere in this volume supports this contention; rather than remaining perpetually angry, some disadvantaged people will adjust their expectations downward, coming, eventually, to view their low status as legitimate.

However, the results of the group deprivation research suggest that, under some conditions, different patterns of response will occur. Some members of disadvantaged groups, particularly those whose ideology does not justify their disadvantaged status, will make upward comparisons and find between-group inequality to be expected, dissatisfying, and unjust. A realistic assessment of behavioral options might lead these victims of discrimination to conclude that voice would be unlikely to trigger organizational change, or exit to yield a better paying job, since most organizations exhibit similar patterns of segregation. Furthermore, collective action might seem unlikely, given the absence of mobilization resources. Under these conditions, victims of discrimination might stay on the job and continue to make upward, dissimilar comparisons and to feel keenly the injustice of their low pay and lack of promotion opportunities. The only behavioral sign of their feelings might be the individual-level responses catalogued by Jermier, including crushed aspirations, political indifference, family disintegration, physical and mental illness, and drug and alcohol dependency.

This creates a picture of chronic discontent and alienation rather than the image of placid acceptance of inequality implicit in assumptions regarding the legitimacy of customary reward allocation rules. The difference is crucial because festering feelings of group deprivation could erupt into violent protest or other collective actions challenging the legitimacy of an entire system of reward distribution. Even if collective behavior does not occur, individual behavioral reactions to chronic feelings of deprivation (such as alcohol and drug abuse) can create severe difficulties for individuals and organizations.

The group deprivation research summarized in this chapter indicates the importance of including the perspectives of those who are members of disadvantaged groups in our theory and research. Compared to other kinds of organizational studies, justice research has been relatively careful to avoid or minimize managerial bias. Nevertheless, justice research is not immune to these limitations. When justice research assumes that common systems of reward allocation are considered legitimate, or when perceptions of justice are studied in contexts unlikely to arouse chronic, intense feelings of injustice, we represent the viewpoints of those who benefit from those systems of reward distribution rather than the perspectives of those who are disadvantaged and find their disadvantaged position to be expected, dissatisfying, and unjust. Theories of justice have more explanatory power when they include the points of view of the "have nots" as well as the "haves." Organizational theories such as institutionalization or internal labor markets would be improved if they drew on distributive justice research for ideas about how to assess the validity of the legitimacy assumptions that lie at their core.

REFERENCES

ADAMS, J. S. (1963). Toward an understanding of inequity. *Journal of Abnormal and Social Psychology, 67*, 422–436.

AZJEN, I., & FISHBEIN, M. (1980). *Understanding attitudes and predicting social behavior.* Englewood Cliffs, NJ: Prentice Hall.

BARON, J. N. (1988). The employment relation as a social relation. *Journal of the Japanese and International Economies, 2*, 492–525.

BARON, J. N., & BIELBY, W. T. (1986). The proliferation of job titles. *Administrative Science Quarterly, 31*, 561–586.

BARON, J. N., & NEWMAN, A. E. (1990). For what it's worth: Organizations, occupations, and the value of work done by women and nonwhites. *American Sociological Review, 55*, 155–175.

BARON, J. N., & PFEFFER, J. (1991). *The social psychology of organizations and inequality.* Unpublished manuscript, Stanford University.

BERKOWITZ, L., & WALSTER, E. (Eds.). (1976). *Advances in experimental social psychology* (Vol. 9). New York: Academic Press.

BIELBY, W. T., & BARON, J. N. (1983). Organizations, technology, and the firm. *Research in Social Stratification and Mobility, 2*, 77–113.

BIELBY, W. T., & BARON, J. N. (1984). A woman's place is with other women: Sex segregation within organizations. In B. Reskin (Ed.), *Sex segregation in the workplace: Trends, explanations, remedies* (pp. 27–55). Washington, DC: National Academy Press.

BIES, R. J. (1987). The predicament of injustice. The management of moral outrage. *Research in Organizational Behavior, 9*, 289–319.

BLAU, P. (1964). *Exchange and power in social life.* New York: Wiley.

BLINDER, A. S. (Ed.). (1990). *Paying for productivity: A look at the evidence.* Washington, DC: The Brookings Institution.

BRICKMAN, P., FOLGER, R., GOODE, E., & SCHUL, Y. (1981). Microjustice and macro-justice. In M. J. Lerner & S. C. Lerner (Eds.), *The justice motive in social behavior* (pp. 173–202). New York: Plenum Press.

BROCKNER, J. (1990). Scope of justice in the workplace—How survivors react to co-worker layoffs. *Journal of Social Issues, 46,* 95–105.

BROCKNER, J., GROVER, S., REED, T., DeWITT, R., & O'MALLEY, M. (1987). Survivors' reactions to layoffs: We get by with a little help for our friends. *Administrative Science Quarterly, 32,* 526–541.

CALÁS, M. B., & SMIRCICH, L. (1992). Using the "F" word: Feminist theories and the social consequences of organizational research. In A. J. Mills & P. Tancred (Eds.), *Gendering organizational theory* (pp. 222–234). Newbury Park, CA: Sage.

CAPLAN, N., & PAIGE, J. M. (1968). A study of ghetto rioters. *Scientific American, 219,* 15–22.

CASPER, J. D., TYLER, T., & FISHER, B. (1988). Procedural justice in felony cases. *Law & Society Review, 22,* 483–507.

CLEGG, S., & DUNKERLY, D. (Eds.). (1977). *Critical issues in organizations.* London, England: Routledge and Kegan Paul.

CROSBY, F. J. (1976). A model of egoistical relative deprivation. *Psychological Review, 83,* 85–113.

DAVIES, J. (1962). Toward a theory of revolution. *American Sociological Review, 27,* 5–18.

deCARUFEL, A. (1981). The allocation and acquisition of resources in times of scarcity. In M. J. Lerner & S. C. Lerner (Eds.), *The justice motive in social behavior* (pp. 317–341). New York: Plenum Press.

DEUTSCH, M. (1975). Equity, equality, and need: What determines which value will be used as a basis for distributive justice? *Journal of Social Issues, 31,* 137–150.

DiMAGGIO, P. (1988). Interest and agency in institutional theory. In L. G. Zucker (Ed.), *Institutional patterns and organizations* (pp. 3–21). Cambridge, MA: Ballinger Publishing Co.

DiMAGGIO, P., & POWELL, W. W. (1983). The iron cage revisited: Institutional isomorphism and collective rationality in organizational fields. *American Sociological Review, 48,* 147–160.

DOERINGER, P. B., & PRIORE, M. J. (1971). *Internal labor markets and manpower analysis.* Dexington, MA: D. C. Heath.

ELSBACH, K., & SUTTON, R. (1991). *Enhancing organizational legitimacy through illegitimate actions: A marriage of institutional and impression management theory.* Unpublished manuscript, Stanford University.

FANON, F. (1968). *The wretched of the earth.* New York: Grove Press.

FOLGER, R. (1977). Distributive and procedural justice: Combined impact of "voice" and peer opinions on responses to inequity. *Journal of Personality and Social Psychology, 35,* 108–119.

FRUG, G. (1986). The ideology of bureaucracy in American law. *Harvard Law Review, 97,* 1276–1388.

GARTRELL, D. (1987). Network approaches to social evaluation. In W. R. Scott & J. F. Short (Eds.), *Annual review of sociology* (Vol. 13, pp. 49–66). Palo Alto, CA: Annual Reviews Inc.

GOULDNER, A. W. (1970). *The coming crisis in western sociology.* New York: Basic Books.

GREENBERG, J., & COHEN, R. (Eds.). (1982). *Equity and justice in social behavior.* New York: Academic Press.

GREENBERG, J., & FOLGER, R. (1983). Procedural justice, participation, and the fair process effect in groups and organizations. In P. Paulus (Ed.), *Basic group processes* (pp. 235–258). New York: Springer-Verlag.

GUIMOND, S., & DUBÉ–SIMARD, L. (1983). Relative deprivation theory and the Quebec nationalist movement: The cognition-emotion distinction and the personal-group deprivation issue. *Journal of Personality and Social Psychology, 44,* 526–535.

GURR, T. R. (1970). *Why men rebel.* Princeton, NJ: Princeton University Press.

HABERMAS, J. (1979). *Communication and the evolution of society.* Boston: Beacon Press.

HALABY, C. (1986). Worker attachment and workplace authority. *American Sociological Review, 51,* 634–649.

HERNES, G. (1976). Structural change in social processes. *American Journal of Sociology, 82,* 513–547.

HIRSCHMAN, A. (1970). *Exit, voice, and loyalty: Responses to decline in firms, organizations and states.* Cambridge, MA: Harvard University Press.

HOMANS, G. (1974). *Social behavior: Its elementary forms.* New York: Harcourt Brace Jovanovich.

ISRAEL, J., & TAJFEL, H. (Eds.). (1972). *The context of social psychology: A critical assessment.* New York: Basic Books.

JASSO, G. (1983). Specifying the conflict between the micro and macro principles of justice. *Social Psychology Quarterly, 46,* 185–199.

JERMIER, J. (1982). Infusion of critical social theory into organizational analysis: Implications for studies of work adjustment. In D. Dunkerly & G. Salaman (Eds.), *The international yearbook of organization studies 1981* (pp. 195–211). Boston: Routledge and Kegan Paul.

KOMORITA, S. S. (1977). Negotiating from strength and the concept of bargaining strength. *Journal for the Theory of Social Behavior, 7,* 65–79.

KOMORITA, S. S., & CHERTKOFF, J. M. (1973). A bargaining theory of coalition formation. *Psychological Review, 7,* 65–79.

LANE, R. (1962). *Political ideology: Why the American common man believes what he does.* New York: Free Press.

LERNER, M. J., & LERNER, S. C. (Eds.). (1981). *The justice motive in social behavior.* New York: Plenum.

LIND, E. A., MACCOUN, R. J., EBENER, P. A., FELSTINER, W. L. F., HENSLER, D. R., RESNIK, J., & TYLER, T. R. (1990). In the eye of the beholder: Tort litigants' evaluations of their experiences in the civil justice system. *Law & Society Review, 24,* 953–996.

MARTIN, J. (1982). The fairness of earning differentials: An experimental study of the perceptions of blue collar workers. *Journal of Human Resources, 17,* 110–122.

MARTIN, J. (1986a). The tolerance of injustice. In J. M. Olson, C. P. Herman, & M. P. Zanna (Eds.), *Relative deprivation and social comparison: The Ontario symposium* (Vol. 4, pp. 217–242). Hillsdale, NJ: Erlbaum.

MARTIN, J. (1986b). When expectations and justice do not coincide: Blue-collar visions of a just world. In H. W. Bierhoff & R. L. Cohen (Eds.), *Justice in social relations* (pp. 317–335). New York: Plenum.

MARTIN, J., BRICKMAN, P., & MURRAY, A. (1984). Moral outrage and pragmatism: Explanations for collective action. *Journal of Experimental Social Psychology, 20,* 484–496.

MARTIN, J., & HARDER, J. (1990). *Bread and roses: Justice and the distribution of financial and socio-emotional rewards in organizations.* Unpublished manuscript, Stanford University.

MARTIN, J., & MURRAY, A. (1983). Distributive injustice and unfair exchange. In K. S. Cook & D. M. Messick (Eds.), *Theories of equity: Psychological and sociological perspectives* (pp. 95–139). New York: Praeger.

MARTIN, J., & MURRAY, A. (1984). Catalysts for collective violence: The importance of a psychological approach. In R. Folger (Ed.), *The sense of injustice: Social psychological perspectives.* New York: Plenum.

MARTIN, J., PRICE, R. L., BIES, R. J., & POWERS, M. E. (1987). Now that I can have it,

I'm not so sure I want it: The effects of opportunity on aspirations and discontent. In B. A. Gutek & L. Larwood (Eds.), *Women's career development* (pp. 42–65). New York: Sage.

MARTIN, J., SCULLY, M., & LEVITT, B. (1990). Injustice and the legitimation of revolution: Damning the past, excusing the present, and neglecting the future. *Journal of Personality and Social Psychology, 59,* 281–290.

MAYHEW, B. H. (1980). Structuralism versus individualism (Part 1): Shadowboxing in the dark. *Social Forces, 59,* 335–375.

McCARTHY, J. D., & ZALD, M. N. (1977). Resource mobilization and social movement: A partial theory. *American Journal of Sociology, 82,* 1212–1241.

MESSICK, D. M., & COOK, K. S. (Eds.). (1983). *Theories of equity: Psychological and sociological perspectives.* New York: Praeger.

MESSICK, D. M., & SENTIS, K. (1983). Fairness, preference, and fairness biases. In D. M. Messick & K. S. Cook (Eds.), *Equity theory: Psychological and sociological perspectives* (pp. 61–94). New York: Praeger.

MEYER, J. W., SCOTT, W. R., & DEAL, T. E. (1981). Institutional and technical sources of organizational structure. In H. D. Stein (Ed.), *Organization and the human services.* Philadelphia, PA: Temple University Press.

MOORE, B. (1978). *Injustice: The social bases of obedience and revolt.* White Plains, NY: Sharpe.

MUMBY, D. K. (1988). *Communication and power in organizations: Discourse, ideology, and domination.* Norwood, NJ: Ablex Publishing Corp.

OBERSCHALL, A. (1978). Theories of social conflict. *Annual Review of Sociology, 4,* 291–315.

OSSOWSKI, S. (1963). *Class structure in the social consciousness.* New York: Free Press.

PATCHEN, M. (1961). *The choice of wage comparisons.* Englewood Cliffs, NJ: Prentice Hall.

PETERSON, T., SPILERMAN, S., & DAHL, S. (1989). The structure of employment terminations among clerical employees in a large bureaucracy. *Acta Sociologica, 32,* 319–338.

PETTIGREW, T. F. (1967). Social evaluation theory: Convergence and applications. In D. Levine (Ed.), *Nebraska symposium on motivation* (Vol. 15, pp. 241–311). Lincoln, NE: University of Nebraska Press.

POWELL, W., & DiMAGGIO, P. (Eds.). (1991). *The new institutionalism in organizational analysis.* Chicago: University of Chicago Press.

PRICE, J. L. (1981). *Professional turnover.* New York: Spectrum Publications.

ROSENBAUM, J. E. (1984). *Career mobility in a corporate hierarchy.* Orlando, FL: Academic Press.

RUNCIMAN, W. G. (1966). *Relative deprivation and social justice: A study of attitudes to social inequality in twentieth century England.* Berkeley, CA: University of California Press.

SCOTT, W. R. (1987). The adolescence of institutional theory. *Administrative Science Quarterly, 32,* 493–511.

SCULLY, M. (in preparation). *Meritocratic ideology and the imperfect legitimation of inequality in internal labor markets.* Unpublished doctoral dissertation, Stanford University.

SENNETT, R., & COBB, J. (1972). *The hidden injuries of class.* New York: Knopf.

SKOCPOL, T. (1979). *States and social revolutions: A comparative analysis of France, Russia and China.* Cambridge, England: Cambridge University Press.

SMELSER, N. (1980). Theoretical issues of scope and problems. In M. D. Pugh (Ed.), *Collective behavior: A source book* (pp. 7–11). St. Paul, MN: West.

SPENCE, J. T., HELMREICH, T., & STAPP, J. (1973). A short version of the attitudes toward women scale (AWS). *Bulletin of the Psychonomic Society, 2,* 219–220.

STABLEIN, R., & NORD, W. (1985). Practical and emancipatory interests in organizational symbolism: A review and evaluation. *Journal of Management, 11,* 13–28.

STARK, W. (1958). *The sociology of knowledge: An essay in aid of a deeper understanding of the history of ideas.* London, England: Routledge and Kegan Paul.

STRANG, D., & BARON, J. N. (1990). Categorical imperatives: The structure of job titles in California State agencies. *American Sociological Review, 55,* 479–495.

STRAUSS, G. (1974). Workers: Attitudes and adjustments. In M. Rosow (Ed.), *The worker and the job* (pp. 73–98). Englewood Cliffs, NJ: Prentice Hall.

TOUGAS, F., BEATON, A. M., & VEILLEUX, F. (in press). Why women approve of affirmative action. *International Journal of Psychology.*

TOUHEY, J. (1974). Effects of additional women professionals on ratings of occupational prestige and desirability. *Journal of Personality and Social Psychology, 29,* 86–89.

TYLER, T., & BIES, R. (1990). Beyond formal procedures: The interpersonal context of procedural justice. In J. S. Carroll (Ed.), *Advances in applied social psychology: Business settings* (pp. 77–98). Hillsdale, NJ: Erlbaum.

TYLER, T. R. (1990). *Why people obey the law.* New Haven, CT: Yale University Press.

VANNEMAN, R., & PETTIGREW, T. (1972). Race and relative deprivation in the urban United States. *Race, 13,* 461–486.

WEDDERBURN, D. (Ed.). (1974). *Poverty, inequality, and class structure.* Cambridge, England: Cambridge University Press.

WILLIAMSON, O. E. (1975). *Markets and hierarchies.* New York: Free Press.

WORCHEL, S., LEE, J., & ADEWOLE, A. (1975). Effects of supply and demand on ratings of object value. *Journal of Personality and Social Psychology, 32,* 906–914.

WORTMAN, C. B., & BREHM, J. W. (1975). Responses to uncontrollable outcomes: An integration of the reactance theory and the learned helplessness model. In L. Berkowitz (Ed.), *Advances in experimental social psychology* (Vol. 8, pp. 278–332). New York: Academic Press.

ZUCKER, L. G. (Ed.). (1988). *Institutional patterns and organizations.* Cambridge, MA: Ballinger Publishing Co.

CHAPTER FIFTEEN

The Multiple Cognitions and Conflicts Associated with Second Order Organizational Change*

JEAN M. BARTUNEK

Boston College

This chapter addresses several dynamics often associated with organizational change: the likely presence of groups operating out of multiple schemata, conflict among holders of these different schemata, and changes aimed at fostering movement away from a particular schema toward a new one (second-order change). The beginning of the chapter describes some of the history of organization development (OD) as a basic approach to organizational change. An example of an OD intervention in the 1970s and some problems it encountered is given. Then three illustrations of organizational change projects—in a religious order, food processing plant, and school—are woven into a discussion of dynamics of second-order change. Analysis of the illustrations indicates that organizational change that involves potential shifts in schemata is often initiated due to important external changes that cause organization members to experience a sense of crisis. Change agents' attempts to alter organizational members' shared schemata provide the stage for the development of multiple schemata as well as for conflicts among holders of the different schemata. How these conflicts are addressed affects the outcome of organizational change. The chapter concludes with several proposals regarding likely processes of second-order change.

The two books written in the late 1960s about the social psychology of organizations, Katz and Kahn (1966) and Weick (1969), took different approaches to the topic of organizational change. Weick devoted little formal attention to change, although his description of deviation-amplifying and deviation-countering feedback loops suggested that change was an integral element of the organizing process. Katz and Kahn devoted a chapter to the topic, applying systems thinking

*I am grateful to Jeanne Brett, Joyce Fletcher, Linda Ginzel, Rod Kramer, Joanne Martin, Fred Meyer, and Richard Nielsen for their helpful suggestions at various points in the preparation of this chapter.

to the understanding of organizational change attempts. The issues they discussed included participation in decision making, survey feedback, and sociotechnical systems design. These are three important dimensions of organization development (OD).

In the late 1960s and early 1970s, most attention to organizational change came from scholars and practitioners identified with organization development. The OD division of the Academy of Management was founded in 1971, partly to make planned organizational change a salient part of academic discourse on organizations. In the 1970s, although OD practitioners allied themselves with a number of scholarly disciplines in the social sciences, the one they most relied on for theory relevant to organizational change was social psychology (e.g., Schmuck & Miles, 1971). In fact, some intervention strategies were simply social psychological experiments adapted to applied settings (e.g., Johnson, 1967).

Links between organizational change, social psychology, and organizational behavior have changed in many ways during the last 20 years. For example, there is a tendency now to speak of "Organizational change and development" rather than OD as an appropriate title for the field (e.g., Woodman & Pasmore, 1987). Social psychology is now seen as one of many sources of training for OD practitioners. With the radical changes in organizational research methods that have been occurring since the late 1970s, action research, the primary research method of OD practitioners, is now recognized as having the potential to contribute to scholarship in addition to serving as a problem-solving method (e.g., Brief & Dukerich, 1991; Pasmore & Friedlander, 1982; Susman & Evered, 1978). Lewin's often-cited dictum that the best way to learn about something is to try to change it is finding increasing acceptance.

This chapter addresses organizational change. The work that is the focus of the chapter initially grew out of OD but encompasses a broader range of approaches to change than those typically associated with OD. The chapter examines important complex dynamics of change that have seldom been addressed: the presence of groups operating out of differing perspectives, conflict between these groups, and types of change that might be affected by conflicts between the groups. All three topics are integral to the intersection of social psychology and organizational change.

After presenting some overview material about OD in the late 1960s and early 1970s, I will describe a typical intervention of that time, one that introduces the issues that are the focus of the chapter. I will interweave these issues with discussion of several organizational change attempts—a reorganization in a religious order (Bartunek, 1984), a Quality of Work Life (QWL) project in a food processing facility (Bartunek & Moch, 1987, 1991; Moch & Bartunek, 1990), and an attempt to increase coordination in a school by implementing a new position (Bartunek & Reid, 1992). The QWL intervention clearly falls under the rubric of OD; the other two are organization-initiated change attempts carried out without the assistance of a consultant. I also discuss a change attempt that sheds light on some of these projects' findings: the implementation of a new dispute system in a coal mine (Ury, Brett, & Goldberg, 1988). I conclude by offering proposals that link multiple cognitions, conflict, and types of change in a new understanding of processes of organizational change, an understanding important for both scholars and practitioners of change.

ORGANIZATIONAL CHANGE AND DEVELOPMENT IN THE EARLY 1970S

In 1969 Addison-Wesley initiated its Organization Development series. These popular books helped define both OD and organizational change.

While many of the series' books defined organization development, Beckhard's (1969, p. 9) definition has been used most often: "an effort (1) *planned*, (2) *organization-wide*, and (3) *managed* from the *top* to (4) increase *organization effectiveness* and *health* through (5) *planned interventions* in the organization's 'processes,' using *behavioral science* knowledge" (italics in original). This definition identified OD as a comparatively conservative change strategy; others were more revolutionary in purpose and/or focused on change from the bottom up rather than from the top down (e.g., Hornstein, Bunker, Burke, Gindes, & Lewicki, 1971). Beckhard conceptualized OD as having a systems (rather than individual) focus, as planned rather than emergent, and as encompassing such organizational processes as decision making and conflict handling. For Beckhard, conflict handling in successful systems included ongoing clashes of ideas about tasks. His approach for resolving conflicts included having participants in an intervention air their conflicts and manage them using means such as role negotiation and third-party intervention (Schmuck, Runkel, Saturen, Martell, & Derr, 1972; Walton, 1969).

AN OD INTERVENTION IN THE 1970S

Project START (Schools That Are Renewing Themselves) was a fairly typical OD effort of the early 1970s. It was initiated in the Archdiocese of Chicago schools in 1973. Eight elementary schools and one high school were matched with a control group to determine the project's effectiveness. Several intervention activities were implemented during the project, and questionnaires and interviews assessed its effectiveness between 1973 and 1975. The intervention was initiated because new programs being implemented in the school system often failed to diffuse due to interpersonal friction, lack of planning skill, or some other "people problem" (Keys, Martell, Peltz, Bartunek, & Szaflarski, 1975).

The intervention began with a decision retreat to orient interested schools to the project and to OD. Based on their actions during the decision retreat, the nine schools that seemed most ready for an intervention were chosen to participate. Eight members of the administration and faculty from each of these schools participated in two in-service training workshops and then, with assistance, acted as intervention teams in their schools. The first workshop covered process issues (e.g., giving feedback to other team members) and task issues (e.g., identifying major problems in the day-to-day functioning of the school). Teams practiced skills in team building, conflict management, listening, force field analysis, and needs assessment. In the second workshop each school team brought its own lists of concerns, such as confronting interpersonal friction among members or diagnosing school problems. The focus was on developing problem-solving skills to address the school's concerns.

During the 1973–1974 school year, the faculty and administration from each participating school formulated shared goals that were the basis for educational changes to be implemented the following year. In May 1974 each school presented its goals statement in a common meeting. A 2-day workshop on communication and feedback was conducted in late August 1974, and during the 1974–1975 school year the schools obtained further training and consultation on either organizational and interpersonal issues or curriculum development.

Evaluation of the intervention

The evaluation of the project focused on whether it affected organizational outcomes that were related to its goals. The first two studies (Bartunek & Keys, 1982; Keys & Bartunek, 1979) assessed whether participating schools developed agreement on their goals, whether teachers thought they had developed skills in participation and conflict utilization, and whether the comparative power of the participating teachers and principals had become more equalized. These were all expected outcomes of the intervention.

The results were favorable on most counts. Repeated measures analyses of questionnaire data indicated that participating teachers in the experimental schools agreed on goals and perceived increased participation in decision making and increased airing of conflict. Moreover, the power of the principals and teachers became more equal during the intervention, with power equalization related to amounts of participation in decision making. However, the project had no impact on teachers' perceptions of their skill in resolving intergroup conflict in the schools.

Both of these studies indicated short-term positive effects. But what of the longer term impacts of the intervention? Three years after the program began, Bartunek (1980) assessed the joint effects of the intervention and the experience of conflict during group decision making on the teachers' ratings of the value of participation in decision making. Experimental and control school teachers were asked to rate two decision-making cases, one with a high degree of conflict, the other with no conflict. They were asked to indicate how much participation they would like to have and how much participation was needed to achieve high-quality decisions and acceptance of the decisions. If the OD intervention was achieving its intended results, the presence of conflict should not affect the experimental school teachers' ratings of participation or desires to participate.

However, the results indicated an interaction between the intervention and the presence of conflict. Experimental school teachers rated participation in decision making in the no-conflict cases significantly more positively than control school teachers did. Conversely, when conflict was present, the control school teachers rated participation in decision making significantly higher. This interaction suggested that the intervention may have had contradictory effects. Increasing participation increased conflict, because the teachers became more willing to state their disparate views. But conflict decreased desire for participation.

A final study (Brown, Bartunek, & Keys, 1985) assessed whether the intervention affected the distribution of power among the teachers. The vertical distribution of power between faculty and administration had become more equal (Bartunek & Keys, 1982), but what about the horizontal distribution? Was there less disparity in power among teachers? This effect was an implicit goal of OD.

The results indicated that the disparity of power among the experimental school teachers was not affected by the intervention; it was as great as the disparity among control school teachers. In addition, comparatively powerless teachers in both sets of schools perceived teachers as a group as significantly less influential than powerful teachers did.

Several aspects of this intervention and its effects, as well as other studies being conducted at the time (e.g., Mirvis & Berg, 1977), raised questions about standard approaches to OD. In the studies reported here, two issues were raised. The first was the role of conflict: Even though the participating teachers had been trained to handle conflict, it still discouraged them from participating in decision making. The second was the varied perceptions of subgroups: The perceptions of the less powerful teachers were very different from those of the more powerful teachers.

An additional issue was neither explicitly addressed nor considered. The schools in these studies were chosen for the intervention because of their "readiness" for OD. Indeed, OD practitioners realize that OD works most effectively with people who already have an orientation consistent with its basic values (cf. Neilsen, 1984). What would have happened if readiness had not been a criteria for choice of the schools, if schools with different perspectives from the OD practitioners had been selected? Issues related to these questions underlie the investigations described next.

INTRODUCTION TO WORK
ON SECOND ORDER CHANGE

OD has developed considerably and in a number of different directions since the mid-1970s. For example, some OD practitioners have developed much more explicit links with organizational strategy (Jelinek & Litterer, 1988) and corporate restructuring (Johnson, Hoskisson, & Margulies, 1990). Others have sought to elaborate the original personal and interpersonal orientation of OD in new and creative ways (Mirvis, 1990). Although OD's range of application has expanded,

OD and other change scholars have not attended to a number of complex dynamics associated with change (e.g., Porras & Robertson, 1987). The research described next addresses some of these dynamics, focusing on multiple perspectives, conflict, and two types of change—change that reinforces already present organizational schemata and change that includes shifts in schemata.

What are schemata, and how are they important to organizational change? Literature in the cognitive sciences suggests that individuals do not experience the world as events that are meaningful in themselves. Rather, organizing frameworks—which have been variously labeled as interpretive schemes (Bartunek, 1984; Hinings & Greenwood, 1988; Ranson, Hinings, & Greenwood, 1980), frames of reference (e.g., Goffman, 1974), or, most frequently, schemata (Bartunek & Moch, 1987; Markus & Zajonc, 1985; Schneider, 1991; Weick, 1979)—guide understanding of events. Schemata are best understood as generalized cognitive structures or frameworks that people use to impose structure on and impart meaning to some particular event or domain. Schemata are data reduction devices derived from the perceiver's past experience. They guide people to attend to some aspects of their current experience and ignore others (Bartunek & Moch, 1987); they also guide subsequent behavior (Schneider, 1991).

While individuals have their own schemata, group- and organizational-level schemata represent shared meanings or frames of reference for the organization as a whole or for its subgroups. They guide organizational members' interpretations and behavior and are affected by the events that organizational members experience (e.g., Dutton & Dukerich, 1991).

Interventions and other change projects are bound to affect organizational members' shared schemata, either by *reinforcing* or *challenging* them. These are two very different types of organizational change.

Watzlawick, Weakland, and Fisch (1974) discussed these two types of change for family therapy and labeled them *first order* and *second order* change. First order change (or alpha change, cf. Golembiewski, Billingsley, & Yeager, 1976) consists of incremental modifications that make sense within an organization's already shared schemata. It is quantitatively measured by changes in mean scores on some scale. Second order change (or gamma change, cf. Golembiewski et al., 1976) refers to qualitative, discontinuous shifts in the schemata organizational members use to understand significant dimensions of their organization.[1] A second order change in participative decision making, for example, might imply that people's ideas of adequate participation would shift. Employees might have initially considered consultation as participative. Due to an organizational change, the understanding of participation might shift for

---

[1]Third order change (Moch & Bartunek, 1990) is a rarely attempted alternative to first and second order change. Briefly, third order change can be understood as "the training of organizational members to be aware of their present schemata and, therefore, more able to change these schemata as they see fit" (Bartunek & Moch, 1987, p. 486). In first or second order change, group members are not necessarily aware of their schemata, even if the schemata change. Some ways this type of change might be introduced are suggested by Moch and Bartunek (1990, chapter 7).

them. For example, they might require a stock ownership plan to feel they are participating meaningfully.[2]

Although some theorists suggest that OD should be transformational (e.g., Beer & Walton, 1987; Mirvis, 1990), and researchers have described QWL interventions as reflecting a novel "paradigm" (Mohrman & Lawler, 1985), organizational members' shared schemata and the relationship of schemata to change have not received much attention (cf. Bartunek & Louis, 1988). Discussions of change in OD (and most other) theorizing typically assume that organizational change is first order change—organizational members getting "better at" or developing "more" of some organizational characteristic. For example, participants in an intervention may participate in decision making more effectively or find their power more equalized. Most assessments of organizational change (with the exception of work inspired by Golembiewski et al., 1976—e.g., Randolph & Elloy, 1989) have assumed that the "meanings" of various organizational events (i.e., the schemata regarding them) remain relatively constant during organizational change. However, whether explicitly stated or not, many important change initiatives involve attempts to change, rather than reinforce, organizational members' schemata. In all of the studies described next, the intent of the change was to achieve such a schematic shift. And in all of these studies the dynamics associated with multiple schemata and conflict played a central role in change.

RESTRUCTURING IN A RELIGIOUS ORDER

In 1979 the U.S. leaders of an international religious order decided to merge its five U.S. provinces (geographical districts) into one national province with a new organizational structure. The new structure was designed over a three-year period, and the provinces were formally merged in 1982. While the overt change occurred in organizational structure, there were other changes occurring at the same time that made the structure change possible. The primary shifts were in members' schemata regarding the order's educational mission. In fact, discussion of both the educational mission and the order's structure had been occurring simultaneously for several years prior to the restructuring decision. To understand the form of the ultimate change, it is necessary to understand the shifts in order members' schemata regarding the order's educational mission.

From its founding early in the nineteenth century until the early 1960s, members had shared an assumption that the order's educational mission centered in its schools. This understanding, or schema, was reflected in "plans of

---

[2]The concept of second order change overlaps somewhat with punctuated equilibrium models of organizational change (Gersick, 1991; Tushman & Romanelli, 1985); both involve major qualitative shifts that are frequently accompanied by other types of organizational change. However, second order change refers to more types of change than punctuated equilibrium models do. In addition, much of the research on punctuated equilibrium models in organizations investigates occasions when such change has been known to occur (cf. Gersick, 1991, p. 31). As is evident in this chapter, much of the research on second order change addresses whether or not such changes occur.

studies" that were used as a basis of instruction in the order's schools throughout the world.

The Second Vatican Council in the mid-1960s substantially changed the Catholic Church's sense of its relationship to world events and corresponding sense of social responsibility. The Council also established much more participative structures within religious orders than had existed before, structures that allowed members to take more individual initiative than previously. One of the effects of these changes was that members' understanding of the order's educational mission was challenged, especially when some members advocated that the order be more concerned about and allow members to work directly for social justice movements rather than in the order's schools. Other members believed that the original focus should continue and that the primary emphasis should be within the order's schools.

Conflicts between these groups continued over several years. Eventually, some members began to realize that education and justice were potentially complementary. Jobs (in the order's schools or social justice work) might conflict in that members could only take one job, but underlying concepts regarding education and justice did not necessarily conflict.

During the late 1970s, a new schema regarding the educational mission began to emerge. Order members began to perceive an integral link between education and justice: Education did not have to be limited to the order's schools to "count" as part of the order's mission; it could also take place in social justice work. Moreover, members in social justice work could take an educational and developmental approach. This change represented a qualitative shift in understanding, a second order change that seemed unifying for many order members. The decision to unify the U.S. provinces by merging them followed the formalization of this new understanding.

This change process shared some characteristics with dialectical processes. There had been an original thesis, a taken-for-granted shared schema that the order's educational mission resided within its schools. The antithesis was a focus on social justice work outside the schools, a focus that was originally seen as incompatible with work in the original schema. The conflict between proponents of these two schemata led to a somewhat paradoxical outcome in that, on one level at least, the incompatibility between the perspectives was dissolved (cf. Murnighan & Conlon, 1991). A new, more complex shared schema evolved, one that allowed for a conceptual interplay of education and social justice.

A similar pattern took place in a very different type of setting and change intervention: an attempt to introduce a new dispute resolution system into a coal mine (Ury et al., 1988). The change project is too complex to be described fully here. However, a brief summary shows that the process of second order change that occurred in the order may generalize to other situations.

In 1980, conflict between union and management in a coal mine in Eastern Kentucky had reached monumental proportions. This caused considerable anxiety on the part of national management and union officials, who asked three consultants, Ury, Brett, and Goldberg, to assist in dealing with the conflict.

In their diagnosis of existing conditions at the mine, the consultants learned that the miners' understandings of potentially satisfactory options (schemata) for resolving grievances were very constrained: They felt that the only way they could get what they wanted was to strike (thesis). As a consequence, strikes were frequent. To deal with this problem, the consultants introduced a new schema. They designed and introduced a system that allowed and encouraged disputing parties to talk about disagreements rather than striking (antithesis). This new dispute system involved a number of elements, including structural procedures for the use of consultation and negotiation at early stages of a conflict and training in skills for using these new procedures. Ury and his colleagues introduced the new system through negotiation processes in which they worked out drafts of the new procedure with union and plant officials until the procedure was satisfactory to all parties. In addition, Ury was present at the plant throughout the new system's implementation to coach and train people in its use. Ury and his colleagues expected that the new procedure would become a formal amendment to the union contract in the plant.

At the last moment, their formal plan was aborted; the miners voted against incorporating it as an amendment to the contract. Nevertheless, largely because they had had a say in its design, plant and local union officials implemented the new system informally, even without the contract. Once the plan was put into effect, many fewer strikes occurred at the mine, especially strikes over minor issues.

The changes that occurred in the order and the coal mine contribute to an initial process model of the underlying dimensions of second order change. This model is outlined in Figure 1.

A process model of second order change

The model starts with an assumption that second order change is very difficult to achieve: Both individual and shared schemata, once established, tend to endure (e.g., Gersick & Hackman, 1990; Ury et al., 1988). Starbuck (1982, 1983), for example, suggests that shared organizational schemata often remain long after they have outlived their usefulness.

However, some conditions can initiate schematic change, including poor organizational performance, unsuccessful management practices, shifts in power, or, most likely, major environmental changes that make past practice infeasible (Greiner, 1972; Miller & Friesen, 1984). For the change process to begin, these conditions must lead to a sense of crisis. Otherwise, there will not be sufficient impetus to begin change (e.g., Bartunek, 1984, 1988; Ury et al., 1988).

A sense of crisis and the perceived inadequacy of a particular shared schema, however strong, are insufficient for achieving change. For the process to move forward, some organizational members or involved outsiders must develop alternative, conflicting, frameworks or schemata, just as order members developed a social justice approach to challenge the traditional emphasis on schools, and Ury et al. developed a qualitatively different dispute resolution system. These alternatives must be presented strongly and clearly to have an im-

FIGURE 1   A Preliminary Model of the Second Order Change Process

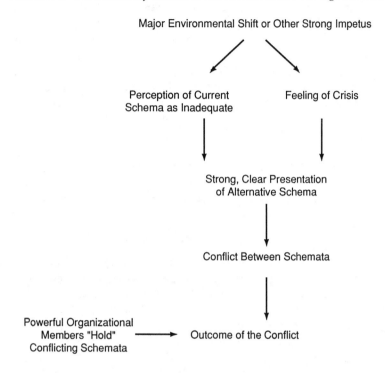

pact, since people who are accustomed to one particular schema often have great difficulty adopting or even understanding a new one. Rather than immediately accepting a new perspective, even when there are problems with an old one, people often try to fit information that seems ambiguous to them into their preexisting schemata to preserve their existing cognitive structures (e.g., Griffin, Dunning, & Ross, 1990; Kahn & Kramer, 1990; Schneider, 1991; Taylor & Brown, 1988). Unless a new approach is forcefully and coherently presented, it will have little chance of making an impact.

When an alternative schema surfaces, the change process typically centers around the interaction of old and new schemata. The conflict may take a variety of forms. Powerful proponents of a new schema may simply impose their definition (e.g., Poole, Gioia, & Gray, 1989). In contrast, a more creative, paradoxical outcome (cf. Smith & Berg, 1987; Murnighan & Conlon, 1991; Quinn & Cameron, 1988) assumes the simultaneous validity of the conflicting schemata and allows a more complex schema to evolve from them. This type of outcome is analogous to creative outcomes in a variety of fields that assume the simultaneous validity of apparently incompatible elements. In music, for example, such an outcome would be illustrated by a musical score that includes simultaneous movement and rest in the chords (Rothenberg, 1979).

The creation of a shared, more complex schema requires that at least some powerful organizational members or consultants "hold" both sides of the conflict and both schemata, excluding neither. This role combines the characteristics of a mediator with those of a committed disputant (Jones, 1988) and requires fostering both integration and differentiation of the different groups' schemata. Ury et al. (1988, p. 119) described this role well when they said of their activities in the coal mine that "we were not only mediators, but also designers and advocates of a particular procedure. This required a balancing act among disparate roles" (i.e., an ability to be both advocates for a specific dispute resolution system and facilitators who could allow the mine personnel to retain or revise their own schemata).

Changes accompanying shifts in schemata

Schematic shifts do not occur in a cognitive vacuum: They are accompanied by strong feelings and by actions that enact them (cf. Bartunek, 1988; Gersick, 1991). As noted earlier, the beginning of change is typically accompanied by a sense of crisis, which is accompanied by tension, anger, and a strong sense of loss. If the original schema does not seem adequate and a new one is not apparent, feelings of anxiety or hopelessness may surface. The proposal of a new schema is accompanied by a different kind of anxiety, one concerned about whether the new schema will work. Conflict and tension are usually directed toward people with different perspectives. If a new shared schema is finally achieved, those who concur with it typically experience a sense of clarity and satisfaction.

Ranson et al. (1980) noted that schemata are often manifested in such activities as organizational resource allocation, and that such activities reinforce the schemata they reflect (also see Gersick & Hackman, 1990, and Giddens, 1979). Thus, when schemata are changing, the changes are reflected in organizational activities that make further change possible. The schema shift within the religious order illustrated this relationship between schematic change and organizational action. The Second Vatican Council mandated an increase in participation in decision making. Increased participation opened the way for discussions of a new orientation toward social justice, which helped foster the change in definition of the order's educational mission (Bartunek, 1984). When there is satisfaction with rather than attempts to change a shared perspective, activities tend to reinforce the present understanding rather than challenge it (e.g., Tushman, Newman, & Romanelli, 1986).

The primary focus thus far has been on a shift in schemata that involved conflict between two groups, one of which emerged during the course of change (e.g., those oriented toward social justice in the religious order, the consultants designing the new dispute system in the coal mine). The next study explored the impact of a more complicated interaction, where long-established groups with different schemata were confronted with an intervention that implied a new shared schema for everyone.

QWL PROGRAM

This study assessed a Quality of Work Life intervention at a medium-sized food processing plant, part of a *Fortune* 500 company called "FoodCom" (Bartunek & Moch, 1987, 1991; Moch & Bartunek, 1990). In this study schemata were considered not simply as content about some topic (e.g., focus on social justice), but also as "causal maps" (cf., Weick & Bougon, 1986). Schemata often imply causal relationships among variables, and this complicates the ways that schemata held by different groups can differ. Schemata may (1) involve different variables (e.g., they may treat different types of events as important or salient); (2) attach different values to the same variables (e.g., they may place different values on the same concept); (3) have different meanings attached to the same variables (e.g., they may include conflicting definitions of a particular term); and (4) specify different relationships among variables (e.g., in one schema, cause x may be positively related to outcome y, while in another schema, x and y are unrelated; Bartunek & Moch, 1989). The overall combination of schematic variables and their linkages is reflected in what Anderson and Godfrey (1987) called a "script imagination," an imagined sequence of events leading to some particular outcome that is highly salient to those who hold it. In the QWL intervention we can see the impact of different script imaginations on attempted second order change processes.

Description of the intervention

QWL interventions are designed to improve both productivity and the quality of working life (Cammann, Lawler, Ledford, & Seashore, 1984; Drexler & Lawler, 1977). The interventions include well-articulated causal maps or scripts to achieve these goals: By fostering improved communication and mutual problem solving, QWL interventions are expected to reconcile corporate productivity needs with employees' needs for challenging and satisfying work (e.g., Mohrman & Lawler, 1985). In standard designs (Nadler, 1978), several union members and management representatives form a joint labor–management committee (LMC) that works cooperatively to determine ways of improving productivity and the quality of working life. The committee is expected to address shared labor–management interests beyond the scope of the bargaining contract, assuming that management and labor in a plant have a number of shared interests. The LMC is typically assisted by outside consultants it has chosen. Top-level corporate and union officials act as overseers of the program, and outside evaluators assess it.

The schematic conflict at FoodCom was that the concepts "productivity" and "a high quality of working life" had different value and different meanings to various groups. The different groups also had different understandings of how to achieve these ends. A summary of important aspects of the schemata held by five of the major groups in the intervention, the consultants, top-level corporate management, plant management, line employees, and machinists is presented in Table 1 and summarized next (Moch & Bartunek, 1990).

Five schemata present during the QWL intervention

The consultants worked from a cooperative schema: They placed a high value on achieving both a high quality of working life (improved relationships among plant personnel marked by communication, trust, and respect) and increased productivity. They felt that these aims could be achieved if they facilitated cooperation among the LMC members, who would share joint responsibility for decision making (Porras & Hoffer, 1986). They also felt fairly confident that the intervention would have positive effects.

The firm's corporate managers, who were responsible for all the plants around the country, worked from a control schema. Their most important aim was increased productivity; a higher quality of working life was valuable only if it helped increase employees' productivity. Corporate management agreed with the consultants that labor–management cooperation through the LMC could achieve increased productivity, but they were concerned that the LMC might take actions that would inadvertently have an adverse impact on productivity. Consequently, they took several actions during the intervention designed to

TABLE 1 Chart Summarizing the Schemata of the Different Groups at FoodCom

GROUPS	LABEL FOR SCHEMA	VALUED OUTCOME(S)	EXPRESSED CONCERNS	MEANS TO ACHIEVE DESIRED ENDS
Consultants	Cooperation	Productivity and QWL (QWL = mutual respect and communication)	None	LMC cooperation (cooperation = shared responsibility for decisions)
Corporate management	Control	Productivity	Productivity might decrease	LMC cooperation and corporate management control
Local management	Paternalism	Productivity and QWL	Decreased productivity and decreased QWL	LMC cooperation (cooperation = employees request, management decides)
Line employees	Dependence	QWL (QWL = acquisition of amenities)	None	LMC cooperation (cooperation = employees make requests, management grants requests)
Machinists	Competition	Maintain influence and pay differential	Influence and pay differential might decrease	Refuse to participate in the intervention

maintain control and to ensure that the committee's actions would achieve higher productivity.

Local plant management and union officials agreed that increased productivity and a high quality of work life were desirable. They worked from a paternalistic schema: They felt that a high quality of working life was achieved by treating the plant as a family in which management took a parental concern for employees. They agreed that the LMC was likely to increase productivity and the quality of working life. But, like top corporate management, they were concerned that the work of the committee might raise the visibility of longstanding problems in the plant, and they knew that if productivity did not increase there would be declining corporate support for the program regardless of its impacts on the quality of working life.

Line employees operated out of a dependence schema, a term that illustrates their dependent relationship on plant management. They were primarily concerned with improving the quality of their working life; productivity remained a managerial responsibility. They seemed to believe that productivity increases would result from a high quality of working life. They viewed a high quality of working life primarily as an acquisition of amenities (such as improved food and a non-smoking area in the cafeteria, synchronized clocks, and improvements in the parking lot). Like local plant management, but unlike the consultants, line employees understood cooperation to mean that employees would make requests to top management. Unlike local plant management, however, they felt that cooperation also implied that top management should grant their requests.

The machinists belonged to a different union than the line employees. They took pride in the differential between their wages and those of the line employees as well as their greater influence in the plant. The machinists worked from a competitive schema. They saw the LMC as likely to take actions that would increase productivity by increasing the quality of working life of the line employees. Because these scenarios posed a threat to the machinists' power, they refused to participate in the QWL program. Since the machinists had to implement many of the amenities projects desired by the line employees, they were in a position to interfere with the intervention by being slow to implement the amenities projects.

Many of the schematic differences between groups had been present in the plant long before the QWL intervention. However, the consultants' attempt to facilitate cooperation between the different groups made them much more salient.

The consequences of interaction among the groups holding multiple schemata

For both management and line employees, cooperation meant that employees should make requests (Table 1). Employee requests, especially for amenities, substantially increased during the intervention, as did employee expectations that these requests would be granted. This situation led to a very large number of requests to management and a complicated pattern of implementation, since the machinists were needed to do most of the work for the amenities. Management tried to solve the problem by asking the LMC members to do much of the preliminary work for their requests, such as learning city specifications about widening the parking lot. The employees saw this move as a violation of the co-operative spirit of the intervention because management was not granting their requests. They began to tally management's frequent failures as political ammunition to use against plant management during the corporate oversight group's first visit to the plant.

When the corporate oversight group visited the plant, they agreed that it was local management's responsibility to respond to the initiatives of the LMC, and they arranged for consultants to help with several specific improvements such as renovating the parking lot. In doing so, the corporate oversight group and the LMC isolated the plant manager as a central figure in the problems occurring during the intervention; they implicitly ignored the different schemata among the various groups at the plant.

The oversight group expected that their assistance to the LMC would result in greater productivity, not just more amenities or higher employee satisfaction. During the following year, however, the plant experienced decreases in productivity. As a result, corporate management's support declined considerably, and they became willing to support only the projects that they expected to have a positive impact on productivity. Many line employees saw these projects as a management concern that was outside the scope of an improved quality of working life project, and so did not want to support them. In fact, over 300 (out of approximately 800) employees signed a petition to the oversight group requesting that the program be terminated. Corporate management agreed that the program had not improved productivity. Rather than terminate it, however, they quietly took steps to absorb it as a managerial function.

Implications of the intervention
for the model of change

The outcomes of this intervention suggest some additions to the model of second order change shown in Figure 1. Multiple schemata due to a differentiation of positions (Lawrence & Lorsch, 1967) are likely to generate ongoing conflict that may be more or less public, but will certainly be present beneath the surface. Indeed, one of the major functions of bureaucratic structures (such as the one at FoodCom) is to contain conflict among different groups in different functional areas (Mintzberg, 1979).

What are the underlying issues in this type of conflict, especially as it relates to attempted organizational change? As noted in Table 1, each of the different groups at the plant was operating out of its own schema regarding the QWL intervention, its own understanding of the important variables involved in change, and its own perception of the likely sequence of events once LMC cooperation was initiated. However, the participants were unaware that the different groups saw the situation so differently. Instead, each group overestimated the commonness of its own beliefs (i.e., the extent to which others saw things the same way they did; Griffin & Ross, 1991). Thus, their actions increased the underlying conflict. The consultants, for example, overestimated the groups' views of cooperation in the LMC as consistent with joint responsibility for decision making, and neither plant management nor the line employees realized they had different understandings of decision making. None of the groups really appreciated the different perspectives of the other groups.

A second issue is also relevant. As noted in Table 1, the consultants were initially optimistic about the success of the intervention. Such optimism is typical of people introducing radically different perspectives into an organizational or other type of setting (e.g., Dunning, Griffin, Milojkovic, & Ross, 1990; Griffin & Ross, 1991; Griffin et al., 1990). Change agents (and people in general) frequently overestimate similarities between their own and other groups' schemata and thus are unprepared for conflict. This issue is particularly problematic for change projects such as QWL interventions that attempt to foster cooperative relationships in settings previously marked by competition. When multiple groups are present, a cooperative, facilitative intervention that assumes shared interests and schemata is more likely to generate competitive conflict than foster dialectical means of dealing with differences. When such conflict occurs, a comparatively powerful perspective, such as one held by corporate management, is likely to dominate. A negotiation approach such as that used by Ury et al. (1988) in the coal mine, or any type of approach that consciously builds on different perspectives, is more likely to succeed.

INCREASING COORDINATION IN A SCHOOL

In the studies of the religious order and FoodCom, conflict had been integral to the course of change (or lack of change), even though the relationship between conflict and change had not been the central focus of the research. In a third study of the implementation of a new position in a school (Bartunek & Reid, 1992), the relationship between conflict and attempted second order change was a central focus. This study explored (1) how organizational members understood conflicts that involved schematic differences during an attempted second order change, (2) how they handled these conflicts, and (3) how conflict handling affected the course of change.

The study hypothesized that organizational members would be unlikely to recognize differences in schemata. Instead, they would be likely to see schematic differences as personality conflicts. At FoodCom, for example, employees had blamed the plant manager for the problems they encountered. This fundamental attributional bias (Ross, 1977) or lay dispositionism (Griffin & Ross, 1991) occurs in many organzational settings. It is particularly likely when there are surprising effects (especially negative ones) associated with change.

How are schematic conflicts likely to be handled? I noted earlier that organizational schemata tend to be expressed in actions that reinforce them (e.g., Ranson et al., 1980). Black (1990) has recently suggested that patterns of conflict handling are likely to be isomorphic with an organization's schema. For example, in an organization characterized by autonomy, a normal conflict-handling pattern is likely to be avoidance of conflict. This pattern, which discourages confronting differences directly, maintains the separateness of the different organizational parts.

If conflict-handling patterns reflect schemata, then the ways conflict is handled during an organizational change attempt have important implications for second order change. Based on the previous theorizing, any conflict-handling process (or other behavioral pattern) is likely to affect change in organizational schemata, either challenging or reinforcing a particular schema. If a second order change process is going to succeed, some organizational members must not only propose alternative schemata (Figure 1) but initiate new ways of handling conflict that are consistent with the new schema. For example, it was very important at the coal mine that Ury coached and trained participants in new forms of dispute resolution rather than simply advocating them (Ury et al., 1988). Previous conflict-handling patterns that reinforce the original schema should lead that schema to become more entrenched, rather than open to change.

The next study examined an attempted second order change in a private school in which the principal wanted to foster an atmosphere of coordination among groups in a system with a strong tradition of autonomy. She created a new position, Academic Director, hoping that it would facilitate collaboration among academic units. This new position replaced a curriculum coordinator role and gave its incumbent considerably more power and discretion than the previous curriculum coordinators had had. The questions raised in the study concerned how conflict would affect the change process.

Patterns prior to the implementation of the new position

Departmental autonomy had been a strong shared schema at the school for years and had consistently led to significant problems in coordinating the curriculum. For example, it was not unusual for students to have overlapping homework assignments and tests because the departments would not coordinate their assignments with each other.

Interviews with the previous curriculum coordinators at the school indicated that there were consistent patterns for dealing with conflict regarding coordination. The most prominent was passive resistance; school personnel often simply operated as they pleased and ignored the curriculum coordinators' requests. One curriculum coordinator said response to her coordination attempts was like "shadow boxing . . . never like active resistance." Curriculum coordinators had no sense of decision-making power and felt like failures in their positions.

The academic director position

The new academic director's job description was much stronger than previous job descriptions for curriculum coordinators. Moreover, the person appointed to the position was a good friend of the principal, had worked at the school as a teacher and administrator for several years and, more than the other administrators, valued collaboration among the different units. Consequently, the principal was optimistic that she would be more effective in achieving coordination than the curriculum coordinators.

During her first year in the new position, the academic director attempted several means of coordinating the curriculum. But, as had happened with the curriculum coordinators, her influence attempts led to passive (and sometimes active) resistance. She was often excluded from departmental and administrative decisions that she believed were included in her job description. In addition, she and the principal experienced ongoing conflict and a breakdown in their friendship. During the course of the year, the academic director came to perceive a lack of support from the principal for the initiatives she was taking, and the principal came to perceive the academic director as developing excessive demands for personal attention. The principal commented at one point that even though the academic director had been at the school for more than 10 years, school personnel had misjudged her personality. In response to feeling that the principal was not supporting her, the academic director began to solicit support against the principal, escalating the conflict between them. The conflict came to a head during an accrediting evaluation near the end of the year, when the evaluating team spent much of its time examining the academic director role and eventually recommended that the principal clarify the role.

The events of the year had several effects. The academic director began to realize that the responses to coordination attempts had not changed and began to sense how little authority she had. She started referring to herself as "borderline stupid" and eventually gave up attempts to coordinate. At the end of the year, several administration members agreed that nothing had changed.

Implications of the study for the model of change

In this study, as in the QWL study, an attempted change project did not succeed. Two dimensions of the relationship between conflict and change stood out. First, conflicts that resulted from differences in schemata were perceived by school personnel to be due to personalities. As in other cases (Griffin & Ross, 1991; Griffin et al., 1990), it is likely that personality attribution occurred because the change process was not proceeding as expected, and participants lacked the ability to take each others' perspectives. This type of personality attribution is frequent in organizational settings during times of conflict (e.g., Kolb, 1987; Ury et al., 1988).

A second dimension that emerged was the conflict-handling pattern. The original pattern for conflict handling, the strong "passive resistance" script, continued to be enacted despite the change in role. No attempts were made to change it, probably because it was not recognized. This pattern expressed and reinforced the schema regarding autonomy. In particular, it led to avoidance of overt conflict between autonomy and coordination. As a result of this pattern and the personality attributions, the change objectives were not achieved. Rather, the original pattern was reinforced.

The studies at FoodCom and at the school suggest several ways the original model of change presented in Figure 1 might be elaborated. Prior to elaborating this model, however, it is important to raise two other issues that are the subjects of contemporary discussion and have implications for this chapter—dialectical processes and the other with the role of continuity in change.

SOME CONTEMPORARY ISSUES REGARDING ORGANIZATIONAL CHANGE

The problematic role of dialectical processes

Figure 1 indicates that a primary mechanism for schema change is conflict that may be expressed in multiple ways—through domination of one perspective by another, for example, or through more equal, dialectical processes in which different subgroups can inform each other. I have suggested that the dialectical approach is the one most likely to achieve creative new shared schemata.

Some recent authors have challenged the value of a dialectic-based model, questioning whether dialectical processes (1) truly enable participants to have equal power, (2) allow adequately for the experience of ambiguity, and (3) narrow the type of outcome possible in a change process. With regard to the first point, Calás and Smircich (1992) and Martin (1992) have both noted that when separate categories (e.g., race or gender or espoused perspective) are created in organizations or elsewhere, there is a strong tendency in practice to create a hierarchy wherein one category (male rather than female, one schema rather than another) is favored. This power disparity may interfere with creative use of differing perspectives; it is likely to foster the domination of one perspective by another. Thus, these authors question whether processes that simultaneously value contradictory perspectives are likely in organizations.

This point is important. Power differentiation is likely to occur whenever more than one group exists—during organizational change, and at other times. Thus, powerful organizational members or consultants who value and are able to hold multiple perspectives are critical for the success of the approach to second order change described here. They can balance the power between the different perspectives and help move the interaction toward a creative outcome. However, as Ury et al. (1988) noted, that role is likely to be very difficult. Many people who believe they are not favoring one side more than another may actually be doing so.

The second issue is whether all groups in an organization work from a schema. Perhaps some groups do not have any particular coherent schema (Martin, 1992; Martin & Meyerson, 1988), no particular shared perspective on the issue that is the subject of change. How would this affect the second order change process? If this is the case, either individual schemata will take the place of group schemata during conflict or organizational members who lack a strong perspective on an issue may remain tangential to the conflict. Conflict and change may only involve those who have a stake in the outcome. It might be comparatively easy for change agents who hold strongly to a particular schema to introduce it in a group without a strong shared schemata; it should encounter much less coordinated opposition (Bartunek, 1988).

A third issue concerns the outcomes of dialectical processes. While the thesis–antithesis process may awaken organizational members to new perspectives and schemata, a synthesis stifles this expanded awareness, imposing a comparatively narrow understanding that will become entrenched and will need to be challenged again.

In this chapter, I have suggested that the type of synthesis developed as a result of second order change should not engender a narrow schema, equivalent in scope to the original one, but a more cognitively complex understanding, one that builds on prior schemata. This type of outcome may not be a synthesis in the way the term is often understood, though it reflects a synthesis in terms of prior understandings. It might arise through explicit negotiation processes over a brief period of time (Ury et al., 1988) or through an interplay of schemata and their behavioral expressions over a multiyear period (Bartunek, 1984).

Relationship between continuity and change

Some authors assume clear disjunctures between organizational change and stability. They argue that organizations are likely either to maintain the status quo with some incremental adjustments or undergo rapid transformational change that touches virtually all dimensions of their existence (e.g., Tushman et al., 1986). The implication is that second order change and continuity are almost mutually exclusive.

However, it seems more likely that continuity and change coexist and are interdependent. For example, Walsh and Ungson (1991) have proposed that organizations whose members remember the organization's history are more likely to make effective decisions about new organizational challenges than organizations whose members have no historical perspective. In their analysis of a major transformation at Cadbury Limited, Child and Smith (1987) and Smith, Child, and Rowlinson (1990) emphasized that major change is often interwoven with continuity. The transformational processes there included several major discontinuities with previous practices in new product marketing, productivity strategies, and relationships with employees. However, throughout the multiyear transformation, the traditional priority given to mechanization continued, as did some dimensions of the company's ideology of "Cadburyism." Child and Smith and Smith et al. argued that this continuity was necessary for the transformation to occur, and that continuity and change cannot be temporally disconnected.

Gergen (1990, p. 23) has recently proposed a way of thinking of the integral links between continuity and change. She notes that the usual sequence in auto-biographies is linear progression, often of achievements. However, this pattern is less likely to be followed in women's autobiographies, where "various plot lines are juxtaposed and interconnected. Progressive, regressive, and stability narratives are interrelated."

Organizations also have multiple juxtaposed plot lines. They involve mul-tiple products or services and multiple relationships among individual members and groups. Major change in one of these is likely to affect the others, but not entirely. Moreover, continuity in one dimension is likely to create an important context for the experience of change in others. Just as a woman with a stable home life might change her career activities, so too might an organization that employs a relatively stable technology diversify into new ventures. Indeed, con-tinuity along some dimensions may be crucial for second order change in others.

EXPANDED PROPOSALS REGARDING
SECOND ORDER CHANGE

The work reported in this chapter suggests that second order change processes involve a number of complex elements extending beyond the issues identified in Figure 1. The work reported here can be formulated as specific proposals about second order change processes and factors that affect their success. These pro-posals are outlined and discussed here.

*   Second order change is typically initiated in response to major environmental shifts or equivalent events that lead powerful organizational members to perceive estab-lished schemata as inadequate.
*   An experience of crisis is necessary for the process to begin; otherwise there will not be sufficient impetus to change. Likely feelings after the initiation of change include tension, anger, and a sense of loss.

Second order change does not begin easily. Some strong, potentially trau-matic event or series of events within the organization, or—more likely—in its environment, are necessary for powerful organizational members to question their established schemata. The event must be strong enough to cause a sense of crisis in the organization. Otherwise organizational members are unlikely to feel a strong enough impetus to develop alternative schemata. One of the problems at FoodCom, for example, was the lack of a sense of urgency about implement-ing the QWL program.

*   Some organizational members develop alternative (conflicting) schemata with causal maps that include expectations of the success of the new schema.

For the process to move beyond initial perceptions and feelings, powerful organizational members or outsiders (such as consultants) need to develop a new and different schema, which will usually include a causal map, an image of the sequence of events for successful schema enactment. Change agents who develop this alternative perspective may, at least initially, be overly optimistic about the success of its implementation; they may not understand how differently others view events or how conflict may result.

*   Alternative schemata need to be presented strongly and clearly to foster change. They also need to be enacted within new conflict-handling patterns.

The alternative schema needs to be introduced clearly and forcefully into the organization. Otherwise, other organizational members may assimilate the new information into their existing schemata; they will not experience the schema as something new.

The clarity of the presentation requires both articulation of the new schema and the development of new ways of acting, especially new conflict-handling patterns. Otherwise organizational members will be familiar only with patterns that reinforce the original schema, and will act in ways that make it difficult to implement something new. At the school, for instance, there were already strong behavioral scripts associated with the original schema, and no conflict-handling pattern developed that expressed the new schema in a way that was equally powerful. At the coal mine, however, training in new dispute patterns helped to foster the change process.

*   The process of change typically centers around the conflict of old and new schemata.
*   Several outcomes of this conflict may occur, including
    —imposition of the new schema
    —reversion to the original schema
    —creation of a different schema that extends beyond previous ones.
*   For the conflict to be maximally productive, some powerful organizational member(s) or consultants must hold both sides of the conflict.

New, alternative schemata are unlikely to be accepted easily, no matter how well developed they are. Unless those who develop the schema are extraordinarily powerful (e.g., Poole et al., 1989), proposals of new schemata are likely to lead to conflict among proponents of different schemata—either among original and emergent ones (as in the religious order) or among existing multiple schemata (as at FoodCom). It is standard practice during a change process for individual groups to attempt to impose their schemata on other groups. Another possible process is a dialectical interaction between holders of the different schemata, in which the simultaneous validity of multiple schemata is assumed. Dialectical interaction may involve an explicit negotiation approach such as that used by Ury et al. (1988) or, as in the case of the religious order, a long-term conflict in which people with different schemata interacted in a way that deepened understanding and led to a change in everyone's understanding of the order's educational mission. In both cases, the eventual resolution of the conflict was a more complex, creative understanding than had been present before. The outcomes occurred in part because powerful people were able to hold the different schemata, to respect both their own and others' understandings.

* Conflicts regarding schemata are typically experienced as personality conflicts rather than conflicts between schemata.

When schemata conflict, groups are unlikely to see the conflict as one of different perspectives; they are unlikely to have an in-depth sense of the groups' differing schemata. Instead, they are likely to attribute conflict to personalities. The stronger this perception, the more difficult it should be for them to appreciate the other party's perspective, making an outcome of conflict that reconciles perspectives more difficult.

* Continuity in some organizational dimensions is likely to help major change occur in others.

Major transitions are likely to be intertwined with continuity. In the school study, for example, the attempted change toward coordination occurred in the context of relative stability in other dimensions of schooling. At FoodCom, attempts to create major shifts in relationships occurred amidst relative stability in production. Stability in some organizational dimensions makes major shifts in others more likely.

These proposals are based on an examination of relatively few cases, although each case represented a long-term change attempt. The generalizability of these proposals needs to be explored in a much broader array of changes and attempted changes. As the Ury et al. (1988) study makes clear, it is not necessary that these situations be defined from the outset as organizational change attempts. Rather, the situations may focus on the content of the change—such as the introduction of a new dispute system. Such foci may illustrate particular alternative schemata and thus foster second order change more easily than change attempts that are primarily facilitative in nature, implicitly assuming shared understandings.

CONCLUSION: SOME IMPLICATIONS FOR STUDIES OF ORGANIZATIONAL CHANGE AND DEVELOPMENT

This chapter has focused on some of the dynamics that result when organizational members or consultants attempt a second order change. It stresses the importance of members' multiple cognitions and conflict as typical components of this type of change.

The types of issues explored here differ from theorizing about OD. Although the notion has been advanced that QWL practitioners have their own paradigm (Mohrman & Lawler, 1985), and some potential participants are more or less "ready" for OD (Neilsen, 1984), discussion rarely addresses the dynamics of change agents who hold a schema that differs from participants'. It is important, therefore, for change agents to take these dynamics into account. In particular, consultants need to realize that they frequently represent only one perspective or schema among many within an organizational setting. Moreover, their perspective likely differs from others over whom they may have little formal power. Their most helpful contribution may be to help organizational members develop new, more complex schemata that build on rather than negate their differences (Smith & Berg, 1987). When multiple schemata are present, successful consultation can only result when consultants initiate second order change processes rather than facilitate participants' achievement of first order change.

Some of the early interventions for resolving conflict developed by OD practitioners such as Beckhard's (1969) confrontation meeting and Blake, Mouton, and Sloma's (1965) imaging exercise constitute ways of exploring different perceptions held by organizational groups. However, the conceptual bases of these exercises and ways they might be expanded to encompass different schemata have never been very fully developed. The research reported in this chapter suggests the value of developing this conceptual understanding and developing ways of dealing with multiple cognitions in more depth.

While this chapter has some specific implications for planned change attempts, such as those of OD practitioners, it also has more general implications for studies of organizational change. Many significant organization changes, especially those that fall under the rubric of organizational transformation, involve second order shifts. While attention has been paid to the general nature of these types of change, such as the number of organizational aspects affected by them, their more micro processes have received little attention. The material described in this chapter suggests some of the crucial dynamics of this type of change and a way of approaching them. The ideas discussed here need to be explored in more depth and in other organizational change projects, and other important dynamics and processes of second order change should also be surfaced. This type of work has considerable potential for expanding our knowledge of the experiences of, and types of events, necessary for major organizational change.

REFERENCES

ANDERSON, C. A., & GODFREY, S. S. (1987). Thoughts about actions: The effects of specification and availability of imagined behavioral scripts on expectations about oneself and others. *Social Cognition, 5*, 238–258.

BARTUNEK, J. M. (1980). Participation training, agreement, and teacher participation in decision-making. *Group and Organization Studies, 5*, 491–504.

BARTUNEK, J. M. (1984). Changing interpretive schemes and organizational restructuring: The example of a religious order. *Administrative Science Quarterly, 29*, 355–372.

BARTUNEK, J. M. (1988). The dynamics of personal and organizational reframing. In R. E. Quinn & K. S. Cameron (Eds.), *Paradox and transformation: Towards a theory of change in organization and management* (pp. 137–162). Cambridge, MA: Ballinger.

BARTUNEK, J. M., & KEYS, C. B. (1982). Power equalization in schools through organization development. *Journal of Applied Behavioral Science, 18*, 171–183.

BARTUNEK, J. M., & LOUIS, M. R. (1988). The interplay of organization development and organizational transformation. In R. Woodman & W. Pasmore (Eds.), *Research in organizational change and development* (Vol. 2, pp. 97–134). Greenwich, CT: JAI Press.

BARTUNEK, J. M., & MOCH, M. K. (1987). First order, second order, and third order change and organization development interventions: A cognitive approach. *Journal of Applied Behavioral Science, 23*, 483–500.

BARTUNEK, J. M., & MOCH, M. K. (1989, August). *Organizational schemata which specify and affect intergroup relationships within organizations.* Paper presented at the Working Conference on Managerial Thought and Cognition, Washington DC.

BARTUNEK, J. M., & MOCH, M. K. (1991). Multiple constituencies and the quality of working life intervention at FoodCom. In P. J. Frost, L. F. Moore, M. R. Louis, C. C. Lundberg, & J. Martin (Eds.), *Reframing organizational culture* (pp. 104–114). Newbury Park: Sage.

BARTUNEK, J. M., & REID, R. D. (1992). The role of conflict in a second order change attempt. In D. M. Kolb & J. M. Bartunek (Eds.), *Hidden conflict in organizations: Uncovering behind-the-scenes disputes* (pp. 116–142). Newbury Park: Sage.

BECKHARD, R. (1969). *Organization development: Strategies and models.* Reading, MA: Addison-Wesley.

BEER, M., & WALTON, R. (1987). Organization change and development. *Annual Review of Psychology, 38,* 339–367.

BLACK, D. (1990). The elementary forms of conflict management. In Arizona School of Justice Studies, Arizona State University (Eds.), *New directions in the study of justice, law, and social control* (pp. 43–69). New York: Plenum Press.

BLAKE, R. R., MOUTON, J. S., & SLOMA, R. L. (1965). The union-management intergroup laboratory: Strategy for resolving intergroup conflict. *Journal of Applied Behavioral Science, 1,* 25–57.

BRIEF, A. P., & DUKERICH, J. M. (1991). Theory in organizational behavior: Can it be useful? In L. L. Cummings & B. M. Staw (Eds.), *Research in organizational behavior* (Vol. 13, pp. 327–352). Greenwich, CT: JAI Press.

BROWN, S. J., BARTUNEK, J. M., & KEYS, C. B. (1985). Teachers' powerlessness: Peer assessments and own perceptions. *Planning and Changing, 16,* 22–34.

CALÁS, M. B., & SMIRCICH, L. (1992). Re-writing gender into organizational theorizing: Directions from feminist perspectives. In M. I. Reed & M. D. Hughes (Eds.), *Rethinking organization: New directions in organizational research and analysis* (pp. 227–253). London: Sage.

CAMMANN, C., LAWLER, E. E., III, LEDFORD, G. E., & SEASHORE, S. E. (1984). *Management-labor cooperation in quality of worklife experiments: Comparative analysis of eight cases.* Ann Arbor, MI: The University of Michigan.

CHILD, J., & SMITH, C. (1987). The context and process of organizational transformation: Cadbury Limited in its sector. *Journal of Management Studies, 24,* 565–593.

DREXLER, J. A., & LAWLER, E. E. (1977). A union management cooperative project to improve the quality of work life. *Journal of Applied Behavioral Science, 13,* 373–387.

DUNNING, D., GRIFFIN, D. W., MILOJKOVIC, J. D., & ROSS, L. (1990). The overconfidence effect in social prediction. *Journal of Personality and Social Psychology, 58,* 568–581.

DUTTON, J. E., & DUKERICH, J. M. (1991). Keeping an eye on the mirror: Image and identity in organizational adaptation. *Academy of Management Journal, 34,* 517–554.

FRENCH, W. L., & BELL, C. H. (1990). *Organization development* (4th ed.). Englewood Cliffs, NJ: Prentice Hall.

GERGEN, M. (1990, December). *Baskets of reed and arrows of steel: Stories of chaos and continuity.* Presented at the Symposium on Executive and Organizational Continuity, Case Western Reserve University, Cleveland, OH.

GERSICK, C. (1991). Revolutionary change theories: A multilevel exploration of the punctuated equilibrium paradigm. *Academy of Management Review, 16,* 10–36.

GERSICK, C., & HACKMAN, J. R. (1990). Habitual routines in task-performing groups. *Organizational Behavior and Human Decision Processes, 47,* 65–97.

GIDDENS, A. (1979). *Central problems in social theory.* Berkeley, CA: University of California Press.

GOFFMAN, E. (1974). *Frame analysis.* Cambridge, MA: Harvard University Press.

GOLEMBIEWSKI, R. T., BILLINGSLEY, K., & YEAGER, S. 1976. Measuring change and persistence in human affairs: Types of change generated by OD designs. *Journal of Applied Behavioral Science, 12,* 133–157.

GREINER, L. (1972). Evolution and revolution as organizations grow. *Harvard Business Review, 50*(4), 37–46.

GRIFFIN, D. W., DUNNING, D., & ROSS, L. (1990). The role of construal processes in overconfident predictions about the self and others. *Journal of Personality and Social Psychology, 59,* 1128–1139.

GRIFFIN, D. W., & ROSS, L. (1991). Subjective construal, social inference, and human misunderstanding. In L. Berkowitz (Ed.), *Advances in experimental social psychology* (Vol. 24, pp. 319–359). New York: Academic Press.

HININGS, C. F., & GREENWOOD, R. (1988). *The dynamics of strategic change.* New York: Blackwell.

HORNSTEIN, H. A., BUNKER, B. B., BURKE, W. W., GINDES, M., & LEWICKI, R. J. (1971). *Social intervention: A behavioral science approach.* New York: Free Press.

JELINEK, M., & LITTERER, J. A. (1988). Why OD must become strategic. In R. Woodman & W. Pasmore (Eds.). *Research in organizational change and development* (Vol. 2, pp. 135–162). Greenwich, CT: JAI Press.

JOHNSON, D. B. (1967). Use of role reversal in intergroup competition. *Journal of Personality and Social Psychology, 7,* 135–141.

JOHNSON, R. A., HOSKISSON, R. E., & MARGULIES, N. (1990). Corporate restructuring: Implications for organization change and development. In R. Woodman & W. Pasmore (Eds.), *Research in organizational change and development* (Vol. 4, pp. 141–166). Greenwich, CT: JAI Press.

JONES, T. S. (1988). Phase structures in agreement and no-agreement mediation. *Communication Research, 15,* 470–495.

KAHN, R. L., & KRAMER, R. M. (1990). Untying the knot: De-escalatory processes in international conflict. In R. L. Kahn & M. N. Zald (Eds.), *Organizations and nation states: New perspectives on conflict and cooperation* (pp. 139–180). San Francisco: Jossey-Bass.

KATZ, D., & KAHN, R. L. (1966). *The social psychology of organizations.* New York: Wiley.

KEYS, C. B., & BARTUNEK, J.M. (1979). Organization development in schools: Goal agreement, process skills, and diffusion of change. *Journal of Applied Behavioral Science, 15,* 61–78.

KEYS, C. B., MARTELL, R. T., PELTZ, J., BARTUNEK, J. M., & SZAFLARSKI, T. (1975). *An evaluation of Project Start: Assessment of organization renewal.* Unpublished report, University of Illinois at Chicago Department of Psychology.

KOLB, D. M. (1987). Who are organizational third parties, and what do they do? In R. S. Lewicki, B. H. Sheppard, & M. H. Bazerman (Eds.), *Research on negotiation in organizations* (Vol. 1, pp. 207–227). Greenwich, CT: JAI Press.

LAWRENCE, P. R., & LORSCH, J. W. (1967). *Organization and environment: Managing differentiation and integration.* Boston: Division of Research, Graduate School of Business Administration, Harvard.

MARKUS, H., & ZAJONC, R. B. (1985). A cognitive perspective in social psychology. In G. Lindzey & E. Aronson (Eds.), *The handbook of social psychology* (3rd ed., Vol. 1, pp. 137–230). New York: Random House.

MARTIN, J. (1992). *Cultures in organizations: Three perspectives.* New York: Oxford University Press.

MARTIN, J., & MEYERSON, D. (1988). Organizational cultures and the denial, channeling, and acknowledgment of ambiguity. In L. R. Pondy, R. J. Boland, & H. Thomas (Eds.), *Managing ambiguity and change* (pp. 93–125). Chichester, England: Wiley.

MILLER, D., & FRIESEN, P. (1984). *Organizations: A quantum view.* Englewood Cliffs, NJ: Prentice Hall.

MINTZBERG, H. (1979). *The structuring of organizations.* Englewood Cliffs, NJ: Prentice Hall.

MIRVIS, P. H. (1990). Organization development: Part II—a revolutionary perspective. In W. H. Pasmore & R. W. Woodman (Eds.), *Research in organizational change and development* (Vol. 4, pp. 1–66). Greenwich, CT: JAI Press.

MIRVIS, P. H., & BERG, D. N. (1977). *Failures in organization development and change.* New York: Wiley-Interscience.

MOCH, M. K., & BARTUNEK, J. M. (1990). *Creating alternative realities at work: The quality of work life experiment at FoodCom.* New York: Harper Business.

MOHRMAN, A. M., & LAWLER, E. E. III. (1985). The diffusion of QWL as a paradigm shift. In W. G. Bennis, K. D. Benne, & R. Chin (Eds.), *The planning of change* (4th ed., pp. 149–159). New York: Holt, Rhinehart and Winston.

MURNIGHAN, J. K., & CONLON, D. (1991). The dynamics of intense work groups: A study of British string quartets. *Administrative Science Quarterly, 36,* 165–186.

NADLER, D. A. (1978). Consulting with labor and management: Some learnings from quality of work life projects. In W. W. Burke (Ed.), *The cutting edge: Current theory and practice in organization development* (pp. 262–277). La Jolla, CA: University Associates.

NEILSEN, E. (1984). *Becoming an OD practitioner.* Englewood Cliffs, NJ: Prentice Hall.

PASMORE, W., & FRIEDLANDER, F. (1982). An action-research program for increasing employee involvement in problem-solving. *Administrative Science Quarterly, 27,* 343–362.

POOLE, P., GIOIA, D. A., & GRAY, B. (1989). Influence modes, schema change, and organizational transformation. *Journal of Applied Behavioral Science, 25,* 271–289.

PORRAS, J. I., HOFFER, S. J. (1986). Common behavior changes in successful organization development efforts. *Journal of Applied Behavioral Science, 22,* 477–494.

PORRAS, J. I., & ROBERTSON, P. J. (1987). Organization development theory: A typology and evaluation. In R. W. Woodman & W. A. Pasmore (Eds.), *Research in organizational change and development* (Vol. 1, pp. 1–57). Greenwich, CT: JAI Press.

QUINN, R. E., & CAMERON, K. S. (1988). *Paradox and transformation: Towards a theory of change in organization and management.* Cambridge, MA: Ballinger.

RANDOLPH, W. A., & ELLOY, D. F. (1989). How can OD consultants and researchers assess gamma change? A comparison of two analytical procedures. *Journal of Management, 15,* 633–648.

RANSON, S., HININGS, B., & GREENWOOD, R. (1980). The structuring of organizational structures. *Administrative Science Quarterly, 25,* 1–17.

ROSS, L. (1977). The intuitive psychologist and his shortcomings: Distortions in the attribution process. In L. Berkowitz (Ed.), *Advances in experimental social psychology* (Vol. 10, pp. 337–400). New York: Academic Press.

ROTHENBERG, A. (1979). *The emerging goddess.* Chicago: University of Chicago Press.

SCHNEIDER, D. J. (1991). Social cognition. *Annual Review of Psychology, 42,* 527–561.

SCHMUCK, R. A., & MILES, M. B. (Eds.). (1971). *Organization development in schools.* Palo Alto: National Press Books.

SCHMUCK, R. A., RUNKEL, P.J., SATUREN, S. L., MARTELL, R. T., & DERR, C. B. (1972). *Handbook of organization development in schools.* Palo Alto: National Press Books.

SMITH, C., CHILD, J., & ROWLINSON, M. (1990). *Reshaping work: The Cadbury experience.* Cambridge: Cambridge University Press.

SMITH, K. K., & BERG, D.N. (1987). *Paradoxes of group life.* San Francisco: Jossey-Bass.

STARBUCK, W. H. (1982). Congealing oil: Inventing ideologies to justify acting ideologies out. *Journal of Management Studies, 19*, 3–27.

STARBUCK, W. H. (1983). Organizations as action generators. *American Sociological Review, 48*, 91–102.

SUSMAN, G. I., & EVERED, R. D. (1978). An assessment of the scientific merit of action research. *Administrative Science Quarterly, 23*, 582–603.

TAYLOR, S. E., & BROWN, J. D. (1988). Illusion and well-being: A social psychological perspective on mental health. *Psychological Bulletin, 103*, 193–210.

TUSHMAN, M. L., NEWMAN, W. H., & ROMANELLI, E. (1986). Convergence and upheaval: Managing the unsteady pace of organizational evolution. *California Management Review, 29*(1), 29–44.

TUSHMAN, M. L., & ROMANELLI, E. (1985). Organizational evolution: A metamorphosis model of convergence and reorientation. In L. L. Cummings & B. M. Staw (Eds.), *Research in organizational behavior* (Vol. 7, pp. 171–122). Greenwich, CT: JAI Press.

URY, W. L., BRETT, J. M., & GOLDBERG, S. B. (1988). *Getting disputes resolved: Designing systems to cut the costs of conflict.* San Francisco: Jossey-Bass.

WALSH, J. P., & UNGSON, G. R. (1991). Organizational memory. *Academy of Management Review, 16*, 57–91.

WALTON, R. E. (1969). *Interpersonal peacemaking: Confrontations and third party consultation.* Reading, MA: Addison-Wesley.

WATZLAWICK, P., WEAKLAND, J. H., & FISCH, R. (1974). *Change: Principles of problem formation and problem resolution.* New York: Norton.

WEICK, K. E. (1969). *The social psychology of organizing.* Reading, MA: Addison-Wesley.

WEICK, K. E. (1979). *The social psychology of organizing* (2nd ed.). Reading, MA: Addison-Wesley.

WEICK, K. E., & BOUGON, M. C. (1986). Organizations as cognitive maps. In H. Sims & D. Gioia (Eds.), *The thinking organization* (pp. 102–135). San Francisco: Jossey-Bass.

WOODMAN, R. W., & PASMORE, W. A. (Eds.). (1987). *Research in organizational change and development* (Vol. 1). Greenwich, CT: JAI Press.

CHAPTER SIXTEEN

Macro Organizational Psychology*

Barry M. Staw   Robert I. Sutton

University of California at Berkeley   *Stanford University*

This chapter outlines the area of macro organizational psychology. This subfield comprises theory and research in which individual traits and states play a central role in explaining behavior at the organizational level of analysis. Past research indicates that psychological forces can be used without reference to, in combination with, or as a replacement for more traditional explanations for behavior at the organizational level, especially for explanations based on sociological theory. We consider three ways that psychological forces influence the behavior of organizations: (1) Autonomous agents can represent the organization to outside publics; (2) powerful members can influence organizational structures, reputations, and performance; and (3) the aggregation of individual traits, emotional states, and beliefs can reflect organizational attributes and can shape the behavior of organizations. We then illustrate how these psychological mechanisms combine to shape organizational outcomes and discuss how future macro psychological research can influence the field of organizational behavior.

The micro–macro continuum is perhaps the most frequently used and influential distinction in organizational research over the past two decades. Many scholars have held public debates about whether the macro or micro perspective is superior for explaining behavior. The titles of doctoral, masters, and undergraduate courses have typically indicated whether the focus is on micro or macro organizational behavior. And, in recent years, when there has been a job opening for a faculty member in organizational behavior, the first question is usually, "Are you looking for a macro or a micro person?"

Even though the micro–macro dimension is a ubiquitous theme in the field of organizational behavior, its meaning is muddled. There is particular confusion about whether this dimension refers to the unit of analysis in which behav-

*We wish to acknowledge that some of the ideas in this chapter build on Staw's (1991) earlier paper "Dressing Up Like an Organization: When Psychological Theories Can Explain Organizational Action," *Journal of Management, 17,* 805–819.

ior is explained or to the discipline from which explanatory concepts are derived. If only the unit of analysis were involved, its meaning would be fairly clear. Research in organizational settings can usually be arrayed on a continuum ranging from the study of individual members, groups, departments, organizations, to populations of organizations. Yet when disciplinary labels are applied, the micro–macro dimension is often used in an inappropriate or even misleading fashion. The word *micro* is interpreted narrowly to indicate that psychological theory is used to explain the behavior of individuals (or, at most, dyads and groups). The word *macro* is often interpreted to mean that sociological (or perhaps economic) theory is used to explain behavior at the organizational or population level of analysis. The implication is that researchers who use psychological theory do not have a valid claim to the macro high ground, nor do sociologists have something to say about individual behavior.[1]

An unfortunate consequence of the alignment of academic fields and units of analysis has been a loss of interdisciplinary research on organizations. In our view, the contributions of both psychologists and sociologists are now being understated. For example, the work of sociologists like Goffman, Mead, and Simmel are rarely used to explain the behavior of individuals in organizational behavior. And, despite the promising earlier efforts by Katz and Kahn (1966, 1978) and by Weick (1969, 1979) to apply social psychology to organizations, researchers currently only make occasional use of psychological theories to understand organization-level behavior. This provincialism has led to a waste of conceptual leverage for explaining complex behaviors in and of organizations. It has also contributed to an overly bifurcated field, one in which the micro–macro dimension drives rather orthodox psychological and sociological research rather than more interdisciplinary work with flexibility in theory and method.

The goal of this chapter is to map an area that we call "macro organizational psychology." It is, we contend, an underdeveloped linkage between micro and macro organizational research and a territory sorely in need of study. One could, of course, argue that sociological work also needs to be extended to the individual level (see Pfeffer, 1991, for an initial effort in this regard) or that additional resources should be placed in small group research. We agree wholeheartedly with these aims. Though we address only the psychological approach to macro organizational behavior, each of these efforts could help restore organizational studies to the interdisciplinary field it once was. Each could help enlarge the common ground where multiple perspectives are used to explain behavior in and of organizations.

---

[1]In recent years, economic perspectives have had a growing impact on theory building and research at the organizational level of analysis. Although we occasionally refer to economics, our examples focus primarily on the relationship and competition between sociological and psychological perspectives because this volume's subject is the social psychology of organizations. Moreover, most of our colleagues who believe that psychological theory and research "isn't macro" have been those who draw primarily on sociological theory. As a result, we have thought more carefully (and engaged in more arguments) about psychological versus sociological explanations of behavior at the organizational level of analysis than psychological versus economic arguments.

DEFINING MACRO ORGANIZATIONAL PSYCHOLOGY

Before outlining the domain of macro organizational psychology, it may be useful to revisit the basic distinction between psychological and sociological inquiry. According to a dictionary definition, the discipline of psychology is concerned with "mental states and processes" within persons (*Random House Dictionary*, 1987, p. 1561). William James (1963, p. 17, originally published in 1892) referred to such mental states and processes as "states of consciousness as such," or more specifically "sensations, desires, emotions, cognitions, reasonings, decisions, violations, and the like." James went on to say that psychology was concerned with explaining the "causes, conditions, and immediate consequences" of these states. Psychological theory is thus concerned primarily with states and traits that reside within individuals. In contrast, sociology is concerned with the "origin, development, organization, and functioning" of the "the fundamental laws of social relations," rather than "psychological or personal characteristics" (*Random House Dictionary*, 1987, p. 1812). Sociology is concerned with how structural, environmental, and cultural forces explain the behavior of collectivities of human beings.

The area of macro organizational psychology is concerned with using states and traits that reside within individuals as explanations of collective behavior, specifically collectivities known as organizations. It examines how qualities that reside within individuals, especially thoughts and feelings, can play a central role in explaining the behavior of organizations as a whole. The dictionary definitions suggest that macro organizational psychology is not properly labeled a sociological perspective because of its emphasis on psychological or personal characteristics. Instead, this area is a branch of social psychology because it considers the influence of individuals on social systems.

RATIONALE FOR A MACRO ORGANIZATIONAL PSYCHOLOGY

We outline several alternative explanations of macro organizational behavior to demonstrate how psychological theory can explain the behavior of organizations. We start with the most radical: that organizational actions may in fact be individual behavior. Then, we consider two more conciliatory viewpoints: that powerful individuals often shape the way organizations function, and that the aggregation of individual traits, emotional states, and beliefs can determine the behavior of an organization. Once these arguments have been posed, we provide an example of how these psychological forces can combine to shape macro organizational behavior. Finally, we discuss the limitations of macro organizational psychology as well as additional directions that such work might take.

Autonomous individuals can pose as organizations

We have all received letters from organizations bringing bad news: "It is not corporate policy to give refunds," or "Your skills do not fit the company's current needs," or "The organization's current priorities unfortunately prevent it from participating in your interesting study." As Staw (1991) points out, if we probe each of these organizational actions, we will probably find that an individual has represented and responded as the organization. The person in charge is usually a low- or middle-level employee, acting autonomously, who does not like pushy customers who demand refunds, does not want to offer us a job, or does not want to waste time on our valuable study. Individual and organizational actions are not just parallel in these instances; they are the same thing. Organizational actions can thus be individual actions in the guise of a larger and more impersonal entity.

If many organizational actions actually reflect autonomous individuals posing as organizations, then psychological theories are useful for explaining the behavior of organizations. Psychological theories are especially pertinent when employees have discretion in how they deal with external constituencies. For example, an investment banker at Solomon Brothers, a buyer for K-Mart, or an admissions officer at Stanford University may each represent the organization and function without close supervision. Like most middle- and upper-level employees, only general guidelines constrain such representatives' behavior; the details of their actions are self-determined and motivated.

A ready argument against using psychological theory to explain behavior at the organizational level proceeds as follows: Because organizations are such strong situations that overwhelm weak individual dispositions (Davis–Blake & Pfeffer, 1989) and are laced with potent socialization practices (Kanter, 1977), employees may absorb the organization's norms and goals as their own. As a result, their behavior simply reflects the standards and goals of the larger system. We would argue that psychological theories still apply even when this is true. Just as in the case of altruistic behavior, where one seeks benefits for another with whom one identifies closely (Batson, O'Quin, Fultz, Vanderplas, & Isen, 1983), psychological theories are useful for explaining organizational behavior. In performing their organizational roles, individuals may sometimes behave altruistically so that the institution's interests are furthered, even at their own expense (Staw, 1983). More often, however, behavior is determined by a confluence of loyalties, where individuals and organizational interests sometimes coincide, sometimes conflict, and at other times are irrelevant to one another. In such a complex world, variations of motivation theory, personality theory, role theory, and identity theory would likely provide as many research leads as conventional sociological theories of organizational action.

Powerful individuals can sway organizations

Individuals are sometimes more than agents of organizations: They may exert control over their organizations. The greatest influence of this kind occurs in small, one-person businesses where organizational action is individual action. Newly founded organizations are also strongly influenced by individual preferences and actions. How a new business is organized and managed is a product of the founder's ideas and predilections. Certainly other factors like the type of market, the availability of external role models, and prevailing social norms can influence how the new business is organized (Aldrich & Mueller, 1982). Yet there is usually enough ambiguity in the organization's environment and equifinality in organizational structure for the individual to come shining (or glaring) through. Schein (1983) argues that a firm's founder is the major instigator of its culture. At first, personal preferences are translated into the management of a few employees in ways that are comfortable to the founder. As the firm grows, the management style of the founder is likely to become embodied in the firm's symbols, interaction style, procedures, and formal structure. And the founder's legacy may even endure long after he or she departs. Just as the vestiges of an arbitrary norm can persist in small groups over time and through changes in membership (Jacobs & Campbell, 1961; Zucker, 1977), one would expect that the modes of internal operation and strategies of dealing with the environment would likely persist in organizations.

Individuals other than founders may also shape organizations through leadership (Kets de Vries & Miller, 1986). The strongest effects would be expected in small firms because the leader's preferences can be more directly translated into organizational actions, without dilution and buffering by middle management. One might also expect that leaders would have a greater effect on younger firms, in which behavior patterns are less strongly institutionalized than in firms with older and more established patterns of behavior. These expectations are supported by Miller and Dröge's (1986) findings that Chief Executive Officers' need for achievement predicted organizational formalization, integration, and centralization, and that these relationships were strongest in smaller and younger firms.

The possible effects of leadership on organizations have been a subject of much controversy. Some have argued that the environment is what shapes the actions of organizations (Pfeffer & Salancik, 1978) or that leadership is an overly romanticized explanation of events that have other causes (Meindl, Ehrlich, & Dukerich, 1985). Yet recent research, even studies by some of the most severe critics of leadership, have uncovered evidence that leaders can influence outcomes in organizations. For example, Pfeffer and Davis–Blake (1986) found that although simply replacing the coach is generally not related to changes in team performance, the past win–loss records of basketball coaches do predict the performance of coaches who take over new teams. A similar effect of successor competence is also suggested by Smith, Carson, and Alexander's (1984) research on new methodist ministers and church performance. Likewise, after correcting for methodological problems in a study often cited for showing little impact of leadership on organizational outcomes (Lieberson & O'Connor, 1972), Thomas (1988) demonstrated that leadership could explain more than 50 percent of the variance in the financial performance of large firms in both the United States and the United Kingdom. Finally, Bass's (1990) encyclopedic leadership handbook describes a number of studies supporting the view that leaders' actions shape organizations. Although leaders are not all-powerful in their ability to influence organizations, there is overwhelming evidence that they can have a significant impact. We propose four ways that leaders and other powerful individuals can influence organizations.

BY SHAPING STRATEGIC DECISIONS.   Powerful people can influence organizations through strategic decisions. For example, Zajac and Bazerman (1991) use psychological theory on behavioral decision making to develop hypotheses about why and how decision makers in competitive situations will make nonrational judgments. These poor judgments stem primarily from insufficiently considering the contingent decisions of an opponent and result in blind spots including nonrational escalation of commitment to decisions, overconfidence in judgment, and limited perspective and problem framing.

Zajac and Bazerman blend theory concerning cognitive shortcomings with insights from the strategy literature to explain the persistence of poor strategic decisions that result in industry overcapacity, new business failures, and acquisition premiums (i.e., buying new businesses at excessive costs). For example, Porter (1980, p. 355) observed that there are often "irrational bidders" when two or more firms are competing to buy the same firm. Zajac and Bazerman argue that the cognitive biases of decision makers play an important role in explaining why excessive prices are often paid by the "winner" of these competitive games:

> If a bidding firm believes it has some distinctive ability to improve the acquired firm, but fails to consider the likelihood that other bidders also see themselves as having similar abilities, this insufficient consideration can manifest itself in the judgment of competing potential acquirers. Such overconfidence in a competitive bidding situation can lead to excessively high bids and is consistent with Roll's observation that top management "hubris" can lead to acquisition premiums. (p. 49)

Zajac and Bazerman's perspective exemplifies how the cognitive limitations of a powerful leader, or a small group of powerful top managers and advisors, can cause them to make decisions that change organizational attributes such as size (e.g., the organization may become larger as a result of acquisitions), mission (e.g., the organization may enter new markets and sell new products), organizational conflict (e.g., acquisitions may lead to battles between members of the acquiring and acquired companies), and performance (e.g., the organization may decline as a result of overcapacity, new business failures, cash reserves that are wasted, or excessive debts that are serviced to pay acquisition premiums).

BY SHAPING ORGANIZATIONAL ATTRIBUTES.   Powerful people can influence organizations by making and implementing decisions about relatively stable features of the organization, including structures, procedures, and technologies. The impact of leaders is suggested by Kets de Vries's research on the psychodynamics of leaders' personalities (e.g., Kets de Vries, 1980; Kets de Vries & Miller, 1984). This clinical research suggests that pathological leaders shape organizational structures and procedures in ways that are congruent with their disorders. For example, leaders who suffer from feelings of persecution may try to exercise excessive control through close supervision, formal procedures and controls, and reward systems that emphasize punishment rather than rewards as consequences.

As we noted, the influence of leaders on organizational attributes appears to be especially strong in young and small organizations, where institutional forces have not yet led to widely accepted structures and practices (Scott, 1987). These effects of leadership are perhaps best illustrated by Kimberly's (1979) case study of the birth of a medical school. He found that the ambition and vision of the first dean led to procedures for training medical students that were at odds with the practices at other schools. These practices followed directly from the dean's beliefs. Students learned basic sciences at their own pace rather than at a predetermined pace, reflecting the dean's belief that not all students learn at the same pace. The curriculum was disease centered rather than science centered (e.g., students learned the biochemistry needed to understand cancer rather than studying general biochemistry), reflecting his belief that the traditional science-centered approach was flawed. Students began working with patients during their first year, which reflected his belief that traditional medical education did not expose students to patients early enough in their training. These practices illustrate how the founder of an organization profoundly influenced its initial structures and procedures.

BY SHAPING THE PERCEPTIONS OF KEY ORGANIZATIONAL EXCHANGE PARTNERS. Much has been written in the past decade about leaders as managers of meaning who interpret events in ways that protect and enhance the images of their organizations. Weick and Daft (1983) provide perhaps the most extreme argument along these lines, asserting that "the job of management is to interpret, not to get the work of the organization done" (p. 90–91) and that, in doing so, leaders "must wade into the swarm of events that constitute and surround the organization and actively try to impose some order on them" (p. 74). Even writers who argue that the substantive effects of leaders on organizational attributes and performance are fairly trivial do acknowledge that the symbolic function of leadership can have important effects, especially on an organization's reputation and legitimacy, which can in turn influence organizational resource levels and survival (Pfeffer, 1981, 1982; Pfeffer & Salancik, 1978).

Meindl and his colleagues (Meindl et al., 1985; Meindl & Ehrlich, 1987) suggest that observers of an organization, including key exchange partners, place particularly great weight on leaders' interpretations of organizational events. They argue that observers have a romanticized view that leadership "is a central organizational process and the premier force in the scheme of organizational events and activities" (Meindl et al., 1985, p. 79). Meindl and his colleagues, along with others (Pfeffer, 1977), suggest that this exaggerated perception of leaders' efficacy is caused by the endemic properties of human sensemaking, which cause people to embrace leadership as a simple, vivid explanation for organizational actions rather than engaging in the distressing task of trying to come to grips with the multitude of variables that shape organizations.

Regardless of whether one believes that people place great weight on leadership because they hold a romanticized view of leaders or because leaders do actually influence organizations, the conclusion is the same. Individuals who are potential or current exchange partners pay attention to the interpretations that leaders place on events within and surrounding an organization. As a result, leaders whose interpretations protect and enhance the organization's reputation among its network of exchange partners will, all other forces being equal, lead organizations that are widely endorsed and that receive ample support from their external network (Pfeffer, 1981; Pfeffer & Salancik, 1978).

A number of studies have examined how leaders and other organizational representatives attempt to impose interpretations on the stream of events occurring within and around organizations. Three investigations examined the attributions for corporate financial performance appearing in annual stockholder reports (Bettman & Weitz, 1983; Salancik & Meindl, 1984; Staw, McKechnie, & Puffer, 1983). These reports are signed, if not necessarily written, by chief executive officers. These studies suggest that, in much the same way that individuals use self-serving causal attributions to explain their own behavior, annual reports tend to attribute successful organizational performance to internal organizational actions and unsuccessful performance to events outside of the organization. Staw and his colleagues also found that the use of such self-serving attributions was related to increases in future stock prices. The additional twist added by Salancik and Meindl's (1984) study was that when organizations were in environments that were unstable and difficult to control, leaders tended to try to create the illusion that they were in control by claiming responsibility for both positive and negative outcomes and by claiming that although environmental forces caused financial problems, management was "taking steps to wrestle with its unruly environment" (p. 238).

Recent qualitative research provides additional insights into the means that leaders use to interpret events to protect organizational images. Sutton and Callahan's (1987) case studies of bankrupt firms found that leaders relied on impression management strategies identified by psychologists. Leaders' interpretations of events were meant to eliminate or reduce the stigma of bankruptcy and help maintain the participation and support of key exchange partners such as creditors, suppliers, employees, and customers. Their impression management strategies included concealing that the firm had declared bankruptcy, defining the bankruptcy filing as both a socially acceptable act and a good business decision, and denying that the current management was responsible for causing the bankruptcy. Sutton and Callahan also found, similar to Salancik and Meindl (1984), that leaders took responsibility for the organization's bankruptcy more often than might be expected from the psychological literature on self-serving attributions.

Sutton and Callahan's research provided insights into the nuances of how leaders implement impression management strategies, but it did not consider the effectiveness of such strategies. Sutton and Kramer's (1990) analysis of the 1986 Iceland Arms Control talks between President Reagan and Chairman Gorbachev provides a graphic example of the effects of impression management strategies. This example also illustrates how a small number of representatives, rather than a single leader, can serve as the managers of meaning for an organization.

Just after the Iceland talks ended, members of the Reagan administration, especially Secretary of State George Schultz, glumly conveyed that a failure had occurred because neither side could agree on the status of the Star Wars missile defense system. The perception that the administration had failed was further fueled by Gorbachev's eloquent attack on Reagan and his advisors. Speaking without benefit of notes, Gorbachev offered detailed, compelling arguments that the talks had failed because the Reagan administration was unwilling to compromise on the Star Wars issue. The next day, however, three top Reagan aides began a vigorous campaign to reinterpret the talks in a way that was favorable to the administration. Led by White House chief of staff Donald Regan, these three spokespersons held 44 briefings and interviews "on the record" and dozens of other meetings "off the record" in the week following the talks. Rather than using the excuses and justifications that people employ when a negative event has occurred, they focused instead on using impression management techniques that are typically employed after a positive event has occurred (Tedeschi & Reiss, 1981). They sought to change the meaning of the event by arguing that Reagan had made the most sweeping arms control proposal in history and that Gorbachev had turned it down. They also continually emphasized that Reagan and his advisors deserved credit for developing and proposing this path-breaking proposal, not Gorbachev. In the language of impression management theorists (Tedeschi & Reiss, 1981), they used "enhancements" to increase the positiveness of the event and "entitlings" to gain credit for the event.

Evidence that these talks were subsequently interpreted by the American public as a positive event is found in numerous supportive editorials and even in a grudging acknowledgment from administration rival Senator Edward Kennedy that the Iceland talks enhanced Reagan's reputation. Opinion polls showed that most Americans believed that Gorbachev, not Reagan, was to blame for the failure to reach agreement and that although only 28 percent of Americans had "a lot" of confidence in Reagan's ability to negotiate an arms control agreement before the Iceland talks, 53 percent had "a lot" of confidence after the talks. As Donald Regan put it on November 16, 1986 in the *New York Times*,

> "Some of us are like a shovel brigade that follow a parade down Main Street cleaning up," Mr. Regan said with a laugh. "We took Reykjavik and turned what was a sour situation into something that turned out pretty well." (p. 1)

In sum, the psychological literature on attribution and impression management provides useful conceptual grounding for identifying the means that leaders and other organizational spokespersons use to shape the reactions of key exchange partners to the organization. And, as Weick and Daft (1983) suggest, given the importance of maintaining an organization's reputation and the associated importance of maintaining a set of favorable exchange relationships, there is good reason to believe that the interpretations provided by leaders and other organization members are crucial to organizational effectiveness and survival.

BY SHAPING THE INDIVIDUALS WHO COMPOSE THE ORGANIZATION.   Research conducted at the individual level suggests that organizations may become reflections of their leaders' enduring characteristics. Social psychological research on interpersonal attraction (Schneider, Hastorf, & Ellsworth, 1979) and industrial psychology research on selection interviews (Arvey & Campion, 1982) provide consistent evidence that people are attracted to and are likely to select job candidates who are similar to themselves. In the same way, leaders may select followers who are similar to themselves in gender, physical attributes, race, and personality. This proposition suggests a mechanism by which organizations, or at least top management teams, become clones of their founders and top executives. It also may help explain why the top executives of *Fortune* 500 companies are almost all older white males.

In addition to shaping the set of members who compose an organization, leaders can also create conditions that influence their subordinates' emotions, cognitions, and behaviors. We consider two means of such influence: self-fulfilling prophecies and charismatic leadership.

Research on the self-fulfilling prophecy, or the Pygmalion effect, has been conducted primarily in classrooms. Typically teachers are told by a credible source that a subset of their students has great potential for high achievement. Although these "high potential" students are randomly selected and have no more or less ability than other members of a class, research suggests that teachers create conditions that lead to a self-fulfilling prophecy because the so-called high potential students improve more over time than their peers (Rosenthal & Jacobsen, 1978).

Eden and his colleagues have studied the Pygmalion effect in organizations. Eden and Shani (1982) found that when instructors at an Israeli boot camp were convinced that a randomly selected subset of their trainees had exceptional "command potential," this expectancy induction explained 73 percent of the variance in trainee performance, 66 percent of the variance in trainee attitudes, and 28 percent of the variance in trainee leadership. On the basis of this and other studies, Eden (1984) proposed that when a leader believes subordinates will perform exceptionally well, he or she communicates those expectations to subordinates and provides resources and advice that help this come true. Acts of leadership cause increased subordinate performance, which reinforces both the leaders' and the subordinates' expectations further, creating a self-fulfilling prophecy.

The power of leaders' expectations to determine organizational performance is implied, but not demonstrated by, Eden's work. For example, if a leader expects all subordinates to do well, the organizational performance should be higher than when a leader expects an otherwise identical set of subordinates to do poorly or has no expectations at all. This overall effect is also implied by King's (1974) quasi-experiment in which job rotation was introduced in two plants and job enlargement was introduced in two other plants. Expectations of improved output were created in one job enlargement and one job enrichment plant, but not in the other two. King's findings suggest that expectancy effects were associated with a far greater improvement in output than differences between job enrichment and job enlargement.

In addition to expectation effects, the literature on charismatic leadership also suggests that leaders shape the cognitions, emotions, and behaviors of their followers. Weber defined charismatic authority as that to which "the governed submit because of their belief in the extraordinary quality of the specific person" (Weber, 1947, p. 295). There is controversy about whether the ideas, influence tactics, theatrical skills and/or appearance of charismatic leaders create dedicated and excited followers or whether leaders are selected to symbolize and reflect the thoughts, emotions, actions, and desired actions of their followers (Conger, Kanungo et al., 1988; Lindholm, 1990). Bass (1990, p. 188) presents the most reasonable position in this debate, arguing that both a charismatic leader and the strong desire by followers to identify with him or her must be present if a "charismatic relationship" is to emerge.

Despite this controversy, some research suggests that leaders who convey ideologically appealing ideas and missions while simultaneously demonstrating a high degree of linguistic ability, emotional expressiveness, and confidence in themselves and their followers will influence both the cognitions and emotions of their followers (Conger et al., 1988; House, 1977; Howell & Frost, 1988; Lindholm, 1990). Emotional effects include increased self-esteem and excitement and devotion to and trust toward the leader. Cognitive effects include emulating leaders' value and goals and having an exceptionally high degree of confidence in the correctness of the leaders' beliefs.

The emotional and cognitive effects of charismatic leadership can sometimes be disastrous. Lindholm (1990) documents how charismatic relationships, including Adolf Hitler and the Nazi Party, Charles Manson and his Family, and Jim Jones and the People's Temple all culminated in morally reprehensible acts and in the demise of the leader and his social system. But a modest body of research in organizational settings suggests that charismatic leaders can produce increased commitment and effort. For example, a laboratory study by Howell and Frost (1988) found that charismatic leaders generated more productivity in followers, even when those followers were discouraged from working hard by confederate co-workers. In contrast, leaders who lacked charisma and instead were high in consideration (i.e., likeable and emotionally supportive) or in initiating structure (i.e., focused on the details of task accomplishment) were unable to sway followers when a discouraging confederate was present.

There are also qualitative studies on the effects of charismatic leaders on organizational success. For example, Biggart's (1989) extensive case studies of direct sales organizations suggest that having a charismatic founder who can create excitement, commitment, and effort in followers is essential for the success of these organizations. Biggart (1989) provides a revealing summary of how one charismatic leader, Mary Kay Ash of Mary Kay Cosmetics, influenced her followers:

> Mary Kay Ash acts in a caring and nurturing way toward the women in her organization. She sends them cards on their birthdays and on their anniversaries in the organization. She replies personally to letters from any of the 150,000 beauty consultants. Whenever she hears of illness or suffering, she expresses concern, according to her beauty consultants. At the 1986 seminar, she told the assembly that she was worried about their health and asked every woman present, as a favor to her, to learn how to do a breast self-examination to fight cancer, their common enemy. (p. 143)

Most of the organizations that Biggart studied had charismatic founders, and all of these founders used their emotional expressiveness, linguistic ability, confidence, and vision to help build their corporations. This link between charismatic leadership and organizational growth and prosperity is also suggested in other case studies (Bass, 1990; Conger et al., 1988).

Quantitative studies of the influence of charismatic leaders on organizations are rare. But the House, Spangler, and Woycke (1991) study of United States Presidents provides some interesting data on the potential influence of charismatic leaders on followers. On the basis of data from political historians, cabinet members' biographies, and *New York Times* editorials written immediately after inaugural addresses, they developed a measure of presidential charisma that predicted performance in the economy and domestic and foreign affairs.

A NOTE ON THE INFLUENCE OF LESS POWERFUL INDIVIDUALS.   Though we have outlined how powerful people can influence organizational outcomes, one need not be a top manager to influence the organization. Middle managers also influence how decisions, policies, and procedures are implemented. For example, political appointees who head U.S. governmental agencies often cannot implement policies that threaten the security of middle-level civil servants or that clash with the agency's historical goals. Middle-level bureaucrats can find ways to stall the implementation of directives from the political appointee, who is likely to leave after the next national election. Similar tactics are used in the private sector. A CEO who proposes sweeping organizational changes can meet either resistance or support from people who are asked to make the changes.

As Mechanic (1962) observed long ago, and as March (1981) noted more recently, those lower in the hierarchy have more power than organizational theorists, or top managers, usually realize. Because lower level employees are the people who complete the product or execute the service, the organization depends on their efforts to perform in the marketplace (Bowen & Schneider, 1988). The influence of lower level employees is especially high when there is discretion in the way that tasks are carried out. At the extreme, behavior at the organizational level can be viewed as the collection of efforts by a set of quasi-independent actors. In many universities, for example, each professor conducts courses in a nearly independent manner and the educational process is an additive product of these loosely coordinated individual efforts. When the organization employs a set of professionals, the product of the organization may consist of an amalgam of individual behaviors.

The aggregation of individual behavior

We have argued thus far that individuals can singly determine an organization's structure and its internal and external actions. There are degrees of truth to this assertion, depending on whether individuals act as founders, leaders, autonomous agents, or functionaries who are constrained by the structure and rules of the firm. Yet all of our arguments have been based on the notion that individual actions can, by themselves, be organizational actions or can, on their own, influence organizational actions. Now we turn to the idea that organizations are basically an aggregation of their individual parts, and that by knowing more about these individuals, we can better explain macro organizational behavior. Specifically, we discuss the aggregation of stable attributes, emotional states, and beliefs.

AGGREGATION OF STABLE ATTRIBUTES.   Perhaps the clearest statement of the aggregation argument is Schneider's (1987) observation that "the people make the place." Rather than viewing individuals as passive products of organizations, Schneider sees organizations as a reflection of the individuals who compose them. The culture, prevailing values, structure, and basic strategies of a firm are all, he argues, dependent on the aggregation of individuals making up the organization. Moreover, the composition of organizations may be self-sustaining. People who are similar to the current membership of an organization are more likely to be attracted to the organization and, in turn, selected by those doing the hiring. Once in the organization, socialization practices tend to yoke individuals in the direction of existing norms; those who hold out or exhibit deviant behavior are likely to leave the firm. Organizations have a tendency to become homogeneous, with a prevailing set of personality traits and behavioral tendencies (O'Reilly, Chatman, & Caldwell, 1991). Organizations' internal policies as well as their strategies in dealing with environments may be a reflection of this dominant set of characteristics.

To study how a set of individual characteristics can influence organizational action, some researchers have drawn on the literature of organizational culture. Presumably, culture is the set of values, beliefs, and behavioral tendencies that are shared by an organization's membership (Schein, 1985). These individual attributes, aggregated over a collectivity, can be studied with both qualitative and quantitative data.

Sutton's (1991) ethnographic study showed how a bill collection agency attracted and selected members who were inclined to display the "right" emotions and induced attrition among members who were inclined to display the "wrong" emotions in order to maintain organizational norms about emotions that ought to be expressed to debtors. Supervisors tried to hire new collectors who, like themselves, had intensity. Supervisors described intense collectors as "being fired-up," "having fire in the belly," or having the ability to "sound like they mean what they say." They believed that intense people were best suited for convincing recalcitrant debtors to pay their bills. On the basis of careful monitoring of their behavior, intense collectors were more likely to be promoted; people who were not intense enough were either fired or were criticized until they left the organization voluntarily.

Chatman (1991) conducted a quantitative longitudinal study of 171 newly recruited auditors in Big Eight accounting firms and, like Sutton (1991), provided evidence that organizations tend to retain employees who have similar personalities and drive away employees with dissimilar personalities. She used a Q-sort methodology to assess 54 dimensions (e.g., quality, respect for individuals, flexibility, and risk taking) that characterized the values shared by organization members and held by individual new auditors. Recruits who had values similar to most other members of the firm adjusted to their roles more quickly, expressed greater commitment to the firm, were more satisfied with their jobs, were given higher performance evaluations by their supervisors, and were less likely to turn over. Just as Schneider (1987) proposes, attrition of the "wrong types" and retention and reward of the "right types" is one way that organizations maintain their shared values.

Both Sutton's and Chatman's studies suggest that the tendency to pick "right types" may enhance organizational performance. But the tendency to base selection decisions on similarity carries risks. For example, Perkins, Nieva, and Lawler's (1983) study examined how production workers were hired for a new plant. Newspaper ads encouraged applications from people who were willing to accept responsibility, to constantly learn new skills, and who wanted to work as members of a team. Plant supervisors interviewed 172 applicants and hired 38 new employees who presumably fit this profile. The data, however, reveal an interesting twist. Although the company advertised for "team players," supervisors tended to pick new people like themselves who were individualistic and not particularly concerned about relationships at work. The subsequent conflict in the plant and associated performance problems may have been exacerbated because the work force was composed of aggressive individualists rather than team players.

Theory and research on the demographic composition of an organization suggests various ways in which the aggregation of enduring attributes of members can influence organizations. For example, both Staw (1980) and Pfeffer (1982) have noted that there may be an inverted U-shaped relationship between tenure and job performance. New employees lack the skill and experience to do their jobs well, while senior employees have greater experience but may lack motivation. Research by Katz (1982) finds some support for this notion. His study of 50 project groups found a curvilinear relationship between the average tenure of the group and performance at research and development tasks. He also found that long-tenured groups tended to be characterized by behavioral stability and a greater emphasis on internal social relations, but lower contact with external sources of information and a reduced emphasis on task performance. Transported to the organizational level of analysis, these findings suggest that the demographic composition of the organization may influence its internal functioning as well as adaptation to environmental changes.

To illustrate how the demography of an organization can affect its overall mission and operating strategies, Pfeffer (1982) discusses cohorts that compose organizations. He argues that there will likely be conflict between cohorts and solidarity and attraction within cohorts. Pfeffer draws on Gusfield's (1957) study of the Woman's Christian Temperance Union to show how conflict arose between older members, who wanted to continue efforts used during the prohibition period to outlaw and restrict the sale of liquor, and newer members who wanted to use more socially desirable tactics such as persuasion and education. This conflict appeared to affect the organization's size and effectiveness: Older members retained control of the organization, leading to a reduction in membership and other signs of organizational decline.

Recent demographic research suggests that tenure, age, and gender composition may affect organizational turnover rates (O'Reilly, Caldwell, & Barnett, (1989), innovation (Bantel & Jackson, 1989; O'Reilly & Flatt, 1989), and communication patterns (Zenger & Lawrence, 1989). These results are often interpreted in sociological terms because demographic variables are generally treated as structural constructs. In our view, however, explanations of the effects of organizational demography should be broadened to include the enduring values, preferences, and behaviors for which demographic variables now serve as a rather broad or imperfect proxy. The research by O'Reilly et al. (1991) provides a useful conceptual basis for helping to explain the impact of demographic variables. It aggregates personal characteristics across the membership of the organization and provides a more detailed accounting of these dimensions than more traditional demographic variables such as age and sex. Using the methods developed by O'Reilly and his colleagues to measure differences between the values held by different cohorts that compose an organization, one could trace how and why the age composition of an organization's membership affects structure and functioning. If we are to understand what demographic effects really mean, it is useful to move toward such fine-grained analysis.

AGGREGATION OF EMOTIONAL STATES.   In addition to the aggregation of stable individual attributes, it may also be useful to examine the aggregation of organizational member's more ephemeral emotional states, which may combine to influence how organizations function.

Hochschild's (1979, 1983) conceptual and empirical work, along with subsequent work by Rafaeli and Sutton (Rafaeli & Sutton, 1987, 1989; Sutton & Rafaeli, 1988), suggests that emotions may be meaningful descriptors of organizations. Organizations maintain norms about the emotions that employees ought to feel ("feeling rules") and norms about the emotions that employees ought to express ("display rules"). These collective emotions constitute the "front" or facade presented to an organization's clients or external public. Similarly, a study of retail stores by George (1990) found that, as with expressed emotions, individual measures of felt emotion could be aggregated and transformed into useful measures of positive and negative affective tone. Such aggregate emotions may influence organizational outcomes. For example, George (1990) found that, in stores where employees reported having more negative feelings, less prosocial behavior was evident and that in stores where employees reported more positive feelings there was less absenteeism. Furthermore, because positive emotion is associated with decision-making patterns including more rapid and efficient problem-solving strategies and the tendency to take small risks more frequently and large risks less frequently (Isen & Baron, 1991), collective emotions may influence how efficiently an organization makes decisions and the riskiness of those decisions.

As noted by Hochschild and Rafaeli and Sutton, an organization's marketing strategy can cause organizations to require or encourage their employees to express certain emotions and to conceal other emotions. For example, many retail stores may try to project an image of helpfulness and positive emotion. And banks may wish to project an air of efficiency and prudence. But the emotions typically expressed by organization members may not always be determined by organizational policies or leaders' preferences. Instead, the composition of the organization may determine the organization's strategy. Organizations may, for instance, be composed largely of employees who generally feel either happy or sad, or calm or angry, due to either the mix of personnel in the firm or to the way the business is run. If the work force happens to be composed mostly of people who experience positive emotion the organization may, in turn, emphasize customer service because smiling at and helping others comes more naturally to people in positive moods. In contrast, an organization with low morale may not only present a more negative posture to outside publics but may also choose strategies (e.g., become "defenders" rather than "innovators" in the market) that are reflective of their collective emotional states. In this way, the aggregation of individual states may influence organization-level functions and characteristics.

In addition, the presence of strong collective emotion can influence organizational action in more dramatic ways. For example, Weick's (1990) analysis of an airplane crash at Tenerife, in which communication problems between the crews of two 747s and the air traffic controllers led to 583 deaths, suggests that system-wide rigidities may arise from the aggregate effects of arousal and anxiety among the individuals who compose a system. Weick proposes that this accident was caused partly because time urgency and bad weather generated high arousal and anxiety in the air traffic controllers and crew members of the two planes. Strong negative feelings apparently caused these interdependent people to engage in rigid behaviors including excessive reliance on prior knowledge, inability to emit less well-known—and safer—behaviors correctly or at all, and centralization of decision making. Weick demonstrates how, as a result of the tight coupling of these rigid individual behaviors, the system was vulnerable to disaster.

AGGREGATION OF INDIVIDUAL BELIEFS.   One could also argue that organizations reflect the sum of their members' individual cognitive tendencies and beliefs. Some theory and research suggests strong parallels between how individual and organizations "think." Much of March and Simon's (1958) classic book treats organizational information processing as identical to or a direct aggregation of individual information processing. For example, in summarizing their influential chapter on cognitive limits on rationality, March and Simon assert "Because of the limits of human intellective capacities in comparison with the complexities of the problems that individuals and organizations face, rational behavior calls for simplified models that capture the main features of a problem without capturing all of its complexities" (p. 169). Note that individual and organizational information processing are treated as identical in this quote. Following in this tradition, Louis and Sutton (1991) propose that individuals and organizations are both likely to switch cognitive gears from automatic, schema-based information processing to active, conscious thinking when they encounter novel stimuli. Louis and Sutton's arguments also suggest that organizations switch from automatic to active thinking through the aggregation of individual beliefs. Similarly, Walsh and Ungson (1991) suggest that because individuals remember information and maintain records as memory aids, an organization's memory is determined partly by the aggregation of such information. Walsh and Ungson note that individuals who compose an organization are not only sources of retained information; they also "largely determine what information will be acquired and then retrieved from other memory stores" (p. 78) such as culture, structures, and exernal archives. The notion that individual and aggregate cognitive tendencies are parallel is also reflected in some writings on group processes, including Bazerman's (1990) suggestion that symptoms exhibited by decision-making bodies suffering from groupthink parallel the overconfidence observed in individual decision makers.

The assumption that aggregate action reflects the simple sum of individual cognitive tendencies may, however, not always hold. Some theory and data suggest that, when joined together in groups and organizations, individual cognitive tendencies can be accentuated. The notion that individual tendencies are accentuated when people band together can be traced to Le Bon's (1895, cited in Freud, 1959) early writings on the "group mind." Research on group polarization provides evidence for accentuation: If most people share a bias or opinion, then the decision coming from the larger entity will be even more extreme (Moscovici & Zavalloni, 1969). Accentuation of individual biases is also suggested by Argote, Seabright, and Dyer's (1986) findings that groups tend to make judgments about which category a person belongs to on the basis of vivid qualitative information that is consistent with their stereotypes of such persons and to ignore more valid base rate information about the likelihood that the individual belongs to a given category (i.e., exhibit use of the representativeness heuristic) to an even greater degree than do individuals. And, although the mean level of escalation to commitment to a nonrational course of action was similar in the individuals and groups studied by Bazerman, Giuliano, and Appleman (1984), they found that there were more extreme responses in groups. A higher proportion of groups than individuals were able to avoid escalation, but those groups that made this error in judgment escalated to a greater degree than individuals.

In contrast to these examples of accentuation, Tetlock's (1985) work suggests conditions under which groups and organizations may blunt individual response tendencies. He points out that research indicating that groups magnify individual cognitive biases has all been conducted in artificial groups assembled for brief experiments rather than in real organizations. Tetlock suggests that, because of organizational pressures for accountability, many of the flaws in information processing observed in experimental subjects may be attenuated in organizational settings. Organizations counteract individual cognitive biases through structural devices (e.g., organizations may have one group that hires people and a separate group that evaluates the progress of new employees) and the checks and balances of competing political forces in organizations (e.g., those who can effectively solve organizational problems will gain power in the system). In short, given that organizations can magnify and blunt individual cognitive processes, it is important to conduct research on the effects of aggregated beliefs on organizational actions rather than to just assume that such effects will occur because they have been demonstrated in individuals or groups operating outside of the organizational context.

So far, we have noted how organizational action can be determined by autonomous agents, by powerful individuals, and by the aggregation of members' enduring attributes, emotional states, and beliefs. These three explanations of organization-level behavior are not always independent, however. Indeed, we suspect that organizational action is typically determined by a combination of these forces. We use Sutton's (1987) model of organizational death to illustrate the more complex processes that occur when some of these forces combine.

MORE COMPLEX PROCESSES:
THE EXAMPLE OF DYING ORGANIZATIONS

Sutton's model of organizational death describes the sequence of events as organizations make the transition from what is first thought to be a permanent entity, to a temporary organization, and finally to a defunct organization. This model is grounded in interview and archival data gathered from eight dying organizations in the public and private sectors in Southeastern Michigan in the early 1980s.

The influence of leaders on members played a central role in each of the dying organizations. Sutton identified a three-stage process in which the interpretations provided by leaders helped bring about pronounced and rapid shifts in the cognitions and actions of members. In the first stage, when members believed that they were still part of an ongoing organization, leaders reinforced these collective views by denying rumors that a closing was imminent, although they often acknowledged that such an action was being considered. Because the possibility of organizational death was in the air, members tried to avert the demise of the organization through various means, from working to carry out routine tasks more effectively to presenting arguments to powerful exchange partners such as banks and parent organizations that the organization was a viable enterprise.

The second stage was launched when legitimate authorities (i.e., leaders of the organization or its parent) announced the decision to close the organization and that the decision could not be reversed. Such announcements typically provoked widespread anger and sadness. These emotions helped members make a cognitive shift from viewing their social system as a permanent entity to a temporary entity with a known "date of death." This shift in shared beliefs helped members perform the tasks required to disband the organization and to reconnect to more viable organizations. The third stage was launched when leaders announced that disbanding and reconnecting were complete and that the organization was officially defunct. The statements that organizational death had occurred helped facilitate a shift in shared beliefs among former members and other exchange partners from viewing the organization as temporary to viewing it as defunct.

Leaders took specific actions that shaped the process of organizational death such as developing plans for carrying out disbanding and reconnecting. Leaders also played a key symbolic role in changing members' beliefs about the viability of their social system. Finally, leaders' actions seemed to trigger other psychological forces that shaped widely observed emotions, cognitions, and behaviors in these dying organizations. The most surprising finding was that, contrary to leaders' expectations, the quality and quantity of work carried out by members of these organizations did not decrease—and more often increased—after the announcement that the organization would die. Some members held out lingering beliefs that if they just worked harder, the organization would be saved. Some members reported that the tasks of disbanding and reconnecting were more motivating than the often boring jobs they had in the permanent organization. Some worked especially hard after the closing announcement because they needed a recommendation from their former bosses. These emotional states and beliefs appeared to lead to increased individual effort that, in the aggregate, seemed to maintain and even increase the performance of these eight dying organizations.

MULTILEVEL PROCESSES

Not only can micro level processes combine to explain organizational functioning, but as suggested in our discussion of aggregate beliefs, they may trigger other more macro processes along the way. Consider escalating commitment to a course of action. Early studies in this area examined the effect of self-justification motives on the commitment of resources to a losing course of action (e.g., Staw, 1976; Tegar, 1980). Analogous research applied such decision biases as the tendency to be influenced by sunk costs (Arkes & Blumer, 1985) and negative framing (Tversky & Kahneman, 1981) to decision situations involving losses. Most escalation research has been at the individual level. But one could argue that this research is relevant to organizations when leaders make strategic blunders due to escalation effects. In addition, more recent research has uncovered other, indirect means by which escalation tendencies can affect organizations as a whole.

Staw and Ross (1987) traced escalation dynamics across different levels of analysis. They observed that projects are typically proposed and launched by individual administrators who see bright promise in a new product or enterprise. Yet when negative or mixed results start to appear, these same administrators often try to defend the endeavor to both themselves and to others. Downplaying adversity and asserting that "success is around the corner" are typical responses by administrators who are responsible for a losing course of action. Yet an escalation episode rarely ends with this kind of individual rationalization. After a course of action is taken by an organization, it can take on political overtones, with defenders mobilizing to defend their interests in the venture. A project or product can also become so absorbed into the goals, procedures, role structure, and politics of an organization that—despite compelling evidence of failure—it persists because it has become an institutionalized part of the firm. Thus, what starts as an initial decision bias can end up as an important feature of the organization itself.

Discontinuing an institutionalized venture is difficult. Consider the example of Pan American Airlines' actions over the past two decades as it underwent a slow, steady decline. When losses first mounted, Pan Am sold its profitable Intercontinental Hotel chain. The valuable Pan Am building in New York was sold when losses persisted. Then, when business again soured, the profitable Asian routes were sold to United Airlines. Pan Am is now defunct and competitors have purchased the remainder of its routes. In hindsight, it would have been more prudent for top managers to sell the airline and keep the profitable hotel and real-estate businesses. But prospective rationality of this kind is unlikely when there is an institutionalized form of escalation (that is, when the political core of the firm depends on the continuation of a given course of action and when the mission and ideology of the firm make it difficult to even imagine the organization in another line of business). Thus, what starts as an initial decision bias can end up as a near-permanent feature of the organization itself.

Escalation research also illustrates how psychological tendencies may prompt organizations to set up countervailing structures. Many banks, for example, have recognized that the officer responsible for originating a bad loan is not the one who can best extricate the bank from the losing situation. The responsible loan officer tends to be overly prone to support the failing client with further investment to "save" the prior investment or turn the situation around. As a result, some banks have set up workout groups devoted solely to salvaging troubled loans. When a client's financial situation deteriorates, responsibility is shifted away from the original lending officer to an elite group of loan officers whose sole job is to provide a fresh and detached perspective. In a fashion parallel to debiasing techniques at the individual level (Bazerman, 1990; Fischhoff, 1982), organizations may learn to offset psychological biases with countervailing structural mechanisms.

Longitudinal case studies of escalation (e.g, Ross & Staw, 1986) have delineated some important linkages between psychological processes and organizational actions. But escalation is not the only arena where such cross-level effects are likely to operate. Take, for example, the hypothesis that people are subject to optimistic biases and illusions of control. A direct translation of these hypotheses to the organizational level would mean that companies generally overestimate their performance and their prowess in the market place. As Zajac and Bazerman (1991) propose, such overconfidence may have disastrous effects, such as leading executives to pay excessive prices when acquiring another firm. Yet, similar to Taylor and Brown's (1988) proposals about individuals, a high degree of confidence might also positively contribute to an action orientation on the part of an organization.

To illustrate such dual consequences on organization-level behavior, consider the problems associated with managing new product innovation. On the one hand, substantial bravado is necessary to push a risky product through the organization and into the marketplace. Without some (typically illusory) beliefs of control and very positive (and often unrealistic) expectations, little energy may be expended on new products. On the other hand, as the innovation literature indicates (Amabile, 1988; Kanter, 1988), some filtering of projects is necessary to sort the good ideas from the absurd as well as difficult goals from the impossible. As Staw (1989) suggests, successfully innovative firms may be those that can both stimulate a diversity of ideas and filter these varied ideas into a few viable projects. To do so, organizations may supply seed money for many speculative products but require that an increasingly difficult set of financial hurdles be surmounted before substantial levels of resources are expended. Such procedures avoid crushing the energy to push new ideas and harness this energy in productive directions. The most innovative firms may therefore be those that have best learned to channel the psychological tendency to be optimistic into appropriate organization-level actions. And, as illustrated by this example, a psychological tendency may trigger a more macro structural device to capitalize on useful aspects of the individual-level process, while selecting out the more deleterious effects.

CONDUCTING MACRO PSYCHOLOGICAL RESEARCH

This chapter has sought to define, map, and provide examples of an area that we label macro organizational psychology. This area comprises theory and research that uses psychological constructs, especially constructs reflecting individual cognitions and emotions, to explain the attributes and behavior of organizations.

We identified three mechanisms through which such psychological forces shape the behavior of organizations: (1) actions by autonomous agents of the organization; (2) the influence of powerful members; and (3) the aggregation of members' enduring attributes, emotional states, and beliefs. We then discussed how a combination of these forces may influence organizations and how micro forces may engender structural properties of organizations.

Although we have outlined a number of psychological forces that may affect organization-level outcomes, we have said little about the range of these macro consequences. Figure 1 provides a simple mapping of the territory of macro organizational psychology and shows a variety of potential linkages between psychological causes and organizational outcomes.

As shown in Figure 1, autonomous agents of the organization often represent the firm to the outside world. They are primarily located in boundary role positions and have flexibility to negotiate terms for the organization or to present a product, image, or service to the outside public. Leaders and other powerful people sway organizations in more varied ways. They may directly influence the internal functioning of the firm through new policies or directives, they may structure the firm in various organizational shapes and forms, and they may serve as primary decision maker in formulating market and environmental strategies. Finally, the aggregation of member attributes can also have effects on the

FIGURE 1   The Domain of Macro Organizational Psychology: Linkages between Micro Causes and Macro Consequences

Organization-level Consequences

	Internal Organizational Functioning	Organizational Structure	Market Strategies	Representation to Organizational Environment
Autonomous Agents				
Powerful Individuals				
Aggregated Traits, Emotional States, & Beliefs				

Psychological Causes

way the firm is organized and performs, because as we have argued, the form and functioning of an organization may follow from the aggregate characteristics of its membership. As one can see from the linkage of micro causes with macro consequences shown in Figure 1, macro organizational psychology comprises a vast domain.

Because of the broad scope of macro organizational psychology, one must ask where the most advantageous research openings lie. Though it may be tempting to understand all the psychological dynamics of firms and their effects on organizations, this is a far too ambitious research agenda. Yet we do need to go beyond the present stage of research in this area. We need to go beyond existing surveys of employee attributes and occasional plant-wide interventions that may affect organization-level measures of performance (e.g., Pasmore & Friedlander, 1982; Pritchard, Jones, Roth, Stuebing, & Ekeberg, 1988). We also need to go beyond the few experiments showing individual-level effects that may be relevant for organizational strategy (e.g., Staw & Ross, 1980). We hope to stimulate an increase in the linkage of micro and macro variables by mapping the subfield of macro organizational psychology.

Studying top managers as a starting point

In our view, the study of top organizational decision makers would be one especially lucrative source of research. Current macro theory dubs this collection of policy makers as the "dominant coalition" or "elite groups," depersonalizing them into sociological entities. Nonetheless, it is possible (indeed, usually easy) to identify key players in important organizational decisions. Psychological theory and research can be used to explain how organizational actions are shaped by these individuals.

DISPOSITIONAL FACTORS.   We have already mentioned Miller and Dröge's (1986) application of personality theory to the relationship between CEO characteristics and organization structure. After controlling for traditional macro variables, chief executives' need for achievement predicted centralization and formalization in a sample of 100 Canadian firms. This research could be extended to other personality dimensions as predictors of organizational characteristics. For example, executives who are low in interpersonal trust and who have difficulty dealing with others may make less use of "hands-on" interaction and make greater use of impersonal and formal means of coordination and control, such as written reports from subordinates, written orders to subordinates, and written procedures. More broadly, one could examine the link between the CEO's personality profile (or profiles of the group of top managers) and the organization's cultural profile (O'Reilly et al., 1991). Research of this kind may reveal that firms with aggressive versus passive or competitive versus cooperative CEOs have instituted organizational structures that reflect these values.

Leaders' personalities may also predict external organizational actions.

Consider the scheme developed by Miles and Snow (1978) that depicts firms as "prospectors," "analyzers," "reactors," or "defenders." Firms that work to develop new products and stay ahead of the market ("prospectors") would, it seems reasonable to propose, have CEOs that are creative and risk taking. Conversely, firms that strive to retain their market niche ("defenders") may have more passive or cautious CEOs. Research by Miller, Kets de Vries, and Toulouse (1982) provides tentative support for these arguments: CEOs scoring higher on a measure of locus of control were more likely to lead organizations that innovated in terms of product technology and new product introduction. That is, leaders who believed they could exert effective control over the events in their own lives ("internals") headed more risk-taking and dynamic organizations than CEOs who believed that they had little control over their personal fates ("externals"). These findings are correlational rather than causal. But moderator variable analysis provides additional evidence that CEO personality helped shape organizational attributes. The smaller the firm and the longer the CEO's tenure, the stronger the relationships between locus of control and innovation.

Staw (1991) proposes that research using manager's dispositions to predict organizational characteristics and actions must confront two issues. The first is how to choose the proper personality dimensions as predictors. Should researchers concentrate on the most commonly studied aspects of personality and examine their macro consequences? This route appears to be dangerous because, despite the promising findings by Miller and his colleagues (Miller et al., 1982; Miller & Dröge, 1986), many low and nonsignificant correlations may be found even if researchers follow the precepts of modern personality research in gathering multiple measures of personality as well as the behavior to be explained (e.g., Weiss & Adler, 1984). Most personality measures have been designed to predict individual behavior over an array of family and school situations rather than behavior in organizations. Stronger predictions are likely to be obtained by tailoring dispositional measures to organizational settings. For example, instead of using a general scale of competitiveness, one could assess the importance of career advancement or being the highest paid CEO in one's industry. In addition to grounding measures to the setting, it may be beneficial to make our dispositional scales more behaviorally based. For example, rather than using abstract scales such as moral reasoning (Kohlberg, 1976) to predict organizational violations of the law, one might construct an index of prior infractions (even minor ones) as a measure of predisposition to break the law. One might expect, for instance, that leaders (such as sports coaches) who have previously been suspected or charged with violations are more likely to head organizations that will be charged with violations in the future, even if they change jobs or organizations.

We might also generalize the entire notion of behavioral disposition to the organization level. The result would be to treat organizations *as if* they were living, breathing entities with predictable behavioral tendencies. This point was made explicitly in early writings by Selznick (1957), where he described an organization's character as analogous to an individual's personality. More recent work uses the same logic, but only implicitly. Categorization schemes such as Miles and Snow's (1978) depiction of the firm's market orientation (i.e., prospector versus defender) suggest that, like individuals with stable personalities, organizations will respond consistently over time. This assumption is also implicit in the population ecology literature, where it is hypothesized that organizations pursue a given market strategy at birth and that this tendency persists over time (Hannan & Freeman, 1984). Though rarely measured and sometimes questioned (e.g., March, 1981; Meyer, 1990), firms are assumed to die because they lack flexibility to meet changing market conditions; their strong disposition to behave consistently over time contributes to their eventual extinction.

PSYCHOLOGICAL PROCESSES.   Bazerman's (1990) writings suggest that decision heuristics, including representativeness, framing, availability, anchoring, hindsight bias, and overconfidence, influence managerial behavior. More traditional psychological processes such as conformity, stereotyping, and cognitive consistency may also be useful for anticipating how top managers will act. For example, individual conformity processes may explain why firms tend to blindly adopt practices and structures used by other firms, as institutional theorists (e.g., Scott, 1987) have observed. Similarly, establishing that top managers try to reduce or avoid cognitive dissonance may help explain why firms tend to base strategy on the organization's past actions rather than on future opportunities, as researchers who study organizational decline propose (see Sutton, 1990; Whetten, 1987). Of course, as noted in our discussion of the aggregation of individual beliefs, structural and political forces in organizations may stifle or magnify the impact of individuals on organizations. Rather than just assuming such effects, it is important to conduct research on the consequences of psychological processes for organizations.

Psychological versus economic explanations

Although this chapter has focused primarily on the competition between sociological and psychological perspectives, recent data on CEO compensation have created a lively debate between psychologists and economists. This research suggests that psychological explanations for organizational behavior may compete with economic explanations, thus extending the domain of macro organizational psychology.

In a study of 105 *Fortune* 500 firms, O'Reilly, Main, and Crystal (1988) examined conventional economic determinants of CEO compensation such as size and profitability of the firm. They also examined a recent economic model (Lazear & Rosen, 1981) proposing that CEO compensation reflects the outcome of a tournament in which executives competing for the corporate throne are willing to forfeit some of their current compensation to increase the attractiveness of the prize (CEO salary) for which they are all vying. O'Reilly and his colleagues found no evidence to support the tournament theory. Instead they found that CEO salary was predicted by the salaries of the members of the compensation committee, who are usually CEOs of other large companies. Thus, social comparison processes are strongly implicated as causes of management compensation.

The study by O'Reilly and his colleagues indicates that when boards of directors or top management teams make decisions that affect or shape the organization, they may be influenced by psychological factors as strongly or even more strongly than economic factors. In addition to CEO salary, social comparison processes may, for example, influence the board in making decisions about such issues as plant location, layoffs, or centralization of decision making. And norms of reciprocity may cause organizational decisions to be made on the basis of social agreements or even favors owed among board members.

Going beyond the organization level

If psychological theory can be used to explain the behavior of collectivities as large as organizations, then it is reasonable to assume that the domain of macro organizational psychology may extend to even higher levels of aggregation. Some recent work demonstrates how psychological perspectives may help explain the behavior of industries and markets. Consider an example at each of these levels of analysis.

Zajac & Bazerman's (1991) conceptual work helps explain how the cognitive limitations of top managers in an industry can have aggregate effects that lead to excessive capacity in that industry. They suggest that members of each top management team, in the automobile industry, for example, may believe that their company has a special ability to manufacture a superior product at a lower price and to market that product in a superior way. Bazerman and Zajac further suggest that managers may not take into account that the management of other companies can also have the same overconfidence. As a result, each company's management will think it can dominate the market or at least increase its market share. The result may be that many or all of the firms will decide to manufacture more cars than they can sell, and too many automobiles will be produced by the industry.

At the market level of analysis, Abolafia and Kilduff's (1988) study of the fluctuation in silver prices relies on the aggregation and transmission of emotional states. They examined the silver futures market in 1980 (which swung from $10.00 to $50.00 and back to $10.00 in several months) and showed how this "speculative bubble" occurred through three emotional phases. The socially constructed reality in each of these phases of mania, distress, and panic appeared to change, and then remain constant for a time, and then changed again, partly through emotional reactions and attributions that were spread among a few powerful actors. Kindleberger (1978) has hypothesized that, rather than through the actions of a few powerful actors, the phases of mania, panic, and distress observed in speculative bubbles can spread through a process of contagion among the members of a market, in much the same way as symptoms are spread in mass psychogenic illness (Singer, Baum, Baum, & Thew, 1982).

Borrowing metaphors

Even if macro organizational psychology does not succeed in promoting truly interdisciplinary research, we hope it will at least stimulate the borrowing of theoretical metaphors. As Staw (1991) notes, there are substantial parallels between macro and micro models, but these similarities go largely unrecognized. For instance, structural contingency theories imply that there is some impetus toward efficiency or energy minimization (e.g., Lawrence & Lorsch, 1969; Thompson, 1967; Woodward, 1965). And resource dependence theory (Pfeffer & Salancik, 1978) proposes that organizations strive to minimize sources of external control and uncertainty. These models parallel those of goal setting, control theory, and expectancy theory, formulations that similarly emphasize how people move toward valued end states. These models also parallel psychological theories of personal control and reactance that emphasize motives of freedom and choice. In institutional theory, another sociological perspective, central assumptions are that organizations attempt to manage their public image to secure external support and legitimacy and that organizations are adept at implementing structures and procedures that mimic other institutions (Meyer & Rowan, 1977; Meyer & Scott, 1983). Such reasoning is close to psychological theories of impression management (Schlenker, 1980) and modeling (Bandura, 1977).

Why are there such close parallels between micro and macro theories? Some system theorists have noted that all social entities have similar properties and predilections (e.g., Miller, 1978). Economists might also argue that, because organizations are fundamentally utility-maximizing entities, many of their behaviors are similar to self-interested people. Finally, as we have already noted, because organizations are composed of people, personal predilections are likely to have an aggregate effect on organizational actions.

Our position is that it does not matter why organizations tend to behave like people. Because they do, individual psychology is useful in developing theories to explain organizational action.

We contend that many sociologists are already implicitly using psychological concepts in macro models. They seem to have asked, "What would I do if I were an organization?" The psychological theories mentioned here—contingency theory, resource dependence theory, and institutional theory—were developed well after the publication of parallel psychological theories. Perhaps psychological theories have influenced the development of these macro perspectives. If psychological concepts are implicit in these theories, why not use them to the fullest extent, capitalizing on their ability to explain organizational behavior?

We might also reverse the process and ask how individuals would act if they were organizations. Decision making is one topic that could benefit from such a shift in perspective. Decision researchers frequently study the failure of individuals to follow expected value logic in their economic choices. Ambiguity about preferences, lack of information, and uncertainty about states of nature are common explanations for deviations from economic norms. Taking an organizational perspective might cast new light on the problem. Like an organization, people may not be in the business of finding perfect or economically rational solutions; instead, they may try to satisfy both internal (personal) and external (referent other) constituencies. Likewise, as in the garbage can model of organizations (March & Olsen, 1976), individuals may have a set of skills and preferences looking for expressive outlets. When examined from a more macro theoretical lens, "irrational" behavior may become both less surprising and more easily studied as a subset of organizational action.

Final thoughts

By arguing in this chapter for the relevance of macro organizational psychology, we do not intend to provoke a "turf war" in which each subdiscipline is vying for an enlarged conceptual space. We are calling for a broadening of common ground in which various approaches can be compared and combined to explain complex organizational problems. We are also not simply arguing for more middle-level or meso-organizational research, but would like to see organizational problems both reduced and enlarged in their levels of analysis. That is, caveats should be dropped against both reductionism and contextualism in organizational research.

In our view, reductionism is not just a way to pick up additional variance missed by macroscopic models. Psychological theories can strengthen and add theoretical substance to macro models by providing the underlying rationale or missing mechanisms to explain the behavior of organizations. We do not deny the power of macro models but view them as incomplete solutions. This argument also implies that reductionism is a process without logical limits. For example, one could try to explain the strategic actions of a firm, not only by the cognitive limits of its decision makers but by their psychophysiology. This may sound like an almost absurd assertion at first blush. But it could be an interesting lead. Connections could be made between chemical bases of aggression in CEOs and their organization's participation in the hostile takeover of other firms, or perhaps between the physiology of workers and their efforts. The limitations on such research stem from cost and feasibility, not from the legitimacy of reductionism.

If reductionism is a legitimate enterprise, then so is contextualism—the explanation of peoples' behavior using the organizational context, be it the person's immediate work surroundings or wider influences in the industrial and social world impinging on the individual (e.g., Pfeffer, 1991). We generally prefer psychological to sociological explanations in our own research work, but applaud efforts to apply macro models to traditional micro research issues.

CONCLUSION

This chapter started with the observation that organizational research has evolved over the past two decades into two distinct subfields: micro and macro organizational behavior. The aim of this chapter has been to stall this bifurcation. We have tried to take tangible steps toward renewed integration of the field by using psychological theories to explain organizational action. We have argued that psychological models can be relevant when individuals act as autonomous agents of organizations, when they are powerful leaders, and when individuals' enduring attributes, emotional states, and beliefs aggregate to the organizational level. We have shown how psychological research might be applied to macro problems that involve several of these components and how micro processes might influence macro variables. Finally, we have worked through several examples of macro organizational research to illustrate what is now missing or has often gone unnoticed in current work in the field. In essence, we believe that more work in macro organizational psychology can help provide the interdisciplinary focus that is needed in organizational research. By weaving together multiple theoretical perspectives, macro organizational psychology may be able to enrich our understanding of organizations and provide more powerful solutions to organizational problems. Of course, whether these hopes can be realized will depend on sustained empirical efforts to link psychological causes with organizational outcomes. This chapter is but one step in that direction.

REFERENCES

ABOLAFIA, M. Y., & KILDUFF, M. (1988). Enacting market crisis: The social construction of a speculative bubble. *Administrative Science Quarterly, 33,* 177–193.

ALDRICH H., & MUELLER, S. (1982). The evolution of organizational forms: Technology, coordination, and control. In B. M. Staw & L. L. Cummings (Eds.), *Research in organizational behavior* (Vol. 4, pp. 33–87). Greenwich, CT: JAI Press.

AMABILE, T. M. (1988). A model of creativity and innovation in organizations. In B. M. Staw & L. L. Cummings (Eds.), *Research in organizational behavior* (Vol. 10, pp. 123–167). Greenwich, CT: JAI Press.

ARGOTE, L., SEABRIGHT, M. A., & DYER, L. (1986). Individual versus group: Use of base rate versus individuating information. *Organizational Behavior and Human Decision Processes, 38,* 124–140.

ARKES, H. R., & BLUMER, C. (1985). The psychology of sunk costs. *Organizational Behavior and Human Performance, 35,* 124–140.

ARVEY, R. P., & CAMPION, J. E. (1982). The employment interview: A summary and review of recent research. *Personal Psychology, 35,* 281–322.

BANDURA, A. (1977). *Social learning theory.* Englewood Cliffs, NJ: Prentice Hall.

BANTEL, K. A., & JACKSON, S. E. (1989). Top management innovations in banking: Does the composition of the top team make a difference? *Strategic Management Journal, 10,* 1078–1124.

BARKER, R. G., & GUMP, P. V. (1964). *Big school, small school: High school size and student behavior.* Stanford, CA: Stanford University Press.

BASS, B. M. (1990). *Bass & Stogdill's handbook of leadership.* Free Press: New York.

BATSON, C. D., O'QUIN, K., FULTZ, J., VANDERPLAS, M., & ISEN, A. M. (1983). Influence of self-reported distress and empathy on egoistic versus altruistic motivation to help. *Journal of Personality and Social Psychology, 45,* 706–718.

BAZERMAN, M. H. (1990). *Judgment in managerial decision making.* New York: Wiley

BAZERMAN, M. H., GIULIANO, T., & APPLEMAN, A. (1984). Escalation in individual and group decision-making. *Organizational Behavior and Human Performance, 33,* 141–152.

BETTMAN, J., & WEITZ, B. (1983). Attributions in the board room: Causal reasoning in corporate annual reports. *Administrative Science Quarterly, 28,* 165–183.

BIGGART, N. W. (1989). *Charismatic capitalism: Direct selling organizations in America.* Chicago: University of Chicago Press.

BOWEN, D. E., & SCHNEIDER, B. (1988). Services marketing and management: Implications for organizational behavior. In B. M. Staw & L. L. Cummings (Eds.), *Research in organizational behavior* (Vol. 10, pp. 43–80). Greenwich, CT: JAI Press.

CAMPBELL, D. T. (1975). On the conflicts between biological and social evolution and between psychology and moral tradition. *American Psychologist, 30,* 1103–1126.

CHATMAN, J. A. (1991). Matching people and organizations: Selection and socialization in public accounting firms. *Administrative Science Quarterly, 36,* 459–484.

CIALDINI, R. B. (1984). *Influence: The new psychology of modern persuasion.* New York: Quill.

CONGER, J. A., KANUNGO, R. N., et al. (1988). *Charismatic leadership.* San Francisco: Jossey-Bass.

DAVIS–BLAKE, A., & PFEFFER, J. (1989). Just a mirage: The search for dispositional effects in organizational research. *Academy of Management Review, 14,* 385–400.

EDEN, D. (1984). Self-fulfilling prophecy as a management tool: Harnessing Pygmalion. *Academy of Management Review, 9,* 64–73.

EDEN, D., & SHANI, A. B. (1982). Pygmalion goes to boot camp: Expectancy, leadership, and trainee performance. *Journal of Applied Psychology, 67,* 194–199.

FISCHHOFF, B. (1982). Debiasing. In D. Kahneman, P. Slovic, & A. Tversky (Eds.), *Judgment under uncertainty: Heuristics and biases.* New York: Cambridge University Press.

FREUD, S. (1959). *Group psychology and the analysis of ego.* New York: W. W. Norton & Company. (Originally published in 1921).

GEORGE, J. M. (1990). Personality, affect, and behavior in groups. *Journal of Applied Psychology, 75,* 107–116.

GUSFIELD, J. R. (1957). The problems of generations in a social structure. *Social Forces, 35,* 323–330.

HANNAN, M. T., & FREEMAN, J. H. (1984). Structural inertia and organizational change. *American Sociological Review, 49,* 149–164.

HARRIS, S. C., & SUTTON, R. I. (1986). The functions of parting ceremonies in dying organizations. *Academy of Management Journal, 29,*(1), 5–30.

HOCHSCHILD, A. (1979). Emotion work, feeling rules and social structure. *American Journal of Sociology, 85,* 551–575.

HOCHSCHILD, A. R. (1983). *The managed heart.* Berkeley: University of California Press.

HOUSE, R. J. (1977). A 1976 theory of charismatic leadership. In J. G. Hunt & L. L. Larsen (Eds.), *Leadership: The cutting edge* (pp. 189–273). Carbondale, IL: Southern Illinois University Press.

HOUSE, R. J., SPANGLER, W. D., & WOYCKE, J. (1991). Personality and charisma in the U.S. Presidency: A psychological theory of leader effectiveness. *Administrative Science Quarterly, 36,* 364–396.

HOWELL, J. M., & FROST, P. J. (1988). A laboratory study of charismatic leadership. *Organizational Behavior and Human Decision Processes, 43,* 243–269.

ISEN, A. M., & BARON, R. A. (1991). Positive affect as a factor in organizational behavior. In L. L. Cummings & B. M. Staw (Eds.), *Research in organizational behavior* (Vol. 13, pp. 1–53). Greenwich, CT: JAI Press.

JACOBS, R. C., & CAMPBELL, D. T. (1961). The perpetuation of an arbitrary tradition through several generations of a laboratory subculture. *Journal of Abnormal and Social Psychology, 62*, 649–658.

JAMES, W. (1963). *Psychology.* Greenwich, CT: Fawcett. (Originally published in 1892).

KANTER, R. M. (1977). *Men and women of the corporation.* New York: Basic Books.

KANTER, R. M. (1988). When a thousand flowers bloom: Structural, collective, and social conditions for innovation in an organization. In B. M. Staw & L. L. Cummings (Eds.), *Research in organizational behavior* (Vol. 10, pp. 169–211). Greenwich, CT: JAI Press.

KATZ, D., & KAHN, R. L. (1966). *The social psychology of organizations.* New York: John Wiley.

KATZ, D., & KAHN, R. L. (1978). *The social psychology of organizations* (2nd ed.). New York: John Wiley.

KATZ, R. (1982). The effects of group longevity on communication and performance. *Administrative Science Quarterly, 27*, 81–104.

KETS DE VRIES, M. F. R. (1980). *Organizational paradoxes: Clinical approaches to management.* London: Tavistock.

KETS DE VRIES, M. F. R., & MILLER, D. (1984). Group fantasies and organizational functioning. *Human Relations, 37*, 11–134.

KETS DE VRIES, M. F. R., & MILLER, D. (1986). Personality, culture, and organization. *Academy of Management Review, 11*, 266–279.

KIMBERLY, J. R. (1979). Issues in the creation of organizations: Initiation, innovation, and institutionalization. *Academy of Management Journal, 22*, 437–457.

KINDLEBERGER, C. P. (1978). *Manias, panics, crashes: A history of financial crises.* New York: Basic Books.

KING, A. S. (1974). Expectation effects in organizational change. *Administrative Science Quarterly, 19*, 221–230.

KOHLBERG, L. (1976). Moral stages and mobilization: The cognitive-developmental approach. In T. Lichona (Ed.), *Moral development and behavior* (pp. 31–53). New York: Holt.

LAWRENCE, P. R., & LORSCH, J. W. (1969). *Organization and environment.* Boston: Graduate School of Business Administration, Harvard University.

LAZEAR, F., & ROSEN, S. (1981). Rank-order tournaments as optimum labor contracts. *Journal of Political Economy, 89*, 841–864.

LIEBERSON, S., & O'CONNOR, J. F. (1972). Leadership and organizational performance: A study of large corporations. *American Sociological Review, 37*, 117–130.

LINDHOLM, C. (1990). *Charisma.* Cambridge, MA: Basil Blackwell.

LOUIS, M. R., & SUTTON, R. I. (1991). Switching cognitive gears: From habits of mind to active thinking. *Human Relations, 44*, 55–76.

MARCH, J. G. (1981). Footnotes to organizational change. *Administrative Science Quarterly, 26*, 563–577.

MARCH, J. G., & SIMON, H. A. (1958). *Organizations.* New York: Wiley.

MARCH, J. G., & OLSEN, J. P. (1976). *Ambiguity and choice in organizations.* Bergen, Norway: Universitelsforlaget.

MECHANIC, D. (1962). Sources of power of lower participants in complex organizations. *Administrative Science Quarterly, 7*, 349–362.

MEINDL, J. R., & EHRLICH, S. B. (1987). The romance of leadership and the evaluation of organizational performance. *Academy of Management Journal, 30*, 91–109.

MEINDL, J. R., EHRLICH, S. B., & DUKERICH, J. M. (1985). The romance of leadership.

Administrative Science Quarterly, 30, 78–102.

MEYER, J. W., & ROWAN, B. (1977). Institutionalized organizations: Formal structure as myth and ceremony. *American Journal of Sociology, 83,* 340–363.

MEYER, J. W., & SCOTT, W. R. (1983). *Organizational environments: Ritual and rationality.* Beverly Hills, CA: Sage Publications.

MEYER, M. W. (1990). Notes of a skeptic: From organizational ecology to organizational evolution. In J. V. Singh (Ed.), *Organizational evolution* (pp. 298–314). Newbury Park, CA: Sage.

MILES, R. E., & SNOW, C. C. (1978). *Organizational strategy, structure, and process.* New York: McGraw-Hill.

MILLER, J. G. (1978). *Living systems.* New York: McGraw-Hill.

MILLER, D., & DRÖGE, C. (1986). Psychological and traditional determinants of structure. *Administrative Science Quarterly, 31,* 539–560.

MILLER, D.,KETS DE VRIES, M. F. R., & TOULOUSE, J. M. (1982). Top executive locus of control and its relationship to strategy making, structure, and environment. *Academy of Management Journal, 25,* 237–253.

MOSCOVICI, S., & ZAVALLONI, M. (1969). The group as a polarism of attitudes. *Journal of Personality and Social Psychology, 12,* 125–135.

O'REILLY, C. A., CALDWELL, D. F., & BARNETT, W. P. (1989). Work group demography social integration, and turnover. *Administrative Science Quarterly, 34,* 21–37.

O'REILLY, C. A., CHATMAN, J. A., & CALDWELL, D. M. (1991). People and organizational culture: A Q-sort approach for assessing person-organization fit. *Academy of Management Journal, 34,* 487–516.

O'REILLY, C. A., & FLATT, S. (1989). *Executive team demography, social integration, and turnover.* Working paper, University of California at Berkeley.

O'REILLY, C. A., III, MAIN, B. G., & CRYSTAL, G. S. (1988). CEO compensation as tournament and social comparison: A tale of two theories. *Administrative Science Quarterly, 33,* 257–274.

ORGAN, D. W. (1988). *Organizational citizenship behavior: The good soldier syndrome.* Lexington, MA: Lexington Books.

PASMORE, W., & FRIEDLANDER, F. (1982). An action research program for increasing employee involvement in problem-solving. *Administrative Science Quarterly, 27,* 343–362.

PERKINS, D. N. T., NIEVA, V. F., LAWLER, E. E., III (1983). *Managing creation: The challenge of building a new organization.* New York: John Wiley.

PFEFFER, J. (1977). The ambiguity of leadership. *Academy of Management Review, 2,* 104–112.

PFEFFER, J. (1981). Management as symbolic action. In L. L. Cummings & B. M. Staw (Eds.), *Research in organizational behavior* (Vol. 3, pp. 1–52). Greenwich, CT: JAI Press.

PFEFFER, J. (1982). *Organizations and organization theory.* Boston: Pitman.

PFEFFER, J. (1983). Organizational demography. In L. L. Cummings & B. M. Staw (Eds.), *Research in organizational behavior* (pp. 1–46). Greenwich, CT: JAI Press.

PFEFFER, J. (1991). Organizational theory and structural perspectives on management. *Journal of Management. 17,* 789–803.

PFEFFER, J., & DAVIS–BLAKE, A. (1986). Administrative succession and organizational performance. How administrator experience mediates the succession effect. *Academy of Management Journal, 29,* 72–83.

PFEFFER, J., & SALANCIK, G. R. (1978). *The external control of organizations: A resource dependence perspective.* New York: Harper & Row.

PORTER, M. E. (1980). *Competitive strategy.* New York: Free Press.

PRITCHARD, R. D., JONES, S. D., ROTH, P. L., STUEBING, K. K., & EKEBERG, S. E.

(1988). Effects of group feedback, goal setting, and incentives on organizational productivity. *Journal of Applied Psychology, 73,* 337–358.

RAFAELI, A., & SUTTON, R. I. (1987). The expression of emotion as part of the work role. *Academy of Management Review, 12,* 23–37.

RAFAELI, A., & SUTTON, R. I. (1989). The expression of emotion in organizational life. In L. L. Cummings & B. M. Staw (Eds.), *Research in organizational behavior* (Vol. 11, pp. 1–42). Greenwich, CT: JAI Press.

The Random House Dictionary of the English Language. (1987). Second edition, unabridged. New York: Random House.

ROSENTHAL, R., & JACOBSEN, D. B. (1978). Interpersonal expectancy effects: The first 345 studies. *Behavioral and Brain Studies, 3,* 377–415.

ROSS, J., & STAW, B. M. (1986). Expo 86: An escalation prototype. *Administrative Science Quarterly, 31,* 274–297.

SALANCIK, G. R., & MEINDL, J. R. (1984). Corporate attributions as strategic illusions of management control. *Administrative Science Quarterly, 29,* 238–254.

SALANCIK, G. R., & PFEFFER, J. (1978). A social information processing approach to job attitudes and task design. *Administrative Science Quarterly, 23,* 224–253.

SCHENKLER, B. R. (1980). *Impression management.* Monterey, CA: Brooks/Cole.

SCHEIN, E. H. (1983). The role of the founder in creating organizational culture. *Organizational Dynamics* (Summer), 13–28.

SCHEIN, E. H. (1985). *Organizational culture and leadership: A dynamic view.* San Francisco: Jossey-Bass.

SCHNEIDER, B. (1987). The people make the place. *Personnel Psychology,* 40:437–453.

SCHNEIDER, D. J., HASTORF, A. H., & ELLSWORTH, P. C. (1979). *Person perception.* Reading, MA: Addison-Wesley.

SCOTT, W. R. (1987). The adolescence of institutional theory. *Administrative Science Quarterly, 32,* 493–511.

SELZNICK, P. (1957). *Leadership in administration.* Evanston, IL: Row, Peterson.

SINGER, J. E., BAUM, C. S., BAUM, A., & THEW, B. D. (1982). Mass psychogenic illness: The case for social comparison. In M. J. Colligan, J. W. Pennebaker, & L. R. Murphy (Eds.), *Mass psychogenic illness: A social psychological analysis* (pp. 155–170). Hillsdale, NJ: Erlbaum.

SMITH, J. E., CARSON, K. P., & ALEXANDER, R. A. (1984). Leadership: It can make a difference. *Academy of Management Journal, 27,* 765–776.

STAW, B. M. (1980). The consequences of turnover. *Journal of Occupational Behavior, 1,* 253–273.

STAW, B. M. (1976). Knee-deep in the big muddy: A study of escalating commitment to a chosen course of action. *Organizational Behavior and Human Performance, 16,* 27–44.

STAW, B. M. (1983). Motivation research versus the art of faculty management. *The Review of Higher Education, 6,* 301–312.

STAW, B. M. (1989). An evolutionary approach to creativity and innovation. In M. A. West & J. L. Farr (Eds.), *Innovation and creativity at work* (pp. 287–308). London: Wiley.

STAW, B. M. (1991). Dressing up like an organization: When psychological theories can explain organizational action. *Journal of Management, 17,* 805–819.

STAW, B. M., McKECHNIE, P. I., & PUFFER, S. M. (1983). The justification of organizational performance. *American Science Quarterly, 28,* 582–600.

STAW, B. M., & ROSS, J. (1980). Commitment in an experimenting society: An experiment on the attribution of leadership from administrative scenarios. *Journal of Applied Psychology, 65,* 249–260.

STAW, B. M., & ROSS, J. (1987). Behavior in escalation situations: Antecedents, prototypes, and solutions. In L. L. Cummings & B. M. Staw (Eds.), *Research in organizational behavior* (Vol. 9, pp. 39–78). Greenwich, CT: JAI Press.

SUTTON, R. I. (1987). The process of organizational death: Disbanding and reconnecting. *Administrative Science Quarterly, 32,* 542–569.

SUTTON, R. I. (1990). Organizational decline processes: A social psychological perspective. In B. M. Staw & L. L. Cummings (Eds.), *Research in organizational behavior* (Vol. 12, pp. 205–253). Greenwich, CT: JAI Press.

SUTTON, R. I. (1991). Maintaining norms about emotional expression: The case of bill collectors. *Administrative Science Quarterly, 36,* 245–268.

SUTTON, R. I., & CALLAHAN, A. L. (1987). The stigma of bankruptcy: Spoiled organizational image and its management. *Academy of Management Journal, 30,* 405–436.

SUTTON, R. I., & KRAMER, R. M. (1990). Transforming failure into success: Impression management, the Reagan Administration, and the Iceland arms control talks. In R. L. Kahn, R. I. Sutton, & M. N. Zald (Eds.), *International cooperation and conflict: Perspectives from organizational theory* (pp. 221–245). San Francisco: Jossey-Bass.

SUTTON, R. I., & RAFAELI, A. (1988). Untangling the relationship between displayed emotions and organizational sales: The case of convenience stores. *Academy of Management Journal, 31*(3), 461–487.

TAYLOR, S. E., & BROWN, J. D. (1988). Illusion and well-being: A social psychological perspective on mental health. *Psychological Bulletin, 103,* 193–210.

TEDESCHI, J. T., & REISS, M. (1981). Identities, the phenomenal self, and laboratory research. In J. T. Tedeschi (Ed.), *Impression management theory and social psychological research* (pp. 3–22). New York: Academic Press.

TEGAR, A. I. (1980). *Too much invested to quit.* New York: Pergamon Press.

TETLOCK, P. E. (1985). Accountability: The neglected social context of judgment and choice. In L. L. Cummings & B. M. Staw (Eds.), *Research in organizational behavior* (Vol. 7, pp. 297–332). Greenwich, CT: JAI Press.

THOMAS, A. B. (1988). Does leadership make a difference to organizational performance? *Administrative Science Quarterly, 33,* 338–400.

THOMPSON, J. D. (1967). *Organizations in action.* New York: McGraw-Hill.

TVERSKY, A., & KAHNEMAN D. (1981). The framing of decisions and the psychology of choice. *Science, 211,* 453–463.

WALSH, J. P., & UNGSON, G. R. (1991). Organizational memory. *Academy of Management Review, 16,* 57–91.

WEBER, M. (1947). *The theory of social and economic organization.* New York: Free Press.

WEICK, K. E. (1969). *The social psychology of organizing.* Reading, MA: Addison-Wesley.

WEICK, K. E. (1979). *The social psychology of organizing* (2nd ed.). Reading, MA: Addison-Wesley.

WEICK, K. E. (1990). The vulnerable system: An analysis of the Tenerife air disaster. *Journal of Management, 16,* 571–593.

WEICK, K. E., & DAFT, R. L. (1983). The effectiveness of interpretation systems. In K. S. Cameron & D. A. Whetten (Eds.), *Organizational effectiveness: A comparison of multiple models* (pp. 71–93). New York: Academic Press.

WEISS, H. M., & ADLER, S. (1984). Personality and organizational behavior. In B. M. Staw & L. L. Cummings (Eds.), *Research in organizational behavior* (Vol. 6, pp. 1–50). Greenwich, CT: JAI Press.

WHETTEN, D. A. (1987). Growth and decline processes in organizations. *Annual Review of Sociology, 13,* 335–358.

WOODWARD, J. (1965). *Industrial organization: Theory and practice.* London: Oxford University Press.

ZAJAC, E. J., & BAZERMAN, M. H. (1991). Blind spots in industry and competitor analysis: Implications of interfirm (mis)perceptions for strategic decisions. *Academy of Management Review, 16,* 37–56.

ZENGER, T. R., & LAWRENCE, B. S. (1989). Organizational demography: The differential effects of age and tenure distributions on technical communication. *Academy of Management Journal, 32,* 353–376.

ZUCKER, L. G. (1977). The role of institutionalization in cultural persistence. *American Sociological Review, 42,* 726–743.

CHAPTER SEVENTEEN

Emergent Themes in Organizational Research

Robert L. Kahn

University of Michigan

INTRODUCTION

A book that has the word *advances* in its title issues an invitation to critics as well as a promise to readers. As a partner in this joint enterprise, I cannot claim disinterested objectivity, but as a longtime student of organizations I will attempt an examination of the claimed advances. We will consider the extent to which the chapters of this book take us into new and important organizational domains, suggest new approaches to territories already explored, demonstrate improvements in design and methods, and thus deepen our understanding of why the words *social psychology* and *organizations* belong in the same sentence. Finally, having examined the things these chapters do, we will conclude by discussing some things that social psychologists who choose to study organizations still need to do.

SOCIAL PSYCHOLOGY AND ORGANIZATIONS

Two chapters in this book, Chapter 2 and Chapter 16, deal directly with the question of why social psychology is relevant for understanding human organizations. Weick's answer, counterintuitive but powerfully developed, is that the defining properties of organizations are social psychological. Organizations, he tells us, are "collections of people trying to make sense of what is happening to them." This continuous effort at sensemaking is not a solitary cerebral activity; it proceeds by means of interactions with others. The building block of organizations is thus the double interact, an episode in which one person acts and another acts in response.

The familiar patterns and visible signs of organizational life—statements of goals and mission, for example—are thus products rather than first causes in Weick's view. They are the result of sensemaking, and sensemaking is essentially a retrospective process.

The basic sequence that Weick develops to explain the creation and continuing life of an organization begins with interaction that is voluntary, visible to others, explicit, and irreversible. These are the conditions under which action generates commitment, which the innate human need for sensemaking then requires to be justified. The process of justification or rationalization leads to norms, and on to social structure. What begins as reification ends as reality.

Thus sensitized to the sequence of organization-creating events that begins with individual commitment and small-scale interactions, we may reasonably ask the probable consequences if we were to commit ourselves to this conceptualization of human organizations. One answer is implied by the subtitle of Weick's chapter: small structures with large consequences. We would acknowledge in organizations the phenomenon that chaos theorists call "the butterfly effect," the possibility that the mere fluttering of a butterfly's wings can initiate a chain of meteorological changes at great distance and on a very large scale (Gleick, 1987). To the extent that human organizations, like the weather, are characterized by a sensitive dependence on initial conditions, the formulations and mathematics of chaos theory become relevant.

Weick's conception of organizations as the continuing product of efforts at sensemaking under changing environmental conditions brings another problem to the agenda of organizational researchers, the virtual impossibility of attaining a steady state. This problem is not new; Ashby (1952) believed that all living systems of great complexity and interconnectedness were at risk for becoming "ultra-stable," intrinsically unable to attain equilibrium.

Other theorists have remarked the difficult but unavoidable organizational task of adjusting to a changing environment. Emery and Trist (1965, 1973) proposed four categories of increasing complexity to characaterize organizational environments and asserted that the fourth of these has become dominant, that most organizations exist in a turbulent field, which because of its complexity and multiple interconnections generates its own dynamic and unpredictable properties. Their remedy, proposed more in a spirit of hopefulness than optimism, was to create overarching societal values that would simplify environmental complexities by means of universally held prescriptions and proscriptions. Still others (Lawrence & Lorsch, 1967) have argued that in order to adjust to their environments, organizations must acquire the dominant environmental characteristics. If the environment is complex and rapidly changing, the successfully adapted organization will be similarly complex and dynamic. This is a solution that presents organizations with a daunting prospect, a never-ending contest with their surround.

Weick's definition of organizations as the constructions of a continuous effort at sensemaking suggests a different way of linking external to internal events. Whether investigation of organizational sensemaking would then suggest adaptive solutions or merely reveal more of the social and cognitive processes by which environmental changes generate internal demands remains to be discovered.

The possibility that equilibrium may be beyond organizational grasp need not lead us to define the organizational world as unpredictable. Chaos theory not only speaks to the butterfly effect in Weick's schema, it suggests that we look for patterns and periodicities in the life cycle of organizations and it gives us a mathematics for doing so. The lack of theory and research on organizational life cycles has been noted before. Haire (1959) made an early proposal that they be studied in terms of biological models, a lead that has not been followed and that probably strained a less than robust analogy. Weick's conception of organizations as the product of the psychological need to make sense of the world and the resulting social interactions by which sensemaking proceeds does not in itself address the issue of organizational life cycles. In combination with the suggestion of looking for periodic and repetitive patterns in organizational life cycles, however, Weick's theory of sensemaking offers us another approach to understanding the dynamic relationship of organizations to their environments.

Chapter 16, like Chapter 2, deals directly with the special relevance of social psychology to organizations and with the potentiality for increasing our understanding of organizational behavior. Staw and Sutton begin by noting the paradoxical state of organizational theory and research with respect to the treatment of micro and macro organizational phenomena. We organizational scholars have transformed—or at least allowed our universities to transform—early arguments about conceptual levels and units of analysis into occupational specialties and individual subidentities. Departmental search committees announce unselfconsciously that they are seeking only micro or macro recruits to their organizational faculties, and newly minted organizational scholars, on being introduced, ask each other seriously, "Are you micro or macro?"

This sorry state of affairs, as Staw and Sutton note, in part reflects the retreat of social psychology to its two parent disciplines and the consequent creation (or re-creation) of two social psychologies, psychological and sociological. Both are apparently viable if not optimal subdisciplines, but neither satisfies the requirements of organizational studies. Staw and Sutton propose macro organizational psychology, defined as the use of individual states and traits to explain collective behavior, as a way of integrating the macro and micro levels. Their proposal is thus explicitly social psychological and unabashedly reductionistic, with the psychological level used to explain the social.

Staw and Sutton identify three main ways in which we can think about the organizational effects of individual characteristics. The most straightforward—and perhaps the most primitive—is to regard organizations as aggregations of individual characteristics. It follows that knowing more about the parts will enable us to know more about the whole. Stated in those conservative terms, the argument is almost unassailable. It is also limited, however. Organizations are of course the sum of their parts, but they are more than that, as Staw and Sutton appreciate. The method of aggregation is an acceptable beginning, provided that its use does not mislead us into mistaking its partial truths for larger revelations.

The second causal link from micro to macro phenomena is formed when semiautonomous members of an organization give organizational explanations for—and thus legitimacy to—what are really individually determined decisions and choices. Many prejudices and idiosyncrasies masquerade as policy.

Finally, and perhaps most important, Staw and Sutton remind us that psychological explanations for organizational behaviors are important because powerful individuals shape and influence organizations. This assertion emphasizes the importance of doing research at times when such influences are likely to be most strongly felt, in the development of new busienss, for example, or during the process of succession at top levels.

The argument that powerful individuals shape organizations represents a point of convergence between this chapter and Weick's. The processes by which founders and other persons in key positions shape organizations are explicit in Weick's treatment of sensemaking. His hypothetical sequence from individual action, commitment, and justification to macro organizational properties can be regarded as a specification of the third connection between micro and macro levels as proposed by Staw and Sutton. In combination, these authors make a strong case for the role of social psychology in explaining organizational behavior.

VENTURING INTO NEW DOMAINS

One way of advancing social psychological theory and research is to demonstrate that the social psychological approach can illuminate areas of significance in organizational life that other approaches have either ignored or found inaccessible. The dividing line between wholly new territory and the significant extension of areas already charted is admittedly arbitrary, but several chapters in this book address topics that seldom or never appear in earlier work.

The Brockner–Wiesenfeld chapter (6), which deals with the effects of layoffs on co-workers not laid off, is an obvious example. Research on unemployment, of course, is not new. Quantitative work on the subject goes back at least 60 years, to the time of the Great Depression, and each prolonged downturn in the business cycle since has produced its own set of unemployment studies.

Viewed as a single research literature, these studies show a remarkable convergence in major findings. Jahoda's early research in Austria (Lazarsfeld–Jahoda & Zeisel, 1933), *Seven Stranded Coal Towns* and the other monographs of the WPA Division of Research and Statistics (now lost beyond the reach of bibliographic retrieval), case studies like those of the U.S. Senate Committee on Unemployment Problems (Sheppard, Ferman, & Faber, 1960), and the more recent psychosocial epidemiological work of Cobb and Kasl (1977) combine with many other studies to document the psychological and physical damage of job loss.

We know, for example, that people rate job loss as one of life's most stressful events, less disturbing than death or divorce but more so than almost anything else. We know that in most cases savings are quickly exhausted, that their exhaustion is followed by borrowing, and that when unemployment is prolonged a significant proportion of families have depended on public relief programs.

The psychological and physical effects of unemployment are carefully described in the research by Cobb and Kasl (1977), which was unusual in several important respects. It was longitudinal rather than cross-sectional and retrospective; it utilized biomedical as well as self-reported data; and its quantitative findings were supplemented by intensive case studies of some of the unemployed workers (Slote, 1969).

This research showed that men who lost their jobs in plant closings, compared to those in similar plants that did not close, were more likely to be depressed, low in self-esteem, anxious and tense, irritable, easily angered, and suspicious. Moreover, these symptoms became more intense as the period of unemployment increased. The physiological findings were consistent with these psychological results. Even during the period of anticipated unemployment, there were increases in blood pressure, and they persisted until stable new jobs were acquired. Cholesterol levels and pulse rates showed similar patterns, and there were significant elevations in blood sugar. Days of disability for reasons of illness or injury went down for workers who found stable new jobs and up for those who did not.

It is remarkable, at least in retrospect, that this large literature of unemployment includes almost nothing about the effects of job loss on workers in the same organizations who keep their jobs. This is the subject of the work by Brockner and Wiesenfeld, and it is an important subject. Its importance becomes clear when we consider that most reductions in force involve a small proportion of workers laid off and a large proportion of survivors. Moreover, the purpose of the layoff is to strengthen the economic position of the organization; to the extent that the layoff has negative effects on the performance of survivors, the purpose of the layoff is defeated.

The Brockner–Wiesenfeld research on the ramifying effects of unemployment reminds us that organizational researchers too often stop at the organizational boundary, so to speak. There is some work, still inconclusive, on the effects of job characteristics on off-the-job activities (for example, Gardell, 1976) and some recent Swedish work on the physiological spillover effects of work on men and women (Frankenhaeuser, 1991), but these are rare examples. The system theorists' dictum that organizational boundaries are permeable is no longer disputed, but its implications are still to be realized. As social psychologists, we must remember that the lines of causation in organizational life are boundary crossers; they lead between roles, between persons, and between organizations.

Another venture into territory largely unexplored is the work on research collaboration by Northcraft and Neale (Chapter 10). The several separate strands that are combined in their work are familiar to social psychologists: The dramatic increase in jointly authored articles is well documented; there is a visible if thin line of research on voluntary cooperation in organizational life, and negotiation has generated a large literature of its own. The integration of these subjects is original, however, and the research findings have implications far beyond the collaboration of coauthors.

The underlying assumption of this research is that varied capabilities, when successfully combined, produce better science. This is an argument in favor of diversity, familiar in political as well as scientific affairs. The collaborative benefit is greatest, of course, when the diverse research inputs are complementary and the collaborators' preferences about outputs (research rewards such as order of authorship) are happily congruent. Since these ideals are seldom met, the process of collaboration is also a process of negotiation in which the partners must struggle against the tendency to underestimate the integrative benefits of collaboration and overestimate the perceived costs.

Contractual agreements, external research grants, and friendship are discussed as factors that enhance the prospects for successful collaboration. Contractual agreements have the advantage of decreasing uncertainties and enlarging the time frame, so that compromise and reciprocity become easier. Research grants, since they bring external resources to the collaboration over some specified time period, facilitate negotiation both by extending the time frame and "increasing the pie." Friendships also alter the time frame but more important, because of the intrinsic importance of the relationship itself, they reduce the relative importance of the bargained issues. That in turn makes it easier to reach agreements and thus to concentrate on the scientific task.

All this has relevance for formal organizations, but for me the most intriguing of the organizational leads comes in the discussion of renewal. Organizations, unlike individuals, are not bound to a life cycle of fixed (or modestly varying) length. Organizations can last indefinitely, but only so long as they continue to solve the never-ending problem of renewal. John Gardner (1981) has written insightfully on this issue at the individual and societal levels, but little research has been done at the organizational level.

As Northcraft and Neale see it, the need for renewal in the collaborative relationships of authors arises because of a gradual and unavoidable loss of diversity. This is a pernicious disease, not only because its onset is unnoticed, its damage gradual, and its ultimate effects fatal, but also because it is a side effect of collaborative success. The collaborative process itself gradually reduces diversity, and the partners are likely to experience their increasing similarity of conceptual vocabulary and conceptual viewpoint as increasingly comfortable. Moreover, proposals to introduce new members into an already successful collaboration confront the partners with choosing between a certain temporary process loss, at least, and a potential but uncertain larger benefit. People confronted by such choices, as Tversky and Kahneman (1981) have demonstrated, are characteristically short sighted and loss aversive.

The Northcraft–Neale chapter is more theoretical than empirical and more interpersonal than organizational, unless we regard the collaborative dyad as a mini-organization. But the organizational implications of their approach to collaboration are many and important. Organizations can be regarded as formal structures for facilitating collaborative effort, and conventional decisions about succession, recruitment, promotion, and transfer can be assessed in terms of their effects on collaborative relationships. For organizations that make use of matrix theories and task force strategies, which are devices for increasing collaborative effort, the relevance of the Northcraft–Neale chapter is still greater. In short, I read the chapter as a source of researchable hypotheses on an important and neglected topic, and I look forward to the empirical work that will test the Northcraft–Neale framework and extend it to the larger collaborative settings of organizational life.

The theme of voluntary cooperation in organizational life is represented directly in the chapter by Roderick Kramer (12), who notes the general neglect of this topic by organizational scholars. Kramer is primarily interested in the determinants of cooperation and his hypotheses are characteristically social psychological: Willingness to cooperate depends on identification with others, which in turn depends on the relative salience of group/organizational identities as compared to those that are personal/individual.

Kramer and his colleagues (for example, Brewer & Kramer, 1984) conducted a series of experiments to test the effects of group identification on the choices subjects make when group identification is manipulated and they are confronted with tasks representing several classic organizational problems. One of these is a resource management dilemma, in which individuals must decide how much to draw on a shared budget without knowing what others are doing, but with the final outcome affected by the overall restraint of the participants. Another experiment involves a free-loader problem, in which individuals engaged in a collective task know in advance that they will share equally in the resulting reward but each must decide how much effort to invest in its accomplishment. The experimental findings confirm the hypotheses; when group identification is salient, subjects reduce their consumption of resources from the common pool and constrain the tendency to free-load.

As Kramer notes, economists are not alone in making the assumption of self-interest the bedrock of their theoretical constructions. Agency theory, transaction-cost perspectives, and most theories of collective action also take self-interest as the prime mover in human affairs. Social psychology, on the other hand, recognizes that people are affiliative as well as calculative, emotional as well as rational, and communal as well as individualistic. Kramer concludes with Perrow's (1986) injunction that social researchers must treat self-interest as a variable to be explained, not as an assumption, and get away from "atomistic, undersocialized conceptions of human action."

These three chapters—Brockner and Wiesenfeld, Northcraft and Neale, and Kramer—are by no means the only exemplars of bringing social psychology into new or neglected organizational territory. They are, however, excellent examples of that venturesome process.

NEW APPROACHES TO CLASSIC PROBLEMS

Advances in research do not consist mainly of ventures into new substantive territory. Equally important are the explorations and corrections that enlarge our understanding of issues that have long been apparent. At least five such issues are addressed in the preceding chapters. They have to do with units of analysis, exercise of influence, fairness and justice, the role of affect, and the induction of organizational change. We consider each of these briefly, with illustrative material from chapters for which these topics are central.

Units of analysis

Organizations are complex systems; no one level of analysis is adequate to explain their complexities, nor is any one unit of analysis uniquely appropriate for explanation. Carroll's choice of the decision as the unit of analysis (Chapter 3) allows him to tap into a body of theory and research already well developed at individual and small group levels. With some notable exceptions (for example, Janis & Mann, 1977), however, social psychologists have not taken decision theory into the context of organizations.

Especially rare is organizational research in which large numbers of decisions of a single type can be assessed in the light of unambiguous outcomes. Parole decisions in the criminal justice system permit such assessment against the criteria of recidivism and new imprisonment. Moreover, the involvement of successive hierarchical levels in the decision to grant parole, and the availability of records of the decision-making process at each of those levels, presented Carroll with an unusual research opportunity and one that he has used well.

The results of the research are more enlightening than encouraging. A comparison of the decision-making data with prisoner outcomes one year after parole generates only low correlations between recommendations and subsequent behavior (recidivism)—negligible for case analysts and clinical psychologists, somewhat better for interviewers. As the main source of decisional error, Carroll identifies the process of causal attribution, its evocation of strongly held cognitive schemas, and a reciprocal process in which the attributions are shaped by the repertoire of available alternatives. The explication of these processes increases what we know of decision making in the organizational context and makes more understandable its characteristic limitations.

Ancona's work (Chapter 11) provides a second example of research in which the unit of analysis is a central issue. Here the analytic unit is more tangible than decision events; it is the primary workgroup. The research is built around the assumption that workgroups in organizations are much concerned with their external relations (that is, their relations with other groups within the organization).

This idea is not new. Ancona recognizes its origins in the work of Homans (1950), Lewin (1951), and Hackman (Hackman, Brousseau, & Weiss, 1976). To these names I must add those of Emery and Trist (1960), who in their early exposition of the sociotechnical approach proposed that one of the prime functions of leadership in any organizational unit is to manage that unit's relationship with others.

This proposition has not been much disputed, but neither has it been as influential in organizational research as it should have been; detailed conceptualizations of the relational process have been few. Ancona and Caldwell's typology of groups according to dominant functional pattern includes the ambassadorial, technical scouting, isolationist, and comprehensive. These types came initially from careful logging of the external activities of 38 new product teams. They are related in turn to performance as appraised by management and (differently) as perceived by group members, to the internal life of the group, and to goodness of fit between a group and its organizational environment.

As Carroll has done with decision making, Ancona has taken a familiar conceptual generalization—that external relations of primary workgroups are important for their internal life and their rated effectiveness—and gone systematically about unpacking it. It is an approach that deserves testing in other settings.

Equity, justice, and fairness

It would be fair to say that issues of equity and justice were brought into organizational research by social psychologists. Adam's (1965) chapter on inequity in social exchange was included among the advances in experimental social psychology in that year (Berkowitz, 1965), and within a decade, more or less, studies of distributive and procedural justice were being conducted in ongoing organizations as well as laboratories.

The substantive core of this work is equity theory, which Martin (Chapter 14) considers inherently biased in favor of existing organizational arrangements, because they are assumed to be legitimate. The appropriateness of that assumption depends, of course, on one's definition of legitimacy. If it means merely recognizing the rules of the game, so to speak, and accepting those rules as a condition for remaining a player, the assumption seems appropriate. It does not follow, however, that those rules are personally satisfying or that they meet some external criterion of justice or fairness.

Martin prefers a definition of legitimacy that includes considerations of justice and fairness, and she has ample authority for doing so (for example, Habermas, 1979). The considerable importance of her chapter, however, lies in its careful distinction between justice, equality, and legitimacy per se. Moreover, a series of studies by Martin and her colleagues bear out the importance of the distinctions she proposes.

The first of these, done with blue-collar workers in seven manufacturing plants, required the subjects to design three pay plans for managers and workers—one to be expected, one satisfying, and one just. The plans differed in the resulting gap between worker and managerial pay—greatest in the expected plan and least in the just plan, with the satisfying plan falling between. Subsequent studies replicated and extended these findings with other occupational categories and industries. And in all of them, individual differences in designing plans to these several criteria were explained to a significant degree by ideological factors—identified as meritocratic versus skeptical, feminist versus nonfeminist, and the like.

The data support the argument: Organizational theory can gain by unpacking the concept of legitimacy, differentiating the issue of equity from those of equality and justice, and thus making value assumptions accessible to test.

Bazerman (Chapter 9) is concerned with some of the same issues, and his chapter, like Martin's, enlarges our understanding of them. His emphasis is on the processes of social comparison that generate judgments of fairness and on the forms of "irrationality" that affect such judgments. As equity theory proposes, people use the rewards of others as a basis for evaluating their own and reaching a conclusion about "fairness," but the process of comparison is complex.

The resulting deviations from any of several criteria of rationality—the immediate maximization of personal reward, of Pareto-model efficiency, and consistency of preference—are substantial and deserve to be understood. In exploring the reasons for such differences, Bazerman moves us beyond the generalized notion of social comparison on which most equity research has depended.

Exercise of influence

Three chapters in this book deal in detail with the exercise of influence, although they come at the subject in the context of different issues—Chapter 5 (Meindl) on leadership, Chapter 7 (Tyler) on authority, and Chapter 13 (Lawler) on social power. All three deal with concepts that are familiar in organizational theory, but each of these chapters brings something new to the investigation.

Meindl calls his approach to leadership radical, and it is. Its radicalism expresses Meindl's two main criticisms of more conventional approaches—the treatment of leadership as so inclusive that it becomes "everything and nothing," and the concentration on leader-centered explanations of an interactive process. With some notable exceptions—Fiedler's work (1967), for example—I concur with Meindl's criticisms. Nevertheless, I find the antidote hard to swallow; to correct for overconcentration on the leader, it substitutes an almost total concentration on followers. Leadership is defined at one point as "an experience undergone by followers."

For our present purpose, however, the important point is the number of new and researchable questions that this approach to leadership suggests. By what processes of attribution do certain leaders come to be seen as charismatic? By what processes of interaction and contagion do followers reach near consensus on such attributions? To what extent is the emergence of charismatic leadership dependent on the social perception of crisis?

Tyler's chapter (7) can be regarded as an attempt to explicate the ambivalence that people report and express toward those who exercise authority—that is, power that is conferred by the formal rules of an organization and backed by its rewards and sanctions. Tyler believes that acceptance of authority is based on the recognition that rules and direction are necessary to solve problems, meet crises, and get on with the business of interdependent production.

The opposition to authority, or at least the reluctance to accept the decisions of authorities, Tyler finds rooted in questions of fairness, partly with respect to allocation of tangible rewards but partly with respect to status or standing, the acknowledgment by authorities of one's value to the group.

He is led therefore to develop a "relational model" (Tyler & Lind, in press) that includes the variables of standing, trust, and neutrality. These involve, respectively, information regarding one's status, confidence in the benevolent intentions of the authorities, and belief that the authorities provide equal opportunities to group members.

The empirical data to test this model by no means contradict the importance of resource outcomes in determining loyalty and its behavioral expression, but they demonstrate the concurrent importance of the three relational elements. It is perhaps ironic that organizational researchers should need to be reminded that neither economic nor interpersonal explanations of organizational behavior suffice, but the need is difficult to deny.

Lawler's chapter (13) presents the results of a 20-year programmatic effort to enlarge social psychological understanding of a fundamental organizational process—the exercise of power. Almost 40 years ago, Cartwright (1953) had accused social psychologists of being "soft on power," a fault that he described as "a major deficiency of our theories." It was a justifiable criticism, and one that was particularly serious for social psychologists who studied organizations. In the decades since, many organizational researchers have addressed issues of power and a few (Tannenbaum, 1968, 1974, for example) have put power and control at the center of their work. Lawler's research, much of it done in collaboration with Bacharach, is perhaps the most sustained and influential of such efforts still under way.

Lawler bases his work on the proposition that power in organizations is a nonzero-sum phenomenon. That idea is not new, as he points out, but much organizational theorizing has continued to depend, explicitly or implicitly, on zero-sum formulations. Acceptance of the nonzero-sum formulation in principle has not led to its general incorporation in empirical research.

Lawler has done just that, in the laboratory and in the field. There is an impressive progression apparent in the five stages of his research during the past two decades. He began with a specific question about "revolutionary coalitions"—under what conditions will subordinates form a coalition against their formal leader? That led to the related issue of how leaders forestall such revolts, and then to a more general theory of power dependence and its effect on tactics of influence. Exploring the link between structurally determined power dependence and tactical choice led in turn to hypotheses that predict bilateral deterrence.

Lawler's model, which involves separate measurement of absolute (total amount) and relative power, is successful in explaining many phenomena of organizational life—conflict and conciliation, deterrence and escalation (conflict spiral), co-optation and rebellious coalition. The implications and, in my view, the applicability of these findings extend beyond organizations to the level of nation-states, where the need for insight and innovation in the exercise of power is uniquely urgent.

Affect: the search for intervening variables

Most social psychological research in organizations involves some part of a hypothetical causal sequence that leads from the environment of organizations to their structural properties, the behavioral expression of those properties by people in positions of authority, the perception and cognition of those behaviors by other organizational members, the short-term responses (physiological, psychological, and behavioral) thus evoked, and the consequences for the individual, the organization, and the larger society. Of the psychological responses of members to their organizational experiences, the dimension of satisfaction–dissatisfaction has been the most thoroughly researched.

The emphasis of early human relations researchers on job satisfaction reflected both their humanistic values and the hopeful hypothesis that satisfaction was an intervening variable between organizational properties, especially supervisory behavior, and productivity. This is a hypothesis so user friendly, to use a term less venerable than the hypothesis itself, that its demise before an onslaught of disconfirming data (Vroom, 1964, for example) was remarkably slow. No other universalistic proposal for an affective link in the causal chain has replaced it, which is probably good for our science. On the other hand, no serious observer of organizations can doubt that organizational life is warm with emotion. The chapters by Baron (4) and Folger (8), in different ways, take us into the domain of affective responses, their antecedents, and their consequences.

Baron's work over a period of more than 20 years shows a sustained interest in aggression and the factors that evoke or moderate its expression. His investigations have included environmental factors (temperature, odor, lighting), demographic factors (race, gender), and the concomitant induction of affective states (humor, sexual arousal) hypothesized to be aggression incompatible. The link to organizational behavior was suggested by the fact that managers reported spending up to 25 percent of their time dealing with conflict problems, the assumption that many such conflicts have interpersonal causes, and the hypothesis that they might yield to psychological rather than structural interventions. The result was a series of laboratory experiments in which subjects demonstrated increased willingness to collaborate after conflict when humor or sympathy was induced.

As always, these interesting research findings generated a list of new research questions, which are well summarized in the concluding pages of Baron's chapter. For our purposes, the most relevant of them have to do with the importance of different affective states for predicting organizational behavior, and with the mechanisms by which affect influences behavior.

Folger's work (Chapter 8) concentrates on a single affective state, resentment, which he regards as a negative side effect of the basic exchange involved in paid employment. It is not an inevitable side effect, however, but one induced by the perception of significant loss, absolute or in comparison with relevant others. It is affected also by circumstances surrounding the imposition of such losses. In hierarchical organizations these circumstances are under the control of people in positions of authority. The behavior of people in these positions determines, for example, the adequacy of explanation for imposed losses.

Laboratory experiments dealing with such issues were followed by three field studies, one of workers laid off and two of the survivors of such layoffs. Folger interprets the results in terms of a two-factor theory (his dual-obligation model) that closely parallels the distinction between distributive and procedural justice. Absence of either predicts resentment and a consequent lack of organizational commitment.

Together these chapters constitute a strong argument for the explanatory value of affective elements in organizational life. Social psychology, more than any other discipline, is concerned with the role of affect in interpersonal relations but, except for the ubiquitous measures of satisfaction, there has been little evidence of that concern in organizational research. We can hope that these chapters encourage additional and wider ranging explorations of affective factors in organizational life.

Organizational change

Organizational change has been much researched and even more widely discussed, advocated, and attempted. The induction of some changes and the prevention of others absorb much time and effort among managers, and no less in the deliberations of labor unions. Change is of course the main business of organizational consultants and the preoccupation of popular authors.

There is general recognition that all organizational change is not of one kind, and various typologies of change have been proposed. Some are based on the primary target of change (Katz & Kahn, 1978), some on the mode of intervention (Kahn, 1981), and others on still other criteria. Bartunek's (Chapter 15) main concern is with the distinction between first order and second order change. First order change is typically incremental, quantitative rather than qualitative, but its defining property is cognitive; it makes sense within schemata (organizing frameworks) that are already understood and shared within the organization. Second order change, in contrast, is qualitative, discontinuous, and requires new schemata. Similar distinctions appear elsewhere in Bartunek's work (Bartunek & Louis, 1988, and Bartunek & Moch, 1989, for example) and in the work of others whom she cites (Golembiewski, Billingsley, & Yeager, 1976; Mohrman & Lawler, 1985). Her formulation reminded me also of Argyris's distinction between single loop and double loop learning (Argyris & Schon, 1978).

The power of the chapter and its implications for other investigations stem in part from Bartunek's deep involvement in, and sustained observation of, organizational efforts at creating second order change. One example of insights that come out of such experience is the connectedness of organizational change and conflict. A significant environmental demand or a crisis of some other kind may bring many different organizational groups into agreement on the need for change, but they are likely to disagree on what changes will answer that need, with the result that two or more new schemata for the organization are in active conflict. The creative solution to such intraorganizational conflicts, as Bartunek puts it and Hegel might have, is neither thesis nor antithesis, but synthesis.

Social psychological research in organizations needs to discover the conditions under which such creative outcomes are likely to occur, and social psychological theories of organizational change need to be integrated with theories of conflict and conflict management. Bartunek's work, like that of Bazerman (Chapter 9), moves these issues forward on our common agenda.

A COMMENT ON METHODS

This book is primarily concerned with matters of substance rather than method. In one crucial respect, however, the work described in the preceding chapters breaks significantly—and for the better—with earlier methodological habits in our field. Past research in social psychology, at least as it has addressed organizational issues, reflects a condition that can reasonably be termed methodological addiction.

Fortunately for the discipline and for progress in understanding organizations, not all researchers have been addicted to the same method. Nevertheless, the image of methods in search of a problem is not reassuring. One would prefer a stage of development in which the problem to be explored or the hypothesis to be tested would suggest the method of choice, and the methodological repertoire of the researcher would be large enough to respond appropriately. Experimental or nonexperimental designs, laboratory or field research, qualitative or quantitative methods of investigation are choices that should be determined by the needs of the science rather than the limitations of the scientist.

I must add that the monocular view of methodological choice that has characterized much of organizational research has been apparent as well in application and practice by social scientists. If you were to tell me the names of the organizational researchers consulted by a number of different corporations, I believe that in most cases I could tell you whether the instruments of organizational therapy were qualitative or quantitative, surveys or experiments, individual counsel or modified encounter groups. In short, for much of their history both research and practice in organizational behavior show a pattern of single methods and sovereign remedies. The same could have been said once of medicine, but not since the net effect of medical practice on life expectancy has become positive. It is with such reflections and prejudices in mind that I celebrate the methodological variety and depth of the preceding chapters.

The examples are many, and I will cite only a few. Carroll pursues the topic of decision making, as his chapter title suggests, "out of the lab and into the field." The series of studies he reports are both experimental and nonexperimental. The data sources range from self-report and behavior under simulated conditions to the protocols of parole boards and decisions in nuclear power plants.

Lawler's studies of power and its exercise are based both on data from field studies and laboratory experiments. Martin's studies of justice and its limitations in organizational life include design characteristics seldom found in combination; they are truly experimental and of limited duration but they were conducted with different populations (blue-collar and white-collar) in ongoing organizations. Folger's studies of the negative side effects of the characteristic organizational exchange (effort for tangible reward) have been done in both field and laboratory. And Staw and Sutton, in their proposal for macro organizational psychology, utilize studies of impression management and organizational death that involve both qualitative and quantitative research, and depend on materials that range from traces of international events in the media to intensive interviews with key informants about the demise of their organizations.

Variety of method for its own sake, of course, is no virtue. The methodological versatility of these investigations, however, has contributed both to their insights and to the strength of their conclusions.

FOUR PROPOSALS FOR FURTHER RESEARCH

Advances in the social psychology of organizations, satisfying as they are in many respects, lead to the question, "What next?" Organizational theory is not so unitary nor so fully developed that the answers to that question, were we to ask it of a representative group of researchers, could be expected to reveal some marvelous consensus. I suspect that answers might be more interesting for their idiosyncratic differences than for their convergence. With that likelihood in mind, I offer four topics that I believe deserve serious attention from social psychologists who study organizations:

1. Sociotechnics revisited
2. Organizational renewal
3. Coherence in loosely coupled systems
4. Organizational perspectives on international relations.

Sociotechnics revisited

The concept of productive organizations as sociotechnical systems is more than 30 years old, and it has had a substantial influence on organizational theory and research. I believe, however, that our use of the sociotechnical approach has been very limited, and it is for that reason I propose it now deserves to be revisited.

The basic idea, of course, is that any productive system includes both a technological organization—layout of equipment and specification of process—and a social organization that specifies individual tasks and the relationships of individuals who perform them (Emery & Trist, 1960; Rice, 1958; Trist & Bamforth, 1951). Two questions of goodness of fit are thus raised: the fit between the social and technical aspects of an organization, and the fit between the resulting sociotechnical structure and the human characteristics of the people who enact it.

Research in the sociotechnical tradition has addressed these questions by accepting the technology as given and attempting to discover which of the organizational possibilities compatible with that technology was most acceptable to members of the organization. The early work in the British coal mines, for example, was an empirical comparison of two socially different methods of using the then-new equipment (Trist & Bamforth, 1951). Both methods were in use, and the research task was essentially one of comparison.

Other work in the same tradition, most of it later, was more ambitious; research workers proposed innovations in the social organization of work rather than limiting themselves to the observation of differences already in existence (Davis & Cherns, 1975; Rice, 1958; Thorsrud, Sørensen, & Gustavsen, 1976). But this work continued to take the technology as a starting point, to accept the limitations that it set, and then to ask how fully the needs of individuals could be met within those technological limits. Major modifications in existing technologies for the purpose of improving the psychosocial aspects of work are rare, and cases in which a new technology was invented for that purpose are almost nonexistent. The introduction of an alternative to assembly-line production of automobiles in the Volvo plant at Kalmar (Sweden) generated sustained public interest precisely because it was a unique event: an attempt to invent and adapt technology to the needs of individuals (Agurén, Hansson, & Karlsson, 1976).

Decades of organizational research have documented quite thoroughly the psychosocial conditions that affect the quality of working life—challenge, variety, autonomy, affiliative bonds, adequate material rewards, and the like. Some key determinants of those conditions, however, lie beyond the boundaries of the social sciences. To discover them and to improve the quality of working life therefore requires a kind of interdisciplinary collaboration that has yet to be created, the collaboration of social psychologists with engineers and architects. Members of these latter professions, jointly with managers, determine the technology with which employees work and define the space within which they work. In so doing, members of these professions determine in large part the quality of working life. Collaborative relationships between engineers and social scientists are thus necessary to launch an era of studies—largely experimental in both laboratory and field—that will for the first time show how nearly the goals of production and consumption can be made to converge. It was with such research in mind that I chose the subhead "sociotechnics revisited."

Organizational renewal

This is an area that has already been suggested by the work of Northcraft and Neale (Chapter 10) on research collaboration. I am convinced of its importance for organizational theory and its special timeliness for the United States and the major organizations that it comprises.

Most organizations and most civilizations whose histories we know about appear to have had a life span—a beginning, a period of growth, perhaps of flourishing, a period of decline, and a death. It is impossible to see one's own historical moment with the perspective conferred by time and distance. Nevertheless, in the eyes of some astute observers (Gardner, 1978, for example) and by many standards—income per capita, longevity, absence of domestic violence, worker productivity, and others—the United States appears to be nearing the end of a long period of unequalled national success.

The meaning of national renewal and even the need for it may still be a matter for political debate. The need for organizational renewal is less debatable; its meaning is easier to grasp, and the process is more readily researchable. Moreover, the issue of organizational renewal has been addressed by some organizational theorists, although not all of them have used that term. Examples include Argyris's emphasis on double-loop learning and strategic change (Argyris, 1982; Argyris & Schon, 1978) and Bennis's discussion of transformational leadership (Bennis & Nanus, 1985). Lawrence and Dyer's (1983) book, *Renewing American Industry,* proposes a theory of organizational adaptation and a set of specific hypotheses that await testing.

These authors, and others whom they cite, see a widespread need for organizational change of a kind more profound than most practitioners and scholars contemplate. I believe that organizational researchers should search out the substantive commonalities and differences in such approaches, work past the terminological differences, and initiate a sequence of studies that will advance the theory and practice of organizational change of this special kind.

Coherence in loosely coupled systems

Maintaining bonds of sufficient strength to keep a large complex system together and at the same time provide the autonomy that its component subsystems demand has become one of the most visible and important organizational dilemmas of our time. As this chapter is written, a period of unprecedented organizational combination and agglomeration is being followed by a time of divestment and decomposition. These latter processes are driven not only by the burden of recklessly assumed debt, but also by the frequent organizational discovery that the acquired parts could not be successfully integrated into the larger whole. The reasons for such failures are not well understood, and the conspicuous rarity of satisfying post hoc explanations is exceeded only by the absence of their earliest prediction.

Sociology and psychology are not without conceptual resources to study these organizational phenomena. The concepts of differentiation and integration are familiar to both disciplines, and systems theorists have long been concerned with both concepts as developmental processes. Von Bertalanffy (1956) proposed that all open systems move toward increasing differentiation, but that as differentiation proceeds, it is countered in viable systems by processes that prevent disintegration. Georgopoulos (1975) distinguished two such processes, integration and coordination, the former maintaining organizational unification through shared norms and values, the latter through the imposition of controls and regulations. Katz and Kahn (1978) discussed differentiation and integration as opposing and complementary processes that are unavoidable aspects of organizational growth and argued that the costs of coordination set limits to such growth.

These theoretical generalities have their counterparts in network theory and its organizational applications (Aldrich & Whetten, 1981), but we lack the body of sustained empirical investigation that the subject demands. Current organizational ideologies speak in praise of diversity, and the increasing diversity of American society is widely remarked. Biological theories are explicit about the importance of diversity as an evolutionary mechanism of survival. We lack data, however, about how, in the most successful human organizations, the needs and demands of diverse components are made compatible with the need of the organization as a whole for coherence.

The importance of this issue for nation-states as well as for organizations is too obvious to require elaboration. Civil wars, the fractionation of continents into untenable quasi-national units, the effort to create a commonwealth of former soviet republics, and the hopeful development of the European community on land where ancient enemies fought for centuries—all exemplify the effort to reconcile unavoidable interdependencies with unquenchable needs for autonomy of individuals and the groups with which they identify. Social psychologists committed to the study of organizations can find no more challenging set of problems on which to work.

Organizational perspectives
on international relations

The preceding discussion of coherence in loosely coupled systems exemplifies a more general point—the possibility that organizational theory and research may have special relevance for international affairs. Among the organizational phenomena that seem important at the international level are the management of interdependence between autonomous units and the making of decisions by organizational systems consisting of unequal components.

MANAGING INTERDEPENDENCE BETWEEN AUTONOMOUS UNITS.   Political scientists tell us that the dominant paradigm in international affairs is realist theory, a rather self-congratulatory title selected by those who take that point of view. The basic premise of the realists is Hobbesian; it assumes that the anarchic state of each against all is inevitable in the absence of a hegemon, and that the security and sovereign survival of each nation therefore depends on its ability to defend itself against attack (Mares & Powell, 1990).

An alternative paradigm would begin with the premise that nations are interdependent, that technological developments are rapidly increasing that interdependence, and that the existence of nuclear weapons has made national security itself a problem in learning to manage unavoidable interdependencies.

That task, the management of interdependence, is what organizations and organizational theory are about, at levels from the interpersonal to the international. Recognition of interdependence between individuals at the level of the workgroup was central to the early work of the human relations school (Argyris, 1957; Likert, 1961; Mayo, 1933; McGregor, 1960; Roethlisberger & Dickson, 1939), which treated the management of interdependence within the workgroup as the central task of supervision and regarded participative decision making as the most effective way of accomplishing that task. One of the main elements in sociotechnical theory was an analogous proposition at the organizational level: "Similarly, the primary task in managing the enterprise as a whole is to relate the system to its environment and is not in internal regulation per se" (Emery & Trist, 1973, p. 220).

Over the years, other organizational scholars have emphasized the relationships between each organization and its environment of others (Evan, 1966; Lawrence & Lorsch, 1967), and this emphasis has been continued in resource-dependence models of organizational behavior (Hannan & Freeman, 1977; Scott, 1981). The concept of interdependence is fundamental in such models; without significant interdependence there would be no incentive to assume the risks and costs of conflict or the effort of cooperation.

A persisting question for every organization, therefore, is how best to manage interdependencies—that is, how to minimize the costs and maximize the benefits of existing and potential interdependent relationships. Elsewhere, my colleagues and I (Kahn & Zald, 1990) have proposed that this question be approached in terms of a hypothetical continuum in which the scale points represent specific structural arrangements for the management of interdependence between two organizations. Arranged in order of increasing proportions of managed as compared to "unmanaged" interdependence, we than have an ordinal scale anchored at one end by total combination (merger or absorption) and at the other by no-holds-barred conflict. Between these extremes are markets, informal agreements, spot contracts, continuing contracts, and joint ventures.

So far as I know, no systematic data are available on the relative costs and benefits of these various modes of interorganizational relations, each of which seems to have its counterpart at the international level. Nor have systematic comparisons been made within categories. For example, we do not know what factors differentiate successful joint ventures from those that fail, those that endure from those whose lifelines are short, those that tend to induce further cooperation between their principals and those that do not. Research of these kinds would be important both for understanding organizations and for realizing the potential contributions of organizational research to international relations.

FORMAL DECISIONS IN ORGANIZATIONS WITH UNEQUAL COMPONENTS.   International organizations, from the United Nations to those least ambitious in numbers and purpose, almost always consist of units (nations) that differ greatly in size and power, a fact that makes it extremely difficult to reach agreement about the formal basis for making decisions. The principle of national sovereignty implies that decisions of such multinational bodies be made on the basis of one nation, one vote. This principle is predictably unacceptable to nations of great size or power, which are likely to prefer procedures weighted to take account of these characteristics. Bicameral solutions to such problems are variously successful, and the UN invention of the Security Council, with its rotating and permanent members, cannot be considered a total success. In short, the question of how units of unequal size and power can reach joint decisions that are acceptable to all the participating units and that maximize their long-term collective good remains a serious international dilemma.

I do not think that organizational scholars have resolved this problem in theory or that organizational practitioners have solved it in practice. I do believe, however, that most large organizations encounter this problem in some form, that they have evolved many different ways of dealing with it, and that these different approaches are not equally successful. Research to document the ways in which organizational collectivities made up of unequal components reach joint decisions, and to evaluate the costs and benefits of these different mechanisms, could add significantly to organizational theory and contribute to solving the decisional dilemma at the international level.

CONCLUSION

Writing a conclusion to a concluding chapter is by definition an exercise in iteration, but it is also a useful test of the material. Arguments and expositions that depend on style rather than substance tend to vanish under the pressure of summarization. And for content that is stress resistant, a conclusion serves a purpose like that of summary statistics for a baseball or football game; it gives readers a convenient basis for reevaluating what they have already seen in greater detail.

As the subheads of this chapter suggest, I have found that the chapters of this book advance the social psychological study of organizations in three ways: (1) by deepening our understanding of why social psychology is essential for explaining and predicting organizational phenomena, (2) by bringing social psychology to bear on organizational questions not previously investigated in these terms, and (3) by adding to what is known about organizational domains already studied by social psychologists.

Social psychology and organizations

The first of these functions is exemplified especially in the chapters by Weick (2) and by Staw and Sutton (16). Weick's thesis is radical; he asserts that social psychology is not merely relevant for understanding organizations, it is central. In contrast to the usual definitions of organizations, which emphasize their economic functions, Weick's definition is explicitly social psychological: Organizations are collectivities of people trying to make sense of what is happening to them. From this starting point, Weick develops a line of argument so closely reasoned that readers are enlightened, whether or not they are wholly persuaded.

Staw and Sutton propose a new term, *macro organizational psychology*, to designate the heartland of organizational research. Research in this field uses individual characteristics as its independent variables and collective behavior as its dependent variable, thus integrating the micro and macro levels of discourse that have become illogically separated as subspecialties. I regard this proposal as compatible with Weick's framework, and in a sense derivative from it. It exemplifies the process of explaining organizational outcomes by building from individual states, traits, and behaviors.

My own research interests also involve the integration of micro and macro levels, but in a direction that complements Staw and Sutton. I am concerned with the effects of organizational (macro) attributes on individual health and well-being. I hope that research along these lines can be included in their macro organizational psychology.

Venturing into new domains

We discussed three main examples of such ventures in the chapters of this book—(1) the extension of unemployment research to include effects on those still employed in the same organizations; (2) a dynamic theoretical framework for studying intellectual collaboration; and (3) experimental studies on the determinants of cooperation in organizational life.

The first of these, research on "survivors" of in-plant layoffs (Brockner & Wiesenfeld, Chapter 6) begins to fill a gap that is obvious as soon as it is pointed out. Studies of unemployment have produced a large literature, but it has focused almost entirely on the unemployed themselves. The extension to survivors is important not only because they are affected, but because the organizational rationale for layoffs assumes zero or positive effects on those who retain their jobs.

Intellectual collaboration in research and writing has been rapidly increasing, at least as measured by the frequency of joint authorship. I believe that the trend is real, not some epiphenomenon of cultural drift or changing etiquette. It is driven by the increasing complexity of scientific technology and the requirement for large-scale scientific enterprise. Northcraft and Neale (Chapter 10) have opened this topic for study by organizational researchers, who have every reason to become interested in the organizational properties of science-making itself.

Kramer's chapter (12) can be read as an attempt to correct the common assumption that self-interest is the dominant motive in human behavior. The attempt is successful, as I read the evidence, which consists mainly of experimental work by Kramer and his colleagues. Those experiments, which model some classic organizational problems, demonstrate that self-interest is more appropriately treated as a variable than a constant and that its variability depends on group identification.

New approaches to classic problems

Research advances in any field consist mainly of new approaches to familiar problems or new findings that amplify the answers to such problems. The chapters of this book address five of these problem areas: units of analysis, exercise of influence, fairness and justice, the role of affect, and the induction of organizational change. The relevance of different units and levels of analysis for explaining organizational behavior is illustrated in the work of Carroll (Chapter 3) and Ancona (Chapter 11), the former using organizational decisions as the analytic unit and the latter built around a typology of workgroups.

Martin (Chapter 14) and Bazerman (Chapter 9) deal with equity, justice, and fairness in organizational life. Martin's experiments in organizations demonstrate that workers distinguish between reward allocations that are "expected," satisfying, and just—distinctions that are lacking in most equity research. Bazerman illuminates the complex social comparisons by which organization members make such distinctions and the ways in which their judgments deviate from criteria of rationality.

Exercise of influence

Three chapters report work in this domain: Meindl on leadership (Chapter 5), Tyler on authority (Chapter 7), and Lawler on social power (Chapter 13). All three chapters can be read as corrections to the prolonged overemphasis of organizational scholars on the downward exercise of influence (that is, hierarchical influence as viewed from above). Meindl concentrates on acts of leaders as they are perceived by followers; Tyler deals with authority and the response to those who exercise it; Lawler's cumulative research program begins with the challenge to authority by coalitions of subordinates.

Affect: the search for intervening variables

Baron (Chapter 4) and Folger (Chapter 8) share an interest in affective states as variables that are evoked by characteristics of the work situation and are among the immediate determinants of behavior at work. Both report research that began as an attempt to explain a negative response—aggression in Baron's case and resentment in Folger's. Together they go far toward correcting the tendency of organizational researchers to restrict the study of affect to global measures of satisfaction and dissatisfaction.

Organizational change

No research topic in our field has a longer lifeline than organizational change and few, if any, are more important. Organizational leadership involves continuing efforts to induce some changes and prevent others, and organizational opposition can be described in exactly the same terms. Bartunek (Chapter 15) recognizes the consequent linkage of organizational change to conflict, especially when the changes are profound, and she shows the potentialities for creative outcomes.

I ended my review of the preceding chapters with four proposals for further research. To put it another way, I ended an appreciation of advances in organizational research by asking for more. Both the review and the proposals reflect the vigor of social psychology in organizations. At a time when scholars in some fields are critical of recent stagnation and uncertain about the remedy, it is encouraging to find organizational researchers excited about their current work and no less so about their agenda for the future. I look forward to the next generation of social psychological advances in the study of human organizations.

REFERENCES

ADAMS, J. S. (1965). Injustice in social exchange. In L. Berkowitz (Ed.), *Advances in experimental social psychology* (Vol. 2, pp. 267–299). New York: Academic Press.

AGURÉN, S., HANSSON, R., & KARLSSON, K. G. (1976). *The impact of new design on work organization.* Stockholm: The Rationalization Council SAF-LO.

ALDRICH, H. E. (1979). *Organizations and environments.* Englewood Cliffs, NJ: Prentice Hall.

ALDRICH, H. E., & WHETTEN, D. A. (1981). Organization-sets, action-sets, and networks: Making the most of simplicity. In P. C. Nystrom and W. H. Starbuck (Eds.), *Handbook of organizational design* (pp. 385–408). London: Oxford University Press.

ANCONA, D. G., & CALDWELL, D. F. (1987). Management issues facing new-product teams in high technology companies. In D. Lewin, D. Lipsky, & D. Sokel (Eds.), *Advances in industrial and labor relations* (Vol. 4, pp. 199–221). Greenwich, CT: JAI Press.

ARGYRIS, C. (1957). *Personality and organization.* New York: Harper.

ARGYRIS, C. (1985). Making knowledge more relevant to practice: Maps for action. In E. E. Lawler et al. (Eds.), *Doing research that is useful for theory and practice* (pp. 79–125). Beverly Hills, CA: Sage.

ARGYRIS, C., & SCHÖN, D. A. (1978). *Organizational learning: A theory of action perspective.* Reading, MA: Addison-Wesley.

ASHBY, W. R. (1952). *Design for a brain.* New York: Wiley.

BARTUNEK, J. M., & LOUIS, M. R. (1988). The interplay of organization development and organizational transformation. In R. Woodman & W. Pasmore (Eds.), *Research in organizational change and development* (Vol. 2, pp. 97–134). Greenwich, CT: JAI Press.

BARTUNEK, J. M., & MOCH, M. K. (1989, August). *Organizational schemata which specify and affect intergroup relationships within organizations.* Paper presented at the working conference on managerial thought and cognition, Washington, DC.

BENNIS, W., & NANUS, B. (1985). *Leaders: The strategies for taking charge.* New York: Harper & Row.

BERKOWITZ, L. (Ed.). (1965). *Advances in experimental social psychology* (Vol. 2). New York: Academic Press.

BREWER, M. B., & KRAMER, R. M. (1984, August). *Subgroup identity as a factor in conservation of resources.* Paper presented at the American Psychological Association annual convention, Washington, DC.

CARTWRIGHT, D. (1953, September). *Toward a social psychology of groups.* Presidential address delivered before the Society for the Psychological Study of Social Issues, Cleveland, OH.

COBB, S., & KASL, S. (1977). *Termination: The consequences of job loss.* U.S. Department of Health, Education and Welfare. Washington, DC: U.S. Government Printing Office.

DAVIS, L. E., & CHERNS, A. B. (1975). *The quality of working life* (Vols. 1–2). New York: Free Press.

EMERY, F. E., & TRIST, E. L. (1960). Socio-technical systems. In *Management science models and techniques* (Vol. 2). London: Pergamon.

EMERY, F. E., & TRIST, E. L. (1965). The causal texture of organizational environments. *Human Relations, 18,* 21–32.

EMERY, F. E., & TRIST, E. L. (1973). *Toward a social ecology.* New York: Plenum.

EVAN, W. M. (1966). The organization-set: Toward a theory of interorganizational relations. In J. D. Thompson (Ed.), *Approaches to organizational design* (pp. 173–188). Pittsburgh: University of Pittsburgh Press.

FIEDLER, F. E. (1967). *A theory of leadership effectiveness.* New York: McGraw-Hill.

FRANKENHAEUSER, M. (1991). The psychophysiology of sex differences as related to occupational status. In M. Frankenhaeuser, U. Lundberg, & M. Chesney (Eds.), *Women, work, & health* (pp. 39–61). New York: Plenum.

GARDELL, B. (1976). *Job content and quality of life.* Stockholm: Prisma.

GARDNER, J. W. (1978). *Morale.* New York: Norton.

GARDNER, J. W. (1981). *Self-renewal: The individual and the innovative society* (rev. ed.). New York: Norton.

GEORGOPOULOS, B. S. (1975). *Hospital organization research: Review and source book.* Philadelphia: W. B. Saunders.

GLEICK, J. (1987). *Chaos: Making a new science.* New York: Viking.

GOLEMBIEWSKI, R. T., BILLINGSLEY, K., & YEAGER, S. (1976). Measuring change and persistence in human affairs: Types of change generated by OD designs. *Journal of Applied Behavioral Science, 12,* 133–157.

HABERMAS, J. (1979). *Communication and the evolution of society.* Boston: Beacon Press.

HACKMAN, J. R., BROUSSEAU, K. R., & WEISS, J. A. (1976). The interaction of task design and group performance strategies in determining group effectiveness. *Organizational Behavior and Human Performance, 16,* 350–365.

HAIRE, M. (1959). Biological models and empirical histories of the growth of organizations. In M. Haire (Ed.), *Modern organization theory* (pp. 272–306). New York: Wiley.

HANNAN, M. T., & FREEMAN, J. H. (1977). The population ecology of organizations. *American Journal of Sociology, 82,* 929–964.

HOMANS, G. (1950). *The human group.* New York: Harcourt Brace Jovanovich.

JANIS, I. L., & MANN, L. (1977). *Decisionmaking: A psychological analysis of conflict, choice, and commitment.* New York: Free Press.

KAHN, R. L. (1981). *Work and health*. New York: Wiley.

KAHN, R. L., & ZALD, M. N. (1990). *Organizations and nation-states: New perspectives on conflict and cooperation*. San Francisco: Jossey-Bass.

KATZ, D., & KAHN, R. L. (1978). *The social psychology of organizations* (2nd ed.). New York: Wiley.

LAWRENCE, P. R., & DYER, D. (1983). *Renewing American industry*. New York: Free Press.

LAWRENCE, P. R., & LORSCH, J. W. (1967). *Organization and environment*. Boston: Harvard Business School, Division of Research.

LAZARSFELD–JAHODA, M., & ZEISEL, H. (1933). *Die Arbeitslosen von Marienthal*. Leipzig: S. Hirzel.

LEWIN, K. (1951). *Field theory in social science: Selected theoretical papers*. D. Cartwright (Ed.). New York: Harper & Brothers Publishers.

LIKERT, R. (1961). *New patterns of management*. New York: McGraw-Hill.

MARES, D. R., & POWELL, W. W. (1990). Cooperative security regimes: Preventing international conflicts. In R. L. Kahn & M. N. Zald (Eds.), *Organizations and nation-states: New perspectives on conflict and cooperation* (pp. 55–94). San Francisco: Jossey-Bass.

MAYO, E. (1933). *The human problems of an industrial civilization*. New York: Macmillan.

McGREGOR, D. (1960). *The human side of enterprise*. New York: McGraw-Hill.

MOHRMAN, A. M., & LAWLER, E. E. III. (1985). The diffusion of QWL as a paradigm shift. In W. G. Bennis, K. D. Benne, & R. Chin (Eds.), *The planning of change* (4th ed., pp. 149–159). New York: Holt, Rhinehart and Winston.

PERROW, C. (1986). *Complex organizations* (3rd ed.). New York: Random House.

RICE, A. K. (1958). *Productivity and social organization: The Ahmedabad experiment*. London: Tavistock Publications.

ROETHLISBERGER, F. J., & DICKSON, W. J. (1939). *Management and the worker*. Cambridge MA: Harvard University Press.

SCOTT, W. R. (1981). *Organizations: Rational, natural, and open systems*. Englewood Cliffs, NJ: Prentice Hall.

SHEPPARD, H. L., FERMAN, L. A., & FABER, S. (1960). Too old to work—too young to retire: A case study of a permanent plant shutdown. U.S. Senate. Special Committee on Unemployment Problems. Washington, DC: U.S. Government Printing Office.

SLOTE, A. (1969). *Termination: The closing at Baker Plant*. New York: Bobbs-Merrill.

TANNENBAUM, A. S. (1968). *Control in organizations*. New York: McGraw-Hill.

TANNENBAUM, A. S. (1974). *Hierarchy in organizations*. San Francisco: Jossey-Bass.

THORSRUD, E., SØRENSEN, B. S., & GUSTAVSEN, B. (1976). Sociotechnical approach to industrial democracy in Norway. In R. Dubin (Ed.), *Handbook of work, organization, and society* (pp. 111–142). Chicago: Rand McNally.

TRIST, E. L., & BAMFORTH, K. W. (1951). Some social and psychological consequences of the long-wall method of coal-getting. *Human Relations, 4,* 3–38.

TVERSKY, A., & KAHNEMAN, D. (1981). The framing of decisions and the psychology of choice. *Science, 211,* 453–458.

TYLER, T. R., & LIND, E. A. (in press). A relational model of authority in groups. In M. Zanna (Ed.), *Advances in experimental social psychology*.

VON BERTALANFFY, L. (1956). General system theory. *General systems*. Yearbook of the Society for General Systems Theory, 1, 1–10.

VROOM, V. H. (1964). *Work and motivation*. New York: Wiley.